2ND CANADIAN EDITION

Management Information S

FOR THE INFORMATION A

FOR THE INSTRUCTOR

- Want an easy way to test your students prior to an exam that ***doesn't*** create more work for you?
- Want to access your supplements ***without*** having to bring them all to class?
- Want to integrate current happenings into your lectures ***without*** all the searching and extra work?
- Want an ***easy*** way to get your course on-line?
- Want to ***free up more time*** in your day to get more done?

Of course you do!

Then check out your

Online Learning Centre!

- Downloadable Supplements
- Extra Quizzes and Solutions
- PageOut
- Online Resources

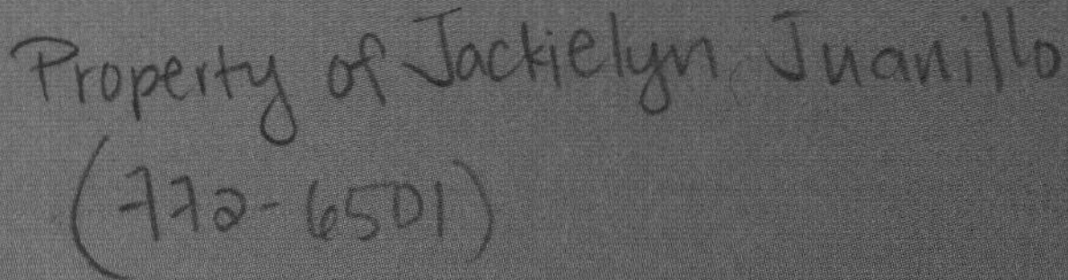

2ND CANADIAN EDITION

Management Information Systems

FOR THE INFORMATION AGE

Stephen Haag

DANIELS COLLEGE OF BUSINESS
UNIVERSITY OF DENVER

Maeve Cummings

PITTSBURG STATE UNIVERSITY

Donald J. McCubbrey

DANIELS COLLEGE OF BUSINESS
UNIVERSITY OF DENVER

Alain Pinsonneault

McGILL UNIVERSITY

Richard Donovan

McGILL UNIVERSITY

Toronto Montreal Boston Burr Ridge, IL Dubuque, IA Madison, WI New York San Francisco
St. Louis Bangkok Bogotá Caracas Kuala Lumpur Lisbon London Madrid Mexico City
Milan New Delhi Santiago Seoul Singapore Sydney Taipei

The McGraw-Hill Companies

Management Information Systems for the Information Age
Second Canadian Edition

ISBN: 0-07-091120-7

2 3 4 5 6 7 8 9 10 TCP 0 9 8 7 6 5 4

Printed and bound in Canada

Vice President, Editorial and Media Technology: Pat Ferrier
Sponsoring Editor: Catherine Koop
Developmental Editor: Darren Hick
Marketing Manager: Kim Verhaeghe
Senior Supervising Editor: Margaret Henderson
Copy Editor: Rodney Rawlings
Production Coordinators: Kelly Selleck/Madeleine Harrington
Composition: Bookman Typesetting
Inside Design: Mary Christianson
Cover Design: Sharon Lucas
Cover Image: Photographer: Oliver Burston (Debut Art)/Taxi
Printer: Transcontinental Printing Group

National Library of Canada Cataloguing in Publication Data

Management information systems for the information age / Stephen Haag ... [et al.]. — 2nd Canadian ed.

Includes index.
ISBN 0-07-091120-7

1. Management information systems. 2. Information technology.
I. Haag, Stephen

T58.6.M34 2003 658.4'038'011 C2003-900121-0

ABOUT THE AUTHORS

STEPHEN HAAG is a professor in and Chair of the Department of Information Technology and Electronic Commerce in the Daniels College of Business at the University of Denver. Stephen holds a B.B.A. and M.B.A. from West Texas State University and a Ph.D. from the University of Texas at Arlington. Stephen has been teaching in the classroom since 1982 and publishing books since 1984. He has also written numerous articles appearing in such journals as *Communications of the ACM*, *Socio-Economic Planning Sciences*, and the *Australian Journal of Management*.

Stephen is the co-author of numerous books including *Interactions: Teaching English as a Second Language* (with his mother and father), *Information Technology: Tomorrow's Advantage Today* (with Peter Keen), *Excelling in Finance*, and over 20 books within the *I-Series*. Stephen lives with his wife, Pam, and their three sons—Indiana, Darian, and Trevor—in Highlands Ranch, Colorado.

For my father, Carl. If I could achieve only one goal in life, I would want to be like him.

MAEVE CUMMINGS is a professor of Information Systems at Pittsburg State University. She holds a B.S. in Mathematics and Computer Science and an M.B.A from Pittsburg State, and a Ph.D. in Information Systems from the University of Texas at Arlington. She has published in various journals including the *Journal of Global Information Management* and the *Journal of Computer Information Systems*. She serves on various editorial boards and is a co-author of *Case Studies in Information Technology* and the concepts books of the *I-Series*, entitled *Computing Concepts*. Maeve has been teaching for 20 years and lives in Pittsburg, Kansas, with her husband, Slim.

To Clodagh and Jerry, whose presence in my life is like warm sunshine and a gentle breeze.

DONALD J. McCUBBREY is a professor in the Department of Information Technology and Electronic Commerce and Director of the Center for the Study of Electronic Commerce in the Daniels College of Business at the University of Denver. He holds a BSBA in Accounting from Wayne State University, a Master of Business from Swinburne University of Technology in Victoria, Australia, and a Ph.D. in Information Systems from the University of Maribor, Slovenia.

Prior to joining the Daniels College faculty in 1984, he was a partner with Andersen Consulting/Arthur Andersen & Co. During his career as an IT consultant, he participated in client engagements in the United States and several other countries in the Americas and Europe. He has published articles in *Communications of the Association for Information Systems*, *Information Technology and People*, and *MIS Quarterly*, and co-authored the Systems Analysis and Design text entitled *Foundations of Business Systems*. He is a co-founder and director emeritus of the Colorado Software and Internet Association and serves on the board of the EC Institute. He lives in the Colorado foothills with his wife, Janis.

To Jani: My wife, best friend, and favourite marathon runner.

CANADIAN AUTHORS

ALAIN PINSONNEAULT is the Imasco Professor of information systems in the Faculty of Management at McGill University. He holds a B.Comm. from Concordia university, an M.Sc. in Information Systems from École des Hautes Études Commerciales de Montréal, and a Ph.D. from the University of California, Irvine. Prior to joining McGill University in June 1999, he was an Associate Professor at the École des Hautes Études Commerciales (Montréal).

Alain Pinsonneault won numerous awards for both his research and teaching, including the Doctoral Award of the International Center for Information Technology and MCI Communications in 1990, the Person of the Week of *La Presse* Newspaper in 1991, Promising HEC Graduate Award in 1993, Gaëtan Morin Research Award at HEC in 1995, and the CDROM-SNI Award for his use of information technology in teaching in 1997.

He has published papers in *Management Science, Management Information Systems Quarterly, Information Systems Research,* the *Journal of Management Information Systems, Small Group Research, Organization Science, Decision Support Systems*, and the *European Journal of Operational Research.*

To: My love France, whose love and friendship energize my life.
To: My wonderful children, Alexe, Camille, and Loïc. You are my heroes.
To: Isalie and Jean-Marc.

RICHARD G. DONOVAN is the Associate Dean of the Bachelor of Commerce program within the Faculty of Management at McGill University. He holds a B.Comm. with a

Major in Information Systems and a Concentration in Marketing as well as a Certificate in Public Relations from McGill University. In addition, he has earned a Graduate Diploma in Instructional Technology from Concordia University.

Prior to joining McGill in July 1997, he worked at a top Canadian life insurance company for eight years, where he held positions such as Systems Consultant, Senior Training and Development Consultant, and Production Manager supervising a staff of 18. Since his arrival at McGill, he has won outstanding teaching awards and student life awards on nine occasions.

Prior to being appointed Associate Dean of the Undergraduate Program in January 2001, Richard was the area coordinator for the Information Systems area. He continues to design and teach courses in the I.S. and Strategy areas. He teaches executives at both the International Masters Program in Practicing Management and the McGill International Executive Institute. Richard works regularly as an information technology consultant for private industry and also sits on the advisory board of a dot-com company based in Montreal.

To Carmelina: You are the Love of my Life, my very Best Friend and #1 fan.
To Adamo and Justino: You will always keep me young and proud.

ABOUT THE CONTRIBUTORS

PAIGE BALTZAN is a professor in the Department of Information Technology and Electronic Commerce in the Daniels College of Business at the University of Denver. Paige holds a B.S.B.A from Bowling Green State University and an M.B.A. from the University of Denver. Paige's primary concentration focuses on object-oriented technologies and systems development methodologies. Paige has been teaching Systems Analysis and Design, Telecommunications and Networking, and Software Engineering at the University of Denver for the past three years. Paige has published supplemental materials for several McGraw-Hill publications including *Using Information Technology*.

Prior to joining the University of Denver Paige spent three years working at Level 3 Communications as a Technical Architect and four years working at Andersen Consulting as a Technology Consultant specializing in the Telecommunications industry. Paige lives in Lakewood, Colorado with her husband, Tony, and daughter, Hannah.

AMY PHILLIPS is a professor in the Department of Information Technology and Electronic Commerce in the University of Denver's Daniels College of Business. Amy has a B.S. degree in Environmental Biology and a M.Ed. degree in Educational Technology. She has been teaching for more than 18 years: 5 years in public secondary education and 13 years in higher education. Amy has also been an integral part of both the academic and the administrative functions within the higher educational system in Colorado and New Hampshire.

Amy's main concentration revolves around database-driven Web sites focusing on dynamic Web content; specifically ASP and XML technologies. Some of the main core course selections that Amy teaches at the University of Denver include XML, Systems Analysis and Design, Database Management Systems, Using Technology to Communicate Information, and Using Technology to Manage Information. Amy has offered many workshops and seminars as well as been invited to guest-speak at various conferences on Web development. She has just finished writing her first book *Internet Explorer 6.0* with Stephen Haag and James Perry. This book is part of the well-received *I-Series* from McGraw-Hill.

MERRILL WELLS The caption in Merrill Wells' eighth-grade yearbook noted that she wanted to teach college and write books. Although she spent several years after completing an M.B.A. at Indiana University developing business applications, in the end teaching and writing won out. She began her career as an application software developer (programmer) and then progressed to the systems analyst and finally the project manager roles, gaining invaluable experience in business, database design, application design, technical writing, and programming languages.

Merrill returned to academia after classroom experience training users on the software that her team had developed reignited the urge to teach. For ten years she was a computer technology faculty member at Red Rocks Community College developing and teaching courses in emerging technologies. She is now a professor in the Department of Information Technology and Electronic Commerce at the University of Denver, Daniels College of Business. Other publications include *An Introduction to Computers*, *Introduction to Visual Basic*, *Programming Logic and Design*, *Microsoft Access 2002* (Brief, Introductory, and Complete), and *Microsoft PowerPoint 2002* (Brief and Introductory), *Microsoft Office XP Volume I*, and *Microsoft Office XP Volume II*.

BRIEF CONTENTS

CONTENTS

PREFACE

As a group of authors and contributors working together, we carefully pored over the insightful reviews we gathered from instructors throughout Canada and the United States. This resulted in an expanded and improved Second Canadian Edition of *Management Information Systems for the Information Age*.

The Canadian Environment

Examples of Canadian companies, government policies, health care issues, and more pervade the text. Throughout, you will find new or updated opening and closing Canadian case studies, Industry Perspective boxes, The Global Perspective boxes, Assignments and Exercises, Real HOT Group Projects, and Team Work and On Your Own projects, as well as new or expanded coverage of such topics as intelligent agents and statistical tools (Chapter 3), groupware (Chapter 4), the role of the Canadian government (Chapter 5), payment systems (Chapter 5), privacy and Canadian law (Chapter 8), and new and emerging technologies (Chapter 9).

Organization and Structure

The Second Canadian Edition provides you with the ultimate flexibility in tailoring content to the exact needs of your MIS or IT course. This text, consisting of nine chapters, two integrated Extended Learning Modules (XLMs or modules), four additional XLMs at the end of the text, and four Skills Modules on the CD-ROM, allows you to decide the extent to which you want to cover technical topics, application/programming topics and business/managerial topics. Each of the Extended Learning Modules and the Skills Modules is a self-contained unit, and can be easily covered by instructors at any point in their courses, or not at all.

A NEW LOOK

All of the text's content updates and new pedagogical features are presented in a visually appealing, streamlined format. Moving to a much cleaner, single-column format, with overhauled palette and design of pedagogical boxes, the new Canadian edition is sure to appeal to instructors and students alike.

ENGAGING PEDAGOGY

The Second Canadian Edition has been approached with active learning and real-world examples in mind. Grounded in content, the text has been designed to facilitate student learning through several learning tools created with this in mind:

- New *Skills Modules* on the text CD-ROM and Online Learning Centre focus on skill-based learning in Excel, Access, HTML, and building e-portfolios.
- *Opening* and *Closing Case Studies* from Canada and abroad give a real-world context for the topics at hand.
- *Industry Perspective* and *The Global Perspective* focus boxes throughout the text bring real-world Canadian and international context to the subjects at hand.

- *Student Learning Outcomes* and *Summaries* act as a road map to knowledge, focusing students on what they should know or be able to do upon completing each chapter and module.
- *Team Work* and *On Your Own* projects are integrated into the text.
- *Assignments and Exercises* at the end of each chapter help students apply what they have learned.
- *Real HOT Electronic Commerce* projects at the end of each chapter broaden student horizons by requiring them to explore the Web.

COMPLETE TEACHING/LEARNING PACKAGE

- **Instructor's Manual.** Provided to instructors in an effort to help prepare class presentations. Beyond providing an outline of the chapters and modules and answers to the various projects, exercises, and assignments, the IM includes *Concept Reinforcement* boxes to guide use of the text's pedagogy and modules, and facilitate class participation. The IM is available in Word format through the Online Learning Centre at www.mcgrawhill.ca/college/haag.
- **Test Bank.** Instructors receive special software to select both multiple-choice questions and problems requiring full solutions from the bank of over 2000 questions tied to the text material. These questions and problems may be selected according to topic and degree of difficulty criteria. Instructors may edit test items and add new questions to the test bank.
- **Videos.** A complete set of *CBC videos* including segments from *The National* and *UNDERcurrents*, as well as a set of six original videos tied to topics in the text, are available to instructors.
- **Text CD-ROM.** Accompanying this text is a CD-ROM containing four new Skills Learning Modules, data sets, additional focus boxes, Real HOT Group Projects, glossary, and over 1000 Web links to relevant sites.
- **Online Learning Centre.** Can be found at www.mcgrawhill.ca/college/haag.
- **Instructor Resources.** A secured area for instructors stores essential course materials, including the Instructor's Manual, PowerPoint presentations, solutions to Real HOT Group Projects, and more.
- **Student Resources.** The student area of the OLC stores videos, PowerPoint presentations, data files, and online quizzes that follow each chapter and module in the text. Plus, students can find additional content, including Skills Learning Modules, additional focus boxes, Real HOT Group Projects, a searchable glossary, and over 1000 Web links to relevant sites.

Grateful Appreciation

In preparing this Second Canadian Edition, it has become obvious that a close collaboration between the authors and numerous groups of people is essential in making a high-quality book such as this one. Within McGraw-Hill Ryerson, there are numerous people who have made this project successful, including Editorial (Patrick Ferrier, Vice President, Editorial and Media Technology; Catherine Koop, Senior Sponsoring Editor; and Darren Hick, Developmental Editor), Production (Kelly Dickson, Margaret Henderson, and Rodney Rawlings), and Sales and Marketing (Jeff MacLean, Michael Ryan, and Kim Verhaeghe).

As well, we would like to acknowledge all of the work done by the staff at McGraw-Hill/Irwin, publisher of the U.S. edition, which forms the basis of this one.

We would also like to take this time to especially acknowledge the wonderful efforts of our Research Assistant, Daniel Tomiuk. Daniel has brought to the table unique research and writing talents, helping to make this text truly Canadian.

Last, but certainly not least, we would offer our gratitude to our reviewers. They took on a thankless job that paid only a portion of its true worth and contributed in countless ways to the development of the Second Canadian Edition. They include:

Deborah Compeau, *University of Western Ontario*
Ralph Deters, *University of Saskatchewan*
Allan Dyer, *University of Guelph*
Felix Ernst, *Camosun College*
Len Fertuck, *University of Toronto*
Dale Foster, *Memorial University of Newfoundland*
Bob Goldstein, *University of British Columbia*
Rob Hollis, *Dalhousie University*
Leo Kerklaan, *McGill University*
Jocelyn King, *University of Alberta*
Dennis Kira, *Concordia University*
Ron Murch, *University of Calgary*
Anne Banks Pidduck, *University of Waterloo*

As well, we would like to thank the reviewers of the U.S. edition, whose insight helped to shape not only the American edition, but the Canadian as well:

Ron Lemos, *California State University—Los Angeles*
Alicia Fetters, *De Moines Area CC—Ankeny*
Morris Pondfield, *Towson University*
David Bradbard, *Winthrop University*
Bennie D. Waller, *Francis Marion University*
Sumit Sircar, *University of Texas at Arlington*
Mike Raisingani, *University of Dallas*
Harold Wise, *East Carolina University*
Lawrence Andrew, *Western Illinois University*
Craig Tyran, *Western Washington University*
Ross A. Malaga, *University of Maryland*
Bryan Foltz, *East Carolina University*
Laurette Simmons, *Loyola University—Maryland*
Ron Berry, *University of LA at Monroe*
Kenneth R. Lee, *Delaware Valley College*
Dennis Williams, *Cal Poly—San Luis Obispo*
Robert J. Mills, *Utah State University*
James Waegelein, *University of Kansas—Lawrence*
Brian Kovar, *Kansas State University*
Kent Whitman, *Franklin Pierce College*
Joy M. Perrine, *Penn State University—Shenango*
Denise Nitterhouse, *DePaul University*

Features and Supplements

The Second Canadian Edition of *Management Information Systems for the Information Age* is filled with robust features to connect core concepts to examples in the real world, facilitate student activities, and otherwise enhance student learning. Each of the following elements has been created and reviewed by instructors in Canada and abroad to create the best learning tools possible for students.

Features

CASE STUDIES

Each chapter in the text opens with a real-world Canadian or international case study to introduce the topic, and closes with two case studies that focus application through student discussion questions.

DATABASES AND DATA WAREHOUSES

Building Business Intelligence

CASE STUDY:
DATA WAREHOUSING—PART OF THE INFORMATION LOOP AT SCOTIAMcLEOD

If you ever contact ScotiaMcLeod (www.scotiamcleod.com—formerly Charles Schwab Canada) to inquire about their financial services such as individual retirement accounts (IRAs), do not be surprised if the call centre agent tries to capture as much information about you as possible. Not only will your name, address, and request for information be entered into the company's central database (a.k.a. the core production system), but so will any information you provide such as whether you currently own stocks or equities and whether you consider yourself a beginning investor. During subsequent calls, the agent

affluence, trading activity, contact channel preference, etc. The data warehouse then feeds different data marts (a subset of a data warehouse) used by ScotiaMcLeod's various business units. Marketing analysts, for instance, use these data marts for reporting and analysis purposes and to make inferences about your needs and preferences as a customer. As such, if the request you made concerning IRAs is also made by several other customers sharing similar characteristics, Schwab will attempt to increase its marketing efforts for IRAs to your segment.

The benefits of data warehousing at ScotiaMcLeod do not stop there. In fact, the information fed into the data warehouse by the core production system goes full circle and is made available to all of the different channels (Internet, call centre, and branch office), dramatically

support business activities and decision-making tasks, not transaction processing

6. **Define the four major types of data mining tools in a data warehouse environment.** The four major types of data mining tools in a data warehouse environment are:

information?

- How will changes in technology affect organizing and managing information?
- Is information ownership a consideration?
- What are the ethics involved in managing and organizing information?

CLOSING CASE STUDY ONE

WE'VE GOT OLTP COVERED; LET'S GO ON TO OLAP

In business environments today, you'll find rich, technically correct, and very supportive databases that meet transaction processing needs (OLTP or online transaction processing). But many of those same organizations have failed to implement the necessary technologies that support business analysis and decision-making needs (OLAP or online analytical processing). And it makes sense. It's far easier to implement a database for processing something like sales transactions than it is to provide the necessary technology tools and information that would support someone, for example, in determining where to build a new distribution centre.

So we've pretty well got OLTP covered. We need now to focus on OLAP. Consider these three companies and their efforts in supporting OLAP. They are not unique situations, nor are they bad ones. In fact, we would say that these are leading-edge companies because they are willing to acknowledge their problems, face them, and strive to do something about them.

EASTMAN CHEMICAL COMPANY

As Jerry Hale, CIO at Eastman, explains it, managers don't have easy access to the information they need to make effective decisions. He further explains that there is a variety of reasons for this problem—too much information is available, much of the information is in incompatible formats, and most of the decision support software is too difficult for managers to use. According to Jerry, "A high percentage of the data is there. The challenge is extracting it and presenting it in a way that's useful for managers to make decisions."

STUDENT LEARNING OUTCOMES AND SUMMARIES

The content of each chapter and module begins with a list of items that students should know or should be able to do upon completing their reading. At the conclusion of each chapter and module, we revisit the Student Learning Outcomes for students to confirm their understanding and knowledge, as well as to prepare for tests and exams.

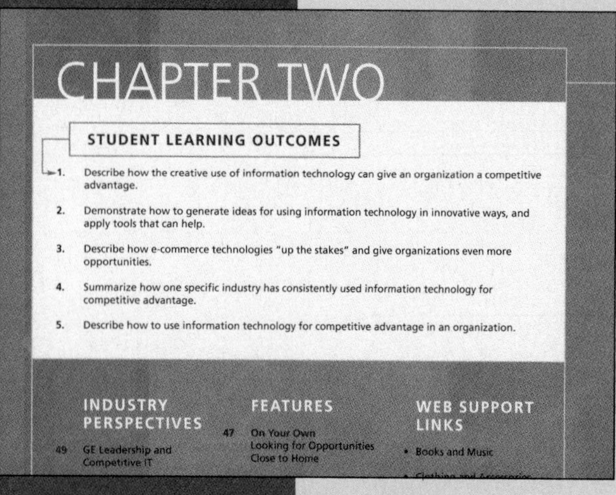

CHAPTER TWO

STUDENT LEARNING OUTCOMES

1. Describe how the creative use of information technology can give an organization a competitive advantage.
2. Demonstrate how to generate ideas for using information technology in innovative ways, and apply tools that can help.
3. Describe how e-commerce technologies "up the stakes" and give organizations even more opportunities.
4. Summarize how one specific industry has consistently used information technology for competitive advantage.
5. Describe how to use information technology for competitive advantage in an organization.

INDUSTRY PERSPECTIVES

49 GE Leadership and Competitive IT

FEATURES

47 On Your Own Looking for Opportunities Close to Home

WEB SUPPORT LINKS

- Books and Music

Summary: Student Learning Outcomes Revisited

1. **Describe how the creative use of information technology can give an organization a competitive advantage.** Smart companies spend a lot of time, money, and effort in designing and installing it systems because they realize a competitive advantage when it systems deliver creative solutions to business problems. A **competitive advantage** can be gained by providing a product or service in a way that customers value more than the competition's. Some concepts related to IT systems are:
   - **Temporary advantage**—whatever you do, sooner or later the competition duplicates what you've done, but a temporary advantage can linger in customers' minds and have lasting effects.
   - **First mover**—first to market with a new IT-based product or service can gain competitive advantage.
   - **Information partnership**—two or more companies acting in cooperation by integrating their IT systems provide customers with the best of what each can offer.
   - **Alliance partner**—companies that you do business with on a regular basis in a cooperative fashion.
   - **Business to Business (B2B)**—IT-enabled business with other businesses.
   - **Business to Consumer (B2C)**—IT-enabled business with individual customers.
2. **Demonstrate how to generate ideas for using information technology in innovative ways, and**

   - Rivalry among existing competitors
   - The **three generic strategies**:
     - Cost leadership
     - Differentiation
     - Focused strategy
   - The **value chain**—a view of the organization as a chain—or series—of processes, each of which adds value to the product or service for the customer.
3. **Describe how e-commerce technologies "up the stakes" and give organizations even more opportunities.** E-commerce makes it even more important for you to focus on competitive advantage. The main reason for this is that the Internet and related technologies provide new capabilities to establish more effective information partnerships along the supply and distribution chains and to forge closer relationships with customers. This can be achieved through:
   - **Mass customization**—occurs when a business gives its customers the opportunity to have its product or service tailored to the customer's specifications
   - **Personalization**—occurs when an Internet site can know enough about your likes and dislikes that it can fashion offers more likely to appeal to you (supported by techniques such as **collaborative filtering**)
   - **Disintermediation**—occurs when, with the

PERSPECTIVE BOXES

Each chapter contains feature boxes titled Industry Perspective and The Global Perspective, providing students with real-world application of the concepts of MIS in Canada and abroad.

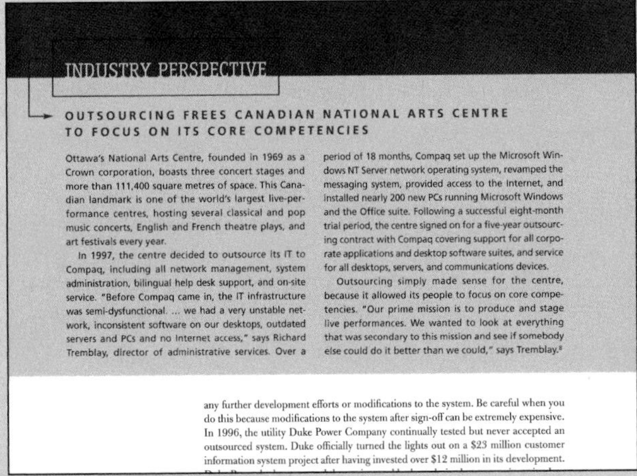

INDUSTRY PERSPECTIVE

OUTSOURCING FREES CANADIAN NATIONAL ARTS CENTRE TO FOCUS ON ITS CORE COMPETENCIES

Ottawa's National Arts Centre, founded in 1969 as a Crown corporation, boasts three concert stages and more than 111,400 square metres of space. This Canadian landmark is one of the world's largest live-performance centres, hosting several classical and pop music concerts, English and French theatre plays, and art festivals every year.

In 1997, the centre decided to outsource its IT to Compaq, including all network management, system administration, bilingual help desk support, and on-site service. "Before Compaq came in, the IT infrastructure was semi-dysfunctional. ... we had a very unstable network, inconsistent software on our desktops, outdated servers and PCs and no Internet access," says Richard Tremblay, director of administrative services. Over a period of 18 months, Compaq set up the Microsoft Windows NT Server network operating system, revamped the messaging system, provided access to the Internet, and installed nearly 200 new PCs running Microsoft Windows and the Office suite. Following a successful eight-month trial period, the centre signed on for a five-year outsourcing contract with Compaq covering support for all corporate applications and desktop software suites, and service for all desktops, servers, and communications devices.

Outsourcing simply made sense for the centre, because it allowed its people to focus on core competencies. "Our prime mission is to produce and stage live performances. We wanted to look at everything that was secondary to this mission and see if somebody else could do it better than we could," says Tremblay.[8]

any further development efforts or modifications to the system. Be careful when you do this because modifications to the system after sign-off can be extremely expensive. In 1996, the utility Duke Power Company continually tested but never accepted an outsourced system. Duke officially turned the lights out on a $23 million customer information system project after having invested over $12 million in its development.

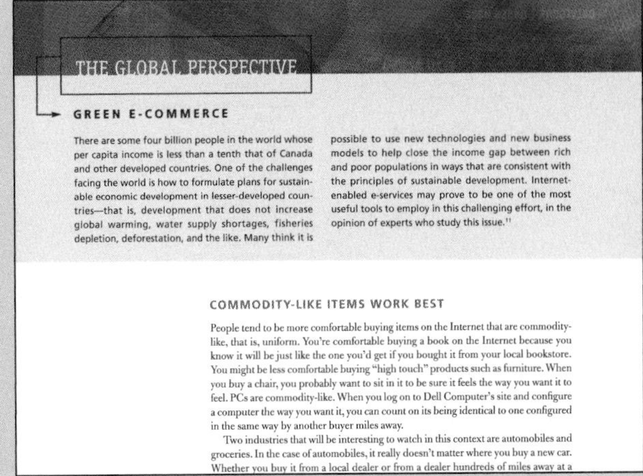

THE GLOBAL PERSPECTIVE

GREEN E-COMMERCE

There are some four billion people in the world whose per capita income is less than a tenth that of Canada and other developed countries. One of the challenges facing the world is how to formulate plans for sustainable economic development in lesser-developed countries—that is, development that does not increase global warming, water supply shortages, fisheries depletion, deforestation, and the like. Many think it is possible to use new technologies and new business models to help close the income gap between rich and poor populations in ways that are consistent with the principles of sustainable development. Internet-enabled e-services may prove to be one of the most useful tools to employ in this challenging effort, in the opinion of experts who study this issue.[11]

COMMODITY-LIKE ITEMS WORK BEST

People tend to be more comfortable buying items on the Internet that are commodity-like, that is, uniform. You're comfortable buying a book on the Internet because you know it will be just like the one you'd get if you bought it from your local bookstore. You might be less comfortable buying "high touch" products such as furniture. When you buy a chair, you probably want to sit in it to be sure it feels the way you want it to feel. PCs are commodity-like. When you log on to Dell Computer's site and configure a computer the way you want it, you can count on its being identical to one configured in the same way by another buyer miles away.

Two industries that will be interesting to watch in this context are automobiles and groceries. In the case of automobiles, it really doesn't matter where you buy a new car. Whether you buy it from a local dealer or from a dealer hundreds of miles away at a

PROJECT BOXES

As well, Team Work and On Your Own boxes are spread throughout the chapters and modules of the text and CD-ROM to give students hands-on application of the concepts of MIS, whether in group projects or individual assignments.

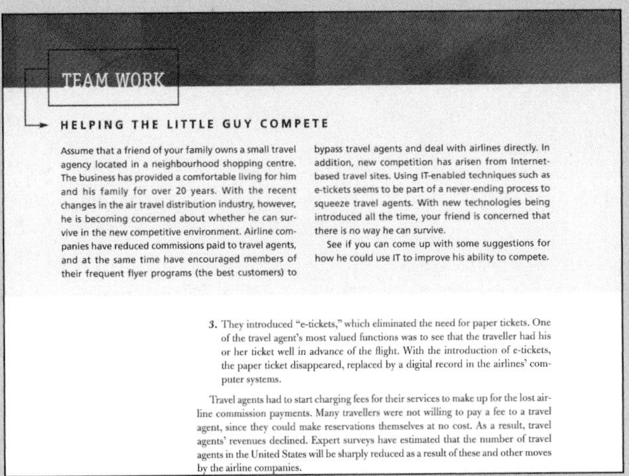

TEAM WORK

HELPING THE LITTLE GUY COMPETE

Assume that a friend of your family owns a small travel agency located in a neighbourhood shopping centre. The business has provided a comfortable living for him and his family for over 20 years. With the recent changes in the air travel distribution industry, however, he is becoming concerned about whether he can survive in the new competitive environment. Airline companies have reduced commissions paid to travel agents, and at the same time have encouraged members of their frequent flyer programs (the best customers) to bypass travel agents and deal with airlines directly. In addition, new competition has arisen from Internet-based travel sites. Using IT-enabled techniques such as e-tickets seems to be part of a never-ending process to squeeze travel agents. With new technologies being introduced all the time, your friend is concerned that there is no way he can survive.

See if you can come up with some suggestions for how he could use IT to improve his ability to compete.

3. They introduced "e-tickets," which eliminated the need for paper tickets. One of the travel agent's most valued functions was to see that the traveller had his or her ticket well in advance of the flight. With the introduction of e-tickets, the paper ticket disappeared, replaced by a digital record in the airlines' computer systems.

Travel agents had to start charging fees for their services to make up for the lost airline commission payments. Many travellers were not willing to pay a fee to a travel agent, since they could make reservations themselves at no cost. As a result, travel agents' revenues declined. Expert surveys have estimated that the number of travel agents in the United States will be sharply reduced as a result of these and other moves by the airline companies.

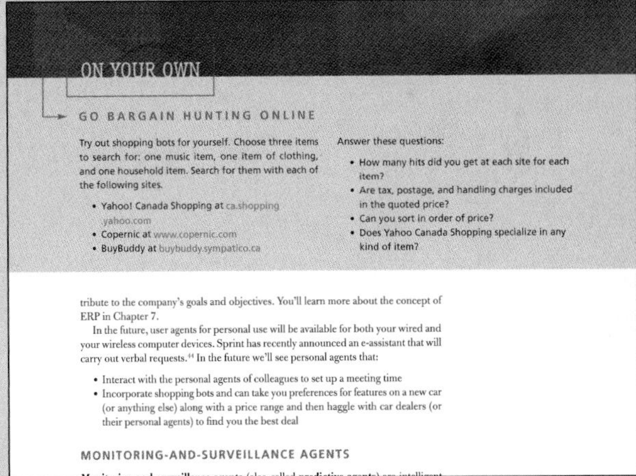

ON YOUR OWN

GO BARGAIN HUNTING ONLINE

Try out shopping bots for yourself. Choose three items to search for: one music item, one item of clothing, and one household item. Search for them with each of the following sites.

- Yahoo! Canada Shopping at ca.shopping.yahoo.com
- Copernic at www.copernic.com
- BuyBuddy at buybuddy.sympatico.ca

Answer these questions:

- How many hits did you get at each site for each item?
- Are tax, postage, and handling charges included in the quoted price?
- Can you sort in order of price?
- Does Yahoo Canada Shopping specialize in any kind of item?

tribute to the company's goals and objectives. You'll learn more about the concept of ERP in Chapter 7.

In the future, user agents for personal use will be available for both your wired and your wireless computer devices. Sprint has recently announced an e-assistant that will carry out verbal requests.[44] In the future we'll see personal agents that:

- Interact with the personal agents of colleagues to set up a meeting time
- Incorporate shopping bots and can take you preferences for features on a new car (or anything else) along with a price range and then haggle with car dealers (or their personal agents) to find you the best deal

MONITORING-AND-SURVEILLANCE AGENTS

KEY TERMS AND CONCEPTS

Key terms are bolded within the text and listed at the end of each chapter for easy reference. They are also defined in the Glossary.

SHORT-ANSWER QUESTIONS

These review questions (between 12 and 20 per chapter) cover key topics from the chapter.

Key Terms and Concepts

alliance partner, 47
application architect, 44
B2B marketplace, 51
business process, 53
business to business (B2B), 47
business to consumer (B2C), 47
buyer power, 49
collaborative filtering, 58
competitive advantage, 44
disintermediation, 58
distribution chain, 46
entry barrier, 51
first mover, 46
five forces model, 49
global reach, 59
information partnership, 47
mass customization, 57
permission marketing, 62
personalization, 58
rivalry among existing competitors, 50
supplier power, 50
switching costs, 50
temporary advantage, 46
threat of new entrants, 50
threat of substitute products or services, 50
three generic strategies, 52
value chain, 53

Short-Answer Questions

1. What are the two things you need, as a minimum, in order to design an information system that gives an organization a competitive advantage?
2. What do "application architects" do?
3. Why are competitive advantages achieved through IT usually only temporary?
4. What do we call a company which is the first to market with a product or service?
5. What is meant by "B2B" and "B2C"?
6. When is buyer power high?
7. When is supplier power high?
8. Why is it important to view the business problem from another perspective?
9. What is a B2B marketplace?
10. What is CPFR? How do companies who use it get a competitive advantage?
11. What is the *value chain*? How is it used?
12. What is an example of a value-added process not discussed in the chapter?
13. What is an example of a value-reducing process not discussed in the chapter?
14. What is the difference between mass customization and personalization? See if you can give some examples not included in the chapter.
15. What is meant by *global reach*? Why might it be important for an importer in Saskatoon, Saskatchewan to be concerned about it?

Assignments and Exercises

1. **EVALUATING TELEMEDICINE.** The Industry Perspective "Remote Surgery: A New Export Industry?" mentioned that perhaps health care could someday become an export industry. Assume that you work for a university-based medical centre and have been given the assignment to evaluate whether remote medicine, in general, is likely to be more common in the coming years and, if so, how your medical centre and its health care professionals should respond to such a trend.
   To get you started on this assignment, you might try to find out what is being written about "telemedicine"—the term often used to describe the remote delivery of health care services, enabled, of course, by computer and telecommunications technologies. For example, a small town in a remote part of the country typically does not have access to skilled medical specialists such as radiologists. If someone is injured and requires an X-ray for diagnosis, it is possible to take an X-ray locally and then transmit the results to your medical centre where it would be reviewed and evaluated by a radiologist. Of course, if the X-ray can be

we noted that even governments can get a competitive advantage with IT. This holds true for state and local governments as well as national governments. For example, our lives as citizens would be much easier if certain governmental services could be had them over the Internet instead of us having to visit an office and stand in line. Visit your city or town's Web site, and note what services (e.g., licences, traffic tickets, utility services, information on recreational facilities, etc.) are offered to citizens over the Internet. How well are they doing?

Discussion Questions

1. What is meant by the term "competitive advantage"? Why is competitive advantage important? Give some examples of companies you deal with which you think have achieved competitive advantage, and explain the technique(s) they used to achieve it. Next, give some examples of companies you deal with, or know of, that have used IT in creative ways to get a competitive advantage. Try to come up with at least three examples not discussed in the chapter.
2. How does Dell get a competitive advantage from its "sell, source, and ship" model? Why do you suppose other manufacturers of personal computers let Dell get and maintain a first-mover advantage with its business model and not simply do business the same way as Dell as soon as they saw how effective it was?
3. The chapter states that it is important to view the business problem from another perspective if

ASSIGNMENTS AND EXERCISES

At the end of each chapter, these longer student exercises are created to challenge student understanding and enhance critical thinking in a real-world context.

DISCUSSION QUESTIONS

These sets of review questions cover key concepts of the chapter and can be used to generate classroom discussion or for individual review.

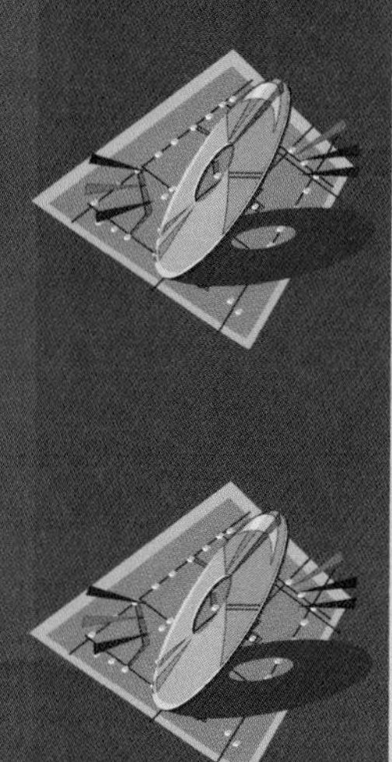

REAL HOT ELECTRONIC COMMERCE

Each chapter concludes with Real HOT (Hands on Technology) exercises for students to explore the Web and see what it's like to be on each end of business-to-consumer electronic commerce. Over 1000 links can be found on the text CD-ROM and at the Online Learning Centre (www.mcgrawhill.ca/college/haag) to provide a starting point for students.

REAL HOT GROUP PROJECTS

On the text CD-ROM and at the Online Learning Centre (www.mcgrawhill.ca/college/haag), students can access Real HOT Group Projects and accompanying data files, which require them to roll up their sleeves and use technology to take advantage of an opportunity or solve a problem.

REAL HOT Electronic Commerce

Living Life on the Internet

Real HOT Links

The personal computer is quickly becoming a household necessity similar to a stove or a fridge. The primary reason the personal computer has become such an important part of our lives is the Internet. There are literally thousands of ways people use the Internet to perform tasks.

Do you have a personal computer with Internet connectivity in your home? How often do you use it and why? We bet you use it all the time to perform tasks ranging from sending e-mails to finding driving directions. There are so many great Web sites available, and all of them can help you accomplish things such as finding movie times, cooking a delicious meal, and seeking medical advice.

In this section we'll provide you with a few key Web sites you can use to help you live your life, and you can find many more sites on the Web site that supports this text (www.mcgrawhill.ca/college/haag).

ONLINE MAGAZINES

Every year, people spend an incredible amount of money buying magazines. Many of these magazines are received through the mail and never read, ending up in a giant pile a giant recycling plant. Do you receive magazines through the mail or buy them while doing your grocery shopping? How much are you paying for them, and do you actually find the time to read them? Did you know that many magazines are available online for free? That's right, free. Save yourself some money by using the Internet to

REAL HOT Group Projects

CASE 1:
ASSESSING THE VALUE OF INFORMATION

TREVOR TOY AUTO MECHANICS

Trevor Toy Auto Mechanics is an automobile repair shop in Lindsay, Ontario. Over the past few years, Trevor has seen his business grow from a two-bay car repair shop with only one other employee to a 15-bay car repair shop with 21 employees.

Up to now, Trevor has advertised that he will perform any work on any vehicle. But that's becoming problematic as cars are becoming increasingly more complex. Trevor has decided he wants to create a more focused repair shop, and is asking for your help. He has provided you with a spreadsheet file that contains a list of all the repairs his shop has completed over the past year. The file contains the fields provided in the table here.

Column	Name	Description
A	MECHANIC #	A unique number assigned to the mechanic who completed the work
B	CAR TYPE	The type of car on which the work was completed
C	WORK COMPLETED	What type of repair was performed on the car
D	NUM HOURS	How long in hours it took to complete the work
E	COST OF PARTS	The cost of the parts associated with completing the repair

Student Supplements

Students using this *Management Information Systems for the Information Age* are provided with robust media supplements created to provide tools for test preparation, to teach MIS-related skills, to connect students to real-world applications of MIS, and to otherwise strengthen their understanding and enhance their abilities in MIS.

TEXT CD-ROM

All copies of this text are packaged with a special CD-ROM that includes:

- Skills Modules on the topics of Microsoft® Excel, Access, HTML, and e-portfolios
- Real HOT Group Projects
- Data files
- Added content, including extra cases, added-value boxes, and projects
- Glossary
- Hundreds of Web links

... and *more*!

When the CD-ROM icon appears in the margin of the text, the student can go to the text CD-ROM to access relevant data files, links, added content, or Skills Modules to enhance learning.

ONLINE LEARNING CENTRE

The Online Learning Centre (OLC) is a Web site—www.mcgrawhill.ca/college/haag—that follows the text chapter by chapter, with additional materials and quizzing, that enhance the text and classroom experience. As students read the text, they can go online to take self-grading quizzes, link to hundreds of relevant Web sites, access videos and PowerPoint presentations, and work through Skills Modules on the topics of Microsoft Excel, Access, HTML, and e-portfolios.

Instructor Supplements

The Second Canadian Edition of *Management Information Systems for the Information Age* is accompanied by a robust package of supplements for instructor use, created to enhance classroom activities, facilitate student testing, and otherwise augment the tools provided by the text.

INSTRUCTOR'S MANUAL

A manual is provided to instructors in an effort to help prepare class presentations. Beyond providing an outline of the chapters and modules and answers to the various projects, exercises, and assignments, the IM includes Concept Reinforcement boxes to guide use of the text's pedagogy and modules and facilitate class participation. The IM is available in Word format through the Online Learning Centre (www.mcgrawhill.ca/college/haag).

COMPUTERIZED TEST BANK

Instructors receive special software to select both multiple-choice questions and problems requiring full solutions from the bank of over 2000 questions tied to the text material. These questions and problems may be selected according to topic and degree of difficulty criteria. Instructors may edit test items and add new questions to the test bank. A printed copy of the test bank is also available upon request from your McGraw-Hill Ryerson i-Learning Sales Specialist.

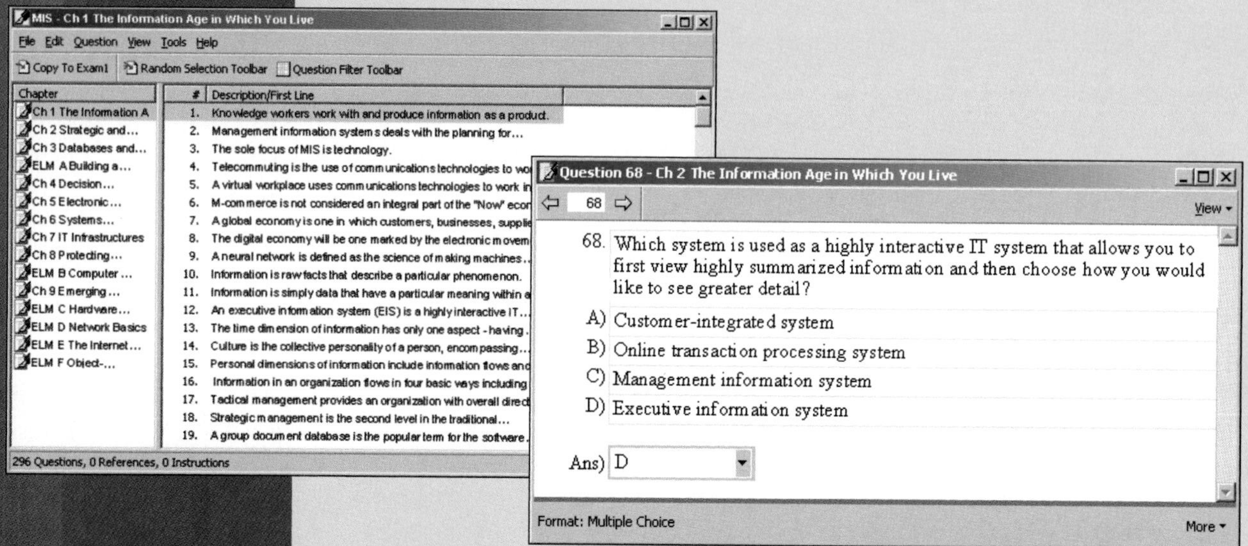

ONLINE LEARNING CENTRE

The Online Learning Centre (OLC) is a Web site (www.mcgrawhill.ca/college/haag) that follows the text chapter by chapter, with additional materials and quizzing, that

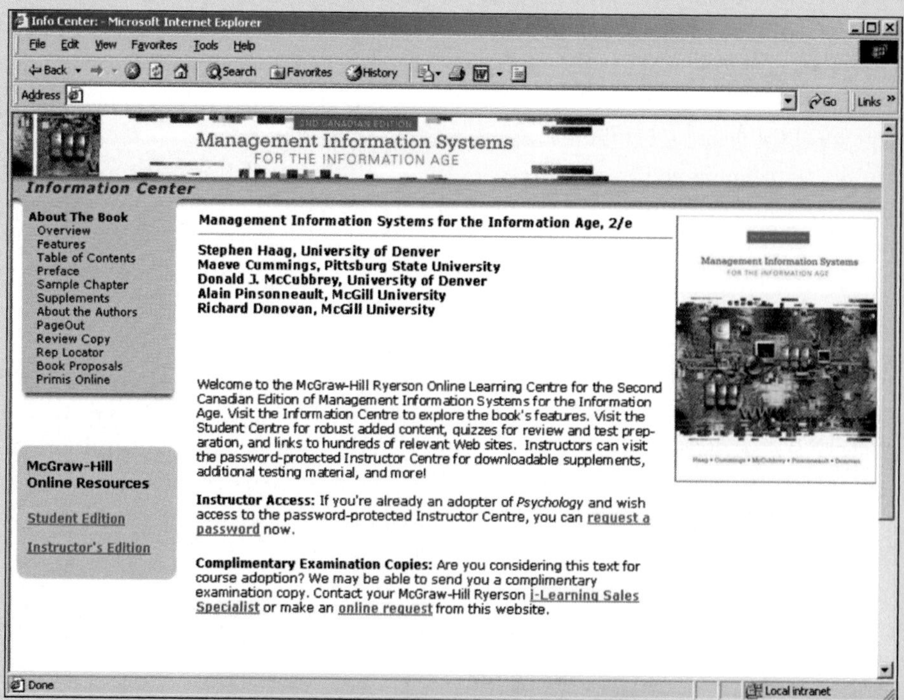

enhance the text and classroom experience. As students read the text, they can go online to take self-grading quizzes, link to over 1000 relevant Web sites, access videos and PowerPoints, and work through Skills Modules on the topics of Microsoft Excel, Access, HTML, and e-portfolios. Instructors and students can access the OLC directly through the text Web site, through PageOut, or within a course management system (e.g., WebCT or Blackboard).

CBC VIDEOS

Two sets of videos are available to instructors using *Management Information Systems in the Information Age*:

- A complete set of **CBC videos**, including segments from *The National* and *UNDERcurrents*, offers instructors the opportunity to highlight such topics as paying for privacy, new technology, and more—all for situational analysis in the classroom.
- A set of six **original videos** created to accompany the U.S. edition of the text and keyed to topic areas in the text can be obtained from your i-Learning Sales Specialist.

PageOut

Create a custom course Website with PageOut, free with every McGraw-Hill Ryerson textbook.

To learn more, contact your McGraw-Hill Ryerson publisher's representative or visit www.mhhe.com/solutions

PageOut, McGraw-Hill's unique point-and-click course Web site tool, enables users to create a full-featured, professional-quality course Web site without knowing HTML coding. PageOut is free for instructors, and lets you post your syllabus online, assign McGraw-Hill OLC content, add Web links, and maintain an online grade book. (And if you're short on time, we even have a team ready to help you create your site.)

PRIMIS ONLINE

You can customize this text and save your students money off bookstore prices by using McGraw-Hill's Primis Online digital database, the largest online collection of texts, readings, and cases. Contact your McGraw-Hill i-Learning Sales Specialist for more information.

WebCT/BLACKBOARD

This text is available in two of the most popular course-delivery platforms—WebCT and Blackboard—for more user-friendly and enhanced features. Contact your McGraw-Hill i-Learning Sales Specialist for more information.

i-LEARNING SALES SPECIALIST

Your Integrated Learning Sales Specialist is a McGraw-Hill Ryerson representative who has the experience, product knowledge, training, and support to help you assess and integrate any of the above products, technology, and services into your course for optimum teaching and learning performance. Whether it's how to use our test bank software, helping your students improve their grades, or how to put your entire course online, your i-Learning Sales Specialist is there to help. Contact your local i-Learning Sales Specialist today to learn how to maximize all McGraw-Hill Ryerson resources!

CHAPTER ONE

STUDENT LEARNING OUTCOMES

1. Describe the information age and the role of knowledge workers within it.
2. Define management information systems (MIS).
3. Describe key factors shaping today's economic environment.
4. Validate information as a key resource and describe both personal and organizational dimensions of information.
5. Define how people are the most important organizational resource, their information and technology literacy challenges, and their ethical responsibilities.
6. Describe the important characteristics of information technology (IT) as a key organizational resource.
7. List and describe the six roles and goals of information technology in any organization.

INDUSTRY PERSPECTIVES

FEATURES

WEB SUPPORT LINKS

- Job Databases
- Creating and Posting an Electronic Résumé
- Searching Newspapers the New-Fashioned Way
- Locating That All-Important Internship
- Interviewing and Negotiating
- Going Right to the Source—The Organization You Want

Visit www.mcgrawhill.ca/college/haag

Changing the Face of Business

CASE STUDY:
INFORMATION TECHNOLOGY AT RITZ-CARLTON HOTELS HELPS STAFF DELIVER EXCELLENT SERVICE QUALITY

The Ritz-Carlton manages more than thirty luxury hotels across North America, Europe, Asia, Australia, the Middle East, Africa, and Caribbean. This chain of hotels has become synonymous with elegance and excellent customer service worldwide. About 95% of guests leave its hotels with the impression that they had a "memorable visit." It is the only hospitality organization which is a two-time recipient of the Malcolm Baldrige National Quality Award. Much of the secret to its success lies in its effective management of its knowledge workers in combination with Information Technology to track and fulfill customers' needs.

Each hotel in the chain includes one or two guest recognition coordinators. Their job consists of "preemptively" ensuring superior quality of service personalized to each guest according to his or her preferences. After receiving a list of incoming guests, they link up to the guest-history database. This "guest recognition system" includes the histories and preferences of more than half a million guests. The system is a Windows-based application accessible across a network spanning all of its hotels no matter where they are situated in the world. According to Allison Frantz, corporate manager of training and development for Ritz-Carlton, guest recognition coordinators consult the system and then "tell the manager, and everyone else about VIPs and other guests who may have had previous difficulties coming in that day, as well as any other information on new high-profile guests. Maybe somebody likes chocolate or enjoys having dinner early. This is the time to pass that information along so we can be ready with a box of candy or early dinner time when the guests check in."

The "Ritz" realized that, although technology had to play a key role in providing this high a standard of service, its success crucially depended on getting all knowledge-workers involved. "We try to blend technology with a systematic approach in collecting information. It's important to inspire the staff to hunt for the information" explains Jonathan Campbell, general manager at Ritz-Carlton in Kuala Lumpur, Malaysia. This consists of "active observation" by the hotel's knowledge workers. They discreetly watch hotel guests for particular individual behaviours which may be linked to individual preferences. For instance, a waiter at the Ritz in Montreal, Quebec may notice that a guest prefers one "sweet and low" and no milk with her tea. Immediately, this preference is jotted down as a "guest preference" on a "guest recognition pad" and then entered into the chain's worldwide system. Months later, if this guest ever finds herself ordering a tea in a Ritz-Carlton anywhere else in the world, the waiter will simply confirm whether she still prefers it with one "sweet and low" and no milk.[1]

Introduction

It is the **information age**—a time when knowledge is power. Today, more than ever, businesses are using information (and information technology) to gain and sustain a competitive advantage. You'll never find a business whose slogan is "What you don't know can't hurt you." Businesses understand that what they don't know can become an Achilles' heel and a source of advantage for the competition.

Think about your major. Whether it's marketing, finance, accounting, human resources management, or any of the many other specializations in a business program, you're preparing to enter the business world as a knowledge worker. Simply put, a **knowledge worker** works with and produces information as a product. According to *U.S. News & World Report* in 1994, knowledge workers in North America outnumber all other workers by a four-to-one margin.[2] Unfortunately, we couldn't find a more up-to-date reference for the same statistic, but we would imagine today that knowledge workers outnumber all other types of workers by at least a five-to-one margin.

Sure, you may work with your hands to take notes or use a mouse and keyboard to produce a spreadsheet, but what you've really done is use your mind to work with, massage, and produce more information (hopefully meaningful and useful information). Accountants generate profit and loss statements, cash flow statements, statements of retained earnings, and so on, some of which appear on paper. But you wouldn't say that an accountant produces paper any more than you would say Michelangelo was a commercial painter of churches.

In the information age, management information systems is a vitally important topic. Why? Because it deals with the coordination and use of three very important organizational resources—information, information technology, and people. Formally, we define MIS as follows:

> **Management information systems (MIS)** deals with the planning for, development, management, and use of information technology tools to help people perform all tasks related to information processing and management.

In that definition, you can find three key resources—information, information technology, and people. That is, people or knowledge workers use information technology to work with information. Indeed, if we were not in the information age, information technology would probably still be around but it wouldn't be nearly as important as it is today.

That's what this text is all about—management information systems or MIS. What you need to remember is that the sole focus of MIS is *not* technology. Technology is a set of tools that enables you to work with information. Pragmatically speaking, people and information are the most important resources within MIS, not technology. Of course, every organization today needs all three (and many others such as capital) to compete effectively in the marketplace. So don't think of this as a technology textbook, because it's not. You will read three very technology-focused chapters—Chapter 3 on databases and data warehouses, Chapter 4 on decision support systems and artificial intelligence, and Chapter 7 on technology infrastructures. But all the remaining chapters really focus on how people, information, and information technology work together to help an organization achieve a competitive advantage in the marketplace.

As we move forward in this chapter, let's first talk some more about today's exciting and dynamic market environment. Then, we'll explore information, people, and information technology as key resources. Finally, we'll address the specific roles and goals of information technology in both your life and the life of any business. It is these roles

THE GLOBAL PERSPECTIVE

CUSTOMER MOMENT OF VALUE

Canberra-Packard Canada (CPC), located in Mississauga, Ontario recognizes that managing the customer's "moment of value" is essential to quickly and appropriately responding to customers' varying needs. However, this was always a challenge, because the company specializes in distributing sophisticated scientific and laboratory equipment to clients from a wide range of areas, including government, medicine, and academia. According to president Keith Thompson, responding to individual customers' moments of value means having "the ability to understand the varied problems our customers may encounter, and provide not only the right solution, but the ongoing assistance and quick problem-solving techniques that may be needed. ..." The cornerstone of managing the customers' moment of value at CPC lies in the company's effective use of IT and in the quality of the company's knowledge workers. To better respond to customers' needs whenever and wherever these may occur, CPC has equipped all sales and service staff with laptops giving them immediate access to the CPC's databases. All field service technicians carry a laptop and a portable printer. Customer requests are electronically sent to technicians. These are then able to pull up the complete service history for the customer's instrument directly on their laptop, printing the details right at the customer's location. This kind of attention to service means that CPC has been able to equate value to more than just a low price. The company's focus on customer value has enabled it to effectively use IT and provide optimal solutions and individualized after sales care ensuring that each and every customer is fully satisfied. However, the company recognizes the importance to keep track of new technological developments. "We will continue to adopt the latest technologies within our business to provide this value in the most efficient and cost-effective way possible," Thompson says.[3]

and goals that drive our organization of this text. They also define the ways in which businesses today can and are gaining and sustaining a competitive advantage in the marketplace.

Today's Economic Environment

To be successful in business today, you have to understand and operate effectively within a dynamic, fast-paced, and changing economic environment. As you'll see later in this chapter, many businesses must undergo a sort of transformation just to stay in business and compete effectively. Other businesses remain highly competitive by continuing to innovate product and service characteristics. Whatever the case, today's economic environment is changing at a dramatic pace. As you enter today's economic environment, you must:

- Know your competition, an accomplishment sometimes known as *competitive intelligence*
- Know your customers, through tools such as customer relationship management (CRM)
- Work closely with your business partners, through tools such as supply chain management (SCM)
- Know how each and every part of your organization works together to provide its products and services

Throughout this text, we focus on all these, including many "best business practices" such as CRM and SCM and the technologies that support them. Right now, let's take an overall look at today's economic environment.

THE E.CONOMY

Electronic commerce is certainly the hottest topic in business today, and we've devoted all of Chapter 5 to it, as well as significant portions of other chapters (especially the next chapter). But what exactly is electronic commerce and what does it enable a business to do? Formally defined,

> **Electronic commerce** is commerce accelerated and enhanced by information technology, in particular the Internet. It enables customers, consumers, and companies to form powerful new relationships that would not be possible without the enabling technologies.

Electronic commerce will make winners out of some businesses and losers out of others. Indeed, most of the early dot-com companies are out of business today because of their failure to implement electronic commerce correctly. In short, you can't simply create a Web site and expect your customers to beat a virtual path to your door. You must still follow sound business principles and guidelines. That's why most of the early dot-coms failed. They ignored sound business principles and focused solely on the technology. That's a bad road to travel, and one that will undoubtedly lead to failure. Remember—information technology is indeed a key organizational resource, but it is only one of many.

Electronic commerce is giving rise to many new and innovative "best business practices," such as telecommuting and the virtual workplace (see Figure 1.1). Telecommuting and the virtual workplace go hand in hand:

> **Telecommuting** is the use of communications technologies (such as the Internet) to work in a place other than a central location.

> The **virtual workplace** is a technology-enabled workplace. No walls. No boundaries. Work anytime, anyplace, linked to other people and information you need, wherever they are.[4]

Figure 1.1
Telecommuting—Canadian Statistics[5]

Working from Home
31% of Canadians spend 20 hours or more working from home. 52% of Canadians find that the idea of working at home is either appealing or extremely appealing.
Benefits
68% of Canadians who telecommute report an improvement in overall quality of life. 57% of Canadians who telecommute report an improvement in finances. 60% of Canadians who telecommute report an improvement in standard of living. 36% of Canadians who telecommute report a positive impact on career advancements.
Telecommuting Leaders
Bell Canada: 5000 telecommuters Canadian federal government: 5000 telecommuters IBM Canada: 2300 telecommuters

Today, over 35 million people in North America telecommute, and that figure is expected to grow by 20 percent over the next several years. You may be participating in a form of telecommuting if you're taking this class via *distance learning*. Distance learning essentially enables you to learn in a virtual classroom without going to campus a couple of times of week. Of course, if you are participating in distance learning, your instructor is most probably participating in telecommuting as well. That is, he or she may be sitting at home right now sending you e-mails and leading class discussions in chat rooms.

Telecommuting is popping up in many business sectors—some make obvious sense and some may surprise you. For example, JC Penney has told its telephone service representatives who handle orders over the phone to go home and work there. In each home, JC Penney provides a computer, work space furniture, and a high-speed Internet connection. When you call the 1-800 number for JC Penney to order from its catalogue, your phone call is routed to the home of a telecommuter. The telephone service representative will answer the phone and use the Internet connection to record your order, inform you of a delivery time, and process your credit card. It makes sense when you think about it. If you're handling customer orders over the phone, all you really need is a computer with a connection to a database of product and customer information. You don't need to be sitting in a central office.

THE "NOW" ECONOMY

The "now" economy is one characterized by the immediate access customers have to the ordering of products and services. ATMs are an obvious and simple example. Using an ATM, you have access to your money any time of the day or night and just about anywhere in the world. You don't have to wait for your bank to open to cash a cheque or make a deposit. Business-to-consumer Web sites are also great examples. In the comfort of your home, apartment, or dorm, you can buy books from Amazon.com (www.amazon.com), make airline reservations (at www.aircanada.com for example, Air Canada's Web site), and purchase concert tickets from such sites as Ticketmaster (www.ticketmaster.com) or Admission (www.admission.com).

The truth is we've become a very impatient society. And we've come to expect businesses to provide us with products and services (or at a minimum the ability to order them) whenever and wherever we desire. Technology is certainly an integral facilitator here. **M-commerce**, the term used to describe electronic commerce conducted over a wireless device such as a cell phone or personal digital assistant, now gives you the ability to buy and sell stocks with your cell phone while driving down the road. And, using most Web-enabled personal digital assistants, you can bid on auctions at eBay or obtain up-to-the-minute weather forecasts.

A closely related concept is that of a wants-based economy. Some 30 years ago, people mainly purchased what they needed. Not so today. Consider these two examples. First, there's tennis shoes in which the heels light up with the pressure of each footstep. Now, how many people do you think really need tennis shoes with rear lights? Very few, if any, but if that's what they want, that's what they'll buy. A second example is that of dog bakeries, some of which even offer dog birthday cakes that range in price from $100 to $500. In reality, neither people nor dogs need to eat treats—some dog owners simply want to indulge their pets.

Why is it important to understand that you're in a wants-based economy? Because you will then realize that, while you can fairly easily forecast what your customers will need, you can't always predict what they'll want. So, the better you know your customers, the better you can determine what they might want.

TEAM WORK

I WANT IT!

Tennis shoes with lighted heels are just one of the many wants-based products that have recently surfaced. Take a walk around a mall, see how many wants-based products you can find, and then fill in the table below. Critically think about what information a business must know about its customers to identify potential buyers. Also, stay away from foods—we need very few actual food products, but our taste buds deserve variety.

Now that you've identified a few wants-based products, consider how technology could help you capture and process information relating to people who buy those products. Where would that information come from? Could you use technology to capture that information? Once you have the information, what technologies could you use to process that information?

Product	Price	Why People Want It	What Kind of People Buy It

THE GLOBAL ECONOMY

A **global economy** is one in which customers, businesses, suppliers, distributors, and manufacturers all operate without regard to physical and geographical boundaries.

Consider the table in Figure 1.2. It shows Canada's total import and export figures (in millions of Canadian dollars) from 1998 to 2000 with its top five trading partners. Notice the gradual and consistent increase in the amount of total imports to Canada. Although it's true that there are many foreign companies competing for consumer dollars in the Canadian market, Canadian export figures are also on the rise. So while foreign products and services are entering the Canadian market to an ever-greater extent, in parallel, Canadian companies are increasingly selling their goods and services to a world market of over six billion people worldwide.

You must realize that most large businesses (and even many small businesses) operate as **transnational firms**—firms that produce and sell products and services in countries all over the world. This is a substantial career opportunity for you. Think of how much better your résumé would look if you could speak a foreign language or had knowledge in subjects related to all aspects of international commerce.

THE ARRIVING DIGITAL ECONOMY

Right now, we are in the information age. But we are seeing a transition into the digital age. When we do arrive there, the **digital economy** will be one marked by the electronic movement of all types of information, including physiological information such as voice recognition and synthesization, biometrics (your retina scan and breath for example), and 3D holograms. A hologram is a three-dimensional image projected into the air. If you've ever watched *Star Trek*, then you're familiar with the *holodeck*, a sophisticated technology-based device that allows people to have virtual experiences

Figure 1.2

Total Import and Export Figures, 1998 to 2000 (millions of Canadian dollars)[6]

Canadian Imports in Billions of Dollars				Canadian Exports in Billions of Dollars			
Country	*1998*	*1999*	*2000*	*Country*	*1998*	*1999*	*2000*
United States	203.5	215.4	229.6	United States	269.9	308	359.2
Japan	14	15	16.6	Japan	8.6	8.4	9.1
United Kingdom	6.3	8.1	13	United Kingdom	4.4	4.7	5.7
Mexico	7.6	9.5	12	China and Mongolia	2.4	2.6	3.6
China and Mongolia	7.6	8.9	11.2	Germany	2.7	2.4	3.1
Germany	6	6.9	7.7	South Korea	1	1.9	2.2
Total imports (all countries)	**298.3**	**320.2**	**356.8**	**Total exports (all countries)**	**318.4**	**355**	**412.8**

without the need for today's clunky gloves, headsets, and walkers (found in current virtual reality systems).

Again, we're not there yet. But we are definitely moving in that direction. A few short years ago, pay-per-view movies and sporting events in your home were only a vision of the future. Today, they are a reality and a part of the upcoming digital economy. This represents another substantial career opportunity for you. Don't limit your thinking to the digital movement of just words, numbers, graphs, and photos. Think outside the box and envision moving all types of information electronically. For a rich and thought-provoking discussion of the future digital economy, you might want to read Chapter 9. (This isn't a novel, so reading ahead won't ruin the rest of the story for you.)

Today's economic environment is indeed unique, exciting, and full of opportunities for you. Tomorrow's economic environment will be even more exciting and holds much promise for you in your career. Are you ready to help a business use technology to gain and sustain a competitive advantage?

Information as a Key Resource

Information is important for several reasons today, two of which we've already stated. First, information is one of the three key components of management information systems along with information technology and people. Second, as we have said, we are in the "information age," a time when knowledge is power. And knowledge comes from having timely access to information and knowing what to do with it.

DATA VERSUS INFORMATION

To understand the nature of information and exactly what it is, you must first understand another term—data. **Data** are raw facts that describe a particular phenomenon. For example, the current temperature, price of a movie rental, and your age are all data. **Information** then is simply data having a particular meaning within a specific context.

For example, if you're trying to decide what to wear, the current temperature is information because it's pertinent to your decision at hand (what to wear)—the price of a movie rental, however, is not.

Information may be data that have been processed in some way or presented in a more meaningful fashion. In business, for instance, the price of a movie rental may be information to a checkout clerk, but it may represent only data to an accountant who is responsible for determining net revenues at the end of the month.

PERSONAL DIMENSIONS OF INFORMATION

As a knowledge worker, you work with and produce information. As you do, you can consider it from three points of view or dimensions—time, location, and form (see Figure 1.3).

THE TIME DIMENSION The time dimension of information encompasses two aspects—(1) having access to information when you need it and (2) having information that describes the time period you're considering. The first really deals with timeliness. Information can in fact become old and obsolete. For example, if you want to make a stock trade today, you need to know the price of the stock right now. If you have to wait a day to get stock prices, you may not survive in the turbulent securities market. It's no wonder that over one-third of all stock transactions today occur over the Internet.

The second time aspect deals with having information that describes the appropriate time period. For example, most utility companies provide you with a bill that not only tells you of your current usage and the average temperature but also compares that information with that of the previous month and perhaps the same month last year. This type of information can help you better manage your utilities or simply understand that this month's high utility bill was caused by inclement weather.

THE LOCATION DIMENSION The location dimension of information deals with having access to information no matter where you are. This simply means that you should be able to access needed information from an airplane, in a hotel room, at

Figure 1.3
Personal Dimensions of Information

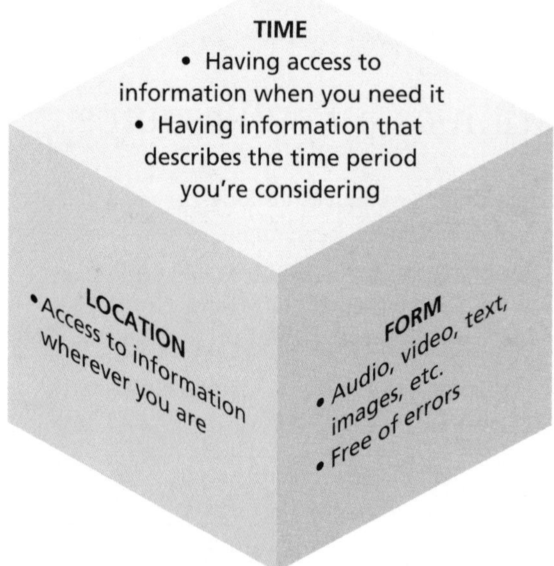

THE GLOBAL PERSPECTIVE

OVERCOMING LANGUAGE BARRIERS ON THE INTERNET

The Internet is certainly a technology that has eliminated geographical and location barriers. With almost one-sixth of the world's population having access to the Internet, "location, location, location" in the physical world is becoming less and less and less important.

However, now we have new issues to deal with, notably that of a language barrier. What happens if you connect to a site that offers information in a language you don't understand? How can you send an e-mail to someone in Japan who doesn't speak English?

One solution is language translation software. And one company leading the way in the development of language translation software is SYSTRAN. SYSTRAN Enterprise is a suite of software tools that enables you to, among other things, translate about 3700 words per minute, translate both e-mail and Web page content, and display Asian fonts.

Is it perfect? Not according to SYSTRAN's disclaimer, which says that although the software is designed to be as accurate as possible, "no automated translation is perfect nor is it intended to replace human translators. Users should note that the quality of the source text significantly affects the translations."

As you might expect, automated translation software has a particularly difficult time with idioms. When Kentucky Fried Chicken wanted to translate its slogan "finger-lickin' good" into Chinese, it came out as "eat your fingers off." Now, KFC wasn't using SYSTRAN's software, but this example does illustrate the difficulty of translating idiomatic expressions. Product names are another example. When General Motors tried to sell the Chevy Nova in South America, people didn't buy it. As it turns out, in Spanish *no va* means "it won't go." GM subsequently changed the name to Caribe for its Spanish markets.

By the way, you might want to try out the software at SYSTRAN's Web site (www.systransoft.com). There is a box into which you can type a phrase or sentence and choose the language into which you would like it translated.[7]

home, in the student centre of your campus, at work, or even driving down the road. Of course, because of the Internet you can be almost anywhere in the world and access almost any information you need.

To keep certain information private and secure while providing remote access for employees, many businesses are creating intranets. An **intranet** is an organization's internal "Internet" guarded against outside access by a special security feature called a *firewall* (which can be software, hardware, or a combination of the two). So if your organization has an intranet and you want to access information on it while away from the office, all you need is Web browser software, a modem, and the password that will allow you through the firewall.

The Canadian design company silverorange has created an award-winning intranet that you can demo at demo.silverorange.com. Employees can connect to the intranet and meet in online chat rooms, exchange documents, and discuss ongoing projects, even with employees located in remote geographical areas. While they are doing this, the firewall ensures that no one outside silverorange can gain access to the intranet-based information.

THE FORM DIMENSION The form dimension of information deals with two primary aspects. The first is simply having information in a form that is most usable and understandable by you—audio, text, video, animation, graphical, and others. The second deals with accuracy. That is, you need information that is free of errors. Think of information as you would a physical product. If you buy a product and it's defective, you become an unsatisfied customer. Likewise, if you receive information that is incorrect, you're very unhappy as well.

For all these various information dimensions, be mindful that you provide your customers with information. Information you provide to your customers should be timely, describe the appropriate time dimension, accessible from anywhere, in the most usable form, and free of errors. Information is a valuable resource and also a commodity you provide to customers. Make sure they get it the way they want it.

ORGANIZATIONAL DIMENSIONS OF INFORMATION

Even if your choice in life is to be an entrepreneur and run your own business, you also need to consider various organizational dimensions of information. These include information flows, what information describes, information granularity, and how information is used (for either mainly transaction processing or analytical processing, which we'll discuss in an upcoming section).

INFORMATION FLOWS Information in an organization flows in four basic directions—up, down, horizontally, and outward. To consider these flows, let's first briefly look at the structure of an organization. Most people view a traditional organization as a pyramid with four levels and many sides (see Figure 1.4). At the top is **strategic management**, which provides an organization with overall direction and guidance. The second level is often called **tactical management**, which develops the goals and strategies outlined by strategic management. The third level is **operational management**, which manages and directs the day-to-day operations and implementations of the goals and strategies. Finally, the fourth level of the organization comprises non-management employees who actually perform daily activities, such as order processing, developing and producing goods and services, and serving customers. If you consider your school as an example, strategic management would include the chancellor, president, and various vice-presidents. Tactical management would include the deans. Operational management would include the department chairs and directors of academic programs. The final level would include instructors who are responsible for teaching the classes.

The *upward flow of information* describes the current state of the organization on the basis of its daily transactions. When a sale occurs, for example, that information

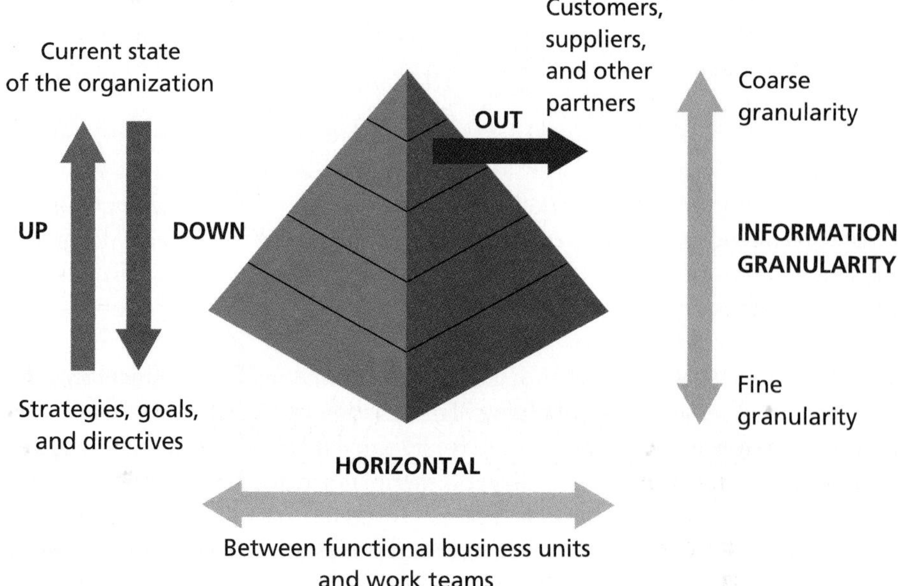

Figure 1.4
An Organization, Its Information Flows, and Information Granularity

originates at the lowest level of the organization and then is passed up through the various levels of management. Information gathered as part of everyday operations is consolidated by information technology and passed upward to decision makers who monitor and respond to problems and opportunities.

The *downward flow of information* involves the strategies, goals, and directives that originate at one level and are passed to lower levels. The *horizontal flow of information* is between functional business units and work teams. For example, at your school, various departments are responsible for scheduling courses. That information is passed horizontally to the registrar's office, which creates a course schedule for your entire campus (which may be online—timely and accessible from anywhere by you).

Finally, there is an *outward flow of information* to customers, suppliers, distributors, and other partners for the purpose of doing business. This (and its corresponding inward flow) is really what electronic commerce is all about. Today, no organization is an island, and you must ensure that your organization has the right information technology tools to communicate outwardly with all types of business partners. In a later section, and in more detail in Chapter 2, we'll discuss this outward flow of information within the context of creating business partnerships and alliances.

INFORMATION GRANULARITY Figure 1.4 also illustrates another dimension of information—granularity. **Information granularity** refers to the extent of detail within the information. On one end of this spectrum is coarse granularity, or highly summarized information. At the other end is fine granularity, or information that contains a great amount of detail. As you might guess, people on the highest levels of the organization deal mainly with a coarse granularity of information, sales by year being an example. People on the lowest levels of the organization, on the other hand, need information with fine granularity. If you consider sales again, nonmanagement employees need information in great detail that describes each transaction—when it occurred, whether by credit or cash, who made the sale, to whom the sale was made, and so on.

So, when transaction information originates at the lowest level of an organization (with fine granularity), it is consolidated to a more coarse granularity as it moves up through the organization (the upward flow of information).

WHAT INFORMATION DESCRIBES Another organizational dimension of information is what the information describes. Information can be internal, external, objective, subjective, or some combination of the four.

- **Internal information** describes specific operational aspects of the organization.
- **External information** describes the environment surrounding the organization.
- **Objective information** describes quantifiably something that is known.
- **Subjective information** attempts to describe something that is unknown.

Consider a bank that faces the decision of what interest rate to offer on a CD. That bank will use internal information (how many customers it has who can afford to buy a CD), external information (what other banks are offering), objective information (what today's prime interest rate is), and subjective information (what the prime interest rate is expected to be several months down the road). As well, what other banks are offering is an example of not only external information (it describes the surrounding environment) but also objective information (it is quantifiably known).

As a general rule, people on the lowest levels of the organization deal mainly with internal and objective information (the price of a movie rental is an example). People on the highest levels of the organization, on the other hand, deal with all types of information.

MICHAEL DELL PREACHES IMMEDIATE INFORMATION ACCESS

We can all learn a lot from Michael Dell, CEO and founder of Dell Computer. In the mid-1980s, Michael couldn't even wait to get out of college to start his own direct-sales computer business. In the 18 years since he started that small operation in his dorm room, Dell Computer has definitely become the market leader, with over $30 billion in revenues in 2001.

Speaking to a group of entrepreneurs recently, Michael had this to say about the importance of timely information: "One of the great things about our business is that we have immediate information; we don't have to wait a week or a month. We get information every day, so that I know that yesterday we sold 77,850 computers. I know it by customer type, by product type, by geography, and what the mix was. So that immediacy of information is incredibly valuable to everything in our business, because it's changing very, very rapidly. We just continue to shrink the time and space and distance between our customers and our suppliers and make that as efficient as we can. We're down to about three to four days of inventory now. We get deliveries every two hours based on what we just sold. You take out the guessing."

That's a powerful set of statements; look closely at them. By having access to timely information, Dell Computer is able to carry only three to four days of inventory. That's remarkable when you compare it to the industry standard of about 45 days. Businesses in the technology sector cannot afford to carry 45 days' worth of inventory when you consider the rapid speed at which technology is changing.

Notice also that timely information takes out the guesswork for Dell. If your business is guessing to determine its next move, you won't be in business very long. Perhaps it's time to get timely information.[8]

People as a Key Resource

The single most important resource in any organization is its people. People (knowledge workers) set goals, carry out tasks, make decisions, serve customers, and, in the case of IT specialists, provide a stable and reliable technology environment so the organization can run smoothly and gain a competitive advantage in the marketplace. This discussion is all about you. You're preparing to be a knowledge worker.

INFORMATION AND TECHNOLOGY LITERACY

In a business environment, your most valuable asset is *not* technology but rather your *mind*. IT is simply a set of tools that help you work with and process information, but it's really just a *mind support* tool set. Technology such as spreadsheet can help you quickly create a high-quality and revealing graph. But it can't tell you whether you should build a bar or pie graph and it can't help you determine whether you should show sales by territory or sales by salesperson. Those are your tasks and that's why your business curriculum includes classes in human resources management, accounting, finance, marketing, and perhaps production and operations management.

Nonetheless, technology is an important set of tools for you. Technology can help you be more efficient and can help you dissect and better understand problems and opportunities. So, it's important for you to learn how to use your technology set. And it's equally important that you understand the information to which you're applying your technology tools.

A **technology-literate knowledge worker** is a person who knows how and when to apply technology. The "how" aspect includes knowing what technology to buy, how to exploit the many benefits of application software, and what technology infra-

POLAROID IS POLAR-PEOPLE

People are really the most important resource in any organization, no matter how big or small and no matter in what industry. People possess *intellectual capital*, and intellectual capital is what enables an organization to innovate.

At Polaroid, film isn't the most important asset—it's simply the product produced. The most important asset are the scientists who know everything about the chemistry of film. So Polaroid has created a very sophisticated model of its hiring requirements.

The model first combines employee-turnover information with forecasts and known trends of its current workforce. For example, Polaroid forecasts probable retirement dates of every scientist and estimates how many people in each given skill area will leave within the next decade.

That information is then used extensively in the interviewing and hiring processes. Where Polaroid sees an intellectual capital vacancy upcoming in the next several years, it focuses its hiring efforts.

How many businesses do you believe have such an elaborate system for hiring new employees?[9]

structure is required to get businesses connected to each other, to name just a few. If you've had a class that deals with learning personal productivity software, then you already know the benefits of application software. In this text, we want to help you decide what technology an organization needs (if any) and how best to use it to support organizational goals and achieve a competitive advantage. If you can do that, then you'll truly be a technology-literate knowledge worker.

In many unfortunate cases, people and organizations have blindly decided to use technology to help solve some sort of business problem. What you need to understand is that technology is not a panacea. You can't simply apply technology to any given process and expect that process to instantly become more efficient and effective. Look at it this way—if you apply technology to a process that doesn't work correctly, then you'll only be doing things wrong millions of times faster. There are cases when technology is not the solution. Being a technology-literate knowledge worker will help you determine when and when not to apply technology.

Information-literate knowledge workers:

- Can define what information they need
- Know how and where to obtain that information
- Understand the information once they receive it
- Can act appropriately on the basis of the information to help the organization achieve the greatest advantage

Consider a unique, real-life example of an information-literate knowledge worker.

Several years ago, a manager of a retail store on the East Coast received some interesting information—diaper sales on Friday evening accounted for a large percentage of total sales for the week. Most people in this situation would immediately jump to the conclusion to make sure that diapers are always well stocked on Friday evening or run a special on diapers during that time to increase sales, but not our information-literate knowledge worker. She first looked at the information and decided it was not complete. That is, she needed more information before she could act.

She decided the information she needed was why a rash of diaper sales (pardon the pun) occurred during that time and who was buying them. That information was not stored within the store's computer system, so she stationed an employee in the diaper aisle on Friday evening who recorded any pertinent information to the situation (i.e., she knew how and where to obtain information). The store manager learned that young businessmen purchased the most diapers on Friday evening. Apparently, they had been instructed to buy the weekend supply of diapers on their way home from work. Her response was to stock premium domestic and imported beer near the diapers. Since then, Friday evening is a big sale time not only for diapers but also for premium domestic and imported beer.

The store manager's information-literate knowledge—her ability to define what information she needed, know how and where to obtain that information, and understand the meaning of the information once she received it—enabled her to determine that diapers and premium beer were complementary products for most young businessmen. Would you have made that connection? By the way, this is an example of a wants-based economic environment. While diapers are a very necessary product (just ask any parent), premium beer is a wants-based product.

YOUR ETHICAL RESPONSIBILITIES

Your roles as a technology-literate and information-literate knowledge worker extend far beyond using technology and information to gain an advantage in the marketplace for your organization. You must also consider your social responsibilities—this is where ethics becomes important. **Ethics** are the principles and standards that guide our behaviour toward other people. Ethics are different from laws. Laws either require or prohibit some sort of action on your part. Ethics are more of a matter of personal interpretation, and thus have a right and wrong outcome according to different people. Consider the following examples:

1. Copying software you purchased, making copies for your friends, and charging them for the copies
2. Making an extra backup of your software just in case both the copy you are using and the primary backup fail for some reason
3. Giving out the phone numbers of your friends and family, without their permission, to a provider of some sort of calling plan so you can receive a discount

Each of these is either ethically or legally incorrect. In the second example, you may have been ethically correct in making an extra backup copy (because you didn't share it with anyone), but according to most software licences you're prohibited by law to make more than one backup copy.

To help you better understand the relationship between ethical and legal acts (or the opposite), consider Figure 1.5. The graph is composed of four quadrants and you

Figure 1.5

Acting Ethically and Legally[10]

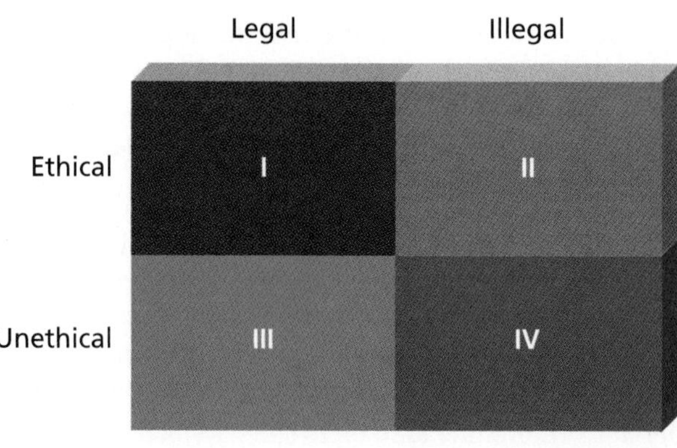

ON YOUR OWN

E-MAIL: ELECTRONIC MAIL OR EXPENSIVE MAIL?

In February 1995, an employee at Chevron came across what he thought was an interesting and funny list—"25 Reasons Why Beer Is Better Than Women." He quickly logged into his e-mail and distributed the list to many people. The only problem was that one of the people who received the e-mail was a woman, and she was offended by it. What followed was a lot of legal mumbo jumbo and an eventual out-of-court settlement worth $2 million that Chevron had to pay to the offended employee—definitely an example of when e-mail becomes expensive mail.

Most people agree that the original sender should not have distributed the list. It was mail that was potentially embarrassing and offensive to some people and, therefore, should not have been distributed as a matter of ethics. What people don't agree on, however, is whether or not the company was at fault for not monitoring and stopping the potentially offensive mail. What are your thoughts? Before you decide, follow the accompanying diagram and consider the consequences of your answers.[11]

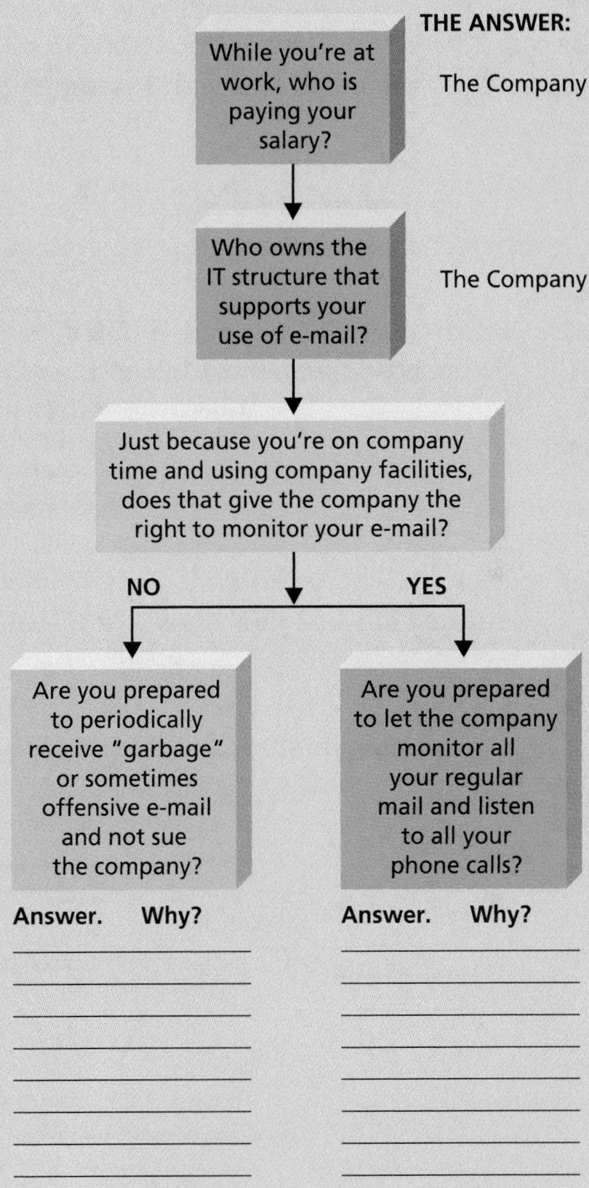

always want your actions to remain in quadrant I. If all your actions fall in that quadrant, you'll always be acting legally and ethically, and this in a socially responsible way.

In business, the question of ethics is an overriding concern because of the widespread use of IT to capture information. For example, if a business invests money to capture information about you as you make a purchase, does that information then belong to the business or do you still have privacy rights regarding its distribution?

Being socially and ethically responsible not only includes the actions you undertake yourself but also dealing with the actions of others, which may involve protecting yourself against cyber-crimes. Hackers are one group of people who commit cyber-crimes. A **hacker** is a very knowledgeable person who uses his or her knowledge to invade other people's computers. There are actually many types of hackers today—white-hat hackers, black-hat hackers, crackers, hacktivists, and script bunnies. Each has different motives and each is largely a different group of people. To protect yourself and your organization from their hacking, you need to understand who they are and what they do. We explore hackers in more detail in Chapter 8.

People, again, are the most valuable resource in any organization. People, like you as a knowledge worker, use IT to work with and massage information. The most successful people understand their information and information processing needs, and they understand the benefits of technology and know how to use technology to facilitate their working with information.

Information Technology as a Key Resource

Within management information systems (MIS), the third key resource is information technology. Formally defined, **information technology (IT)** is any computer-based tool that people use to work with information and support the information and information processing needs of an organization. So IT includes a cell phone or PDA that you might use to obtain stock quotes, your home computer that you use to write term papers, large networks that businesses use to connect to other businesses, and the Internet that almost one in every six people in the world currently use.

KEY TECHNOLOGY CATEGORIES

There are two basic categories of technology—hardware and software (see Figure 1.6). **Hardware** is the physical devices that make up a computer (often referred to as a *computer system*). **Software** is the set of instructions that your hardware executes to carry out a specific task for you. So, if you have a Nintendo GameCube, the GameCube box itself and the controller are hardware devices, while the games you play are software. Let's briefly look at hardware and software; for a more thorough discussion, read Extended Learning Module C.

TECHNOLOGY HARDWARE

All hardware falls into one of six categories—input devices, output devices, storage devices, telecommunications devices, CPU and RAM, and connecting devices. Here's a quick summary.

- An **input device** is a tool you use to capture information and commands; input devices include such tools as a keyboard, mouse, touch screen, game controller, barcode reader, and skimmer (used for swiping credit cards and the like).
- An **output device** is a tool you use to see, hear, or otherwise accept the results of your information processing requests. Output devices include such tools as a printer, monitor, and set of speakers.
- A **storage device** is a tool you use to store information for use at a later time. Output devices include such tools as a floppy disk, hard disk, CD, and DVD.
- A **telecommunications device** is a tool you use to send information to and receive it from another person or location. For example, if you connect to the Internet using a modem, the modem (which could be a telephone, DSL, cable, wireless, or satellite modem) is a telecommunications device.

Figure 1.6

Information Technology Hardware and Software

Description	Examples
Hardware: The Physical Devices That Make Up a Computer	
Input device—tool you use to capture information and commands	• Keyboard, mouse • Touch screen, game controller • Barcode reader, skimmer
Output device—tool you use to see, hear, or otherwise accept the results of your information processing requests	• Printer • Monitor • Set of speakers
Storage device—tool you use to store information for use at a later time	• Floppy disk • Hard disk • CD, DVD
Central processing unit (CPU)—the actual hardware that interprets the software instructions and coordinates how all the other hardware devices work together	• Pentium 4 • AMD Athlon XP Thunderbird
RAM (random access memory)—temporary memory that holds information, application software, and operating system software	• Many manufacturers make RAM that will fit in a variety of computers
Telecommunications device—tool you use to send information to and receive it from another person or location	• Telephone modem • DSL modem • Cable modem • Microwave • Satellite
Connecting devices—tools that connect devices to each other	• Printer cord • Parallel and serial ports
Software—The Set of Instructions That Your Hardware Executes to Carry Out a Specific Task	
Application software—software that enables you to solve specific problems or perform specific tasks	• Word processing software • Payroll software • Spreadsheet software • Inventory management software
Operating system software—system software that controls your application software and manages how your hardware devices work together	• Windows XP • Windows 2000 • Windows Me • Mac OS • Linux • UNIX
Utility software—software that provides additional functionality to your operating system	• Antivirus software • Screensaver • Disk optimization software • Uninstaller software

- The **central processing unit (CPU)** is the actual hardware that interprets and executes the software instructions and coordinates how all the other hardware devices work together. Popular personal CPUs include the Pentium 4 and AMD Athlon XP Thunderbird. **RAM**, or **random access memory**, is temporary storage that holds the information you're working with, the application software you're using, and the operating system software you're using. Together, the CPU and RAM make up the "brains" of your computer.
- *Connecting devices* include such things as parallel ports into which you would connect a printer, connector cords to connect your printer to the parallel port, and internal connecting devices that mainly include buses over which information travels from one device such as the CPU to RAM.

That may be the shortest overview of hardware you've ever read. If you need more detail, please read the Extended Learning Module C on hardware and software.

TECHNOLOGY SOFTWARE

There are two main types of software—application and system. **Application software** enables you to solve specific problems or perform specific tasks. Microsoft Word, for example, can help you write term papers, so it's application software. From an organizational perspective, payroll software, collaborative software such as videoconferencing, and inventory management software are all examples of application software.

System software handles tasks specific to technology management and coordinates the interaction of all technology devices. Within system software, you'll find operating system software and utility software. **Operating system software** is system software that controls your application software and manages how your hardware devices work together. Popular personal operating system software includes Microsoft Windows XP, Microsoft Windows Me, Mac OS X (for Apple computers), and Linux (an open source operating system).

Utility software provides additional functionality to your operating system. It includes antivirus software, screensavers, disk optimization software, uninstaller software (for properly removing unwanted software), and a host of others. Again, in Extended Learning Module C we discuss software in greater detail.

DECENTRALIZED COMPUTING AND SHARED INFORMATION

All organizations use hardware and software to connect people to each other, reach out to customers, distributors, suppliers, and business partners, and to provide a reliable and stable computing environment for smooth operations. Because so many people perform so many different tasks within a business environment, the concepts of decentralized computing and shared information are very important (see Figure 1.7).

Decentralized computing is an environment in which an organization splits computing power and locates it in functional business areas as well as on the desktops of knowledge workers. This is possible because of the proliferation of less expensive, more powerful, and smaller systems including notebooks, desktops, minicomputers, and servers. The Internet is a great example of a decentralized computing environment. You use your computer or perhaps cell phone or PDA to access the information and services of host computers on the Internet. In this case, your computer is called a *client computer*, while the host computers are referred to as *server computers*.

ON YOUR OWN

IDENTIFYING HARDWARE AND SOFTWARE

Pick up a recent copy of your local newspaper or perhaps a computer magazine such as *PC Magazine* or *Wired* and find an ad for a personal computer system. What is the price of the complete system? What hardware devices does it include and to which of the six hardware categories does each belong? What software does it include? Which software, if any, is application software? Which software, if any, is operating system software? Which software, if any, is utility software?

Now compare that system to a similar one that you can find on the Internet (you might want to start at Dell at www.dell.com). Which is cheaper? Does this surprise you? Why or why not?

Shared information is an environment in which an organization's information is organized in one central location, allowing anyone to access and use it as they need to. Shared information enables people in the sales department, for example, to access work-in-progress manufacturing information to determine when products will be available to ship. At your school, the registrar's office can access the information within the financial aid office to determine how much of your tuition bill is covered by a scholarship or loan. To support shared information, most businesses organize information in the form of a database. In fact, databases have become the standard by which businesses organize their information and provide everyone access to it. We've devoted all of Chapter 3 to databases as well as data warehouses, tools for organizing information to support decision-making tasks.

Now that we've provided you with a brief overview of information technology, let's look specifically at the roles and goals of information technology in any business. IT is an essential enabler of business operations. In the information age, all businesses need technology as tools for working with information.

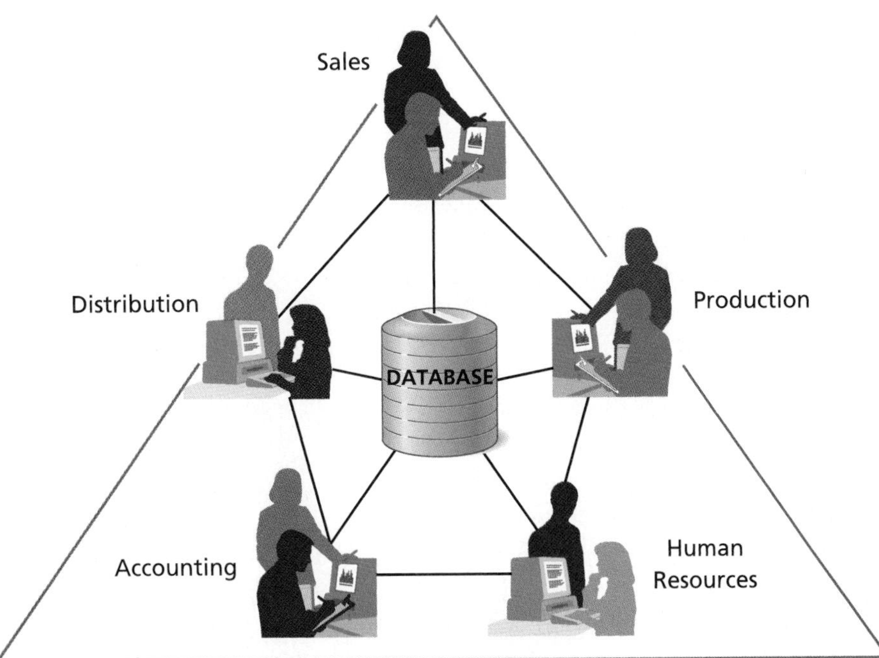

Figure 1.7
Decentralized Computing and Shared Information

Roles and Goals of Information Technology

The roles and goals of information technology are many and varied. Here we introduce you to six important roles and goals. And we will constantly refer back to these throughout the chapter. So they're not only important to learn so you can do well on an exam; they will also help you better organize your view of technology within an organization. The six major roles and goals of information technology include (see Figure 1.8):

1. Increase employee productivity
2. Enhance decision making
3. Improve team collaboration
4. Create business partnerships and alliances

Figure 1.8
The Roles and Goals of Information Technology

Role/Goal	IT Tool Examples	Business Benefits Examples
1. Increase employee productivity	• OLTP • TPS • CIS	• Reduce time • Reduce errors • Reduce costs • Enable customers to process their own transactions
2. Enhance decision making	• OLAP • DSS • GIS • EIS • AI • Data warehouses	• Generate alternatives • Recommend solutions • Drill down through information
3. Improve team collaboration	• WSS • Groupware	• Manage knowledge within the organization • Support geographically dispersed teams • Facilitate communications • Develop applications quickly
4. Create business partnerships and alliances	• IOS • EDI	• Manage supply chains • Share expertise and intellect • Enable B2B e-commerce
5. Enable global reach	• Internet • Translation phones	• Take advantage of a cheaper/larger workforce • Advertise locally made • Tap into global intellectual expertise
6. Facilitate organizational transformation	• Just about any technology you can name, depending on its use	• Stay competitive • Offer new customer interfaces • Enter new markets

5. Enable global reach
6. Facilitate organizational transformation

INCREASE EMPLOYEE PRODUCTIVITY

The original and still most fundamental role of information technology is to increase productivity. In short, because of its great speed and ability to store and process massive amounts of information accurately, IT can greatly reduce the time, errors, and costs associated with processing information in a variety of ways.

For example, if you have an automated payroll system, it can process payroll sheets and generate cheques more quickly than if you were doing it by hand. If your employees can submit time cards and expense reimbursement sheets electronically as opposed to submitting handwritten documents, then the likelihood of an error occurring is reduced. And when you decrease processing times and errors, you decrease costs. When you use technology to process transaction information, it's called **online transaction processing (OLTP)**—the gathering of input information, processing that information, and updating existing information to reflect the gathered and processing information.

IT systems such as our payroll example are called transaction processing systems. A **transaction processing system (TPS)** processes transactions that occur within an organization. Today, we pretty well accept these as rather dull and mundane. But your customers see them differently. If your TPSs don't process information correctly or don't work at all because of a computer outage, your customers may choose to do business with one of your competitors. Indeed, if you call an airline to make a reservation and you're informed that the computers don't work and your reservation cannot be processed, you may call another airline.

A vitally important hybrid of a TPS is a customer-integrated system. A **customer-integrated system (CIS)** is an extension of a TPS that places technology in the hands of an organization's customers and allows them to process their own transactions (see Figure 1.9). ATMs are a good example of a CIS. ATMs provide you with the ability to do your own banking anywhere at anytime. What's really interesting is that ATMs actually do nothing "new," but they give you greater flexibility in accessing and using your money. CISs further decentralize computing power in an organization by placing that power in the hands of customers.

The Web is full of examples of customer-integrated systems. When you use any Web site that allows you to order and pay for products and services, you're using a CIS. Customer-integrated systems are the new popular IT system today. You can use a CIS to scan your groceries, pay for fuel at the pump instead of going inside, and perhaps even register for classes online. When you enter the business world, first make sure your transaction processing systems work correctly and all the time. Then, try to convert them to customer-integrated systems. It's a win-win situation for your organizations and your customers.

ENHANCE DECISION MAKING

The counterpart to online transaction processing is **online analytical processing (OLAP)**—the manipulation of information to support decision making. And IT can definitely play a significantly role here. Some decisions are easy to make. If you're deciding what to wear to school, you'll look at today's weather forecast and decide whether to wear shorts and a T-shirt or perhaps a sweatshirt and pants. However, deciding what to major in or which job to accept upon graduation is

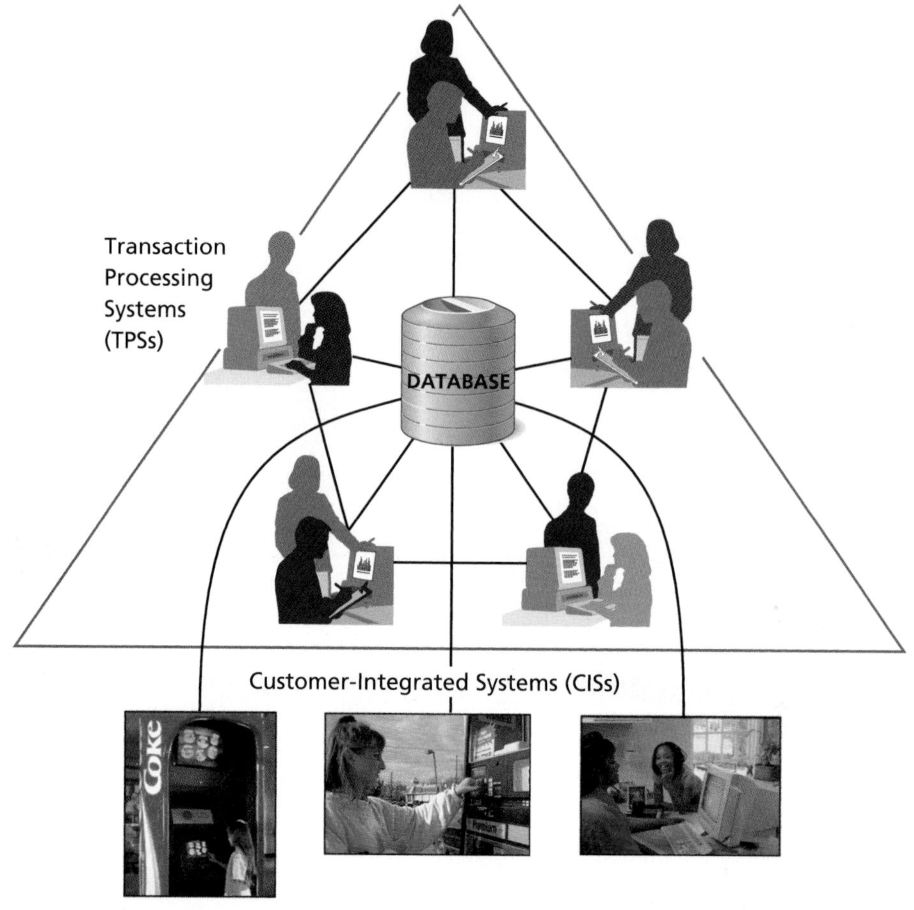

Figure 1.9
Transaction Processing and Customer-Integrated Systems

much more difficult. Likewise, in business, deciding how many inventory units to reorder is relatively simple, while deciding where to build a new distribution centre is not.

Technology to support decision making falls into one of two general categories—(1) those that help you analyze a situation and then leave the decision entirely up to you including decision support systems, executive information systems, and geographic information systems and (2) those that actually make some sort of recommendation concerning what to do. The first category includes such IT tools as decision support systems, executive information systems, and geographic information systems. For example, an **executive information system (EIS)** is a highly interactive IT system that allows you to first view highly summarized information and then choose how you would like to see greater detail, which may alert you to potential problems or opportunities. In Figure 1.10, you can see three graphs which might appear in an EIS. The first one of the left shows sales by year. By clicking on a particular, year, you can then view sales by territory for that year. Then, by clicking on a particular territory, you can view sales by product line for that territory within a given year. These types of IT systems really offer you just great speed in massaging information, developing alternatives, and viewing information from various perspectives. However, they do not make recommendations concerning what you should do.

The second category includes technologies in the area of artificial intelligence. **Artificial intelligence (AI)** is the science of making machines imitate human thinking and behaviour. For example, a **neural network** is an artificial intelligence which is capable of learning to differentiate patterns. Your credit card company probably uses

Figure 1.10

Drilling Down with an Executive Information System

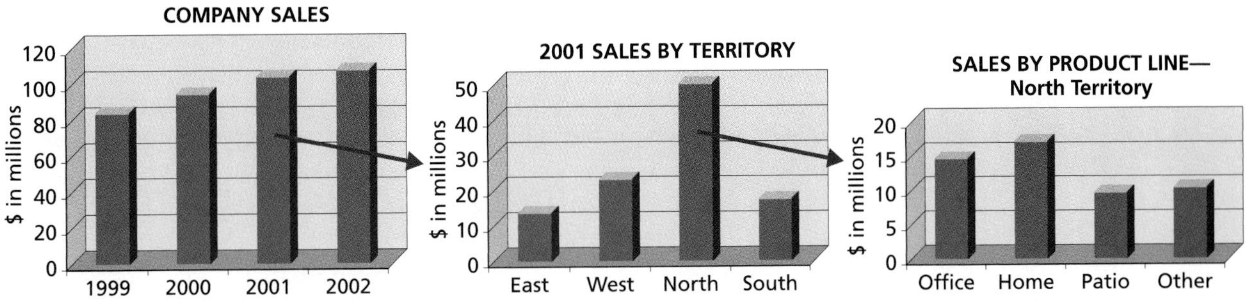

a neural network to monitor your card use and identify potential fraud if someone else happens to steal your card and attempt to use it. In this instance, the neural network has been fed every single credit card transaction you've performed, and it's developed a pattern of how, when, and why you use your card. Then, when a transaction occurs that doesn't fit the pattern of your profile, the neural networks alerts someone that your credit card may have been stolen.

We explore technology support for decision making throughout this text and specifically in Chapter 4.

IMPROVE TEAM COLLABORATION

Teams would certainly be characterized as a "best business practice" today. The adage "Two heads are better than one" does hold true. Of course, teams in the business world are often composed of more than two people with many being spread all over the globe, and that's why information technology plays such an important role in team collaboration. Collaboration-enabling technologies such as chat rooms, the Internet in general, and workgroup support systems are all fundamental to the success of a team.

A **workgroup support system (WSS)** is a system designed specifically to improve the performance of teams by supporting the sharing and flow of information. The foundation of any workgroup support system is **groupware**—the popular term for the software component that supports the collaborative efforts of a team. Popular groupware suites include Lotus/Notes Domino, Microsoft Exchange, Novell GroupWise, and NetSys WebWare.

Groupware contains software components for supporting the following three team functions:

1. Team dynamics—communications among team members and the facilitation and execution of meetings. Specific technologies that support team dynamics include group scheduling software, electronic meeting software, videoconferencing software, and whiteboard software.
2. Document management—a **group document database** that acts as a powerful storage facility for organizing and managing all documents related to specific teams. Most group document database employ multiple levels of security, allowing some teams to access the information of other teams. In these databases, you can store and search information of all kinds—text, graphs, images, audio clips, and even videos.
3. Applications development—facilities that allow a team to develop unique applications quickly, so the teams can literally "get to work."

SPAR AEROSPACE LAUNCHES INFORMATION-SHARING INTRANET

Spar Aerospace, with its major sites in Brampton, Ontario and Sainte-Anne-de-Bellevue, Quebec has opted for an intranet solution to facilitate information sharing between different business units. Each site is dedicated to different product lines (i.e., telerobotics/Canadarm in Ontario and satellites/satellites subsystems in Quebec). Before intranets were introduced, collaboration was difficult. Each site maintained different libraries focused on specific disciplines and on serving the needs of a specific client base. Document sharing between sites was complicated because of incompatible document formats. In early 1995, Spar's management realized that the Internet and the World Wide Web allowed the sharing of numerous files of various formats. Consequently, the company decided to adopt an "internal Internet" solution—as Spar's management called it. The goal became to implement an integrated system giving employees companywide accessibility to the libraries' collections and to other useful information.

Today, when users within the Spar firewall type "biblio.spar.ca," a graphical menu appears offering a choice between the Ontario or the Quebec site. Clicking on either of these links leads the user to a listing of all information available at that site. Furthermore, conferencing capabilities have been added enabling engineering staff at either site to share various data and exchange project information with others.[12]

All of these technology-based tools and many more enable teams to work effectively, even when their members are geographically dispersed. Teams, as you'll learn in later chapters, are vitally important to the success of any organization. But concepts such as the virtual workplace and telecommuting are almost contradictory to the success of teams. If you consider even further that today's economy is a global one, any given team may be composed of people all over the world. In this case, technology, and specifically groupware, is an essential enabler of team innovation.

We'll talk more about the technologies that support team collaboration throughout this text and especially in Chapter 4. Your career opportunity lies in learning how to work effectively in a team environment. Many of your classes in school will probably require that you work in teams; the reason is because teams are such an important part of the business world.

CREATE BUSINESS PARTNERSHIPS AND ALLIANCES

Each and every business contains unique and strategically sensitive expertise and intellect. Wal-Mart, for example, is a premier retailer of home and family products such as clothing. Vanity Fair, on the other hand, is a premier manufacturer of clothing including Lee and Wrangler jeans. So these two organizations have created a strong and highly successful business partnership.

When a customer buys a pair of Wrangler jeans at a Wal-Mart store on a Wednesday, for example, that information is sent that night to Vanity Fair, via computer of course. If Vanity Fair has a replacement pair in stock, it's immediately sent out on Thursday and arrives at Wal-Mart on Saturday. Three days for inventory replenishment is an outstanding feat, and would not be possible without the use of technology.

But speed isn't the only advantage. Vanity Fair's market-response system also takes the guesswork out of reordering and provides retailers with only the best-selling styles and lines. Vanity Fair's extended market response system will even analyze the sales databases of retailers and determine groups of products—for instance, matching jeans, shirts, and jackets—to help retailers forecast ideal inventory supply levels. As you can

TEAM WORK

FINDING BUSINESS PARTNERS AND ALLIANCES ON THE WEB

Like any other type of business, no dot-com on the Web can be an island. Indeed, dot-coms have determined that they must develop business partners on the Web. These partnerships manifest themselves in many different ways. One such way is through a **banner ad**—a small ad on one Web site that advertises the products and services of another business, usually another dot-com.

Visit the Web and go exploring. Find five Web sites on which banner ads appear. Which Web sites did you find with banner ads? For what business was each ad? Did you find any Web sites with more than one? If so, which sites? Now wait a day and visit the same five sites. Did any of the banner ads change? If so, why do you think they changed?

see, business partnerships and alliances enable each participating organization to tap into the intellectual capital of the other participating organizations.

This type of business partnership is enabled by interorganizational systems and is form of business to business (B2B) e-commerce. An **interorganizational system (IOS)** automates the flow of information between organizations to support the planning, design, development, production, and delivery of products and services. A typical IOS includes **electronic data interchange (EDI)**—the direct computer-to-computer transfer of transaction information contained in standard business documents, such as invoices and purchase orders, in a standard format. In short, EDI replaces paper documents with digital records exchanged between business partnerships' computers. R. J. Reynolds uses EDI to order materials from its suppliers. In doing so, R. J. Reynolds has been able to cut order processing costs from $75 per order (using paper) to only 93 cents using EDI.

EDI is becoming so important that most large businesses won't do business with your business if you don't support EDI. For example, General Motors will only order raw materials and parts from suppliers who support EDI capabilities.

Another important concept related to EDI is electronic funds transfer (EFT). EFT allows organizations to complete the full transaction without physically sending anything, including the payment. So EDI supports the electronic transfer of information such as sales invoice, and EFT supports the electronic transfer of the monies to pay the sales invoice amount. Just as EDI is becoming a common business practice, so is EFT. Think about filing your income tax returns electronically. It doesn't make much sense to file the paperwork and then still have to send a personal cheque or receive a refund cheque from the federal government.

ENABLE GLOBAL REACH

As we've already stated, you can characterize today's operating environment as one of a global economy. Because of technology, you now have the ability to market your products and services in countries all over the world and develop partnerships and alliances (which we just discussed) with other businesses throughout the globe. Not only can you do this, you *must* to be successful in the long run. Think about Honda cars for a moment, considered by most people to be manufactured in Japan, its "country" headquarters. Honda actually produces more cars outside than inside Japan. Not only that—Honda exports more cars from the United States than General Motors, Ford, or Chrysler.

A business can gain significant advantages by enabling global reach through technology. It can take advantage of a cheaper and larger workforce; many businesses in

North America locate their back-end office functions (accounting and the like) in Ireland for this reason. It can also tap into the intellectual expertise of a workforce in another country. Many North American software publishers actually write and produce much of their software in such countries as India and Pakistan.

To operate effectively using global reach, businesses must use technology to overcome the barriers of time and location. One simple example is that of translation phones. AT&T is currently perfecting a translation phone that will allow you to call anywhere in the world and use your native language for speaking while the person on the other end hears your speech in his or her native tongue. In between is a powerful automatic speech recognition system that captures your speech, converts it into another language digitally, and then synthesizes the speech in that language to the person on the other end of the line. There are also utilities on the Web that translate Web pages from one language to another.

To also operate effectively using global reach, you must consider the culture of other countries. **Culture** is the collective personality of a nation or society, encompassing language, traditions, currency, religion, history, music, and acceptable behaviour, among other things. For example, in many countries around the world workers take extended breaks at lunch well into the afternoon hours. So you shouldn't schedule a virtual team meeting during those particular hours. It's a simple example, but it does illustrate the fact that you have to consider the culture, in this case the work hours, of your various team members.

FACILITATE ORGANIZATIONAL TRANSFORMATION

And last, but certainly not least, information technology plays a critical role in facilitating organizational transformation. Organizational transformation is necessary to respond to the ever-changing needs (and wants) of today's marketplace. But organizational transformation doesn't have to be like going from a cocoon to a beautiful butterfly (one of nature's most dramatic and wonderful transformations). Businesses today can undergo a transformation by simply changing the way they deliver their products and services.

Consider Blockbuster Video—it has recently undergone one transformation (renting video games as opposed to just movies) and is in the middle of another. Blockbuster has created a business partnership with many cable TV services. Through a cable TV service, Blockbuster is now offering pay-per-view movies. So you don't have to go to a Blockbuster store to rent a video—you can order it from the comfort of your own home for about the same price. Not only that, once you order a movie, you can typically watch it several times within 24 hours.

This transformation for Blockbuster lies in changing how it delivers its products to you. Even more importantly, Blockbuster realizes that pay-per-view movies is the wave of the future, not going to a store to rent a video. Don't be surprised if, in ten years, you can't find a local video rental store. Of course, technology played a key role in Blockbuster's transformation. Without enabling network technologies and large servers that digitally store videos, Blockbuster would have no way of offering pay-per-view service.

Every business today must be willing to change, sometimes in minor ways but often in dramatic and "knee-breaking" ways. Just ask the folks at Kmart. At one point in time, it was considered to be a premier discount retailer. But it failed to transform itself to meet the changing desires of the market, and Kmart filed for bankruptcy in 2002.

As we study business transformations in this text, you'll learn about some information technologies, including enterprise software and object-oriented technologies. As you learn about them, don't focus too much on the technology itself. Instead, focus on how businesses can use those technology to enable organizational transformation.

NOKIA—FROM PAPER, TO RUBBER, TO CELL PHONES AND TELECOMMUNICATIONS

The Nokia Company began over 150 years ago as a producer of paper. In 1967, the Nokia Corporation was formed, through a merger of the Nokia Company (paper), Finnish Rubber Works (rubber), and Finnish Cable Works (telecommunications cables).

As Nokia moved through the remainder of the 1960s, all of the 1970s, and into the 1980s, it saw huge possibilities in the wire-free telephone market. By transforming itself and focusing its energies in that area, Nokia produced the original and first hand-portable telephone in 1987.

You probably know the rest of the story. Today, Nokia is regarded as the premier innovator and manufacturer of cell phones. And it hasn't forgotten its past. For example, while producing rubber as a primary product, Nokia was the first to manufacture and sell brightly coloured rubber boots (you might as well be in fashion while as work). So it's no surprise that Nokia innovated the multicoloured, clip-on facias that literally made cell phones an overnight fashion sensation.

Businesses don't have to go out of business just because the products they manufacture are no longer needed in our society. If your business finds itself in a shrinking market, be bold and innovative. Undertake some sort of dramatic organizational transformation. Nokia went from a premier manufacturer of rubber boots to the world's leading provider of cell phones in less than 15 years. That's a rather dramatic organizational transformation, wouldn't you say?[13]

Summary: Student Learning Outcomes Revisited

1. **Describe the information age and the role of knowledge workers within it.** The **information age** is a time when knowledge is power. That is to say, what you don't know can in fact hurt you and put you out of business. A **knowledge worker**, in the information age, works with and produces information as a product.
2. **Define management information systems (MIS). Management information systems (MIS)** deals with the planning for, development, management, and use of information technology tools to help people perform all tasks related to information processing and management. MIS includes three key resources—information, information technology, and people.
3. **Describe key factors shaping today's economic environment.** Key factors shaping today's economic environment include:
   - The "e.conomy"—characterized by **electronic commerce**, which is commerce accelerated and enhanced by information technology, in particular, the Internet
   - The "Now" economy—immediate access customers have to the ordering of products and services
   - The **global economy**—in which customers, businesses, suppliers, distributors, and manufacturers all operate without regard to physical and geographical boundaries
   - The arriving **digital economy**—the electronic movement of all types of information, not limited to numbers, words, graphs, and photos but including physiological information such as voice recognition and synthesization
4. **Validate information as a key resource and describe both personal and organizational dimensions of information.** Information is not only one of the three key components of management information systems (MIS), we are also in the "information" age, a time when knowledge is power. The personal and organizational dimensions of information include:
   - Personal

- Time—access to information when you need it and information that describes the time period you're considering
- Location—access to information no matter where you are
- Form—information in a form that is most usable and understandable (audio, text, video, animation, graphical, and others) and information that is free of errors
- Organizational
- Information flows—up, down, horizontally, and outward with respect to an organization
- Granularity—the extent of detail within information
- What information describes—**internal** (specific operational aspects of the organization), **external** (the environment surrounding the organization), **objective** (quantifiably describing something that is known), and **subjective** (attempting to describe something that is unknown)

5. **Define how people are the most important organizational resource, their information and technology literacy challenges, and their ethical responsibilities.** People are the single most important resource in any organization, setting goals, carrying out tasks, and making decisions.
   - Technology-literate knowledge workers are people who know how and when to apply technology.
   - Information-literate knowledge workers (1) can define what information they need, (2) know how and where to obtain that information, (3) understand the information once they receive it, and (4) can act appropriately on the basis of the information.
   - Most importantly, knowledge workers must be ethical. **Ethics** are the principles and standards that guide our behaviour toward other people.
6. **Describe the important characteristics of information technology (IT) as a key organizational resource. Information technology (IT)** is any computer-based tools that people use to work with information and support the information and information processing needs of an organization. All technology is either **hardware** (the physical devices that make up a computer) or **software** (the set of instructions that your hardware executes).
7. **List and describe the six roles and goals of information technology in any organization.** The roles and goals of information technology include:
   - Increase employee productivity—reducing the time, errors, and costs associated with processing information
   - Enhance decision making—helping you analyze a situation and then leaving the decision entirely up to you or actually making some sort of recommendation concerning what to do
   - Improve team collaboration—improving the performance of teams by supporting the sharing and flow of information
   - Create business partnerships and alliances—helping organizations work together to provide better and more timely products and services
   - Enable global reach—marketing your products and services in countries all over the world and developing partnerships and alliances with other businesses throughout the globe
   - Facilitate organizational transformation—responding to the ever-changing needs (and wants) of today's marketplace

CLOSING CASE STUDY ONE

YOU AND YOUR INFORMATION

In the opening case study and throughout the chapter, you read about how pervasive and invasive technology is in your life today. No matter what you do or where you go, your information travels with you and is eventually captured and stored by a number of organizations. Many people simply accept this fact and think little beyond it. In this all-encompassing information and IT environment, let's consider two issues—trust and accuracy. As you'll see, they are related.

First, answer (with a simple yes or no) the questions below, which pertain to your everyday life.

1. Do you keep a paper record of all your long-distance phone calls—when you placed them by date and time, to whom, and the length—and then compare that list to your monthly phone bill?
   Yes ☐ No ☐
2. Do you meet with the meter reader to verify the correct reading of your water, gas, or electricity usage?
   Yes ☐ No ☐
3. As you shop, do you keep a record of the prices of your groceries and then compare that record to the register receipt?
   Yes ☐ No ☐
4. Do you frequently ask to see your doctor's medical record on you to ensure that it's accurate?
   Yes ☐ No ☐
5. When you receive a tuition bill, do you pull out your calculator, add up the amounts, and verify that the total is correct?
   Yes ☐ No ☐
6. Have you ever purchased a credit report on yourself to make sure your credit information is accurate?
   Yes ☐ No ☐
7. Have you ever called the police department to verify that no outstanding traffic violations have been inadvertently assigned to you?
   Yes ☐ No ☐
8. Do you count your coin change when you receive it from a store clerk?
   Yes ☐ No ☐
9. Do you verify your credit card balance by keeping all your credit card receipts and then matching them to charges on your statement?
   Yes ☐ No ☐
10. Do you keep all your paycheque stubs to verify that the amounts on your T4 form at the end of the year are accurate?
   Yes ☐ No ☐

To how many of those questions did you answer yes? To how many did you answer no? More than likely, you answered no to almost all the questions (if not all of them). What does that say? Well, basically, that you trust organizations to keep accurate information about you. The real question is "Is that necessarily the case?"

Now answer the set of questions below, which relate to the level of confidence organizations have in the accuracy of information you give them.

1. When interviewing with potential employers, do they take your word that you have a college degree?
   Yes ☐ No ☐
2. If you deposit several cheques into your chequing account at once, does the bank trust you to correctly add the amounts?
   Yes ☐ No ☐
3. When you register for a class that has a prerequisite, does your school assume that you have actually taken the prerequisite class?
   Yes ☐ No ☐
4. When you make a deposit at an ATM and enter the amount, does the bank assume that you entered the correct amount?
   Yes ☐ No ☐
5. When you're buying a house and negotiating a loan, does the bank assume that the price

you're paying for the house is correct and not inflated?

Yes ☐ No ☐

6. When insuring your car, does the insurance company assume that you have a good driving record?

Yes ☐ No ☐

7. When you apply for a parking permit at your school, does it assume that the car belongs to you?

Yes ☐ No ☐

8. When you file your taxes, does the Canada Customs and Revenue Agency assume that you've reported all your income over the past year?

Yes ☐ No ☐

The answer to each of those questions is probably no. And what does that say about the extent to which organizations trust you to provide accurate information? In this instance, it may not be strictly a matter of trust. Organizations today can't afford to have dirty information—information that's not accurate. Because organizations base so many of their decisions on information, inaccurate information creates a real problem that may equate to inefficient processes and lost revenue.

So, on the one hand, you're probably very trusting in your assumptions that organizations are maintaining accurate information about you; on the other, organizations don't really trust you to provide accurate information.

Questions

1. Should you really trust organizations to maintain accurate information about you? In many instances, is it even worth your time and energy to verify the accuracy of that information?
2. What other examples can you think of in which you simply trust that your information is accurate? What other examples can you think of in which specific organizations don't assume that you're providing accurate information?
3. What sort of impact will cyberspace business have on the issues of trust and accuracy? Will it become easier or more difficult for cyberspace business to assume that you're providing accurate information? Will you trust cyberspace business to maintain your information more accurately than traditional organizations?
4. What are the ethical issues involved in organizations sharing information about you? In some instances it may be okay and in your best interest. But what if the shared information about you is inaccurate? What damage could it cause? What recourse do you have, if any?
5. It's a real dilemma—most people think that credit card offerers charge extremely high interest rates. But how many people do you know who actually go through the process of calculating their average daily balances, applying the interest rates, and then verifying that the interest charged on their accounts is correct? Why do people complain that they are being charged excessive interest rates and then fail to check the accuracy of the interest calculations?
6. What about the future? As more organizations maintain even more information about you, should you become more concerned about accuracy? Why or why not?

CLOSING CASE STUDY TWO

HOW MUCH OF YOUR PERSONAL INFORMATION DO YOU WANT BUSINESSES TO KNOW?

The information age has brought about great debates with respect to information availability and privacy. For example, most cities in North America provide searchable Internet-based databases with real estate information. You can type in an address and see what a family paid for a home, when they bought it, and often even how it's financed. You can also type in a person's name and find the same information. Is that good or bad? Probably depends on your perspective. You can also use special search engine utilities such as Yahoo! People Search (people.yahoo.com) to find the phone numbers and addresses of people all over the world. You might want to try and see if you can find yourself.

From an organizational perspective, businesses need information about you to provide the best possible products and services. The more a business knows about you, the more it can tailor its offerings to you. In many ways, this is good. We all want personalized service. But, in a way, it could also be bad. Just how much of your personal information do you want businesses to know? Consider these examples.

MITCHELLS OF WESTPORT

Mitchells is an upscale old-fashioned clothing retailer that's exploiting technology and information to create one-to-one customer service. With a database of more than 50,000 customers and ten years of transaction data, Mitchells can sift through information to better serve its customers. As CEO Jack Mitchell explains, "What that means in real terms is that we can look at historical preferences of our customers, and, for instance, see if a customer who used to buy American suits likes a more contemporary European look in his clothing."

Mitchells even tracks information on its high-revenue customers such as the company they work for, their position, birthdays, anniversaries, and kids' name and ages. Mitchells uses this type of information to constantly communicate with its customers and create a very real one-to-one relationship.

ACXIOM CORP.

Most people have never heard of Acxiom Corp., but it is most certainly aware that you exist, even to the extent that it may know your height and weight. Acxiom specializes in providing information to organizations that want to market products and services. Since the mid-1980s, Acxiom has been gathering information and building a special file called InfoBase. InfoBase contains some or all of the following facts on over 200 million people: home ownership, age, estimated income, cars owned, occupation, buying habits, types of credit cards used, children, and even height and weight.

For a fee, you can buy any or all of this information from Acxiom on any customer demographic (perhaps just the people who live in your neighbourhood). And Acxiom does sell this information to other organizations. For example, Allstate Corp. buys information concerning insurance applicants' credit reports, driving records, claims histories, and family relationships (just in case you have a relative who likes to speed) from Acxiom.

In today's world, information is big business, and the use of it is definitely enabled by information technology. Perhaps the real question isn't "How much information is too much?" but rather "Who has access to that information and for what purposes are they using it?"

These are the sorts of questions you'll face throughout the rest of your life. And you'll do so from two perspectives. The first is a personal one. How much of your information do you want others to be able to access? If you fill out sweepstakes entries on the Internet or even a warranty card for a new product you've recently purchased, you are giving up a great deal of privacy.

The second perspective deals with how you'll use information in the business world. Will you check on your potential customers by using the Internet to see if and when they've purchased a home? Is that legal? Certainly. Is it ethical? That depends on you—ethics, after all, are a matter of personal interpretation.[14]

Questions

1. What is the role of information technology at Acxiom? Could it still maintain and provide such a wealth of information without using IT? Acxiom's InfoBase holds 350 terabytes of information. How much information is that? How many double-spaced pages of text would it take to hold all that information?

2. How has Mitchells used information and information technology to enable organizational transformation? Consider how Mitchells operated before it gathered and kept such a wealth of information and how it operates now in the information age.

3. Acxiom and Mitchells have two entirely different sets of business goals—Acxiom uses information to sell as a product (or commodity if you wish) to other businesses, while Mitchells uses information to better serve individual consumers. For each, discuss the flows of information relative to upward, downward, horizontally, and outward.

4. What are the ethical and legal issues relating to the fact that Acxiom may know your height and weight and is certainly willing to sell that information to the highest bidder? Can Acxiom legally own that information and sell it to any and every organization?

5. From where do you think Acxiom gathers its information? Could it establish a partnership with other organizations such as Mitchells and buy personal information? How do you feel about this?

6. Many people dream of having a close personal relationship with a clothing retailer such as Mitchells. You simply walk in and the salesperson seems to know everything about you (and remembers you well). However, Mitchells communicates extensively with its customers by e-mail. Would you ever get tired of receiving e-mails that solicit your business? How many of those e-mails do you receive now on a weekly basis? What steps can you take to avoid them?

7. Overall, what's your view of the information age in which we live? Are we better off because we have access to a wealth of information, including personal information? Should organizations such as Acxiom and Mitchells exploit their information for all its worth? Should they consider your feelings?

Key Terms and Concepts

application software, 20
artificial intelligence (AI), 24
banner ad, 27
central processing unit (CPU), 20
culture, 28
customer-integrated system (CIS), 23
data, 9
decentralized computing, 20
digital economy, 8
electronic commerce, 6
electronic data interchange (EDI), 27
ethics, 16
executive information system (EIS), 24
external information, 13
global economy, 8
group document database, 25
groupware, 25
hacker, 17
hardware, 18
information, 9
information age, 4
information granularity, 13
information technology (IT), 18
information-literate knowledge worker, 15
input device, 18
internal information, 13
interorganizational system (IOS), 27
intranet, 11
knowledge worker, 4
m-commerce, 7
management information systems (MIS), 4
neural network, 24
objective information, 13
online analytical processing (OLAP), 23
online transaction processing (OLTP), 23
operating system software, 20
operational management, 12
output device, 18
RAM (random access memory), 20
shared information, 21
software, 18
storage device, 18
strategic management, 12
subjective information, 13
system software, 20
tactical management, 12
technology-literate knowledge worker, 14
telecommunications device, 18
telecommuting, 6
transaction processing system (TPS), 23
transnational firm, 8
utility software, 20
virtual workplace, 6
workgroup support system (WSS), 25

Short-Answer Questions

1. How does a knowledge worker differ from other types of workers?
2. What is management information systems (MIS)?
3. What is electronic commerce?
4. How are telecommuting and the virtual workplace related?
5. How is today's economy wants-based?
6. What will follow the information age?
7. What is the relationship between data and information?
8. What are the personal dimensions of information?
9. What are the three levels of management in an organization?
10. What is information granularity? How does it differ according to the levels of an organization?
11. What is the difference between internal and external information?
12. What are the two basic categories of information technology (IT)?
13. What are the six categories of information technology (IT) hardware?
14. How are decentralized computing and shared information related to each other?
15. What are the six roles and goals of information technology?

Assignments and Exercises

1. **SURVEYING THE GLOBAL ECONOMY.** Visit a local store in your area that sells clothing and perform a small survey. Pick up ten different pieces of clothing (shoes, shirts, pants, belts, etc.) and note the country in which they were made. Do your results support or contradict our assertion that we now live in a global economy? Why?
2. **FINDING TRUST IN TRUSTe.** TRUSTe (www.truste.org) is an organization on the Web that has created specific guidelines for the use of your private information by Web sites to whom you offer it. If a site adheres to all of TRUSTe's guidelines, that site can then display the TRUSTe logo. That way you know you're private information is protected. TRUSTe has four main guidelines or principles that Web sites displaying its logo must follow. Connect to TRUSTe. What are the four guidelines? Are any or all of these guidelines important to you as an individual? If so, which one or ones and why? Should the government require that all Web sites follow these guidelines or a similar set? Why or why not?
3. **REPORTING ON INTERNET STATISTICS BY BUSINESS SECTOR.** NUA (www.nua.com) claims to be the world's leading resource for Internet statistics and trends. Connect to NUA and choose one of the business sectors located along the left side of the page. Pick a specific article discussing that particular business sector and prepare a short report for class. Which business sector did you choose? What was the focus of the article you chose? Did some of the statistics surprise you? Considering that you might be interested in working in a business sector on which NUA tracks Internet statistics, would you find NUA's site useful in preparing to go into that business sector? Why or why not?
4. **LEARNING ABOUT AN MIS MAJOR.** Using your school's catalogue of majors and courses (or the catalogue of another school), briefly outline what classes you would have to take to major in management information systems (MIS). Do any of the courses mention specific technology tools such as Java or Oracle? If so, which technology tools are listed? Now, do some searching on the Internet for salaries in the MIS field. What did you find? Does this particular major appeal to you? Why or why not?
5. **REVIEWING THE 100 BEST COMPANIES TO WORK FOR.** Every year *Fortune* magazine devotes an issue to the top 100 best companies to work for. Find the most recent issue of *Fortune* that does this. First, develop a

numerical summary that describes the 100 companies in terms of their respective industries. Which industries are the most dominant? Pick one of the dominant industries (preferably one in which you would like to work) and choose a specific highlighted company. Prepare a short class presentation on why that company is among the 100 best to work for.

6. **REDEFINING BUSINESS OPERATIONS THROUGH IT INNOVATION.** Many businesses are building customer-integrated systems (CISs) as a way of redefining their operations through the use of information technology. We discussed several in this chapter, with the most notable and obvious example probably being that of banks offering ATMs. Identify how each of the eight types of businesses below are using technology to offer customer-integrated systems. As you describe a CIS for each type, be sure to include what advantages you receive as a customer. Also, describe how you would have to interface with each type of business if it did not offer a CIS.

   - Airlines
   - Grocery stores
   - Phone companies
   - Hotels
   - Fuel stations
   - Utility companies
   - Cable TV providers
   - Universities and colleges

Discussion Questions

1. Knowledge workers dominate today's business environment. However, many industries still need workers who do not fall into the category of knowledge workers. What industries still need skilled workers? Can you see a time when these jobs will be replaced by knowledge workers? Can you envision circumstances that would actually cause our economy to do an "about face" and begin needing more skilled workers than knowledge workers?

2. Consider today's economic environment—we have characterized it as the e.conomy, the "now" economy, the global economy, and the arriving digital economy. For each of these characterizations, identify why it's an effect causing the remaining three. That is, how is the "e" causing the "now," global, and arriving digital economies, how is the "now" economy causing the "e," global, and arriving digital economies, etc.

3. The three key resources in management information systems (MIS) are information, information technology, and people. Which of these three resources is the most important? Why? The least important? Why?

4. Telecommuting, like all things, has a good and a bad side. What are some of the disadvantages or pitfalls of telecommuting? How can these be avoided?

5. As an information-literate knowledge worker for a local distributor of imported foods and spices, you've been asked to prepare a customer mailing list that will be sold to international cuisine restaurants in your area. If you do so, will you be acting ethically? If you don't consider the proposal ethical, what if your boss threatens to fire you if you don't prepare the list? Do you believe you would have any legal recourse if you didn't prepare the list and were subsequently fired?

6. How is your school helping you prepare to take advantage of information technology? What courses have you taken that included teaching you how to use technology? What software packages were taught? To best prepare to enter the job market, how can do you determine what software you need to learn?

7. Consider the ATM system now in place worldwide. How does it address your personal dimen-

sions of time, location, and form? Besides just tracking what transactions you've completed using an ATM, what other information might your bank want to know and use concerning your use of the system?

8. Information granularity changes according to the level of an organization. Consider your school, the classes it offers, and the number of students who register in those classes. What sort of information exhibiting coarse granularity would people at the highest levels of your school want to know? What sort of information exhibiting fine granularity would people at the lower levels of your school want to know? As a consumer (student), do you need fine or coarse information? Or perhaps both?

9. In addition to using neural networks to monitor credit card fraud, the same companies also use neural networks to determine whether you are a credit risk. By feeding in thousands of credit card applications, the neural network develops a pattern of who is and isn't creditworthy. Basically, the neural network compares your credit application to past ones and makes a recommendation. How do you feel about that? Should you be given or denied a credit card on the basis of what others have done (or failed to do)? Why or why not?

10. Many schools use groupware to offer distance learning classes. Instead of going to class, you communicate with your instructors and classmates via technology. Would you like to take distance learning classes? What are the advantages? Can you learn as much without going to class and personally interacting with your instructor and classmates? What might be some of the disadvantages of distance learning? Is there a happy medium? How about going to school for only one class session per week and then attending the other virtually via technology? Good or bad idea?

11. We often say that hardware is the *physical* interface with a technology system while software is the *intellectual* interface. How is your hardware your physical interface with your computer? How is your software your intellectual interface with your computer? Do you see technology progressing to the point where we may no longer distinguish between hardware and software and thus no longer perceive differing physical and intellectual interfaces?

REAL HOT Electronic Commerce

Using the Internet as a Tool to Find a Job

Real HOT Links

Electronic commerce is a great new business horizon. And it's not "just around the corner" any more. Electronic commerce is already here and businesses all over the world are taking advantage of it. Today, information technology can help you land a job. You can use your knowledge of IT and IT itself to help you find potential employers, place your résumé in their hands, locate summer internships, and learn the art of selling yourself during the interview and negotiation process. How? By simply cruising the Internet and using online job database and service providers as well as accessing information about how to prepare for an interview (among other things).

Are you taking advantage of the Internet to find a job? If you're not, we'd like to help you by introducing you to just a few of the thousands of Web sites that can help you find a job. In this section, we've included a number of Web sites related to finding a job through the Internet. On the Web site that supports this text (www.mcgrawhill.ca/college/haag), select "Electronic Commerce Projects." Here, we've provided direct links to all these Web sites as well as many, many more. These are a great starting point for completing this Real HOT section. We would also encourage you to search the Internet for others.

JOB DATABASES

There are—quite literally—thousands of sites that provide you with databases of job postings. Some are better than others. Some focus on specific industries; others offer postings only for executive managers. For the best review of job Web sites, connect to two different places. The first is The 100 Top Network (www.100.com, choose "Career"). The second is the Career Resource Homepage at www.careerresource.net. This site provides the most comprehensive list of the available job Web sites such as Monster.ca. There, you'll find a list of over 1000 job Web sites.

Think for a moment about the job you want. What would be its title? In which industry do you want to work? In what part of the country do you want to live? What special skills do you possess? (For example, if you're looking for an accounting job, you may be specializing in auditing.) Is there a specific organization for which you would like to work?

Connect to a couple of different databases, search for your job, and answer the following questions for each database.

A. What is the date of last update?

B. Are career opportunities abroad listed as a separate category or are they integrated with domestic jobs?

C. Can you search for a specific organization?

D. Can you search by geographic location? If so, how? By province? By city? By postal code?

E. Does the site provide direct links to e-mail addresses for those organizations posting jobs?

F. Can you apply for a position online? If so, how do you send your résumé?

G. Can you search by a specific industry?

CREATING AND POSTING AN ELECTRONIC RÉSUMÉ

Skills Module 4
E-Portfolio

Most, if not all, job databases focus on two groups—employers and employees. As a potential employee, you search to find jobs that meet your qualifications and desires. Likewise, employers search job databases that contain résumés so they can find people (like you) who meet their qualifications and desires. In this instance, you need to build an electronic résumé (an *e-résumé* or *e-portfolio*, which we discuss in Skills Module 4 on the CD-ROM accompanying this text) and leave it at the various job database sites as you perform your searches. That way, organizations performing searches can find you.

Almost all the job database sites we've listed give you the ability to create and post an electronic résumé. Visit two new job database sites (different from those you visited to find a job). In each, go through the process of creating an e-résumé, posting it, and making some sort of modification to it. As you do, answer the following questions for each of the sites.

A. Do you have to register as a user to build an e-résumé?

B. Once a potential employer performs a search that matches your e-résumé, how can that employer contact you?

C. What valuable tips for building a good e-résumé are available?

D. Once you build your e-résumé, can you use it to perform a job search?

E. When you modify your e-résumé, can you update your existing e-résumé or must you delete the old one and create a new one?

F. How many key terms concerning your qualifications can you include in your e-résumé?

G. For what time frame does your e-résumé stay active?

SEARCHING NEWSPAPERS THE NEW-FASHIONED WAY

One of today's most popular ways to find a job is to search the classified sections of newspapers. Every Sunday (if your library is open) and Monday you can visit your local library and find a gathering of people searching through the classified sections of the *National Post*, *Globe and Mail*, and *Halifax Chronicle Herald* in hopes of finding a job. Most of these people are attempting to find a job in a specific geographic location. For example, a person looking in the *Halifax Chronicle Herald* is probably most interested in finding a job in Nova Scotia or the Maritimes.

And as you might well guess, newspapers are not to be left off the Internet bandwagon. Today you can find hundreds of online editions of daily newspapers. And the majority of these provide their classified sections in some sort of searchable electronic format. Pick several newspapers, perform an online search for a job that interests you at each newspaper, and answer the following questions.

A. Can you search by location/city?

B. Can you search back issues or only the most recent issue?

C. Does the newspaper provide direct links to Web sites or provide some other profile information for those organizations posting jobs?

D. Does the newspaper provide direct links to e-mail addresses for those organizations posting jobs?

E. Is the newspaper affiliated with any of the major job database providers? If so, which one(s)?

LOCATING THAT ALL-IMPORTANT INTERNSHIP

Have you ever noticed that a large number of jobs require experience? That being the case, how does someone gain such experience through a job when experience is required to get the job? As it turns out, that's always been a perplexing dilemma for many students, and one way to solve it is by obtaining an internship. Internships provide you with valuable knowledge about your field, pay you for your work, and offer you that valuable "experience" you need to move up in your career.

On the Online Learning Centre (www.mcgrawhill.ca/college/haag), we've provided you with a number of Web sites that offer internship possibilities. Visit a few of them. Did you find any internships in line with your career? What about pay—did you find both paying and nonpaying internships? How did these internship sites compare to the more traditional job database sites you looked at earlier? Why do you think this is true?

INTERVIEWING AND NEGOTIATING

The Internet is a vast repository of information—no doubt more information than you'll ever need in your entire life. During the job search process however, the Internet can offer you very valuable specific information. In the area of interviewing and negotiating, for example, the Internet contains over 5000 sites devoted to interviewing skills, negotiating tips, and the like.

Interviewing and negotiating are just as important as searching for a job. Once you line up that first important interview, you can still not land the job if you're not properly prepared. If you do receive a job offer, you may be surprised to know that you can

negotiate such things as moving expenses, signing bonuses, and allowances for technology in your home.

We've provided Web sites for you that address the interviewing and negotiating skills you need in today's marketplace. Review some of these sites (and any others that you may find). Then, develop a list of dos and don'ts for the interview and a list of tips to increase your effectiveness during negotiation. Once you've developed these two lists, prepare a short class presentation.

GOING RIGHT TO THE SOURCE— THE ORGANIZATION YOU WANT

Today, many organizations are posting open positions on their own Web sites. Their idea is simple: if you like an organization enough to visit its Web site, you just might want to work there. For example, if you connect to The Bay at www.hbc.com and buy clothes online, you might consider working there if the opportunity is right.

Choose several organizations that you'd be interested in working for. For each, connect to its Web site, look for job opportunities, and answer the following questions:

A. Are you able to find job opportunities?

B. How difficult is it to find the job opportunities?

C. Are positions grouped or categorized by type?

D. Is a discussion of career paths included?

E. How do you obtain an application form?

F. Are there international opportunities available? Do the job descriptions include a list of qualifications?

G. Are there direct links to e-mail addresses for further questions?

Go to the Online Learning Centre at www.mcgrawhill.ca/college/haag for quizzes, extra content, a searchable glossary, and more! Click on "Electronic Commerce Projects" for links to hundreds of Web sites.

Go to the text CD-ROM for data files, extra content, and Skills Modules on Microsoft Excel, Microsoft Access, HTML, and e-portfolios.

CHAPTER TWO

STUDENT LEARNING OUTCOMES

1. Describe how the creative use of information technology can give an organization a competitive advantage.
2. Demonstrate how to generate ideas for using information technology in innovative ways, and apply tools that can help.
3. Describe how e-commerce technologies "up the stakes" and give organizations even more opportunities.
4. Summarize how one specific industry has consistently used information technology for competitive advantage.
5. Describe how to use information technology for competitive advantage in an organization.

INDUSTRY PERSPECTIVES

FEATURES

WEB SUPPORT LINKS

- Books and Music
- Clothing and Accessories
- Auction Houses
- Automobiles

Visit www.mcgrawhill.ca/college/haag

Using IT for Competitive Advantage

CASE STUDY:

ZARA: FASHION FAST FORWARD

At Zara's flagship apparel store in downtown Madrid, the store manager scans the racks holding the latest fashions. Quickly, she notes which items are selling well and which are not. Currently, leather items—particularly the short skirts—are selling briskly; so are the tailored jeans, the black sequined shirts, and the red and blue gabardine blazers.

Making her bet on which items will be next week's hot sellers, she pulls out her handheld computer and enters an order that is transmitted over the Internet to Zara headquarters in the northwestern Spanish town of La Coruña.

There, Zara's designers and product managers are deciding what to create. Every day they gather suggestions from the flagship store in Madrid and 518 other store managers worldwide. Importantly, however, they don't just want specific orders. They ask for and get ideas for cuts, fabrics, or even a new line.

After evaluating the store managers' input, the team in La Coruña decides what to make. Designers draw up the latest ideas on their computers and send them over Zara's Intranet to one of its nearby factories. Within days, the cutting, dyeing, stitching, and pressing begin. And in just three weeks, the clothes will hang in stores from Barcelona to Berlin to Beirut. Zara isn't just a bit faster than rivals such as The Gap, whose lead time is nine months. It's 12 times faster!

What sets Zara apart from its competitors is a computerized network that ties the stores to the design shops and company-owned factories in real time. The Zara model may be unique, but at its heart is a perfectly simple principle: in fashion, nothing is as important as time to market.

For years, apparel companies have manufactured their garments in lesser-developed countries in pursuit of lower costs. Zara decided against that. The company believed that the ability to respond quickly to shifts in consumer tastes would create far greater efficiencies than outsourcing to low-cost countries could. "The fashion world is in constant flux and is driven not by supply but by customer demand," says one of the company's executives. "We need to give consumers what they want, and if I go to South America or Asia to make clothes, I simply can't move fast enough."

Once the company decided it would have the world's most responsive supply chain, the pieces of its operating model fell logically into place. Zara has a twice-a-week delivery schedule that not only restocks old styles but brings in entirely new designs; rival chains tend to receive new designs only once or twice a season. "It's like you walk into a new store every two weeks," noted one prominent retail industry executive. The advantages of world-beating time to market, according to Zara, more than offset manufacturing costs that run 15 to 20 percent higher than those of its rivals. For example, Zara almost never needs to absorb inventory writeoffs to correct merchandising blunders. And the company maintains steady profit margins of 10 percent—in line with the best in the industry.[1]

Introduction

There are many examples of ways that organizations have used and are using information technology creatively to give themselves a competitive advantage. A company gains a **competitive advantage** by providing a product or service in a way that customers value more than what the competition is able to do. We'll give you some examples in a moment. First, it's important for you to get the right perspective about it. It's not the technology that gives a company a competitive advantage; it's the *way* people use the technology that makes the difference. For example, let's assume that there is a Porsche Boxster S parked outside and there are two people available to drive it, a trained professional racecar driver and a senior citizen who usually drives a six-year-old Buick, as shown in Figure 2.1. Although both people would have access to the same technology, there's probably no question in your mind that the professional racecar driver would do a better job of utilizing the technology embodied in the Boxster.

In a way, it's the same with information technology. With the widespread availability and ever-decreasing cost of computers, telecommunications and the Internet, the same technology is available to just about everyone. The real difference comes in the way that different people use the technology. Those who are well trained, proficient, and creative in its use are going to be able to get the most out of it and give their organizations a competitive advantage. These people are the knowledge workers we discussed in Chapter 1.

Designing an information system that gives a competitive advantage requires an understanding of at least two things: the business problem you're trying to solve or the situation in which you're trying to get a competitive advantage; and available technologies, to know which ones to use in designing a creative solution for the business situation. This is why studying management information systems (MIS) is so important. MIS emphasizes both business processes and technical solutions.

If you want to build a house, it's important to design it before you start. Otherwise, there's no telling what you might end up with. Most people hire an architect for the job. It's similar with information systems. As we discuss in Chapter 7, it's important to design a system before you build it. This job is done by **application architects**—information technology professionals who can design creative technology-based business solutions, working hand-in-hand with their business management counterparts from marketing, manufacturing, accounting, and human resources, for example. Skilled application architects are in short supply. They are among the most sought-after of knowledge workers.

Figure 2.1
Who Can Get the Most out of the Boxster S?

Competitive Advantage Examples

Seeing competitive advantage in action is perhaps the best way for you to learn how to implement it in your organization. As we look at the following examples, we'll introduce you to some "best business practices" as well.

FEDERAL EXPRESS

It used to be that if you wanted to track a package you'd shipped somewhere via FedEx you had to call an 800 number and listen to some music for a while until a customer service representative came on the line. Then you had to give him or her the tracking number from the receipt you got when you shipped the package. The customer service representative would enter the tracking number into a computer system that would access a database containing up-to-date information on the whereabouts of your package. You could find out whether or not it had been delivered, and if so when it had been delivered and who signed for it.

Someone at FedEx got the idea that with today's technology, life could be much easier for the customer. So, FedEx designed a system that lets you access that same database through your Internet connection and Web browser. Now, all you have to do is go to the FedEx Web site (www.fedex.ca), find your way to the tracking screen and key in your tracking number. The system will respond by giving you the same information you used to get from a customer service representative (see Figure 2.2).

The FedEx tracking system, and similar systems that benefit both the customers and the company, are often called "win-win" systems. It's better for customers because it's easier and faster; they no longer have to spend time waiting in voicemail jail. It's better for FedEx because it's cheaper; the company doesn't need nearly as many customer

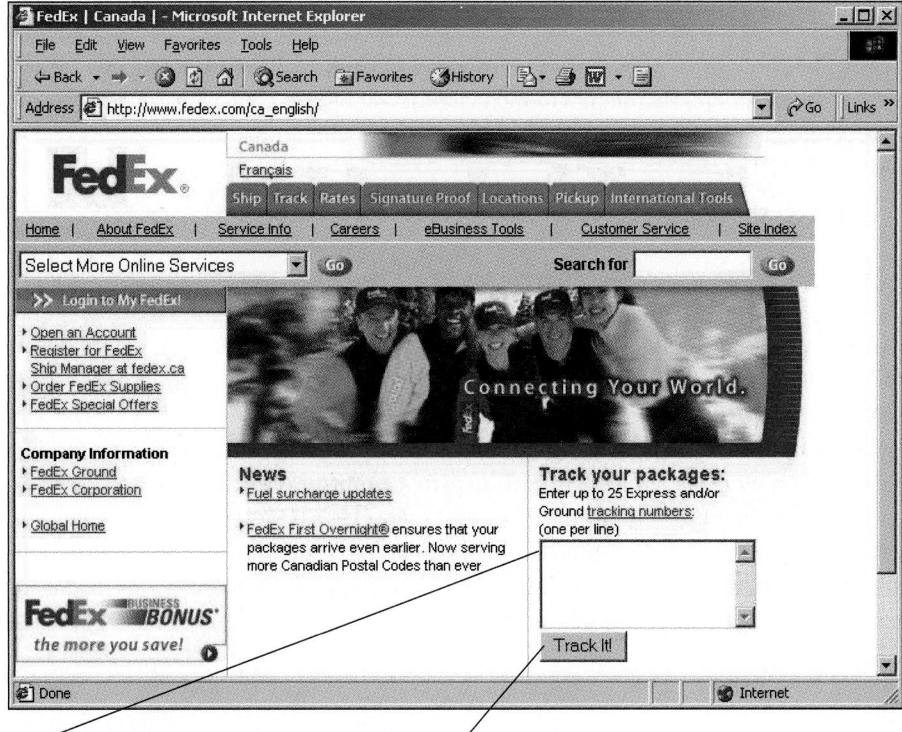

Figure 2.2
FedEx Package Tracking Screen

service representatives to handle the incoming calls. Plus, it gets a competitive advantage by delivering superior customer service—at least until the competition develops a similar system, as UPS and other competitors soon concluded they had to do.

This illustrates an important point about using information technology for competitive advantage. A competitive advantage you achieve for your company usually turns out to be temporary, because the competition soon figures out that they have to offer a similar system to their customers or risk losing them to you. Even a temporary advantage can make a difference, however, because the first mover usually makes some gains at the expense of the competition. **Temporary advantage** simply means that whatever you do, sooner or later the competition duplicates what you've done, or even leapfrogs you with an even better system. Despite this, the **first mover**, the company first to market with a new IT-based product or service, may well capture new customers that it never loses, and it often gains additional benefits by being viewed as a market leader.

CHARLES SCHWAB

Charles Schwab was a pioneer in the discount brokerage business. The company began operations more than 25 years ago serving investors who were comfortable making their own trades and did not need the advice and counsel provided by full-service brokers who charged a higher commission. Over the years, the company evolved into one that offers services to independent investors as well as investors who prefer to have more in the way of professional guidance. Schwab (www.schwab.com) was a first mover in offering stock trades over the Internet, along with other online brokers like E*TRADE. Using the latest in Internet and telephone technologies, Schwab offers its customers around-the-clock personal services. Its three million online customers manage over $250 billion in assets and trade more than $11 billion in securities every week. Schwab is not only the largest, it's perceived as the best. Gomez (www.gomez.com) is a highly regarded company in the "Internet quality measurement" (IQM) business, and Schwab appears at the top of their list of 29 discount brokers.[2] The willingness of Schwab's management to embrace the Internet early on as a way of serving their customers more efficiently and effectively has made Schwab the largest online broker, and one of world's most successful e-businesses.

DELL COMPUTER

Dell computer has a direct sell model that gives them a huge advantage over any competitor still using a traditional model of selling through retailers. The traditional way PC manufacturers get their product to customers is to build a bunch of PCs and ship them to wholesalers, distributors, or maybe directly to retailers. The PCs sit on the retailers' shelf or in a warehouse until you come in and buy one. If you looked at a typical distribution chain you would see that there are a lot of PCs in inventory. (A **distribution chain** is simply the path followed from the originator of a product or service to the end consumer.) In a typical distribution chain you'd find inventory at the manufacturer's warehouse, at the wholesalers, at the distributors, and at the retailers. Holding on to all of this inventory costs money, because whoever owns the inventory has to pay for it and pay for the operation of the warehouses or stores while waiting for someone to buy it.

Dell's model is different.[3] It sells computers directly from its Web site. They make it easy for you to log on and configure a computer just the way you want it. Once you've done that and given Dell your credit card number, you click to order and your

ON YOUR OWN

LOOKING FOR OPPORTUNITIES CLOSE TO HOME

You don't have to be a part of a traditional for-profit organization in order to get into the habit of looking for ways to use IT for competitive advantage. Not for profits and governmental agencies can get benefits from IT as well. For example, most universities are considered to be not for profit. See if you can come up with ways that your college or university could get a competitive advantage from the way it uses IT. You might try taking the customer's perspective (yours) as a point of departure. Other candidates could be your state or local government. How complicated is it to get your driver's licence renewed? How difficult is it to get information on various governmental services? How could information access be improved with the creative use of IT systems?

computer arrives in a few days. Shortly after you click to order, Dell has your money! Then it gets busy sending electronic orders to other companies, their alliance partners, who assemble and ship your computer. An **alliance partner** is a company you do business with on a regular business in a cooperative fashion, usually facilitated by IT systems. Dell pays its alliance partners for their efforts a bit later. An arrangement such as this, called an **information partnership**, lets two or more companies cooperate by integrating their IT systems (supported by interorganizational systems which we introduced in Chapter 1), thereby providing customers with the best of what each can offer.

This is a win-win-win situation. You win because you get a computer made expressly for you, which arrives in good shape in a couple of days. Dell wins because all this occurs without it having to tie up a lot of money in inventory in the distribution chain. Dell's alliance partners win because they get a lot of business from Dell. The differences between Dell's "sell, source, and ship" model with the traditional "buy, hold, and sell" model are illustrated in Figure 2.3.

CISCO SYSTEMS

Dell Computer is in both the "business to business" and the "business to consumer" space. **Business to business (B2B)** refers to companies whose customers are primarily other businesses, while **business to consumer (B2C)** is the term used for companies whose customers are primarily individuals. (Some companies, like Dell Computer, have both B2B and B2C lines of business.)

Cisco Systems sells switches and routers, machines that manage information flowing through telecommunications networks in the B2B space. Cisco has been a leader in utilizing the direct sell model over the Internet. It currently sells over $1 billion a year this way. Customers like the system because it lets them log on to a home page that they can customize to reflect the particular way they deal with Cisco. Then, they can order Cisco products and configure them to their exact specifications. Cisco likes the system because it puts the management of the customer order process in the hands of the customer, freeing up Cisco employees for other tasks.

Recently, Cisco announced a partnership with Ariba, one of the leading suppliers of Web-based purchasing tools.[4] Ariba's software, which manages buying, selling, and e-commerce processes, will be combined with Cisco Web-based ordering tools, which provide pricing and configuration capabilities. Cisco says that its newly streamlined order entry process will increase customer productivity by as much as 20 percent. So,

Figure 2.3

Buy-Hold-Sell Versus Sell-Source-Ship

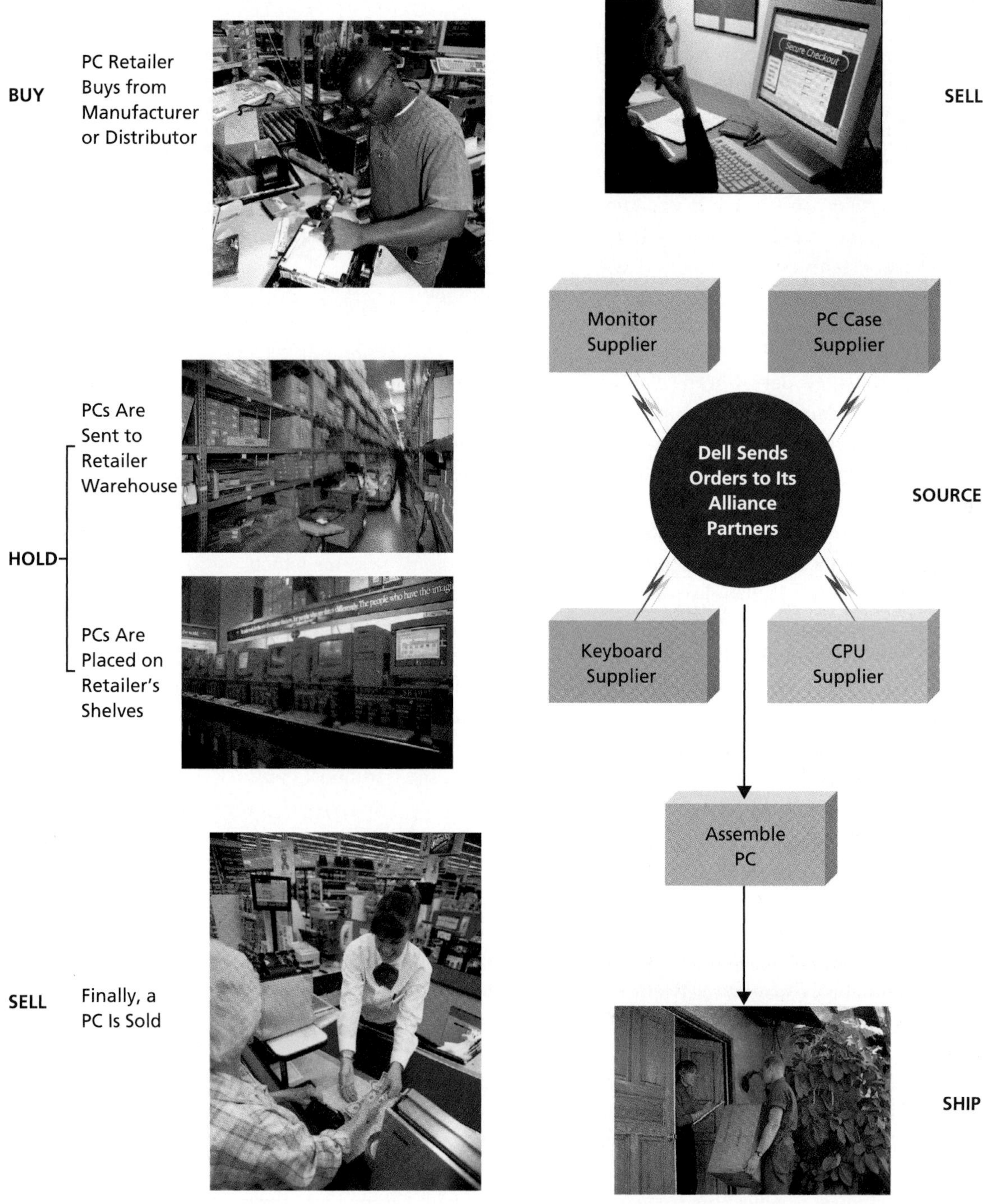

you see, Cisco has found a couple of ways to get a competitive advantage through the creative use of information technology.

First, Cisco made it easy to turn the management of the customer ordering process over to the customers themselves, and then it formed a software alliance with Ariba to increase the productivity of the customer ordering process even more. As you might expect, both Cisco and its customers are pleased with the results.

GE LEADERSHIP AND COMPETITIVE IT

Jack Welch retired as chairman and CEO of the world's largest company in 2001, but his legacy survives. Welch's accomplishments at the head of General Electric (GE), a company which both *Forbes* and the *Financial Times* declared the most admired company in 2000, earned him wide recognition as an outstanding manager. During his 20-plus years at the helm of GE, he raised the corporation's profits from $1.6 billion to more than $110 billion. Under his leadership, GE created a business culture regarded as the best in the world.

While many executives and traditional businesses were slow to react to the competitive advantages made possible by the Internet, Jack Welch and GE were not among them. He recognized that the potential of the Internet would bring new threats and opportunities that GE could not afford to ignore.

He urged his managers to examine their competitive positions and think "destroyyourbusiness.com." In other words, he asked them to see how a competitor could use the Internet to make inroads into their markets or gain a competitive advantage over them. Thinking that way, GE managers would be able to innovate and change their businesses before a new competitor arrived on the scene.

Welch also led by example, unlike many of his peers at other companies. He assigned young mentors to himself and 3000 other top GE executives to teach them how to use the Web.

Welch was serious about changing the culture at GE from a traditional one to one that is Internet-driven. He saw the potential for using the Web to eliminate unnecessary layers of middle management, promote teamwork, improve customer service, and make GE more competitive.

Jack Welch continues to be a great example of the kind of vision, leadership, and understanding that winning corporations need from their CEOs if they are going to be able to thrive in the information economy.[5]

Developing a Strategy for the Internet Age

Among the useful tools for business people thinking about business strategy, the "three frameworks" of Professor Michael Porter have long been accepted. Several of his colleagues, Professor Warren McFarland among them, showed how they also be used in coming up with ideas of how information technology could be harnessed to create a competitive advantage. In a recent article, Professor Porter observed that the Internet provides better opportunities for companies to establish distinctive business strategies than previous generations of information technology.[6]

Porter's three frameworks are:

1. The five forces model
2. The three generic strategies
3. The value chain

THE FIVE FORCES MODEL

The **five forces model** was developed to determine the relative attractiveness of an industry. Porter's intention was that it be used as a tool for business managers to use when they were trying to decide if they should enter a particular industry or expand their operations if they were already in it. As illustrated in Figure 2.4, the five forces are:

- *Buyer power.* **Buyer power** is high when buyers have many choices of whom to buy from, and low when the choices are few. If the buyers in a particular industry hold a lot of the power, the industry is less attractive to enter.

Figure 2.4
The Five Forces Model

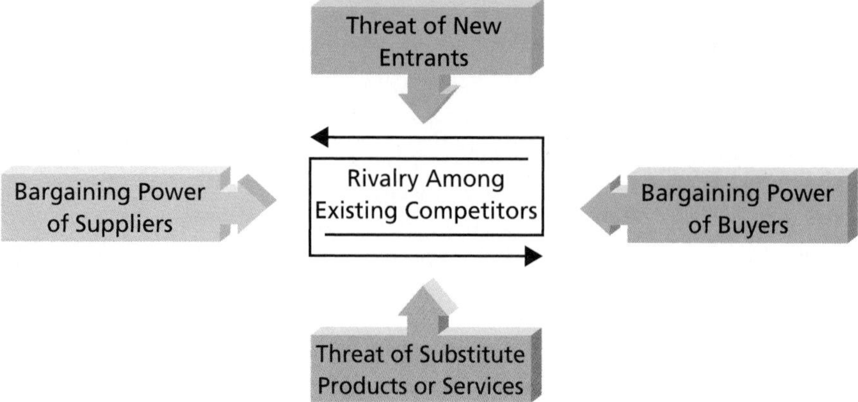

- *Supplier power.* **Supplier power** is high when buyers have few choices of whom to buy from, and low when there are many choices. If the suppliers in a particular industry hold a lot of the power, the industry is also less attractive to enter.
- *Threat of substitute products or services.* If there are very few alternatives to using the product or service the **threat of substitute products or services** is low, and it is an advantage to the supplier. Or, if there are switching costs associated with the product or service, it is an advantage to the supplier as well. **Switching costs** are costs that can make customers reluctant to switch to another product or service. For example, you may decide to keep your virus protection software even if a slightly better one becomes available because you don't want to invest the time and money to install and learn the new package.
- *Threat of new entrants.* The **threat of new entrants** is high when it is easy for competitors to enter the market. If it's easy, that's not good, for pretty soon you'll have a ton of competitors going after your customers. If it's difficult for others to enter the market, that's good news for those who are already there.
- *Rivalry among existing competitors.* An industry is less attractive when the **rivalry among existing competitors** is high and more attractive when it is low. Competition is more intense in some industries than in others. The intensity of competition in the industry is another factor that you should consider before entering an industry.

USING THE FIVE FORCES MODEL

Warren McFarland had the idea that a company could use information technology to alter one of or more of the five forces in their favour. When he shared this idea with business people, they quickly found that it worked. Some good examples of where it worked are provided next.

BUYER POWER Because there are many hotels competing for the business traveller's business, buyers have many choices, and therefore hold power over the suppliers of hotel rooms. To counteract this, most hotel chains have created loyalty programs which give points for each stay that can be cashed in for free hotel stays at one of their resort hotels, for example, or for other rewards. Such programs, supported by state-of-the-art information systems, have the effect of increasing the likelihood that a traveller will stay at a single chain.

SUPPLIER POWER One of the best ways to decrease supplier power is to locate alternative sources of supply. The B2B marketplaces on the Internet can have the effect of doing this. A **B2B marketplace** is an Internet-based service that brings together many buyers and sellers. One example is Covisint, the cooperative Internet purchasing venture established by the automotive industry. It uses Internet technology to "speed the flow of material through the supply chain, increase response to consumer demand, and deliver new products to market faster than ever before."[7]

Another way of reducing supplier power is to find a way to put more information in the hands of the buyer. The Internet has played a huge role in this in many industries. Probably the best example is the retail automobile industry. It used to be that when you wanted to buy a new car you really put yourself at the mercy of the dealer. Only the salesperson knew what the car cost the dealer, how much your trade-in was really worth, and how much money the dealership could make on optional equipment, extended warranties, and financing. Now, all this information is freely available on the Internet. The buyer can thus begin negotiations having roughly the same amount of information as the dealer. Supplier power is effectively reduced.

THREAT OF SUBSTITUTE PRODUCTS OR SERVICES Many professionals find that their normal way of making a living is threatened by the introduction of new IT-enabled products or services. One example would be the local chartered accountant who used to make a good portion of her living doing tax returns for individuals; her income has been substantially reduced now that inexpensive and easy-to-use tax return software packages such as QuickTax® or TAXWIZ® are generally available. One of the challenges for professionals is to find a way to counter threats to their livelihoods. Can you think of other professionals who might be threatened by such alternatives?

THREAT OF NEW ENTRANTS It is not a good thing to be trying to survive in an industry where it is very easy for others to enter. All that does is make it more crowded with competitors. Successful companies try to use information technology to erect "barriers" to entry. An **entry barrier** is a product or service feature that customers have come to expect from companies in a particular industry. Entry barriers make it more difficult for competitors to enter a particular market. A good example of an entry barrier is what we have come to expect from banks. We want to be sure our bank can offer us an ATM card that works at lots of locations locally and even around the world. We'd also like to be able to view our account and pay bills on the Internet. When one bank in a region first introduced such information technology services, it gained a competitive advantage. Other banks saw that they had to introduce similar services or face the loss of some of their customers to the bank that was more advanced. Now, such services are entry barriers to anyone who thinks of starting a new bank.

RIVALRY AMONG EXISTING COMPETITORS There are many ways that information technology can make one company better prepared than its rivals in an intensely competitive setting. For example, many retailers compete on the basis of price, particularly with products that are commodity-like in nature. It probably doesn't matter where you buy a six-pack of Diet Pepsi, at a convenience store or at a discount chain. The Pepsi will taste the same. What will likely be different is the price you paid for that six-pack. Probably it will be quite a bit cheaper at the discount chain store than at the convenience store. The reason it's cheaper at the discount chain store is because of the way the chain store uses information systems to make itself more efficient. Having information systems that let a retailer be more efficient and lower its costs so that it can offer lower prices to its customers is a definite competitive advantage.

THE GLOBAL PERSPECTIVE

EVEN NATIONS CAN GAIN A COMPETITIVE ADVANTAGE WITH IT

Using IT for competitive advantage is not restricted to companies. Singapore is a well-known example that a nation can use IT for competitive advantage as well.

As a small island nation with few natural resources, Singapore concluded that its most valuable resource was its people. The government decided that the wave of the future was IT, and that it should invest in training a cadre of IT workers and focus on becoming what they called "The Intelligent Island." Singapore subsequently became well known for the way it used IT to speed up the flow of goods through its port facilities by replacing cumbersome paperwork processes with e-commerce techniques.

As stated on its Web site, "Singapore will continue to reinvent itself and add value to businesses here as it develops into a vibrant and robust knowledge-driven global economy."[8]

THE THREE GENERIC STRATEGIES

Porter says that a business should adopt only one of **three generic strategies:** cost leadership, differentiation, or a focused strategy. As illustrated in Figure 2.5, a focused strategy can focus on either cost leadership or differentiation. According to Porter, trying to follow more than one of these strategies at the same time is almost always unsuccessful.

Taking examples from retailers, Wal-Mart is following a broadly targeted cost leadership strategy. Nordstrom's, with its emphasis on superior customer service and in-store experience, is following a broadly targeted differentiation strategy. Rite-Aid is pursuing a cost leadership strategy, but is focused on drugstore items.

USING THE THREE GENERIC STRATEGIES

Companies use the three generic strategies and information technology to change the basis of competition in ways that are favourable to them. For example, if they find that they are embroiled in a fierce competitive marketplace where all of the players are competing on the basis of price, they could use information technology to develop and support a strategy based on differentiation. Amazon.com deals with many commodity-like products where competition (as we saw with the Diet Pepsi example) is usually based on who can sell a product for the lowest price. New books, CDs, and

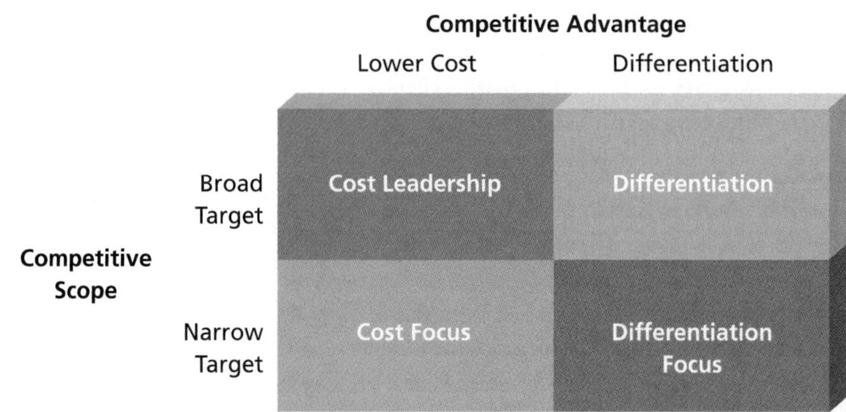

Figure 2.5
The Three Generic Strategies[9]

REMOTE SURGERY: A NEW EXPORT INDUSTRY?

Recently, two doctors removed the gall bladder of a 69-year-old patient lying on an operating table in Strasbourg, France. The most unusual aspect of this otherwise routine operation was that the surgeons were in New York.

They used joysticks and voice commands to direct three robotic arms in the operating room and watched their work on monitors. France Telecom provided a secure fibre-optic line to connect the control console to the robotic arms and instruments, while surgeons and nurses in France monitored the patient and switched the instruments as needed.

Such technology could eventually save the lives of patients who need a surgeon but can't reach one in person. Even sooner, remote robotic surgery systems will offer surgeons the chance to collaborate and teach new techniques without having to travel.[10]

videos are all commodity-like products. It doesn't really matter where you buy them, they will all be the same.

You may have noticed that, while Amazon.com has good prices, its price is often not the lowest. What Amazon.com has done well, however, is make its site informative and easy to navigate and use sophisticated software to personalize the site for each customer. It has used information technology to pursue a differentiated strategy in what would otherwise be a low-cost marketplace.

THE VALUE CHAIN

Once you have an understanding of how IT can help you develop a business strategy, it's important that you reinforce this view by ensuring IT support for all important business processes. A **business process** is a standardized set of activities that accomplishes a specific task, such as processing a customer's order. One important graphical tool that helps you identify those important processes is Michael Porter's **value chain**—which views the organization as a chain, or series, of processes, each of which adds value to the product or service for the customer. Customers patronize your organization because of the value that it adds to its products and services. If you view your organization as a value chain, you can identify the important processes in adding value for customers and, thus, identify IT systems that support those processes.

Figure 2.6 depicts the components of a value chain. The chain of primary value processes along the bottom half takes the raw materials and makes, delivers, markets and sells, and services your organization's products or services. Processes along the top half of the chain, such as management, accounting, finance, legal, human resources, research and development, and purchasing, support the primary value processes. Your organization requires these support value processes to ensure the smooth operation of the primary value processes.

All value processes process an individual value. However, these processes combined have a total value greater than the sum of their individual values. We call this additional value *value added*, and it's depicted on the far right of the value chain. The larger the value added, the more value customers place on an organization's product or service. To the organization, this can mean a competitive advantage and often greater profits. Let's look at how a firm might use the value chain to identify both value-added and value-reducing processes.

Figure 2.6
The Components of a Value Chain

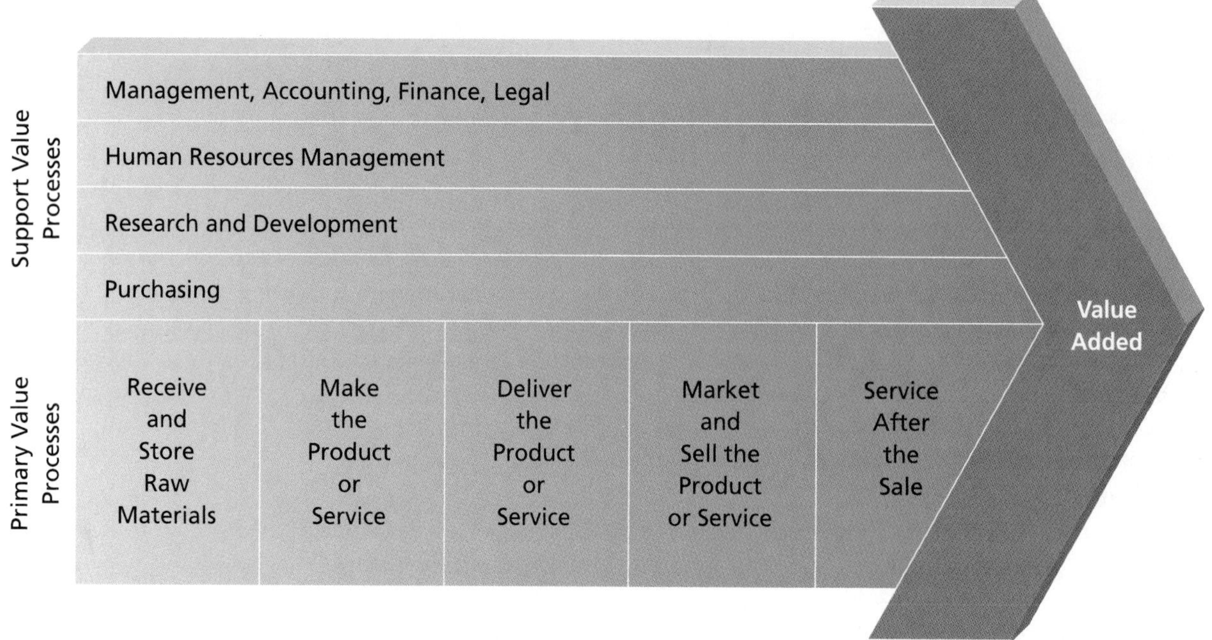

USING THE VALUE CHAIN

If you've ever purchased a necktie, you may have heard of the Robert Talbott company.[11] Talbott is one of the premier necktie manufacturers in North America. Talbott has always shunned technology—all of its tie orders, historically, were written on paper forms.

That used to work fine, because Talbott's has always ensured added value by utilizing high-quality workmanship, and unique designs and fabrics. However, customer "wants" drive their demand, and that demand is always changing in nature. Today customers want constantly updated styles and more of them. In fact, Talbott now creates four neckwear lines for Nordstrom every year with up to 300 designs per line. Given this situation, how could the value chain help Talbott plan for a better way of meeting customer demands?

Well, it would begin by identifying both value-added and value-reducing processes. Let's look at the identification of value-added processes first.

IDENTIFYING PROCESSES THAT ADD VALUE Talbott should begin by looking at the firm's business processes and identifying, with help from customers, those processes that add the most value. These include manufacturing high-quality ties and purchasing quality materials. Then Talbott should graphically depict the customer responses on a value chain. Figure 2.7 is one possible result. Notice how the processes are sized to depict the value that customers attribute to those processes. The largest value-added source is the high-quality manufacturing process. Still, a close second is the purchasing process that provides access to high-quality silks and other fabrics. As these processes are the ones that are most visible to the customers, they will quickly add even more value when supported by new IT systems. Therefore, Talbott created a computer-aided design system to reduce the time it takes to create and manufacture new ties.

IDENTIFYING PROCESSES THAT REDUCE VALUE In addition to identifying valued-added processes, it's important to identify those processes that reduce value for

Figure 2.7
The Value-Added View of a Necktie Manufacturer

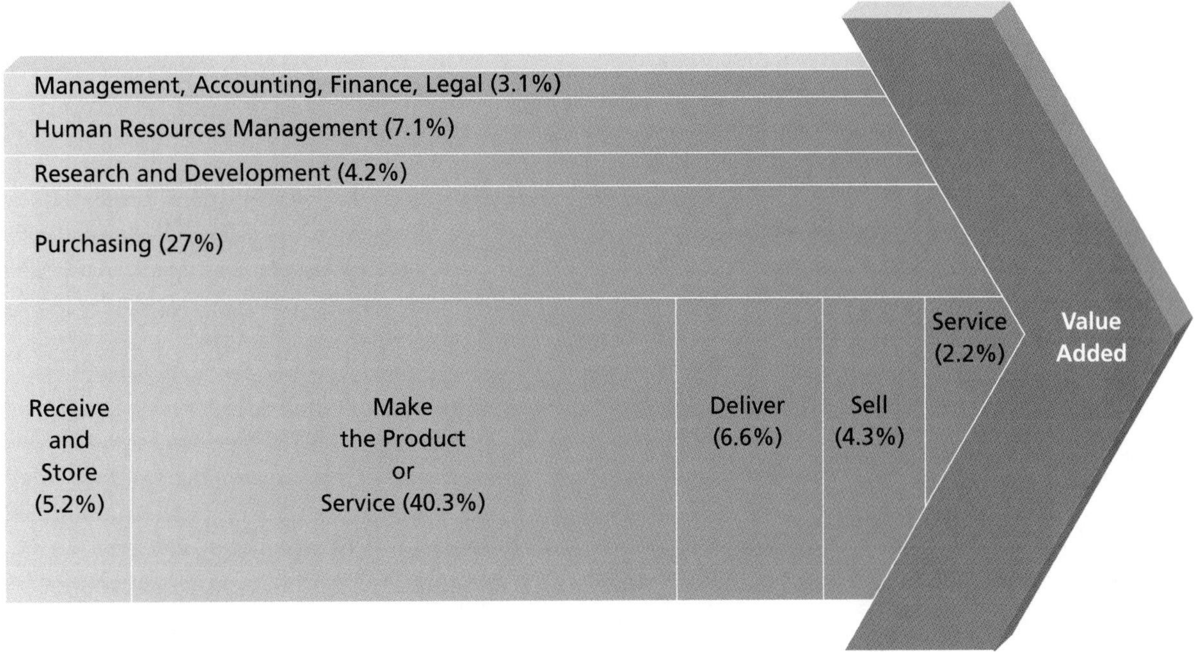

the customer. Using the same technique to gather this information from the customers, Talbott should create a value-reducing value chain. Talbott identified the sales process as the process that reduced value the most, as shown in Figure 2.8. It found sales were lost because salespeople were promising neckties that were out of stock. Customers were beginning to lose faith in Talbott's ability to deliver high-quality ties. They saw this process failure as one that reduced Talbott's value to them as customers.

Figure 2.8
The Value-Reduced View of a Necktie Manufacturer

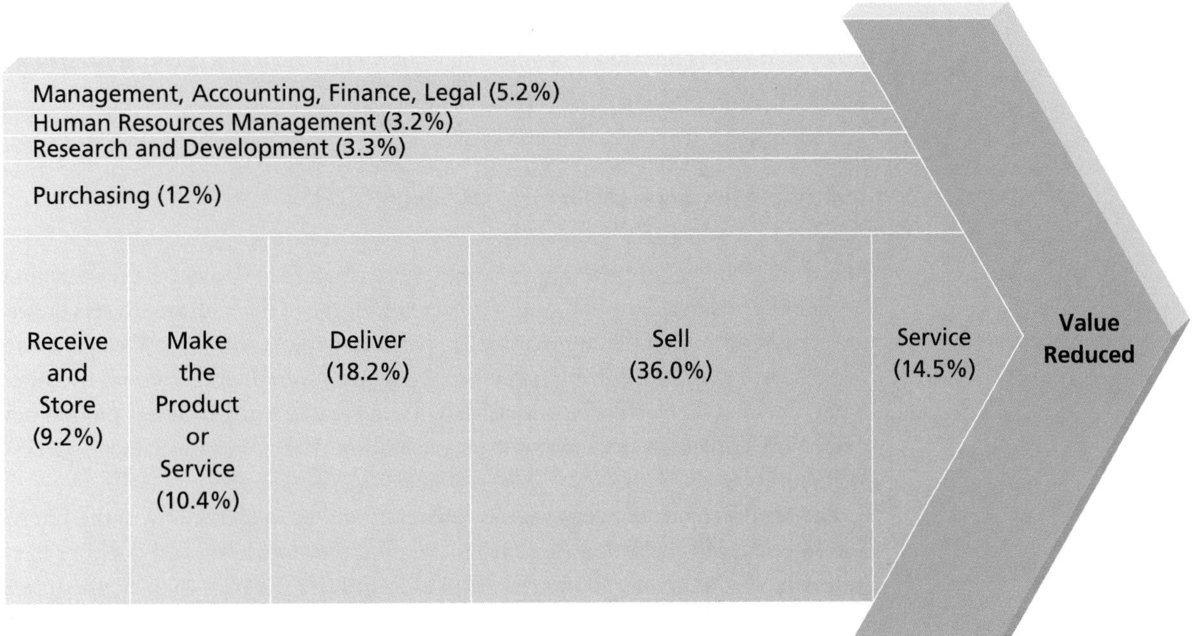

TEAM WORK

FINDING THE BEST IT STRATEGY FOR YOUR INDUSTRY

Regardless of which of Michael Porter's tools you select to use in developing IT solutions, it is crucial that they be appropriate for your organization. To simplify the selection process even further, you might consider which tools work best with some of the industries profiled in the Industry Perspective boxes in each chapter of this book.

In the grid here, match the tool on the left with the most appropriate industry across the top. Each tool can match more than one industry. For each match, write at least one reason why this match is appropriate.

	Industries								
Porter's Tools	Hospitality & Leisure	Financial Services	Health Care	Retail	IT & Telecommunications	Transportation	.com	Entertainment & Publishing	Manufacturing
Reduce buyer power									
Reduce supplier power									
Increase switching costs									
Increase entry barriers									
Switch to a cost leader strategy									
Switch to a differentiated strategy									
Switch to a focused strategy									
Enhance value-added activities									
Lower value-reducing activities									

To correct its sales process deficiencies, Talbott implemented a new IT system to get timely product information to the sales force. Using laptop computers, the sales force now carries product-line custom CD-ROMs on the road with them. They place orders over their computers from their hotel rooms and receive inventory updates at the same time. As a result, customers have new faith in an old friend who now adds more value than ever.

Key E-Commerce Strategies

There are many examples where companies have created competitive advantage through the creative use of IT, and we discussed some of them above. In recent years, however, the advent of the Internet and, in particular, the World Wide Web gave rise to a new burst of creative entrepreneurship. New ways were found to reach out to customers and suppliers. New businesses have been created using business models never seen before. It has been a time of experimentation with some spectacular successes and failures.

The big difference between the new economy and the old economy is the Internet. The Internet is global in scope, can now be found everywhere, and is either free or quite inexpensive in many countries. Three capabilities made possible by the Internet that companies should keep in mind when searching for ways to use new economy technologies for competitive advantage are:

1. Mass customization and personalization
2. Disintermediation
3. Global reach

Let's examine how each of these works.

MASS CUSTOMIZATION AND PERSONALIZATION

Mass customization and personalization are two different concepts that are sometimes confused. With **mass customization**, a business gives its customers the opportunity to tailor its product or service to the customer's specifications. For example, if you order an automobile from the factory, you can have it made with exactly the list of options and colours you wish. The way Dell sells computers, as we discussed earlier in this chapter, is an example of mass customization in an Internet business. Another example is the customized CDs you can order through Hamaracd.com (www.hamaracd.com), a company based in India. Usually when you buy a CD there are around twelve tracks on it and you're lucky if you like three of them. So you end up playing the tracks you like and skipping the ones you don't. Hamaracd.com and others now let you create your own CD containing only tracks you like, as illustrated in Figure 2.9. You pick them and then the CD is created for you. (Of course, in this example, it helps if you like music that is popular in India.)

Choose your artists and select your favourite tracks.

Figure 2.9
Create Your Own Custom CD at Hamaracd.com

Personalization has a different twist—it is the idea that a Web site can know enough about your preferences to fashion offers likely to appeal to you. Imagine opening up the daily newspaper and seeing only ads for products or services you were really interested in—no more ads for mattresses, wireless phones, or sofas. Personalization techniques try to do the same thing online.

One of the best examples is the books Amazon.com will suggest to you when you log onto its site. It keeps track of your taste in books with **collaborative filtering**, a technique to enable a Web site to support personalization. On the basis of buying patterns you establish over time, the site puts you into an *affinity group*, which consists of people who like the same sort of topics. Then it tracks the buying patterns of both you and the group, and suggests books the affinity group is buying that you have not yet bought. This creative use of IT gives you the kind of personal service you might expect from a small bookstore in your home town whose owner knew your tastes.

DISINTERMEDIATION

Disintermediation simply means that with the Internet as a delivery vehicle, intermediate players in a distribution channel such as wholesalers and retailers can be bypassed, as illustrated in Figure 2.10. For example, if you buy a book from Amazon.com, the bookstore on Main Street is not involved. Many Internet business models take advantage of disintermediation to reach the consumer directly. Good advice for anyone who occupies an intermediary position in a distribution channel is to think

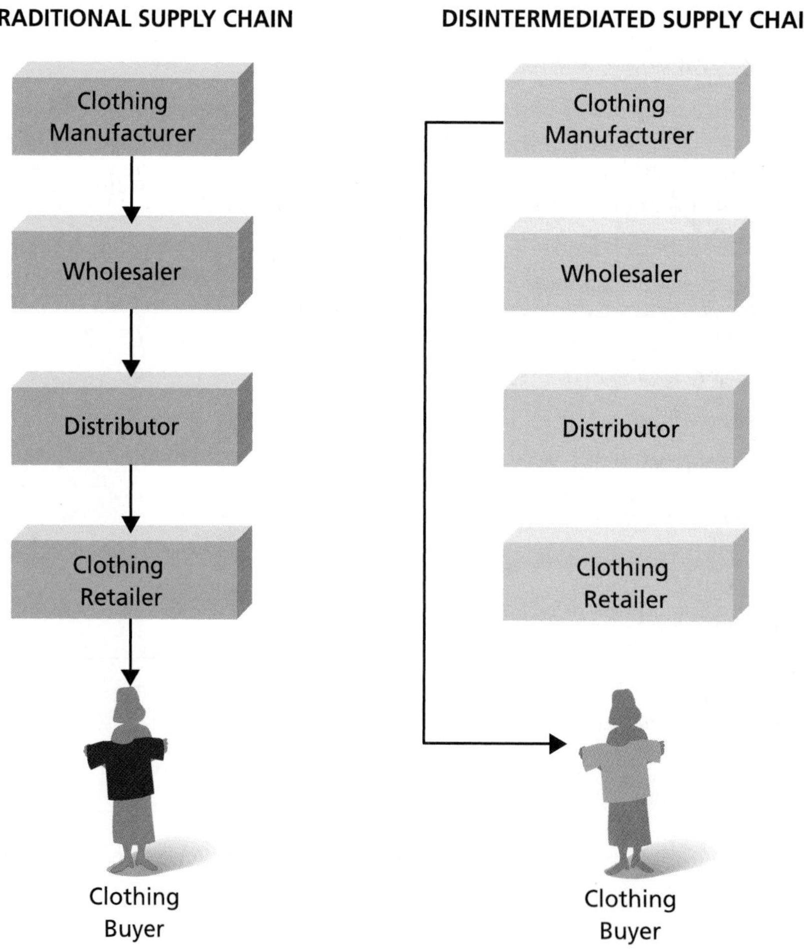

Figure 2.10
Disintermediation at Work

through how an e-business might enter the market and take customers away from them. There are scores of examples of this happening to people such as stockbrokers, insurance agents, real estate agents, mortgage brokers, and merchants selling commodity-like items such as books, videos, and CDs.

One interesting example is Egghead Software, which used to have stores in strip malls in many cities. It soon found that it was being disintermediated by the Internet. Customers who might normally come into an Egghead store and buy a shrink-wrapped package off the shelf were finding it more convenient to buy from a Web site and download software immediately. What did Egghead finally do? It closed its brick-and-mortar stores and set up shop in cyberspace.

Unfortunately, this refocusing came too late. On August 15, 2001 Egghead filed for bankruptcy, and in late November 2001 Amazon.com bought the rights to its domain name and intellectual property. Now, if you type "www.egghead.com" into your browser, you'll be directed to an Amazon.com page displaying the Egghead logo.[12]

GLOBAL REACH

Sausage Software (www.sausagetools.com) is a software developer located outside of Melbourne, Australia. It makes a pretty good Web editor called HotDog. If you want to try it out, you can log on to its Web site and download a copy you can use free for 30 days. At the end of the 30-day trial period, if you want to continue to use HotDog, you just log on to the Web site and give your credit card number. Sausage will send you by return e-mail a code that opens up the software for you to use forever, just as if you had bought it at a store.

Think about this: you buy software, have it delivered, and pay for it, all online. Without the Internet, if Sausage wanted to reach you, it would have had to put salespeople on an airplane, and they would have had to find a software retailer such as CompuServe and convince them to add copies of HotDog to their shelves. Since shelf space is limited and HotDog is not well known, Sausage would probably have had to pay the retailer $20,000 or so as a "stocking fee" just to get HotDog into a few stores. The Internet gives even small companies like Sausage Software **global reach**—the ability to extend their reach to customers anywhere there is an Internet connection, and at a much lower cost. And if the product is digital, so much the better, for then it can be both sold and delivered over the Internet.

The U.S. Airline Industry: A Great Example

To give you a feel for how much of what we have been discussing in this chapter can come together in a single industry, it's hard to think of a better example than the U.S. air travel industry. The large U.S. airlines in particular have given ample evidence over a number of years that they know how to use information technology for competitive advantage. Let's show you how.

AIRLINE RESERVATION SYSTEMS

The airlines really got started using IT in a significant way when American Airlines and United Airlines introduced the first airline reservation systems, SABRE and APOLLO. At the time they pretty much divided up the market between them. They

THE GLOBAL PERSPECTIVE

HOW DO YOU SAY "COOL" IN JAPANESE? TSUTAYA

Tsutaya is Japan's largest purveyor of movies, recorded music, and game software. Its 1100 shops reflect the fashion and culture that appeal to Japanese youth. The most popular outlets offer movie theatres and Starbucks coffee and symbolize all that's cool today in Japan. Founder Muneaki Masuda says he owes much of his success to an early bet on information technology. Tsutaya has systems that can analyze trends hourly at each store. They also track demographics, consumer tastes, and other data in every major urban district—information that helps managers decide what software to stock or where to open a new outlet.

Tsutaya's online site is the most popular destination on i-mode, a mobile Internet service run by NTT DoCoMo. Some 2.4 million users regularly log on to conduct searches and order movie and music titles.[13]

marketed the systems to travel agents who got a special computer terminal from either SABRE or APOLLO when they signed up. Typically, a travel agent signed up for one or the other system, but not both. Airline companies who did not have their own reservation systems, Frontier Airlines for example, paid for the privilege of being a "co-host" on SABRE or APOLLO, which permitted their flights to be listed on the systems, and available to travel agents. American and United got a tremendous competitive advantage from being the owners of the reservation systems. First, they were very profitable. Second, American and United had access to information on the sales volumes of their competitors such as Frontier because it was all available in the reservation systems database. If Frontier wanted to have special competitive analyses prepared they could request special reports, but they had to pay and wait for them to be prepared. Also, SABRE and APOLLO were accused by their co-hosts of "screen bias."[14] This meant that when a travel agent keyed in a request for available flights between Montreal and San Francisco, for example, the first flights shown were those of the airline who owned the reservation system.

FREQUENT FLYER PROGRAMS

When the airlines introduced frequent flyer programs (the airline industry's form of loyalty program), it was to increase the likelihood that their most valued customers, their frequent business travellers, would fly them instead of the competition. Until frequent flyer programs were introduced, business people had no particular incentive to fly the same airline all the time.

After frequent flyer programs came into being, with their mileage and other perks, air travellers saw that it made sense to concentrate their travel with a single airline as much as possible in order to get free trips and upgrades to first class. Frequent flyer programs became very popular and now almost every airline in the world has some sort of program. Frequent flyer programs require complex computer systems to handle all of the record keeping and reporting. They are a good example of using IT to alter Porter's five forces in the airlines' favour. They reduced buyer power by making it less likely a traveller would choose another airline; they reduced the threat of substitute products or services by increasing switching costs; and they erected entry barriers by making a frequent flyer program a practical necessity for any airline to compete effectively.

YIELD MANAGEMENT SYSTEMS

Yield management systems are designed to maximize the amount of revenue an airline generates on each flight.

Basically, what they do is alter the price of available seats on a flight minute by minute as the date of the flight approaches, depending on the number of seats that have been sold compared to an estimate of what was expected. So, if fewer seats have been sold, more low-cost seats are made available for sale. If more seats have been sold than what was estimated, fewer low-cost seats will be made available for sale. The objective is to have the airplane take off full at the highest possible average cost per seat, as illustrated in Figure 2.11. (Airlines would rather make something on a low-cost seat than make nothing on an empty seat.)

Yield management systems are the reason an airfare you're quoted over the phone can be $100 higher when you call back an hour later. Yield management systems are also why you should never ask your seatmate what she paid for her ticket unless you're prepared to be disappointed. They're a good example of how the *value chain* concept uses IT to add value to the sales and marketing process.

DISINTERMEDIATING THE TRAVEL AGENT

Travel agents used to get a commission from the airlines on every ticket they sold. Airlines, realizing that agents' commissions were their third-highest cost after payroll and fuel, decided to first reduce and finally eliminate travel agents' commissions. At the same time, they made it easier for air travellers to make reservations directly with the airlines either through a Web site or by using a toll-free 800 number. They encouraged their frequent flyers to bypass the travel agents by doing three additional things:

1. They offered up to 1000 frequent flyer miles to travellers who made their reservations on the Web.
2. They gave out restricted toll-free 800 numbers to members of frequent flyer "elite" groups, with shorter waiting times and specially trained reservationists.

Figure 2.11

The Payoff from Yield Management

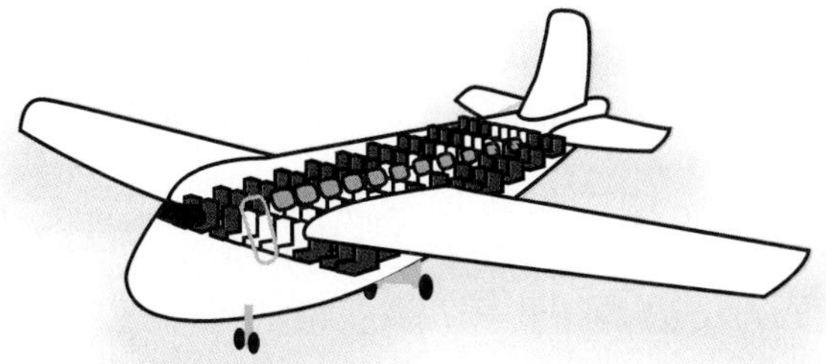

Average seat = $420
Yield = $50,400

120 seats occupied at average price of $420 per seat = $50,400 total yield for the flight.

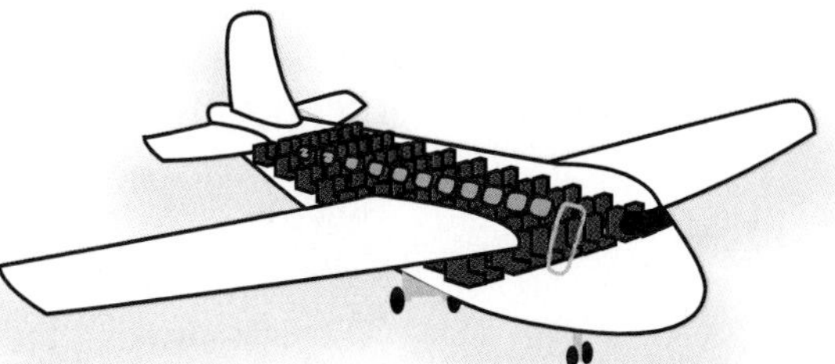

Average seat = $325
Yield = $65,000

200 seats occupied at average price of $325 per seat = $65,000 total yield for the flight.

TEAM WORK

HELPING THE LITTLE GUY COMPETE

Assume that a friend of your family owns a small travel agency located in a neighbourhood shopping centre. The business has provided a comfortable living for him and his family for over 20 years. With the recent changes in the air travel distribution industry, however, he is becoming concerned about whether he can survive in the new competitive environment. Airline companies have reduced commissions paid to travel agents, and at the same time have encouraged members of their frequent flyer programs (the best customers) to bypass travel agents and deal with airlines directly. In addition, new competition has arisen from Internet-based travel sites. Using IT-enabled techniques such as e-tickets seems to be part of a never-ending process to squeeze travel agents. With new technologies being introduced all the time, your friend is concerned that there is no way he can survive.

See if you can come up with some suggestions for how he could use IT to improve his ability to compete.

3. They introduced "e-tickets," which eliminated the need for paper tickets. One of the travel agent's most valued functions was to see that the traveller had his or her ticket well in advance of the flight. With the introduction of e-tickets, the paper ticket disappeared, replaced by a digital record in the airlines' computer systems.

Travel agents had to start charging fees for their services to make up for the lost airline commission payments. Many travellers were not willing to pay a fee to a travel agent, since they could make reservations themselves at no cost. As a result, travel agents' revenues declined. Expert surveys have estimated that the number of travel agents in the United States will be sharply reduced as a result of these and other moves by the airline companies.

One of more interesting aspects of this trend (unless, of course, you happen to be a travel agent) is that the airlines made no secret about the fact that they were trying to eliminate the travel agents from the distribution chain. Usually, the originators of a product or service are more subtle about disintermediation strategies. When Levi Strauss announced that it was going to sell "501" jeans only over its Web site, retailers told Levi Strauss they were going quit selling Levi's jeans altogether. Levi Strauss quickly backed off on that particular disintermediation strategy.[15]

UTILIZING EMERGING TECHNOLOGIES

Note, however, that the competitive landscape in the air travel industry continues to change as tech-savvy entrepreneurs come up with new business ideas. Internet-based travel services such as Expedia, Travelocity, and Trip.com have entered the market, as has Priceline.com, whose customers can name their own price. Last-minute deals to be sure all those seats are filled are sent out by personalized e-mails every Wednesday. You've told the airline's Web site that you want to know when there are last-minute bargain fares to Toronto, and given the airline permission to send you those e-mails. **Permission marketing** is when you have given a merchant your permission to send you special offers. Auction sites such as Bid4vacations.com are another approach. Wireless applications are on the way. It will not be long before your airline will call your cell phone and tell you to sleep in for another hour because your flight has been delayed. Mechanics will soon be able to locate spare parts quickly using wireless devices. Airlines are experimenting with smart card solutions that will speed up the

RIVALWATCH: KEEPING AN EYE ON THE COMPETITION

In the physical world, monitoring the competition down the street or across town is a relative snap, but keeping track of a global base of online competitors is all but impossible. The problem is that there can be so many competitors and so much information on each of them. Adding to the problem is that information on their prices and products can change several times a day. Keeping tabs on what they are doing can be very useful to your company, however, and might even give you some valuable insight into one of your competitor's next moves.

Trying to keep track of them without some expert help, using IT, would be next to impossible. This is where a company called RivalWatch (www.rivalwatch.com) comes to the rescue. Using its proprietary software, RivalWatch will keep a close eye on as many competitors as a company can identify. It keeps its clients up to date on the competition's pricing, product assortment, availability, and even promotional activities. RivalWatch has software that downloads information for its customers from competitors' Web sites and then uses it to produce reports, accessible securely over the Web. RivalWatch focuses on adding some analysis and presenting information in a useful form. It specializes in surveying digital commerce sites so customers can be sure they're pricing their merchandise competitively.

"We present the data in a form [that lets you] make a business decision," says Ann Hsu, vice-president for business development and a co-founder of RivalWatch. "Just giving you a spreadsheet with the prices of 10,000 products is not helpful. Only 5000 are a direct overlap with your site, and out of these, we summarize the price differences. So you can see [that one group of] products is competitive, but these [others] are 25% higher."

As you might imagine, the growing availability of software like RivalWatch has generated interest in developing software products that block electronic snooping. It will be interesting to see the way intelligence gathering and intelligence blocking products evolve.[16]

check-in process and improve security at the same time. Iris scan and facial-recognition devices offer alternative solutions.

You can see how the airlines have employed (and continue to employ) Michael Porter's frameworks as well as some of the other approaches discussed in this chapter: taking the customers' perspective, demanding creativity, personalization, disintermediation, and coming up with new ways to relate to customers and suppliers.

Summing It Up

We've talked about ideas for using IT for competitive advantage, discussed tools companies use to generate such ideas, and given several examples of IT systems that have given their organizations a competitive advantage. Now, we'll summarize some of the most important considerations you should keep in mind as you work to bring an IT competitive advantage to your organization. These include:

- Be efficient and effective.
- Competition is all around you.
- Push the state-of-the-art technology.
- IT competitive advantages are only temporary.

First, remember that what you are trying to do is to make your organization more efficient and more effective. That means you should be applying IT to solving an important business problem. It's the difference between doing something right and doing the right thing. IT resources are limited in most organizations so it's important

ON YOUR OWN

BUILDING ON THE STATE OF THE ART

It's good to get into the habit of noticing the ways that companies are using or not using IT effectively. You can start to build up your own catalogue of ideas for your own organization. It's always good to use to use a state-of-the-art application and see if you can build on it to come up with something even better. Pick a company that you think is getting a competitive advantage from IT and try to suggest ways that it could be improved. This is the time to let your imagination run free and to consider using some of the new emerging technologies.

that they be applied to solving the most important business problems or exploiting the opportunities with the highest potential payoff.

Second, remember that your organization is in a competitive environment. The reason we emphasize competitive advantage is that you and your competitors are both trying to attract and retain the same customers. You are all competing for that customer's business. We all tend to buy from the company that gives us the best product or service at the price we want to pay, and the customers of your organization are no different. Companies should strive to "delight the customer," by giving them more value than what they were expecting to receive. Keep that in mind when you're reviewing proposals for new IT systems. Will they help you to delight your customers? It's always smart to try and anticipate how your competitor might use IT for competitive advantage. Why let them get a first-mover advantage?

Third, in addition to the other suggestions we made in this chapter, if an IT system is going to give you a competitive advantage it must push the state of the art. In order to push the state of the art, you must find out what a state-of-the-art IT system is for the business problem you're trying to solve. Do a little research to find out which company has the best solution and then try to surpass it. And don't restrict your search to just your industry. A state-of-the-art system for a hospital, for example, might find some ideas in a manufacturing control system. Don't let your imagination be limited by just considering technologies that are currently available, or discard currently available technologies because they're too expensive. If you place artificial boundaries like these on candidate solutions, you may inhibit creativity unnecessarily. You can always bring an overly ambitious solution back to reality, but if you don't evaluate it, the opportunity will be lost.

Finally, it's worth reemphasizing is that using IT for competitive advantage usually provides only a temporary advantage. This is because your competitors are forced to duplicate (or to better) what you have. This means your organization must be continually looking for ways to use IT for competitive advantage so you stay ahead of, or don't fall behind, the competition.

That may sound like a lot of work, and a never-ending cycle, but the reassuring reality is that there will be continuing opportunities for you to come up with creative IT solutions to business problems.

Summary: Student Learning Outcomes Revisited

1. **Describe how the creative use of information technology can give an organization a competitive advantage.** Smart companies spend a lot of time, money, and effort in designing and installing it systems because they realize a competitive advantage when it systems deliver creative solutions to business problems. A **competitive advantage** can be gained by providing a product or service in a way that customers value more than the competition's. Some concepts related to IT systems are:
   - **Temporary advantage**—whatever you do, sooner or later the competition duplicates what you've done, but a temporary advantage can linger in customers' minds and have lasting effects.
   - **First mover**—first to market with a new IT-based product or service can gain competitive advantage.
   - **Information partnership**—two or more companies acting in cooperation by integrating their IT systems provide customers with the best of what each can offer.
   - **Alliance partner**—companies that you do business with on a regular basis in a cooperative fashion.
   - **Business to Business (B2B)**—IT-enabled business with other businesses.
   - **Business to Consumer (B2C)**—IT-enabled business with individual customers.
2. **Demonstrate how to generate ideas for using information technology in innovative ways, and apply tools that can help.** Creating an IT system that gives you a competitive advantage is not merely a technical challenge. Important considerations include:
   - Bridging the gap between business people and technical people
   - Viewing the business problem from another perspective
   - Demanding a creative design
   - Looking beyond the four walls of the company

   Concepts to remember and tools that can help include:
   - The **five forces model**:
     - Buyer power
     - Supplier power
     - Threat of substitute products or services
     - Threat of new entrants
     - Rivalry among existing competitors
   - The **three generic strategies**:
     - Cost leadership
     - Differentiation
     - Focused strategy
   - The **value chain**—a view of the organization as a chain—or series—of processes, each of which adds value to the product or service for the customer.
3. **Describe how e-commerce technologies "up the stakes" and give organizations even more opportunities.** E-commerce makes it even more important for you to focus on competitive advantage. The main reason for this is that the Internet and related technologies provide new capabilities to establish more effective information partnerships along the supply and distribution chains and to forge closer relationships with customers. This can be achieved through:
   - **Mass customization**—occurs when a business gives its customers the opportunity to have its product or service tailored to the customer's specifications
   - **Personalization**—occurs when an Internet site can know enough about your likes and dislikes that it can fashion offers more likely to appeal to you (supported by techniques such as **collaborative filtering**)
   - **Disintermediation**—occurs when, with the Internet as a delivery vehicle, intermediate players in a distribution channel are bypassed
   - **Global reach**—the ability to extend reach to customers anywhere there is an Internet connection, and at a much lower cost
4. **Summarize how one specific industry has consistently used information technology for competitive advantage.** The U.S. air travel industry is a good industry for you to study to see how companies can consistently use IT for competitive advantage over a period of many years to both reduce costs and create differentiation. For example, the airlines' frequent flyer programs increase customer loyalty by encouraging frequent flyers to take most or all of their flights on a single airline. Using Porter's five forces framework, frequent flyer programs reduce buyer power and increase

switching costs. And frequent flyers like them! Because they do, frequent flyer programs are also an example of an entry barrier. If you want to be in the airline business you pretty much have to have a frequent flyer program. Frequent flyer programs also illustrate how a competitive advantage is often only temporary as competitors race to duplicate innovative IT systems. Other examples of the use of IT for competitive advantage include the airline reservation systems, yield management systems, and the airline companies' e-commerce initiatives.

5. **Describe how to use information technology for competitive advantage in an organization.**

Try to get into the habit of looking for ways that IT could be used to solve a business problem in your organization. Work with IT professionals to get their ideas and look around to see what the state of the art is, not only in your industry but in others as well. Keep in mind that you are operating in a competitive environment and that it will be useful for you to try to anticipate what your competition's next move in the IT arena might be. Remember that the nature of a competitive environment is that there are winners and losers. IT *can* give you a competitive advantage, but "If you snooze you lose!"

CLOSING CASE STUDY ONE

GM TRIES TO LURE CUSTOMERS WITH ONSTAR

General Motors Corp. has suffered a loss in market share in the past few years. Partly this is because many of its cars are viewed as boring by consumers. GM recently added an in-car cellular service to many of its cars in an attempt to update its image and increase sales.

The service, called OnStar, was originally offered in Cadillacs as an emergency concierge and road service. It uses a global positioning system (GPS) combined with a cellular telephone and a 24-hour call centre where highly trained "virtual advisors" are on duty. Drivers can access a virtual advisor whenever they wish and get specialized services such as the latest news, sports information, and stock quotes. The virtual concierge can also help you plan trips, make restaurant reservations, tell you what's playing at the movies, and give you driving directions. Of course, you can also make a hands-free cellular telephone call.

Have you ever been stuck in a traffic jam and wondered what in the world was going on up ahead? Or have you ever been late for an appointment and wondering if there was a traffic problem on your normal route? Well, with OnStar, drivers in metropolitan areas can also get information on traffic conditions such as accidents, delays, and construction within a five-mile radius of their vehicle.

OnStar subscribers can also get emergency roadside assistance if they have car trouble on the road. The integrated GPS combined with the cellular connection to the call centre provides assurance that a vehicle can be located no matter what. OnStar can even run a diagnostic check of your car's engine while you drive. And, if you ever have the bad luck to have your car stolen (or forget where you left it in a huge shopping centre parking lot), the OnStar virtual concierge can track it and guide the police (or you) to its location.

Fees for the OnStar service start at $199 for an annual subscription. You may have seen ads on television showing a driver calling the OnStar centre because he has locked his keys in his car. The operator tells him not to worry and unlocks his car doors with a remote signal from the centre. Problem solved. As one more example, emergency assistance is automatically dispatched if the OnStar system detects that the car's airbags have been deployed.

Industry analysts have commented that adding services like OnStar is something GM had to do in order to improve its brands' images in the minds of consumers. GM is betting that being the leader with an onboard technology such as OnStar will show that it is once again technology leader rather than a follower.

OnStar is one of the many ways GM President Rick Wagoner wants to keep the company innovative. As another example, former Chrysler executive Bob Lutz was recently hired to revitalize GM's product lines. Known in the industry as a "car guy," Lutz is sharpening GM's focus on design and finding ways to get new products to market faster. Under the new business process for designing and manufacturing cars that Lutz is overseeing, design moves to the forefront. For every vehicle idea, three teams will compete to create what will eventually make it to market. Lutz held just such a contest to develop the Pontiac Solstice concept car—a two-seat roadster that has been lauded for its looks at auto shows. Lutz views OnStar as a technology that can only add value to the innovative car designs he intends to develop and introduce.

OnStar is now installed in about 1.7 million vehicles. It is available in 36 GM models and is also licensed to Acura, Audi, and Lexus. While some automobile manufacturers are already talking about offering similar products in their cars, others may find it more economical to license OnStar from GM than develop an offering of their own as Acura, Audi, and Lexus did.

Some industry analysts remain skeptical about the OnStar initiative. They agree that OnStar offers some interesting features that will be valued by consumers; on the other hand, they point out that GM must continue to focus on its fundamental problem, the style of its cars. Perhaps the combination of OnStar and Bob Lutz will go a long way toward solving some of GM's problems.[17]

Questions

1. The chapter discussed several examples of companies that have used IT for competitive advantage. Is there anything about the OnStar system that makes it a good example as well? Is OnStar a feature that is likely to give GM a competitive advantage for an extended period of time or is it likely to give, if anything, a temporary advantage?

2. Evaluate the OnStar system from the perspectives of the five forces model and the three generic strategies. Explain how OnStar might alter the five forces in GM's favour. Where would you place the OnStar system in the three generic strategies grid illustrated in Figure 2.5?

3. Is OnStar a good example of a company incorporating emerging technologies into its product strategies? Why or why not? What features do you think a system such as OnStar might offer five years from now? Is GM taking any risks by placing such a large bet on OnStar's being accepted by the marketplace? What are those risks, if any?

4. If you were a product designer for Ford Motor Company, what would your reaction be to GM's rollout of OnStar? Do you think systems such as OnStar will become an entry barrier? Log on to the Internet and see if you can find out what the other major automobile manufacturers, both U.S. and non-U.S., are doing in response to the OnStar system. Draw a conclusion as to which responses you think will be most effective.

5. What would your reaction to OnStar be if you were a marketing strategist for a cell-phone, Internet Portal, or GPS service provider? Would you consider OnStar a competitive threat to your company? If so, why, and what would your response be? If not, why not?

CLOSING CASE STUDY TWO

SPEEDPASS: THROW AWAY YOUR PLASTIC?

Speedpass is an idea that has been around since 1996 but it is now beginning to take off. Speedpass offers a short plastic cylinder, called a Key Tag, that contains an RFID (radio frequency identification) transponder. The Key Tag is very lightweight, short, and can be placed on your key ring. It communicates wirelessly with receiving devices over short distances. It was developed by Mobil Oil Corporation (now part of ExxonMobil) as a substitute for using a credit card at the gasoline pump. Instead of waiting for a credit card authorization, Speedpass users simply wave their Key Tag at the gasoline pump and their billing information is transmitted and recorded for subsequent billing. Speedpass is not available in all areas yet, but if it's available in your area, you can get a Speedpass transponder for free.

In some areas, you can get a Speedpass Car Tag as well as a Key Tag. The Car Tag is a device placed inside the rear window of your car. In the same way as the Key Tag, the Car Tag activates Speedpass technology. You can sign up and also learn more about Speedpass and the way the technology works at www.speedpass.com.

The advantage of the Car Tag version is that you don't have to wave it at anything. When you get close enough to the gasoline pump, the Car Tag transmits your billing information to the pump. You still have to get out of your car and pump the gasoline, however. But wait; there is another technology on the horizon that will make your life even easier. One of the other big oil companies has been developing a "smart" gasoline pump. It can recognize the make and model of automobile you are driving, and on the basis of that know where the fuel door is located and what grade of gasoline you should use. Just think of the day, not that far away, when we will be able to pull up to a gasoline station, "fill 'er up" and pay without getting out of the driver's seat by using Speedpass combined with smart pumps. Great for late nights or rainy days!

Speedpass can also be used at properly equipped cash registers as well. With cash register purchases, not only is there no waiting for authorization, there is also no need for customers to sign a paper receipt.

McDonald's Restaurants is testing Speedpass, so if it works there, you may soon find that you will be able to buy a Big Mac, fries, and a Coke with your Key Tag or Car Tag. Not only that, if it works at McDonald's, it will surely be adopted by other retailers who would like to take advantage of the technology. There are currently over five million users of Speedpass in North America with more being added every day. Customers are signing up because they like its convenience. This will encourage more retailers to offer the technology because they can see that customers will be more likely to shop at their stores if they can offer them Speedpass in addition to cash, credit, and debit cards.

Another interesting variation is the new Speedpass-enabled Timex Watch, which is also undergoing market testing. Whereas the traditional Car Tag is attached to a user's key ring, this watch looks and functions just like a regular watch. Inside it, however, is a Speedpass transponder that works just like the Car Tag. The new Speedpass-enabled watch will give customers a hands-free option that enables them to pay for purchases by simply positioning their watch in front of an electronic reader located at a gasoline pump, the checkout counter, or the drive-thru window. The Timex version of Speedpass is not available yet, but should be soon if the testing goes as well as expected.

Speedpass earns revenue by taking a small portion of each transaction as a fee, like a credit card company. In some ways, it acts like a loyalty program, because it encourages customers to return to shop at retailers who offer the Speedpass technology. However, it differs from traditional loyalty programs in that it does not offer free tickets or other incentives. The incentive to Speedpass' customers seems to be the sheer convenience of it, and maybe that's enough to make Speedpass a market success.[18]

Questions

1. With over five million users signed up already, Speedpass seems to have a pretty good first-mover advantage. In addition, it seems to be embarked on a strategy of continuous innovation that will keep it in the lead. What sort of companies can you imagine as likely competitors to Speedpass and what sort of strategies might they use to overcome the lead Speedpass has established?

2. Speedpass has its critics, who claim that its technology, particularly the Car Tag, has some serious security problems in comparison to credit cards. For example, with a credit card, there is a signature on the back that a merchant can use to compare with the purchaser's signature if the sale is made at a cash register. If you were promoting Speedpass' solution, how would you respond to this issue?

3. Evaluate Speedpass using as many elements of Porter's five forces model as you think are appropriate. For example, consider the threat of substitute products. What are the substitute products (or services) for Speedpass? Are they serious threats? If so, how could they be overcome? Can you think of other technologies that might be threats?

4. The case stated that Speedpass had no plans at the moment to incorporate elements of a loyalty program into its strategy. Do you agree with this decision? If so, why? If not, can you come up with an approach that would let Speedpass merchants incorporate features of a loyalty program for users?

5. Pick another country that you have visited or perhaps one that you have lived in for awhile. (It could be your country of origin.) Using the Internet, see if you can find out if Speedpass is being used in that country. If not, try and determine why it is not. Is it just that the technology is not known there yet? Is there a competing technology that is well accepted or in the process of becoming so? Are there some elements of the culture in the country you have chosen that make Speedpass a bad bet for that country? Is the level of technology development such that it is too soon to try to introduce Speedpass?

Key Terms and Concepts

alliance partner, 47
application architect, 44
B2B marketplace, 51
business process, 53
business to business (B2B), 47
business to consumer (B2C), 47
buyer power, 49
collaborative filtering, 58
competitive advantage, 44
disintermediation, 58
distribution chain, 46
entry barrier, 51
first mover, 46
five forces model, 49
global reach, 59
information partnership, 47
mass customization, 57
permission marketing, 62
personalization, 58
rivalry among existing competitors, 50
supplier power, 50
switching costs, 50
temporary advantage, 46
threat of new entrants, 50
threat of substitute products or services, 50
three generic strategies, 52
value chain, 53

Short-Answer Questions

1. What are the two things you need, as a minimum, in order to design an information system that gives an organization a competitive advantage?
2. What do "application architects" do?
3. Why are competitive advantages achieved through IT usually only temporary?
4. What do we call a company which is the first to market with a product or service?
5. What is meant by "B2B" and "B2C"?
6. When is buyer power high?
7. When is supplier power high?
8. Why is it important to view the business problem from another perspective?
9. What is a B2B marketplace?
10. What is CPFR? How do companies who use it get a competitive advantage?
11. What is the *value chain?* How is it used?
12. What is an example of a value-added process not discussed in the chapter?
13. What is an example of a value-reducing process not discussed in the chapter?
14. What is the difference between mass customization and personalization? See if you can give some examples not included in the chapter.
15. What is meant by *global reach*? Why might it be important for an importer in Saskatoon, Saskatchewan to be concerned about it?

Assignments and Exercises

1. **EVALUATING TELEMEDICINE.** The Industry Perspective "Remote Surgery: A New Export Industry?" mentioned that perhaps health care could someday become an export industry. Assume that you work for a university-based medical centre and have been given the assignment to evaluate whether remote medicine, in general, is likely to be more common in the coming years and, if so, how your medical centre and its health care professionals should respond to such a trend.

   To get you started on this assignment, you might try to find out what is being written about "telemedicine"—the term often used to describe the remote delivery of health care services, enabled, of course, by computer and telecommunications technologies. For example, a small town in a remote part of the country typically does not have access to skilled medical specialists such as radiologists. If someone is injured and requires an X-ray for diagnosis, it is possible to take an X-ray locally and then transmit the results to your medical centre where it would be reviewed and evaluated by a radiologist. Of course, if the X-ray can be transmitted to your medical centre, it could be transmitted to a medical centre anywhere in the world. Prepare a brief analysis on the possibilities for telemedicine and recommend whether your medical centre should begin to evaluate its competitive opportunities and threats.

2. **COMPARING PARCEL DELIVERY SERVICES.** The chapter mentioned that, almost always, competitive advantages gained through the creative use of information technology are temporary. The need for continuous innovation is always present. If companies stand still, time and time again we have seen their competitors leapfrog them with further innovations. In the FedEx example discussed in the chapter, we described their package tracking system as a good example of using IT for competitive advantage. Recently, FedEx introduced additional features to its package tracking system that make it more useful and convenient to its customers. You can see what they have done by going to www.fedex.ca and navigating to the "FedEx Insight" page. Note the features that it offers customers compared to the basic package tracking service described in the chapter. Now go to one of the competitor sites, UPS, at www.ups.ca. Note what it is offering its customers in the way of tracking services and compare them with those of FedEx. Prepare a short comparison of the features of each and pick the company you would prefer if your selection were to be made strictly on the basis of tracking services.

3. **DISINTERMEDIATION IN THE TRAVEL AGENT INDUSTRY.** We discussed the concept of disintermediation in the chapter and gave several examples. One of the examples discussed at some length was the air travel distribution industry and how it has affected smaller travel agents in particular. There is probably a small travel agency located either on or near your campus. It would be interesting for you to hear from its owner or manager just exactly how the use of IT by the airlines and by Internet travel services has affected them personally, and how business has changed as a result. Find and visit a the owner of a small local travel agency who would be willing to spend a little time giving you his or her impressions of how the business has changed, and what he or she had to do to react to the new competitive pressures.

   This is an assignment you may have to undertake in groups of two or three, and you may have to do a little pre-planning so that not everyone is imposing on the time of the same agency. If there are only one or two travel agents nearby, see if you can arrange a telephone interview, or perhaps choose one of the other professions mentioned in the chapter.

4. **EVALUATING GOVERNMENT SERVICES ON THE INTERNET.** In one of the Global Perspectives in this chapter, we noted that even governments can get a competitive advantage with IT. This holds true for state and local governments as well as national governments. For example, our lives as citizens would be much easier if certain governmental services could be had them over the Internet instead of us having to visit an office and stand in line. Visit your city or town's Web site, and note what services (e.g., licences, traffic tickets, utility services, information on recreational facilities, etc.) are offered to citizens over the Internet. How well are they doing?

Discussion Questions

1. What is meant by the term "competitive advantage"? Why is competitive advantage important? Give some examples of companies you deal with which you think have achieved competitive advantage, and explain the technique(s) they used to achieve it. Next, give some examples of companies you deal with, or know of, that have used IT in creative ways to get a competitive advantage. Try to come up with at least three examples not discussed in the chapter.

2. How does Dell get a competitive advantage from its "sell, source, and ship" model? Why do you suppose other manufacturers of personal computers let Dell get and maintain a first-mover advantage with its business model and not simply do business the same way as Dell as soon as they saw how effective it was?

3. The chapter states that it is important to view the business problem from another perspective if

you are to develop an IT system that gives your organization a competitive advantage. Why is this important? What are some of the other perspectives that you could use in order to generate fresh ideas for solving a business problem?

4. In the chapter we gave examples of some common entry barriers in the banking industry such as ATMs and Internet banking. Pick an industry you are familiar with and give an example of an entry barrier that was created using IT. See if you can think of other examples of companies who have used IT to alter Porter's five forces model in their favour.

5. In the Industry Perspective "GE Leadership and Competitive IT" we discussed how Jack Welch urged GE managers to come up with new ideas for using the Internet to improve the efficiency and effectiveness of their business units. He urged them to think "destroyyourbusiness.com," or, in other words, to drop old ways of doing business in favour of new ways before the competition did. How important do you suppose it is for presidents and CEOs to act in similar ways if an organization is going to be able to use IT for competitive advantage? For example, do you think it will be likely that a company's managers will make the effort to find ways to use IT for competitive advantage if IT seems to be about number 23 on the CEOs' priority list?

6. See if you can think of a make and model of automobile that would be properly placed in each quadrant of Michael Porter's three generic strategies model as illustrated in Figure 2.5. For example, where would you place the Honda Civic? How about a Ferrari?

7. Can you think of why a process in the value chain would be value-reducing? Do you really think that organizations operate with processes that are value-reducing? How could that happen?

8. The chapter makes the statement that the big difference between the old economy and the new economy is the Internet. Can you think of additional factors that can or will make the way business will be done in the future different from the way it is being done today? Do you think that we will reach a point during the next ten years when business people will not have to be concerned about technological changes affecting the way they do business? Why or why not?

9. Assume you are in business as a real estate agent. Should you feel threatened by the possibility of being disintermediated? Right now, you get a handsome commission for every house that you sell, perhaps as much as 6 or 7 percent. You know that some tech-savvy entrepreneurs are placing listings of homes for sale on the Internet. Many of their Web sites have search engines that let prospective buyers look for the kinds of homes they want in neighbourhoods where they want to live. Some of the sites offer virtual home tours as well. You realize that the technology is only going to get better, and that buyers may feel they can get along without at least some of the services you offer and either bypass you completely or negotiate a reduced commission for fewer services. Is it time to start looking for another career?

10. Think of other good examples of industries in which companies have used IT for competitive advantage the way the U.S. airline industry has. Come up with examples of both industries that seem to be ahead in the way they use IT and industries that are behind the curve. Why do you suppose some industries are lagging behind?

REAL HOT Electronic Commerce

Ordering Products on the Internet

Real HOT Links

For most people, electronic commerce is all about business-to-consumer; that is, most of us think of electronic commerce as an essential enabler for allowing businesses to interact with its individual consumers (you and me). The B2C aspect is certainly well known right now. On the Internet, you (as an individual consumer) can purchase groceries, clothes, computers, automobiles, music, antiques, books, and much more. If you want it, there's probably an Internet site selling it. What's more, there are probably hundreds of Internet sites selling it, giving you the opportunity to shop around.

We would offer a couple of words of caution before you begin this project. Those words are "*Caveat emptor*" or "Let the buyer beware." You can indeed find almost anything you want to buy on the Internet; however, you should carefully consider the person or organization from whom you're making the purchase. You want to be sure you are doing business with someone you can trust. This is especially true if you have to provide a credit card number to make the purchase.

BOOKS AND MUSIC

Books and music make up one category of products you can readily find to purchase on the Internet. Chapters offers several million book, movie, and music titles for sale at www.chapters.indigo.ca.

Of course, as with all products you buy online, you need to consider price and the amount you'll save on the Internet compared to purchasing books and music from

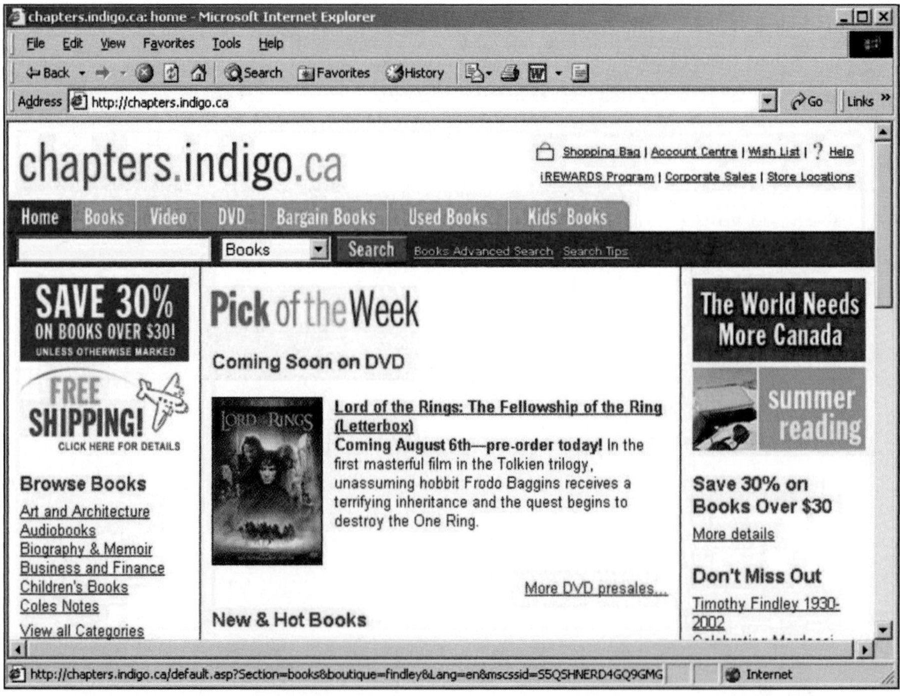

local stores. Sometimes, prices are higher on the Internet, and you can certainly expect to pay some sort of shipping and handling charges. So don't blindly purchase any product on the Internet without first checking local stores.

Make a list of books and music CDs or cassettes you're interested in purchasing. Find out their prices at a local store. Next, visit three Web sites selling books and music and answer the following questions:

A. What are the books or music albums you're interested in?

B. What are their prices at a local store?

C. Can you find them at each Internet site?

D. How does each site categorize its books and music?

E. Are the local prices higher or lower than the Internet prices?

F. How do you order and pay for your products?

G. How long is the shipping delay?

H. What is the shipping charge?

I. Overall, how would you rate your Internet shopping experience compared to your local store shopping experience?

CLOTHING AND ACCESSORIES

It might seem odd, but many people purchase all types of clothing on the Internet—from shoes to pants to all kinds of accessories (including perfume). The disadvantage in shopping for clothes on the Internet is that you can't actually try them on and stand in front of the mirror. However, at sites such as www.lesailes.com, you can browse and purchase clothing with the help of a "virtual stylist."

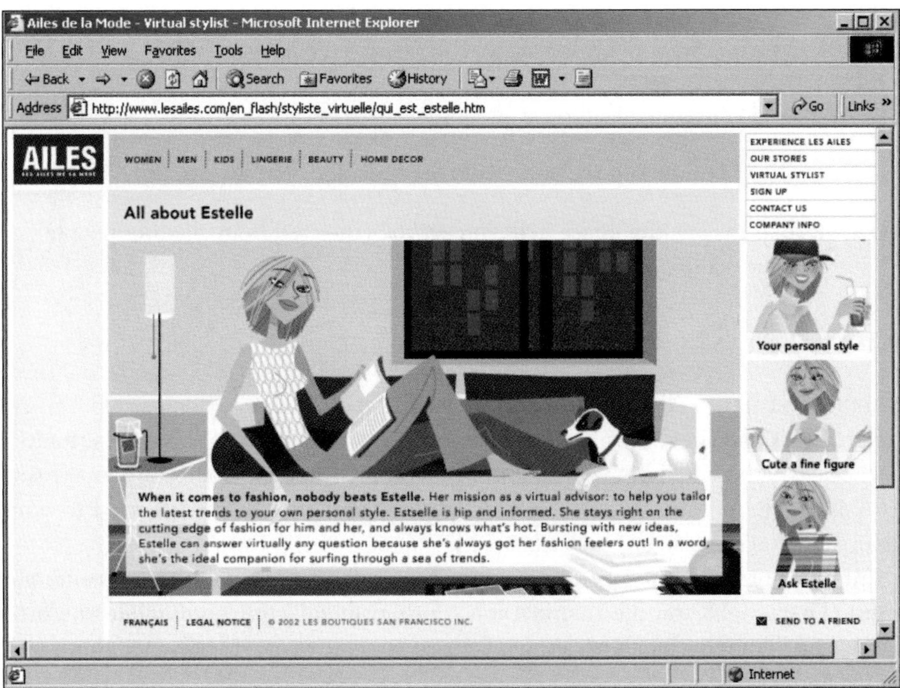

Connect to several clothing and accessory sites and experience cyber-clothing shopping. As you do, consider the following. How do you order and pay for merchandise? What sort of description is provided about the clothing—text, photos, perhaps 3D views? What is the return policy for merchandise that you don't like or doesn't fit? Finally, is shopping for clothes on the Internet as much fun as going to the mall? Why or why not?

AUCTION HOUSES

As you search for products on the Internet, you'll find a lot of traditional organizations such as Grand & Toy selling their wares. You'll also come across a variety of Internet auction houses. These act as clearing stations on which you can sell your products or purchase products from other people in an auction format (essentially, consumer-to-consumer or C2C electronic commerce). Auction houses represent some serious electronic commerce on the Internet. eBay, one of the more popular auction houses, boasts an amazing ten million items for sale.

It works quite simply. First, you register as a user at a particular auction house. Once you do, you'll have a unique user ID and password that allow you to post products for sale or bid on other products. When the auction is complete for a particular product (time limits typically last from one to ten days), the auction house will notify the seller and the winning bidder. Then it's up to you and the other person to exchange money and merchandise.

So think of a product you'd like to buy or sell—perhaps a rare coin, a computer, a hard-to-find collectible, or a car. Connect to a couple of different Internet auction houses and answer the following questions for each.

A. What is the registration process to become a user?

B. Do you have to pay a fee to become a user?

C. Is your product of interest listed?

D. How do you bid on a product?

E. What does the auction house charge you to sell a product?

F. What is the duration of a typical auction?

G. Can you set a minimum acceptable bid for a product you want to sell?

H. How does the auction house help you evaluate the credibility of other people buying and selling products?

AUTOMOBILES

On the Internet, you'll find a lot of products for sale that almost don't seem to fit the "electronic commerce" environment. We've already discussed clothes and perfume—you can't try them out, but you can buy them on the Internet. There are actually several sites where you can place grocery orders and have them delivered to your doorstep. You can also buy real estate from photos.

Another product category you may not expect to find on the Internet is automobiles. That's right—on the Internet you can find literally any automobile you'd be interested in purchasing. Muscle cars, Jaguars, Rolls Royces, Hondas, and thousands more are for sale.

Try connecting to a few of these sites and browse for an automobile you'd like to own. As you do, think about these issues. What variety can you find (colour, engine size, interior, etc.)? Are financing options available? How do you "test-drive" a car for sale on the Internet? What happens if you buy a car and then don't like it? What about used cars—can you trust people selling a used car on the Internet? How do you pay for a car, typically a relatively large purchase?

You can find a variety of sites that provide competitive pricing information concerning cars. Many of these sites are for all cars in general, not just those for sale on the Internet. One of the best is AutoSite (www.autosite.com). If you're ever shopping for a new or used car, you should definitely check out that site.

Go to the Online Learning Centre at www.mcgrawhill.ca/college/haag for quizzes, extra content, a searchable glossary, and more! Click on "Electronic Commerce Projects" for links to hundreds of Web sites.

Go to the text CD-ROM for data files, extra content, and Skills Modules on Microsoft Excel, Microsoft Access, HTML, and e-portfolios.

CHAPTER THREE

STUDENT LEARNING OUTCOMES

1. Describe business intelligence and its role in an organization.
2. Differentiate between databases and data warehouses with respect to their focus on online transaction processing and online analytical processing.
3. List and describe the key characteristics of a relational database.
4. Define the five software components of a database management system.
5. List and describe the key characteristics of a data warehouse.
6. Define the four major types of data mining tools in a data warehouse environment.
7. List key considerations in managing the information resource in an organization.

INDUSTRY PERSPECTIVES

FEATURES

WEB SUPPORT LINKS

- Financial Aid Resources
- Libraries
- Consumer Information
- Demographics
- Real Estate

Visit: www.mcgrawhill.ca/college/haag

DATABASES AND DATA WAREHOUSES
Building Business Intelligence

CASE STUDY:
DATA WAREHOUSING—PART OF THE INFORMATION LOOP AT SCOTIAMcLEOD

If you ever contact ScotiaMcLeod (www.scotiamcleod.com—formerly Charles Schwab Canada) to inquire about their financial services such as individual retirement accounts (IRAs), do not be surprised if the call centre agent tries to capture as much information about you as possible. Not only will your name, address, and request for information be entered into the company's central database (a.k.a. the core production system), but so will any information you provide such as whether you currently own stocks or equities and whether you consider yourself a beginning investor. During subsequent calls, the agent knows exactly what took place during the initial contact and is also provided with an idea of your needs on the basis of the information ScotiaMcLeod's analysts retrieved from the company's data warehouse.

What makes this possible? Well, all customer contact information, including the information on all clients' active accounts, is replicated in the company's data warehouse, which is used to sort customers into segments according to gender, affluence, trading activity, contact channel preference, etc. The data warehouse then feeds different data marts (a subset of a data warehouse) used by ScotiaMcLeod's various business units. Marketing analysts, for instance, use these data marts for reporting and analysis purposes and to make inferences about your needs and preferences as a customer. As such, if the request you made concerning IRAs is also made by several other customers sharing similar characteristics, Schwab will attempt to increase its marketing efforts for IRAs to your segment.

The benefits of data warehousing at ScotiaMcLeod do not stop there. In fact, the information fed into the data warehouse by the core production system goes full circle and is made available to all of the different channels (Internet, call centre, and branch office), dramatically improving customer interaction in an almost seamless way. As Beth Devin, senior VP of retail technology, puts it—"It's a loop really." Information about customer interactions is captured into the central database and automatically fed into the data marts. This enables the marketing department to analyze it and to create new information, which is then fed back into the central database weekly and used by specialists while interacting with clients.[1]

Introduction

Imagine that you're the inventory manager for a multimillion-dollar firm and that you can accurately predict selling trends by the week, territory, salesperson, and product line. Imagine that you own an accounting firm and can accurately predict which and how many of your clients will file for tax extensions. Imagine that you're an accounts manager and can accurately determine creditworthy risks. Sound impossible? Not really—it's quite possible that you could make these predications with a 95 percent accuracy rate, or even higher.

How? Obviously your education has a lot to do with it. But so does access to and the ability to work with two resources that every organization owns today—information and business intelligence. *Access to* information and business intelligence implies that they are organized in such a way that you can easily and quickly get to them. *Working with* information and business intelligence implies that you have the right information processing tools. That's what this chapter is all about—organizing information and business intelligence and having the right tools to work them.

Throughout this chapter, we focus on (1) databases and data warehouses as methods for organizing and managing information and business intelligence and (2) database management systems and data mining techniques as IT tools you use to work with information and business intelligence.

Business Intelligence

"Business intelligence" sounds like a great term. But what exactly is it? **Business intelligence** is knowledge—knowledge about your customers, your competitors, your partners, your competitive environment, and your own internal operations. Business intelligence comes from information. It enables your organization to extrapolate the true meaning of information to take creative and powerful steps to ensure a competitive advantage. So business intelligence is much more than just a list of the products you sell. It would, for example, combine your product information with your advertising strategy information and customer demographics to help you determine the effectiveness of various advertising media on demographic groups segmented by location (see Figure 3.1).

Of course, business intelligence doesn't just magically appear. You must first gather and organize all your information. Then, you must have the right IT tools to define and analyze various relationships within the information. In short, knowledge workers such as you use IT tools to create business intelligence from information. The technology won't simply do it for you. However, technology such as databases, database management systems (DBMSs), data warehouses, and data mining tools can definitely help you build and use business intelligence.

As you begin working with these tools (which we'll discuss in great detail throughout this chapter), you'll be performing the two types of information processing we alluded to in Chapter 1—online transaction processing and online analytical processing. **Online transaction processing (OLTP)** is the gathering of input information, the processing of that information, and the updating of existing information to reflect the gathered and processed information. Databases and DBMSs are the technology tools that directly support OLTP. Databases that support OLTP are most often referred to as **operational databases**; inside these is valuable information that forms the basis for business intelligence.

Figure 3.1
Building Business Intelligence

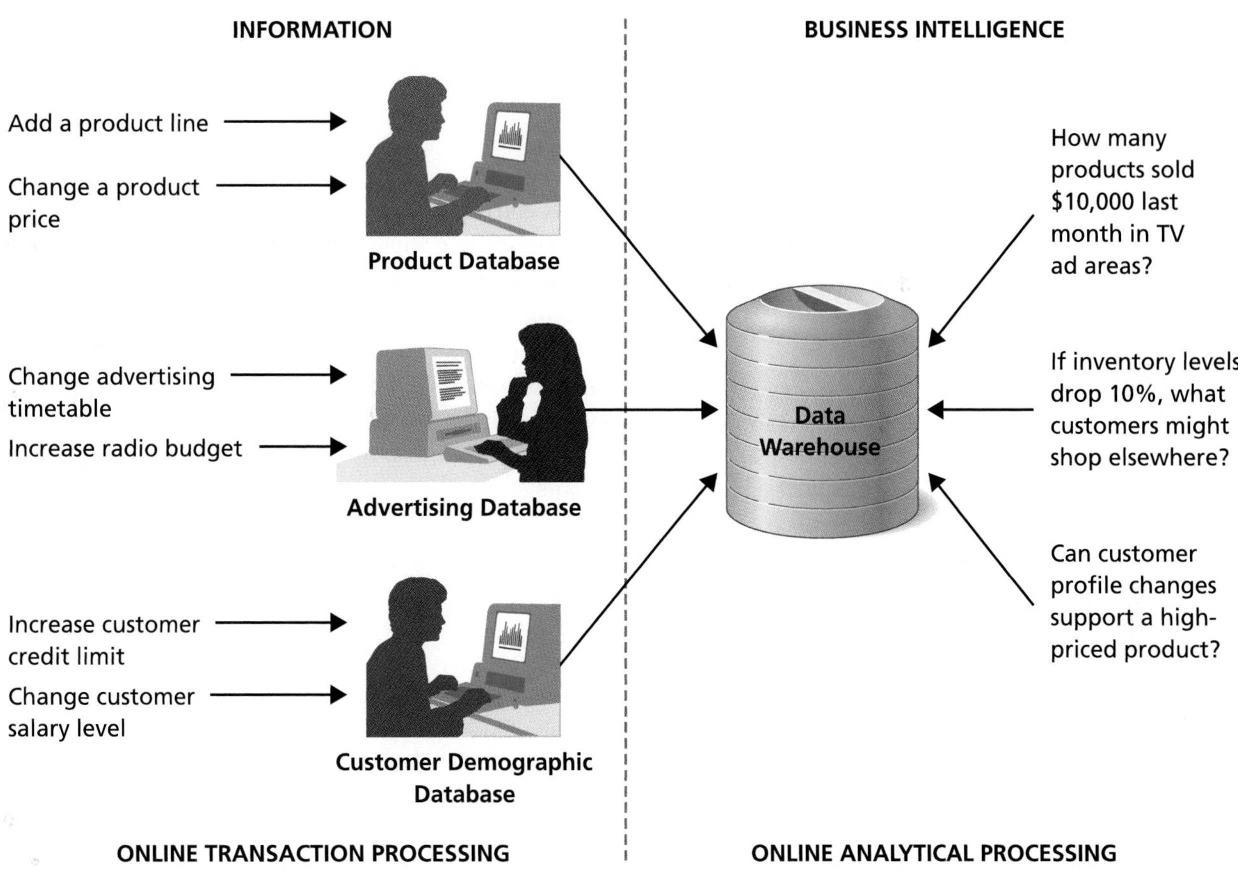

Online analytical processing (OLAP) is the manipulation of information to support decision making. At Mervyn's, a subdivision of Dayton Hudson Corp., OLAP is a must and a definite improvement over the way things used to work.[2,3] According to Sid Banjeree, "Mervyn's had people who spent hours pouring over shopping carts full of paper reports ... to gather product information by units, by dollars, by a single store, by season, by region, and by ad zone. Now, those same people spend just a few seconds to perform the same tasks with OLAP and a data warehouse. As Sue Little, Mervyn's manager of merchandise planning and logistics systems, points out, "We're finally comparing apples to apples, and now we're spending only 10 percent of our time gathering data and 90 percent acting upon it, instead of the other way around."

A data warehouse is, in fact, a special form of a database that contains information gathered from many operational databases for the purpose of supporting decision-making tasks. When you build a data warehouse and use data mining tools to manipulate the data warehouse's information, your single goal is to create *business intelligence.* So data warehouses support only OLAP—they do not at all support OLTP.

As this chapter unfolds, we'll look specifically at (1) databases and database management systems and (2) data warehouses and data mining tools. Databases today are the foundation for organizing and managing information, and database management systems provide the tools you use to work with a database. Data warehouses are explosive, relatively new technologies that help you organize and manage business intelligence, and data mining tools help you extract that vitally important business intelligence.

The Relational Database Model

For organizing and storing basic and transaction-oriented information (eventually used to create business intelligence), businesses today use databases. There are actually four primary models for creating a database. The object-oriented database model is the newest and holds great promise—we'll talk more about the entire object-oriented genre in Chapter 7 and Extended Learning Module F. Right now, let's focus on the most popular database model—the relational database model.

As a generic definition, we would say that any **database** is a collection of information that you organize and access according to the logical structure of that information. In reference to the **relational database model**, we say that it uses a series of logically related two-dimensional tables or files to store information in the form of a database. The term **relation** often describes each two-dimensional table or file in the relational model (hence the name *relational* database model). A relational database is actually composed of two distinct parts: (1) the information itself—stored in a series of two-dimensional tables, files, or relations (people use these three terms interchangeably) and (2) the logical structure of that information. Let's look at a portion of an *Inventory* database to further explore the characteristics of the relational database model.

COLLECTIONS OF INFORMATION

In Figure 3.2 we've created a view of a portion of an *Inventory* database. Notice that the *Inventory* database contains two files: *Part* and *Facility*. (In reality, it would contain many more files including *Orders*, *Distributors*, and so on). A facility is simply a storage place for parts (similar to a warehouse). The *Part* and *Facility* files are related for two reasons. First, parts are stored in various facilities, so each file contains a common field—*Facility Number*. Second, you would use both files to manage your inventory, a common function in almost any business.

Within each file, you can see specific pieces of information (what we often call *attributes*). For example, the *Part* file contains *Part Number*, *Part Name*, *Cost*, *Percentage Markup*, *Distributor ID*, *Facility Number*, and *Bin Number*. *Bin Number*, in this case, describes the physical location of a given part in a facility. In the *Facility* file, you can see specific information including *Facility Number*, *Facility Name*, *Phone Number*, *Street Location*, and *Manager Number*. These are all important pieces of information that an inventory database would need to maintain. Moreover, you would need all this information (and probably much more) to effectively manage your inventory.

CREATED WITH LOGICAL STRUCTURES

Skills Module 2
Database Design—
Access

Using the relational database model, you organize and access information according to its logical structure, not its physical position. So you don't really care in which row of the *Part* file 50' tape measures appear. You really only need to know that the *Part Number* is 1003 or—for that matter—that the name of the part is 50' tape measure. In the relational database model, a **data dictionary** contains the logical structure for the information. When you create a database, you first create the data dictionary. The data dictionary contains important information or logical properties about your information. The screen in Figure 3.2 shows how you can build the data dictionary for the *Part* file using Microsoft Access (a popular personal database package). Notice that the data dictionary identifies all field names, types (Currency for *Cost*, for example), sizes, formats, default values, and so on.

Figure 3.2

A Portion of an Inventory Database and Data Dictionary

Part Number is the primary key because of the key icon beside it.

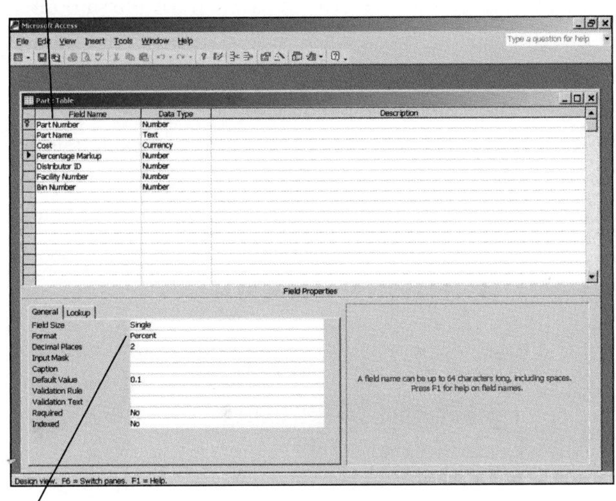

For *Percentage Markup*, we defined its format as "Percent" and its number of decimal places as 2.

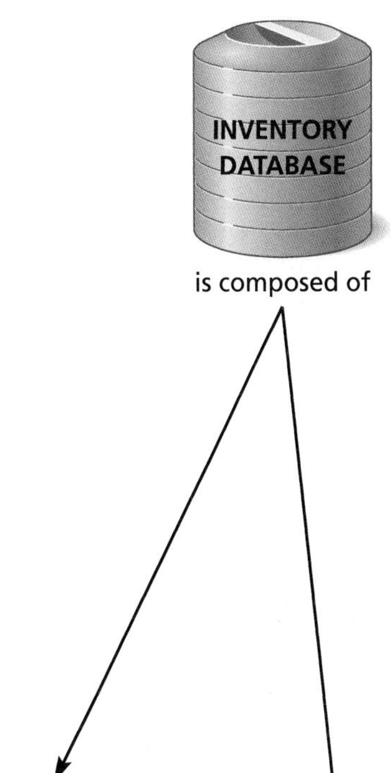

PART FILE

Part Number	Part Name	Cost	Percentage Markup	Distributor ID	Facility Number	Bin Number
1003	50' Tape Measure	$11.90	40.00%	10	291	2988
1005	25' Tape Measure	$9.95	40.00%	10	291	3101
1083	10 Amp Fuse	$0.07	50.00%	14	378	3984
1109	15 Amp Fuse	$0.07	50.00%	14	378	3983
2487	25 Amp Fuse	$0.08	50.00%	14	378	3982
2897	U.S. Socket Set	$29.75	25.00%	12	411	8723
3789	Crimping Tool	$14.50	30.00%	13	411	3298
3982	Claw Hammer	$9.90	30.00%	10	291	2987
4101	Metric Socket Set	$23.75	25.00%	12	411	4123
5908	6" Pliers	$7.45	25.00%	11	411	4567
6743	8" Pliers	$7.90	25.00%	11	411	4385

FACILITY FILE

Facility Number	Facility Name	Phone Number	Street Location	Manager Number
291	Pegasus	378-4921	3578 W. 12th St.	123456
378	Medusa	379-2981	4314 48th Ave.	234567
411	Orion	298-8763	198 Red Ln.	345678

This is quite different from other ways of organizing information. For example, if you want to access information in a certain cell in most spreadsheet applications, you must know its physical position—row number and column letter. With a relational database, however, you need only know the field name of the column of information (e.g., *Percentage Markup*) and its logical row, not its physical row. As a result, in our *Inventory* database example, you could easily change the percentage markup for part number 1003, without knowing where that information is physically stored (by row or column).

And with spreadsheet software, you can immediately begin typing in information, creating column headings, and providing formatting. You can't do that with a database. Using a database, you must first clearly define the characteristics of each field by creating a data dictionary. So you must carefully plan the design of your database before you can start adding information.

WITH LOGICAL TIES AMONG THE INFORMATION

In a relational database, you must create ties or relationships in the information that show how the files relate to each other. Before you can create these relationships among files, you must first specify the **primary key** for each file—a field (or group of fields in some cases) that uniquely describes each record. In our *Inventory* database, *Part Number* is the primary key for the *Part* file and *Facility Number* is the primary key for the *Facility* file. That is to say, every part in the *Part* file must have a unique *Part Number* and every facility in the *Facility* file must have a unique *Facility Number*.

As well, when you define that a specific field in a file is the primary key, you're also stating that the field cannot be blank. That is, you cannot enter the information for a new part in the *Part* file and leave the *Part Number* field blank. If that were possible, you could potentially do it for more than one part. If so, you would have two parts with identical primary keys (blank), which is not possible in a database environment.

Again, this is quite different from working with spreadsheets. Using a spreadsheet, it would be almost impossible to ensure that each field in a given column (e.g., *Part Number* in the *Part* file) is unique. This points up the fact that, while spreadsheets work with information according to physical location, databases work with information logically.

If you look back at Figure 3.2, you can see that *Facility Number* also appears in the *Part* file. This creates the logical relationship between the two files and is an example of a foreign key. A **foreign key** is a primary key of one file that appears in another file. Now look at Figure 3.3. In it, we've added the *Distributor* file and the *Employee* file in the *Inventory* database. In doing so, we can illustrate two more examples of foreign keys.

Notice *Distributor ID* in the *Distributor* file—it is the primary key for that file. It also appears in the *Part* file—this enables us to track from whom we get our parts. So *Distributor ID* is the primary key in the *Distributor* file and also a foreign key that appears in the *Part* file. Now, take a look at *Employee Number* in the *Employee* file—it is the primary key for that file. And it also appears in the *Facility* file (as *Manager Number*). This enables us to track the manager for each facility. So *Employee Number* is the primary key in the *Employee* file and also a foreign key in the *Facility* file.

Foreign keys are essential in the relational database model. Without them, you have no way of creating logical ties among the various files. As you might guess, we use these relationships extensively to create business intelligence because they enable us to track the logical relationships between many types of information.

WITH BUILT-IN INTEGRITY CONSTRAINTS

By defining the logical structure of information in a relational database, you're also developing **integrity constraints**—rules that help ensure the quality of the informa-

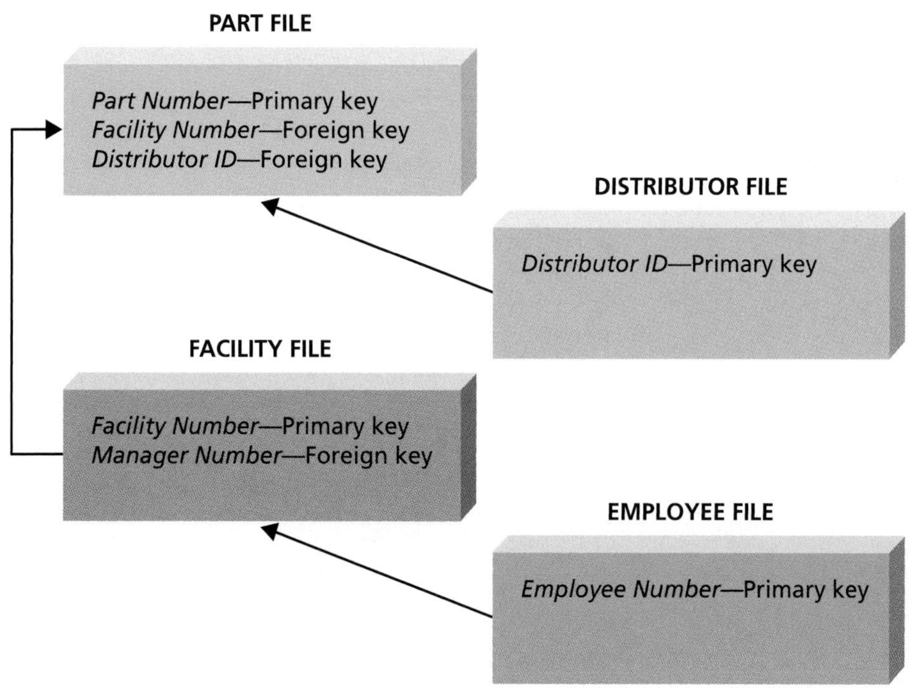

Figure 3.3

Creating Logical Ties with Primary and Foreign Keys

tion. For example, by stating that *Facility Number* is the primary key of the *Facility* file and a foreign key in the *Part* file, you're saying (1) that no two facilities can have the same *Facility Number* and (2) that a part in the *Part* file cannot be assigned to a facility number that does not exist in the *Facility file*. So, as you add a new part to the inventory, you must specify a facility in which it will be located that already exists in the *Facility* file. Likewise, you can't choose to eliminate a facility if parts are still assigned to it. This makes perfect sense. If you want to close a certain facility, you must first move all of the parts in it to a different facility.

Consumer Reports has rated the Ritz-Carlton first among luxury hotels.[4] Why? As outlined in the opening Case Study in Chapter 1, Ritz-Carlton has created a powerful guest preference database to provide customized, personal, and high-level service to guests in any of its hotels. Using a unique customer ID for you that creates logical ties to your various preferences, the Ritz-Carlton transfers your information to all the other hotels. The next time you stay in a Ritz-Carlton hotel, your information is already there and the hotel staff immediately knows of your desires.

For the management at Ritz-Carlton, achieving customer loyalty starts first with knowing each customer individually. To store and organize all this information, Ritz-Carlton uses a relational database, and employees use it to fill your every need (or whim).

Database Management System Tools

When working with word processing software, you create and edit a document. When working with spreadsheet software, you create and edit a workbook. The same is true in a database environment. A database is equivalent to a document or a workbook because they all contain information. And, while word processing and spreadsheet are the software tools you use to work with documents and workbooks, you use database management system software to work with databases. A **database management system (DBMS)** helps you specify the logical organization for a database and access and

TEAM WORK

PRIMARY KEYS, FOREIGN KEYS, AND INTEGRITY CONSTRAINTS

Let's consider the information that your school tracks for a class. In this instance, a class is a scheduled course. For example, your school may have FINA 2100—Introduction to International Financial Markets as a course. If it offers it in the fall, it becomes a class. Below, we've provided many pieces of information that your school probably tracks about the class. First, which is the primary key (put an X in the second column)? Second, for each piece of information, identify if it's a foreign key (a primary key of another file). If it is, write down the file name in the third column. Finally, in the fourth column for each piece of information, write down any integrity constraints you can think of. For example, can it be blank or must it contain something? Can it be duplicated across multiple records (classes)? If it's a number, does it have a specific range in which it must fall? There are many others.

Information	Primary Key?	Foreign Key?	Integrity Constraints
Department designation (e.g., FINA)			
Course number (e.g., 2100)			
Course name			
Course description			
Prerequisite			
Number of credit hours			
Lab fee			
Instructor name			
Room number			
Time of day			
Day of week			

use the information within a database. A DBMS contains five important software components (see Figure 3.4):

1. DBMS engine
2. Data definition subsystem
3. Data manipulation subsystem
4. Application generation subsystem
5. Data administration subsystem

The DBMS engine is perhaps the most important—yet seldom recognized—component of a DBMS. The **DBMS engine** accepts logical requests from the various other DBMS subsystems, converts them into their physical equivalent, and actually accesses the database and data dictionary as they exist on a storage device. Again, the distinction between *logical* and *physical* is important in a database environment. The **physical view** of information deals with how information is physically arranged, stored, and accessed on some type of storage device such as a hard disk. The **logical view** of information, on the other hand, focuses on how you as a knowledge worker need to arrange and access information to meet your particular business needs.

Figure 3.4
Software Subsystems of a Database Management System

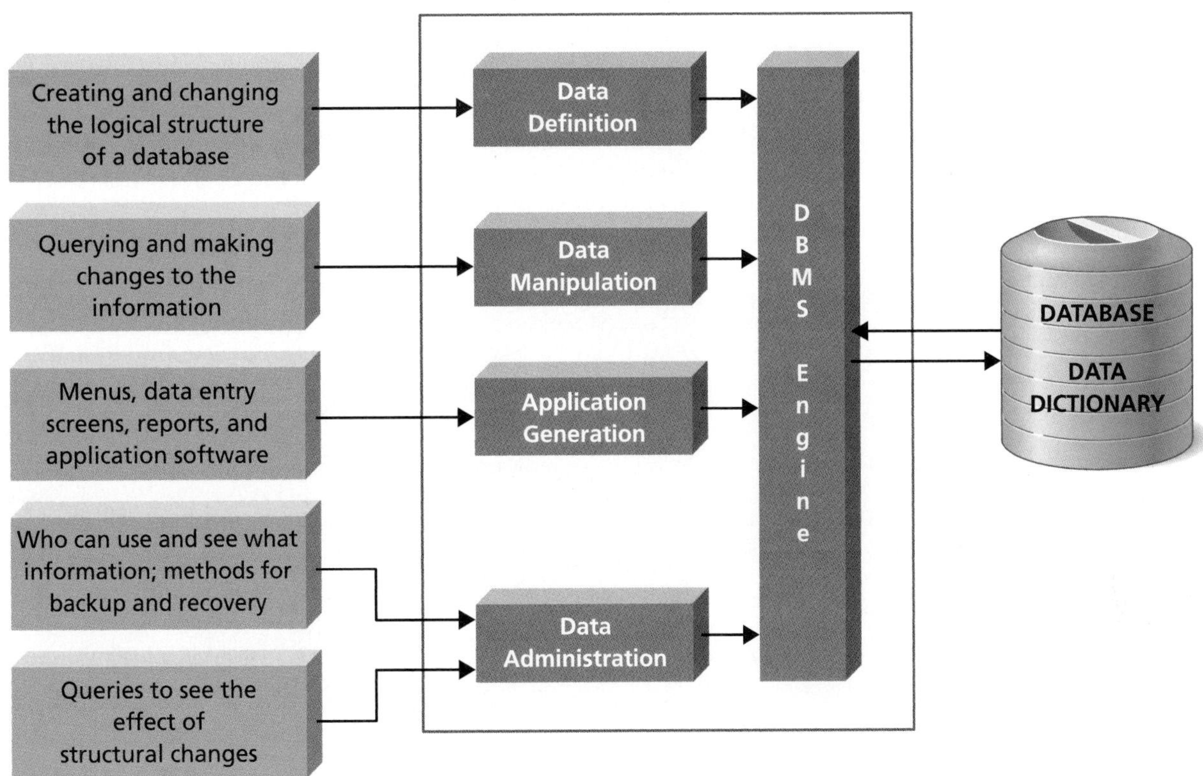

Databases and DBMSs provide two really great advantages in separating the logical from the physical view of information. First, the DBMS handles the physical tasks, so you, as a database user, can concentrate solely on your logical information needs. Second, although there is only one physical view of information, there may be numerous knowledge workers who have different logical views of the information in a database. That is, according to what business tasks they need to perform, different knowledge workers logically view information in different ways. The DBMS engine can process virtually any logical information view or request into its physical equivalent.

DATA DEFINITION SUBSYSTEM

The **data definition subsystem** of a DBMS helps you create and maintain the data dictionary and define the structure of the files in a database. In Figure 3.2, we provided a screen capture of the data definition subsystem using Microsoft Access. In that screen, we created the data dictionary and defined the structure of the *Part* file of our *Inventory* database.

Skills Module 2 Database Design—Access

When you create a database, you must first use the data definition subsystem to create the data dictionary and define the structure of the files. This is very different from using something like spreadsheet software. When you create a workbook, you can immediately begin typing in information and creating formulas and functions. You can't do that with a database. You must define its logical structure before you can begin typing in any information. Typing in the information is the easy part—defining the logical structure is more difficult. In Extended Learning Module A, which follows this chapter, we take you through the process of defining the logical structure for a database. We definitely recommend you read that Module—knowing how to define the correct structure of a database can be a substantial career opportunity for you.

If you ever find that a certain file needs another piece of information, you have to use the data definition subsystem to add a new field in the data dictionary. Likewise, if you want to delete a given field for all the records in a file, you must use the data definition subsystem to do so.

As you create the data dictionary, you're essentially defining the logical properties of the information that the database will contain. Logical structures of information include the following:

Logical Properties	Examples
Field name	*Part Number, Bin Number*
Type	Alphabetic, numeric, date, time, etc.
Form	Is an area code required for a phone number?
Default value	If no percentage markup is entered, the default is 10%.
Validation rule	Can percentage markups exceed 100%?
Is an entry required?	Must you enter a *Facility Number* for a part, or can it be blank?
Can there be duplicates?	Primary keys cannot be duplicates, but what about percentage markups?

These are all important logical properties to a lesser or greater extent depending on the type of information you're describing. For example, a typical address might have a field name of *Customer Address* and a type of alphanumeric (allowing for both numbers and letters). Beyond those, the logical properties are not quite as important, with the possible exception of requiring that the field cannot be blank.

However, if you're describing something like *Percentage Markup* in our *Inventory* database, you'll want to define such logical properties as a default value and perhaps some sort of validation rule.

DATA MANIPULATION SUBSYSTEM

The **data manipulation subsystem** of a DBMS helps you add, change, and delete information in a database and mine it for valuable information. Software tools within the data manipulation subsystem are most often the primary interface between you as a user and the information contained in a database. So, while the DBMS engine handles your information requests from a physical point of view, it is the data manipulation tools within a DBMS that allow you to specify your logical information requirements. Those logical information requirements are then used by the DBMS engine to access the information you need from a physical point of view.

In most DBMSs, you'll find a variety of data manipulation tools, including views, report generators, query-by-example tools, and structured query language.

VIEWS A **view** allows you to see the contents of a database file, make whatever changes you want, perform simple sorting, and query to find the location of specific

COMPANY PUSHES TO PUT MORE CANADIAN CONTENT ON THE WEB

Micromedia Limited is Canada's largest publisher and distributor of proprietary and third-party directories and CD-ROM database products for the business and library markets. Since 1999, the company has committed itself to ensuring Canadian content on the Internet by making its CBCA database, Canada's largest and most comprehensive full-text and bibliographic electronic reference database, available online. To do so, Macromedia has relied on LexisNexis Butterworths Canada (www.lexis-nexis-canada.com), a division of Butterworths Canada Ltd. and the world's foremost provider of online business, legal, and news information reaching over 1.5 million professionals worldwide.

When you subscribe to LexisNexis Butterworths online (it's not free, unfortunately), you have access to more than three billion documents, and new ones are being added at the rate of approximately 6.8 million documents per week—that's about 11 new documents each and every second! Not only is the breadth of information available at LexisNexis Butterworths unparalleled, but the system offers numerous functionalities. For example, you can build and customize your own LexisNexis Butterworths home page. So, when you log on, you see exactly what you want in the form of local news, market news, and sources you frequently search and read. You can even request that customized late-breaking news be sent to you via e-mail.

You can also build your own source list. So you can easily perform searches of just certain magazines—no longer do you have to read thousands of search results from obscure and meaningless (to you) sources. You can find articles from only the sources you choose.

You can also get up-to-the-minute market news and other news-related items from around the world. You can build a portfolio of stocks you want to track and read press releases on a daily basis from those companies.

If you spend a great deal of time on the Web finding information, LexisNexis Butterworths may be just what you're looking for. You can research term papers. You can read the news online instead of subscribing to a newspaper. Whatever information you need, LexisNexis Butterworths probably has it.

information. Views essentially provide each file in the form of a spreadsheet workbook. The screen in Figure 3.5 shows a view in Microsoft Access for the *Part* file of our *Inventory* database. At this point, you can click on any specific field and change its contents. You could also point at an entire record and click on the Cut icon (the scissors) to remove a record. If you want to add a record, simply click in the *Part Number* field of the first blank record and begin typing.

Skills Module 2 Database Design—Access

Notice, we've sorted the file in ascending order by *Part Number*. You can easily achieve this by clicking on the A→Z sort button in the view window. If you want to sort in descending order by *Percentage Markup*, simply point to any *Percentage Markup* field and click on the Z→A sort button. You can also perform searches within views. For example, if you wanted to find all parts that have the term "pliers" in the *Part Name* field, simply point anywhere in that column, click on the "find text" button (the binoculars) and enter "pliers." Access will respond by highlighting each *Part Name* field where the word "pliers" appears.

As with most other types of personal productivity software, DBMSs support such functions and tasks as cutting and pasting, formatting (e.g., bolding a field), spell checking, hiding columns (just as you would do using spreadsheet software), filtering, and even adding links to Web sites.

REPORT GENERATORS **Report generators** help you quickly define formats of reports and what information you want to see in a report. Once you define a report, you can view it on the screen or print it. Figure 3.6 shows two intermediate screens in

Figure 3.5

A View in Microsoft Access

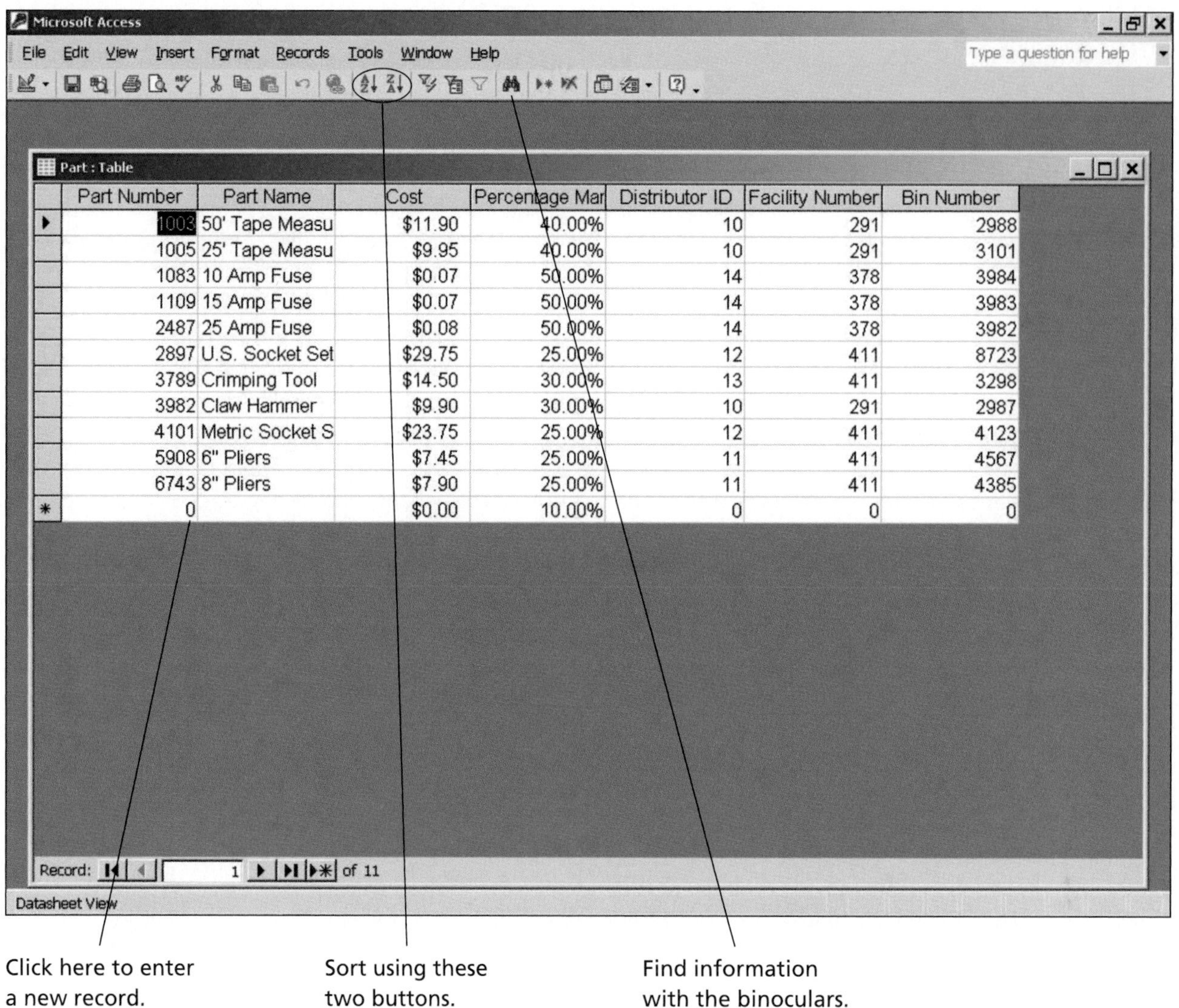

Part Number	Part Name	Cost	Percentage Mar	Distributor ID	Facility Number	Bin Number
1003	50' Tape Measu	$11.90	40.00%	10	291	2988
1005	25' Tape Measu	$9.95	40.00%	10	291	3101
1083	10 Amp Fuse	$0.07	50.00%	14	378	3984
1109	15 Amp Fuse	$0.07	50.00%	14	378	3983
2487	25 Amp Fuse	$0.08	50.00%	14	378	3982
2897	U.S. Socket Set	$29.75	25.00%	12	411	8723
3789	Crimping Tool	$14.50	30.00%	13	411	3298
3982	Claw Hammer	$9.90	30.00%	10	291	2987
4101	Metric Socket S	$23.75	25.00%	12	411	4123
5908	6" Pliers	$7.45	25.00%	11	411	4567
6743	8" Pliers	$7.90	25.00%	11	411	4385
0		$0.00	10.00%	0	0	0

Microsoft Access. The first allows you to specify which fields of information are to appear in a report. We have chosen to include *Part Number*, *Part Name*, *Cost*, and *Percentage Markup*. The second allows you to choose from a set of predefined report formats. Following a simple and easy-to-use set of screens (including the two in Figure 3.6) we went on to specify that sorting should take place by *Part Name* and that the name of the report should be "Part Report." The completed report is also shown in Figure 3.6. Notice that it only displays those fields we requested, that it's sorted by *Part Name*, and that the title is "Part Report."

A nice feature of report generators is that you can save a report format that you use frequently. For example, if you think you'll use the report in Figure 3.6 often, you can save it by giving it a unique name. Later, you can request that report and your DBMS will generate it, using the most up-to-date information in the database. You can also choose from a variety of report formats (we chose a simple one for our illustration). You can even choose report formats that create intermediate subtotals and grand totals, which can include counts, sums, averages, and the like.

Figure 3.6

Using a Report Generator

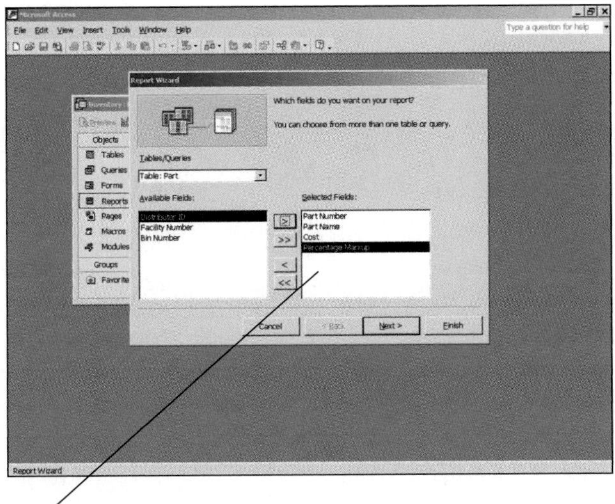

Selected fields from the *Part* file

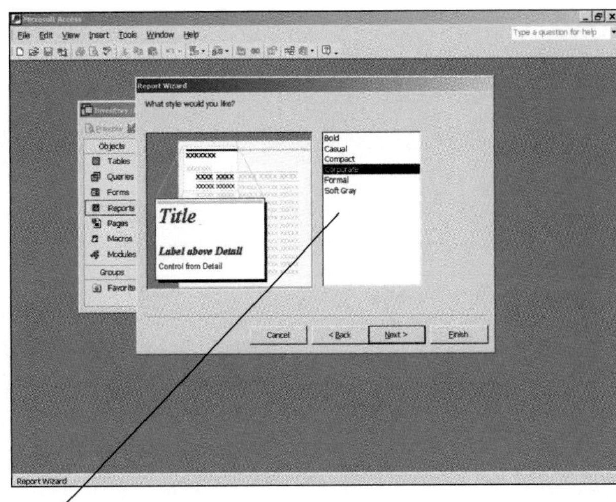

Report formats

PART REPORT

Part Number	Part Name	Cost	Percentage Markup
1003	50' Tape Measure	$11.90	40.00%
1005	25' Tape Measure	$9.95	40.00%
1083	10 Amp Fuse	$0.07	50.00%
1109	15 Amp Fuse	$0.07	50.00%
2487	25 Amp Fuse	$0.08	50.00%
2897	U.S. Socket Set	$29.75	25.00%
3789	Crimping Tool	$14.50	30.00%
3982	Claw Hammer	$9.90	30.00%
4101	Metric Socket Set	$23.75	25.00%
5908	6" Pliers	$7.45	25.00%
6743	8" Pliers	$7.90	25.00%

QUERY-BY-EXAMPLE TOOLS **Query-by-example (QBE) tools** help you graphically design the answer to a question. In our *Inventory* database, for example, "What are the names and phone numbers of the facility managers who are in charge of parts that have a cost greater than $10?" The question may seem simple considering that we have very few parts and even fewer facilities and managers in our database. However, can you imagine trying to answer that question if 100 facilities and 70,000 parts were involved? It would not be fun.

Figure 3.7

Using a Query-by-Example to Find Information

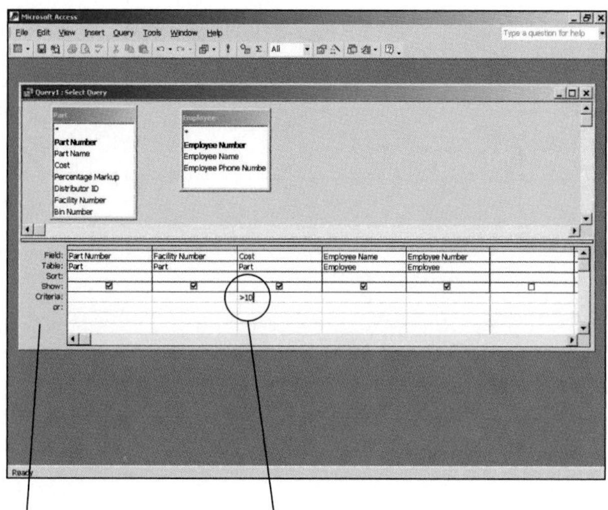

Part Number	Cost	Employee Name	Employee Phone Number
4101	$23.75	James Riley	376-2900
3789	$14.50	James Riley	376-2900
1003	$11.90	Greg Nelson	376-2455
2897	$29.75	James Riley	376-2900

Fortunately, QBE tools can help you answer this question and perform many other queries in a matter of seconds. In Figure 3.7, you can see a QBE screen that formulates the answer to our question. When you perform a QBE, you (1) identify the files in which the information is located, (2) drag any necessary fields from the identified files to the QBE grid, and (3) specify selection criteria.

For names and phone numbers of facility managers in charge of parts with costs over $10, we first identified two files—*Part* and *Employee*. Second, we dragged *Part Number*, *Facility Number*, and *Cost* from the *Part* file to the QBE grid and dragged *Employee Name* and *Employee Phone Number* from the *Employee* file to the QBE grid. Finally, we specified in the Criteria box that we wanted to view only those parts with costs exceeding $10. Access did the rest and provided the information in Figure 3.7.

QBEs rely heavily on the logical relationships within a database to find information. For example, part 4101 has a cost exceeding $10. So, the QBE tool took the *Facility Number* from the *Part* file and found a match in the *Facility* file. It then used the *Manager Number* in that matching record and performed another search of the *Employee* file to find another match. When it found a match, it then gathered the *Employee Name* and *Employee Phone Number*. Without the logical relationships correctly defined, this QBE query would never have worked.

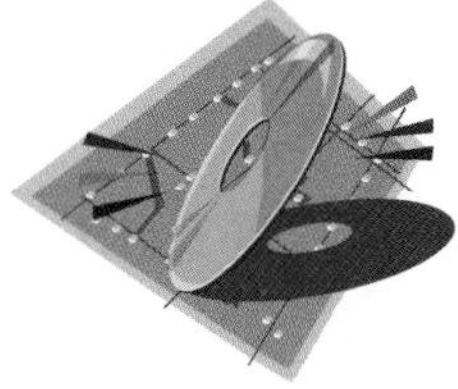
SQL

STRUCTURED QUERY LANGUAGE **Structured query language (SQL)** is a standardized fourth-generation query language found in most DBMSs. SQL performs the same function as QBE, except that you perform the query by creating a statement instead of pointing, clicking, and dragging. The basic form of an SQL statement is:

```
SELECT ... FROM ... WHERE ...
```

After the SELECT, you list the fields of information you want; after the FROM, you specify what logical relationships to use; and after the WHERE, you specify any selection criteria. If you consider our QBE above of "What are the names and phone numbers of the facility managers who are in charge of parts that have a cost greater than $10?" the SQL statement would look like this:

THE GLOBAL PERSPECTIVE

FLOATING DATABASES ABOARD ROYAL CARIBBEAN CRUISE SHIPS

Databases are not a "landlocked" technology, as anyone at Royal Caribbean Cruises will tell you. With floating hotel-like structures that include restaurants, casinos, duty-free shops, and Internet cafes, Royal Caribbean has sophisticated database technologies aboard each ship. According to Thomas Murphy, Royal Caribbean CIO, "The technology is becoming so much more important in running a cruise ship. Customer satisfaction depends on it, but so does the basic operation of the ship."

Aboard a cruise ship, databases track everything including general customer information, customer complaints and inquiries, on-demand movie requests, Internet cafe use, shopping purchases, meal purchases, and pay-for-use services such as massages and haircuts. The system even tracks male customers according to what size of tuxedo they reserve. That information can be used again if the same passenger takes another cruise on a Royal ship.

Royal Caribbean is also planning to build a centralized land-based data warehouse. Each ship, as it records information in its database, will use wireless telecommunications technologies to upload information into the data warehouse. Service planners will then be able to better predict what types of services will be needed on future cruises. For example, by time of year and cruise destination, service planners will know what sizes of tuxedos to stock and approximately how many massages will be performed. (What fields of information would you have in a "massage" record?)

If you're on land and want to take a virtual tour of a Royal Caribbean cruise ship, you can do that. Just connect to Royal Caribbean's Web site (www.royalcaribbean.com) and you can view estate rooms, eating facilities, spa facilities, and general entertainment areas. Of course, Royal Caribbean ultimately wants you to enjoy your virtual experience so much that you book a cruise.

But if you're not quite ready yet, the company would like you to leave some contact information at its Web site. It will then store that information in its database and, from time to time, send you some cruise information.[5,6]

```
SELECT Part.[Part Number], Part.Cost, Employee.[Employee Name],
Employee.[Employee Number]
FROM Part, Employee
WHERE (((Part.Cost)>10));
```

Thoroughly introducing you to the syntax of SQL statements is outside the scope of this text and would easily require almost 100 pages of material. But you should be aware that SQL does exist. If you're majoring in IT or MIS, you'll undoubtedly take a course in SQL.

APPLICATION GENERATION SUBSYSTEM

The **application generation subsystem** of a DBMS contains facilities to help you develop transaction-intensive applications. These types of applications usually require that you perform a detailed series of tasks to process a transaction. Application generation subsystem facilities include tools for creating visually appealing and easy-to-use data entry screens, programming languages specific to a particular DBMS, and interfaces to commonly used programming languages that are independent of any DBMS.

As with SQL, application generation facilities are most often used by IT specialists. We recommend that you, as a knowledge worker, leave application generation to IT specialists as much as you can. You need to focus on views, report generators, and QBE tools. These will help you find information in a database and perform queries so you can start to build and use business intelligence.

ON YOUR OWN

DBMS SUPPORT FOR OLTP, OLAP, INFORMATION MANAGEMENT

In the table below, we've listed the various DBMS subsystems or tools. For each of these, identify whether it supports online transaction processing, online analytical processing, both online transaction and analytical processing, or the management of a database.

DBMS Tool	OLTP	OLAP	Both	Management
DBMS engine				
View				
Report generator				
QBE				
SQL				
Data entry screen				
DBMS programming language				
Common programming language				
Data administration subsystem				

DATA ADMINISTRATION SUBSYSTEM

The **data administration subsystem** of a DBMS helps you manage the overall database environment by providing facilities for backup and recovery, security management, query optimization, concurrency control, and change management. The data administration subsystem is most often used by a data administrator or database administrator—people responsible for assuring that the database (and data warehouse) environment meets the entire information needs of an organization.

Backup and recovery facilities provide a way for you to (1) periodically back up information contained in a database and (2) restart or recover a database and its information in case of a failure. These are important functions you cannot ignore in today's information-based environment. Organizations that understand the importance of their information take precautions to preserve it, often by running backup databases, a DBMS, and storage facilities parallel to the primary database environment. In Chapter 6, we talk specifically about "contingency planning "—how to develop plans and strategies in the event of some sort of failure.

Security management facilities allow you to control who has access to what information and what type of access those people have. In many database environments, for example, some people may only need "view" access to database information, but not "change" access. Still others may need the ability to add, change, and/or delete information in a database. Through a system of user specification and password levels, the data administration subsystem allows you to define which users can perform which tasks and what information they can see. At car dealership JM Family Enterprises (JMFE), security management facilities are an absolute must because its technology is highly decentralized and includes users of mobile technologies.[7] JMFE's system sup-

SHOULD YOU HAVE ACCESS TO MEDICAL MALPRACTICE DATABASES?

Should patients in Canada have the right to know whether physicians have ever been disciplined for sex offences, substance abuse, incompetence, etc.? Dr. Sidney Wolfe thinks so. He is the author of the report published in the United States—*16,638 Questionable Doctors.* Many patients want access to "bad doctor databases," and several organizations, including some state and provincial medical boards, are responding. For instance, in Ohio, residents can visit the state medical board (www.state.oh.us/med) which allows visitors access to doctors' credentials, status of the physician's licence, and whether any malpractice suits were ever filed.

In Canada, provincial licensing bodies have not yet made their complete records open to Internet searchers; online public access to the thousands of complaints against doctors may continue to be limited for some time. Yet there is a trend toward more openness. Recently, the College of Physicians and Surgeons of Ontario (www.cpso.on.ca) and the Alberta College of Physicians and Surgeons (www.cpsa.ab.ca) have made available some basic information about their provinces' physicians.

What are your thoughts? In today's information-based environment, you can find almost any information you want. But should you really have access to all of it? Should you be able to look up instructors according to their student-evaluation rankings? Will this always help you determine which class to take? Should instructors be able to look up all your grades? Can an instructor use that information to decide whether to let you enroll in his or her class?

Is there such a thing as too much information? Can too much information actually be detrimental?[8]

ports encryption and passwords to protect databases, files, and many hardware resources. The system even supports automatic logoffs after a certain amount of time if users accidentally leave their system running.

Query optimization facilities often take queries from users (in the form of SQL statements or QBEs) and restructure them to minimize response times. In SQL, for example, you can build a query statement that might involve working with as many as ten different files. As you might well guess, when working with ten different files, there may be several different solutions for combining them to get the information you need. Fortunately, you don't have to worry about structuring the SQL statement in an optimized fashion; the optimization facilities will do that for you and provide you with the information you need in the fastest possible way.

SQL

Reorganization facilities continually statistics concerning how the DBMS engine physically accesses information. In maintaining those statistics, reorganization facilities can optimize the physical structure of a database to further increase speed and performance. For example, if you frequently access a certain file by a specific order, the reorganization facilities may maintain the file in that order to create an index that maintains the order in that file. What's really nice is that you don't have to be aware of the changes to your database with respect to physical locations—the DBMS engine will take care of it for you.

Concurrency control facilities ensure the validity of database updates when multiple users attempt to access and change the same information. This is crucial in today's networked business environment. Consider your school's online registration system. What if you and another student try to register for a class with only one seat remaining at the exact same time? Who gets enrolled? What happens to the person excluded? These are important questions, and once answered they must be defined in the database environment using concurrency control facilities.

Change management facilities allow you to assess the impact of proposed structural changes to a database environment. For example, if you decide to add a character identifier to a numeric part number, you can use the change management facilities to see how many files will be affected. Recall that *Part Number* would be the primary key for a *Part* file and that it would also be a foreign key in many other files. Some structural changes (such as adding a postal code extension) may not have much effect on the database, but others can cause widespread changes that you must assess carefully.

All of these—backup and recovery, security management, query optimization, reorganization, concurrency control, and change management—are vitally important facilities in any DBMS and thus any database environment. As a user and knowledge worker, you probably won't deal with these facilities specifically as far as setting them up and maintaining them is concerned. But how they're set up and maintained will affect what you can do. So knowing that they do exist and their purposes are important.

Data Warehouses and Data Mining

Suppose you, as a manager at Victoria's Secret, wanted to know the total revenues generated from the sale of shoes last month. That's a simple query, which you could easily implement using either SQL or a QBE tool. But what if you wanted to know "By actual vs. budgeted, how many size 8 shoes in black did we sell last month in the southeast and southwest regions, compared with the same month over the past five years?" That task seems almost impossible, even with the aid of technology. And, if you were actually able to build a QBE query for it, you would probably bring the organization's operational database environment to its knees.

This example illustrates the two primary reasons so many organizations are opting to build data warehouses. First, while operational databases may have the needed information, the information is not organized in such a way that lends itself to building business intelligence within the database or using various data manipulation tools. Second, if you could build such a query, your operational databases, which are probably already supporting the processing of hundreds of transactions per second, would seriously suffer in performance when you hit the start button to perform the query.

To support such intriguing, necessary, and complex queries to create business intelligence, many organizations are building data warehouses and providing data mining tools. A data warehouse is simply the next step (beyond databases) in the progression of building business intelligence. And data mining tools are the tools you use to mine a data warehouse and extrapolate the business intelligence you need to make a decision, solve a problem, or capitalize on an opportunity to create a competitive advantage.

WHAT IS A DATA WAREHOUSE?

A **data warehouse** is a logical collection of information—gathered from many different operational databases—used to create business intelligence that supports business analysis activities and decision-making tasks (see Figure 3.8). Sounds simple enough on the surface, but data warehouses represent a fundamentally different way of thinking about organizing and managing information in an organization. Consider the following key features of a data warehouse.

DATA WAREHOUSES ARE MULTIDIMENSIONAL In the relational database model, information is represented in a series of two-dimensional tables. Not so in a data warehouse—most data warehouses are multidimensional, meaning that they con-

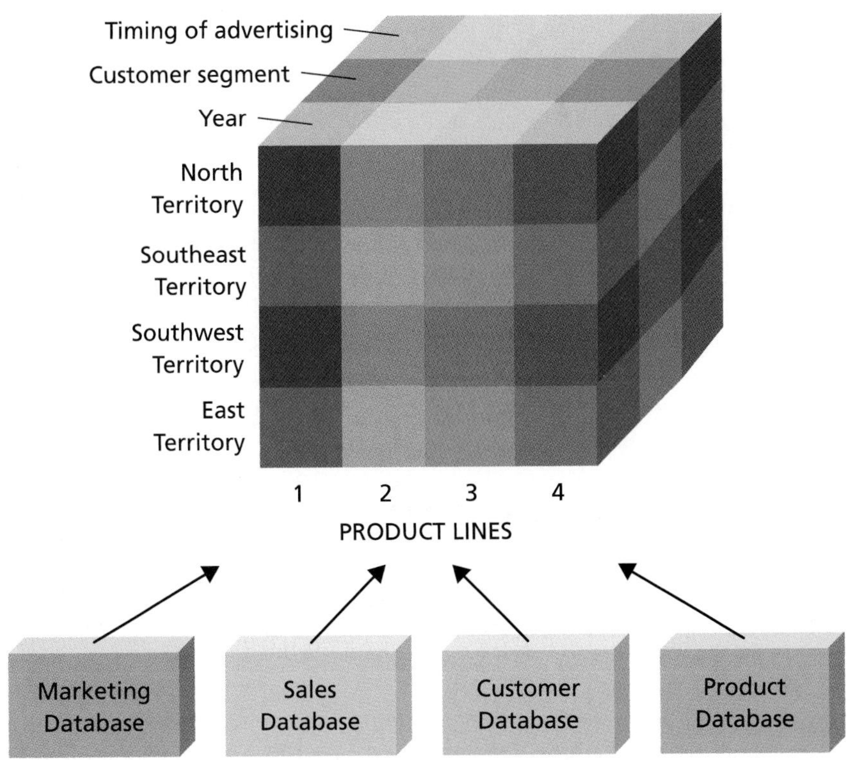

Figure 3.8
A Multidimensional Data Warehouse with Information from Multiple Operational Databases

tain layers of columns and rows. For this reason, most data warehouses are really *multi-dimensional databases*. The layers in a data warehouse represent information according to different dimensions. This multidimensional representation of information is referred to as a *hypercube*.

In Figure 3.8, you can see a hypercube that represents product information by product line and region (columns and rows), by year (the first layer), by customer segment (the second layer), and by the timing of advertising media (the third layer). Using this hypercube, you can easily ask, "According to customer segment A, what percentage of total sales for product line 1 in the southwest territory occurred immediately after a radio advertising blitz?" The information you would receive from that query constitutes business intelligence.

Any specific sub-cube within the larger hypercube can contain a variety of summarized information gathered from the various operational databases. For example, the forwardmost and top left sub-cube contains information for the North territory, by year, for product line 1. So it could contain totals, average, counts, and distributions summarizing in some way that information. Of course, what it contains is really up to you and your needs.

DATA WAREHOUSES SUPPORT DECISION MAKING, NOT TRANSACTION PROCESSING In an organization, most databases are transaction-oriented. That is, they support online transaction processing (OLTP) and, therefore, are operational databases. Data warehouses are not transaction-oriented—they exist to support decision-making tasks in your organization. Therefore, data warehouses support only online analytical processing (OLAP).

As we just stated, the sub-cubes within a data warehouse contain summarized information. So, while a data warehouse may contain the total sales for a year by product line, it does not contain a list of each individual sale to each individual customer for a given product line. Therefore, you simply cannot process transactions with a data warehouse. Instead, you process transactions with your operational databases and then use the information contained within the operational databases to build the summary information in a data warehouse.

WHAT ARE DATA MINING TOOLS?

Data mining tools are the software you use to query information in a data warehouse. These tools support the concept of OLAP—the manipulation of information to support decision-making tasks. Data mining tools include query-and-reporting tools, intelligent agents, multidimensional analysis tools, and statistical tools (see Figure 3.9). Essentially, data mining tools are to data warehouse users what data manipulation subsystem tools are to database users.

QUERY-AND-REPORTING TOOLS **Query-and-reporting tools** are similar to QBE tools, SQL, and report generators in the typical database environment. In fact, most data warehousing environments support simple and easy-to-use data manipulation subsystem tools such as QBE, SQL, and report generators. Most often, data warehouse users use these types of tools to generate simple queries and reports.

INTELLIGENT AGENTS Intelligent agents utilize various artificial intelligence tools such as neural networks and fuzzy logic to form the basis of "information discovery" and building business intelligence in OLAP. For example, Bay Street financial analysts can use OLAP software called Data/Logic, which incorporates neural networks to generate rules for a highly successful stock and bond trading system.[9] Other OLAP tools, such as Data Engine, incorporate fuzzy logic to analyze real-time technical processes.

Intelligent agents represent the growing convergence of various IT tools for working with information. Previously, intelligent agents were considered only within the context of artificial intelligence and were seldom thought to be a part of the data organizing and managing functions in an organization. Today, you can find intelligent agents not only being used for OLAP in a data warehouse environment but also for searching for information on the Web. In Chapter 4, we'll explore artificial intelligence techniques such as intelligent agents.

Figure 3.9
The Data Miner's Tool Set

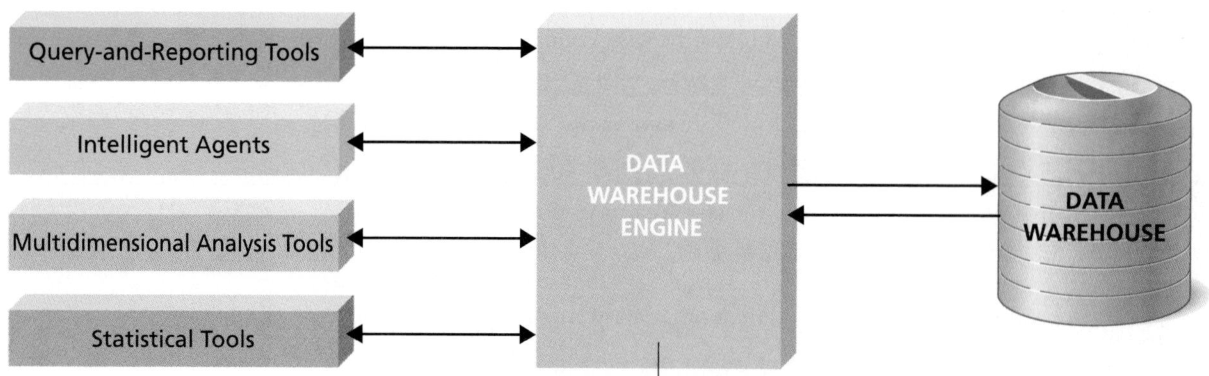

THE GLOBAL PERSPECTIVE

CROSS-SELLING INSURANCE PRODUCTS IN AUSTRALIA

Selling insurance products is competitive all over the world, mainly because of the push by financial services companies into the insurance businesses. Of course, insurance companies can respond by providing more and better products, but that's only part of the solution.

So, many insurance companies, such as Australian P&C Direct, are developing strategies on the basis of customer relationship management, data warehouses, and cross-selling. To achieve those strategies, P&C is creating a customer information data warehouse that includes the typical customer information coupled with census data and lifestyle codes. In doing so, the company can better cross-sell to its customers (e.g., selling a life insurance policy to a customer who has also purchased a health insurance policy from P&C).

P&C is also incorporating its marketing campaign information into the data warehouse. That way, P&C agents can view all of the products a given customer has purchased and more accurately determine what marketing campaigns the customer is likely to respond to.[10]

MULTIDIMENSIONAL ANALYSIS TOOLS **Multidimensional analysis (MDA)** tools are slice-and-dice techniques that allow you to view multidimensional information from different perspectives. Within the context of a data warehouse, we refer to this process as "turning the cube." That is, you're essentially turning the cube to view information from different perspectives.

This "turning of the cube" allows you to quickly see information in different subcubes. If you refer back to the data warehouse in Figure 3.8, you'll notice that information by customer segment and timing of advertising are actually hidden. Using MDA tools, you can easily bring those to the front of the data warehouse for viewing. What you've essentially done is to slice the cube vertically by layer and bring some of the background layers to the front. As you do this, the values of the information are not affected.

STATISTICAL TOOLS Statistical tools help you apply various mathematical models to the information stored in a data warehouse to discover new information. For example, you can perform a time series analysis to project future trends. You can also perform a regression analysis to determine the effect of one variable on another.

Sega, one of the largest publishers of video games, uses a data warehouse and statistical tools to effectively distribute its more than $50+ million a year advertising budget.[11,12] With its data warehouse, product line specialists and marketing strategists "drill" into trends of each retail store chain. Their goal is to find buying trends that will help them better determine which advertising strategies are working best (and at what time of the year) and how to reallocate advertising resources by medium, territory, and time. Sega definitely benefits from its data warehouse, and so do retailers such as Toys "R" Us, Zellers, and Sears—all good examples of customer relationship management through technology.

DATA MARTS—SMALLER DATA WAREHOUSES

Data warehouses are often perceived as organizationwide, containing summaries of all the information that an organization tracks. However, some people need access to only a portion of that data warehouse information. In this case, an organization can create one or more data marts. A **data mart** is a subset of a data warehouse in which only a focused portion of the data warehouse information is kept (see Figure 3.10).

Figure 3.10
Data Marts Are Subsets of Data Warehouses

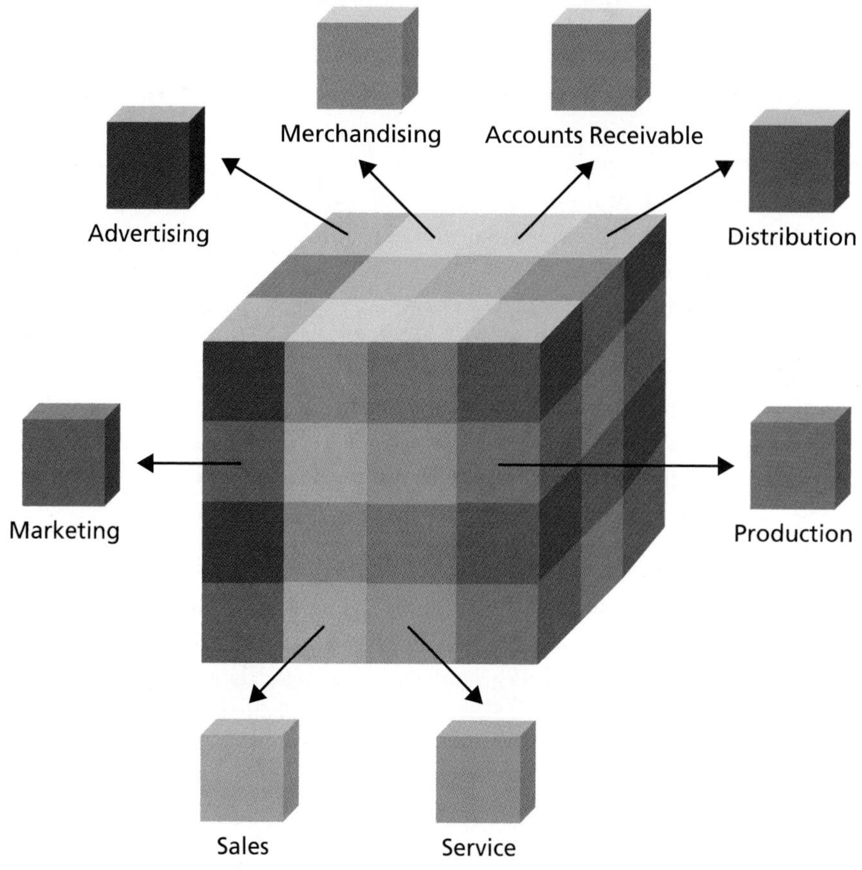

Lands' End first created an organizationwide data warehouse for everyone to use, but soon found out that there can be "too much of a good thing."[13] In fact, many Lands' End employees wouldn't use the data warehouse because it was simply too big and complicated, and included information they didn't need. So Lands' End created several smaller data marts. For example, Lands' End created one for just the merchandising department. That data mart contains only merchandising-specific information and not any information, for instance, that would be unique to the finance department.

Because of the smaller, more manageable data marts, knowledge workers at Lands' End are making better use of information. If some of your employees don't need access to organizationwide data warehouse information, consider building a smaller data mart for their particular needs.

If you do choose to build smaller data marts for your employees, the data mining tools are the same. That is, data marts support the use of query-and-reporting tools, intelligent agents, multidimensional analysis tools, and statistical tools. This yields efficiency in an organization with respect to training. Once you've trained your employees to use any or all data mining tools, they can apply them to an organizationwide data warehouse or smaller data marts.

IMPORTANT CONSIDERATIONS IN USING A DATA WAREHOUSE

As with all types of technology, you can't simply implement a data warehouse and use data mining tools just because they're a "hot" set of technologies. Let your business

FUTURE SHOP IMPLEMENTS DATA WAREHOUSING WITH THE HELP OF BURNTSAND INC.

With more than 90 stores, Future Shop (www.futureshop.ca), Canada's largest and fastest-growing retailer of consumer electronic products, was having trouble making sense of the data it was collecting. Although customer and supplier data were being gathered at the operational level, they remained decentralized and were not synthesized and distributed to improve corporate decision-making. Future Shop contacted Burntsand Inc. (www.burntsand.com), a leading North American e-business solutions integrator, to provide them with a fast and reliable system to support their strategic and tactical business functions. They implemented a data warehouse to centralize all of Future Shop's data which were spread across several databases on different hardware platforms.

Today, Future Shop still gathers all of its crucial data from its decentralized systems, but now applies central business rules to standardize, clean, and unify the data, and then store them in its data warehouse. Bill Akam, Director of Strategic Programs at Future Shop, stated that "the business benefit of having all of our operational and strategic decisions aligned with one single unified set of data is creating efficiency and accuracy previously unachievable." According to Burntsand's president and CEO Paul Bertin, the data warehouse now enables Future Shop "to develop a solid foundation for business intelligence, turning this data into useful information about their business and their customers. ... This use of the company's information asset allows Future Shop to positively impact their dealings and relationships with their suppliers and customers and gain a real competitive advantage."[14]

needs drive your technology decisions. With respect to data warehouses and data mining tools, below are some questions to answer.

DO YOU NEED A DATA WAREHOUSE? If you ask most people in the business world if they need a data warehouse, they'll immediately say yes. But they may be wrong. Although data warehouses are a great way to bring together information from many different databases and data mining tools are a great way to manipulate that information, they're not necessarily the best technologies for all businesses. Why? For three reasons:

- Data warehouses and data mining tools are expensive. These are among the most expensive of all technologies, and your organization will devote considerable time in creating a data warehouse. Training in the use of data mining tools is also expensive.
- Some organizations simply don't need a data warehouse. You may find that you can easily extract necessary information to support decision making from operational databases. If so, don't use a data warehouse.
- Many IT departments suffer from supporting too many applications and application tools. As David Tanaka, a DSS manager at Hospital Health Plan Management Corp., points out, "Right now, we are support-strapped. If we introduce something like OLAP, we will have to give it a lot of support."[15] Technology and its use requires constant support. If you can't support it, don't implement it.

DO ALL YOUR EMPLOYEES NEED AN ENTIRE DATA WAREHOUSE? As we've already discussed, some of your employees may not need access to an organization-wide data warehouse. If this is the case, definitely consider building data marts. Data

TEAM WORK

HOW UP-TO-DATE SHOULD DATA WAREHOUSE INFORMATION BE?

Information timeliness is a must in a data warehouse—old and obsolete information leads to poor decision making. Below is a list of decision-making processes that people go through for different business environments. For each, specify whether the information in the data warehouse should be updated monthly, weekly, daily, or by the minute. Be prepared to justify your decision.

1. To adjust class sizes in a university registration environment
2. To alert people to changes in weather conditions
3. To predict scores for professional football games
4. To adjust radio advertisements in the light of demographic changes
5. To monitor the success of a new product line in the clothing retail industry
6. To adjust production levels of foods in a cafeteria
7. To switch jobs to various printers in a network
8. To adjust CD rates in a bank
9. To adjust forecasted demands of tires in an auto parts store

marts are smaller than data warehouses, and therefore more manageable and easier to access. The easier technology is to use, the more your users will take advantage of it.

HOW UP-TO-DATE MUST THE INFORMATION BE? Data warehouses contain information from other databases. From an operational perspective, it's important to consider how often you should extract information from those databases and update the data warehouse. "Instantaneously" is usually not feasible in most organizations because of communications costs and performance considerations. Some organizations take "snapshots" of databases every 30 minutes and update the data warehouse; others perform updates nightly or even weekly.

WHAT DATA MINING TOOLS DO YOU NEED? User needs should always drive what data mining tools are necessary—query-and-reporting tools, intelligent agents, multidimensional analysis tools, statistical tools, or some combination of the four. Whatever you choose, training is key. It's important for your organization to first make users aware of the capabilities of the entire data mining tool set. Then, once they decide on which tools are best, you'll need to provide training. If your users can fully exploit all the features of their chosen data mining tools, your entire organization will reap the benefits.

Managing the Information Resource in an Organization

As you prepare to enter today's fast-paced, exciting, and information-based business world, you must be prepared to help your organization manage and organize its information. After all, you will be a knowledge worker—a person who works primarily with information. Your organization will be successful, in part, because of your ability to organize and manage information in the way that best moves the organization toward its goals. Below is a list of questions to keep in mind. The answers to some are definitely moving targets. As business and technology change, your answers may have to change as well.

DO YOU WANT TO BE A CIO?

Regardless of your industry or business sector, one of the highest-paid IT jobs is that of chief information officer. According to *InformationWeek Research*'s 2002 National IT Salary Survey, managers in IT earn a median base salary of $83,000, while staffers earn a median base salary of $61,000. Those numbers actually sound pretty good.

But compared to the median salary of CIOs ($119,000), those numbers fall well short.

So what does it take to be a CIO? We know of two things for sure. The first is an intricate knowledge of how a business environment works; the second is an intricate understanding of how information technology can help a business work more efficiently and effectively. Those are givens.

If we were to offer a third requirement, we would say that the new generation of CIOs will come out of the data warehousing arena. Why? Because data warehousing specialists must understand the entire business in great detail, and they must know how to use information technology.[16]

WHO SHOULD OVERSEE THE ORGANIZATION'S INFORMATION?

In organizations today, you find chief executive officers (CEO), chief operating officers (COO), and chief financial officers (CFO), among others. You also find another title—**chief information officer (CIO)**, who is responsible for overseeing an organization's information resource. A CIO's responsibilities may range from approving new development activities for data warehouses and data marts to monitoring the quality and use of information within those data warehouses and data marts.

Two important functions associated with overseeing an organization's information resource are data and database administration. **Data administration** is the function in an organization that plans for, oversees the development of, and monitors the information resource. It must be completely in tune with the strategic direction of the organization to assure that all information requirements can and are being met.

Database administration is the function in an organization that is responsible for the more technical and operational aspects of managing the information contained in organizational databases (which can include data warehouses and data marts). Database administration functions include defining and organizing database structures and contents, developing security procedures, developing database and DBMS documentation, and approving and monitoring the development of databases and database applications.

In organizations of any great size, both functions are usually handled by a steering committee rather than a single individual. Steering committees are responsible for their respective functions and reporting to the CIO. It's definitely a team effort to manage most organizational resources—information is no different in that it needs careful oversight and management.

However, information is different from many "typical" organizational resources. For example, information is intangible, so it becomes extremely difficult to measure its worth or value. What dollar value would you attach to a customer record? Can a business realistically do that? The answer to the latter question is no. So, if you can't put a value on information, how can you know how much you should be spending on information technology tools? It is a difficult question to answer.

ON YOUR OWN

CRUD—DEFINING INFORMATION OWNERSHIP

One easy way to determine information ownership is to think in terms of CRUD—*c*reate, *r*ead, *u*pdate, and *d*elete. If you can create, update, and/or delete information, then in some way you own that information because you are responsible for its quality.

Here again, let's consider your school as an example and focus on your personal and transcript information. That information includes your student ID, name, address, phone number, GPA, declared major, declared minor (if you have one), and courses completed (this is your transcript).

For each of those pieces, first identify who has create, update, and delete privileges. There may be many individuals or departments that have these sorts of information privileges. If so, who is ultimately responsible for your personal and transcript information? Second, identify all the groups of people at your school who can only view your information.

Since information is intangible, it can also be shared by numerous people and not actually be "consumed." Money is different. If you have money in your department budget and spend it on travel, you can't very well use that same money for paying for employee education expenses. In a way, then, the intangibility of information is good because many people can use it. But, as we've alluded to many times, there are unique considerations in the security of information that do not exist for other organizational resources such as money.

HOW WILL CHANGES IN TECHNOLOGY AFFECT ORGANIZING AND MANAGING INFORMATION?

If there ever has been a moving target that businesses are trying to hit, it's most probably information technology. It seems that every day businesses are faced with new technologies that are faster, better, and provide more capabilities than the those of yesterday. Chasing technology in a business environment can be very expensive, and it is not what we would consider to be a best business practice.

What you have to remember is that technology is simply a set of tools for helping you work with information, including organizing and managing it. As new technologies become available, you should ask yourself whether those technologies will help you organize and manage your information *better*. You can't simply say, "A new technology is available that will allow us to organize and manage our information in a different way, so we should use it." The real question is whether that different way is better than what you're currently doing. If the answer is yes, you should seriously consider the new technology in the light of the strategic goals of the organization. If the answer is no, stay with what you've got until a tool comes along that allows you to do a *better* job.

One of the greatest technological changes that will occur over the coming years is a convergence of different tools that will help you better organize and manage information. Environment Canada's Ice Services, for example, is providing a combination of a data warehouse and Internet-based information resources seafarers can use.[17] This new system gathers ice charts stored on the Internet and logically organizes them in the form of a data warehouse. Using this new system, seafarers can obtain updated maps and charts that reflect changing ice conditions every four instead of twelve hours. Who knows? The *Titanic* might still be here today if this system had been available in 1912.

DO MOVIES AFFECT YOUR VIEW OF ETHICS?

Many movies today deal with ethical issues. It's not that movie producers make movies just so you'll think about your own ethics. But, if a movie does have within it an ethical dilemma, you'll want to discuss it with your friends. That, in turn, makes your friends want to pay to see the movie. It's a simple matter of providing the viewing public with a story that raises significant questions and encourages more people to see the movie.

Consider *Gattica*, a movie about the future. In its version of the future, a person's DNA determined his or her entire future. DNA was used to determine the type of job and whether the person would go to school. Of course, everyone's DNA was stored in a large central database that organizations and the government accessed often.

In one scene, a young woman met a young man at a nightclub. She was quite taken by him. So she stole a small strand of his hair and went to a nearby booth. The person working the booth analyzed the hair, accessed the young man's DNA, and provided the young woman with his complete biological profile. She used that information, of course, to determine whether to pursue a relationship with him.

Although it may seem like a rather outlandish view of the future, it does raise some important questions. Should we, as a society, be tracking that kind of information? If so, who should have access to it and for what reasons? Should you be able to pay (as the young woman did) to access someone else's medical information?

These are important questions that you cannot ignore. You may not have to deal with them right now, but you certainly will in the future. How will you respond?

IS INFORMATION OWNERSHIP A CONSIDERATION?

Information sharing in your organization means that anyone—regardless of title or department—can access and use whatever information he or she needs. But information sharing brings to light an important question—does anyone in your organization own any information? In other words—if everyone shares information, who is ultimately responsible for providing that information and assuring the quality of the information? Information ownership is a key consideration in today's information-based business environment. Someone must accept full responsibility for providing specific pieces of information and ensuring its quality. If you find out that wrong information is stored in the organization's data warehouse, you must be able to determine the source of the problem and whose responsibility it is.

This issue of information ownership is present in other management functions: if you manage a department, you're responsible for the work in the department as well as expenses and people. The same is true for information. If information originates in your department, you essentially own that information because you're providing it to those who need it and ensuring its quality.

WHAT ARE THE ETHICS INVOLVED IN MANAGING AND ORGANIZING INFORMATION?

Throughout this text, we address many ethical issues associated with information and information technology. Many of our discussions focus on your organization's societal obligations with respect to customers. Within the organization, those same issues are a concern. By bringing together vast amounts of information into a single place (a database or data warehouse) and providing software (a DBMS or data mining tools) that anyone can use to access that information, ethics and privacy become key concerns.

For example, as a manager of marketing research, should you be able to access the salaries of people in distribution and logistics? Should you be able to access medical profiles of those in accounting? Should you be able to access counselling records of those in manufacturing? The answer to some of these questions is obviously no. But how does an organization safeguard against the unethical use of information within the organization?

While most DBMSs provide good security facilities, it's far easier for someone within your organization to obtain information than it is for someone outside the organization. So what's the key? Unfortunately, we don't know the answer, and neither does anyone else. But it all starts with each person always acting in the most ethical way with respect to information. Ethics, security, and privacy will always be great concerns. You can do your part by always acting ethically. Remember, being sensitive to the ethics of other people is an important challenge that you must meet.

Summary: Student Learning Outcomes Revisited

1. **Describe business intelligence and its role in an organization.** Business intelligence is knowledge—knowledge about your customers, your competitors, your partners, your competitive environment, and your own internal operations. Business intelligence is much more than just a list of your products or to whom you've sold them. It would combine your product information perhaps with your advertising strategy information and customer demographics to help you determine the effectiveness of various advertising media on demographic groups segmented by location.
2. **Differentiate between databases and data warehouses with respect to their focus on online transaction processing and online analytical processing.** A database is a collection of information that you organize and access according to the logical structure of that information. Databases support both online transaction processing (OLTP) and online analytical processing (OLAP). Databases that support OLTP are often referred to as **operational databases**. These databases contain detailed information about transactions that have taken place. And using various data manipulation tools, you can query a database to extract meaningful information. A **data warehouse** is a collection of information—gathered from many different operational databases—used to create business intelligence that supports business analysis activities and decision-making tasks. Data warehouses support only OLAP, not OLTP.
3. **List and describe the key characteristics of a relational database.** The **relational database model** uses a series of logically related two-dimensional tables or files to store information in the form of a database. Key characteristics are:
   - A collection of information—composed of many files or table of information that are related to each other
   - Contain logical structures—you care only about the logical information and not about how it's physically stored or where it's physically located
   - Have logical ties among the information—all the files in a database are related in that some primary keys of certain files appear as foreign keys in others
   - Possess built-in integrity constrains—when creating the data dictionary for a database, you can specify rules by which the information must be entered (e.g., not blank, etc.)
4. **Define the five software components of a database management system.** The five software components of a database management system are:
   - **DBMS engine**—accepts logical requests from the various other DBMS subsystems, converts them into their physical equivalent, and actually accesses the database and data dictionary as they exist on a storage device
   - **Data definition subsystem**—helps you create and maintain the data dictionary and define the structure of the files in a database

- **Data manipulation subsystem**—helps you add, change, and delete information in a database and mine it for valuable information
- **Application generation subsystem**—contains facilities to help you develop transaction-intensive applications
- **Data administration subsystem**—helps you manage the overall database environment by providing facilities for backup and recovery, security management, query optimization, concurrency control, and change management

5. **List and describe the key characteristics of a data warehouse.** The key characteristics of a data warehouse are:
   - Multidimensional—while databases store information in two-dimensional tables, data warehouses include layers to represent information according to different dimensions
   - Support decision making—data warehouses, because they contain summarized information, support business activities and decision-making tasks, not transaction processing
6. **Define the four major types of data mining tools in a data warehouse environment.** The four major types of data mining tools in a data warehouse environment are:
   - **Query-and-reporting tools**—similar to QBE tools, SQL, and report generators in the typical database environment
   - **Intelligent agents**—utilize various artificial intelligence tools such as neural networks and fuzzy logic to form the basis of "information discovery" and building business intelligence in OLAP
   - **Multidimensional analysis (MDA) tools**—slice-and-dice techniques that allow you to view multidimensional information from different perspectives
   - **Statistical tools**—help you apply various mathematical models to the information stored in a data warehouse to discover new information
7. **List key considerations in managing the information resource in an organization.** Key considerations in managing the information resource in an organization are:
   - Who should oversee the organization's information?
   - How will changes in technology affect organizing and managing information?
   - Is information ownership a consideration?
   - What are the ethics involved in managing and organizing information?

CLOSING CASE STUDY ONE

WE'VE GOT OLTP COVERED; LET'S GO ON TO OLAP

In business environments today, you'll find rich, technically correct, and very supportive databases that meet transaction processing needs (OLTP or online transaction processing). But many of those same organizations have failed to implement the necessary technologies that support business analysis and decision-making needs (OLAP or online analytical processing). And it makes sense. It's far easier to implement a database for processing something like sales transactions than it is to provide the necessary technology tools and information that would support someone, for example, in determining where to build a new distribution centre.

So we've pretty well got OLTP covered. We need now to focus on OLAP. Consider these three companies and their efforts in supporting OLAP. They are not unique situations, nor are they bad ones. In fact, we would say that these are leading-edge companies because they are willing to acknowledge their problems, face them, and strive to do something about them.

EASTMAN CHEMICAL COMPANY

As Jerry Hale, CIO at Eastman, explains it, managers don't have easy access to the information they need to make effective decisions. He further explains that there is a variety of reasons for this problem—too much information is available, much of the information is in incompatible formats, and most of the decision support software is too difficult for managers to use. According to Jerry, "A high percentage of the data is there. The challenge is extracting it and presenting it in a way that's useful for managers to make decisions."

To combat such problems, Eastman is currently considering several alternatives. The first is to create a simple menu of reports from which managers can choose. And, upon choosing a specific report, managers will also have the ability to request to see the aggregated information in more detail. Eastman is also planning to incorporate external information into its data warehouse. This will allow managers to compare external information such as economic and chemical industry leading-indicator information to internal information such as production and forecasted demand. The goal, according to Jerry, is "to bring this to another level of access and ease of use." Sounds good.

TEXAS INSTRUMENTS

Texas Instruments faces equally difficult challenges. For example, it has a semiconductor fabrication plant in Kilby, Texas. That plant tests and manufactures new semiconductor products and streamlines the production and yield processes before manufacturing the chips at high volume. The plant tracks huge amounts of performance information from production equipment and prototype semiconductors. That information is then ideally used to make design and production decisions for the chips.

But, as Joe Lebowitz, TI's yield and product engineering director at the plant, explains it, the information needed to make those decisions must be pulled from multiple databases. One database contains semiconductor defect data, another database tracks and maintains process equipment history, and yet another database tracks and maintains electrical test data. As Joe describes it, "One of the big tasks at hand is tying those databases together and extracting the data we need."

Currently, several IT specialists do nothing all day except build data extraction programs and reports to provide managers with the information they need. And that time could be better spent making decisions instead of just extracting the information.

CIGNA CORPORATION

Cigna Corporation, an employee benefits company with $85 billion in revenues, is actually half-pleased with its efforts to provide information that supports OLAP. According to Marc Bloom, Cigna's insurance division business technology and information services director, "I think they get more than half of what they need." The challenge now is to get the other half.

Within the insurance division, managers make daily decisions on managing based on financial and operational information. This information primarily shows fluctuations in financial and operating metrics such as an increase or decrease in claims processing. Managers can receive this information in a variety of ways—through ad hoc facilities that allow them to build their own reports, though report templates already prepared by the IT staff, and though complete reports delivered to their desktop and notebook computers.

It really all depends on the skill set of the manager. As Marc explains it, "Everybody's got a different skill set. It's a question of having the right people and the right tools to access it, turning that data into useful information, and being able to do it quickly enough to make a timely decision."[18]

Questions

1. In your view, what is the single most important factor that hinders all organizations in general from providing good online analytical processing (OLAP) support? Why is it so much easier for organizations to provide good online transaction processing support (OLTP)?

2. Consider Eastman. According to Jerry, most of the decision support software is too difficult for managers to use. One identified solution is to provide a menu of predefined reports. Will that completely solve the problem? What other steps should Eastman take so that managers don't find the decision support software too difficult to use?

3. Now consider Texas Instruments. Its managers need information for decision making that resides in several different databases. One potential solution here is to build a data warehouse and extract the necessary information from the various databases. Will this solve the problem? Why or why not? If Texas Instruments does indeed build a data warehouse, what sort of training will its managers need? How can Texas Instruments convince its managers that learning how to use yet another technology tool will be beneficial?

4. Finally, consider Cigna. According to Marc, Cigna is halfway home in providing OLAP support. If you have only half the information you need to make a decision, how effective do you think you'll be? Can you expect to make the right decision 50 percent of the time if you have only 50 percent of the information you need? What if you have 90 percent of the information you

need? Will you be 90 percent correct in making your decisions? Why or why not?

5. Neil Hastie, CIO at TruServe Corp., describes most decision making in all types of businesses as "a lot of by-guess and by-golly, a lot of by-gut, and a whole lot of paper reports." That statement is not kind to managers in general nor IT specialists charged with providing the right people with the right technology to make the right decisions. What's the key to turning Neil's statement into a positive one? Is it training? Is it providing timely information access? Is it providing easy-to-use tools? Other solutions? A combination of several?

CLOSING CASE STUDY TWO

MINING DINING DATA

Restaurants, fast food chains, casinos, and others use data warehouses to determine customer purchasing habits and what products and promotions to offer and when to offer them. Some of the leading data warehouse users include Red Robin International (a 135-unit casual-dining chain); Harrah's Entertainment (owner of 26 U.S. casinos); and Maxwell Pizza.

RED ROBIN INTERNATIONAL

Red Robin's terabyte-sized data warehouse tracks hundreds of thousands of POS transactions, involving millions of menu items and over 1.5 million invoices. As Howard Jenkins, Red Robin's vice-president of information systems, explains it, "With data mining in place, we can ask ourselves, 'If we put the items with high margins in the middle of the menu, do we sell more versus putting it at the top or bottom, [and if so] to whom and where?' We can also tell if something cannibalizes the sale of other items and can give the marketing department an almost instant picture of how promotions are being sold and used."

The placement of items on a menu is strategic business, just as the placement of promotional items in a grocery store can mean increased sales for one item and reduced sales for another. The job of finding the right mix is definitely suited to mining a data warehouse.

HARRAH'S ENTERTAINMENT

Harrah's uses its data warehouse to make decisions for its highly successful "Total Gold" customer-recognition program. Depending on their spending records, Total Gold members often receive free vouchers for dining, entertainment, and sleeping accommodations. Knowing which rewards to give to which customers is key.

John Boushy, senior vice-president of entertainment and technology for Harrah's, says, "We can determine what adds value to each customer and provide that value at the right time." For example, dining vouchers, not sleeping accommodations or free tickets for shows, are awarded to day visitors; and customers who consistently visit a particular restaurant and order higher-end foods receive free dinners and cocktails, not vouchers for free (and cheaper) breakfasts.

MAXWELL PIZZA

Maxwell Pizza uses its data warehouse to apply the "80/20" rule. That is, it can determine which 20 percent of its customers contribute to 80 percent of its sales and adjust menus and promotions to suit top patron preferences. These changes can often lead to converting some of the other 80 percent of Pizzeria Uno's customers to the more profitable 20 percent.

Questions

1. Consider the issue of timely information with respect to the businesses discussed in the case. Which of the businesses must have the most up-to-date information in its data warehouse? Which business can have the most out-of-date information in its data warehouse and still be effective? Rank the three businesses discussed with a "1" for the one that needs the most up-to-date information and a "3" for the one that is least sensitive to timeliness of information. Be prepared to justify your rankings.

2. Harrah's Entertainment tracks a wealth of information concerning customer spending habits. If

you were to design Harrah's Entertainment's data warehouse, what dimensions of information would you include? As you develop your list of dimensions, consider every facet of Harrah's business operations, including hotels, restaurants, and gaming casinos.

3. Visit a local grocery store and walk down the breakfast cereal aisle. You should notice something very specific about the positioning of the various breakfast cereals. What is it? On the basis of what information do you think grocery stores determine cereal placement? Could they have determined that information from a data warehouse or from some other source? If another source, what might that source be?

4. Suppose you're opening a pizza parlour in the town where you live. It will be a "take and bake" pizza parlour in which you make pizzas for customers but do not cook them. Customers buy the pizzas uncooked and take them home for baking. You will have no predefined pizza types but will make each pizza to the customer's specifications. What sort of data warehouse would you need to predict the use of toppings by time of day and day of the week? What would your dimensions of information be? If you wanted to increase the requests for a new topping (such as mandarin oranges), what information would you hope to find in your data warehouse that would enable you to do so?

Key Terms and Concepts

application generation subsystem, 91
business intelligence, 78
chief information officer (CIO), 101
data administration, 101
data administration subsystem, 92
data definition subsystem, 85
data dictionary, 80
data manipulation subsystem, 86
data mart, 97
data mining tool, 96
data warehouse, 94
database, 80
database administration, 101
database management system (DBMS), 83
DBMS engine, 84
foreign key, 82
integrity constraint, 82
logical view, 84
multidimensional analysis (MDA) tool, 97
online analytical processing (OLAP), 79
online transaction processing (OLTP), 78
operational database, 78
physical view, 84
primary key, 82
query-and-reporting tool, 96
query-by-example (QBE) tool, 89
relation, 80
relational database model, 80
report generator, 87
structured query language (SQL), 90
view, 86

Short-Answer Questions

1. What is business intelligence? Why is it more than just information?
2. What is online analytical processing (OLAP)? Why is it different from OLTP?
3. What is the most popular database model?
4. What is the role of a data dictionary in a database environment?
5. How are primary and foreign keys different? How are they the same?
6. What are the five important software components of a database management system?
7. What part of a DBMS helps you manage the overall database environment?
8. What is a data warehouse? How does it differ from a database?
9. What are the four major types of data mining tools?
10. What database tools are similar to data mining query-and-reporting tools?

11. What is a data mart? How is it similar to a data warehouse?
12. How often should you update information in a data warehouse?
13. What is the role of a chief information officer (CIO)?
14. How do the functions of data administration and database administration differ?

Assignments and Exercises

1. **FINDING "HACKED" DATABASES.** The Web site *The Happy Hacker* (www.happyhacker.org/news/index.shtml) is devoted to "hacking"—the breaking into of computer systems. When people hack into a system, they often go after information in databases. There, they can find credit card information and other private and sensitive information. Sometimes, they can even find designs of yet-to-be-released products and other strategic information about a company. Connect to *The Happy Hacker* and find an article that discusses a database that was hacked. Prepare a short report for your class detailing the incident.
2. **DEFINING QUERIES FOR A VIDEO RENTAL STORE.** Consider your local video rental store. It certainly has an operational database to support its online transaction processing (OLTP). The operational database supports such things as the adding of new customers, the renting of videos (obviously), the ordering of videos, and a host of other activities. Now, assume that the store also uses that same database for online analytical processing (OLAP) in the form of creating queries to extract meaningful information. If you were the store manager, what kinds of queries would you build? What answers would you be hoping to find?
3. **RESEARCHING DB2—A POPULAR BUSINESS DBMS.** IBM provides one of the most well-known DBMSs for the business world, called DB2. Connect to IBM's site (www.ibm.com) and search for "DB2." Read the product overview. What sort of data manipulation tools does it support? What sort of security management does it support? Does IBM claim that you can easily perform OLAP using DB2? If so, how and using what kinds of tools?
4. **THE PHYSICAL VIEW OF A FLOPPY DISK.** Floppy disks are one of the most common storage devices in a computer system. Although they don't store a lot of information (about 1.44 megabytes), they do offer information portability and a means of creating a quick backup of an important file or two. Your task is to research and describe the complete physical view of how information is stored on a floppy disk. As you do, you'll come across such terms as FAT (file allocation table), sides, tracks, sectors, and clusters. In fact, you should be able to provide a brief description of each of those five terms. Is it really that important that you know all of them?
5. **CREATING A QUERY.** On the Web site that supports this text (www.mcgrawhill.ca/college/haag), we've provided the Inventory database (in Microsoft Access) we illustrated in this chapter. Connect to the site and download that database (choose "Chapter 3" and then "Inventory database"). Now create three queries using the QBE tool. The first should extract information from only one file (your choice); the second should extract information found in at least two files; the third should include some sort of selection criteria. How easy or difficult was it to perform these queries? Would you say that a DBMS is just as easy to use as something like word processing or spreadsheet software? Why or why not? By the way, Skills Module 2 on the CD-ROM accompanying this text takes you through the step-by-step process of creating a query in Access.
6. **CAREER OPPORTUNITIES IN YOUR MAJOR.** Knowledge workers throughout the business world are building their own desktop databases (often called end-user databases or knowledge worker databases). To do so, they must understand both how to design a database and how to use a desktop DBMS such as Microsoft Access or FileMaker (made by FileMaker). The ability to design a database and use a desktop DBMS offer you a great career advantage. Research your chosen major by looking at job postings (the Web is the best place to start). How many of those jobs want you to have some database knowledge? Do they list a specific DBMS

package? What's your take on this—should you expand your education and learn more about databases and DBMSs? Why or why not?

7. **SALARIES FOR DATABASE ADMINISTRATORS.** Database administrators (DBAs) are among the highest-paid professionals in the information technology field. Many people work for 10 to 20 years to get a promotion to DBA. Connect to Monster.ca (www.monster.ca) or another job database or your choice and search for DBA job openings. As you do, select all locations and job categories and then use "dba" as the keyword search criterion. How many DBA job postings did you find? In what industries were some of the DBA job openings? Read through a couple of the job postings. What was the listed salary range (if any)? What sort of qualifications were listed?

Discussion Questions

1. Databases and data warehouses clearly make it easier for people to access all kinds of information. This has led to growing debates in the area of privacy. Should organizations be left to police themselves with respect to providing access to information, or should the government impose privacy legislation? Answer this question with respect to (1) customer information shared by organizations, (2) employee information shared within a specific organization, and (3) business information available to customers.

2. Business intelligence sounds like a fancy term potentially with a lot of competitive advantage rolled into it. What sort of business intelligence does your school need? Specifically, what business intelligence would it need to predict enrollments in the coming years? What business intelligence would it need to determine what curricula to offer? Do you think your school gathers and uses this kind of business intelligence? Why or why not?

3. Consider your school's registration database that enforces the following integrity constraint: to enroll in a given class, the student must have completed or currently be enrolled in the listed prerequisite (if any). Your school, in fact, probably does have that integrity constraint in place. How can you get around that integrity constraint and enroll in a class for which you are not taking nor have completed the prerequisite? Is this an instance of when you should be able to override an integrity constraint? What are the downsides to being able to do so?

4. When credit card companies make the decision of whether to issue you a credit card, they go through what is essentially a list of integrity constraints (such as your having a job for a given period of time) or rules. If you don't meet the integrity constraints, you're often denied a credit card. Put yourself in the shoes of a credit card company. What sort of integrity constraints would you follow? Would be willing to forgo any of them in certain situations? What would be the nature of those situations?

5. Some people used to believe that data warehouses would quickly replace databases for both online transaction processing (OLTP) and online analytical processing (OLAP). Of course, they were wrong. Why can data warehouses not replace databases and become "operational data warehouses?" How radically would data warehouses (and their data mining tools) have to change to become a viable replacement for databases? Would they then essentially become databases that simply supported OLAP? Why or why not?

6. Information ownership in an organization is critical. It defines who has responsibility for the quality of the information. When was the last time you got the runaround from a business because no one seemed to know who or why some of your information was changed? As a customer, how did that make you feel? Were you inclined to find a substitute product or service (think back to Chapter 2)? Is it really that difficult of a task for an organization to clearly define who has responsibility for each and every piece of information? Why or why not?

7. Imagine that you work in the human resources management department for a local business and that many of your friends work there also.

Although you don't personally generate payroll cheques, you still have the ability to look up anyone's pay. Would you check on your friends to see if they're earning more money than you? For that matter, would you look up their pay out of simple curiosity, knowing that you would never do anything with the information or share it with anyone else? Why or why not? People working at the IRS have been caught just curiously looking up the reported incomes of movie stars and other high-profile public figures. Is this acceptable? Why or why not?

8. As we discussed in the Industry Perspective "Do Movies Affect Your View of Ethics?," movies such as *Gattica* do play a role in our view of ethics. Make a list of the movies you've recently seen that raise ethical questions. Which questions do they raise? Did any of them, by chance, change your ethical views? Why or why not?

REAL HOT Electronic Commerce

Searching Online Databases and Information Repositories

The world of information is at your fingertips on the Internet. As you've already seen in the Real HOT project in Chapter 1, you can search the Internet for jobs and leave your résumé for employers to find. Almost any type of information you want you can find on the Internet.

As you locate sites that provide information, you'll find many of them do so in the form of a database—a searchable grouping of information that allows you to find specific information by entering keywords and phrases. These words and phrases are in fact a kind of keys (similar to the primary and foreign keys we discussed in this chapter) that are used as matching criteria in a field of the database.

In this section, you'll explore a variety of information topics that you can find on the Internet. To help you, we've included a number of Web sites related to searching online database and information repositories. On the site that supports this text (www.mcgrawhill.ca/college/haag), we've provided direct links to all these other sites and many, many more. These are a great starting point for completing this Real HOT Electronic Commerce section.

FINANCIAL AID RESOURCES

On the Internet, you can find valuable databases that give you access to financial aid resources as you attend school. These resources can be in the form of scholarships, money you don't have to pay back, and standard student loans. And there are a variety of financial aid lenders, ranging from traditional banks and the government to private parties wanting to give something back to society.

Find at least three Web sites that provide a financial aid database and answer the following questions for each.

A. Do you have to register as a user to access information?

B. Do you have to pay a fee to access information?

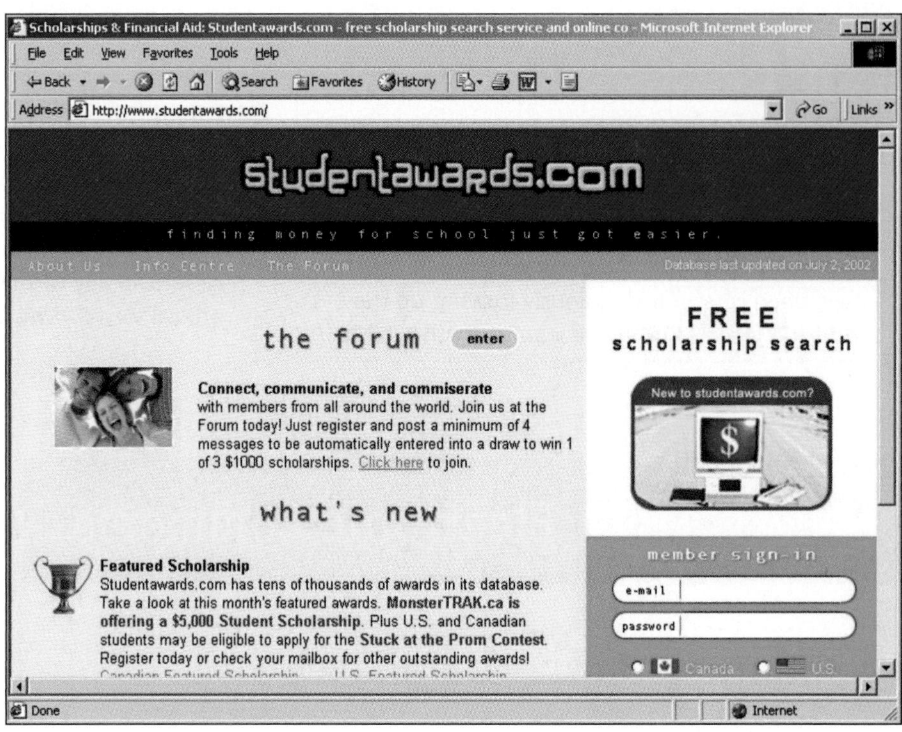

C. Can you build a profile of yourself and use it as you search?

D. Can you apply for aid while at the site or must you request paper applications that you need to complete and return?

E. By what sort of categories of aid can you search?

F. Does the site seem sincere in offering aid to you?

LIBRARIES

LexisNexis Butterworths is now completely on the Internet. Many libraries and other such sites even offer full books online for you to read. You may never have to go to the "physical" library again.

Think for a moment about a term paper you're currently writing or may have to write soon. What is the major topic? Now connect to a couple of different library sites and try to find some of the information you'll need. As you do, answer the following questions for each site.

A. What organization supports the site? Is the organization reputable?

B. Do you have to pay a subscription fee to access the information provided?

C. How good are the search capabilities?

D. How can you obtain printed versions of information you find?

E. Are you able to search periodicals? If so, how up-to-date are the issues?

F. Is finding information in libraries on the Internet easier or more difficult than finding information in a traditional library?

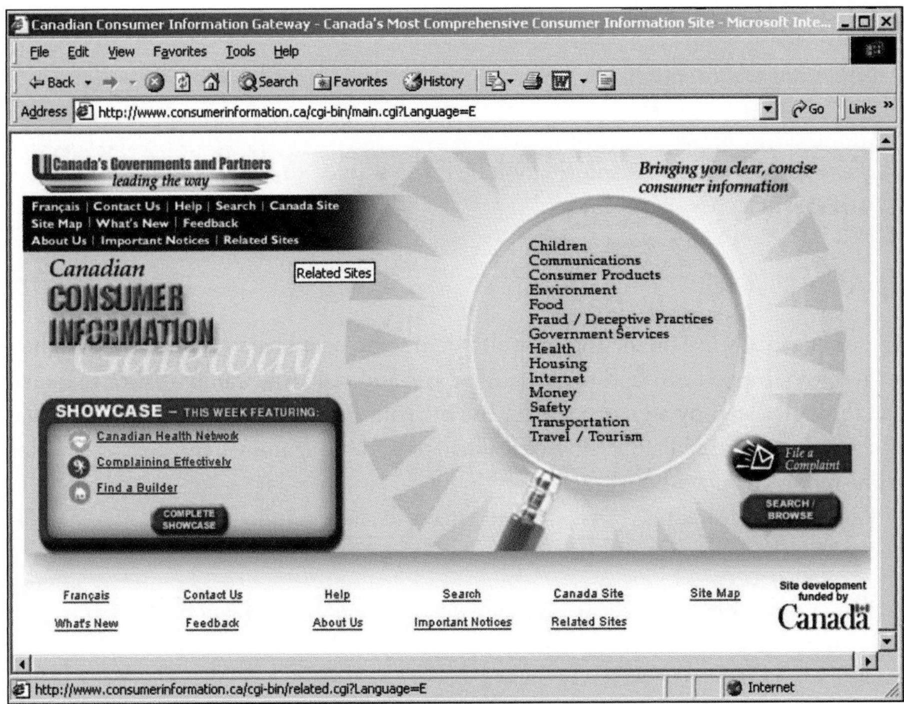

CONSUMER INFORMATION

Many consumer organizations also provide databases of information on the Internet. At those sites, you can read about the latest product reviews, search for new pharmaceuticals that cure diseases (or alleviate symptoms of them), and access safety information for products such as automobiles and children's toys.

Connect to several consumer organization sites and do some digging around. As you do, think about a product you're considering buying or perhaps have just bought. Is the information helpful? Is the information opinion only, completely factual, or a combination of the two? How important will this type of consumer information become as electronic commerce becomes more widespread on the Internet?

DEMOGRAPHICS

Recall from Chapter 1 that we characterized our economy today as "wants-driven." That is, a large portion of purchases are made on the basis of what people *want* and not necessarily what they need. This presents a real marketing and product development challenge.

For organizations focusing on meeting those wants or desires, the demographic makeup of the target audience is key. It's simple—the more you know about your target audience, the better equipped you are to develop and market products based on wants.

And you can find all sorts of demographic information on the Internet. Connect to a couple of different demographic-related Web sites and see what they have to offer. As you do, answer the following questions for each.

A. Who is the target audience of the site?

B. Who is the provider of the site?

C. Is the provider a private (for-profit) organization or a not-for-profit organization?

D. How often is the demographic information updated?

E. Does the site require that you pay a subscription fee to access its demographic information?

F. How helpful would the information be if you wanted to start a new business or sell various types of products?

REAL ESTATE

You can't actually live on the Internet, although some people may seem as though they want to try. But you can find real estate for sale and rent. You can find sites that take you through a step-by-step process for buying your first home, that provide mortgage and interest rate calculators, that offer financing for your home, and that even offer crime reports by neighbourhood.

Connect to several real estate–related sites and see what they have to offer. As you do, answer the following questions for each.

A. What is the focus of the site (residential, commercial, rental, and so forth)?

B. Does the site require you to register as a user to access its services?

Real HOT Links

C. Can you request that e-mail be sent to you when properties become available that you're interested in?

D. How can you search for information (by province, by postal code, by price range, by feature such as swimming pool, etc.)?

E. Does the site offer related information such as loans and mortgage calculators?

Go to the Online Learning Centre at www.mcgrawhill.ca/college/haag for quizzes, extra content, a searchable glossary, and more! Click on "Electronic Commerce Projects" for links to hundreds of Web sites.

Go to the text CD-ROM for data files, extra content, and Skills Modules on Microsoft Excel, Microsoft Access, HTML, and e-portfolios.

EXTENDED LEARNING MODULE A

DESIGNING DATABASES AND ENTITY-RELATIONSHIP DIAGRAMMING

Student Learning Outcomes

1. Identify how databases and spreadsheets are both similar and different.
2. List and describe the four steps in designing and building a relational database.
3. Define the concepts of entity class, instance, primary key, and foreign key.
4. Given a small operating environment, build an entity-relationship (E-R) diagram.
5. List and describe the steps in normalization.
6. Describe the process of creating an intersection relation to remove a many-to-many relationship.

Introduction

As you learned in Chapter 3, databases are quite powerful and can aid your organization in both transaction and analytical processing. But you must carefully design and build a database for it to be effective. Relational databases are similar to spreadsheets in that you maintain information in two-dimensional files. In a spreadsheet, you place information in a cell (the intersection of a row and column). To use the information in a cell, you must know its row number and column letter. For example, cell C4 is in row 4 and column C.

Databases are similar and different. You still create rows and columns of information. However, you don't need to know the physical location of the information you want to see or use. For example, if cell C4 in your spreadsheet contained sales for Able Electronics (one of your customers), to use that information in a formula or function you would reference its physical location (C4). In a database, you simply need to know you want *sales* for *Able Electronics*. Its physical location is irrelevant—that's why we say that a **database** is a collection of information that you organize and access according to the logical structure of that information.

So you do need to carefully design your databases for effective utilization. In this Module, we'll take you through the process of designing and building a relational database, the most popular of all database types. A **relational database** uses a series of logically related two-dimensional tables or files to store information in the form of a database. There are well-defined rules to follow, and you need to be aware of them.

As far as implementation is concerned, you then just choose the DBMS package of your choice, define the tables or files and the relationships among them, and start entering information. We won't deal with the actual implementation in this Module. However, we do show you how to implement a database using Microsoft Access in Skills Module 2 on the CD-ROM accompanying this text.

Once you've implemented your database, you can change the information as you wish, add rows of information (and delete others), add new tables, and use simple but powerful reporting and querying tools to extract the exact information you need.

Designing and Building a Relational Database

Using a database amounts to more than just using various DBMS tools. You must also know *how* to actually design and build a database. So, let's take a look at how you would go about designing a database. The four primary steps include:

1. Defining entity classes and primary keys
2. Defining relationships among entity classes
3. Defining information (fields) for each relation (the term *relation* is often used to refer to a file while designing a database)
4. Using a data definition language to create your database

Let's assume you own a small business and are interested in tracking employees by the department in which they work, job assignments, and number of hours assigned to each job. Below is a list of important business rules that you follow:

1. Each employee must be assigned to one and only one department.
2. A department may have many employees but also may not have any.

3. Each employee must be assigned to at least one job and can be assigned to many jobs.
4. A job can have many different employees assigned to it but a given job does not have to have any employees assigned to it.

Figure A.1 contains a sample Employee Report you would like to generate. Let's briefly look at it and review some of the business rules in action.

First, notice that each employee is assigned to only one department. For example, Mills is assigned to only department number 43. Second, notice that several employees are assigned to department number 43—these employees include Jones, Joslin, and Mills. Third, notice that each employee is assigned to at least one job and that several employees have more than one job. Finally, notice that more than one employee is assigned to the same job. For example, Jones, Mills, and Smith are assigned to the job "Acct" (its job number is 14).

Even before you begin the process of designing a database, it's important that you first understand the business rules. These business rules will help you define the correct structure of your database.

STEP 1: DEFINING ENTITY CLASSES AND PRIMARY KEYS

The first step in designing a relational database is to define the various entity classes and the primary keys that uniquely define each record or instance within each entity class. An **entity class** is a concept—typically people, places, or things—about which you wish to store information and that you can identify with a unique key (called the primary key). A **primary key** is a field (or group of fields in some cases) that uniquely describes each record. Within the context of database design, we often refer to a record as an **instance**—an occurrence of an entity class that can be uniquely described.

From the Employee Report you want to generate, you can easily identify the entity classes *Employee*, *Job*, and *Department*. Now, you have to identify their primary keys. For most entity classes, you cannot use names as primary keys because duplicate names may exist. For example, you have two employees with the last name Jones. However, our sample report does show that each employee has a unique *Employee ID*. So, *Employee ID* should be the primary key for the *Employee* entity class.

Figure A.1

A Sample Report for Your Employee Database

Employee ID	Name	Department Num	Department Name	Num of Employees	Job Number	Job Name	Hours
1234	Jones	43	Residential	3	14 23	Acct Sales	4 4
2345	Smith	15	Commercial	1	14	Acct	8
6548	Joslin	43	Residential	3	23 46	Sales Admin	6 2
9087	Mills	43	Residential	3	23 14	Sales Acct	5 3
8797	Jones	69	Non-profit	1	39	Maint	8

TEAM WORK

DEFINING ENTITY CLASSES AND PRIMARY KEYS

Learning how to design a relational database really requires that you roll up your sleeves and practise, practise, practise. It's not actually that difficult, and practice will make you proficient. To help with this, you'll be designing a database that might be used at your school while we go carefully through the process of designing the one for your employee information. Below is a description of a hypothetical relational database that might be used at your school.

Suppose that in conjunction with taking an introductory computer concepts course, your school has decided to test the idea of offering weekend seminars to cover the basics of the Internet and the Web. Initially, your school will offer two such seminars: Web101—The Basics of the Web; and Internet and Web205—Building a Web Site. Web101 will have five different sections, and Web205 will have four.

Although not required to, students can enroll in one or both seminars. The seminars are held for eight hours on a single day. There is no cost associated with taking the seminars. One teacher, from a pool of qualified teachers, will be assigned to each section of each seminar. Some teachers will obviously not be assigned to teach any sections, and some teachers may be assigned to several different sections. The system should track the final grade assigned to each student.

One more thing. Your school is simply testing this idea in this particular term. So don't worry about the term (e.g., Fall, Winter, Spring, or Summer) or the year.

In the table below, list all the entity classes you can find in the above description. Next to each, identify a potential primary key. Finally, below the table, record as many business rules as you can find provided in the description above.

Entity Class	Primary Key

Business Rules

If you consider *Department* as an entity class, you'll find three pieces of information describing it in the report—*Department Num*, *Department Name*, and *Num of Employees*. The logical choice for a primary key here is *Department Num*. Although each *Department Name* is unique, we would still suggest that you not use names.

Likewise, if you consider *Job* as an entity class, you'll find two pieces of information describing it—*Job Number* and *Job Name*. Again, we recommend that you use *Job Number* as the primary key.

For each of these entity classes, you can also easily identify instances. Smith is an instance of the *Employee* entity class, Residential is an instance of the *Department* entity class, and Sales is an instance of the *Job* entity class.

As you begin the process of designing a database, perhaps the easiest way to define entity classes and their primary keys is to do what we have just done—build a sample report that you would like to generate and use it find entity classes and their primary keys.

STEP 2: DEFINING RELATIONSHIPS AMONG THE ENTITY CLASSES

The next step in designing a relational database is to define the relationships among the entity classes. To help you do this, we'll use an entity-relationship diagram. An **entity-relationship (E-R) diagram** is a graphical method of representing entity classes and their relationships. An E-R diagram includes five basic symbols:

1. A rectangle to denote an entity class
2. A dotted line connecting entity classes to denote a relationship
3. "|" to denote a single relationship
4. A circle to denote a zero or optional relationship
5. A "crow's foot" symbol to denote a multiple relationship

To use these symbols, you must first decide among which entity classes relationships exist. If you determine that two particular entity classes have a relationship, you simply draw a dotted line to connect them and then write some sort of verb that describes the relationship.

In Figure A.2, you can see the E-R diagram for your employee database. Let's take some time to explore it. To determine where the relationships exist, simply ask some questions and review your business rules. For example, is there a relationship between employees and departments? The answer is yes, because employees are assigned to departments. Likewise, employees are assigned jobs (another relationship). However, there is no logical relationship between departments and jobs. So we drew dotted lines between *Employee* and *Department* and between *Employee* and *Job*. We then added some verbs to describe the relationships. For example, an *Employee* is assigned to a *Department*, and an *Employee* performs a *Job*.

It should also make sense (both business and logical) when you read the relationships in reverse. To do this, simply flip the location of the nouns in the sentence and change the verb accordingly. For example:

- *Employee-Department*: An *Employee* is assigned to a *Department*.
- *Department-Employee*: A *Department* has an *Employee* assigned to it.
- *Employee-Job*: An *Employee* undertakes a *Job*.
- *Job-Employee*: A *Job* is performed by an *Employee*.

Each of the above statements makes logical sense, follows the relationships we identified in Figure A.2, and reflects the business rules given above. Again, we stress the

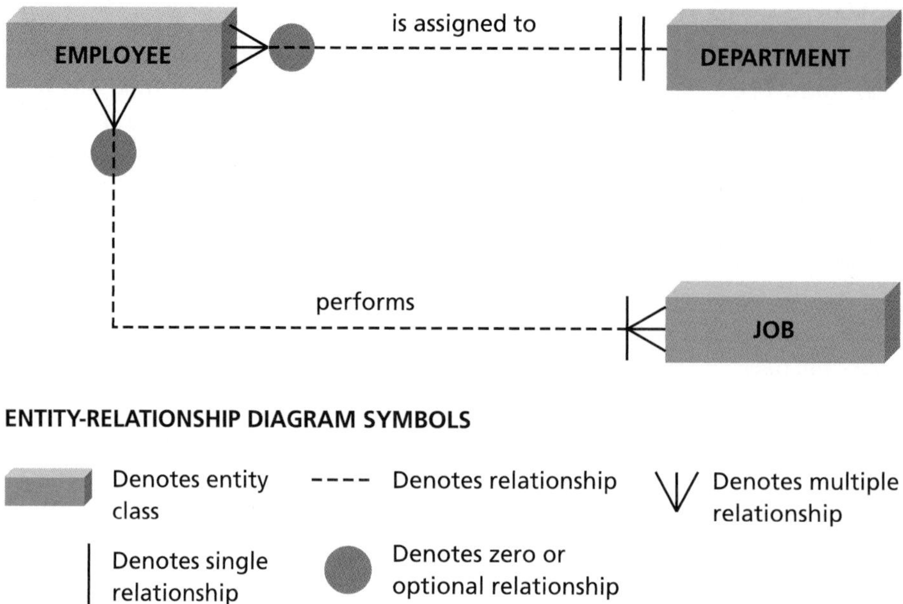

Figure A.2
An Entity-Relationship Diagram

importance of using business rules. Technology (databases, in this instance) is a set of tools that you use to process information. So your implementations of technology should match the way your business works. If you always start by defining business rules and using those rules as guides, your technology implementations will hopefully mirror how your business works. And that's the way it should be.

Once you determine that a relationship does exist, you must then determine the numerical nature of the relationship, what we refer to as minimum and maximum *cardinality*. To describe this, you use a "|" to denote a single relationship, a circle to denote a zero or optional relationship, and/or a "crow's foot" symbol to denote a multiple relationship. By way of illustration, let's consider the portion of your E-R diagram in Figure A.3. To help you read the symbols, we've added coloured lines and arrows. Following the line marked "A," you would read the E-R diagram as "An *Employee* is assigned to one *Department* at minimum and one *Department* at maximum." So that part of the E-R diagram states that the logical relationship between *Employee* and *Department* is that an *Employee* is assigned to one and only one *Department*. This is exactly what business rules 1 and 2 above state.

Following the coloured line marked "B," you would read the E-R diagram as, "A *Department* is not required to have any *Employees* assigned to it but may have many *Employees* assigned to it." That statement again reinforces business rules 1 and 2.

Similarly, you can develop statements that describe the numerical relationships between *Employee* and *Job* on the basis of that part of the E-R diagram in Figure A.2. Those numerical relationships would be as follows:

- An *Employee* must be assigned to one *Job* at minimum and can be assigned to many *Jobs* (maximum).
- A *Job* might not have any *Employees* assigned to it but might have many *Employees* assigned to it.

Again, these statements reinforce business rules 3 and 4.

To properly develop the numerical relationships (cardinality) among entity classes, you must clearly understand the business situation at hand. That's why it's so important to write down all the business rules.

TEAM WORK

DEFINING RELATIONSHIPS AMONG ENTITY CLASSES

Let's continue on exploring how to design a relational database for your school and its offering of weekend seminars. If your group correctly completed the tasks in the previous Team Work, you know that there are four entity classes. They include (along with their primary keys):

Entity Class	Primary Key
Seminar	Seminar 3-character identifier and number (e.g., Web101 and Web205)
Seminar Section	Seminar 3-character identifier, number, and section number (e.g., Web101-1 through Web101-5 and Web205-1 through Web205-4)
Student	Student ID (whatever your school happens to use)
Qualified Teacher	Teacher ID (your school may use the social insurance number)

Now, your task is to define among which of those entity classes relationships exist and then write some verbs that describe each relationship, just we did in Figure A.2. Below, we've drawn rectangles for each of the four entity classes. Connect with dotted lines those rectangles between which relationships exist and write in appropriate verbs to describe the relationships.

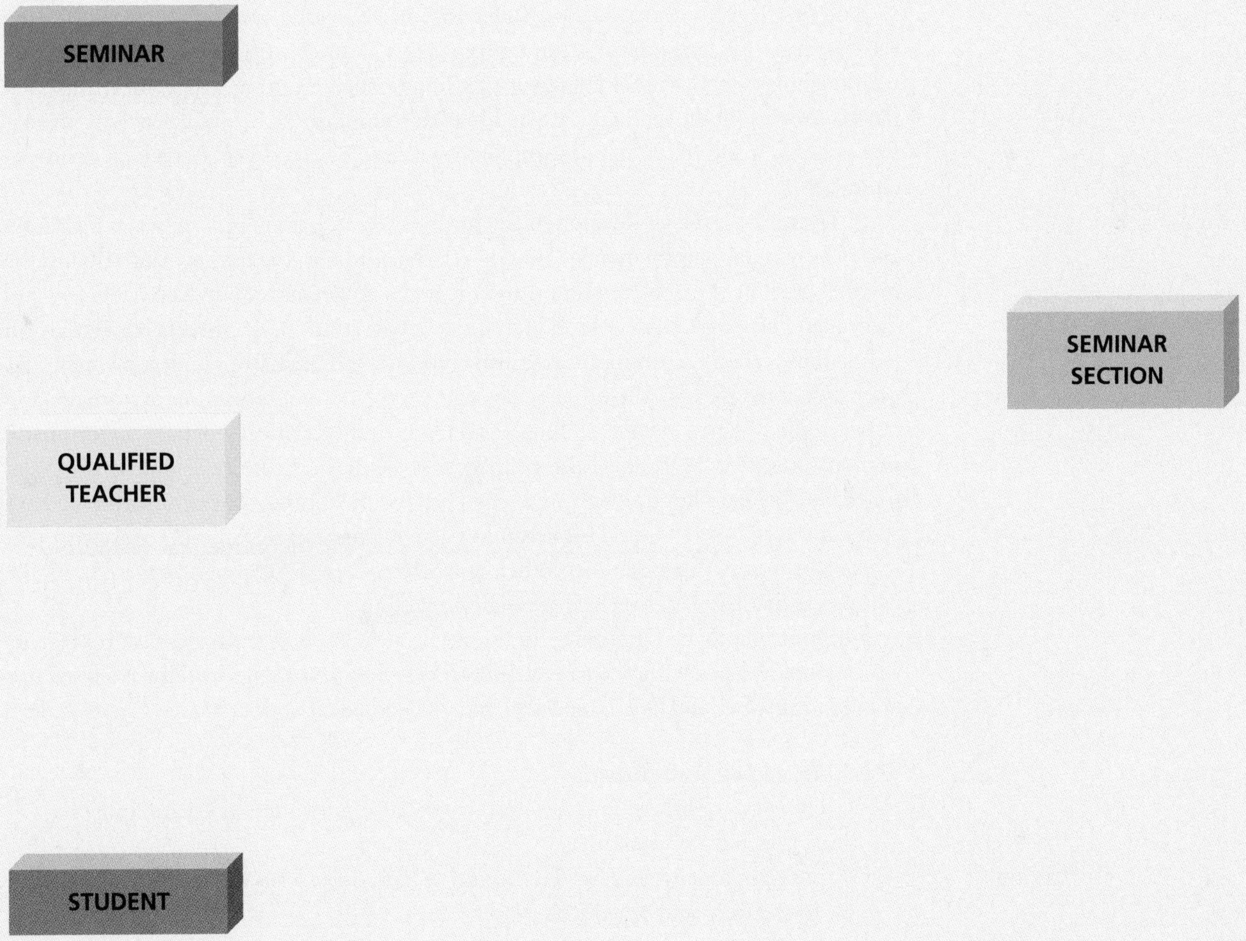

SEMINAR

SEMINAR SECTION

QUALIFIED TEACHER

STUDENT

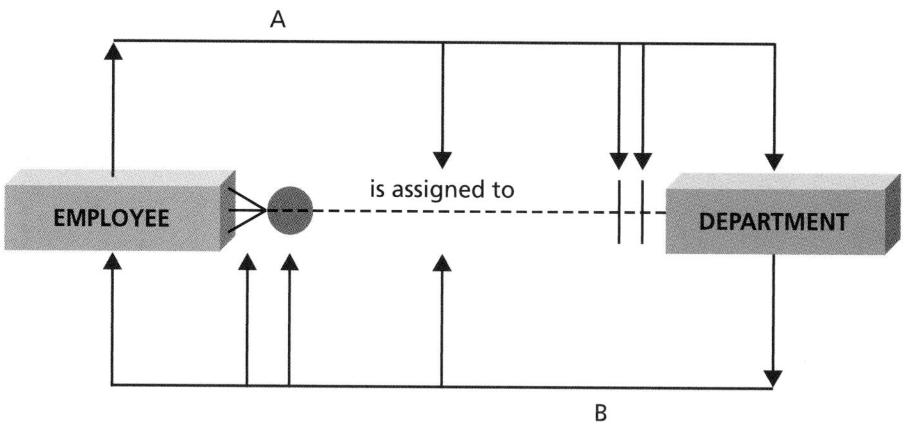

Figure A.3
Reading an Entity-Relationship (E-R) Diagram

Database—Normalization

After developing the initial E-R diagram, it's time to begin **normalization**—a process of ensuring that a relational database structure can be implemented as a series of two-dimensional relations (remember, *relations* are the same as files or tables). The complete normalization process is extensive but quite necessary for developing organizationwide databases. For our purposes, we will focus on the following three rules of normalization:

1. Eliminate repeating groups or many-to-many relationships.
2. Ensure that each field in a relation depends only on the primary key for that relation.
3. Remove all derived fields from the relations.

The first rule of normalization states that no repeating groups or many-to-many relationships can exist among the entity classes. You can find these many-to-many relationships by simply looking at your E-R diagram and noting any relationships that have a crow's foot on each end. If you look back at Figure A.2, you'll see that a crow's foot is on each end of the relationship between *Employee* and *Job*. Let's look at how to eliminate it.

In Figure A.4, we've developed the appropriate relationships between *Employee* and *Job* by removing the many-to-many relationship. Notice that we started with the original portion of the E-R diagram and created a new relation between *Employee* and *Job* called *Job Assignment*, which is an intersection relation. An **intersection relation** (sometimes called a **composite relation**) is a one you create to eliminate a many-to-many relationship. It's called that because it represents an intersection of primary keys between the first two relations. That is, an intersection relation will have a **composite primary key** that consists of the primary key fields from the two intersecting relations. The primary key fields from the two original relations now become foreign keys in the intersection relation. A **foreign key** is a primary key of one file (relation) that appears in another file (relation). When combined, these two foreign keys make up the composite primary key for the intersection relation.

For your employee database, the intersection relation *Job Assignment* represents which employees are assigned to each job. Here is how you would read the relationships between *Employee* and *Job Assignment* and *Job* and *Job Assignment* (see Figure A.5):

Employee-Job Assignment

- From left to right: An *Employee* can have many *Job Assignments* and must have at least one *Job Assignment*.
- From right to left: An *Employee* found in *Job Assignment* must be found and can be found only one time in *Employee*.

TEAM WORK

DEFINING THE CARDINALITY AMONG ENTITY CLASSES

As we continue with the design of the relational database at your school, it's time to define the cardinality among the entity classes. If you correctly completed the previous Team Work project, the relationships among the entity classes are as follows:

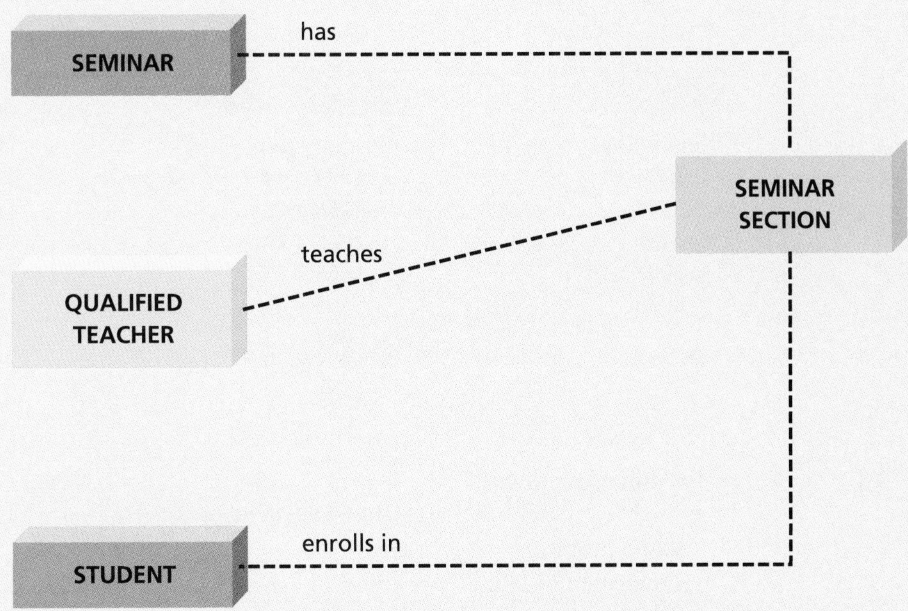

Your task is to create the numerical relationships by adding the cardinality symbols, described earlier, in the appropriate places. Once you do, complete the table below by providing a narrative description of each numerical relationship.

Relationship	Narrative Description
Seminar-Seminar Section	
Seminar Section-Seminar	
Qualified Teacher-Seminar Section	
Seminar Section-Qualified Teacher	
Student-Seminar Section	
Seminar Section-Student	

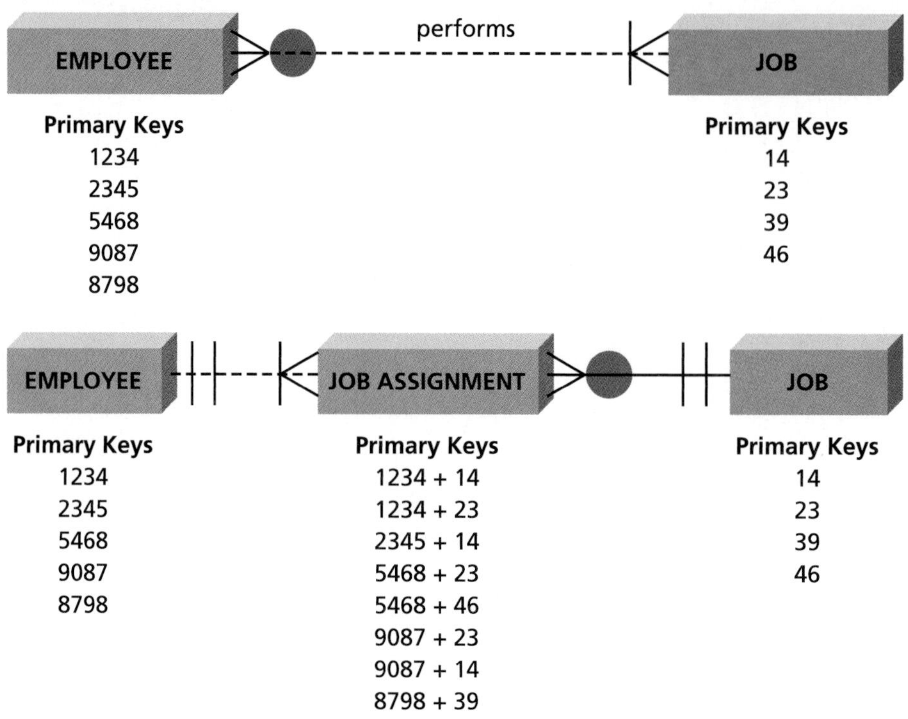

Figure A.4
Creating an Intersection Relation to Remove a Many-to-Many Relationship

Job-Job Assignment

- From left to right: A *Job* can be found in many *Job Assignments* but might not be found in any *Job Assignments*.
- From right to left: A *Job* found in *Job Assignment* must be found and can be found only one time in *Job*.

If you compare the E-R diagram in Figure A.5 to the E-R diagram in Figure A.2, you'll notice that they are very similar. The only difference is that the E-R diagram in Figure A.5 contains an intersection relation to eliminate the many-to-many relationship between *Employee* and *Job*.

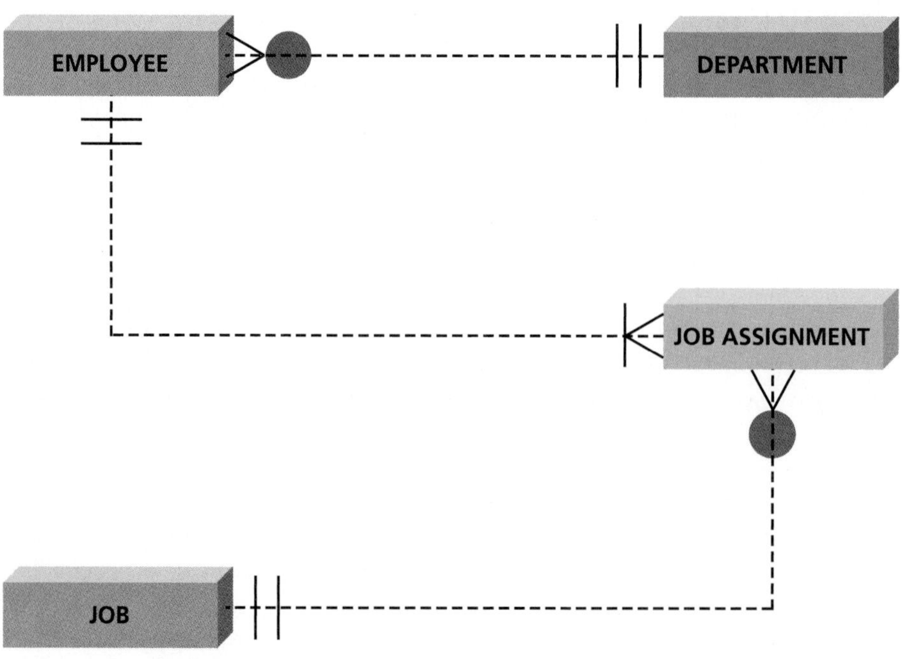

Figure A.5
The Completed E-R Diagram for Your Employee Database

And removing many-to-many relationships is the most difficult aspect when designing the appropriate structure of a relational database. If you do find a many-to-many relationship, here are some guidelines for creating an intersection relation:

1. Just as we did in Figure A.5, start by drawing the part of the E-R diagram that contains a many-to-many relationship at the top of a piece of paper.
2. Underneath each relation for which the many-to-many relationship exists, write down some of the primary keys.
3. Create a new E-R diagram (showing no cardinality) with the original two relations on each end and a new one (the intersection relation) in the middle.
4. Underneath the intersection relation, write down some composite primary keys (these will be composed of the primary keys from the other two relations).
5. Create a meaningful name (e.g., *Job Assignment*) for the intersection relation.
6. Move the minimum cardinality appearing next to the left relation just to the right of the intersection relation.
7. Move the minimum cardinality appearing next to the right relation just to the left of the intersection relation.
8. The maximum cardinality on both sides of the intersection relation will always be "many" (the crow's foot).
9. As a general rule, the new minimum and maximum cardinalities for the two original relations will be one to one.

STEP 3: DEFINING INFORMATION (FIELDS) FOR EACH RELATION

Once you've completed steps 1 and 2, you must define the various pieces of information that each relation will contain. Your goal in this step to make sure that the information in each relation is indeed in the correct relation and that the information cannot be derived from other information—the second and third rules of normalization.

In Figure A.6, we've developed a view of the relations based on the new E-R diagram with the intersection relation. To make sure that each piece of information is in the correct relation, look at each and ask, "Does this piece of information depend only on the primary key for this relation?" If the answer is yes, the information is in the correct relation. If the answer is no, the information is in the wrong relation.

Let's consider the *Employee* relation. The primary key is *Employee ID*, so each piece of information must depend only on *Employee ID*. Does *Name* depend on *Employee ID*? Yes—so that information is in the correct relation. Does *Department Num* depend on *Employee ID*? Yes, because each employee's department designation depends on the particular employee you're describing. In this case, *Department Num* in the *Employee* relation is an example of a foreign key. What about *Department Name*? The answer here is no. The name for a particular department doesn't depend on which employee is in that department.

So the question becomes "In which relation should *Department Name* appear?" The answer is in the *Department* relation, because *Department Name* depends on the primary key (*Department Num*) that uniquely describes each department. Therefore, *Department Name* should not be in the *Employee* relation, but rather in the *Department* relation.

Now, take a look at the intersection relation *Job Assignment*. Notice that it includes the field called *Hours*. *Hours* is located in this relation because it depends on two things—the employee you're describing and the job to which he or she is assigned. So *Hours* does depend completely on the composite primary key *Employee ID* + *Job Number* in the *Job Assignment* relation.

TEAM WORK

CREATING AN INTERSECTION RELATION

Back to work on the project for your school. If you completed the last Team Work project, you are now able to identify a many-to-many relationship between *Student* and *Seminar Section*. That is, a given *Seminar Section* may have many *Students*, and a given *Student* can enroll in many different *Seminar Sections* (two to be exact). So that portion of your E-R diagram looks like this:

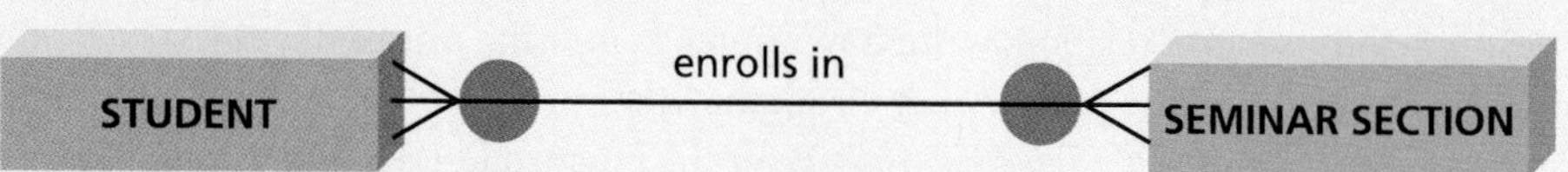

Your task is to eliminate the above many-to-many relationship by creating an intersection relation. As you do, we would encourage you to follow the guidelines given above. What did you name the intersection relation? What does the completed E-R diagram look like?

Figure A.6

A First Look at the Relations in Your Employee Database

EMPLOYEE RELATION

Employee ID	Name	Department Num	Department Name
1234	Jones	43	Residential
2345	Smith	15	Commercial
5468	Joslin	43	Residential
9087	Mills	43	Residential
8798	Jones	69	Non-profit

JOB RELATION

Job Number	Job Name
14	Acct
23	Sales
39	Maint
46	Admin

DEPARTMENT RELATION

Department Num	Department Name	Num of Employees
15	Commercial	1
43	Residential	3
69	Non-profit	1

JOB ASSIGNMENT RELATION

Employee ID	Job Number	Hours
1234	14	4
1234	23	4
2345	14	8
5468	23	6
5468	46	2
9087	23	5
9087	14	3
8798	39	8

Hours belongs in this relation because it depends on a combination of who *(Employee ID)* is assigned to which job *(Job Number)*.

If you follow this line of questioning for each relation, you'll find that all other fields are in their correct relation. Now you have to look at each field to see whether you can derive it from other information. If you can, the derived information should not be stored in your database. When we speak of "derived" in this instance, we're referring to information that you can mathematically derive—counts, totals, averages, and the like. Currently, you are storing the number of employees (*Num of Employees*) in the *Department* relation. Can you derive that information from other information? The answer is yes—all you have to do is count the number of occurrences of each department number in the *Employee* relation. So, you should not store *Num of Employees* in your database (anywhere).

Once you've completed step 3, you've completely and correctly defined the structure of your database and identified the information each relation should contain. Figure A.7 shows your database and the information in each relation. Notice that we have removed *Department Name* from the *Employee* relation (following the second rule of normalization) and that we have removed *Num of Employees* from the *Department* relation (following the third rule of normalization).

Figure A.7

The Correct Structure of Your Employee Database

EMPLOYEE RELATION

Employee ID	Name	Department Num
1234	Jones	43
2345	Smith	15
5468	Joslin	43
9087	Mills	43
8798	Jones	69

JOB RELATION

Job Number	Job Name
14	Acct
23	Sales
39	Maint
46	Admin

DEPARTMENT RELATION

Department Num	Department Name
15	Commercial
43	Residential
69	Non-profit

JOB ASSIGNMENT RELATION

Employee ID	Job Number	Hours
1234	14	4
1234	23	4
2345	14	8
5468	23	6
5468	46	2
9087	23	5
9087	14	3
8798	39	8

ON YOUR OWN

CREATING THE FINAL STRUCTURE FOR YOUR SCHOOL

Now it's time for you to fly solo and try a task by yourself. If your group successfully the completed the previous Team Work project, you should have a relational database model with five relations: *Seminar*, *Seminar Section*, *Student*, *Qualified Teacher*, and *Seminar Section Class Roll*. The first four you identified early on. The last is the result of eliminating the many-to-many relationship between *Seminar Section* and *Student*. We named this intersection relation *Seminar Section Class Roll.* We did so because it represents a list of students enrolling in all of the sections. If you group those students by section, then you get class rolls.

Your task is to complete each table below for each relation. That is, you must first fill in the column headings by identifying what information belongs in each relation. Be sure to follow steps 2 and 3 of normalization. Then, we encourage you to add in some actual data entries.

A word of caution. You could easily identify hundreds of pieces of information that need to be present in this database. For *Qualified Teacher* for example, you could include birth date, rank, office hours, phone number, e-mail address, office location, employment starting date, and many more. Here, simply identify no more than five key pieces of information for each relation. And, by all means, identify the primary and foreign keys for each relation.

Seminar Relation

Seminar Section Relation

Student Relation

Qualified Teacher Relation

Seminar Section Class Roll Relation

STEP 4: USING A DATA DEFINITION LANGUAGE TO CREATE YOUR DATABASE

The final step in developing a relational database is to take the structure you created in steps 1 to 3 and use a data definition language to actually create the relation. Data definition languages are found within a database management system. A **database management system (DBMS)** helps you specify the logical organization for a database and access and use the information within the database. This is the point at which we'll end this Extended Learning Module. But you shouldn't stop learning. We've created Skills Module 2 (on the CD-ROM accompanying this text) that takes you through the process of using the data definition language in Access to create the database we just designed. Keep learning.

Skills Module 2
Database Design—
Access

Summary: Student Learning Outcomes Revisited

1. **Identify how databases and spreadsheets are both similar and different.** Databases and spreadsheets are similar in that they both store information in two-dimensional files. They are different in one key aspect—physical versus logical. Spreadsheets require that you know the physical location of information, by row and column. Databases, on the other hand, require that you know logically what information you want. For example, in a database environment you could easily request total sales for Able Electronics and you would receive that information. In a spreadsheet, you would have to know the physical location—by row and column—of that information.
2. **List and describe the four steps in designing and building a relational database.** The four steps in designing and building a relational database include:
   1. Defining entity classes and primary keys
   2. Defining relationships among entity classes
   3. Defining information (fields) for each relation
   4. Using a data definition language to create your database
3. **Define the concepts of entity class, instance, primary key, and foreign key.** An **entity class** is a concept—typically people, places, or things—about which you wish to store information and that you can identify with a unique key (called a primary key). A **primary key** is a field (or group of fields in some cases) that uniquely describes each record. Within the context of database design, we often refer to a record as an instance. An **instance** is an occurrence of an entity class that can be uniquely described. To provide logical relationships among various entity classes, you use **foreign keys**—primary keys of a file (relation) that also appear in another file (relation).
4. **Given a small operating environment, build an entity-relationship (E-R) diagram.** Building an E-R diagram starts with knowing and understanding the business rules that govern the situation. These rules will help you identify entity classes, primary keys, and relationships. You then follow the process of normalization, eliminating many-to-many relationships, ensuring that each field is in the correct relation, and removing any derived fields.
5. **List and describe the steps in normalization.** **Normalization** is the process of ensuring that a relational database structure can be implemented as a series of two-dimensional tables. The normalization steps include:
   1. Eliminate repeating groups or many-to-many relationships.
   2. Ensure that each field in a relation depends only on the primary key for that relation.
   3. Remove all derived fields from the relations.
6. **Describe the process of creating an intersection relation to remove a many-to-many relationship.** To create an intersection relation to remove a many-to-many relationship, follow these seven steps:
   1. Draw the part of the E-R diagram that contains a many-to-many relationship.
   2. Create a new E-R diagram with the original two relations on each end and a new one (the intersection relation) in the middle.

3. Create a meaningful name for the intersection relation.
4. Move the minimum cardinality appearing next to the left relation to just to the right of the intersection relation.
5. Move the minimum cardinality appearing next to the right relation to just to the left of the intersection relation.
6. The maximum cardinality on both sides of the intersection relation will always be "many."
7. As a general rule, the new minimum and maximum cardinalities for the two original relations will be one and one.

Key Terms and Concepts

composite primary key, 122
composite relation, 122
database, 116
database management system (DBMS), 129
entity class, 117
entity-relationship (E-R) diagram, 119
foreign key, 122
instance, 117
intersection relation (composite relation), 122
normalization, 122
primary key, 117
relational database, 116

Short-Answer Questions

1. How are relational databases and spreadsheets both similar and different?
2. What are the four steps in designing and building a relational database?
3. What are some examples of entity classes at your school?
4. What is the role of a primary key?
5. What is the relationship between an occurrence and a record?
6. What is an entity-relationship (E-R) diagram?
7. What are the five basic symbols found in an E-R diagram?
8. How do business rules help you define minimum and maximum cardinality?
9. What is normalization?
10. What are the three major rules of normalization?
11. What is an intersection relation? Why is it important in designing a relational database?
12. Why must you remove derived information from a database?
13. What is a database management system (DBMS)?

Assignments and Exercises

1. **DEFINING ENTITY CLASSES FOR THE MUSIC INDUSTRY.** The music industry tracks and uses all sorts of information related to numerous entity classes. Find a music CD and carefully review the entire contents of the jacket. List as many entity classes as you can find (for just that CD). Now, go to a music store and pick out a CD for a completely different music genre and read its jacket. Did you find any new entity classes? If so, what are they?
2. **DEFINING BUSINESS RULES FOR A VIDEO RENTAL STORE.** Think about how your local video rental store works. There are many customers, renting many videos, and many videos sit on the shelves unrented.

Customers can rent many videos at one time. And some videos are so popular that the video rental store keeps many copies. Write down all the various business rules that define how a video rental store works with respect to entity classes and their relationships.

3. **CREATING AN E-R DIAGRAM FOR A VIDEO RENTAL STORE.** After completing assignment 2 above, draw the initial E-R diagram on the basis of the rules you defined. Don't worry about going through the process of normalization at this point. Simply identify the appropriate relationships among the entity classes and define the minimum and maximum cardinality of each relationship. By the way, how many many-to-many relationships did you define?

4. **ELIMINATING A MANY-TO-MANY RELATIONSHIP.** Consider the following situation. At a small auto parts store, customers can buy many parts. And the same part can be bought by many different customers. That's an example of a many-to-many relationship. How would you eliminate it? What would you call the intersection relation? This one is particularly tough—you'll have to actually create two intersection relations to model this correctly.

5. **ELIMINATING A DERIVED FIELD.** If you think about it for a moment, your GPA is a derived field—it's a mathematical function of the grade points you've accumulated divided by the credits you've taken. So GPA should not be stored in your school's database. Given that it is not present, in what relations would the information be stored from which you could derive your GPA? What process would a DBMS have to go through to accurately calculate your GPA?

6. **DEFINING THE CARDINALITY AMONG TWO ENTITY CLASSES.** Consider the two entity classes of Student and Advisor at your school. How would you build an E-R diagram to show the relationship between these two entity classes? What is the minimum and maximum cardinality of the relationship?

7. **MODELLING YOUR SCHOOL'S BOOKSTORE.** Your school's bookstore maintains a vast inventory of books (and let's limit this exercise to just books). Consider that your school only orders new books from publishers. Books have a specific category (e.g., math, English, etc.). And books have at least one author and may have several. Focusing just on books, book categories, publishers, and authors, create a normalized relational database that would track key pieces of information. For each relation, define the primary key, any foreign keys, and a few pieces of important information. Did you find any many-to-many relationships? If so, how did you eliminate them?

8. **MAKING SOME CHANGES TO YOUR SCHOOL'S OFFERING OF WEEKEND SEMINARS.** Throughout this Module, you've been creating the correct structure for a database that will support your school's offering of weekend seminars on the Internet and Web. Now, you need to make a few changes. Implement the following business rules: (1) each student must take at least one seminar, (2) each seminar section must be assigned to a building and a room (some rooms won't have any seminar sections scheduled in them), and (3) each qualified teacher is assigned to only one academic department (and each academic department must have at least one qualified teacher in it). What does the new E-R diagram look like?

9. **MAKING SOME CHANGES TO YOUR EMPLOYEE DATABASE.** Throughout this module, you followed along with us as we created the correct structure for a database that will help you manage your employees, their departments, and their job assignments. Implement the following business rules: (1) each department must have one manager who is also an employee (some employees might not be managers) and (2) each employee has at least one of the following skills—team building, project management, and/or follow-up. What does the new E-R diagram look like?

CHAPTER FOUR

STUDENT LEARNING OUTCOMES

1. Define decision support system, list its components, and understand its applications.
2. Describe collaboration systems along with their features and uses.
3. Describe geographic information systems and how they differ from other decision support tools.
4. Define artificial intelligence and list the different types that are used in business.
5. Describe expert systems, their components, and the types of problems to which they are applicable.
6. Define neural networks, their uses, and their strengths and weaknesses.
7. Define genetic algorithms and the concepts on which they are based, and the types of problems they solve.
8. Define intelligent agents, list the four types and identify the types of problems they solve.

INDUSTRY PERSPECTIVES

FEATURES

WEB SUPPORT LINKS

- Learning About Investing
- Researching the Company Behind the Stock
- Finding Other Sources of Company Financials
- Making Trades Online
- Retrieving Stock Quotes

Visit www.mcgrawhill.ca/college/haag

DECISION SUPPORT AND ARTIFICIAL INTELLIGENCE
Brainpower for Your Business

CASE STUDY:
USING AN INTEGRATED DECISION SUPPORT SYSTEM TO HELP TREAT DIABETES AND ASTHMA

A multidisciplinary team of researchers from the Faculty of Medicine, the Faculty of Management, and the Faculty of Pharmacy of McGill University and of Université de Montréal is conducting a research project in which they develop, implement, and study the effects of a decision support system (DSS) that will help to treat patients with asthma and diabetes. The DSS is made of two main components. The drug management module will support the physician in the diagnostic and drug prescription phases. Accessing different databases, the DSS will merge and analyze chronic and chronic episodic health problems of the patient and the current active medications, and it will help in determining therapeutic interventions. For example, on the basis of its historical analysis of the patient condition, the DSS will provide dosing recommendations, and will perform dosing checks relative to recommended doses, drug disease and drug allergy contraindication, drug interactions, therapeutic duplications, and excess duration of therapy alerts.

The second module of the DSS will provide detailed and automatic monitoring data on asthma and diabetes control, and it will alert the physician when needed. Patients will enter information on their condition directly on a Web-based self-management tool. The data will then be analyzed by the inference engine of the DSS, which will perform automatic disease control and provide both the patient and the physician with recommended actions. It is hoped that this integrated DSS will help in improving the quality of care and allowing the patients to better control their diseases, and will result in a higher quality of life for the patients.[1]

Introduction

People in business everywhere regularly make decisions as complex as those that McGill University faces as outlined in the opening Case Study. Information technology can help in the decision-making process, regardless of whether you're running a hospital or a small retailing business.

The big winners in tomorrow's business race will be those organizations, according to *Management Review*, that are "big of brain and small of mass."[2] For example, with only 35 people, the company Adtrack is able to track ten million records (in a data warehouse) of information pertaining to newspaper and magazine ads. These 35 people perform complex tasks to provide newspapers and ad agencies with information on their relative position against competitors.[3,4]

For many years, computers have been crunching numbers faster and more accurately than people can. A computer can unerringly calculate a payroll for 1000 people in the time it takes a pencil to fall from your desk to the floor. Because of IT, knowledge workers have been freed of much of the drudgery of manually handling day-to-day transactions. And now IT power is augmenting brainpower and thought processes in ways previously seen only in science fiction. In some cases, IT power is actually *replacing* human brainpower to a limited degree.

Businesses, like individuals, use brainpower to make decisions, some big, some small, some relatively simple, and some very complex. As an effective knowledge worker, you'll have to make decisions on issues such as whether to expand the workforce, extend business hours, use different raw materials, or start a new product line. IT can help you in most, if not all, of these decisions. The extended brainpower that IT offers you as a decision maker comes in the form of decision support systems and artificial intelligence.

Whether to use a decision support system (there are several variations) or some form of artificial intelligence depends on the type of decision you have to make and how you plan to go about making it. So let's first look at different types of decisions and the process you go through to make a decision. Then we'll discuss decision support systems and artificial intelligence—IT brainpower (see Figure 4.1).

Decisions, Decisions, Decisions

You make many decisions every day from the simplest to the very complex. For example, you may want to made a decision on what mozzarella cheese to buy on the basis of cost. Contrast that decision with the one where you try to decide which job offer to take. Choosing the right job is definitely more complex, because it has multiple decision criteria, not all of which are quantifiable. Therefore, it's much more difficult to select the "best" of the alternatives.

Decision making is one of the most significant and important activities in business. Organizations devote vast resources of time and money to the process. In this section,

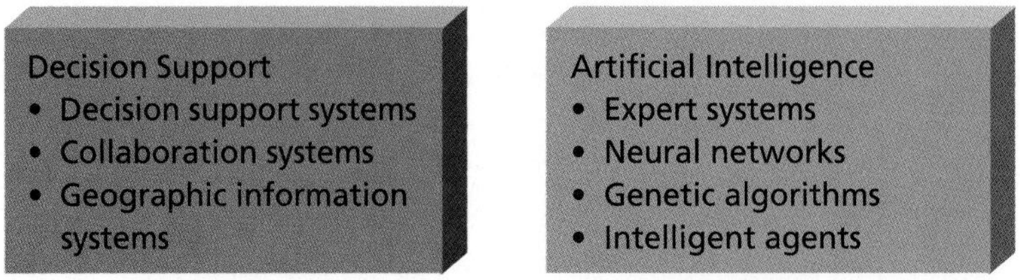

Figure 4.1
The Two Categories of Computer-Aided Decision Support

we'll consider the phases of decision making and different decision types to help you better understand how IT can benefit that process.

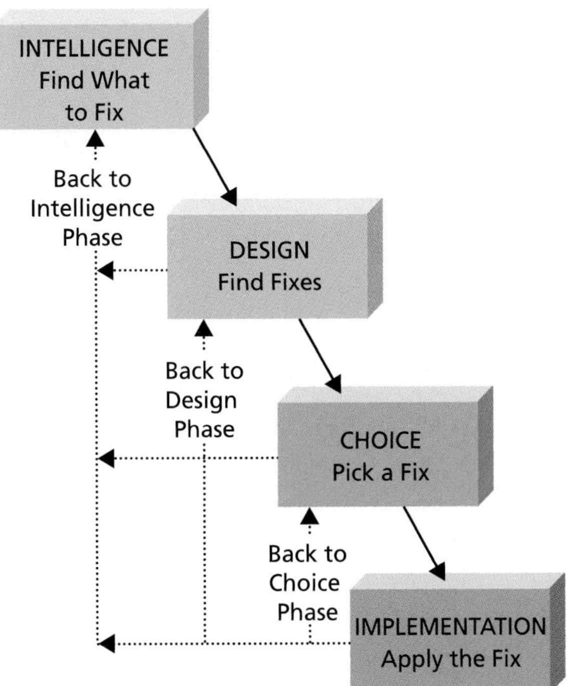

Figure 4.2
Four Phases of Decision Making

HOW YOU MAKE A DECISION

In business, decision making has four distinct phases (see Figure 4.2):[5]

- **Intelligence** *(find what to fix)*. Find or recognize a problem, need, or opportunity (also called the diagnostic phase of decision making). The intelligence phase involves detecting and interpreting signs that indicate a situation which needs your attention. These "signs" come in many forms: consistent customer requests for new-product features, the threat of new competition, declining sales, rising costs, an offer from a company to handle your distribution needs, and so on.
- **Design** *(find fixes)*. Consider possible ways of solving the problem, filling the need, or taking advantage of the opportunity. In this phase, you develop all the possible solutions you can.
- **Choice** *(pick a fix)*. Examine and weigh the merits of each solution, estimate the consequences of each, and choose the best one (which may be to do nothing at all). The "best" solution may depend on such factors as cost, ease of implementation, staffing requirements, and timing. This is the prescriptive phase of decision making—it's the stage at which a course of action is prescribed.
- **Implementation** *(apply the fix)*. Carry out the chosen solution, monitor the results, and make adjustments as necessary. Simply implementing a solution is seldom enough. Your chosen solution will always need fine-tuning, especially for complex problems or changing environments.

These four phases are not necessarily linear—you'll often find it useful or necessary to cycle back to an earlier phase. When choosing an alternative in the choice phase, for example, you might become aware of another possible solution. Then you would go back to the design phase, include the newly found solution, return to the choice phase, and compare the new solution to the others you generated.

TYPES OF DECISIONS YOU FACE

It's pretty clear that deciding which cheese to buy when you want the cheapest is a decision with a simple comparison that leads to a correct answer. Thus it is an example of a structured decision, whereas choosing the right job is an example of a decision with nonstructured and structured elements. That is, some parts are quantifiable and some are not.

A **structured decision** involves processing a certain kind of information in a specified way so that you will always get the right answer. No "feel" or intuition is necessary. These are the kinds of decisions that you can program—if you use a certain set of inputs and process them in a precise way, you'll arrive at the correct result. Calculating gross pay for hourly workers is an example. If hours worked is less than or equal to 40, then gross pay is equal to hours times rate of pay. If hours worked is greater than 40, then gross pay is equal to 40 times rate of pay plus time-and-a-half for every hour over 40. You can easily automate these types of structured decisions with IT.

A **nonstructured decision** is one for which there may be several "right" answers and there is no precise way to get a right answer. No rules or criteria exist that guarantee you a good solution. Deciding whether to introduce a new product line, employ a new marketing campaign, or change the corporate image are all examples of decisions with nonstructured elements.

Figure 4.3

Viewing Structured Versus Nonstructured Decision Making as a Continuum

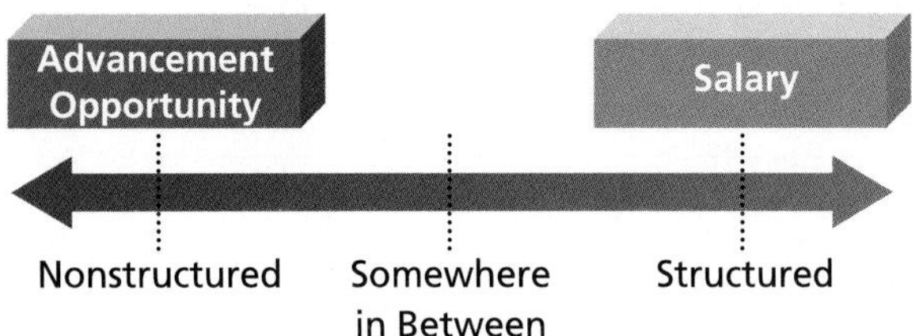

In reality, most decisions fall somewhere between structured and nonstructured. The job choice decision is an example (see Figure 4.3). In choosing the right job, the salary part of the decision is structured, whereas the other criteria involve nonstructured aspects (e.g., your perception of which job has the best advancement opportunity). Stock market investment analysis is another example of "somewhere in-between" because you can calculate financial ratios and use past performance indicators. However, you still have to consider nonstructured aspects of the companies, such as projected prime interest rate, unemployment rates, and competition.

Another way to view decisions is by the frequency with which the decision has to be made. The decision as to which job to take is the sort of decision you don't make on a regular basis—this is a nonrecurring, or ad hoc, decision. On the other hand, determining pay for hourly employees is a routine decision that businesses face periodically. Therefore determining gross pay for hourly employees is a recurring decision.

A **recurring decision** is one that happens repeatedly, and often periodically, whether weekly, monthly, quarterly, or yearly. You will usually use the same set of rules each time. When you calculate pay for hourly employees, the calculation is always the same regardless of the employee or time period. A **nonrecurring**, or **ad hoc**, **decision** is one that you make infrequently (perhaps only once) and you may even have different criteria for determining the best solution each time. A company merger is an example. These don't happen often—although they are becoming more frequent. And if the managers of a company need to make the merger decision more than once, they will most likely have to evaluate a different set of criteria each time. The criteria depend on the needs of the companies considering the merger, the comparability of their products and services, their debt structure, and so on.

Decision Support Systems

In Chapter 3, you saw how data mining can help you make business decisions by giving you the ability to slice and dice your way through massive amounts of information. Actually, a data warehouse with data mining tools is a form of decision support. The term "decision support system," used broadly, means any computerized system that helps you make decisions. However, there's also a more restrictive definition. It's rather like the term "medicine"—it can mean the whole health care industry or it can mean cough syrup, depending on the context.

Skills Module 1 Decision Analysis—Excel

Narrowly defined, a **decision support system (DSS)** is a highly flexible and interactive IT system designed to support decision making when the problem is not structured. A DSS is an alliance between you, the decision maker, and specialized support provided by IT (see Figure 4.4). IT brings speed, vast amounts of information, and sophisticated processing capabilities to help you create information useful in making

What You Bring	Advantages of a DSS	What IT Brings
Experience	Increased productivity	Speed
Intuition	Increased understanding	Information
Judgment	Increased speed	Processing capabilities
Knowledge	Increased flexibility	
	Reduced problem complexity	
	Reduced cost	

Figure 4.4
The Alliance Between You and a Decision Support System

a decision. You bring know-how in the form of your experience, intuition, judgment, and knowledge of the relevant factors. IT provides great power, but you—as the decision maker—must know what kinds of questions to ask of the information and how to process the information to get those questions answered. In fact, the primary objective of a DSS is to improve your effectiveness as a decision maker by providing you with assistance that will complement your insights. This union of your know-how and IT power makes you better able to respond to changes in the marketplace and to manage resources in the most effective and efficient ways possible. Following are some examples of the varied applications of DSSs:

- A national insurance company using a DSS to analyze its risk exposure when insuring drivers who had histories of driving under the influence. The DSS revealed that married male homeowners in their 40s with one DUI conviction were rarely repeat offenders. By lowering its rates to this group the company increased it market share without increasing its exposure.[6]
- The Canadian National Railway regularly tests the rails its trains ride on to prevent accidents. Worn-out or defective rails result in hundreds of derailments every year, so it's important to address the problem. Using a decision support system to schedule rail testing, CN decreased its rail-caused derailments, while other railroad companies had a 16 percent rise in such accidents.[7]
- Customer relationship management (CRM) is an important part of any successful company's strategy. Decision support is an important part of CRM. On Bay Street, retail brokerage companies analyze customers' behaviors and goals with decision support which highlights opportunities and alerts brokers to developing problems.[8]

COMPONENTS OF A DECISION SUPPORT SYSTEM

DSSs vary greatly in application and complexity, but they all share specific features. A typical DSS has three components (see Figure 4.5): data management, model management, and user interface management.

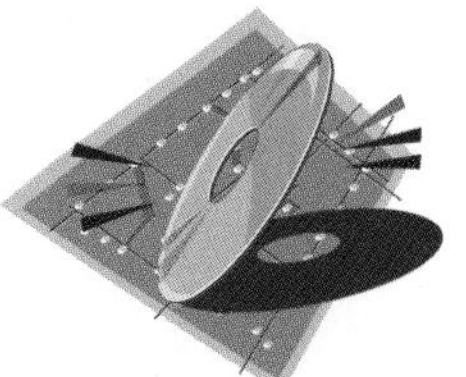

Skills Module 1 Decision Analysis—Excel

Before we look at these three components individually, let's get a quick overview of how they work together. When you begin your analysis, you tell the DSS, using the user interface management component, which model (in the model management component) to use on what information (in the data management component). The model requests the information from the data management component, analyzes that information, and sends the result to the user interface management component, which

Figure 4.5

Components of a Decision Support System

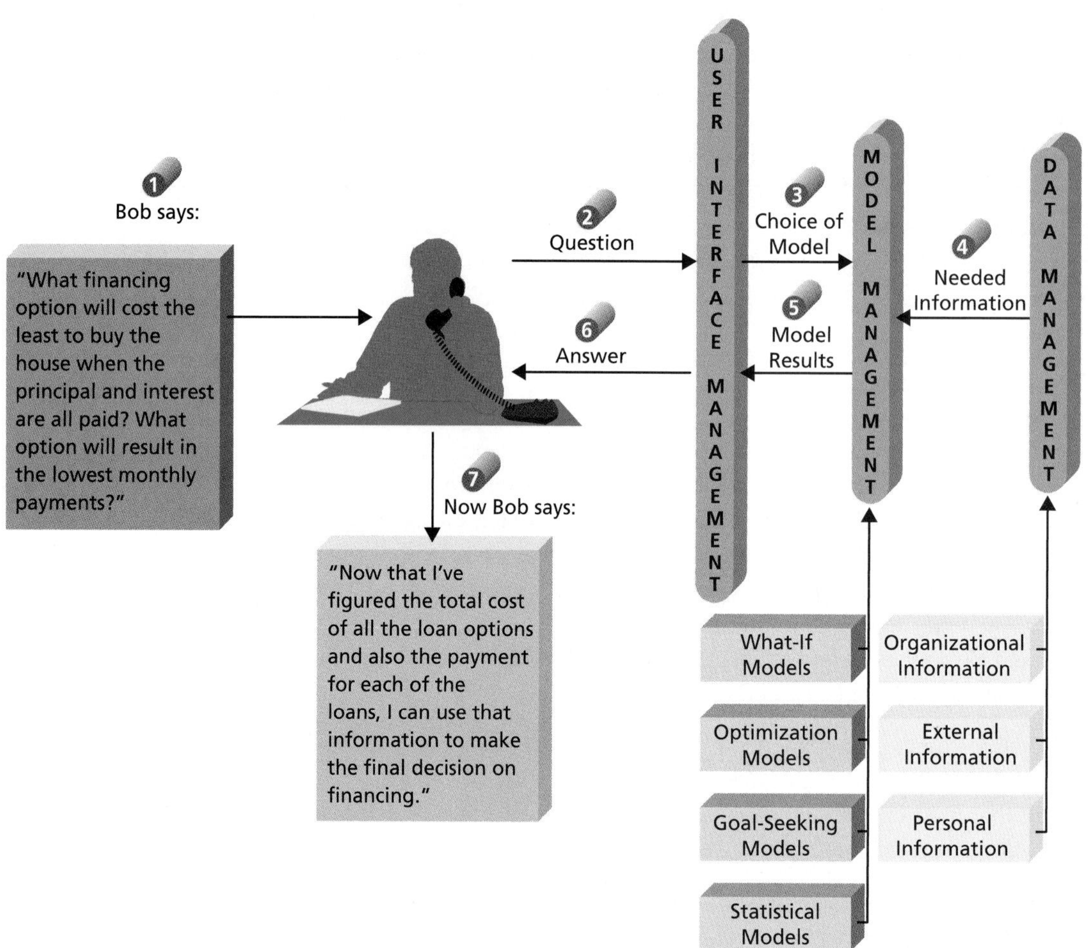

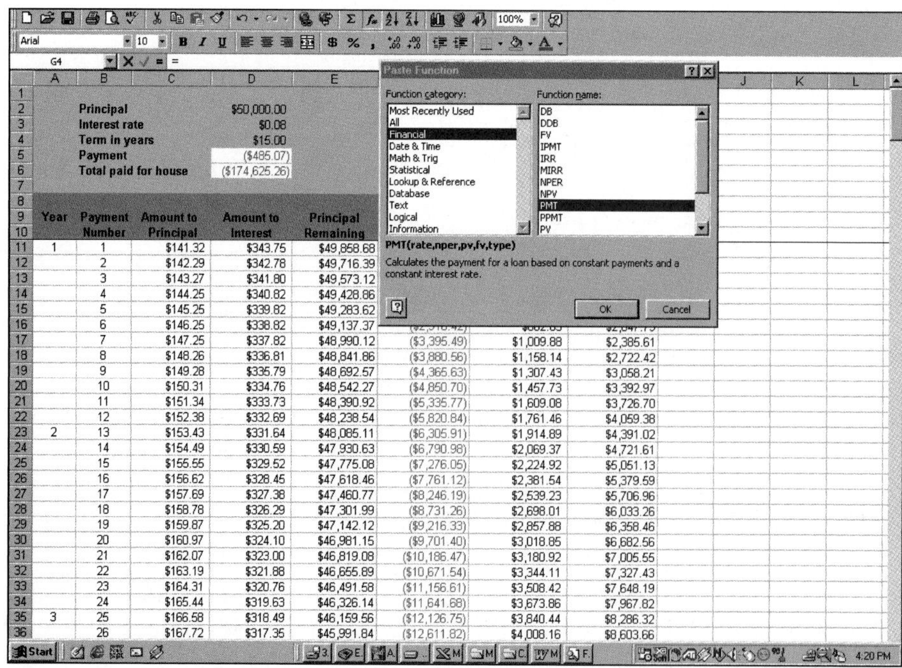

	A	B	C	D	E	F	G	H
2		Principal		$50,000.00				
3		Interest rate		$0.08				
4		Term in years		$15.00				
5		Payment		($485.07)				
6		Total paid for house		($174,625.26)				
9–10	Year	Payment Number	Amount to Principal	Amount to Interest	Principal Remaining			
11	1	1	$141.32	$343.75	$49,858.68			
12		2	$142.29	$342.78	$49,716.39			
13		3	$143.27	$341.80	$49,573.12			
14		4	$144.25	$340.82	$49,428.86			
15		5	$145.25	$339.82	$49,283.62			
16		6	$146.25	$338.82	$49,137.37			
17		7	$147.25	$337.82	$48,990.12	($3,395.49)	$1,009.88	$2,385.61
18		8	$148.26	$336.81	$48,841.86	($3,880.56)	$1,158.14	$2,722.42
19		9	$149.28	$335.79	$48,692.57	($4,365.63)	$1,307.43	$3,058.21
20		10	$150.31	$334.76	$48,542.27	($4,850.70)	$1,457.73	$3,392.97
21		11	$151.34	$333.73	$48,390.92	($5,335.77)	$1,609.08	$3,726.70
22		12	$152.38	$332.69	$48,238.54	($5,820.84)	$1,761.46	$4,059.38
23	2	13	$153.43	$331.64	$48,085.11	($6,305.91)	$1,914.89	$4,391.02
24		14	$154.49	$330.59	$47,930.63	($6,790.98)	$2,069.37	$4,721.61
25		15	$155.55	$329.52	$47,775.08	($7,276.05)	$2,224.92	$5,051.13
26		16	$156.62	$328.45	$47,618.46	($7,761.12)	$2,381.54	$5,379.59
27		17	$157.69	$327.38	$47,460.77	($8,246.19)	$2,539.23	$5,706.96
28		18	$158.78	$326.29	$47,301.99	($8,731.26)	$2,698.01	$6,033.26
29		19	$159.87	$325.20	$47,142.12	($9,216.33)	$2,857.88	$6,358.46
30		20	$160.97	$324.10	$46,981.15	($9,701.40)	$3,018.85	$6,682.56
31		21	$162.07	$323.00	$46,819.08	($10,186.47)	$3,180.92	$7,005.55
32		22	$163.19	$321.88	$46,655.89	($10,671.54)	$3,344.11	$7,327.43
33		23	$164.31	$320.76	$46,491.58	($11,156.61)	$3,508.42	$7,648.19
34		24	$165.44	$319.63	$46,326.14	($11,641.68)	$3,673.86	$7,967.82
35	3	25	$166.58	$318.49	$46,159.56	($12,126.75)	$3,840.44	$8,286.32
36		26	$167.72	$317.35	$45,991.84	($12,611.82)	$4,008.16	$8,603.66

in turn passes the results back to you (see Figure 4.5). Here's an example of a decision support system at the clothing business Lands' End:

- *Model management.* The DSS at Lands' End has to have models to analyze information. The models create new information that decision makers need to plan product lines and inventory levels. For example, Lands' End uses a statistical model called regression analysis to determine trends in customer buying patterns and forecasting models to predict sales levels.
- *Data management.* The DSS's data management component stores Lands' End's customer and product information. In addition to this organizational information, the company also needs external information, such as demographic and industry and style trend information.
- *User interface management.* A user interface enables Lands' End decision makers to access information and specify the models they want to use to create the information they need.

Now we'll examine the three DSS components in more general terms.

MODEL MANAGEMENT COMPONENT The **model management** component consists of both the DSS models and the DSS model management system. A model is a representation of some event, fact, or situation. Businesses use models to represent variables and their relationships. For example, you would use a statistical model called analysis of variance to determine whether newspaper, TV, and billboard advertising are equally effective in increasing sales. DSSs help in various decision-making situations by utilizing models that allow you to analyze information in many different ways. The models you use in a DSS depend on the decision you're making and, consequently, the kind of analysis you require. For example, you would use what-if analysis to see what effect the change of one or more variables will have on other variables, or optimization to find the most profitable solution given operating restrictions and limited resources. You can use spreadsheet software such as Excel to create a simple DSS for what-if analysis. Figure 4.5 has an example of a spreadsheet DSS you might build to compare how much you'd pay for a house at different interest rates and payback periods.

The model management system stores and maintains the DSS's models. Its function of managing models is similar to that of a database management system. The model management component can't select the best model for you to use for a particular problem—that requires your expertise—but it can help you create and manipulate models quickly and easily.

DATA MANAGEMENT COMPONENT The *data management* component performs the function of storing and maintaining the information that you want your DSS to use. The data management component, therefore, consists of both the DSS information and the DSS database management system. The information you use in your DSS comes from one or more of three sources:

- *Organizational information.* You may want to use virtually any information available in the organization for your DSS. You can design your DSS to access this information directly from your company's databases and data warehouses.
- *External information.* Some decisions require input from external sources of information. Various branches of the federal government, S&P/TSX, and the Internet, to mention just a few, can provide additional information for use with a DSS.
- *Personal information.* You can incorporate your own insights and experience—your personal information—into your DSS.

WHICH & WHY?

Are you having difficulty deciding where to advertise? Having trouble choosing a particular health care plan for your employees? Or simply where to go on vacation? Canadian software developer Arlington Software Corp. from Vancouver (www.arlingsoft.com) may not have the solution but certainly promises to help you find one.

The company has developed Which & Why, a decision support system priced at about $350 designed to accelerate and improve managers' decision making. Peter Strum, a senior partner with Deloitte & Touche in Ottawa, while helping a Canadian federal government department select a prime contractor, noted that "using Which & Why reduced the time to complete the project from four months to one month ... the product enabled 15 people with various goals to reach a clear, rational decision." According to Dave Lobley, manager of Arlington Software's Eastern region, the software's strength is that it "guides users through a series of steps, resulting in a carefully thought-out decision." Users are presented with a blank screen on the right called a "model tree" and a "note pad" on the left. All the factors that could possibly affect your decision are typed into the note pad. This includes, for example, such as "contractor's ability to finish project in 10 weeks" and "cost of project should not surpass $2 million dollars." The more important factors are retained and dragged into the model tree while those deemed as extraneous are discarded into the "trash." The DSS then asks the user to rate each of the factors in the tree according to importance. Once all the factors are rated, you simply click on the "build a model" button for a tally of the ratings and analysis of the alternatives under consideration.[9]

USER INTERFACE MANAGEMENT COMPONENT The *user interface management* component allows you to communicate with the DSS. It consists of the user interface and the user interface management system. This is the component that allows you to combine your know-how with the storage and processing capabilities of the computer. The **user interface** is the part of the system you see—through it you enter information, commands, and models. If you have a DSS with a poorly designed user interface—if it's too rigid or too cumbersome to use—you simply won't use it no matter what its capabilities. The best user interface uses your terminology and methods and is flexible, consistent, simple, and adaptable.

Collaboration Systems

Toronto Hydro has 650,000 customers, 1700 employees, and five corporate offices. As you can imagine, the company gets and sends a lot of e-mail messages. The volume was 100 megabytes per day in 1999 and had increased to more than a gigabyte a day by 2002.

E-mail is a simple form of a collaboration system. A **collaboration system** or **collaboration software** is software that allows people to work together (see Figure 4.6). E-mail is, of course, vital to survival, but for many companies it's no longer enough. In fact, almost 60 percent of companies surveyed by *InformationWeek* in February 2002 said that they intended to increase their collaboration initiatives in the near future. Collaboration software takes many forms with many combinations of features with varying degrees of complexity.

ENTERPRISE-WIDE COLLABORATION

Toronto Hydro, for example, found it needed employees also to have access to each other's calendars, group scheduling, imaging, automated workflow, task and docu-

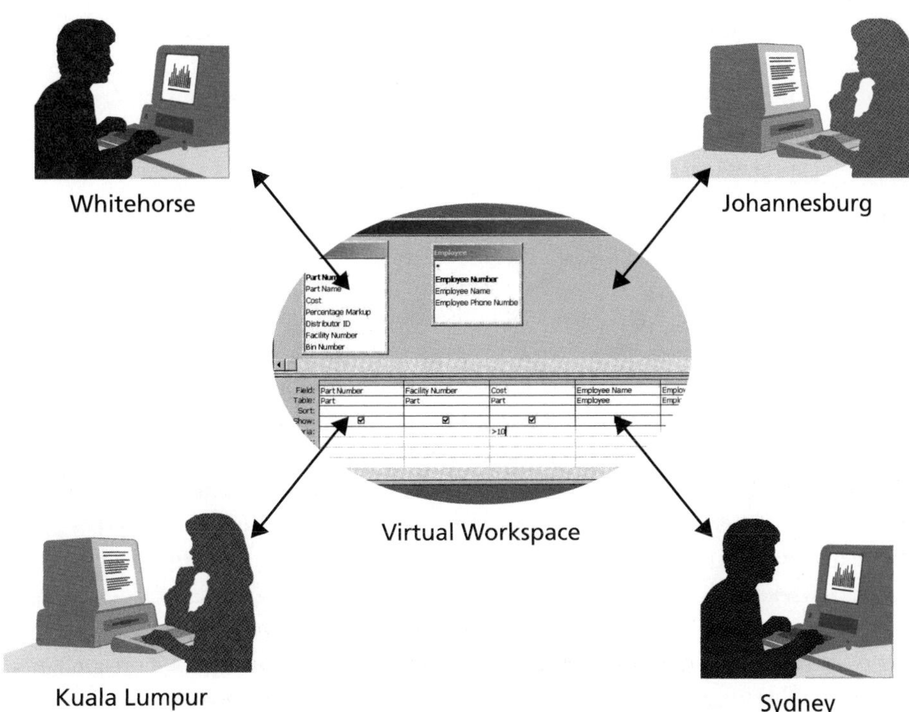

Figure 4.6

Collaboration Software Connects People

ment management, message management, as well as e-mail. For these tasks the company now uses Lotus Notes.[10] Microsoft has a comparable product called Exchange, which allows integration with Access, Excel, Word, and even Visual Basic.

Like the Toronto utility company, many companies first use e-mail and then move on to integrated collaboration systems like Lotus Notes or Exchange. After that, they may need to migrate to more sophisticated collaboration systems that incorporate tele-, video- and Web conferencing in real time, and may even include project management and workflow automation. For example, Ford gets parts for vehicles from places as far apart as France and Singapore, so coordinating ordering, shipping, and delivery with production is very complex, particularly in a just-in-time environment. Electronic collaboration and information sharing are important for any business. But the task becomes particularly critical the more geographically scattered employees, customers, and suppliers are.

SUPPLY CHAIN COLLABORATION

As you already saw in Chapter 2, a supply chain includes the paths reaching out to all of the suppliers of parts and services to a company. It consists not only of a company's suppliers, but of its suppliers' suppliers as well. Supply chain management means working with your suppliers and distributors in all phases of planning, production, and distribution. This involves the routine sharing of information to reduce inventories and improve cash flow.

You might want your suppliers to be able to add or change information. Boeing is a case in point. The company conducts the whole design process for its 777 jets online. All plans, schedules, orders, confirmations, and so on, are online and available to engineers, customers, maintenance staff, project managers, and suppliers all over the world. Changing from physical models and paper blueprints with fax, phone, and travel has cut the time for delivery of a plane from three years to less than 12 months. So Boeing reaps the twin benefits of happier customers and a tripling in its production rate.[11]

You might want to share information with clients too. So you could set up a collaboration system whereby your customers can access information, but can't change or delete it. Ogilvy & Mather, the company that handles advertising for IBM, Ford, and American Express, among others, does this. Ogilvy & Mather has a collaboration system that lets clients view images, text, and multimedia files.[12]

WEB-BASED COLLABORATION

One of the major application areas of collaboration systems is in e-commerce. As you'll see in Chapter 5, e-commerce is simply traditional business in a new form. It's conducted in cyberspace, but is still based on relationships, which means people working together. Web-based collaboration tools use the power of the Internet to enable people to work together effectively and efficiently.

Web-based collaboration software can be wide-open sharing of information on the Internet where anyone can access it, like Lands' End Live where anyone with Web access can interact with representatives of the company. Or it can be a special virtual workspace with access restricted to a select few. For example, CareGroup HealthCare System, a network in six hospitals, uses a collaboration system to permit doctors tending newborns, especially babies that are at risk. While the baby must stay in the hospital, a private Web page, accessible only to the neonatal centre at the hospital and the parents, is set up so that the parents can find out about the baby anytime. The hospital staff put information onto the Web site about feeding, weight, and medical care along with digital photos of the baby. When the new baby goes home, the parents can hold videoconferences with hospital staff so that they can keep a close watch on the baby's progress.[13,14]

Another example of a by-invitation-only virtual workspace is at Intel, the maker of the Pentium chip. More than half of Intel's direct material suppliers are in Asia, so the Internet is a great way for the company to speed up communication and information access. But Intel doesn't necessarily want everyone in the world to be able to snoop into company information. So Intel's suppliers can use passwords to access Intel's demand forecasts, engineering plans, orders, and invoices. Suppliers get demand, inventory, and receipt information automatically from the factory without human intervention. Intel plans to eventually make the company completely electronic.[15]

PEER-TO-PEER COLLABORATION Groove and NextPage are both examples of a special kind of information-sharing software called peer-to-peer collaboration software. It's based on the same principle as Napster, that is, the ability to communicate in real time and share documents between peers without going through a central server. The peer-to-peer file-sharing feature in the collaboration software is combined with the ability to collaboratively create and edit documents, and to send and receive text and voice messages.

Here's an example of how it might work. Let's say you're a representative working at FastTrucks, a company that ships perishable goods all over the country. One of your customers is PotatoSupply, a PEI-based company that grows and distributes potatoes. You're both using the Groove collaboration system. One day a truck filled to the brim with potatoes and other perishables is headed through Niagara Falls—but so is a major winter storm. To avert disaster in the form of rotting potatoes and a stranded truck, you could go online and bring up the virtual workspace that you share with your PotatoSupply counterpart. From there you could check on the potato company's current and past shipments and can access records on routing plans and other pertinent information. This is the file-sharing part of the operation. You could then contact your counterpart at PotatoSupply and negotiate a new route, saving the potatoes and the day.[16]

THE GLOBAL PERSPECTIVE

COLLABORATION TO FIND CURES

Projects that require collaboration between different departments in a company use collaboration software that goes beyond e-mail, instant messaging, and calendar management. Such software would include workflow management, project management, and other tools that improve the efficiently of work processes.

GlaxoSmithKline, a British pharmaceutical company, is a case in point. The company spends $4 billion a year on research, has 4000 researchers whose work is stored in more than a dozen databases in various formats. There are separate databases for chemical and biological information and another for the specimen inventory. In 2001, the company set up an Intranet collaboration system that searches all the company databases and even goes out onto the Web to find any and all research done on a given molecule. By reducing the cost of finding information, the company can spend more time and money developing new medicines.[17]

Geographic Information Systems

Suppose you've decided to go on a two-week vacation that will include camping, sightseeing, and mall touring in Edmonton (after all, Edmonton boasts the largest shopping mall in the world—the West Edmonton Mall). What maps should you buy? Some will show roads for travelling from one place to another; others will show campgrounds in the province; others will pinpoint historic landmarks; still others will detail hotels around the West Edmonton Mall and the locations of the hundreds of stores in the mall.

To get a truly comprehensive picture of your proposed vacation, you'd consolidate the information by redrawing all the maps into a single map. But what about a business that needs to analyze different maps with geographic, demographic, highway, and other information?

Fortunately there's a special type of DSS for just this kind of problem—it's called a geographic information system. A **geographic information system (GIS)** is a decision support system designed specifically to work with spatial information—any information that can be shown in map form, such as roads, the distribution of bald eagle populations, sewer systems, and the layout of electrical lines.

Today GISs are helping businesses perform such tasks as:

- Identifying the best site to locate a branch office based on number of households in a neighbourhood
- Targeting pockets of potential customers in a particular market area
- Repositioning promotions and advertising on the basis of sales
- Determining the optimal location of a new distribution outlet

When businesses combine textual information and spatial information, they are creating a new type of information called *business geography*. GISs are well suited to storing, retrieving, and analyzing business geography to support the decision-making process.

A GIS is actually a combination of sophisticated graphics and database technology. Using a GIS, you can logically link textual and spatial information. For example, you could gather geographic information about the distribution of customers who buy yachts (spatial information). You could also gather information about their colour preferences (textual information) and link it to the spatial information. Then, using queries similar to those illustrated in Chapter 3, you could analyze both the spatial and

Figure 4.7
Geographic Information Systems

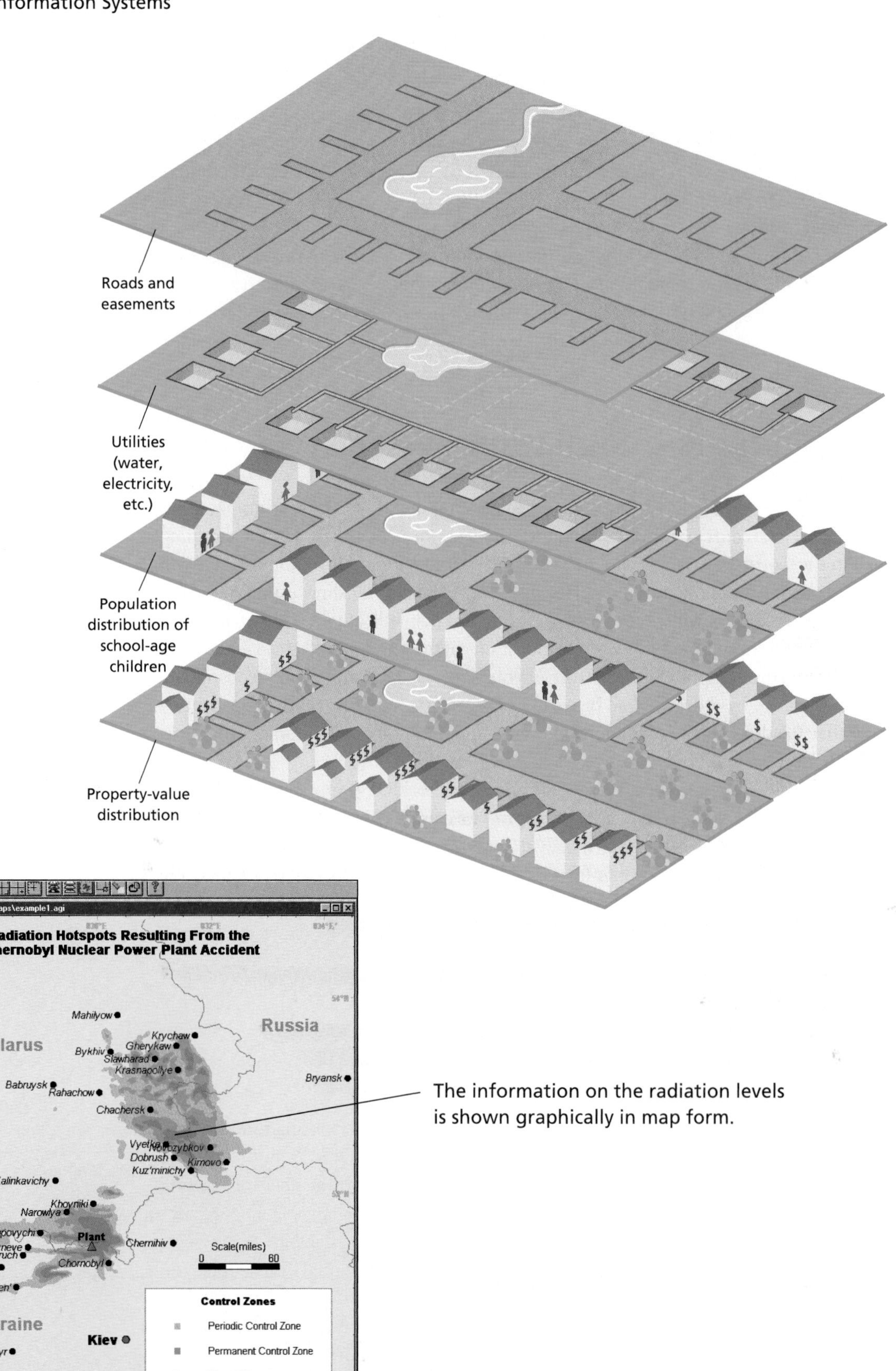

textual information, generating output in the form of maps, graphs, or numeric tables. Some GISs let you load thousands of rows of information from a spreadsheet.

A GIS database represents information thematically. That means that a GIS map is composed of many separate, overlapping information layers, each of which has its own theme. For example, the first layer might be roads, the next might be utilities (water, electricity, etc.), the third school-age children, and the fourth homes within a certain price range (see Figure 4.7). This feature of a GIS, to show map information and attribute information as layers, distinguishes a GIS from other decision support system. Studies show that how information is presented significantly impacts the effectiveness and efficiency of the decision-making process.[18]

Figure 4.8

ArcPad

Figure 4.8 shows a mobile GIS called ArcPad developed by ESRI Canada, a Canadian owned company specializing in GIS products and services. ArcPad operates on Windows CE palm-size computers. It downloads data via a TCP/IP connection such as a wireless LAN, cellular phone, or wireless modem. It has layering features allowing the user to toggle the display of street lights, roads, rail stops, etc.

Here is another example of GISs in use. Clean Harbor Inc. is the company that hauled away the potentially anthrax-tainted debris from the offices of NCB during the anthrax scare toward the end of 2001. Since hazardous waste removal is such a dangerous job, the company had to keep track for the shipment every minute. Clean Harbor used software that incorporated a GIS map and GPS information to watch the trucks along their journey.[19]

Artificial Intelligence

DSSs and GISs are IT systems that augment business brainpower. IT can further expand business brainpower by means of artificial intelligence—the techniques and software that enable computers to mimic human behaviour in various ways. Financial analysts use a variety of artificial intelligence systems to manage assets, invest in the stock market, and perform other financial operations.[20] Hospitals use artificial intelligence in many capacities, from scheduling staff, to assigning beds to patients, to diagnosing and treating illness. Many government agencies use artificial intelligence, including the Canada Customs and Revenue Agency (CCRA) and the armed forces. Credit card companies use artificial intelligence to detect credit card fraud, and insurance companies use artificial intelligence to ferret out fraudulent claims.[21] Artificial intelligence lends itself to tasks as diverse as airline ticket pricing, food preparation, oil exploration, and child protection. It is widely used in the insurance, meteorology, engineering, and aerospace industries and by the military.

Artificial intelligence (AI) is the science of making machines imitate human thinking and behaviour. For example, an *expert system* is an AI system that makes computers capable of reasoning through a problem to reach a conclusion. We use the process of reasoning to find out, from what we already know, something that we don't know.

INDUSTRY PERSPECTIVE

ROBOTS TO THE RESCUE

High-temperature gas samples are invaluable in volcanology, yet scientists are regularly killed attempting to obtain them. Developed by the Carnegie Mellon University Field Robotics Center, the Dante II tethered walking robot explored Mt. Spurr in Alaska, connected by satellite and Internet to the field team. The spider-like robot collected data samples and sent back live video from eight cameras to the scientists, safely away from the heated gases of the active volcano. Though Dante II, like its predecessor, Dante I, lost its footing on the volcano wall and fell to the floor of the crater, it continued to send back video footage. So, while the robot was irreparably damaged during the trek, the project was considered a success.

In the future, robots will have artificial intelligence software to enable them to find their way around rubble or difficult terrain independently without cords.

Search and rescue are not the only applications of robots. You've probably seen RoboMower, Sony's Aibo and Honda's competing Asimo, which are consumer robots. Here are some others.

- The Pentagon has a robot that delivers mail in an automated truck that follows a wire in the floor to move from office to office. As it enters each office, the robot calls the occupants to come and pick up mail.
- For many years the food service industry has used robots to prepare pizza, tacos, and other tasty morsels. Robots also pour drinks and transport food to conveyer belts ready for delivery to customers. Some in the food service industry are predicting that, in the not-too-distant future when better and more sophisticated software that includes wireless and video capabilities is incorporated into robots, a single employee will remotely service multiple robots.
- In London, there's a restaurant that has a robot waiter delivering drinks to customers. The software enables the robot to know the location of different tables.[22,23]

Today computers can see, hear, smell, and, what is important for business, think—in a manner of speaking. Robots are a well-known form of AI. A **robot** is a mechanical device equipped with simulated human senses and the capability of taking action on its own (in contrast to a mechanical device such as an automobile which requires direction from the driver for its every action). Robots are in use in many industries. For example, Piedmont Hospital's Pharmacy Dosage Dispenser is a robotic prescription-filling system. Using barcode technology, the Dispenser receives medication orders online, retrieves prepackaged doses of drugs, and sends them to hospital patients.[24] One of the most exciting new areas of research in robotics is the development of microrobots that can be introduced into human veins and arteries to perform surgery.

Seventy percent of the top 500 companies use artificial intelligence as part of decision support, and the sale of artificial intelligence software is rapidly approaching the $1 billion mark. The artificial intelligence systems that businesses use most can be classified into the following major categories:

- *Expert systems*, which reason through problems and offer advice in the form of a conclusion or recommendation
- *Neural networks*, which can be "trained" to recognize patterns
- *Genetic algorithms*, which can generate increasingly better solutions to problems by generating many, many solutions, choosing the best ones, and using those to generate even better solutions

- *Intelligent agents*, which are adaptive systems that work independently, carrying out specific, repetitive, or predictable tasks

Expert Systems

Suppose you own a real estate business, and you generate over 40 percent of your revenue from appraising commercial real estate. Consider further that only one person in your firm is capable of performing these appraisals. What if that person were to quit? How do you replace that expertise? How fast can you find someone else? How much business would you lose if it took you a month to find a suitable replacement?

In business, people are valuable because they perform important business tasks. Many of these business tasks require expertise, and people often carry expertise in their heads—and often that's the only place it can be found in the organization. AI can provide you with an expert system that can capture expertise, thus making it available to those who are not experts so that they can use it, either to solve a problem or to learn how to solve a problem.

An **expert system**, also called a **knowledge-based system**, is an artificial intelligence system that applies reasoning capabilities to reach a conclusion. Expert systems are excellent for diagnostic and prescriptive problems. Diagnostic problems are those requiring an answer to the question "What's wrong?" and correspond to the intelligence phase of decision making. Prescriptive problems are those that require an answer to the question "What to do?" and correspond to the choice phase of decision making.

An expert system is usually built for a specific application area called a *domain*. You can find expert systems in the following domains:

- *Accounting.* For auditing, tax planning, management consulting, and training
- *Medicine.* To prescribe antibiotics where many considerations must be taken into account (such as the patient's medical history, the source of the infection, and the price of available drugs)
- *Process control.* For example, to control offset lithographic printing
- *Human resources management.* To help personnel managers determine whether they are in compliance with an array of federal employment laws
- *Financial management.* To identify delinquency-prone accounts in the loan departments of banks
- *Production.* To guide the manufacture of all sorts of products, such as aircraft parts
- *Forestry management.* To help with harvesting timber on forest lands

A DSS sometimes incorporates expert systems, but an expert system is fundamentally different from a DSS. To use a DSS, you must have considerable knowledge or expertise about the situation with which you're dealing. As you saw earlier in this chapter, a DSS *assists* you in making decisions. That means that you must know how to reason through the problem. You must know which questions to ask, how to get the answers, and how to proceed to the next step. However, when you use an expert system, the know-how is in the system—you need only provide the expert system with the facts and symptoms of the problem for which you need an answer. The know-how that actually solves the problem came from someone else—an expert in the field. What

PLEASE SEND ALL APPLICATIONS TO THE EXPERT SYSTEM

Companies that hire a lot of hourly workers sometimes use an expert system or some other form of artificial intelligence to sort through the list of candidates and help managers identify the employees who are the best qualified and will stay the longest. Blockbuster, Target, and Universal Studios use a system called Unicru which was developed by psychologists (domain experts) to identify the best applicants.

Applicants sit at a computer and spend a half an hour answering questions, after which a report is sent to the hiring manager with a recommendation of no, maybe, or yes. "Yes" usually results in an interview, "maybe" is accompanied by suggestions on what follow-up questions to ask, and "no" usually results in the application being sent to the recycle bin.

The system has helped Blockbuster cut the time it takes to hire someone from two weeks to 72 hours. The system has also resulted in a reduction in the turnover rate for its users by up to 30 percent, which is very important since the turnover rate in this kind of job can be up to 150 percent per year.

Here's a sample of the type of questions the system asks:

- *True or false?* I was meant to work at Target.
- *True or false?* Slow people irritate me.
- *True or false?* A lot of people do annoying things.
- *True or false?* I like a job that's quiet and predictable.
- *True or false?* I can smile and chat with anyone.
- *True or false?* I am good at taking charge.
- *True or false?* I'd rather do things my way than follow the rules.

When a vice-president of Macy's West was testing the Unicru system, it told him he wasn't qualified to be a clerk in his own store. He was outraged until a Unicru executive explained that with his drive, ambition, and salary requirements, he'd be frustrated and bored to death and would soon quit. The VP had forgotten the difference between being able to do a job and being a good match for the position.[25]

does it mean to have expertise? When someone has expertise in a given subject, that person not only knows a lot of facts about the topic, but also can apply that knowledge to analyze and make judgments about related topics. It's this human expertise that an expert system captures.

Let's look at a very simple expert system that would tell a driver what to do when approaching a traffic light. Dealing with traffic lights is the type of problem to which an expert system is well suited. It is a recurring problem, and to solve it you follow a well-defined set of steps. You've probably gone through the following mental question-and-answer session millions of times without even realizing it (see Figure 4.9).

When you approach a green traffic light, you go on through. If the light is red, you try to stop. If you're unable to stop, and if traffic is approaching from either side, you'll probably be in trouble. Similarly, if the light is yellow, you may be able to make it through the intersection before the light turns red. If not, you will again be faced with the problem of approaching traffic.

Let's say that you know very little about what to do when you come to a traffic light, but you know that there are experts in the field. You want to capture their expertise in an expert system so that you can refer to it whenever the traffic-light situation arises. To gain an understanding of what's involved in the creation and use of an expert system, let's now consider the components of an expert system individually with the traffic-light example in mind.

COMPONENTS OF AN EXPERT SYSTEM

An expert system, like any IT system, combines information, people, and IT components:

Information Types	People	IT Components
Domain expertise	Domain expert	Knowledge base
"Why?" information	Knowledge engineer	Knowledge acquisition
Problem facts	Knowledge worker	Inference engine
		User interface
		Explanation module

These components and their relationships are shown in Figure 4.9, which includes the screen shown at right.

INFORMATION TYPES The traffic-light domain expertise is the core of the expert system, because it's the set of problem-solving steps—the reasoning process that will solve the problem. You'll also want to ask the expert system how it reached its conclusion, or why it asked you a question. The *"Why?" information* included in the expert system allows it to give you the answers. It's information provided by the expert—the traffic expert in our example. With the domain expertise and the "Why?" information, the expert system is now ready to solve traffic-light problems. So now you need to enter the *problem-facts*, the specifics of your traffic-light situation. Problem facts are the symptoms of and assertions about your problem. You'll enter these problem facts as answers to the expert system's questions during your consultation.

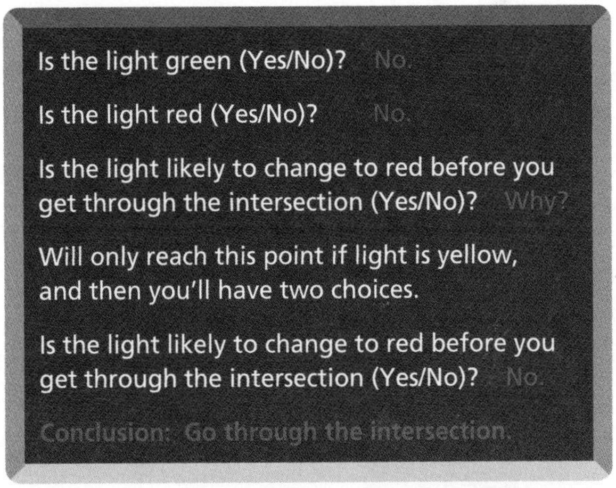

Figure 4.9

Traffic-Light Expert System Rules

Rule	Symptom or Fact	Yes	No	Explanation
1	Is the light green?	Go through the intersection.	Go to Rule 2.	Should be safe if light is green. If not, need more information.
2	Is the light red?	Go to Rule 4.	Go to Rule 3.	Should stop, may not be able to.
3	Is the light likely to change to red before you get through the intersection?	Go to Rule 4.	Go through the intersection.	Will only reach this point if light is yellow, then you'll have two choices.
4	Can you stop before entering the intersection?	Stop.	Go to Rule 5.	Should stop, but there may be a problem if you can't.
5	Is traffic approaching from either side?	Prepare to crash.	Go through the intersection.	Unless the intersection is clear of traffic, you're likely to crash.

PEOPLE Three separate roles must be filled in the development and use of an expert system. The first is that of the domain expert, who knows how to solve the problem. The **domain expert** provides the **domain expertise** in the form of problem-solving strategies. In our traffic-light expert system, the domain expert could be an official from the department of motor vehicles. This official, turned domain expert, would also be able to indicate where to gather further domain expertise, and might direct you to the local police station or give you a booklet with the rules of the road. Eventually, the combination of these sources will produce the five steps that you saw in Figure 4.9.

The domain expert usually works with an IT specialist, a **knowledge engineer**, who formulates the domain expertise into an expert system. In this case, the knowledge engineer might consider it best to represent the five steps in the form of rules, making a **rule-based expert system.** The knowledge engineer will see to it that the rules are in the correct order and that the system works properly.

The knowledge worker or user—that's you—will then apply the expert system to the problem of what to do when approaching a traffic light. When you face the traffic-light problem, you would run a *consultation* (see Figure 4.9) and provide the expert system with the problem facts. You would answer the questions as they appear on the screen, with the expert system applying the appropriate rules and asking you more questions. This process continues until the expert system presents you with a conclusion (telling you what to do) or indicates that it can't reach a conclusion (telling you that it doesn't know what you should do).

Figure 4.10

Developing and Using an Expert System

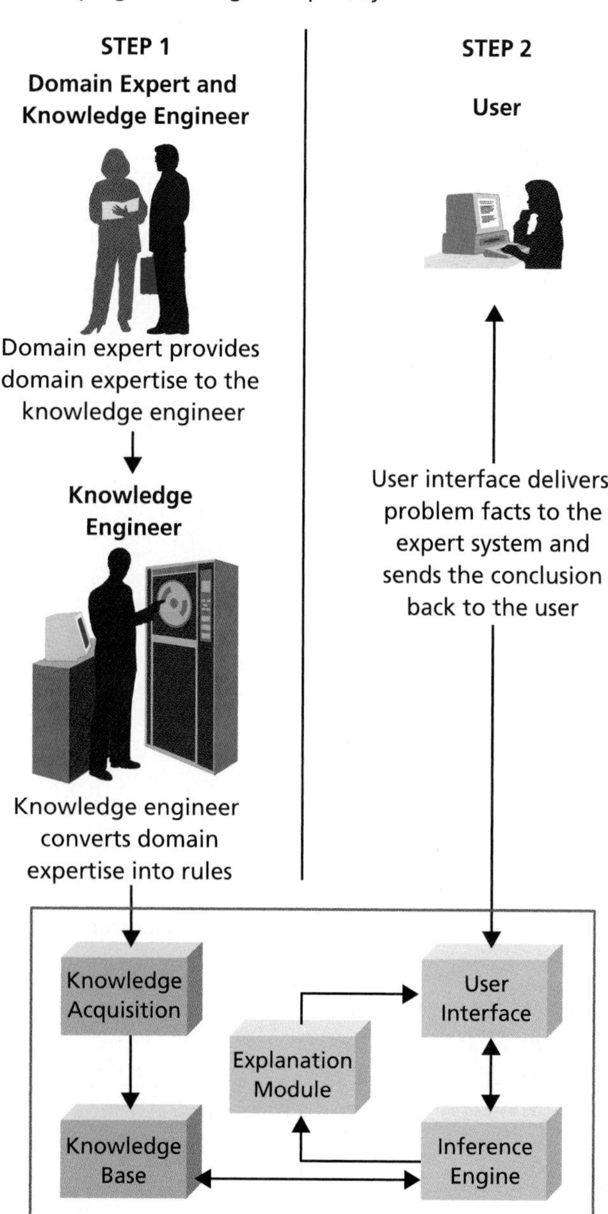

IT COMPONENTS When the knowledge engineer has converted the domain expertise into rules, the **knowledge base** stores the rules of the expert system (see Figure 4.10). All the rules must be in place before a consultation, because the expert system won't be able to offer a conclusion in a situation for which it has no rules. For example, if the traffic light is broken and has been replaced by a four-way stop sign, the expert system, as it stands, would not be able to reach a conclusion. The knowledge engineer could, of course, go back to the domain expert and enter rules about four-way stops. The knowledge engineer uses the **knowledge acquisition** component of the expert system to enter the traffic-light rules. The domain expertise for the rules can come from many sources, including human experts, books, organizational databases, data warehouses, internal reports, diagrams, and so on.

The **inference engine** is the part of the expert system that takes your problem facts and searches the knowledge base for rules that fit. This process is called *inferencing*. The inference engine organizes and controls the rules—it "reasons" through your problem to reach a conclusion. It delivers its conclusion or recommendation on the basis of (1) the problem facts of your specific traffic light situation and (2) the rules that came from the

TEAM WORK

TRAFFIC LIGHTS REVISITED

Create a table similar to the one in Figure 4.9 to extend the traffic-light expert system. Include the following situations in the table:

1. There is a wreck in the middle of the intersection.
2. You are turning left at the intersection.
3. You are turning right at the intersection.
4. A pedestrian is crossing in front of you.
5. A dog has wandered into the intersection.
6. A ball belonging to children playing near the intersection has rolled into the street.
7. The car in front of you has stalled.

domain expert about traffic-light procedures in general. The **user interface** is the part of the expert system that you use to run a consultation. Through the user interface, the expert system asks you questions, and you enter problem facts by answering the questions. In the traffic-light expert system, you would enter "yes" or "no." These answers are used by the inference engine to solve the problem.

The domain expert supplies the "Why?" information, which is entered by the knowledge engineer into the **explanation module**, where it is stored. During a consultation, you—as the knowledge worker or user—can ask why a question was posed and how the expert system reached its conclusion. If you're using the expert system as a training tool, then you'll be very interested in how it solved the problem.

In Figure 4.10 you can clearly see the distinction between the development and use of an expert system. The domain expert and the knowledge engineer develop the expert system, then the knowledge worker can apply the expert system to a particular set of circumstances.

WHAT EXPERT SYSTEMS CAN AND CAN'T DO

An expert system uses IT to capture and apply human expertise. For problems with clear rules and procedures, expert systems work very well and can provide your company with great advantages. An expert system can:

- Handle massive amounts of information
- Reduce errors
- Aggregate information from various sources
- Improve customer service
- Provide consistency in decision making
- Provide new information
- Decrease personnel time spent on tasks
- Reduce cost

You can, however, run into trouble in building and using an expert system:

1. Transferring domain expertise to the expert system is sometimes difficult, because domain experts cannot always explain how they know what they know. Often, experts are not aware of their complete reasoning processes. Experience has given them a feel for the problem, and they "just know."
2. Even if the domain expert can explain the whole reasoning process, automating that process may be impossible. The process may be too complex, requiring an excessive number of rules, or it may be too vague or imprecise. In using an

expert system, keep in mind that it can solve only the problems for which it was designed. It cannot deal with inconsistency or a newly encountered problem situation. An expert system can't learn from previous experience and can't apply previously acquired expertise to new problems the way humans can.

3. An expert system has no common sense or judgment. One of the early expert systems built into an F-16 fighter plane allowed the pilot to retract the landing gear while the plane was still on the ground and to jettison bombs while the plane was flying upside down, both highly dangerous actions.

Neural Networks

Suppose you see a breed of dog you've never encountered before. Would you know it's a dog? For that matter, would you know it's an animal? Probably so—for all of the above. You would know, because you've learned by example. You've seen lots of living things, have learned to classify them, and so can recognize a dog when you see one. A neural network simulates this human ability to classify things without taking prescribed steps leading to the solution. A **neural network** (often called an **artificial neural network** or **ANN**) is an artificial intelligence system that is capable of finding and differentiating patterns. Your brain has learned to consider many factors in combination to recognize and differentiate objects. And this is also the case with a neural network. A neural network can learn by example and can adapt to new concepts and knowledge. Neural networks are widely used for visual pattern and speech recognition systems. If you've used a PDA that deciphered your handwriting, it was probably a neural network that analyzed the characters you wrote.[26]

Neural networks are useful to a variety of other situations too. For example, bomb detection systems in airports use neural networks that sense trace elements in the air indicating the presence of explosives. Some police departments use neural networks to identify corruption within their ranks.[27] In medicine, neural networks check 50 million electrocardiograms per year, check for drug interactions, and detect anomalies in tissue samples that may signify the onset of cancer and other diseases. Neural networks can detect heart attacks and even differentiate between the subtly different symptoms of heart attacks in men and women.[28,29,30] In business, neural networks are very popular for securities trading, fraud detection, real estate appraisal, evaluating loan applications, and target marketing, to mention a few. Neural networks are even used to control machinery, adjust temperature settings, and identify malfunctioning machinery.

Neural networks are most useful for identification, classification, and prediction when a vast amount of information is available. By examining hundreds, or even thousands of examples, a neural network detects important relationships and patterns in the information. For example, if you provide a neural network with the details of numerous credit card transactions and tell it which ones are fraudulent, eventually it will learn to identify suspicious transaction patterns.

Here are some examples of the uses of neural networks:

- Many banks and financial institutions use neural networks. For example, Citibank uses neural networks to find opportunities in financial markets.[31] By carefully examining historical stock market data with neural network software, Citibank financial managers learn of interesting coincidences or small anomalies (called market inefficiencies). For example, it could be that whenever IBM stock goes up, so does Unisys stock. Or it might be that the Canadian dollar is selling for 1 cent less in Japan than it is in Canada. These snippets of information can make a big difference to Citibank's bottom line in a very competitive financial market.

CAUTION! THE NEURAL NETWORK IS WATCHING YOU

Neural networks are used in all sorts of situations where a pattern of conditions or behaviour signals an event, either past or future. For example, there's a neural network that predicts what play a football team is likely to run under a particular set of circumstances.

Mostly, when financial institutions use neural networks for fraud detection, they're looking for certain signals, things that are outside the usual usage pattern of the customer. Sometimes, it's the characteristics of the use of the financial instrument itself that trip the alarm.

For example, many credit card companies send their customers convenience cheques. They encourage card holders to transfer balances from other accounts, and allow you to pay for purchases when the merchant won't accept that credit card. However, convenience cheques are ripe for theft. First, they're easier to steal or counterfeit than credit cards. Second, they're often available in trash cans (tear or shred your convenience cheques if you don't want to use them!). Third, they're easy to order under a false name. Fourth, it's easy for thieves to open a chequing account with a convenience cheque. Fifth, people heading into bankruptcy sometimes use convenience cheques to cover their financial problems.

Neural networks use certain flags to spot possible convenience cheque fraud. For example, if the cheque is written for an unusually large sum, or if multiple cheques are written out of sequence, there might be a problem. If a card holder hasn't used convenience cheques before, or if a particular cheque doesn't fit the card holder's spending patterns, there might be a problem. Another red flag is a higher-than-normal use of automated inquiries to cheque balances followed by several convenience cheques being submitted for payment.[32,33]

- Police use neural network software to fight crime. With crime reports as input, the system detects and maps local crime patterns. Police say that with this system they can better predict crime trends, improve patrol assignments, and develop better crime prevention programs.[34]
- A mail order company has six million people on its customer list. To determine which customers were and were not likely to order from its catalogue, it recently switched to neural network software. The company finds that the new software is more effective and expects to generate millions of dollars by fine-tuning its mailing lists.[35]
- Fraud detection is one of the areas in which neural networks are used the most. Visa, MasterCard, and many other credit card companies use a neural network to spot peculiarities in individual accounts. MasterCard estimates neural networks save them $50 million annually.[36]
- Many insurance companies along with compensation funds and other carriers use neural network software to identify fraud. The system searches for patterns in billing charges, laboratory tests, and frequency of office visits. A claim for which the diagnosis was a sprained ankle and which included an electrocardiogram would be flagged for the account manager.[37]
- FleetBoston Financial Corp. uses a neural network to watch transactions with customers. The neural network can detect patterns that may indicate a customer's growing dissatisfaction with the company. The neural network looks for signs like a decrease in the number of transactions or in the account balance of one of Fleet's high-value customers.[38]

All of the above situations have pattern recognition in common. They all require identification and/or classification, which may then be used to predict a finding or

TEAM WORK

HOW WOULD YOU CLASSIFY PEOPLE?

Some people have suggested that neural networks could be applied to people to indicate how likely they are to develop disease or even become criminals. The idea is to input a child's personal characteristics, demographics, and genealogy into a neural network and it will classify that youngster as being at risk for a disease or aberrant behaviour.

Choose either susceptibility to disease or to criminal behaviour, discuss it with your group, and make the following lists, explaining why you chose each:

1. What personal characteristics would be useful?
2. What demographics factors would strongly influence a person's future?
3. What inherited characteristics can predict a child's future?

Would such classification on a large scale be legal? Would it be ethical? Would it be effective? Why or why not?

outcome. Neural networks are often called predictive systems since they can see patterns in huge volumes of information.

TYPES OF NEURAL NETWORKS

There are two basic types of neural networks; the one you use depends on the problem you're facing. The difference between them is in how the "learning" is done.

The **self-organizing neural network** finds patterns and relationships in vast amounts of data by itself. If you have a lot of experimental data, and you're looking for commonalties, you'd use this type. Self-organizing neural networks often form part of data mining tools for data warehouses (see Chapter 3 for more information on data warehouses and data mining).

A **back-propagation neural network**, on the other hand, is a neural network trained by someone. You'd "teach" the neural network the same way you would a child. That is, you'd show the neural network multiple examples of a dog, a cat, a donkey, etc. until it could correctly identify the animal by itself.

INSIDE A NEURAL NETWORK

Neural networks are so called because they attempt to mimic the structure and functioning of the human brain. Conceptually, neural networks consist of three layers of virtual nerve cells, or neurons. There's an input layer and an output layer and between them are one or more hidden layers. The input and output layers are connected to the middle layer(s) by connections of various strengths called *weights* (see Figure 4.11). If you were to train a neural network to recognize a "good" stock portfolio, you would input many, many examples of good and bad portfolios, telling the neural network which was which. As the neural network is learning to differentiate between good and bad, the weights change. The flow of information to the output layer also changes. After you have fed the system enough examples, the neural network will be able to recognize and classify portfolios and the weights will stabilize so that future portfolios will consistently be correctly classified.

So, you may be asking, how is a neural network different from an expert system, since both can take input and produce an answer as to which group the input belongs to? An expert system, as we saw, can also classify—it asks questions and, on the basis

Figure 4.11
The Layers of a Neural Network

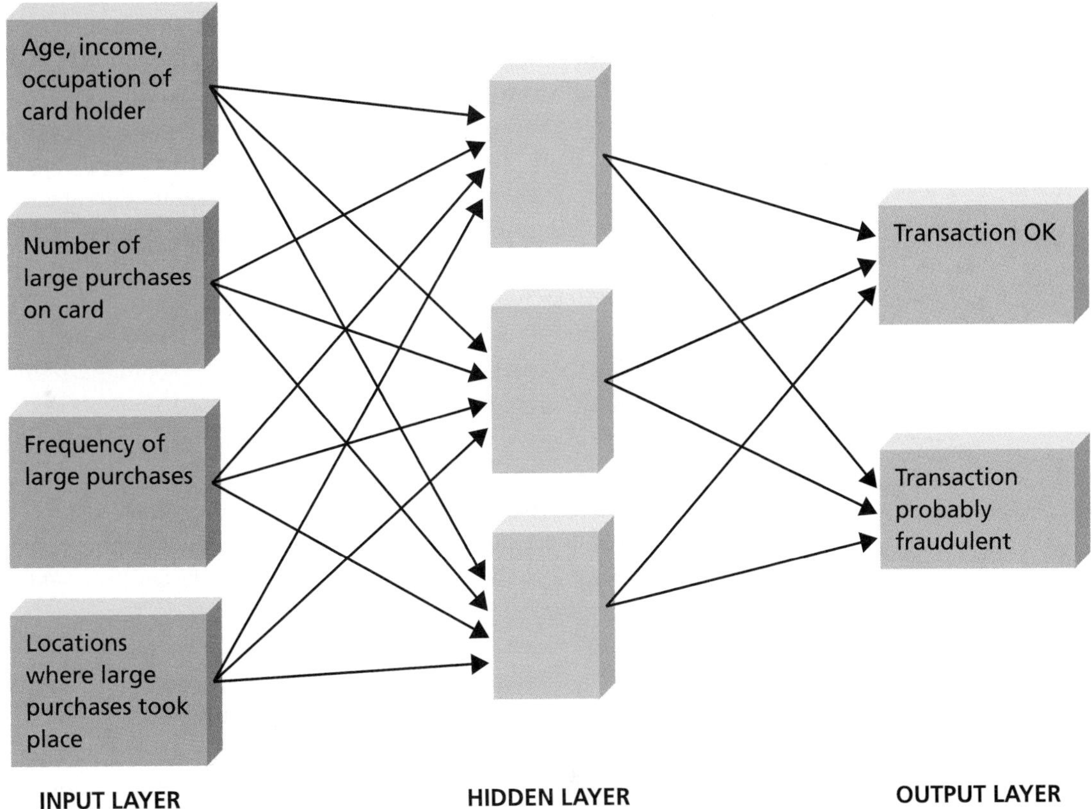

of the answers, can diagnose or prescribe. The difference is that an expert system does not adjust by itself and is too rigid in its application of the rules. For example, if a credit card fraud detection expert system had a rule that said to flag a purchase over a certain amount on certain types of account, the expert system would flag a transaction that was even one penny over. A neural network, on the other hand, would learn the spending behaviour of card holders and would be better able to evaluate whether deviations were large enough to be queried or not. A neural network can even adjust to situations not explicitly used in training. For example, if when the neural network was learning, mortgage rates were between 6 percent and 10 percent, the system could interpolate if the rate dropped to 5 percent.

Neural networks have many advantages:

- They can learn and adjust to new circumstances on their own.
- They lend themselves to massive parallel processing.
- They can function without complete or well-structured information.
- They can cope with huge volumes of information with many dependent variables.
- They can analyze nonlinear relationships in information and have been called fancy regression analysis systems.

The biggest problem with neural networks to date has been the fact that the hidden layers are "hidden." That is, you can't see how the neural network is learning and how the neurons are interacting. Newer neural networks no longer hide the middle layers. With these systems you can manually adjust the weights or connections, giving you more flexibility and control.

Genetic Algorithms

Have you ever wondered how chefs around the world create great recipes? For example, how did the Chinese discover that cashew nuts and chicken taste good when combined? How did Mexican chefs arrive at combining tomatoes, onions, cilantro, and other spices to create pica de gallo? All those great recipes came about through *evolutionary processes*. Someone decided to put together a few ingredients and taste the result. Undoubtedly, many of those combinations resulted in unpalatable concoctions that were quickly discarded. Others were tasty enough to warrant further experimentation of combinations.

Today significant research in AI is devoted to creating software capable of following similar trial-and-error process leading to the evolution of a good result. A **genetic algorithm** is an artificial intelligence system that mimics the evolutionary, survival-of-the-fittest process to generate increasingly better solutions to a problem. In other words, a genetic algorithm is an optimizing system—it finds the combination of inputs that give the best outputs.

Here's an example. Suppose you were trying to decide what to put into your stock portfolio. You have countless stocks to choose from and a limited amount of money to invest. You might decide that you'd like to start with 20 stocks and you want a portfolio growth rate of 7.5 percent.

Probably you'd start by examining historical information on the stocks. You would take some number of stocks and combine them, 20 at a time, to see what happens with each grouping. If you wanted to choose from a pool of 30 stocks, you would have to examine 30,045,015 different combinations. For a 40-stock pool, the number of combinations rises to 137,846,500,000. It would be an impossibly time-consuming, not to mention numbingly tedious, task to look at this many combinations and evaluate your overall return for each one. However, this is just the sort of repetitive number crunching task at which computers excel.

So instead of a pencil, paper, and calculator, you might use a genetic algorithm. You could input the appropriate information on the stocks, like the number of years the company has been in business, the performance of the stock over the last five years, price to earnings ratios, and other information.

You would also have to tell the genetic algorithm your exact "success" criteria. For example, you might use a growth rate in the company over the last year of at least 10 percent, a presence in the marketplace going back at least three years, a connection to the computer industry, etc. The genetic algorithm would simply combine and recombine stocks eliminating any combinations that don't fit your criteria and continuing to the next iteration with the acceptable combinations—those that give an aggregate growth rate of at least 7.5 percent while aiming for as high a growth rate as possible.

Genetic algorithms use three concepts of evolution:

- **Selection** or survival of the fittest. The key to selection is to give preference to better outcomes.
- **Crossover** or combining portions of good outcomes in the hope of creating an even better outcome.
- **Mutation** or randomly trying combinations and evaluating the success (or failure) of the outcome.

Genetic algorithms are best suited to decision-making environments in which thousands, or perhaps millions, of solutions are possible. Genetic algorithms can find

THE EVOLUTION OF FARMING EQUIPMENT

There are an almost infinite number of possible combinations possible for features on a car. This is true for many products, as Deere, a company that makes agricultural equipment, knows all too well. Deere's customers demand all sorts of variations in planters. These different combinations of features make creating a good manufacturing schedule by hand all but impossible. But Deere found that genetic algorithm software not only makes the task manageable, but can compute the best schedule that offers the easiest and fastest way to utilize the production line to optimize production.

The initial stages of the huge project were very expensive, but the software gave the company a way to meet customer demand quickly and to gain competitive advantage. It worked so well for Deere that the company's supplier, Auburn Consolidated Industries, is also using it and Deere is reaping the benefits of improved supply chain management.

As always, technology alone is not the answer. To benefit significantly from technology, the production and business processes have to be efficient and effective.[39]

and evaluate solutions intelligently and can get through many more possibilities more thoroughly and faster than a human can. As you might imagine, businesses face decision-making environments for all sorts of problems like engineering design, computer graphics, strategies for game playing—anything, in fact, that requires optimization techniques. Here are some other examples:

- Genetic algorithms are used by business executives to help them decide which combination of projects a firm should invest in, taking complicated tax considerations into account.
- They're used by investment companies to help in trading choices and decisions.
- In any garment that you buy, the fabric alone accounts for between 35 percent and 40 percent of the selling price. So, when cutting out the fabric to make the garment, it's important that there be as little waste as possible. Genetic algorithms are used to solve this problem of laying out the pieces of the garment and cutting fabric in a way that leaves as little waste as possible.[40]
- US West uses a genetic algorithm to determine the optimal configuration of fibre optic cable in a network that may include as many as 100,000 connection points. By using selection, crossover, and mutation, the genetic algorithm can generate and evaluate millions of cable configurations and select the one that uses the least amount of cable. At US West, this process used to take an experienced design engineer almost two months. US West's genetic algorithm can solve the problem in two days and saves the company $1 million to $10 million each time it's used.[41]

Genetic algorithms are good for these types of problems because they use selection, crossover, and mutation as methods of exploring countless solutions and the respective worth of each.

You have to tell the genetic algorithm what constitutes a "good" solution. That could be low cost, high return, etc., since many solutions are useless or absurd. If you created a genetic algorithm to make bread, for example, it might try to boil flour to create moistness. That obviously won't work, so the genetic algorithm would simply throw away that solution and try something else. Other solutions would eventually be good, and some of them would even be wonderful.

ON YOUR OWN

BE A GENETIC ALGORITHM AND PUT NAILS IN BOXES

This project involves packaging nails so that you make the most profit possible (this is a profit-maximizing problem). Say you have five types of nails and can make as many as you need of each. These are: 4", 3.5", 3", 2.5", 2", and 1.5". The cost of making each type of nail depends on how big it is. Those cost and selling prices are listed in the table below along with the weights. The nails will be sold in boxes of up to 30 nails. There must be no more than 10, but no less than 5, of each of three types of nails in each box. The nails in each box should weigh no more than 20 ounces. You're looking for the combination with the highest profit using trial and error.

A spreadsheet would be helpful in completing this project. You'll most likely find that you identify some promising paths to follow right away and will concentrate on those to reach the best one.

Nail	Weight	Cost	Selling Price
4"	1 oz	4 cents	8 cents
3.5"	0.85 oz	3.5 cents	6 cents
3"	0.7 oz	3 cents	5 cents
2.5"	0.5 oz	2.5 cents	4 cents
2"	0.25 oz	2 cents	3 cents
1.5"	0.1 oz	1.5 cents	2 cents

Intelligent Agents

Do you have a favourite restaurant? Is there someone there who knows you and remembers that you like Italian dressing, but not croutons, on your salad, and ice cream and a slice of cheddar cheese on your apple pie? Does this person familiar with your tastes put a glass of diet cola on your favourite table when you come in the door? If so, he or she has the qualities that artificial intelligence scientists are working on incorporating into intelligent agents. An **intelligent agent** is software that assists you, or acts on your behalf, in performing repetitive computer-related tasks. Future intelligent agents will most likely be autonomous, acting independently, and will learn and adapt to changing circumstances.

You may not realize it, but you're probably already familiar with a primitive type of intelligent agent—the shifty-eyed paper clip that pops itself up when you're using Word. For example, if your document looks as if it is going to be a business letter—that is, you type in a date, name, and address—the animated paper clip will offer helpful suggestions on how to proceed. Another example of a primitive intelligent agent is the software on Amazon.ca's Web site that suggests books to you on the basis of your previous purchases and those of people who bought the books you did.

You can find hundreds of intelligent agents, or *bots*, for a wide variety of tasks. The BotSpot and SmartBots Web sites at www.botspot.com and www.smartbots.com are good places to look for the different types of agents available.

Essentially there are four types of intelligent agents:

- Buyer agents or shopping bots
- User or personal agents
- Monitoring-and-surveillance agents
- Data mining agents

BUYER AGENTS

Buyer agents travel around a network (very likely the Internet) finding information and bringing it back to you. Buyer agents are also called shopping bots. These agents search the Internet for goods and services that you need and bring you back the information.

A **buyer agent** or **shopping bot** is an intelligent agent on a Web site that helps you, the customer, find products and services you want. Shopping bots work very efficiently for commodity products such as CDs, books, electronic components, and other one-size-fits-all products.

Shopping bots make money by selling advertising space, special promotions in cooperation with merchants, or click-through fees, which are payments to the site that provided the link to the merchant site. Some shopping bots give preference to certain sites for a financial consideration. The people who run shopping bot sites have two competing objectives. They want to present as many listings as possible to the consumer in the most useful way, but they also want to make money doing it.

MySimon (www.mysimon.com) is the most successful shopping bot to date, with more than a million visitors a month according to Nielsen/NetRatings. MySimon searches for millions of products on thousands of Web sites.[42] (See Figure 4.12.)

You may have encountered a shopping bot without having specifically requested its services. For example, Amazon.com will offer you a list of books that you might like to buy on the basis of what you're buying now and what you have bought in the past. The Amazon site uses a shopping bot to provide this service. As you saw in Chapter 2, Amazon's agent uses **collaborative filtering**, which consists of matching each customer with a group of users who have similar tastes and presenting choices common in that group.

Figure 4.12

MySimon Shopping Bot Site

You can tell the shopping bot what you're looking for and it will find lots of sources for you.

Collaborative filtering is only one of many techniques that predict your preferences. Here are three more currently being used or considered for use at online shopping sites:

- **Profile filtering** requires that you choose terms or enter keywords. This provides a more personal picture of you and your preferences.
- **Psychographic filtering** anticipates your preferences on the basis of the answers you give to a questionnaire. This method is also more personal than collaborative filtering.
- **Adaptive filtering** asks you to rate products or situations and also monitors your actions over time to find out what you like and dislike.[43]

Collaborative filtering, although it can be quite effective, has two big disadvantages. First, since this method bases your future choices on past purchases of the group to which it deems you to belong, it usually won't offer new or obscure products that might be just what you want. Second, the Web site needs vast amounts of information to be able to use collaborative filtering in the first place. This puts the method out of reach for smaller businesses.

Given these drawbacks, shopping bot designers are experimenting with incorporating the other three methods into shopping agents. Profile filtering, psychographic filtering, and adaptive filtering tend to discover more personal traits of individuals, and therefore if applied well can better anticipate what you'd like to buy.

USER AGENTS

User agents (sometimes called **personal agents**) are intelligent agents that take action on your behalf. In this category belong those intelligent agents that already perform, or will shortly perform, the following tasks:

- Check your e-mail, sort it according to priority (your priority), and alert you when good stuff comes through—like college acceptance letters.
- Play computer games as your opponent or patrol game areas for you.
- Assemble customized news reports for you. There are several versions of these. A CNN Custom News bot will gather news from CNN on the topics you want to read about—and only those.
- Find information for you on the subject of your choice.
- Fill out forms on the Web automatically for you. They even store your information for future reference.
- Scan Web pages looking for and highlighting the text that constitutes the "important" part of the information there.
- "Discuss" topics with you from your deepest fears to sports.

One expanding application of intelligent agent technology is in automating business functions. For example, Mission Hockey, a company that manufacturers and distributes in-line and ice hockey skates and other gear, uses software from Sweden called Movex that has a user agent component. Movex will search a company intranet or extranet to negotiate and make deals with suppliers and distributors. In this case, the intelligent agent is incorporated into an enterprise resource planning system. Enterprise resource planning (or ERP) is a very important concept in today's business world. The term refers to a method of getting and keeping an overview of every part of the business (a bird's-eye view, so to speak), so that production, development, selling, and servicing of goods and services will all be coordinated to con-

ON YOUR OWN

GO BARGAIN HUNTING ONLINE

Try out shopping bots for yourself. Choose three items to search for: one music item, one item of clothing, and one household item. Search for them with each of the following sites.

- Yahoo! Canada Shopping at ca.shopping.yahoo.com
- Copernic at www.copernic.com
- BuyBuddy at buybuddy.sympatico.ca

Answer these questions:

- How many hits did you get at each site for each item?
- Are tax, postage, and handling charges included in the quoted price?
- Can you sort in order of price?
- Does Yahoo Canada Shopping specialize in any kind of item?

tribute to the company's goals and objectives. You'll learn more about the concept of ERP in Chapter 7.

In the future, user agents for personal use will be available for both your wired and your wireless computer devices. Sprint has recently announced an e-assistant that will carry out verbal requests.[44] In the future we'll see personal agents that:

- Interact with the personal agents of colleagues to set up a meeting time
- Incorporate shopping bots and can take you preferences for features on a new car (or anything else) along with a price range and then haggle with car dealers (or their personal agents) to find you the best deal

MONITORING-AND-SURVEILLANCE AGENTS

Monitoring-and-surveillance agents (also called **predictive agents**) are intelligent agents that observe and report on equipment. For example, NASA's Jet Propulsion Laboratory has an agent that monitors inventory, planning, and scheduling equipment ordering to keep costs down.[45] Other monitoring agents work on the manufacturing shop floor, finding equipment problems and locating other machinery that will do the same job.

Monitoring-and-surveillance agents are often used to monitor complex computer networks. Allstate Insurance has a network with 2000 computers. The company uses a network monitoring agent from Computer Associates International called Neugent that watches its huge networks 24 hours a day. Every five seconds, the agent measures 1200 data points and can predict a system crash 45 minutes before it happens. Neugent combines intelligent agent technology with neural network technology to look for patterns of activity or problems. The neural network part can learn what conditions predict a downturn in network efficiency or a slowing of network traffic. Neugent also watches for electronic attacks and can detect them early so that they can be stopped.

Another type of monitoring-and-surveillance agent works on computer networks keeping track of the configuration of each computer connected to the network. It tracks and updates the central configuration database when anything on any computer changes, such as the number or type of disk drives. An important task in managing networks lies in prioritizing traffic and shaping bandwidth. That means sending enough network capacity or bandwidth to the most important tasks over those that are secondary. At a university, for example, processing end-of-semester grades might take precedence over Net surfing.

THE GLOBAL PERSPECTIVE

DATA MINING IN THE BODY SHOP

Have you ever taken a catalogue out of your mailbox and thrown it straight into trash—perhaps even before you brought it into your home? If you're like most people, you probably have. The Body Shop International, like most businesses, knows that. This U.K.-based company would much prefer to send their catalogues only to those who will place orders for products, and so it is using predictive analysis, which is one type of data mining. Data mining involves using technology to find trends and patterns in a vast quantity of information. Predictive analysis consists of forecasting and propensity analysis. Forecasting finds trends and then predicts the future on the basis of those trends. Propensity analysis uses statistical methods such as regression analysis and clustering in combination with neural networks to figure the likelihood that a particular consumer will respond to an offer or buy a product or service. Propensity analysis is also used to predict what customers are most likely to default on a loan or payment plan.

Using data mining, the Body Shop was able to cut in half the number of catalogues it sent out in 2001 after identifying a new 120,000 customers from its Web, store, and customer database. And, not only that, but revenue per catalogue increased 20 percent.

A few years ago, if you wanted to conduct a complex predictive analysis with lots of variables, you'd have to have access to a supercomputer. Today, your desktop computer can do the job.[46]

Some further types of monitoring-and-surveillance agents include:

- Agents that watch your competition and bring back price changes and special offer information
- Agents that monitor Internet sites, discussion groups, mailing lists, and so on, for stock manipulation, insider training, and rumours that might affect stock prices
- Agents that monitor sites for updated information on the topic of your choice
- Agents that watch particular products and bring back price or term changes
- Agents that monitor auction sites for products or prices that you want

DATA MINING AGENTS

A **data mining agent** operates in a data warehouse discovering information. A data warehouse brings together information from lots of different sources. Data mining is the process of looking through the data warehouse to find information that you can use to take action, such as ways to increase sales or keep customers who are considering defecting. Data mining is so called because you have to sift through a lot of information for the gold nuggets that will affect the bottom line. This sort of nugget spotting is similar to what CSIS and the CIA do when they bring together little bits of information from diverse sources and use the overall pattern to spot trouble brewing.

As you learned in Chapter 3, database queries answer questions like "How much did we spend on transportation in March of this year?" Multidimensional analysis is the next step in complexity and answers questions like "How much did we spend on transportation in the southeast during March of the last five years?" Data mining goes deeper and finds answers to questions you may not even have thought to ask like "What else do young men buy on Friday afternoons when they come in to buy diapers?" (The answer, culled by data mining tools, is "beer.")[47]

One of the most common types of data mining is classification, which finds patterns in information and categorizes items into those classes. You may remember that this is just what neural networks do best. So, not surprisingly, neural networks are part of many data mining tools. And data mining agents are another integral part, since data mining agents search for information in a data warehouse.

A data mining agent may detect a major shift in a trend or a key indicator. It can also detect the presence of new information and alert you. Volkswagen uses an intelligent agent system that acts as an early-warning system about market conditions. If conditions become such that the assumptions underlying the company's strategy are no longer true, the intelligent agent alerts managers.[48] For example, the intelligent agent might see a problem in some part of the country that is or will shortly cause payments to slow down. Having that information early lets managers formulate a plan to protect themselves.

COMPONENTS OF AN INTELLIGENT AGENT

To be truly "intelligent" agents, systems must have three qualities: autonomy, adaptivity, and sociability.[49]

- **Autonomy** means that they act without your telling them every step to take. Many of the intelligent agents in use today have this quality. They check networks, index Web pages, retrieve football scores from any information source, tell you when a competitor has an offer you should be aware of, and so on.
- **Adaptivity** is discovering, learning, and taking action independently. This means that the intelligent agent learns about your preferences and makes judgments by itself. If you were to fly to Winnipeg to visit your mother the last weekend of every month, the intelligent agent would discover that it needed to start looking for cheap fares to Winnipeg at least three weeks ahead of time. It would then do this without your intervention.
- **Sociability** is conferring with other agents. For example, a buyer agent, or shopping bot, might go out looking for a product or service. At various branches of a retail store there might be a store agent that knows the merchandise and prices in its own store. The store agents would communicate with each other and the buyer agent to produce results for you. These agents communicate with each other using the Knowledge Query and Manipulation Language (KQML), which has become the de facto standard for interagent communications.

At the moment no intelligent agent software has these qualities. Various agents are autonomous, and some are adaptive with a reasonable amount of success. Sociability is a very hot research area at the moment and more a goal than a reality. Some artificial intelligence scientists believe that lots of one-purpose agents working together are the way to create a very sophisticated artificial intelligence system.

Summary: Student Learning Outcomes Revisited

1. **Define decision support system, list its components, and understand its applications.** A **decision support system (DSS)** is a highly flexible and interactive IT system designed to support decision making when the problem is not structured. It's primarily an analysis tool to support your decision making and you making the final decision. A DSS has three components: data management, model management, and user interface management.
2. **Describe collaboration systems along with their features and uses. Collaboration software** is software that allows people to work together. A basic form of collaboration software is e-mail;

other forms are instant messaging, calendar management, group scheduling, conferencing of various kinds, and workflow, task, and document management. You would use collaboration software whenever members of a team are separated, whether on different floors of a building or on opposite sides of the globe.

3. **Describe geographic information systems and how they differ from other decision support tools.** A **geographic information system (GIS)** is for the analysis of data viewed in map form. Information is stored in layers which can be overlaid as appropriate. It's the layering and presentation that separates a GIS from other decision support tools.
4. **Define artificial intelligence and list the different types used in business.** Artificial intelligence is the science of making machines imitate human thinking and behaviour. The types used in business include: expert systems, neural networks, genetic algorithms, and intelligent agents.
5. **Describe expert systems, their components, and the types of problems to which they are applicable.** An **expert system** (or **knowledge-based system**) is an artificial intelligence system that applies reasoning capabilities to reach a conclusion. An expert system ask the user questions and, on the basis of those questions, asks other questions until it has enough information to make a decision or a recommendation. Expert systems are good for diagnostic (what's wrong) and prescriptive (what to do) problems. For example, you could use an expert system to diagnose illness or to figure out why a machine is malfunctioning. And you could use one to determine what to do about the problem.
6. **Define neural networks, their uses, and their strengths and weaknesses.** A **neural network** (also called an **artificial neural network** or **ANN**) is an artificial intelligence system capable of finding and differentiating patterns. Neural networks are good for finding commonalties in situations that have many variables. The greatest strength of a neural network is that it can learn and adapt. Its greatest weakness is that it's not usually clear how the system reached its result and it's hard, therefore, to verify its solutions.
7. **Define genetic algorithms, the concepts on which they are based, and the types of problems they solve.** A **genetic algorithm** is an artificial intelligence system that mimics the evolutionary, survival-of-the-fittest process to generate increasingly better solutions to a problem. Genetic algorithms borrow the principles of selection, crossover, and mutation from the theory of evolution. These systems are best suited to problems where hundreds or thousands of solutions are possible and you need an optimum solution.
8. **Define intelligent agents, list the four types, and identify the types of problems they solve.** An **intelligent agent** is software that assists you, or acts on your behalf, in performing repetitive computer-related tasks. The four types are:
   - **Buyer agents** (or **shopping bots**) search the Web for products and services.
   - **User agents** (or **personal agents**) take action for you, particularly in repetitive tasks like sorting e-mail.
   - **Monitoring-and-surveillance agents** (or **predictive agents**) track conditions, perhaps on a network, and signal changes or troublesome conditions.
   - **Data mining agents** search data warehouses to discover information.

CLOSING CASE STUDY ONE

USING NEURAL NETWORKS TO CATEGORIZE PEOPLE

Would your banker give you an A, a B, or a C? What about your supermarket? You know you're being graded in your classes, but did you know that you're also being graded by businesses?

Special treatment for certain customers is not new. Airline customers who fly first class have always received preferential treatment, even when flights were cancelled or delayed. You won't find them napping on a stone floor with their backpacks as pillows. This makes business sense to the airlines, since these are the customers who are most profitable.

Although companies have always offered preferential treatment to their more profitable customers, the speed and capacity of computers today is making the segmenting of customers possible to a degree unheard of just a few years ago. Part of the reason for this is neural networks. Using neural network software, businesses now have the ability to look for patterns in their customer information and classify customers into according to how they affect the company's bottom line and thus to gauge whether it's worth the trouble to make them happy.

BANKS

Some banks use software that categorizes people into red, green, and yellow depending on the customer's history and value to the bank. Customers who are "green" might get better credit card rates than customers who are "red" and are judged to add less to the bank's bottom line.

Say you called the bank that issued you your credit card and said that you didn't want to pay the annual fee anymore. The bank could look at your credit card activity and decide whether it's more profitable to the bank to waive your fee rather than risk your not using the credit card anymore.

CREDIT CARD COMPANIES

Visa has saved millions of dollars using neural network software to spot fraud and to determine which of their customers might default or go bankrupt. Neural networks are good at spotting patterns, and if your profile looks like that of people who have defaulted, you'll be tossed into that category.

ROYAL BANK OF CANADA

On a monthly basis, Toronto-based Royal Bank of Canada segments its ten million customers according to credit risk, current and future profitability, demographics (i.e., whether they are young or seniors approaching retirement), channel preference (i.e., call centres, branches, or the Internet), and propensity to purchase other products. The bank's customer segmentation practice has worked so well that it has helped increase the company's response rate to marketing campaigns and sales programs to as high as 30 percent while the banking industry's average remains close to 3 percent.

SUPPLIERS

Neural network classifying software can be applied to finding the best suppliers too. Weyerhaeuser Corporation's door-factory executives have software to rank suppliers and distributors based on price, speed of delivery, and innovation. Using this information Weyerhaeuser doubled its sales and increased its return on net assets from 2 to 24 percent.

MOVIES

Even the movie business is getting in on the act. Twentieth Century Fox slices and dices its information in its databases to determine the most popular movies, actors, and plots in certain theatres, cities, and areas of the country. The aim is to show movies in those areas that will add the most to the bottom line. The result may be that people in certain areas will not get the chance to see certain movies.

There was a time when certain neighbourhoods or geographic regions were "redlined." That meant that banks and other businesses wouldn't deal with anyone who lived there. Some people think that this sort of market segmentation is a new form of redlining. Do you? The following are some questions for you to answer regarding this practice.[50]

Questions

1. A neural network learns to recognize patterns on the basis of past information. One set of people is judged by the behaviour of another. Is this fair or reliable? How accurate is it for a business to predict the future behaviour of customers on the basis of historic information? Don't people change? Have you ever changed your behaviour in the course of your life?

2. Customers are not likely ever to see the information that companies are using to pigeonhole them. Even the company executives may not know what criteria the neural network uses. How important are the assumptions underlying the software (i.e., the facts that the neural network are given about customers)? Even the IT specialists who design neural networks can't vouch for their accuracy or specify exactly how the neural network reaches its conclusions. Is this safe for businesses? What are the possible business consequences of using neural networks without assurances of their reliability?

3. Businesses can use segmenting to suggest products and services to you, or if you request it, to prevent your getting junk mail you don't want. Is that good? Would receiving wanted information or avoiding junk mail be worth the price of being categorized?

4. Say you run a business that supplies medical equipment—wheelchairs, hospital beds, heating packs (not prescription drugs). You're trying to determine which customers you should give preferential treatment to. What assumptions or variables would you use (e.g., age, income, and so on) to segment your customer population?

5. Do you think that this segmentation practice is fair? First consider the business stockholders, then consider the customers. Does it matter whether it's fair or not? Why or why not? Should there be laws against it, or laws controlling it, or none at all? Explain and justify your answer.

6. Does the practice make business sense? If you owned stock in a company, how would you feel about this practice? Do you think you should get better treatment if you're a better customer? Do you think people who are not such good customers should get the same deal that you get? Would it make any difference whether the company collected the information and did the neural network analysis itself, or bought the information or the whole package from a third party?

7. Is this the same as redlining, or is it OK because it looks at behaviour and classifies people rather than assuming characteristics on the basis of membership in a particular group?

CLOSING CASE STUDY TWO

DECISION SUPPORT AND ARTIFICIAL INTELLIGENCE IN HEALTH CARE

Good health care is based largely on good information. Information technology helps with diagnosing illness and treating it. It also aids research in identifying and finding cures for illness. Here are two examples of the use of information technology in health care.

WIRELESS HOME CARE IN NEWFOUNDLAND

In 2001, a pilot project was launched in St. John's, Newfoundland. A revolutionary home care delivery system was developed by AdActus Care Technologies Inc., a Canadian company located in Nova Scotia. The system consists of equipping nurses from the city's Health and Community Services with handheld computers for home visits giving them the ability to capture timely, high-quality data in the course of providing care in the patent's home. Overall, it aims to eliminate the time, effort, and risk of error in documenting visits after the fact.

Highly portable Palm Pilots enable nurses to connect to a packet digital wireless network to receive their daily download which includes appointments for the day, the details of the care to be provided for each patient, patient demographics and current medication, whether the patient has allergies and his/her treatment history. Downloads include "a complete set of protocols for each step of the care prescribed to that patient," explains Keith Sheppard of Collaborative Network Technologies, a St. John's company which helped develop the system. "When they get their download, it comes with a complete set of protocols for each step of the care prescribed for that patient. ... When a bandage has to be checked, for example, it then steps the nurse through examining and describing the wound. Ticked off with the Palm Pilot at each step, the nurse also notes any vital signs or other patient readings taken," adds Sheppard. The handheld also tallies all the syringes, rubber gloves, and other supplies used during daily visits. When each visit ends, nurses need simply reconnect to the network and quickly upload any information about the visit back to the central database without having to physically travel back to the clinic. "You automatically end up with a complete, time-stamped record of all the activities undertaken with the patient," says Sheppard. With the new system, errors in information collection and analysis have been reduced dramatically. All in all, St. John's Health and Community Services is very pleased with the new system.[51]

TECHNOLOGY ENABLES BETTER HEALTH CARE AT SUNNYBROOK

In 2001, MedcomSoft Inc. announced that a Toronto hospital, the Sunnybrook & Women's College Health Sciences Centre, would test their new electronic patient-record software. By using the new system, a physician can now document his or her encounter with a patient as it happens, share this information with colleagues, and even streamline the entire treatment process from initial testing to diagnosis and billing. The system, called MedWorks, was designed to tap into the Medcin database developed by Medicomp Systems Inc. of Chantilly, VA—an extensive database containing more than 200,000 data elements, including symptoms (e.g., "persistent cough" or "blurred vision"), tests, diagnoses and therapies. Each of the data elements is connected via 68 million interrelationships making the system "intelligent." During a consultation, it prompts the physician to answer several questions thereby improving diagnosis speed and accuracy. According to MedcomSoft's president and CEO Dr. Sami Aita, health care professionals can document a patient encounter in 1.5 minutes rather than the typical 15 minutes it used to take using traditional patient record software. The gain in productivity comes from the system's ability to automatically display a series of pop-up choices which can be quickly checked using a stylus or on a keyboard that a physician can use to drill through and quickly create a record of an encounter. Another advantage is that the database is non-static. It is being thoroughly updated every six months, providing physicians with the latest diagnoses and therapies.

A powerful feature of the system is its ability to do outcomes analysis; information over multiple encounters can be loaded into the data warehouse, helping health care managers select the best medical treatments early on, further reducing costs. Moreover, because the encounter information is collected in data form (as opposed to text), it can be easily manipulated, aggregated, graphed, processed, and analyzed. This is significant, according to Dr. Aita, as it allows administrators and other health care professionals to "mine" the data for a range of purposes, including drug utilization evaluation, epidemiological analyses, best-practices assessment, and of course cost/benefit analyses based on outcomes. "We can verify the outcome of various therapies, so we understand whether we're doing the right thing." Moreover, one of the most appreciated features of the MedWorks system is that physicians can customize it. Rather than searching through all 200,000 pieces of information in the database, templates are made for various specialties, such as orthopedics, surgery, critical care, etc.[52]

Questions

1. The two cases had essentially the same goals—to track symptoms, treatment, and outcomes—that require the collection and maintenance of a huge amount of qualitative and quantitative information. What type of software would you recommend for storing this information so that it can be easily accessed and analyzed? What sort of software query tools would you suggest?

2. Would there be a role for a geographic information system help in either of these examples? How could it be useful? Are there extreme cases, perhaps natural disasters, where a GIS would be useful?

3. How could a neural network help the Newfoundland nurses to generate the information it needs? Would it be advisable to automate the medication process for routine illnesses by connecting the pattern recognition abilities of a neural network to a robot that dispenses pills and letting medical staff deal with more complicated cases? Why? Why not?

4. An expert system is designed to ask questions, and then ask more questions based on the answers to the previous questions. Isn't that what medical specialists do when they're diagnosing your illness? Would you, therefore, like to dispense with visiting a doctor and just buy a medical expert system that you could install on your home computer and consult when you don't feel well? Why? Why not?

5. What sort of collaboration might be helpful for the Newfoundland nurses and the doctors at Sunnybrook? What situations can you envisage where a video or a Web conference would be helpful?

6. For both cases, describe tasks that the various types of artificial intelligence software would lend themselves to and state specifically what tasks each AI system is suited to.

7. Part of quality assurance in any organization is the identification and correction of things that went wrong and ways in which processes can be improved. It's no different in health care—errors are inevitable. However, it's part of the mission of health care workers to keep these errors as small and as infrequent as possible. How could a decision support system help in the implementation of safer procedures? What part could expert systems, neural networks, and intelligent agents play?

Key Terms and Concepts

ad hoc decision, 136
adaptive filtering, 160
adaptivity, 163
artificial intelligence (AI), 145
artificial neural network (ANN), 152
autonomy, 163
back-propagation neural network, 154
buyer agent, 159
choice, 135
collaboration software, 140
collaboration system, 140
collaborative filtering, 159
crossover, 156
data mining agent, 162
decision support system (DSS), 136
design, 135
domain expert, 150
domain expertise, 150
expert system, 147
explanation module, 151
genetic algorithm, 156
geographic information system (GIS), 143
implementation, 135
inference engine, 150
intelligence, 135
intelligent agent, 158
knowledge acquisition, 150
knowledge base, 150
knowledge-based system, 147
knowledge engineer, 150
model management, 139
monitoring-and-surveillance agent, 161
mutation, 156
neural network (artificial neural network, ANN), 152
nonrecurring decision, 136
nonstructured decision, 136
personal agent, 160
predictive agent, 161
profile filtering, 160
psychographic filtering, 160
recurring decision, 136
robot, 146
rule-based expert system, 150
selection, 156
self-organizing neural network, 154
shopping bot, 159
sociability, 163
structured decision, 135
user agent, 160
user interface, 140

Short-Answer Questions

1. What are the four types of decisions discussed in this chapter? Give an example of each.
2. What is a DSS? Describe its components.
3. What sort of a system would you use if you wanted to work with your suppliers electronically?
4. What are three of the features that collaborative software might have?
5. What is a geographic information system used for?
6. How is information represented in a geographic information system?
7. What is artificial intelligence? Name the artificial intelligence systems used widely in business.
8. What are the components of an expert system?
9. What three concepts of evolution are used by the genetic algorithm?
10. What are intelligent agents? What tasks can they perform?
11. What do shopping bots do?
12. What do monitoring-and-surveillance agents do?

Assignments and Exercises

1. **COLLABORATIVE WORK.** In a group of two or more students, collaborate on a project to make a list of 100 videos or music CDs. Classify the videos or CDs into groups. For example, if you choose movies, you categories might be adventure, comedy, classic, horror, musicals, etc. All communication about the project must be electronically communicated (but not by phone). You could use e-mail, set up a Web site, use a chat room, or a collaboration e-room, if your university has that facility. Print out a copy of all correspondence on the project and put the correspondence together in a folder in chronological order.

   What this task very different from collaborating face-to-face with your partners? In what ways was it better, in what ways worse? What additional problems or advantages would you expect if the person or people you're working with were in a different hemisphere?

2. **CHOOSE A FINANCING OPTION.** Using a spreadsheet (e.g., Excel), evaluate your options for a $12,000 car. Compare the payments (use the =pmt function in Excel), the total amount of interest, and the total you'll pay for the car under the following four options:
   a. 3 years at 0% interest
   b. 2 years at 1.99% annual percent rate (APR)
   c. 4 years at 5% APR
   d. 6 years at 6% APR

   What other considerations would you take into account, were you to buy a new car? Are there considerations other than the interest rate, and the other parts that can be calculated? What are they? How is a car different from other purchases, like CDs or TV sets or computers?

3. **WHICH SOFTWARE WOULD YOU USE?** Which type or types, of computer-aided decision support software would you use for each of the following situations? Note why you think that those you choose are appropriate. The decision support alternatives are:
   - Decision support system
   - Collaboration software
   - Geographic information system
   - Expert system
   - Genetic algorithm
   - Intelligent agent

Problem	Type of Decision Support
Marketing executives on two continents want to develop a new pricing structure for products.	
A financial expert is trying to find a way to predict when customers are about to take their business elsewhere.	
Filling out a short tax form.	
Determining the fastest route for package delivery to 23 different addresses in a city.	
Deciding where to spend advertising dollars (TV, radio, newspaper, direct mail, e-mail).	
Keeping track of competitors' prices for comparable goods and services.	

4. **FIND SOME NEURAL NETWORKS.** Go to the Internet and find three neural network software packages. Make a short report on the three you find. Be sure to include in your report the following:
   - The applications (finance, manufacturing accounting, fraud detection, etc.)
   - Whether the product is free or, if not, how much it costs (if you can determine this)
   - The operating system required to run the software
   - Any special hardware or software requirements listed

   Do any of those sites explain how the neural network works? Did you have to register to get information?

5. **WHAT SHOULD THE MUSIC STORE OWNER DO?** A music store owner wants to have enough of the hottest CDs in stock so that people who come in to buy a particular CD won't be disappointed—and the store won't lose the profit. CDs that are not sold within a certain length of time go onto the sale table where they may

have to be sold at cost, if they sell at all. She wants to design a decision support system to try and predict how many copies she should purchase and what information will she need.

List some of the considerations that would go into such a system. Here are a couple to start you off:

- The population of the target market
- Sales for particular types of music in similar markets

Discussion Questions

1. Some experts claim that if a business gets 52 percent of its decisions right, it will be successful. Would using a decision support system guarantee better results? Why or why not? What does the quality of any decision depend on? Do you think it matters what type of decisions are included in this 52 percent? For example, would getting the right type of paper clips be as influential a decision as deciding where to locate the business? Can you think of a situation where the type of paper clip matters a great deal?

2. Early systems researchers called expert systems "experts in a box." Today, in most situations, people who consult expert systems use them as assistants in specific tasks and not to totally replace human experts. What sorts of tasks would you feel comfortable about having expert systems accomplish without much human intervention? What sorts of tasks would you not be comfortable having expert systems handle independently? Give examples. The first famous expert system, called MYCIN, was developed to diagnose blood diseases. Would you be comfortable consulting an expert system instead of a live doctor when you're ill? Why or why not? If you knew that expert system "doctors" diagnose illness correctly five times as often as human doctors, would this change your answer? Why or why not?

3. Consider the topic of data warehouses in Chapter 3. In the future, AI systems will be increasingly applied to data warehouse processing. Which AI systems do you think might be helpful? For which tasks, or situations, might they best be applied? Do you think that AI systems will someday play a greater role in the design of databases and data warehouses? Why or why not?

4. Consider the differences and similarities among the four AI techniques discussed in this chapter. Name some problems that might be amenable to more than one type of AI system.

   Say you had a Web site and sold baseballs. What types of AI systems could you use to generate information that would be useful to you in deciding what direction to take your company in the future? Say you were pretty successful at selling baseballs. Would you expect to have the amount of information on customers that, say, Wal-Mart has? Why or why not?

5. AI systems are relatively new approaches to solving business problems. What are the difficulties with new IT approaches in general? For each of the systems we discussed, identify some advantages and disadvantages of AI systems over traditional business processes. Say you were selling specialty teas both in traditional retail stores and on the Internet. Would you use the same type of AI systems for each part of your business? In what way would you use them or why would you not? Is there a place for decision support and artificial intelligence techniques in small specialty businesses? In what way would decision support be value adding? Can you think of how a DSS or an AI system would be value-reducing (in terms of Porter's value chain theory)? What do you see as the major differences between running a mammoth concern and a small specialty business?

6. Neural networks recognize and categorize patterns. If someone were to have a neural network that could scan information on all aspects of your life, where would that neural network potentially be able to find information about you? Consider confidential (doctor's office) as well as publicly available (department of motor vehicles) information.

7. What type of AI systems could your school use to help with registration? Intelligent agents find vast amounts of information very quickly. Neural networks can classify patterns instantaneously. What sort of information might your school administration be able to generate using these (or other AI systems) with all of its student information?

8. Would you be comfortable with your institution allowing a third party (like a credit card company) access to student information? Would it make a difference if there were no identifying information included—if only aggregate or summary information were available to the third party? If this third party got student information (names and all), what sort of AI techniques could it use to generate support for decision making? What sort of third-party companies (apart from credit card companies) would like to be able to get student lists from lots of higher education institutions? Identify ten types of businesses that might be interested in such lists. If these third parties were to get personal information on you, would you like there to be restrictions on what they can and can't do with it? If so, what restrictions would you like to see?

REAL HOT Electronic Commerce

Finding Investment Opportunities on the Internet

When you buy stock in a company, you're betting on the success of that firm. Sometimes that bet is a good one, and sometimes it's not. Finding a company that's a good bet involves lots of research. To further complicate matters, some people prefer investing in large, safe companies, whereas others prefer the higher return of a small, more risky firm. So how do you make sense of all the options? Well, now you have access to financial information that professional investors use to evaluate stocks. The Internet brings together information-hungry investors with companies that have been anxiously looking to reach out to investors online. Over 900 companies now offer investment information on the World Wide Web, and the number is increasing rapidly. Remember, though, you must proceed with caution. Do your best to verify the source of any information.

You'll find many links on the Web site that supports this textbook (www.mcgrawhill.ca/college/haag) and select "Electronic Commerce Projects").

LEARNING ABOUT INVESTING

Investing can be as simple as finding a company that performs well financially and buying some of their stock. Or, if you want to spread your investment over a number of stocks and you don't want to personally select each stock, you can invest in a mutual fund. Of course there are thousands of mutual funds with all types of investment objectives. So, any way you go, you must pick your investment wisely. To help you get up to speed quickly, you'll find many helpful Web sites on the Internet.

For starters, you might explore Advice for Investors (www.fin-info.com). Click on their "Publications" link. Alternatively, go to eNorthern (www.enorthern.com) and click on "Investor Education."

Find three investment reference sites and explore what information is available, and answer the following questions.

A. Is the site designed for first-time investors or those who are more experienced?

B. Can you search for a specific topic?

C. Are specific stocks or mutual funds reviewed or evaluated?

D. Does the site provide direct links to brokerage or stock quoting sites?

E. Is a forum for submitting questions available? If so, are frequently asked questions (FAQs) posted?

F. Who sponsors the site? Does it seem as if the sponsor is using the site to advertise its own products or services?

G. Can you download reference documents to read later?

RESEARCHING THE COMPANY BEHIND THE STOCK

One excellent way to pick a stock investment is to research the company behind that stock. Focusing on items such as sales revenues and profits to pick a stock is called *fundamental research*. So you might choose to invest in Hughes stock because you've discovered their sales revenues have been climbing steadily for the last three years. Or you might initially consider buying some Disney stock but change your mind when you find that Euro Disney revenues have been below expectations.

Now that you're ready to research a stock investment, connect to four different company sites. You can find your own or go to the Web site that supports this text (www.mcgrawhill.ca/college/haag) where you will find a list of many other company sites. As you connect to the four sites, look up each company's financials and answer the questions that follow. You'll probably want to include at least two companies with which you are familiar and two that are new to you. In addition to reviewing company financials, look around each company site and see to what degree the site is investor-oriented.

A. Do all the company sites offer financial information?

B. Is the information targeted at investors? How can you tell?

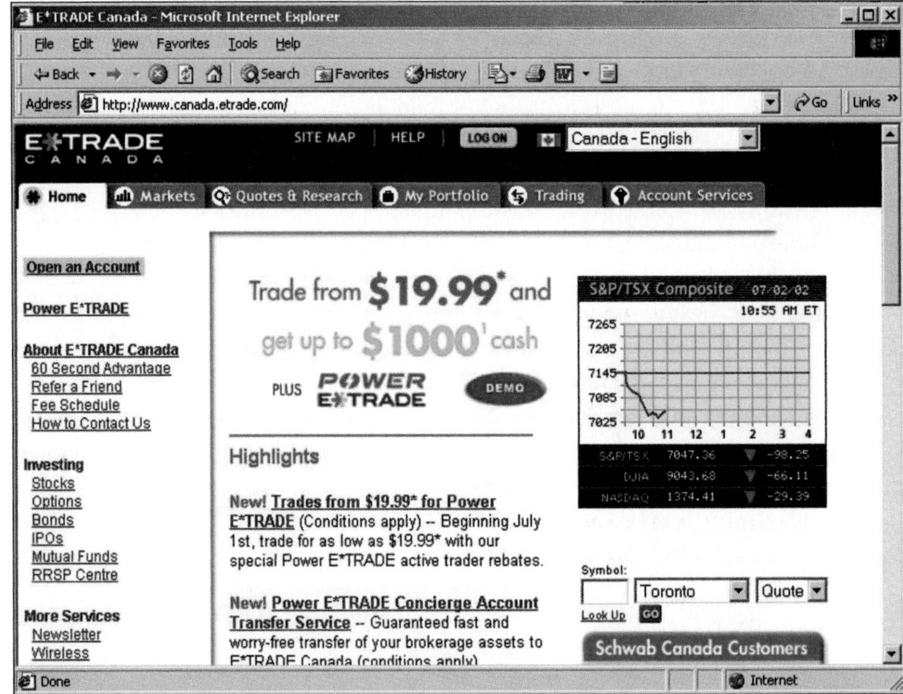

C. Can you download financial information to your computer and use it in a spreadsheet?

D. Can you download the company's annual report? Is it a full-colour version?

E. Does the site provide direct links to e-mail addresses for requesting additional information?

F. Do the companies provide comparisons to others in their industry?

G. Does the site provide stock quotes as well as financials?

H. Can you search the site for financials-related information such as press releases?

I. Was there a charge for retrieving the financial information?

FINDING OTHER SOURCES OF COMPANY FINANCIALS

Searching for a company's financials may be a bit more difficult than you may have first imagined. First you must determine the Internet address for the company either by guessing the address and typing it in or using one of the many search engines available. Both of these methods are fraught with error. For example, if you guessed that "www.amex.com" was the address for American Express you'd be wrong. And even if you did guess a company's address, many companies don't provide their financials on their company-sponsored Web site. Take Adidas Corporation, for example, at www.adidas.com. No financials are available at this site. You'll find that many company Web sites lack information for investors.

The reason many companies don't provide financials on their Web sites is that they view the primary purpose of their sites as reaching consumers, not investors. So many companies elect to post their financials on a financial provider site or simply let investors view the company's submissions to the Securities and Exchange Commission at the SEC's Web site.

Pick three providers of financial information, access their Web sites, and answer the following questions.

A. Is there a charge for retrieving the information?

B. Do you have a choice about the information's format?

C. Are companies listed alphabetically?

D. Does the site offer more than just annual reports?

E. Are there direct links from the site to the desired company's page?

F. Can you find more companies at the site than by searching for individual company Web pages?

G. How many companies are available on each Web site?

H. Are the represented companies mostly large and established or small and relatively unknown?

MAKING TRADES ONLINE

If you want to invest in securities, you might do what a lot of people do, go to a stockbroker. However, many of the same services offered by stockbrokers are now available on the Internet.

Virtually all of the stockbrokers with offices you can visit have Web sites that support online investing and more. These services include account information, financial planning, and online investing services. Before we go online to look at some of these stockbrokers we should be sure we understand the difference between a full-service brokerage house and a discount brokerage house. As the names imply, the full-service brokerage offers many more services than the discount brokerage. And it's important to understand that the price for many of these services is built into the fees to buy and sell stocks and mutual funds. So you pay for having these services available even if you don't use them at a full-service brokerage.

Let's venture online and see what the various brokerages have to offer us. Find three brokerages on the Web, examine what it takes to conduct an online investment transaction, and answer the following questions:

A. Must you already have an investment account with the brokerage to purchase stocks or mutual funds?

B. Which sites are full-service brokerages and which are discount brokerages? How can you tell?

C. Is online research available? Is it free?

D. Can you retrieve stock price quotes for free?

E. If you already have an account with the brokerage, do they offer special services for these customers? What kinds of services are offered?

F. Is the site aimed at experienced investors or new investors?

G. If you are investing for the first time, would you feel comfortable using online investing? Why or why not?

RETRIEVING STOCK QUOTES

Once you find the right stock to buy, you'll be asking yourself, "How much will this stock cost me?" Stocks and mutual funds are both offered by the share and so you can easily buy as much or as little of the stock or mutual fund as you like. Still, some individual shares are priced in the hundreds or thousands of dollars and that alone might make the purchase undesirable to you.

In addition to pricing individual shares to assess the affordability of an investment, you'll probably want to see how the price has varied over time. Even though most financial advisors will tell you that historical price variations provide no indication of future performance, most everyone uses price history to get a feel for whether the investment is trading at all-time highs or lows. So finding a chart of a stock price online might be helpful when making your purchase.

And even after you've made your purchase, you'll probably want to follow how your investment is doing. The thrill of realizing a "paper profit" is enough to keep many investors checking their investments daily. Of course, realizing a "paper loss" can be equally disappointing. And even if daily tracking isn't for you, you'll certainly want to check on your investments regularly and doing so online can be quick and painless.

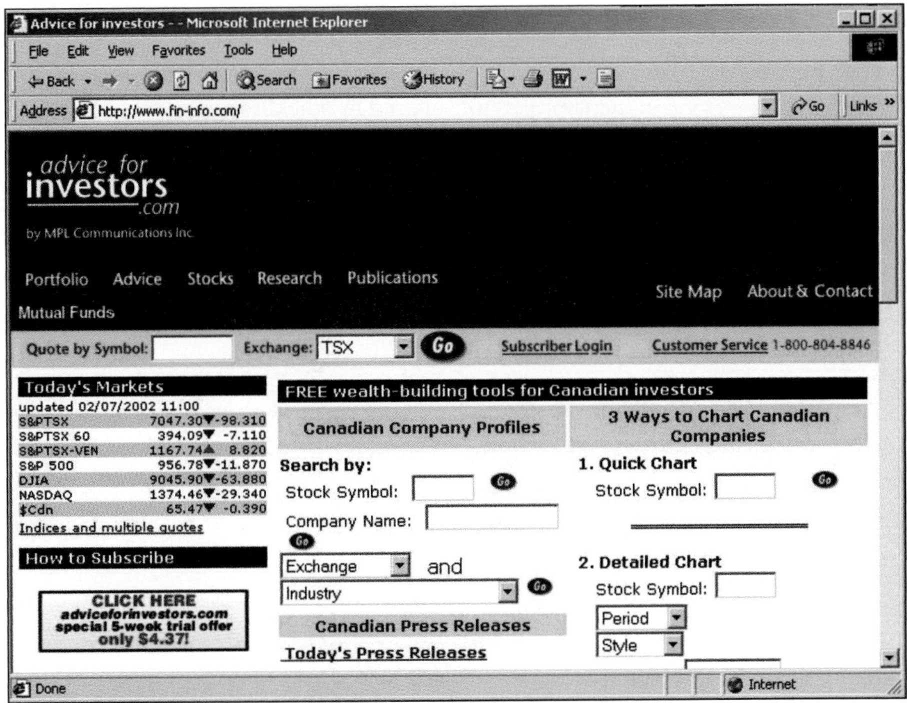

Pick three stock-quoting services, examine what it takes to retrieve a stock or mutual fund quote, and answer the following questions:

A. Are the quotes provided free of charge or for a fee?

B. Does the site require a "ticker" symbol (the abbreviation used by experienced investors) or can you type in a company name?

C. Are the quotes "real-time" or are they "delayed" (15–20 minutes old)?

D. Does the site require registration?

E. Are historical prices available?

F. Are price charts available? Can you customize the chart display?

G. Can you create and save a personal portfolio of stocks?

Real HOT Links

Go to the Online Learning Centre at www.mcgrawhill.ca/college/haag for quizzes, extra content, a searchable glossary, and more! Click on "Electronic Commerce Projects" for links to hundreds of Web sites.

Go to the text CD-ROM for data files, extra content, and Skills Modules on Microsoft Excel, Microsoft Access, HTML, and e-portfolios.

CHAPTER FIVE

STUDENT LEARNING OUTCOMES

1. Describe the four main perspectives of e-commerce, its current status, and the global growth expected in the next few years.
2. Identify the advantages of business-to-consumer (B2C) e-commerce.
3. Describe the techniques that lead to success in B2C e-commerce ventures.
4. Describe the variety of ways that business-to-business (B2B) e-commerce technologies are being used, and describe next-generation models that may widen the adoption of global B2B e-commerce.
5. Identify the unique aspects of e-government applications.
6. Describe the status and options for e-commerce payment systems.

INDUSTRY PERSPECTIVES

FEATURES

WEB SUPPORT LINKS

- Competitive Intelligence
- Storefront Software
- Hosting Services
- Marketing the Site

Visit www.mcgrawhill.ca/college/haag

ELECTRONIC COMMERCE
Strategies for the New Economy

CASE STUDY:
SODAS AND SNACK FOOD ON THE WEB

Cans of soda are probably one of the last things we would think of buying online. They're available on every street corner.

Despite this, Pepsi-Cola Co. has a number of Internet initiatives under way, from music sites to banner ads to Internet sweepstakes. And more are on the drawing board. Even though it is currently spending only 3 percent of its $400 million ad budget on the Internet, Pepsi is placing a lot of emphasis on the medium as an effective way of reaching the most desirable customers. For example, in a deal put together with Yahoo!, Pepsi agreed to put the Yahoo! logo on 1.5 billion cans of Pepsi. In return, Yahoo! encouraged their visitors to visit the Pepsi Stuff site.

Three million consumers logged on to Pepsi Stuff and provided Pepsi with detailed demographic information about themselves. Pepsi's sales volume was up by 5 percent as a result of the promotion at a cost of about one-fifth of a traditional mail-in project.

Pepsi intends to keep using the Web as its medium of choice because it is also the medium of choice for its target market—those under 25. They simply decided that it makes sense to flash the Pepsi logo where their target customers hang out.

As it moves forward, Pepsi will expand its Web-centric marketing efforts. While banner ads and other, more traditional methods have had some success, it's the creation of engaging Pepsi Web sites that has given the brand the best results online. As the technology expands, Pepsi expects the creative potential of what can be done on the Web to explode.

Well, you can't just have a Pepsi without having some snack foods to go with it, and Frito-Lay makes a bunch of them. As a matter of fact, if you go to their Web site (www.frito-lay.com), you'll be able to find their mission statement: "To be the world's favorite snack and always within arm's reach." (Not a bad mission statement when you think about it. After all, they'll sure sell more snack food if they're within arm's reach!) And Frito-Lay has a ton of snack food brands to sell you: Lays and Ruffles potato chips, Doritos tortilla chips, Tostitos, Cracker Jack, and Grandma's cookies among them.

Frito-Lay is a unit of PepsiCo and, as you might expect, also uses the Web as a way to reach out to its customers. They attract customers to their Web site by offering dietary information (to make you feel less guilty about snacking) as well as recipes that may never have occurred to you (such as Lays potato chip cookies). They are also reaching out to a younger audience by operating ePloids (www.eploids.com), the "World's 1st On-Line Auction for Kids." ePloids can be obtained from specially marked snack food packages and used as digital currency for the auction.[1]

Introduction

You've probably heard the ancient Chinese curse, "May you live in interesting times." It's a curse because it is often easier to live in times that are not so interesting, when things move along pretty much as expected, as they always have. The past few years of the new economy introduced by the World Wide Web have certainly been interesting. There has been an entrepreneurial frenzy unlike anything the world has ever seen. Fortunes have been made and lost. Dot-com millionaires and billionaires were created. Some have seen their fortunes increase while others have watched their dot-com business wonders turn into "dot-bombs." Despite all the turmoil, most observers of the e-commerce scene believe that the revolution in business promised by the Internet has just begun. One has said it's "like we're in the first minute of the first period of a hockey game." We have some hint of how e-commerce is going to unfold. We are learning what works and what doesn't work. But there is a lot of uncharted territory ahead. There will be new winners and new losers. That is why it is so important that you learn ways to help your organization develop a winning strategy for the new economy.

The Growth of E-Commerce

Maybe we ought to start with a definition, because there are many definitions of e-commerce. We like this one. **E-commerce** is commerce, but it is commerce accelerated and enhanced by IT, in particular the Internet. It enables customers, consumers, and companies to form powerful new relationships that would not be possible without the enabling technologies.

But let's not forget that, fundamentally, it's all still about *commerce*, people buying and selling products and services from and to each other. The Internet facilitates commerce by its awesome ability to move digital information at low cost.

As illustrated in Figure 5.1, there are four main perspectives for e-commerce, business-to-business (B2B), business-to-consumer (B2C), consumer-to-business (C2B), and consumer-to-consumer (C2C). We'll focus on B2C and B2B in this chapter, but we have also included a short discussion on the roles that the government can play as well.

B2C is what you read about the most in the popular press. These are the e-commerce sites that sell products and services, or provide information services directly to consumers. They include such well-known companies as Yahoo!, Amazon.ca, and LandsEnd.com.

Figure 5.1
Four Categories of E-Commerce[2]

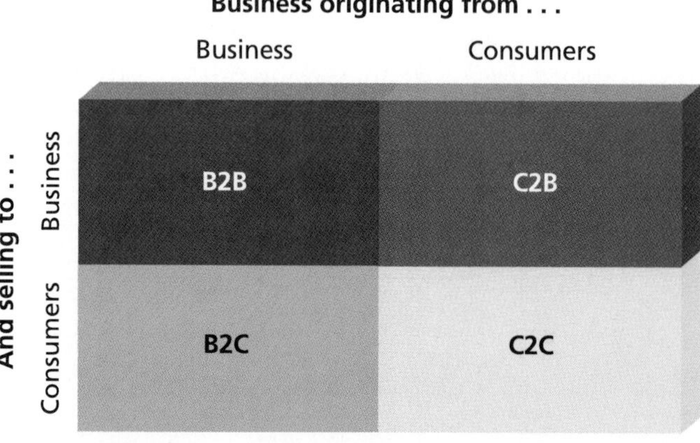

Even though most of the media's attention is focused on B2C, the dollar volume of e-commerce has always been widely expected to be concentrated in the B2B segment, where businesses buy and sell from and to each other. This is because the B2B segment is so much larger, regardless of whether we're talking about e-commerce or traditional commerce.

The C2C sector is where consumers deal with each other. Probably the best examples of C2C e-commerce are the online auction sites. eBay is the most well-known such site and it is one of the real success stories of e-commerce.

Finally, the C2B sector is the one in which the Internet makes it possible for many consumers who want to buy the same or similar products to band together in order to obtain volume discounts from a business. This process is known as demand aggregation. **Demand aggregation** combines purchase requests from multiple buyers into a single large order which justifies a discount from the business. While it's possible to aggregate consumer demand on the Internet, the best-known company to try it, Mercata, was unsuccessful and went out of business. If you'd like to see an example of a company that aggregates demand of consumers interested in high-speed Internet Access, go to Sugarloaf.net (www.sugarloaf.net), a company that brags that it brings "Bandwidth to the Boonies." Demand aggregation is also possible and much more widespread, of course, in the B2B sector (see UniStar LLC at www.unistarllc.com for an example).

GLOBAL E-COMMERCE GROWTH PROJECTIONS

It is estimated that there were 229 million Internet users worldwide in 2000 (see Table 5.1), and that this will rise to 640 million by the year 2004. While growth cannot continue at such a pace for very long, the ultimate number of Internet users worldwide will clearly be an impressive figure. In a survey released early in 2001, Forrester Research estimated that online trade in Canada would reach $272 billion, accounting for 18 percent of all business-to-business transactions by 2005.[3] Later, in May 2002, ElectricNews.Net reported that European business-to-business e-commerce sales are expected to grow from $500 billion in 2002 to $2.3 trillion by 2005.[4] In April 2002, *eMarketer* estimated worldwide e-commerce sales of $557 billion, about 86 percent of it in the B2B space.[5]

You must use growth projections such as the ones cited here with caution, because they are, in fact, estimates. Nevertheless, the consensus of knowledgeable observers of the e-commerce scene is consistent in their expectations that it has nowhere to go but up (and up).

Table 5.1

Active Adult Internet Users (millions)[6]

	2000	2004
Middle East Africa	3.5	10.9
Latin America	3.9	40.8
Asia Pacific	48.7	173.0
Europe	70.1	254.9
North America	97.6	160.6
Total	**229.8**	**640.2**

THE DIGITAL DIVIDE

You will notice from Table 5.1 that the number of Internet users varies from region to region in the world. Less developed regions have fewer users than more developed ones. This phenomenon is called the **digital divide**. The phrase expresses the fact that different peoples, cultures, and areas of the world or within a nation do not have the same access to information and telecommunications technologies. For example, Finland and the other Scandinavian countries have a high population online; these small countries are affluent, with a tradition of good telecommunications systems. Just the opposite is true of Africa and Latin America; many of these areas have large populations, are poor, and do not have state-of-the-art computer and telecommunications infrastructures. This **global digital divide** specifically describes the differences in IT access and capabilities between different countries or regions of the world. Many e-commerce policy experts are concerned that the global digital divide threatens to restrict the benefits of global e-commerce to just the wealthy nations.

The Advantages of Business-to-Consumer E-Commerce

We noted earlier in this chapter that B2C e-commerce was relatively small compared to B2B e-commerce. It is also small compared to the other forms of retail commerce, principally catalogues and retail stores. As we discuss in this section, while retailers based solely on the Internet will continue to exist, the overall trend in the B2C space seems to be one in which retailers increasingly view the Internet as simply another channel by which to reach their customers. As we shall see, however, it is a channel that possesses some unique and powerful advantages over traditional channels when used effectively. Knowing when to use it, how to use it effectively, and when to use it in combination with other channels is key.

In addition to the opportunity to employ the techniques of mass customization and personalization we discussed in Chapter 2, the Internet has several current and potential advantages over the traditional retailing channels of "bricks-and-mortar" stores and catalogue sales. The Internet's most prominent advantages are:

1. Shopping can be faster and more convenient.
2. Offerings and prices can change instantaneously.
3. Call centres can be integrated with the Web site.
4. Broadband telecommunications will enhance the buying experience.

SHOPPING CAN BE FASTER AND MORE CONVENIENT

Some bricks-and-mortar stores are open 24 hours a day, seven days a week, but most are not. Internet sites are open all the time. You've probably experienced the frustration of going from one store to another, from one shopping mall to another, fighting traffic, trying to find a place to park, looking for that one certain item.

Catalogue shopping avoids some of the irritations of bricks-and-mortar shopping by letting you pick out the item you want from a catalogue, dial a toll-free telephone number, and order the item. But though many catalogue retailers such as Sears and Eddie Bauer are open 24 hours a day, seven days a week, many others are not. And although the service of some catalogue retailers is very good, with others you are put on hold and have to listen to music you don't like until the customer service rep comes

TELEMEDICINE IN CANADIAN RURAL AREAS

Providing health care to isolated communities across Canada has always been a challenge. For instance, doctors must regularly be flown in from Vancouver Island on a small Bell JetRanger B206 helicopter to provide health care services to the residents of Zeballos, B.C., one of Canada's more remote settlements. This is often stressful and tiring for doctors. Other health care professionals who have actually established residence in rural communities often complain of low morale, isolation, and burnout. On another stop of the flying circuit called Holberg, local nurse Elizabeth Frost is on call 24 hours a day. "I have no replacement here ... and I get very stressed having no professional colleague to talk to." Yet residents of these communities may still be among the lucky ones. Many rural areas in Canada do not benefit from local service at all. Residents must regularly travel significant distances to consult doctors.

In 1999, while urban centres across Canada boasted a ratio of one doctor for every 200 people, in rural areas the ratio had plummeted to one for every 800, and it was expected that this disparity would become even more pronounced. Not only were rural populations growing because more aging baby boomers chose to retire away from large cities, but provinces were losing rural doctors at an astonishing rate. British Columbia reported an average attrition rate of two country doctors per month. At the time, Dr. Peter Hutten-Czapski of Haileybury, Ontario warned that, at this rate, rural services would likely disappear by 2006.

Today, the provinces are addressing the crisis by increasingly adopting Internet technologies to end rural isolation. In particular, Nova Scotia has been the most aggressive proponent of telemedicine. The province spent $8 million to link its smaller health care facilities to major medical centres in Halifax. Innovations include giving doctors in Halifax the ability to examine patients in rural communities via remote control video camera equipment. Furthermore, small-town physicians across the country are also embracing the Internet. Today, Dr. Patricia Vann, who works in Dryden, 300 kilometres northwest of Thunder Bay, Ontario, heads the Society of Rural Physicians of Canada. The organization, founded in 1993, has flourished in cyberspace, and membership now exceeds 800. The group sponsors online discussion groups that let rural physicians exchange ideas and share experiences.[7]

on the line. In order to comparison-shop, you must hope you have all the right catalogues, and then page through them in a cumbersome fashion.

By contrast, when you shop on the Internet, it can be faster and more convenient. If you don't find what you want at the right price on one merchant's Web site, a click of the mouse will take you to a competitor's. The operator of an Internet retail site is called an **e-tailer**. E-tailers are further divided into pure plays and clicks-and-mortar sites. **Pure plays** are Internet retailers such as Amazon.com that have no physical stores. **Clicks-and-mortar** retailers (also called "bricks-and-clicks") are ones like Nordstrom, which has both an Internet presence and physical stores. They often have catalogues as well. As far as we know, no one has invented a term to describe catalogue retailers such as Lands' End that have an Internet presence but no physical stores. Figure 5.2 illustrates these alternative sales channels.

Compare the convenience of shopping on the Internet to driving from one store to another or flipping from catalogue to catalogue. On the Internet, not only can you go from site to site with the click of a mouse, but there are many sites that offer product and price comparisons for you as well. One of the applications suggested for m-commerce relates to price comparisons. **M-commerce** is e-commerce conducted over a wireless device such as a cell phone or personal digital assistant (PDA). As one example, let's say you're in an electronics store and you notice a DVD player at what seems to be a good price. With m-commerce, you'll be able to find the price at other merchants for the same item simply by using your wireless device. Internet-based services

THE GLOBAL PERSPECTIVE

IF I WANT YOUR ADVICE I'LL ASK FOR IT

PK-35 is an amateur soccer team in a suburb of Helsinki, Finland. Like most sports teams, PK-35 has players and a coach. What makes PK-35 different is that their coach, Janne Viljamaa, asks for suggestions from 300 fans via cell-phone text messages. Every week, Viljamaa provides between three and ten questions to answer about training, team selection, and game tactics. Fans get three minutes to enter responses, and they get the results back three minutes later. (Fan-driven decisions can produce dramatic results, like the decision to use a substitute who scored a last-minute goal in a critical end-of-season game.)

Noting that the concept works for him, Viljamaa went on to say that "because of our high rate of cell-phone use, Finnish soccer can serve as a test bed before taking the concept to the rest of the world."[8]

will search the Web and tell you whether the price you see on the item in front of you is a good deal or not. It will be similar to what you can do now sitting in front of your PC.

The emergence of m-commerce has the potential to create what some call a "freedom economy" wherein commerce is not constrained by location. Buying and selling can be done anywhere, anytime. Access to information in corporate databases will also be easily available from anywhere to employees of corporations as well as to customers and suppliers. As with any emerging technology there are problems to be

Figure 5.2

Alternative Channels for Selling to Consumers

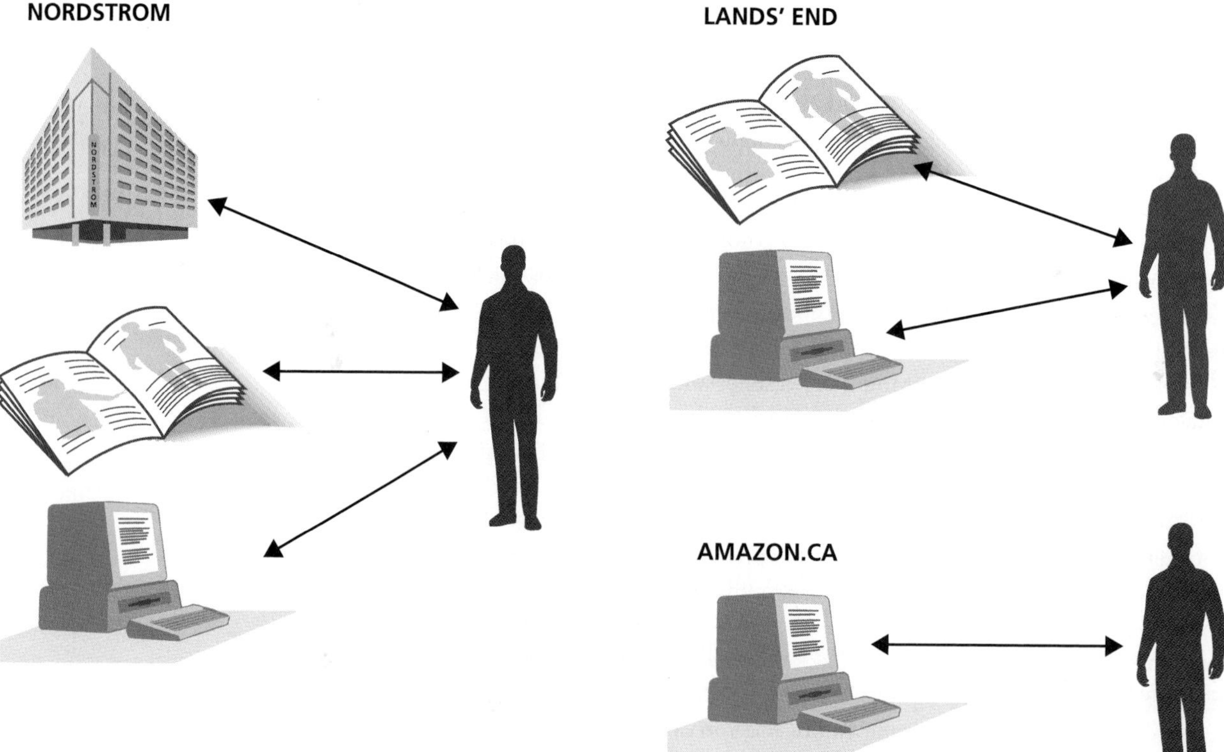

ON YOUR OWN

B2C SERVICES

Just about any product you can imagine is offered for sale to consumers over the Internet—books, videos, CDs, automobiles, clothes, groceries. Not only can you buy products over the Internet, you can buy services. There are sites where you can get financial advice, medical advice, weather reports, and more. See if you can come up with at least ten sites offering *services* (not products) on the Internet. Many of the sites offering services are free. Make five of the ten sites on your list sites where the consumer must pay for the service.

worked out, but in the opinion of experts, the future for m-commerce is bright enough that it cannot be ignored.[9]

If the product you want to buy is digital, such as software, music, and books, it can be delivered *immediately* over the Internet. This, of course, represents a tremendous advantage over both stores and catalogue retailers.

OFFERINGS AND PRICES CAN CHANGE INSTANTANEOUSLY

Another advantage e-tailers have is that product offerings and prices can be changed instantaneously in response to changes in customer demand. One of the most difficult aspects of managing a retail operation, particularly with high-fashion goods, is to know how much to order at the beginning of the selling season. You also need to have enough information to reorder early if sales are better than expected, and to reduce prices early if sales are not up to your expectations. Children's toys, for example, also fall into this category because toys can be "hot" during the critical holiday selling season. One year it's Pokémon and the next year it's the PlayStation 2. In March or April of each year, retail merchandisers try to estimate the number of each item they will sell in November and December, because that's when orders must be placed with manufacturers. When the selling season arrives, actual sales are measured against estimated sales. If sales are taking off, an early order to the manufacturer will make it more likely that more of the hot product can be shipped. If the retailer waits too long, none will be available because everyone else has ordered more and the manufacturer either cannot keep up with the incoming orders or they've moved on to produce products for sale after the holiday season. If sales are slower than expected, the retailer must react quickly to reduce the product's price, or there will be piles of unsold products on the shelves. As you know, sometimes an unpopular item is hard even to give away.

Think about the advantage e-tailers have in managing this process. They can obtain real-time information on how sales are going against expectations. More importantly, they can adjust prices immediately if sales are not going as well as expected. In a way, it's similar to the yield management systems of the airlines we discussed in Chapter 2, but it is a tremendous advantage for the e-tailer. Many e-tailers have "clearance" areas on their sites to alert their customers to last-minute bargains.

If a catalogue retailer wants to reduce its price, what does it have to do? Produce mountains of catalogues to mail to its customers. If a traditional retailer wants to advertise a sale, usually it must incur the expense and delay of newspaper advertising. E-tailers not only can change prices across the board instantly, but, if they wish, they can offer special pricing to their best customers by using the personalization techniques we discussed in Chapter 2.

TEAM WORK

BROADBAND SERVICES: WHERE DO YOU PLACE YOUR BETS?

Assume that your Aunt Millie has just died and left you $10 million in her will. Because you're young, adventurous, and technologically astute, you decide to invest the entire $10 million in stocks of companies in sectors that will be sure to benefit from the coming surge in broadband telecommunications supporting B2C e-commerce applications.

Because there is intense competition in the industry, and several competing technologies, you decide to consult some of your classmates to decide how to allocate the $10 million. You have the option of keeping all or a portion of the $10 million in T-bills while you wait to see how things unfold.

Allocate the $10 million among the following broadband technologies (or T-bills). Which technologies do you feel will be most successful for B2C e-commerce applications in the United States? Pick one other country and do the same. Be prepared to justify your decisions, and feel free to add other technologies:

ISDN
DSL
Cable
Satellite
Fixed wireless
Fibreless optics
Other
T-bills

CALL CENTRES CAN BE INTEGRATED WITH THE WEB SITE

One of the more innovative adaptations in e-tailing has been Web sites that give customers the ability to contact a customer service representative using interactive chat. **Interactive chat** lets you engage in real-time typed exchange of information between you and one or more other individuals over the Internet. LandsEndLive™, on the Lands' End site (www.landsend.com) goes even further, and gives you the option of communicating with a customer service representative using your choice of interactive chat or the telephone. If you choose to use the telephone, you'll need a second line on which the customer service representative can call you back or a direct Internet connection. Soon, you'll be able to connect directly to the customer service representative using Internet telephony as long as your computer has a microphone and speakers. **Internet telephony** is a combination of hardware and software that uses the Internet as the medium for transmission of telephone calls in place of traditional telephone networks.

Before long, speech recognition software will reach the point where the need for call centre representatives will be reduced, particularly for routine inquiries. Speech recognition helps computers identify spoken words (a topic discussed in more detail in the Chapter 9). If you'd like to see how a speech recognition service works in providing information services to consumers, just dial 800-555-TELL in the United States or 408-678-0035 in Canada. You'll be connected with Tell Me, a service that can respond to your spoken commands and provide information on a variety of topics: weather, stock quotes, movie guides, and even driving directions.

BROADBAND TELECOMMUNICATIONS WILL ENHANCE THE BUYING EXPERIENCE

We've already discussed some of the ways in which wireless technologies will enhance e-commerce. When broadband telecommunications become widely available the buy-

HEALTH-RELATED SITES: THE MOST POPULAR WEB SITES FOR CANADIANS

According to Canada's leading market research company, Ipsos-Reid, 55 percent of Canadians with Internet access have visited Web sites containing health-related information. The most popular sites are those offering information about diseases, prevention, and cures, followed in popularity by sites that offer information about nutrition and sites that offer information about prescription drugs. Almost 60 percent of these visitors believe that health-related sites have made them more knowledgeable about their own health. Yet, although interest in health sites is significant, Canadians remain skeptical of the information they find on the Net. More than half of respondents were cynical regarding the credibility of the information. Moreover, it seems that doctors do not particularly endorse these sources. More than 90 percent of doctors do not trust the quality of the health information and 24 percent actually believed that the health information available over the Net was actually doing more harm than good. "This concern over the credibility of health information online suggests that the Net has a long way to go in living up to its full potential in this area," says Steve Mossop, Senior Vice-President of Ipsos-Reid.[10]

ing experience will also be greatly enhanced. You'll be able to purchase a full-length feature film, for example, and downloaded it in minutes. In addition, the inventory of available films will not be limited to what a video store is able to stock on its shelves. You'll be able to choose any film that has ever been made and it will always be available.

Travel sites will offer full-motion video tours of vacation destinations that will let you get a better appreciation of what that beachfront resort in Costa Rica will really be like before you book it. Automobile buying sites will be able to offer virtual test drives to let you narrow down your choices before you take the time to visit an auto dealership. Think of what will be possible with virtual reality (which is, basically, a 3D simulation in which you physically participate—discussed in more detail in the Chapter 9). You will indeed be able to experience "Costa Rica" without spending as much time and money as to actually go there. (Unfortunately—or not—it's unlikely that the relatively inexpensive virtual experience will ever completely match an actual experience.)

Can you think of other ways broadband technologies will enhance the retail e-commerce buying experience?

Keys to Success in Business-to-Consumer E-Commerce

It is important to reflect on what lessons have been learned thus far so that new B2C entrepreneurs (perhaps you and a group of classmates) can increase their chances of being successful. Some of the most important lessons are:

1. Commodity-like items work best.
2. Digital products are the best of all.
3. Attracting and retaining customers.
4. Remember the importance of merchandising.
5. You must execute well.
6. Watch the competition.

THE GLOBAL PERSPECTIVE

GREEN E-COMMERCE

There are some four billion people in the world whose per capita income is less than a tenth that of Canada and other developed countries. One of the challenges facing the world is how to formulate plans for sustainable economic development in lesser-developed countries—that is, development that does not increase global warming, water supply shortages, fisheries depletion, deforestation, and the like. Many think it is possible to use new technologies and new business models to help close the income gap between rich and poor populations in ways that are consistent with the principles of sustainable development. Internet-enabled e-services may prove to be one of the most useful tools to employ in this challenging effort, in the opinion of experts who study this issue.[11]

COMMODITY-LIKE ITEMS WORK BEST

People tend to be more comfortable buying items on the Internet that are commodity-like, that is, uniform. You're comfortable buying a book on the Internet because you know it will be just like the one you'd get if you bought it from your local bookstore. You might be less comfortable buying "high touch" products such as furniture. When you buy a chair, you probably want to sit in it to be sure it feels the way you want it to feel. PCs are commodity-like. When you log on to Dell Computer's site and configure a computer the way you want it, you can count on its being identical to one configured in the same way by another buyer miles away.

Two industries that will be interesting to watch in this context are automobiles and groceries. In the case of automobiles, it really doesn't matter where you buy a new car. Whether you buy it from a local dealer or from a dealer hundreds of miles away at a lower price, you can still get exactly the same car. In theory, you could also log on to the manufacturer's Web site, configure your car just the way you want it, and have it built to your specifications, as if it were a Dell computer. If they could, automobile manufacturers would like to have a process where you do just that because it would help them avoid building cars that sell slowly and sit in dealers' lots. The manufacturers typically subsidize dealers' inventory carrying costs, and on top of that often have to offer rebates to buyers to get rid of surplus cars. The biggest reason the manufacturers have not gone to a direct sell model is the resistance they got from the National Automobile Dealers Association when they floated the idea. The dealers concluded they had no intention of getting disintermediated like the travel agents and had enough clout to force the manufacturers to back down. Don't be surprised if the manufacturers keep trying, however.

The reason grocery sales over the Internet will be interesting to watch is that the things we buy in grocery stores are a mixture of commodity and non-commodity items. Examples of commodity items are laundry detergents or breakfast cereals; examples of non-commodity items are produce and fish. You might not mind having someone else pick a box of breakfast cereal off the shelf for you, but you might prefer to choose your own tomatoes or salmon. One of the most spectacular of the dot-com failures was Webvan, an online grocer. Nonetheless, others, such as Telegrocer (shop.telegrocer.com), are still in business. Groceries may well settle in as an industry where a bricks-and-clicks model ultimately makes the most sense.

DIGITAL PRODUCTS ARE THE BEST OF ALL

The reasons we say that digital products are best suited for B2C e-commerce are:

- They are commodity-like products.
- They can be mass-customized and personalized.
- They can be delivered at the time of purchase.
- They foster disintermediation.
- They have global reach.

We first introduced some of these ideas in Chapter 2 when we gave customized CDs and downloaded software as examples. There are, of course, many other examples: videos (when the necessary bandwidth becomes available) and any text product such as books, newspapers, articles, or manuscripts.

Now, much of the information available on the Internet is free. You can go to the Web sites of many newspapers and magazines and get current information and search the online archives of back issues. At present, most such sites are either losing money or attempting to support themselves with advertising. Some, such as the online version of *Marketing* magazine, charge an annual subscription fee. Others, such as *Maclean's*, make some information free and restrict access to other stories to their print subscribers.

Many observers forecast that, in time, you'll be asked to pay for much of the information you now get for free. One technology that will hasten this is **micro-payments**—techniques to facilitate the exchange of small amounts of money for an Internet transaction. Most B2C transactions today are paid for by credit card. It is not practical to process small payments on credit cards (less than $2) because of transaction processing costs. With micro-payments, however, an online newspaper in London could charge you five cents for a theatre timetable. If you were on your way to London, England and wondering which play to see, you might find that five cents was a bargain. And for the newspaper, five cents here and five cents there could soon add up to some real money. We'll talk more about micro-payments later in this chapter when we discuss smart cards.

ATTRACTING AND RETAINING CUSTOMERS

Designing an attractive Web site that is easy to use is one of the key factors in the success of a B2C venture. As previously mentioned, and as you well know, it's very easy for potential customers to leave your site for a competitor's with a click of the mouse. So, once they've found your site, it's important to keep them there until they purchase something, and once they've purchased something, you need to give them an incentive to return. You must not turn them off with an unattractive or customer-unfriendly Web site. Some tips from a professional Web site designer are listed in Figure 5.3.

Because entry barriers can be lower on the Internet than in traditional retailing, there can be many Web sites competing for the same customers. Successful B2C businesses have learned that attracting and retaining customers is vitally important.

Of course, with a B2C site, it's not simply a case of "Build it and they will come." You have to find a way to let potential customers know that you are there and that, among the many choices they have, your site is the one they should choose to visit. Your Web site needs to be marketed.

When marketing professionals consider how to market and promote a business, they talk about the marketing mix. **Marketing mix** is the set of marketing tools that the firm uses to pursue its marketing objectives in the target market.[14] Bricks-and-mortar

THE SERVICE SECTOR

Today, the service sector accounts for more than 65 percent of Atlantic Canada's gross domestic product. In New Brunswick alone, almost 90 percent of jobs being created are in the service industry. The Internet has played an important role in economically reinvigorating the region after a slump in the fishery and construction sectors. For instance, E-com Inc. (www.e-com.net), a Moncton-based software developer established in 1995, offers business solutions via the Internet to companies located across three continents. "For us, e-commerce is a lean and mean way to expand without incurring mega costs," says president Jean Nadeau. Communicating with both buyers and sellers across the Web avoids the time and travel associated with international travel. The company provides Web-based training and support, and "try before you buy" options using live, online software demonstrations. Furthermore, although the company only has ten employees working out of Moncton, E-com deals electronically with more than 35 freelance graphic designers and programmers. "E-commerce gives you access to the best people at the right price, wherever they are," adds Nadeau.[12]

retailers have traditionally used a combination of techniques such as newspaper advertising, direct mail, radio, and television to attract customers to their stores. Traditional marketing techniques such as those just mentioned are also used by dot-coms. For example, you've probably seen magazine ads with a company's Web address prominently displayed, or seen television ads for a dot-com company.

Figure 5.3

Dos and Don'ts of Web Site Design[13]

Toni Will-Harris has ten dos and don'ts for Web site design. A condensed version appears here. The complete version can be found on her Web site: www.efuse.com/Design/top_10_do_s_and_don_ts.html.

1. Keep graphics files small. The longer a file takes to load, the higher the probability the user will leave before it's done.
2. Keep text files small for the same reason.
3. Design text and backgrounds for easy reading.
4. Design for 256 colours and 640 × 480 resolution. It's the lowest common denominator for older computers.
5. Use ALT tags on graphics. ALT text appears before the graphic does, or in place of the graphic for users who have turned graphics off for speed.
6. Include your company name, address, e-mail address, and phone and fax numbers on every page.
7. Keep your site fresh. It's important to change content frequently so people have something to come back for.
8. Be generous. The more detail you offer, the more reason you give people to visit your site.
9. Be backward-compatible. Using cutting-edge technology may shut out some readers.
10. Test your site as visitors will see it, using all versions of the popular browsers.

To learn how to design your own Web page, go to Skills Module 3 on the CD-ROM accompanying the text.

Skills Module 3
Web Page Design

In the B2C e-commerce space, there are additional techniques for attracting customers using the Internet itself. Some of these are:

1. Registering with search engines
2. Online ads
3. E-mail and viral marketing
4. Affiliate programs
5. Selling to existing customers

REGISTERING WITH SEARCH ENGINES Many Web surfers use searches to find what they need. So one of the first things you should do is to register with the various search engines.

You can register your site with some search engines by filling out some forms on their Web sites. There are services that will do this for you for a fee. For some search engines, it is important to put the keywords people will be using in their search arguments in your Web site text, or in **meta tags**—a part of a Web site text not displayed to users but accessible to browsers and search engines for finding and categorizing Web sites.

ONLINE ADS Many Web sites use **banner ads**, which are small ads on a Web site that advertise the products and services of another business, usually another dot-com. You've probably seen them on many sites that you've visited. According to a recent study published by the Interactive Advertising Bureau,[15] marketers view online advertising as a good way to induce consumers to visit a Web site. Although observers expect the banner ad to be around for a while, you may have noticed that larger ads are becoming more popular. In addition, new technologies such as Flash and DHTML are being employed more frequently and are thought to hold great promise. More interactive advertising is also in the works for the future. Just as with TV now, some of the most entertaining content we see on the Internet may well be the ads.

E-MAIL AND VIRAL MARKETING E-mail marketing has proven to be especially effective for B2C e-commerce. In 2001, for example, e-mail generated 15 percent of online sales in North America, up from only 3 percent in the year 2000.[16] Sites have various ways of asking for your e-mail address. Most commonly, you supply it when you order something so the site can send you a confirmation of your order. Most sites, at the same time, will ask your permission to send you occasional e-mails announcing special sales or information that may be of interest to you about specials from other B2C companies. The more the company knows about you, the more e-mail offers can be personalized to appeal to you. Much of what makes B2C e-commerce potentially so effective is the ability of companies to build customer databases and then use sophisticated data mining software to help in crafting personal appeals.

Most people don't like to receive **spam**—unsolicited e-mail—and immediately delete it from their inboxes without taking the time to read it. Viral marketing is a technique that gets around the need to use spam. **Viral marketing** encourages users of a product or service supplied by a B2C company to ask friends to join in as well. A good example of this technique is that used by MeMail.com and which can be more simply called word-of-mouth recommendation. This Canadian publisher of over 47 e-magazines with more than 400,000 members in 124 countries boasts that 97 percent of its new subscribers come from referrals from existing members. After reading a news story or a joke, subscribers are encouraged to pass these on to a friend or family member, leading them back to MeMail's site and acting as a direct but subtle endorsement for the brand. Contrary to spam, MeMail's "mail this to a friend" feature does not carry the same negative stigma because it is the customer who digitally spreads the word. The principle behind viral marketing is that people are more likely to respond to an invitation that was initiated by a friend than one that comes from persons they are not familiar with.

AFFILIATE PROGRAMS **Affiliate programs** are arrangements made between e-commerce sites that direct users from one site to the other. If a sale is made as a result, the originating site receives a commission. Usually this is done using an online ad in combination with some measure of effectiveness such as **click-throughs**—a count of the number of people who visit one site, click on an ad, and are taken to the site of the advertiser. With click-throughs, software is able to determine the source of visitors to the destination site and give an accurate count of the number who "clicked through" from the source site so that the source can be compensated. For example, Amazon.com has over 500,000 associates, Web sites with ads directing customer traffic to the Amazon.com site. Every time a customer clicking on the Amazon.com ad on an associate's Web site buys something at Amazon.com, the associate receives a commission of up to 15 percent of the amount of the sale. Information on Amazon.com's associate program is available on its Web site (see Figure 5.4).

SELLING TO EXISTING CUSTOMERS One of the keys to success in the B2C space is to encourage customers to continue to buy from you. As in traditional businesses, B2C entrepreneurs call this "repeat business." It doesn't do you much good to spend a lot of money on marketing programs if customers buy from you only once. One of the most effective ways of generating repeat business is to build a customer database and use it for e-mail permission marketing. As you recall, unlike spam, permission marketing entails giving a merchant permission to send you offers.

Now we'll show you how one prominent B2C retailer, eBags (www.ebags.com), is using a combination of techniques on its path to profitability: online ads, affiliate pro-

Figure 5.4

How to Become an Amazon.com Associate

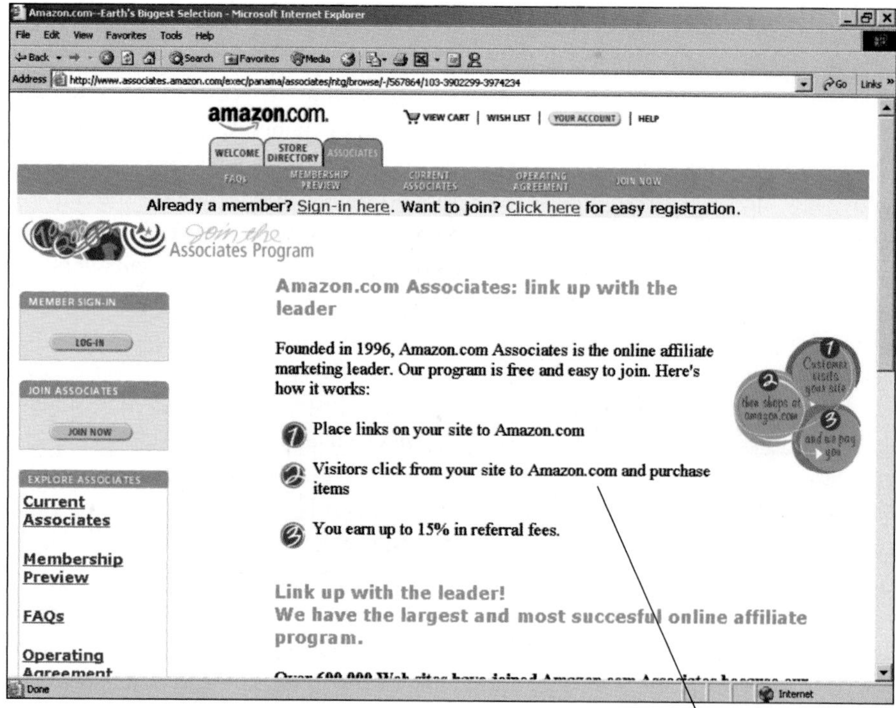

Here's how it works.

grams, and ads in traditional media. Its Web site is well designed, easy to use, and content-rich, with multi-view photos of products, detailed product descriptions, and customer ratings.

It is building a database of customers and asks for permission to e-mail them information on special offerings at reduced prices, using a frequent flyer mileage sweepstakes and viral marketing to help build the database. As customers return to the site, eBags analyzes their usage patterns and learns which products they're most interested in. It adds this information to its database and uses powerful data mining tools to help personalize offers to its customers.

It keeps track of the **conversion rate**—the percentage of customers who visit the site who actually buy something—and the amount of the average sale. Knowing the number of visits it receives each day, as well as the conversion rate and average sale amount, eBags can easily project sales revenue per day. Knowing its costs, it is able to determine where its breakeven point lies. It can also quickly forecast the effect on profits if it's able to increase the number of visitors to the site, increase the conversion rate, or increase the average sale amount.

REMEMBER THE IMPORTANCE OF MERCHANDISING

A B2C business must do an effective job of merchandising. That means it must understand its customer base well enough to be able to select products that will appeal to them and that are attractively displayed. An example of a company that does this well is RedEnvelope (www.redenvelope.com). RedEnvelope is a site that specializes in gifts (see Figure 5.5). It takes its name from the Asian tradition of presenting gifts in a red envelope to signify good fortune, love, and appreciation. It is a site worth visiting to see how an e-tailer has combined attractive design, ease of use, and skillful product selection. It offers a wide variety of products for the giftgiver. One of its most creative features is a category called "Express Gifts," designed to serve procrastinators. If you

Clicking here will take you to the Express Gifts page. Great when you're late!

Figure 5.5
RedEnvelope's Home Page: A Very Well Designed Site

TEAM WORK

EVALUATING COMPETING WEB SITES

Along with two or three classmates, select and compare the Web sites of two local retailers that are in the same business. For example, you might choose two bicycle shops, two musical instrument stores, or two pet shops, but the choice is yours. Use the list of "dos and don'ts" from Figure 5.3 to compare the two sites, along with other criteria you might like to add. Look at the range of information resources and services used in the sites and the ways they are organized, designed, and presented.

The basic question your group should attempt to answer is how well the sites support the conduct of e-commerce. After analyzing the sites, prepare a set of PowerPoint slides comparing the strengths and weaknesses of the two sites. Draw a conclusion as to which one you think does the better job of attracting customers to the Web site and retaining them once they get there. Also comment on how well you think each site does in:

- Offering a fast and convenient shopping experience
- Providing access to help or additional information
- Selecting desirable products and displaying them and describing them in an attractive and easy-to-understand manner
- Describing its method for getting your purchase to you promptly
- Using online ads, affiliate programs, viral marketing, and e-mail marketing

In your presentation, please be sure to highlight important similarities and differences between the two sites. In the conclusion, explain which one your team liked the best, and why, as well as what you learned from this analysis.

order a gift from this category before midnight, RedEnvelope guarantees that it will be delivered the next day.

YOU MUST EXECUTE WELL

Executing well simply means that when a customer places an order on your Web site, you have to follow through and execute the necessary business processes to get the right item to the customer in a timely fashion. A good B2C sites immediately sends an e-mail acknowledgment of the order, containing all of the order details and an estimated shipping date. Thus, the customer is reassured the order is received and is being processed. An order number and instructions for follow-up with customer service is also included. When the order is shipped, the customer receives another e-mail giving details on the shipment such as a carrier tracking number and expected delivery date.

Making it easy to return unwanted items is also important. Some B2C companies include easy cost-free instructions for returning items along with each shipment. Clicks-and-mortar companies have an advantage in this respect if they permit online customers to return items to the local store. Part of the shakeout among online toy retailers began during the holiday selling season in 1999, when toys were not delivered in time for Christmas morning. The reputations of some retailers suffered so much by their failure to execute well that they never recovered.

WATCH THE COMPETITION

Watching the competition is good advice for any business, but it's especially important for B2C businesses. The reason for this is that, as we have previously discussed, retaining customers is one of the keys to e-commerce success. Because it is so easy to lose a customer to a competitor who comes up with a better idea, it's important to be alert to what the competition is up to. You should try to "get inside the heads" of your competitors as a way of anticipating what their next move might be. Put yourself in their place. What would you do next if you were them?

There are a number of ways you can do this. If you're a retailer in the bricks-and-mortar world, it's important to keep an eye on what your competition is doing. For example, if you walk into the conference room of a supermarket's office, you'll likely find the walls plastered with their newspaper ads side by side with those of their competitors. Since the Web has global reach, however, you could have thousands of competitors offering the same products as you. You could spend time on the Web surfing around seeing what's going on in your competitive space by looking at the Web sites of known competitors, or use one of the Web-based shopping comparison services to compare your prices and delivery options to the competition's.

You could also use the services of a company such as RivalWatch (www.rivalwatch.com), which, for a price, will monitor the activities of as many Web-based competitors as your company can identify. It will inform you on the competition's pricing, product assortment, availability, and even promotional activities. RivalWatch is careful to point out that all of the information they gather on behalf of their clients is publicly available. It's just that most clients don't have the software power to gather and analyze the information for themselves.

Business-to-Business E-Commerce

B2B e-commerce is e-commerce that takes place between organizations. As we mentioned earlier in this chapter, B2B is where the most money will be spent. Trade is global; companies do business with other companies in countries all over the world. You probably have an idea how common this is, if you look at the tag inside your blouse or shirt and see Malaysia, Sri Lanka, Peru, or Mongolia.

If you look at the total amount of money that is spent on buying and selling products and services, you'll find that most of it is spent by businesses selling to each other or governments buying from businesses. For example, in order to run an airline, you have to spend a lot of money buying aircraft, fuel, spare parts, and the like. Most such purchases are made from other companies rather than from individuals. To turn it around, by far most of the sales Canadair makes are to airline companies rather than individual consumers. Common estimates are that somewhere between 85 and 90 percent of commerce expenditures are in the B2B space, and that 85 to 90 percent of e-commerce dollars will also be spent in the B2B space. Clearly, B2B e-commerce is worth learning more about.

One of the most important ways that B2B e-commerce contrasts with B2C e-commerce is in the importance of relationships. In B2C e-commerce, establishing a relationship with your customer is important because you want customers to return to your Web site to buy from you again, rather than lose them to a competitor. In the B2B space, relationships are even more important. Businesses tend to form longer-term relationships with some of their most trusted trading partners. Suppose you're the manager of production in a manufacturing firm when you suddenly get an unexpectedly large rush order from one of your best customers. It will be much easier for you to order the necessary materials you need to build and fill that order if your suppliers are people you've done business with over a period of years. They know you, you know them, and just like a friend you can count on them to step in and help you out when you need it. Think of how difficult obtaining those needed materials would be if you tried to obtain them quickly from companies you had never done business with before.

VALUE NETWORKS

Relationships are taking on new forms in the e-commerce environment. Peter Keen and Mark McDonald note that e-commerce "more and more involves a complex network of relationships to operate between the enterprise, its customers, intermediaries, complementors and suppliers"[17] (see Figure 5.6). **Intermediaries** are specialist companies that provide services better than its client companies can themselves. Examples include such categories as call centres and UPS deliveries. **Complementors** provide products and services that complement the offerings of the enterprise and thereby extend its value-adding capabilities to its customers. Yahoo!, for example, has 10,000 complementors providing services such as weather information, financial news, general news, and so forth that add value to the Yahoo! site. Keen and McDonald go on to emphasize the importance of trading partner relationships in forming a company's value network. A **value network** is all of the resources behind the click on a Web page that the customer doesn't see, but that together create the customer relationship—service, order fulfillment, shipping, financing, information brokering, and access to other products and offers. Some of these resources are provided by software, some are outsourced to trusted trading partners, some are provided by electronic links to alliance partners, and others are handled by more efficient and effective business processes. Managers now have many more choices in how to deliver products and services to you when, where, and how you want them. If a trusted trading partner can perform an essential function better than your company can internally, you have the potential for a winning combination for yourself, your trading partner, and your customer.

CORPORATE PURCHASING SEGMENTS

In the B2B space, most attention has traditionally been given to the ways that e-commerce could streamline the purchasing of materials. This does not mean that e-commerce applications such as in sales, transportation, and payments are not important and growing areas; it simply means that attention has been devoted to purchasing because this is where the most money is spent. Purchasing applications are usually divided into three segments:

1. Purchasing of direct materials
2. Purchasing of indirect (MRO) materials
3. Purchasing of services

Figure 5.6
The Value Network

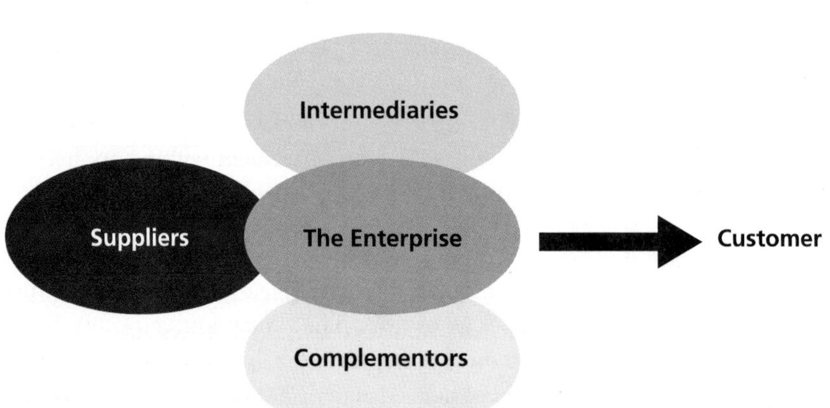

WHAT ABOUT B2C E-BUSINESS?

A report released in 2001 suggests that the Canadian government's plan to "make Canada the most connected nation in the world" may become a reality by 2003 when an estimated 73 out of every 100 Canadians will be connected. This would put Canada at the head of other G7 countries such as the United States and the United Kingdom.

This rapid increase in users is being mirrored by the ever-growing percentage of Canadian households who are purchasing online, which should hit 30 percent by 2003, up from up 12.3 percent in 2000. However, the report warns that while the number of Canadians buying online continues to grow, many Canadian companies are not capitalizing on this. Canadian retail presence over the Internet is actually diminishing, particularly for SMEs. As a result, about 45 percent of Canadian current online purchases are with companies outside of Canada, predominantly with those in the United States.

David Conklin and Marc Trudeau at the School of Business Administration at the University of Western Ontario have suggested that several factors are to blame, including a significant difference in business culture between Canada and the United States. Canadian business leaders tend to be more risk-averse and do not fully appreciate the Internet's potential; they also warn that the future does not look particularly bright. Higher salaries and lower taxes in the United States are leading to an exodus of Canadian entrepreneurial talent. As such, a danger facing Canadian e-tailers and all Canadian e-commerce companies is that American firms will increasingly look north as a land of e-opportunity. In fact, many U.S. companies, such as E*TRADE, are already setting up subsidiaries in Canada.

As a future graduate from a Canadian university and potential e-entrepreneur, what initiatives do you suggest the Canadian government and our business community take to stimulate Canadian retail presence online?[18]

Direct materials are materials used in production in a manufacturing company or placed on the shelf for sale in a retail environment. They are called "direct" because they have a direct relation to the company's primary business. **Indirect materials** (commonly called MRO materials) are materials that are necessary for running a modern corporation, but that do not relate to the company's primary business activities. MRO is an acronym for *m*aintenance, *r*epair, and *o*perations. Examples of MRO materials are ballpoint pens, three-ring binders, repair parts, and lubricating oil.

Examples of purchased services are corporate travel, consulting services, and hiring of part-time workers. Although there are B2B solutions for the purchase of services, most activity in the B2B space is focused on either direct materials or MRO, so this is where we'll focus our discussion.

PURCHASING OF DIRECT MATERIALS One of the most important contributions to a company's effectiveness made by its purchasing department is in the purchase of direct materials: searching out reliable sources of supply, negotiating price, quality, and delivery performance expectations, and monitoring supplier performance. In the typical setting, a purchasing department reaches an agreement with a supplier on the basis of an estimate of quantity required over the course of a year. Then, as goods are needed to satisfy production requirements, the supplier is asked to ship a certain amount to one or more factory or store locations. The requested quantity is determined by the purchasing company's current needs, often by a just-in-time (JIT) or collaborative planning, forecasting, and replenishment (CPFR) system.

The foundation of B2B e-commerce—and in dollar volume the most important form of B2B e-commerce today—is electronic data interchange. **Electronic data interchange (EDI)** is the direct computer-to-computer transfer of transaction

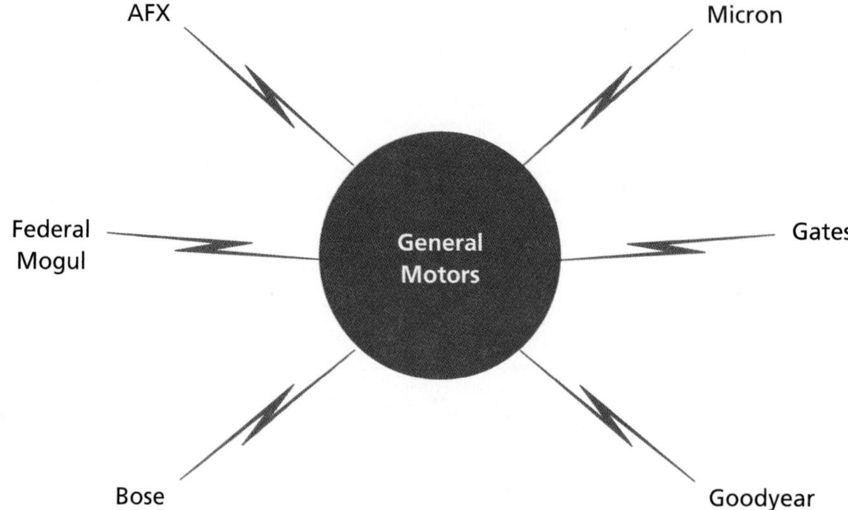

Figure 5.7
An EDI Hub-and-Spoke Arrangement

information contained in standard business documents such as invoices and purchase orders, in a standard format. EDI replaces paper documents with digital records exchanged between trading partners' computers. Although EDI can be and is used to support MRO purchasing, it is most commonly used to support the purchase of direct materials.

EDI data spread in what is called a "hub-and-spoke" manner, as shown in Figure 5.7. For example, suppose a large company such as GM (the hub) decides to use EDI to support a JIT manufacturing process at its assembly plants. The purchasing department at GM notifies its parts suppliers (such as Gates Rubber Company—the spoke) that it expects Gates to be able to use EDI from now on.

While there are other ways to exchange digital information between businesses, EDI practitioners say that if it doesn't meet the three criteria in the definition above it is not EDI. To expand on this:

1. *Computer-to-computer exchange* means just that. It must travel from one company's computer system to another's over a telecommunications network of some sort, be it a private network, a value-added network (VAN), or the Internet. (For more discussion on network options, please see Extended Learning Module D.)
2. *Standard business documents* means that EDI is restricted to standard business forms such as purchase orders, purchase releases, advance shipping notices, invoices, and the like, and not freeform business correspondence such as business letters.
3. *Standard format* means that trading partners have agreed that the digital information exchanged will be in a standard format so that the computer systems at either company can interpret what is being transmitted and use it for further processing without human intervention. Companies using EDI have developed national and international EDI standards so that the same data formats are widely used. The most commonly used standards in North America and Europe are ASC X12 and UN/EDIFACT, respectively.

Value-added networks (VANs) make it easier for trading partners to establish telecommunications links with each other. Rather than sending EDI transactions directly from a hub company to a spoke company, or vice versa, companies usually send a stream of orders to many trading partners directly to a VAN. The VAN places

Figure 5.8
How Value-Added Networks (VANs) Facilitate EDI

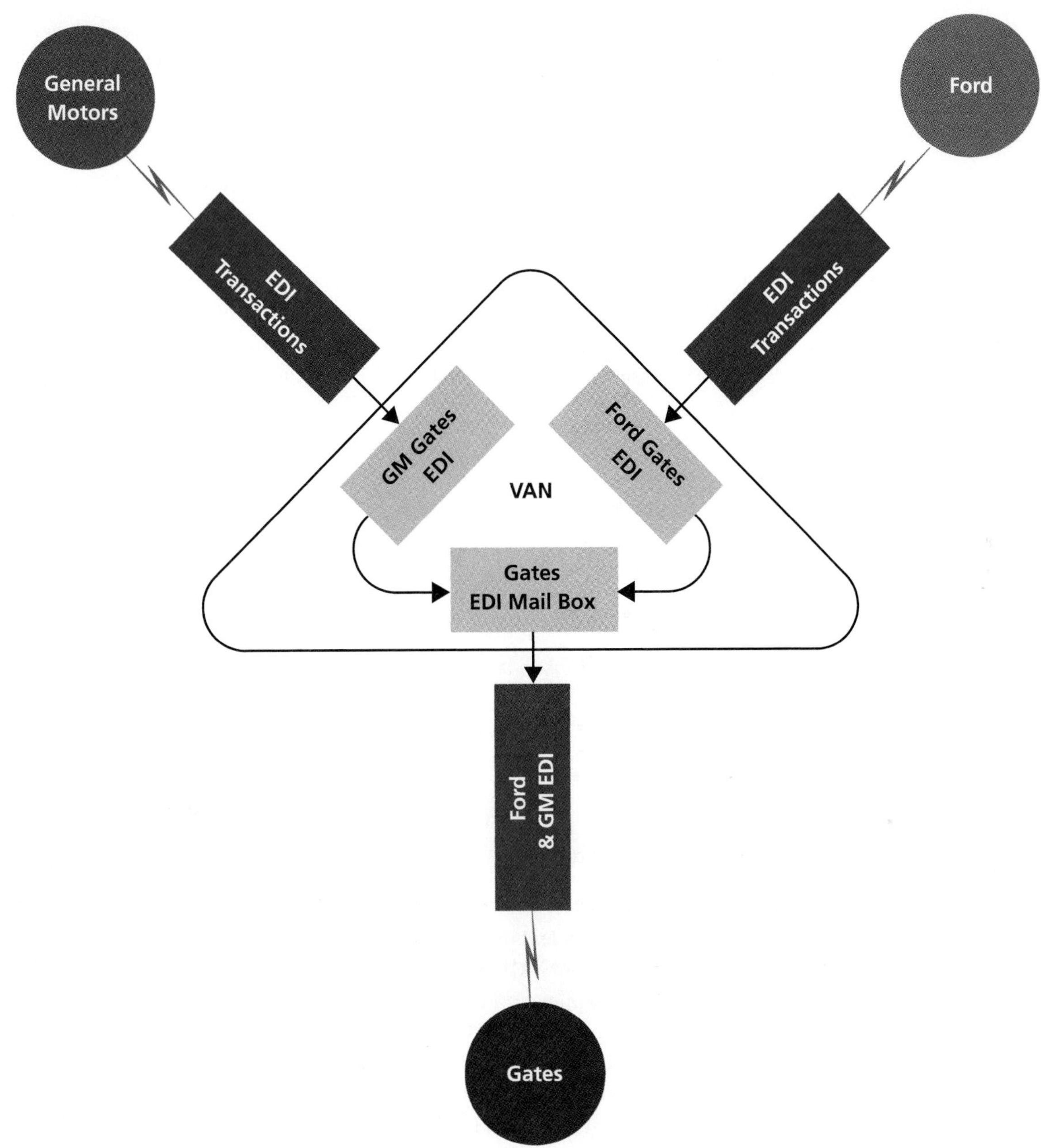

them in an electronic mailbox for each trading partner. Other trading partners do the same thing. Then, once or twice a day, for example, Gates' computer connects with the VAN and downloads all EDI transactions from all of its trading partners at one time, as illustrated in Figure 5.8. VANs also provide translation services between different versions of EDI standards, audit services, and control services, and will even translate EDI messages from hubs to fax messages for smaller spokes who are not prepared to conduct true EDI.

An increasingly popular and less costly alternative to VANs is **virtual private networks (VPNs)**, which use software to establish a secure channel on the Internet for transmitting data.

PURCHASING OF INDIRECT (MRO) MATERIALS Most corporate purchasing departments do not want to be bothered with the paperwork required to process purchase orders for maintenance, repair, and operations (MRO) materials, but at the same time they do not want to let MRO purchases go completely uncontrolled. While the amounts on individual MRO purchase orders are small, collectively they can add up. To deal with this problem, many purchasing departments negotiate with MRO providers for discounted prices on a range of items. Then, the MRO supplier prints a custom catalogue for the company showing the items that can be ordered together with a price sheet. If an administrative assistant needs to order supplies, he or she finds the item in the catalogue and calls the MRO supplier, and the item is delivered.

E-commerce solutions for MRO do about what you would expect them to. The supplier replaces the paper catalogue with an electronic catalogue accessible through a Web browser. Powerful search engines locate the items needed. The administrative assistant orders the MRO item over the Internet in a manner similar to the way he or she orders a B2C item, and it is delivered the next morning.

NEXT-GENERATION SOLUTIONS: XML AND WEB SERVICES

There are several efforts under way now to create a new generation of EDI for B2B transactions that would be easier to set up and use, and more attractive to smaller companies. The vision for the next generation of EDI is one in which a company could create a purchase order on a PC Web form, and send it out over the Internet to a company it has never done business with before. The transaction would contain within itself access to the information a computer at the receiving company needs to interpret it and begin to process it, much the same as if it were a purchase order received in the mail and opened by a human. Most of the next-generation EDI efforts involve the Internet as a substitute for private networks or VANs, because the Internet is cheaper. Also, most of them are built around an emerging technology for creating Web documents called **XML (extensible markup language)**—a coding language for the Web that lets computers interpret the *meaning* of information in Web documents.

Most Web documents now are developed using the HTML coding language. HTML uses tags to tell a browser what a Web page should look like. For example, HTML can tell your browser that a line of text should be capitalized or in colour. XML also uses tags, but the advantage of XML is that its tags define what the text actually means. Compare the two Web snippets in Figure 5.9. The one on the left is coded in HTML; the one on the right is coded in XML. The important thing to notice is that in the XML document, the tags inserted around "Charles" and "Cadwell," for example, let you or a computer know that "Charles" is the person's first name and "Cadwell" is his last name.

XML is more useful than HTML in many ways. As just one example, search engines will find relevant information much more easily if they know the meaning of the text between the tags. For B2B e-commerce, however, the value of XML is that business documents created for the Web can be easily created and understood by trading partners' computers. This makes B2B e-commerce more accessible and affordable to small and medium-sized businesses and will hasten the spread of B2B e-commerce. Two of several possibilities for B2B e-commerce in the spotlight now are ebXML and Web Services.

ebXML (electronic business XML) is a set of technical specifications for business documents built around XML designed to permit enterprises of any size and in any geographical location to conduct business over the Internet.[19,20] Think of it as a replacement for current EDI standards like ASC X12 or UN/EDIFACT. Small companies tend to avoid using EDI unless an important customer insists on it because they find the current standards complex and expensive.

ON YOUR OWN

A RANGE OF POSSIBILITIES FOR NEXT-GENERATION EDI

Below are links to Web sites of some of the companies or groups working on alternatives to traditional EDI where XML plays a role. Take a look at each of them and find one that, in your opinion, holds the most promise for the future. Feel free to seek articles on the Web that compare and contrast the alternative approaches to support your conclusions.

- *Electronic business XML (ebXML).* www.ebxml.org
- *Web Services.* www.w3.org/2002/ws
- *.Net (Microsoft).* www.microsoft.com/net
- *WebSphere (IBM).* www-3.ibm.com/software/info1/websphere
- *Sun ONE (Sun Microsystems).* www.sun.com/sunone

The second approach getting a lot of attention is Web Services. While the Internet makes it easy for anyone with a Web browser to obtain information from Web sites no matter what sort of computer it resides on, it can still be difficult for computer systems to get information from other computer systems that have not be designed to share information widely. This is a problem for many corporations who have separate computer applications for different business units. For example, your college or university may have separate computer systems for registration, student academic records, student financial records, and campus residence information. It can be very difficult to compile a complete profile on you because the individual computer systems do not talk to each other easily. Naturally, separate companies have different computer systems, so it is also difficult for trading partners to easily share information for B2B e-commerce applications. Web Services is designed to address this issue.

Web Services consists of software applications that talk to other software applications over the Internet using XML as a key enabling technology.[21] Initial applications of Web Services are focused on internal applications so a company's computer systems work together more easily. This is because companies want to get some experience with it before extending it to their supply chain partners. The ultimate vision for

Figure 5.9

A Person's Name Coded in HTML and in XML

The Phrase "Mr. Charles Johnson Cadwell IV" in HTML	The Phrase "Mr. Charles Johnson Cadwell IV" in XML
<B>Mr. Charles Johnson Cadwell IV</B>	<PersonName><PersonNameTitle> Mr.</PersonNameTitle>
	<PersonGivenName>Charles</PersonGivenName>
	<PersonMiddleName>Johnson </PersonMiddleName>
	<PersonSurname>Cadwell</PersonSurname>
	<PersonNameSuffix>IV</PersonNameSuffix> <PersonName>

Note how the *XML tags convey the meaning* of the information between the tags. HTML simply presents the information and provides formatting instructions (which XML can do also). For more information on HTML coding, refer to Skills Module 3 on the CD-ROM accompanying this text.

NEW OPPORTUNITIES AND CHALLENGES: OFFICE SUPPLY COMPANIES ATTRACT UNWANTED ATTENTION

Many office supply companies have successfully hit the Net, but so have activist organizations. Established in 1882, Toronto-based Grand & Toy is one of the few genuinely successful online B2B retailers. In 2001, the company reported more than $100 million in sales through its Web site. Yet this Canadian company, like many others in North America, has found that the Internet provides not only new opportunities but new challenges as well. As a Canadian subsidiary of lumber and paper giant Boise Cascade Corp., the company has been on the front lines in a growing battle with forest conservation groups. Boise, Grand & Toy's parent company, has come under heavy fire from the Rainforest Action Network (RAN). This environmental group has successfully used the Internet to gain exposure and to rally support for its cause. Their goal is to use media, including the Web, to put pressure on companies so that they change their business practices. For instance, in 2001, visitors to RAN's site (www.ran.org) were greeted with an unsightly image of a devastated forest with the words "Behind the Scenes at Boise Cascade Office Products."

Previously, after being individually targeted by the group, hundreds of leading companies such as Kinko's, Home Depot, and Lowe's decided to give in and pledged to stop selling products made from endangered forests, but not Boise. The company decided to resist and wage a public relations war against RAN that lasted for more than two years. In an attempt to counteract the group's successful use of the Internet to rally public support, Boise launched its own site aimed at discrediting the group, branding them as environmental extremists (www.ranamuck.org). During the hostilities, organizations such Kinko's, L. L. Bean, and the University of Notre Dame stopped buying paper from Boise rather than feel RAN's wrath. A loss of $50 million resulted from Kinko's defection alone. In the spring of 2002, Boise announced it would stop cutting centuries-old trees by 2004, a practice known as old-growth logging. Although the company continues to deny that it buckled under to RAN's pressure tactics, RAN is taking part of the credit; but it alleges that Boise is still involved in deforestation in many countries. Michael Brune, spokesman for RAN, vows to continue the pressure: "We'll run them out of old-growth or we'll run them out of business."[22]

Web Services, though, is to make it easier for separate companies to do business together electronically.

The next generation of EDI, whatever form(s) it eventually takes, should truly make the benefits of electronic exchange of standard business documents available to companies of all sizes, all over the world. The On Your Own project in this section asks you to compare some of the current ideas for next generation of EDI that are currently in the works.

B2B MARKETPLACES

B2B marketplaces seem to be a natural for the Web. **B2B marketplaces** are Internet-based services which bring together buyers and sellers. They have the potential to bring together large numbers of buyers and sellers, thereby giving buyers more choices and aggregating demand for the sellers. Transaction costs can be reduced, resulting in potential savings for both buyers and sellers. The company operating a marketplace often has software that facilitates matching buyers and sellers and helps them with the transaction. One commonly used technique is to have the marketplace conduct a reverse auction. **Reverse auction** is the process in which a buyer posts its interest in buying a certain quantity of items, and sellers compete for the business by submitting successively lower bids until there is only one seller left. Marketplaces usually make their money by charging a transaction fee for their services. For example, FreeMarkets, Inc. (www.freemarkets.com) is a company that holds auctions so corporations can buy industrial parts, materials, and services from suppliers via the Internet. Recently, one of its customers, Cooper Industries Inc., used FreeMarkets to get bids for its air freight service. It attracted 11 bidders, and the increased competition for their business saved them $1.2 million. More than 19,000 suppliers from more than 70 countries have bid through FreeMarkets since 1995. Of course, companies don't have to use a company like FreeMarkets to conduct an auction. They can arrange one of their own or join together in an industry group, as the automobile companies have done with Covisint (www.covisint.com).

B2B marketplaces are still evolving, and as we have come to see with other e-commerce ventures, not all of them will succeed. They seem to hold the most promise in the MRO space, inasmuch as relationships are often not as important there because the risks of doing business with a new supplier are lower. Working with a new direct materials supplier presents risks of shutting down an assembly line because of late delivery or quality problems. In addition, you have to remember that the legacy EDI systems of many large companies are the way that the supply chain is managed, and these systems, while complicated to set up, are working well. Finally, many suppliers will try to avoid letting anyone get between them and their customers. (Remember in Chapter 2 how we described all the tactics the airlines are using to recapture their best customers from travel agents.)

INTRANETS AND EXTRANETS

An **intranet** is an internal organizational Internet guarded against outside access by special security software called a *firewall* (see Figure 5.10). An **extranet** is an intranet that is restricted to an organization and certain outsiders, such as customers and suppliers. In contrast to intranets and extranets, the Internet can be accessed by anyone, although, of course, many Web sites require user names and passwords for access.

HOW INTRANETS ARE USED Intranets are used to facilitate communication within an organization and to manage many internal business processes. It would be hard for

Figure 5.10
Intranet Structure

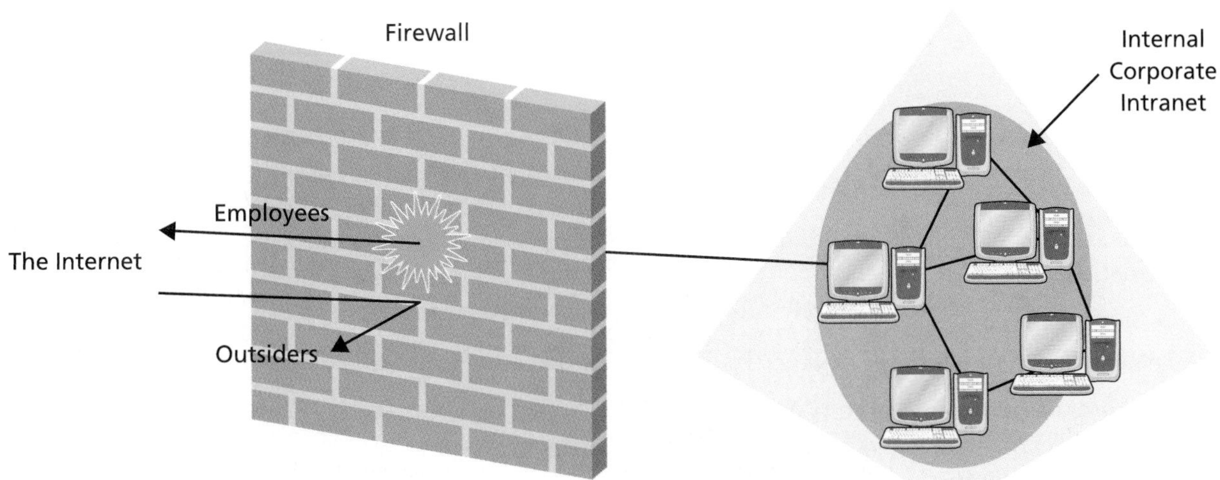

you to go into a modern office today and not see a PC on almost every desk. Giving employees access to information via their Web browsers that used to be available on paper can result in tremendous cost savings as well as provide assurance that the corporate intranet has the most current information available. For example, just about every organization of any size has an employee handbook in which the human resources department expounds policies regarding fringe benefits, vacations, sick leave, and the like. Putting the handbook on the intranet makes it readily accessible to most employees, and when changes are made, a broadcast e-mail can be sent out asking employees to take note. Intranet applications can range from simple ones such as these to putting expense reports and other forms online, as well as newsletters, employee feedback, and sophisticated knowledge management systems.

HOW EXTRANETS ARE USED Extranet applications expand the audience to include persons external to the organization, most often customers and suppliers. Extranets are used to share product, inventory, and other information and news, and as a collaboration platform for joint projects. They can be the vehicle for implementing more advanced supply chain management and customer relationship management systems.

Customer relationship management (CRM) systems use information about customers to gain insight into their needs, wants, and behaviours in order to serve them better. CRM systems can enable a company to obtain a complete picture of all of its relationships with a customer and identify areas where better services are needed. For example, if someone has a mortgage, an auto loan, and a large personal chequing account with one bank, it makes sense for the bank to treat this person well each time it has any contact with him or her. Treating customers well may include giving them personalized access to information on all of their accounts on an extranet.[23]

See Figure 5.11 for a schematic of an extranet.

The Role of E-Government

E-government is the application of e-commerce technologies in governmental agencies. It is a great place to use e-commerce technologies now and could be an employment opportunity for you.

Figure 5.11

Extranet Structure

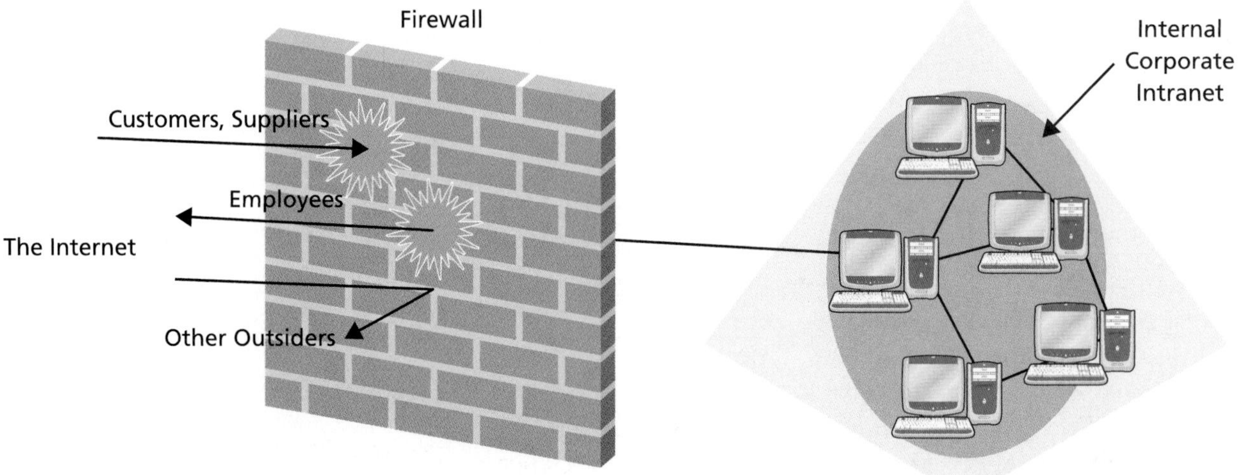

Many government agencies have long been active in using e-commerce technologies in the purchase of direct and indirect materials. Earlier, we talked about how hub companies encourage small and medium-sized companies to adopt e-commerce technologies like EDI. Well, in most countries, the federal government is by far the largest hub of all.

In most cases, governments have lagged behind the private sector in the application of e-commerce technologies. In some areas, however, the government is actually leading the private sector. One example is in the adoption of biometrics for access to secured areas and in the use of face recognition technology for detecting persons who might present security threats at airports.

Currently, there is a lot of activity in the e-government space in using the Internet to provide better services and information to citizens. In a way, you're a customer of your government, but all too often you are not treated as a valued customer. This is changing with e-government initiatives. Governments are asking themselves how they could serve you better, and coming up with ways to do so. Ask yourself how well your government agencies are treating you as a customer. (If they were a company, would you buy their stock?)

One issue that e-government must deal with is the digital divide, discussed earlier in this chapter. Since access to Internet technologies is tilted in favour of citizens at the higher ends of the income scale, governments must devise solutions to be sure that all citizens have access to e-government services. While governments are not likely to give PCs and free Internet access to those who can't afford it anytime soon, they can try to devise solutions that can serve lower-income groups. One example is the use of ATMs to distribute welfare payments instead of sending cheques through the mail or using electronic direct deposits to chequing accounts. (Many welfare recipients do not have bank accounts.)

E-Commerce Payment Systems

Just as there are traditional EDI transactions for purchase orders and other standard business documents, there are EDI transactions for payments. The use of EDI for payments is called **financial EDI (FEDI)**. FEDI has not gained the same acceptance as EDI for one simple reason. Corporate treasurers, who are responsible for managing corporate cash, have not seen it to be advantageous to speed up payments to suppliers. When a payment is dropped into the mail, the payer can earn interest on the money until the cheque is cashed by the supplier. Oftentimes, corporate treasurers will see that a payment is mailed in time to reach the supplier by the due date, but the cheque will be drawn on a bank in another part of the country that will take days to clear. An electronic payment would clear much faster, and the payer would lose the use of that money for those extra few days.

Next-generation EDI approaches include FEDI transactions as a part of their proposed solutions. Still, the obstacle to more widespread acceptance of FEDI is not technical, but the reluctance of human beings to change their business processes. In Canada, the federal government is moving forward aggressively with electronic payments, encouraging them for businesses and for direct deposits to the bank accounts of pension recipients whenever possible.

CREDIT CARDS AND SMART CARDS

In many countries, credit cards are the most common method of payment for e-commerce transactions, particularly in the B2C space. In the early years of B2C, consumers

Figure 5.12

The PayPal Web Site

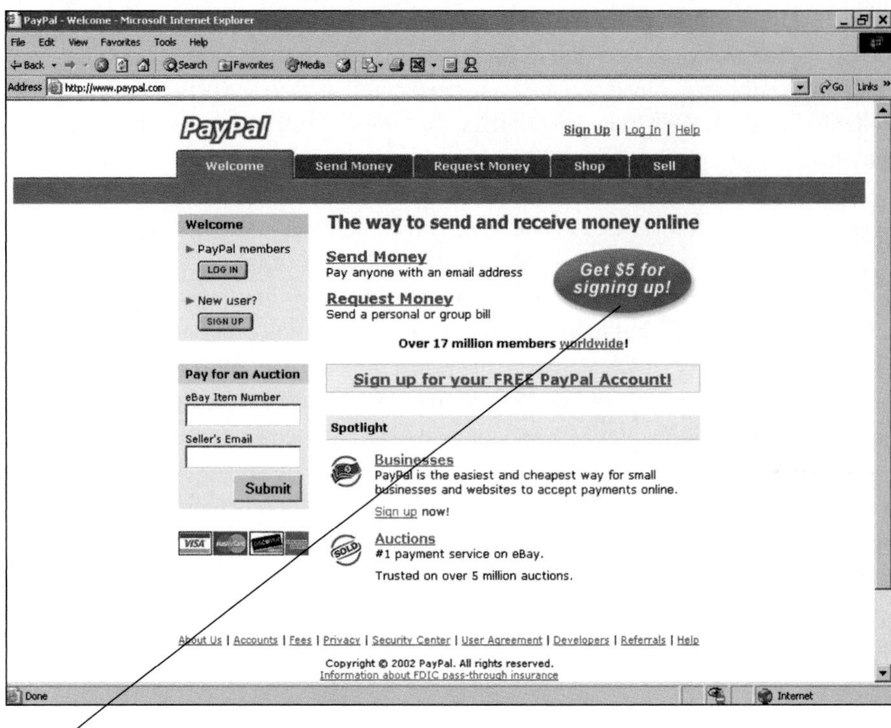

It's easy to sign up, and they'll give you $5 if you do.

were reluctant to enter their credit card numbers on a Web site for fear that they would be stolen. Then it was pointed out that you were much more likely to have your credit card number stolen by a waiter or waitress in a restaurant than by a thief lurking on the Internet. Still, the lack of widespread use of credit cards by consumers in some countries, such as China and India, creates hurdles that B2C companies in such countries will have to overcome.

One option that has been experimented with for some time is **smart cards**—plastic cards the size of a credit card that contain an embedded chip on which digital information can be stored. When the information is monetary, the smart card is called a *stored value card*. One of the best-known smart card initiatives is Mondex (www.mondex.com). The Mondex chip contains an "electronic purse" that is loaded with electronic cash and then spent at retailers who have a Mondex card reader. Electronic cash is transferred from the buyer's card to the seller's device. Electronic cash is added to the card using a telephone connection to your bank.

The Mondex solution is one possible answer to the micro-payments issue we discussed earlier in this chapter, making it possible to purchase low-value items on the Internet. We discuss more about Internet digital cash and smart cards in the Chapter 9.

FINANCIAL CYBERMEDIARIES

Financial cybermediaries are Internet-based companies that make it easy for one person to pay another person over the Internet. One of the best known, and another e-commerce success story, is PayPal (www.paypal.com). PayPal makes it easy for individuals to exchange money for goods or services purchased over the Internet. It is particularly useful in C2C-space electronic auctions, but you can use it anytime you want to send money to another person over the Internet. You create an account by logging on to the PayPal site (see Figure 5.12) and providing personal data and credit card information. When you want to send money, you simply go to the PayPal site and enter the person's name and e-mail address, and the amount you want to send. The payee receives an e-mail notification that the cash has been deposited in his or her PayPal account. They can transfer the cash to a chequing account, request a cheque, send the funds to someone else, or just leave it there awhile.

ELECTRONIC BILL PRESENTMENT AND PAYMENT

We all get bills in the mail every month, from the gas and electric company, the telephone company, the cable TV provider, department stores, and credit card companies. It costs money for the companies to print and mail the bills, and it costs us money to put a cheque in the mail. A technique called **electronic bill presentment and payment (EBPP)** is just beginning to take hold to reduce the time and paper in this process (and save some trees in the process). These systems send us our bills over the Internet and give us an easy way to pay them if the amount looks correct. Electronic bill payment systems available through our local banks or such services as Checkfree and Quicken have been around for a while. What is different about EBPP systems is that our bills appear on a Web site or arrive in our e-mail inboxes instead of our home mailboxes.

Summary: Student Learning Outcomes Revisited

1. **Describe the four main perspectives of e-commerce, its current status, and the global growth expected in the next few years.** There are four main perspectives for e-commerce, business-to-business (B2B), business-to-consumer (B2C), consumer-to-business (C2B), and consumer-to-consumer (C2C). Experts who are in the business of forecasting the growth of global e-commerce may differ in their estimates, but all agree that we can expect to see tremendous growth in the next few years. Most experts think that 85 to 90 percent of e-commerce sales will be in the B2B space.

   Countries in the developed world are more likely to reap the benefits of e-commerce than countries in the lesser developed world. This phenomenon is known as the **digital divide**. Policy experts are searching for ways to close the gap.
2. **Identify the advantages of business-to-consumer (B2C) e-commerce.** B2C e-commerce has several advantages over other methods of retailing, including:
   - Shopping can be faster and more convenient.
   - Offerings and prices can be changed instantaneously.
   - Call centres can be integrated with the Web site.
   - Broadband telecommunications will enhance the buying experience.

   Many traditional retailers are finding that adding the Internet as another channel to their existing channels is a profitable strategy. M-commerce and broadband technologies, when they become more widely available, will offer powerful new ways for retailers to reach their customers.
3. **Describe the techniques that lead to success in B2C e-commerce ventures.** Internet retailers (e-tailers) find that commodity-like products sell best, and that digital products work the best of all, because they can be bought, paid for, and—most of all—delivered immediately. Successful e-tailers have learned the importance of good Web site design and marketing to attract and retain consumers, the importance of merchandising, the importance of executing well, and the need to continuously monitor the competition. E-tailing has become more difficult to succeed in, now that the easy-money early days of the Internet are behind us.
4. **Describe the variety of ways that business to business (B2B) e-commerce technologies are**

being used, and describe next-generation models which may widen the adoption of global B2B e-commerce. While relationships can be important in the B2C space, they tend to be more important in the B2B space because of the interdependencies that exist among trading partners, particularly for direct materials. More complex relationships known as "value networks" are made possible by e-commerce technologies. Relationships tend to be more important in the purchasing of direct materials than in the purchase of indirect materials. Electronic data interchange (EDI) has facilitated the smooth operation of B2B e-commerce, driving paper out of many interorganizational business processes. EDI has not spread beyond large "hub" companies and their smaller "spoke" trading partners, because such a system can be difficult to set up and administer. Next-generation EDI techniques such as ebXML and Web Services hope to address this problem. Internet-based B2B marketplaces using techniques such as reverse auctions hold out the promise of cost savings by making it easier for buyers and sellers to find each other and for buyers to obtain better prices. Their future, however, is as yet unclear. Intranets and extranets are important ways to extend the benefits of Internet technologies to restricted participants such as employees, customers, and suppliers.

5. **Identify the unique aspects of e-government applications.** Many government agencies have fostered the spread of e-commerce by using e-commerce technologies for purchasing and payments. There are tremendous opportunities for governmental bodies to serve citizens better if the potential of the Internet is creatively applied to the provision of governmental services and information.
6. **Describe the status and options for e-commerce payment systems.** Although financial EDI has been available for B2B payments for some time, it has not attained wide acceptance, partly because of corporate treasurers' reluctance to employ it. In B2C space, most e-commerce transactions are paid for with credit cards. Credit card payments have limitations for e-commerce because they are not suitable for small amounts and because there are many countries where the use of credit cards is not so well accepted. **Smart cards** have been proposed as an alternative, but they have not yet achieved widespread acceptance. **Financial cybermediaries** such as PayPal have made significant inroads in making payments over the Internet, particularly in the C2C space. Electronic bill presentment and payment (EBPP) is an emerging technique that holds the promise of driving paper out of the B2C billing process for companies such as utilities, department stores, and credit card companies.

CLOSING CASE STUDY ONE

EBAGS: AN E-COMMERCE SUCCESS STORY

For a real e-commerce success story you don't have to look any further than eBags (www.ebags.com). While many pure-play e-commerce sites have fallen by the wayside, eBags is not only surviving, it is thriving. They are the world's leading online provider of bags and accessories for all lifestyles. With 150 brands and more than 6000 items, eBags has sold more than 1.5 million bags since their launch in March 1999. They carry a complete line of premium and popular brands, including Samsonite, JanSport, North Face, Eagle Creek, and Liz Claiborne. You can buy anything from backpacks and carry-ons to computer cases and handbags at extremely competitive prices from their Web site. You can even do a search, by airline, for bags that meet the airline's carry-on requirements.

They have received several rewards for excellence in online retailing, among them the Bizrate.com "Circle of Excellence Platinum Award," the "Website of the Year" honours at Catalog Age's 16th Annual Catalog/I.Merchant Awards, and the Best Email Marketer Award from ClickZ/Message Media.

A good part of the reason for their success is their commitment to providing each of their customers with superior service, 24 hours a day, 365 days a year. They provide their customers with the ability to contact customer service representatives for personal assistance by telephone or e-mail and also provide convenient, real-time UPS order tracking.

But although you would never know it, this superior customer service is not provided by eBags employees. For the past two years, eBags has outsourced both the handling of phone orders and customer service calls to Finali Corp. (www.finali.com). "The call centre is often the only human contact customers have with our brand," says eBags CEO Jon Nordmark. "By maintaining a call centre staff that can think on its feet, Finali delivers real value to our customers and a measurable return on our call centre investment."

Typically, the conversion rate of inbound customer calls to sales at the call centre has been about 25 percent. But during the 2001 holiday season, special training and incentives for Finali call centre reps servicing the eBags Web site helped raise that number to 44 percent. In addition, the average size of orders placed through the call centre hit $100, topping the average Web order of just over $75. The increased conversion rates and order size meant that for every dollar eBags spent with Finali, Finali generated $3.79 in sales!

eBags announced profits for the first time in December 2001, posting 5.4 percent earnings before interest, taxes, depreciation, and amortization. "Part of that achievement was due to smart outsourcing like the call centre," says eBags CFO Eliot Cobb.

In February 2002, eBags announced a partnership with custom-bag manufacturer Timbuk2 which permits eBags customers to order customized Timbuk2 bags. Timbuk2 (www.timbuk2.com), which launched its e-commerce Web site in 2000, saw its sales over the Internet jump to 50 percent of its total sales. They expect to see their Internet sales climb higher very quickly with the eBags partnership. An option for eBags would have been to simply establish an affiliate relationship with Timbuk2 whereby eBags shoppers would click on a Timbuk2 ad on the eBags site and be taken to the Timbuk2 site to place their order. Instead, eBags chose to integrate Timbuk2's software into its own system and create a feature called "Build a Bag" that allows eBags shoppers to design their own Timbuk2 messenger bags online without leaving the eBags site.

Timbuk2 had already developed the software that let its customers order customized messenger bags, laptop sleeves, and commuter bags. On the messenger bag, for example, customers can specify any one of several sizes, colours, fabrics, and special features such as a centre divider or bottom boot. (A left-handed option is free.)

Before the partnership was established, eBags was already selling Timbuk2's readymade bags on its site. Now, using the Build a Bag option, you can design a Timbuk2 bag to your own specifications from the eBags Web site. If you want to see how it works, just go to www.ebags.com/bagbuilder.

And the partnership is working. Timbuk2 is getting more orders for its customized bags, and eBags customers have even more choices on the eBags site.

Compared to this arrangement, the disadvantage of an affiliate agreement for a retailer the size of eBags is obvious. Why have a setup where a customer must leave your Web site in order to get what she wants? If she stays on your Web site, she might put a few more items in her shopping cart before she leaves.[24]

Questions

1. Pick any two of the advantages of B2C e-commerce discussed in the chapter and describe how eBags has used them to gain a competitive advantage over traditional bricks and mortar retailers of bags and accessories.

2. Do you think that m-commerce or broadband are technologies that could provide an enhanced buying experience for eBags customers when such services become more widely available? Do you see a way that eBags could gain a competitive advantage from being one of the first e-tailers to use one or both of these technologies? Why or why not?

3. This Case Study describes how eBags has chosen to engage a call centre specialist firm, Finali Corp., to handle call centre operations. Refer to the above discussion of value networks and to Figure 5.6. Would you describe Finali Corp.'s relationship with eBags in this venture as a being that of a supplier, an intermediary, or a complementor? Explain the reasons for your choice.

4. This Case Study describes the advantages of the eBags/Timbuk2 relationship over a simple affiliate relationship. What disadvantages are there to this type of relationship to either company?

5. In the chapter, we said that successful B2C e-commerce companies must execute well. Visit eBags at www.ebags.com. What assurances do they give their customers that they will receive the item they ordered when promised? Would you have confidence in ordering from eBags on the basis of what you conclude from examining their site? Why or why not?

CLOSING CASE STUDY TWO

MAKING TOYOTA'S VISION A REALITY

Toyota Motor Corp. has plans to build an IT system that will let it fabricate digitally designed cars and build them in digitally designed factories. When installed, the system will enable Toyota to cut years out of the time it takes to turn concepts into cars. Toyota will use the system to model the entire process of car production, from original design to the development of component parts, to the sequence in which components are assembled, and even to the design of the factory that builds them.

The system is not inexpensive. In order to move forward, Toyota signed a contract worth an estimated $800 million to $1.2 billion for software, hardware, and services. The software is Dassault Systèmes S.A.'s 3D Product Lifecycle Management suite, an integrated set of software that includes design collaboration, product-lifecycle management (PLM), and production-support applications. Implementation will include hardware, software, and services from IBM. Development is expected to take three to five years and will ultimately link Toyota's 56 plants in 25 countries and more than 1000 suppliers. The system will replace Toyota's proprietary CAD platform, Togo, and its homegrown product data management system.

Toyota is revered for quality and efficiency. The fact that it chose third-party software to replace its much-praised, much-studied proprietary production system indicates an acceptance of a core competence strategy and willingness to outsource combined with a strong desire to stay ahead of the car market curve.

In a somewhat unusual series of steps, Toyota visited one of its competitors, DaimlerChrysler, who was already using some of the software they were evaluating and was willing to share their experience with Toyota. Karenann Terrell, director of E-connect, the business-to-business infrastructure group for DaimlerChrysler, said that Toyota was "particularly interested in how DaimlerChrysler was pulling suppliers into the design process using our PLM tools." Dassault's design collaboration software, called Catia, and its PLM management tool, Enovia, cut 60 to 90 percent off the time DaimlerChrysler needed to communicate design changes to suppliers and get back required changes, Terrell said.

The new system will let Toyota's designers collaborate with each other as well as with those 1000 suppliers that will eventually build component parts. Designers from both Toyota and its suppliers will use Catia tools which will permit them to test component designs developed on computers for "manufacturability," that is, how easily they will be able to be manufactured in the first place and, later, installed on cars on the assembly line. To aid in achieving this objective, Toyota intends to start by setting goals for manufacturing efficiency and then work backwards toward a car's concept and design.

The Catia deployment also will let Toyota reuse designs for component parts, such as a hood, in a process known as "morphing." For example, Toyota engineers will be able to search a repository of existing hoods, use Catia's tools to make changes to the design, and automatically test the morphed design for manufacturability.

As engineers work on the design of a new car model, production support software, called Delmia, will let engineering teams use design and manufacturability data to specify the order in which parts should installed in a car as it moves down the production line. Ultimately, engineers will be able to digitally model the entire factory environment, specifying what's done at each stop in the production process; which tools, supplies, and parts will be used; how many people will be stationed at each assembly stop; and exactly what they will do.

Only after all the pieces fit together—the design, the production plan, and the factory-floor strategy—will Toyota roll the specs for the new car model into its production and supply chain management systems. The integration of digital design and digital manufacturing will let Toyota speed new models to market in months rather than years. That's getting increasingly important, because cars have become as much fashion statements as transportation, especially with young people, who buy cars such as the Chrysler PT Cruiser, the Pontiac Vibe, or the Volkswagen Beetle relying on many of the same impulses that guide them when they buy clothes or electronics.

The new system could give Toyota an edge in realizing the ultimate prize for automakers: the ability to build a car to customer specifications and deliver it within days, much as Dell does with computer systems. A marketing model for automobiles that would permit that amount of mass customization is one that would have broad appeal to many buyers. Perhaps someday soon, you'll be able to log on to the Internet, spec out your new car just the way you like it, and have it delivered to your front door.[25]

Questions

1. Refer to the discussion of value networks and to Figure 5.6. Would you describe IBM's relationship with Toyota in this venture as a being that of a supplier, an intermediary, or a complementor? Explain the reasons for your choice.

2. When the new system is implemented, Toyota will get their suppliers involved in the design process earlier than what might normally be the case. In addition, there will be a considerable amount of collaboration all along the way. What are the advantages to the suppliers and to Toyota in doing so?

3. The new system, when operational, will require the use of e-commerce technologies to support the purchase, delivery, and payment for direct materials shipped from Toyota's suppliers to its new plans. Should Toyota plan to use EDI for these purposes or would it be better for them to plan to use one of the next-generation technologies such as ebXML or Web Services? Why or why not?

4. The Case Study mentions that perhaps someday you will be able to mass-customize and order an automobile the way you can mass-customize and order a computer today. Do you think this is a realistic possibility? Is a car really a commodity-like product? What are the obstacles that would need to be overcome to make this idea a reality?

5. Experts have estimated that between 12 and 20 percent of the cost of an automobile is incurred after it is shipped from the factory. Most of this cost is tied up in automobile dealers' inventories. If you could save this amount of money by ordering a new car directly from the factory and bypassing your local dealer, would you do it? Why or why not?

Key Terms and Concepts

affiliate program, 190
B2B marketplace, 200
banner ads, 189
clicks-and-mortar, 181
click-throughs, 190
complementor, 194
conversion rate, 191
customer relationship management (CRM) system, 202
demand aggregation, 179
digital divide, 180
direct material, 195
ebXML (electronic business XML), 198
e-commerce, 178
e-government, 202
electronic data interchange (EDI), 195
electronic bill presentment and payment (EBPP), 205
e-tailer, 181
extensible markup language (XML), 198
extranet, 201
financial cybermediary, 204
financial EDI (FEDI), 203
global digital divide, 180
indirect material, 195
interactive chat, 184
intermediary, 194
Internet telephony, 184
intranet, 201
marketing mix, 187
m-commerce, 181
meta tag, 189
micro-payment, 187
pure play, 181
reverse auction, 200
smart card, 204
spam, 189
value network, 194
viral marketing, 189
virtual private network (VPN), 197
Web Services, 199
XML (extensible markup language), 198

Short-Answer Questions

1. What is the digital divide? What is the global digital divide?
2. In which sector of e-commerce is the greatest dollar volume concentrated?
3. What are four advantages of B2C e-commerce over traditional retailing?
4. Why are digital products the best ones to sell over the Internet?
5. What is meant by the term "the freedom economy"?
6. What is the attraction of affiliate programs to e-tailers?
7. What are three techniques used to attract customers to B2C Web sites?
8. What are value networks?
9. What is spam and how is it used?
10. What is a large EDI buyer company called?
11. What is a supplier to a large EDI buyer company called?
12. What are Internet-based services that bring buyers and sellers together called?
13. What is XML?
14. What is the name for an internal organizational Internet?
15. What is the name for an internal organizational Intranet also open to customers and suppliers?
16. In which areas is the government leading the private sector in the use of e-technology?
17. Why has financial EDI been slow to gain acceptance?

Assignments and Exercises

1. **DEVELOPING M-COMMERCE SCENARIOS FOR GPS CELL PHONES.** Soon, cell phones will be equipped with GPS chips enabling users to be located within a geographical location about the size of a tennis court. The primary purpose for installing GPS chips in phones is to enable emergency services to locate a cell phone user. For example, if you dial an emergency assistance number (911 in North America) from your home now, it is possible for a computer system to use your home telephone number to access a database and obtain your address. This can be very useful in situations where you are unable to give address information to the emergency operator for some reason. The problem with trying to do the same thing with present-day cell phones is that you could be calling from anywhere.

   As you might imagine, marketers have been monitoring this development with great interest. When the new cell phones become available, they can visualize scenarios where they will know who you are (by your telephone number) and where you are (by the GPS chip). One possible way they could use this information, for example, is to give you a call when you are walking past their shop in the mall and let you know of a special sale on items they know you would be interested in buying. Of course, retailers would have to possess IT systems that would permit them to craft such personalized offers, and you would have had to give them permission to call you.

   Find out what at least three e-commerce marketers are saying about personalized marketing using GPS-equipped cell phones and prepare an analysis of how they will likely be used when the technology is widely available.

2. **DEALING WITH THE GLOBAL DIGITAL DIVIDE.** Dealing with the issue of the global digital divide seems to be a task well suited for an international body such as the United Nations.

   Find out what, if anything, the UN is doing about this issue and express whether you believe their efforts will be successful. Determine if there are organizations such as private companies or foundations that have the issue high on their agendas. Do the same thing for any such organizations you find: evaluate their efforts and express an opinion on they will be successful. Finally, search for a lesser-developed country that is making significant local efforts to deal with the digital divide. If you can't find one, prepare a list of the countries you reviewed.

3. **WHY PARTICIPATE IN A COVISINT AUCTION?** Covisint (www.covisint.com) is a B2B exchange for the automotive industry. It was formed by three automobile companies, DaimlerChrysler, Ford, and General Motors. Covisint has received a lot of publicity, both good and bad, and there are different opinions on whether it will ultimately be successful. Go to the Covisint Web site and read about their history and some of their press releases. Then go to sites where others have commented on Covisint's goals and objectives. Try Web sites of magazines such as *Business 2.0* (www.business2.com) and *Context* (www.contextmag.com). Search their archives for articles on Covisint and see what say. Now, put yourself in the place of a supplier to one of the large automobile companies that are running Covisint. What would be the advantages to you of participating in a Covisint auction? What would the disadvantages be? If you had a choice, would you decline to participate? Why or why not?

4. **ALTERNATIVES FOR PERSONALIZED DIGITAL MUSIC.** Sony Music Entertainment and Universal Music Group recently formed a joint venture called PressPlay (www.pressplay.com) that gives subscribers new ways to listen to or buy recorded music. If you visit their Web site, you'll see that you have three options: listen to samples online, download tracks to your hard drive, or burn tracks onto a CD. PressPlay is a subscription service. You sign up for a plan and pay a monthly fee by credit card. Your activity is limited depending on the plan you choose. It offers visitors a free 14-day trial with up to 200 streams or 20 downloads.

   Evaluate PressPlay's business idea in comparison with a company that offers to create a custom CD and mail it to you. Prepare an assessment of the two approaches for presentation in class.

Discussion Questions

1. In what ways can shopping over the Internet be more convenient for consumers? In what ways can it be less convenient? List at least five products you would have no hesitation in buying over the Internet, five products you may want to think about a bit before you do it, and five products you would never consider buying over the Internet. Justify your reasons in each case.

2. Why is the ability to change prices instantaneously considered an advantage for e-tailers? When might the use of personalized pricing be a disadvantage for an e-tailer?

3. There have been a string of e-tailers running out of cash, not being able to attract more money from investors, and going out of business as a result. What are some of the main reasons this happened? What are the keys to success in B2C e-commerce?

4. Under what circumstances would it be appropriate to consider using viral marketing? See if you can think of an organization with an online presence that could benefit from viral marketing but is not currently using it. It could be your school, for example, or it could be an organization you are involved with. How would you suggest it proceed to achieve the desired results? What are some of the other marketing techniques available for an e-tailer to use? Why is it important to consider a mix of techniques rather than just relying on a single one?

5. Some Internet retailers that started as pure plays are now sending catalogues to their customers, opening up another channel. Some are well-known companies; Amazon.com and RedEnvelope are only two of many possible examples. Do you think companies like Amazon.com or RedEnvelope should consider opening up a third channel by establishing stores in your local shopping mall? Why or why not? What factors should they consider in evaluating such a decision? If they decided to do so, how would you suggest they go about it? What factors would do you think it would be important for them to consider in order for them to be successful?

6. Why are relationships between companies said to be more important in the B2B space than between businesses and consumers in the B2C space? Do you agree with this idea? Give an example of an instance in which your company might need to rely on a long-term relationship with a supplier to help you out with a business problem. Give an example of the risk a company might be taking if it chose to buy direct materials

from a supplier they had never done business with before simply on the basis of price.

7. Why has traditional EDI been so slow to gain acceptance with small and medium-sized companies? Do you think that traditional EDI will ever gain enough acceptance with small and medium-sized companies to make widespread B2B e-commerce a global reality? Why or why not? How do some of the ideas for next-generation EDI intend to address this issue? What will it take for some of the new approaches like ebXML and Web Services to be successful? What are some of the things you can think of that would cause them to fail in reaching their objectives?

8. Describe the services provided by value-added networks that make it easier for companies to exchange EDI transactions with each other. What are the pros and cons of using value-added networks for B2B e-commerce instead of the Internet? Why don't more companies use the Internet for EDI, since it is much cheaper than using a value-added network? Assume that you work for a telecommunications company that operates a value-added network (AT&T or GE Information Services). What sort of strategies would you encourage your company to explore to deal with the possibility of losing considerable amounts of revenue as your customers leave you in favour of using the Internet?

9. What are the advantages and disadvantages of B2B marketplaces for buyers? For sellers? How could a supplier company play on the relationships that it has with a long-standing customer to avoid getting pulled in to a reverse auction in an open B2B marketplace? Why do some observers say that B2B marketplaces can be risky ventures?

10. Assume that you have some money to invest in a company in the e-commerce payment systems space and can only choose between Mondex and PayPal. Which one of the two do you think has the best chance of being successful? Be prepared to explain the reasons for your choice.

REAL HOT Electronic Commerce

Getting Your Business on the Internet

Skills Module 3
Web Page Design

Real HOT Links

Let's say you've decided it might be fun (and profitable) to become an e-tailer and establish an Internet-based business. You know that many e-tailers don't make it. You'd like to be one of the successful ones. There are a lot of resources on the Internet that can help you with the task of selecting the right business in the first place, getting the site up and running, deciding who should host your site, marketing your site, understanding privacy issues, and obtaining the funds you need to pay your expenses until your business begins to show a profit. We've provided direct links to many useful Web sites on the site that supports this text (www.mcgrawhill.ca/college/haag, select "Electronic Commerce Projects"). These are a great starting point for completing this Real HOT section. We also encourage you to search the Internet for others.

COMPETITIVE INTELLIGENCE

The first thing you need to have is an idea for the business. What is that you would like to sell? Is it a product or a service? Make sure you have expertise, or something special to offer. After you've come up with a candidate, it's time to check out the competition and what they're up to. One of the things many fail to do is to see how much competition there is out there before they launch their business. They just get what they think is a great idea and move ahead with it. A better tack is to look at what competitors exist in the space you're considering. You may find there are too many and that they would make things tough for you. Or you may find that there are few competitors and they aren't doing a terrific job.

Seek out some of the Web sites of businesses in the competitive space you're thinking of entering. As you do, answer the following questions.

A. How many sites are offering the same product or service as you're planning to offer?

B. How many are in your country and how many are in other countries?

C. Did you come across a site from another country that has a unique approach that you did not see on any of the sites within your own country?

E. Evaluate the competitor sites on the basis of some of the criteria listed in Figure 5.3.

STOREFRONT SOFTWARE

If you decide to sell products, there is software that you can use to make it easy to create a Web site. There are many products to choose from. Some will cost you a lot of money, but others are free. Wired-to-Shop.com, located in North Vancouver, B.C., has a Basic Store for $8.40 per month, a Storefront Package for $60 per month, and an Unlimited Package for $360 per month. What you get in each of these packages is listed in detail on the FreeMerchant.com Web site (www.freemerchant.com). Since there are many options to choose from, it would be worth your while to see if you can find an article that compares current versions of storefront software. A site like ZDNet.com (www.zdnet.com) would be a good place to start your search. Build up a list of features that you would need for your e-tailing site, and then compare your needs with the features offered by the various software packages. They all sound good when you read about them on the vendors' Web sites so be sure you "test-drive" the software before you sign up.

Another possibility would be to sign up for a shopping mall. Find your way to Amazon.com's zShops or Yahoo! Canada Store and see what you think of these alternatives. Finally, you'll need a way for your customers to pay you for what they buy. This involves getting a merchant account which permits you to accept credit cards. Most of the storefront sites will explain how merchant accounts work and will help you get a merchant account (see www.1shoppingcart.com, for example).

A. What features have you decided your storefront software must provide?

B. How have you evaluated the pros and cons of using a storefront software package versus the options offered by Amazon.com and Yahoo!?

C. See if you can track down users of software options you are considering. Send them an e-mail and ask them what they like and dislike about it. You may be surprised at their answers.

HOSTING SERVICES

You've got some options here. You can decide to acquire the necessary computer and communications hardware and software to manage your own technical infrastructure or you can let a specialist firm do it for you. Unless you're really into the technical side of things, it's probably better to work with a firm that specializes in it. They are called

Web hosting services and there are plenty of them around to choose from. Cost, reliability, security, and customer service are some of the criteria you might want to use in selecting a hosting service. If you're planning to have your business located in a country with poor telecommunications services, don't forget that you can choose a hosting service located in a country with a more reliable telecommunications infrastructure, anywhere in the world. There are companies that provide directories that make it easy for you to find and compare prices and features of Web hosting companies, sort of like shopping malls. An example of such a company is CanadaWebsiteHosting.ca (www.canadawebsitehosting.ca). Take a look at its site to see some of the options available. As you consider Web hosting services, answer the following questions.

A. Compare the costs of the various hosting services. Were you able to find one that seems to be within your budget?

B. How can you evaluate the reliability of the various Web hosting services?

C. How can you evaluate the quality of a Web hosting service's customer service? What do you have a right to expect from them in the way of customer service and security, for example?

MARKETING THE SITE

In this chapter, we discussed several options for marketing a Web site: registering with search engines, online ads, viral marketing, affiliate programs, and marketing to existing customers, as well as using traditional media. Deciding on the marketing mix that will be most effective and still permit you to stay within a reasonable budget will be critical to the success of your venture. You may want to consider employing an Internet marketing consultant to help you lay out a marketing plan. One, AdDesigner.com (www.addesigner.com), even offers some free services. Also, you may want to see what marketing services your storefront software or Web hosting service may offer. As you consider how to market your site, answer the following questions.

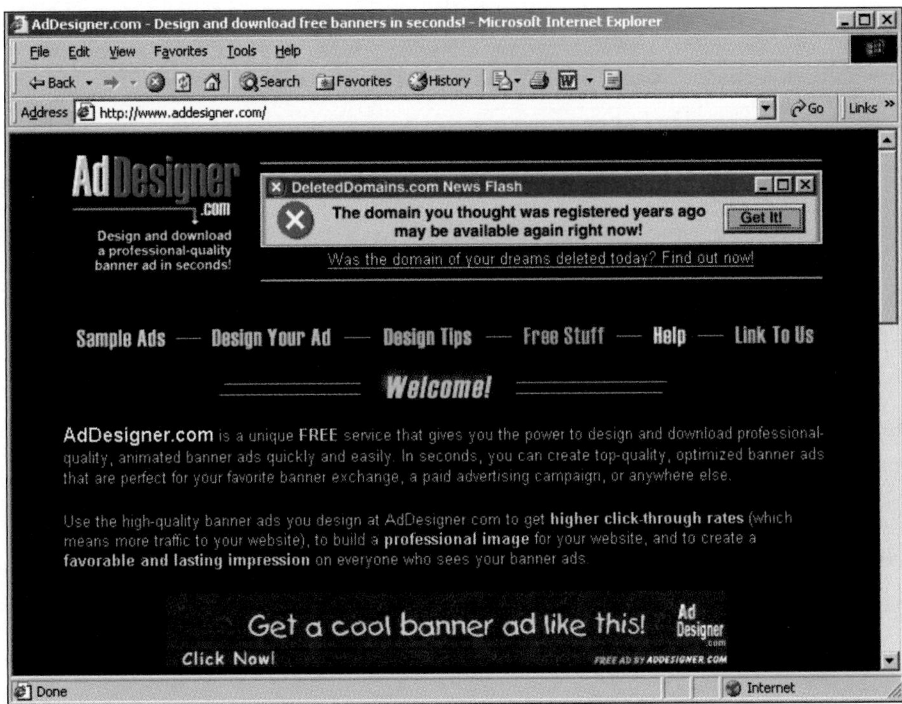

A. How have you defined your target market? Who will be most interested in your product or service?

B. Which of the available marketing techniques have you selected as most appropriate to market your site? Why have you selected this particular marketing mix?

C. What have you decided about using the services of a marketing consultant? How did you justify your decision?

Go to the Online Learning Centre at www.mcgrawhill.ca/college/haag for quizzes, extra content, a searchable glossary, and more! Click on "Electronic Commerce Projects" for links to hundreds of Web sites.

Go to the text CD-ROM for data files, extra content, and Skills Modules on Microsoft Excel, Microsoft Access, HTML, and e-portfolios.

CHAPTER SIX

STUDENT LEARNING OUTCOMES

1. List the seven steps in the systems development life cycle and an associated activity for each step.
2. List four reasons why your participation during the systems development life cycle is critical.
3. Describe three reasons why projects fail.
4. Define the three different ways you can staff a system development project.
5. List two advantages of selfsourcing.
6. Describe prototyping and profile an example of a prototype.
7. Describe two advantages of prototyping.

INDUSTRY PERSPECTIVES

FEATURES

WEB SUPPORT LINKS

- Using Your Computer for More Than Work
- Animating Your Computer Screen
- Protecting Your Computer Investment
- Searching for Freeware and Shareware

Visit www.mcgrawhill.ca/college/haag

SYSTEMS DEVELOPMENT
Steps, Tools, and Techniques

CASE STUDY:
AN ALTERNATIVE TO TRADITIONAL EDI FOR NEWARK ELECTRONICS

Newark Electronics, an American company with offices in Pointe-Claire, Quebec and in London and Mississauga, Ontario, is one of North America's leading distributors of electronic components. Initially, Newark Electronics was connected with most of its large suppliers via traditional electronic data interchange (EDI). However, the bulk of its trading partners remained SMEs unwilling, lacking the skills, or financially incapable to invest into traditional EDI systems. They saw traditional EDI as too expensive and complex to justify the convenience of sending and receiving documents electronically. Only 75 of its approximate 300 suppliers communicated with Newark via traditional EDI. This meant that Newark still needed to rely heavily on faxes, paper, and other various electronic communications to exchange purchase orders (POs), PO acknowledgements, and other important business information. Newark's low rate of acknowledged purchase orders indicated that something needed to be done. In early 2000, it stood at only 33 percent.

Newark wanted to garner the same efficiencies with its small suppliers that traditional EDI made possible with its larger ones. At the same time, Newark was sensitive to its smaller suppliers' concerns. They desperately wanted to avoid the high cost and complexity of traditional EDI solutions. Newark approached ADX—Advanced Data Exchange, a California-based company offering "Internet EDI"—a solution designed to bridge the EDI gap between big and small companies. Based on XML, ADX's Internet EDI represented a powerful, simple, and yet inexpensive alternative to traditional EDI. Users benefit from the advantages of traditional EDI but without its significant initial setup and maintenance costs. It enables companies to exploit the Internet and seamlessly consolidate various formats for exchanging documents. Businesses simply need to install the ADX Desktop Software onto their PCs and access the Internet. Activating the application places an Inbox/Outbox icon on the supplier's desktop similar to those found in many e-mail programs. Sending or receiving electronic documents is just as simple as sending or receiving e-mails. ADX translates the documents into the format that a recipient prefers and delivers them via the Internet to the recipient's inbox.

As of September 2000, Newark had managed to sign up 81 of its suppliers to the ADX option. This number has been increasing ever since. Aside from Newark's low one-time investment of $27,550, suppliers were asked to pay less than $90 per month, on average, to exchange critical business information with Newark via the ADX software. Newark's PO acknowledgement rate has since increased from 33 to 94 percent and other benefits were also realized. Prior to adopting Internet EDI, the data entry tasks alone required four to six temporary clerical staff. With Internet EDI, these were no longer needed. Moreover, Newark's "mountain" of paper was drastically reduced, there were fewer stock outs, improved inventory control, and increased sales from improved fill rates resulting in more business for Newark's suppliers—well worth the average $90 monthly charge these were asked to pay. Overall, Newark realized an impressive 4428 percent three-year ROI and achieved first-year cost savings of more than $1.2 million.[1]

Introduction

Have you ever wondered why businesses build information systems or how a business knows when it's time to replace an old information system? Typically, new systems are created because knowledge workers request the systems in order to help them perform their work. For example, a marketing manager might request a system to produce product information and track customer sales information. A human resources manager might request a system to track employee vacation and sick days. Almost any position you take in a company today will require you to work with information systems because they are one of the most important parts of any business. Information systems supply the support structure for meeting the company's business strategies and goals. It's even common to find that a company's competitive advantage relies heavily on its information systems.

Figure 6.1
The Systems Development Life Cycle

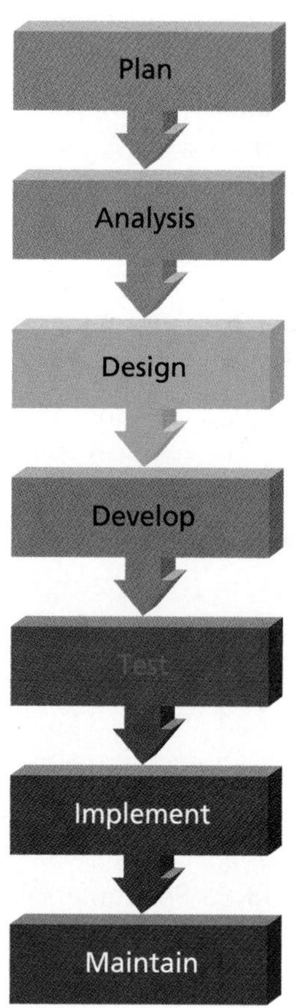

There are many factors that must come together in order to develop a successful information system. This chapter focuses on the **systems development life cycle (SDLC)**, a structured step-by-step approach for developing information systems (see Figure 6.1). Along with covering the SDLC, this chapter provides you with some of the primary activities you'll perform when building an information system. Many individuals make the mistake of assuming they won't benefit from learning about the SDLC because they're not planning on working in an IT department. These individuals are making a giant mistake. As a knowledge worker, or system end user, you and your work will definitely be affected by information systems and you'll be involved in many of the activities performed during the systems development life cycle.

No matter what major you decide to pursue, be it accounting, marketing, or communications, you'll be involved in systems development. In fact, your involvement in developing systems is critical to the success of your company. Information systems that effectively meet your needs will help you be more productive and make better decisions. Systems that don't meet your needs may have a damaging effect on your productivity. Therefore, it's crucial you help your organization develop the best systems possible.

One way to ensure you develop successful information systems is to perform all seven phases in the SDLC. As we move through the SDLC in this chapter, we'll focus on how the overall process works, key activities within each phase, and what roles you might play. We don't expect to make you into a systems development expert. Students majoring in IT or MIS often take as many as seven courses that deal with a different aspect of systems development. However, even if you're not majoring in IT or MIS, and don't plan to be an expert, you'll still have systems development roles and responsibilities throughout your career.

Seven Phases in the Systems Development Life Cycle

There are literally hundreds of different activities associated with each phase in the SDLC. Typical activities are determining budgets, gathering system requirements, modelling, and writing detailed user documentation. The activities you perform during each system development project will vary depending on the type of system you're building and the tools you use to build it. Since we can't possibly cover them all in this brief introduction, we chose a few of the more important SDLC activities detailed in Figure 6.2. These activities are typically performed on every systems development

SDLC Phase	Activities
1. Plan	• Define the system to be developed • Set the project scope • Develop the project plan including tasks, resources, and time frames
2. Analysis	• Gather the business requirements for the system
3. Design	• Design the technical architecture required to support the system • Design system models
4. Develop	• Build the technical architecture • Build the database and programs
5. Test	• Write the test conditions • Perform the testing of the system
6. Implement	• Provide training for the system users • Write detailed user documentation
7. Maintain	• Build a help desk to support the system users • Provide an environment to support system changes

Figure 6.2
Important Activities in the Systems Development Life Cycle

project and chances are high you'll encounter them as a knowledge worker. Let's begin by taking a look at each phase in the SDLC and its associated activities.

PHASE 1: PLAN

The **planning phase** involves determining a solid plan for developing your information system. Planning is the first and most critical phase of any effort your organization undertakes, regardless of whether you're developing a system that allows your customers to order products over the Internet, determining how to create the best logistical structure for warehouses around the world, or developing a strategic information alliance with another organization. If you don't carefully plan your activities (and determine why they are necessary), you're doomed to failure. Let's discuss three of the most important activities involved in the planning phase.

IDENTIFY AND SELECT THE SYSTEM FOR DEVELOPMENT What systems are required to support the strategic goals of your organization? This is an excellent question and if you can answer it correctly then you know which systems you must develop. Answering this question incorrectly will cost your organization a great deal of time and money since you'll be building the wrong systems.

Knowledge workers generate proposals to build new information systems when they are having a difficult time performing their jobs. For example, knowledge workers might have trouble gathering information, generating reports, or producing invoices. Hence, they would request a new information system in order to solve their problems. Unfortunately, most organizations have limited resources and can't afford to develop all proposed information systems. So, they look to critical success factors to help determine which systems to build.

A **critical success factor (CSF)** is simply a factor critical to your organization's success. In order to determine which system to develop, your organization tracks all of the proposed systems and prioritizes them by business impact or critical success factors. This allows the business to decide which problems require immediate attention and which problems can wait.

SET PROJECT SCOPE Once your organization defines the system to be developed you must set the scope for the project. **Project scope** clearly defines the high-level system requirements. Scope is often referred to as the "10,000-foot view" of the system or the most basic definition of the system. A **project scope document** is a written definition of the project scope and is usually no longer than a paragraph. Setting the project scope may seem like a simple and straightforward activity, but it's actually rather difficult. Can you imagine trying to define a scope document, or a single paragraph, to summarize an entire telecommunications billing system including customers, products, charges, taxes, etc.? This is not an easy activity to perform, but it's critical as the project scope sets the boundaries on what will and will not be developed.

DEVELOP PROJECT PLAN Developing a project plan is one of the final activities you'll perform during the planning phase and it's also one of the hardest and most important activities. The **project plan** defines the what, when, and who questions of system development including all activities to be performed, the individuals or resources that will perform the activities, and the time required to complete each activity. The project plan is the guiding force behind ensuring the on-time delivery of a complete and successful information system. It also logs and tracks every single activity that you perform during the project. If you miss one activity, or take longer to complete it than expected, you must adjust the project plan to reflect this change.

Project milestones represent key dates for which you need a certain group of activities performed. For example, completing the planning phase might be a project milestone. If you miss a project milestone then you know the project is experiencing major issues. A **project manager**, an individual who is an expert in project planning and management, defines and develops the project plan and tracks the plan to ensure all key project milestones are completed on time. The project plan is somewhat similar to the syllabus for your course. It tells you what things are due, when they are due, and who is expected to complete them.

PHASE 2: ANALYSIS

Once your organization has decided which systems to develop you can move into the analysis phase. The **analysis phase** involves end users and IT specialists working together to gather, understand, and document the business requirements for the proposed system.

GATHER BUSINESS REQUIREMENTS **Business requirements** are the detailed set of knowledge worker requests that the system must meet in order to be successful. The key activity in this phase is gathering clearly defined business requirements. At this point, you're not concerned with any implementation or technical details. For example, you're not yet defining which types of technology you'll use to implement your solution such as an Oracle database or the Java programming language. You're simply focusing on gathering the true business requirements for the system. A sample business requirement might state, "The system must track all customer sales by product, region, and sales representative." This requirement states what the system must do from the business perspective, giving no details or information on how the system is going to meet this requirement.

Gathering business requirements is similar to performing an investigation. You must talk to everyone who has a claim in using the new system in order to find out

THE TRUTH BEHIND BUSINESS REQUIREMENTS

The Standish Group International (www.standishgroup.com) reported that 31 percent of software projects are cancelled before they ever reach a customer's hands, and 53 percent ultimately cost at least 189 percent more than the original budget. North American corporations that do complete information system projects typically retain only about 42 percent of the features or business requirements that were originally proposed to the knowledge workers. Bad requirements are one of the primary causes for so many system failures. Business requirements are the detailed set of knowledge worker requests that the system must meet in order to be successful. They can include anything from basic functions to a knowledge worker's wish list of extreme functions.

Gathering clear and accurate business requirements is essential to delivering a successful system that meets your knowledge worker's needs. Learning how to gather business requirements has become such an advantage to organizations that there are now several different training programs and certifications a knowledge worker can pursue to ensure their success in this area. Microsoft Training and Certification Center offers several classes on gathering and analyzing business requirements. A knowledge worker can even become Microsoft-certified by passing the Analyzing Requirements and Defining Solution Architectures certification exam. The more knowledge workers know about gathering and analyzing business requirements the greater their chances are at developing successful systems for their company.[2,3]

what is required. An extremely useful way to gather system requirements is to perform a joint application design session. During a **joint application development (JAD)** session knowledge workers and IT specialists meet, sometimes for several days, to define or review the business requirements for the system.

Once you define all of the business requirements, you prioritize them and place them in a formal comprehensive document or the **requirements definition document.** The knowledge workers receive the document for their sign-off. **Sign-off** is the knowledge workers' actual signatures indicating they approve all of the business requirements. One of the first major milestones on the project plan is the knowledge workers' sign-off on business requirements.

PHASE 3: DESIGN

The primary goal of the **design phase** is to build a technical blueprint of how the proposed system will work.

DESIGN THE TECHNICAL ARCHITECTURE The system you build must have a solid technical architecture or else the system will crash or malfunction. The **technical architecture** defines the hardware, software, and telecommunications equipment required to run the system. Most systems run on a computer network with each employee having a workstation and the application running on a server. During this phase, the IT specialists recommend what types of workstations and servers to buy including memory and storage requirements. Along with the server hardware requirements, you define the operating system software. The telecommunication requirements discuss access to the Internet and the ability for end users to dial-in remotely to the server. You typically explore several different technical architectures before choosing the final technical architecture.

The final architecture must meet your needs in terms of time, cost, technical feasibility, and flexibility. It's important to ensure that the final architecture meets not only your current system needs, but also your future system needs. For example, you want to ensure the database is large enough to hold the current volume of customers plus all new customers you expect to gain over the next five years.

DESIGN SYSTEM MODELS **Modelling** is the activity of drawing a graphical representation of a design. You model everything you build including reports, programs, and databases. There are many different types of modelling activities performed during the design phase including GUI screen design.

The **graphical user interface (GUI)** is the interface to an information system. **GUI screen design** is the ability to model the information system screens for an entire system. You must decide many things when modelling a GUI including the placement of items on the screen and the number of items contained in a drop-down list. Figure 6.3 displays two different formats for an information system GUI design. Notice the menu items appear alphabetically in one design and categorically in the other. You base your decision on how and where to display menu items on whatever is easiest for the knowledge workers to use. If the menu items are placed incorrectly on the GUI, knowledge workers could waste a significant amount of time just searching the GUI to find the correct item.

PHASE 4: DEVELOPMENT

During the **development phase**, you take all of your detailed design documents from the design phase and transform them into an actual system. This phase marks the point where you go from logical designs to physical implementation. Activities during this phase include coding the programs, creating the databases, deploying the telecommunication equipment, and installing hardware and software.

Figure 6.3

Graphical User Interface (GUI) Screen Design

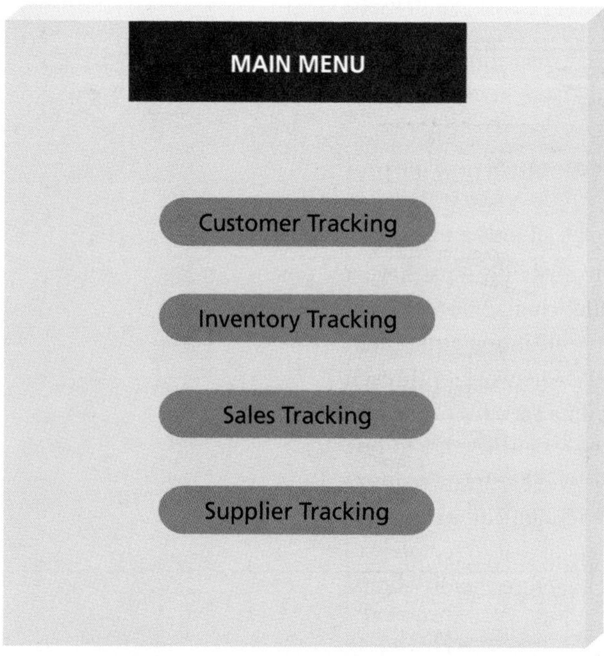

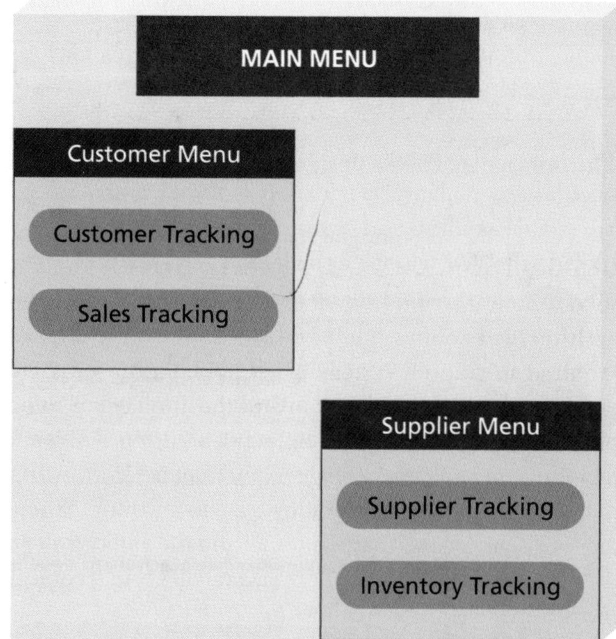

GUI Design: Categorical order of buttons

BUILD THE TECHNICAL ARCHITECTURE In order for you to build your system, you must first build the platform where the system is going to operate. In the design phase, you created a technical architecture blueprint displaying the design of the software, hardware, and telecommunications equipment. In the development phase, you purchase and implement equipment necessary to support the technical architecture.

Most new systems require new hardware and software. It may be as simple as assigning memory to workstations or as complex as setting up a wide area network (WAN) across several states. Whatever the case, the IT specialists, for the most part, are responsible for buying and installing the software, hardware, and telecommunications equipment.

BUILD THE DATABASE AND PROGRAMS Once the technical architecture is built, you begin creating the database and writing the programs required for the system. Refer to Chapter 3 or Extended Learning Module A for additional information on designing and building databases. IT specialists perform these functions, and it may take months or even years to design and create the databases or write all the software.

PHASE 5: TEST

You must perform testing before the knowledge workers begin using the system. The **testing phase** verifies that the system works and meets all of the business requirements defined in the analysis phase.

TEST CONDITIONS—THE PRIMARY TOOL FOR TESTING SUCCESS Testing is critical. You must have excellent test plans and test conditions in order to perform an exhaustive test. **Test conditions** are the detailed steps the system must perform along with the expected results of each step. Figure 6.4 displays several test conditions for testing user logon functionality in a system. The tester will execute each test condition and compare the expected results with the actual results in order to verify that the system functions correctly. Notice how each test condition is extremely detailed and states the result that should occur when executing each test condition. Each time the actual result is different from the expected result you generate a "bug" and the system goes back to development for a bug fix.

Test Condition 6 displays an actual result different from the expected one, because the system failed to allow the user to log on. After this test condition fails, you can determine that the system is not functioning correctly and it must be sent back to development.

A typical system development effort has hundreds or thousands of test conditions. You must execute and verify all of them, which ensures the entire system functions correctly. Writing all of the test conditions and performing the actual testing of the software takes a tremendous amount of time and energy, but it is critical to the successful development of any system. Try not to sacrifice testing time, or your system may not work correctly all the time.

PHASE 6: IMPLEMENT

The goal of phase 6—implementation—is to bring the proposed system to life by placing it in the organization. During the **implementation phase**, you distribute the system to all of the knowledge workers and they begin using the system to perform their everyday jobs.

Figure 6.4
Test Conditions

Test Condition Number	Date Tested	Tester	Test Condition	Expected Result	Actual Result	Pass/Fail
1	1/1/2003	Emily Hickman	Click on System Start button	Main Menu appears	Same as expected result	Pass
2	1/1/2003	Emily Hickman	Click on Logon button in Main Menu	Logon Screen appears asking for username and password	Same as expected result	Pass
3	1/1/2003	Emily Hickman	Type "Emily Hickman" in the User Name field	"Emily Hickman" appears in the User Name field	Same as expected result	Pass
4	1/1/2003	Emily Hickman	Type "Zahara 123" in the Password field	"Zahara 123" appears in the Password field	Same as expected result	Pass
5	1/1/2003	Emily Hickman	Click on OK button	User logon request is sent to database and user name and password are verified	Same as expected result	Pass
6	1/1/2003	Emily Hickman	Click on start	User name and password are accepted and the system main menu appears	Screen appeared stating logon failed and user name and password were incorrect	Fail

USER DOCUMENTATION When you install the system, you must also provide the knowledge workers with information on how to use the system—that is, **user documentation** such as a software program's manual. Knowledge workers find it extremely frustrating to have a new system without documentation.

TRAINING You must provide training for the knowledge workers who are going to use the new system. There are several different types of training you can provide and two of the most popular are online training and workshop training.

Online training is accessed on the Internet or from a CD-ROM; knowledge workers can get the training at any time, on their own computers, at their own pace. **Workshop training** is set up in a classroom-type environment and led by an instructor; it is best for difficult systems where the knowledge workers need one-on-one time with a human instructor.

PHASE 7: MAINTAIN

Maintaining the system is the final sequential phase of any systems development effort. During the **maintenance phase**, you monitor and support the new system to ensure it continues to meet the business goals. Once a system is in place, it must change as your

CATA MONITORS IT SKILLS GAP

According to the Canadian Advanced Technology Association (CATA), an organization which has been monitoring the "IT skills gap," 88 percent of advanced technology companies in Canada believe they face a serious shortage in necessary technology skills and qualifications. Thus, as a student in information systems, your prospects for employment after graduation are very good. According to CATA, more than a million North Americans may be employed in hi-tech jobs by the time you graduate and demand is growing. These are well-paying jobs, with starting salaries ranging from $30,000 to $60,000 per year. The "IT skills gap" is most apparent in "core IT occupations," including computer science, electrical engineering, software design, and systems analysis. CATA estimates that in Ontario alone there will be openings for 56,000 new technology workers over the next five years.[4]

business changes. Constantly monitoring and supporting the new system involves making minor changes (e.g., new reports or information-capturing) and reviewing the system to ensure that it continues to move your organization toward its strategic goals.

HELP DESK To create the best support environment, you need to provide a way for knowledge workers to request changes. One of the best ways to support knowledge workers is to create a help desk.

A **help desk** is a group of people who responds to knowledge workers' questions; typically, there is a phone number knowledge workers can call whenever they have issues or questions about the system. Have you ever found yourself in a situation where you couldn't figure out how to perform a function with a computer program? A help desk is a terrific way to provide comprehensive support for new systems.

SUPPORT CHANGES As changes arise in the ever-changing business environment, you must react by assessing their impact on the system; it may well be that the system needs to change. For example, imagine you work in the manufacturing department of a men's clothing company, and you have a system that design clothes by scanning in different patterns and displaying how they look on different outfits. Now suppose you suddenly decide to start selling women's clothes. Obviously, you will have change the system to design different types of clothes such as skirts and blouses.

Knowledge Workers and Their Roles in the Systems Development Life Cycle

Many people before you have said, and undoubtedly many who will follow will say, "I'm not going to be an IT specialist—so why should I learn about the systems development process?" If you're asking that question, congratulations—you're well on your way to becoming an information-literate knowledge worker. How so? Because you're asking, "Why is this material important to me? What does it mean? How can I use it?"

Your participation in the systems development process is vitally important because you are (or will be):

1. A business process expert
2. A liaison to the customer

THE GLOBAL PERSPECTIVE

MARRIOTT INTERNATIONAL

The hospitality services industry is highly competitive and it's difficult for any one organization in the industry to achieve a competitive advantage. When Marriott International, an international upscale hotel chain, set itself a strategic goal of becoming the world's leader in the hospitality services industry, it took an ingenious idea and transformed it into an information system with the help of Accenture, one of the world's leading outsourcing companies.

Accenture and Marriott teamed up to link Marriott's worldwide financial systems into a single service centre at one location. This allowed Marriott to leverage its operations to provide consistent, cost-effective services, making the organization quicker and more flexible, a competitive advantage that has helped Marriott leap ahead as one of the top worldwide hospitality service providers.[5]

3. A quality control analyst
4. A manager of other people

First and foremost, in business you are the business process expert. You know and understand how the business works better than anyone else in the company does. For example, if you're an administrator at a hospital and the development of a new nursing scheduling system is under way, who knows best how nursing scheduling should occur? That's right—you do. During systems development, knowledge workers know how things should work, what things should happen, how to handle exceptions, and so on. It would be ludicrous to tell a group of IT specialists to develop a new nursing scheduling system when they have no idea how to schedule nurses. You must tell them how the process currently works and how you currently schedule nurses based on certain criteria such as expertise, overload hours, and time of year. In business, you are a business process expert. Without your input, the new system will never meet your needs.

Second, your knowledge of and participation in the systems development process is vitally important because you're a liaison to the customer. That is, you know what a certain customer segment wants, and you can relay that information to the project development team. For example, if you work for a telephone company and manage a call centre that fields billing questions, aren't you qualified to provide information pertaining to the appearance and content of new phone bills? Of course you are. In addition, if you want to make your customers happy, you have to act as a liaison between them and the project development team. The person who deals directly with the customers has the best insight into what the customers want, and that person is you.

Third, your participation is important because you'll act as a quality control analyst during the systems development process. Once you help define the logical requirements of a new system, you can't simply walk away and expect a system that meets your needs. For example, you still need to help review alternative technical solutions, acting as a quality control analyst to assure that the chosen technical alternative meets your logical needs.

Finally, your participation in the systems development process is important because you have ultimate responsibility for the work and productivity of others. In short, you will be a manager of other people, and it's your responsibility to see that new systems will improve the productivity of those you manage.

We have covered the general role knowledge workers play in systems development. Let's take a detailed look at each specific phase and the important role you must play.

PLAN

The most important role knowledge workers play during the planning phase is defining which systems are to be developed. We can't stress the importance of this activity enough. Systems development focuses on either solving a problem or taking advantage of an opportunity. Your new system will only be successful if it solves the right problem or takes advantage of the right opportunity. You must also define the project scope along with the system to be developed. The project scope includes which requirements are in and out of scope for the project.

Developing the project plan is another critical activity where you'll be directly involved. You must help the project manager define the activities for each phase of the systems development life cycle. The project manager is an expert in project management and you are the expert in the business operations, and together the two of you will be able to develop a detailed project plan that meets everyone's needs.

Allocating individuals to work on the different activities is another area where your expertise is critical. There are certain tasks on the project plan that knowledge workers perform and there are certain tasks that IT specialists perform. There are also certain tasks that both knowledge workers and IT specialists perform. You're the expert in your area and you'll be able to provide insight into which individuals have the skills required to perform certain activities. You'll also help define the project milestones, or important dates by which certain activities performed.

ANALYSIS

You're the business process expert—that means you know how current processes and current systems work and you know how things need to change. It's vitally important that you provide this information as the current system model will become the foundation for developing the new system model.

One of the primary activities you'll perform during the analysis phase is reviewing business requirements. One of the key things to think about when you are doing this is the cost for the company to fix errors if the requirements are unclear or inaccurate. Finding an error during the analysis and design phase is relatively inexpensive to fix; all you typically have to do is change a Word document. Finding an error during the testing or implementation phase, however, is incredibly expensive to fix, because you have to change the actual system. Figure 6.5 displays how the cost to fix an error grows exponentially the later the error is found in the SDLC.

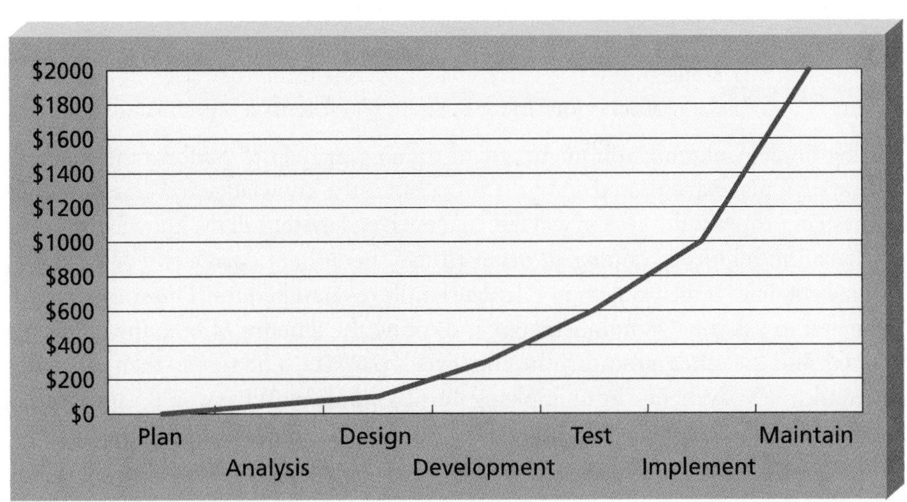

Figure 6.5
The Cost of Finding Errors

Imagine what happens if the following business requirement was supposed to have the word "green" instead of "red": "System must have red GUIs to match colours in company logo." Finding this error during analysis or design would be as simple as changing a Word document. Finding this error during testing or implementation would require the developers to rebuild all of the GUIs with the correct colour. You must take you time and ensure every business requirement is accurate and complete.

DESIGN

During design, your role decreases as a business process expert and increases as a quality control analyst. IT specialists perform most of the activities during the design phase, but quality assurance is a key role for you. The IT specialist will develop several alternative technical solutions. It's your job to analyze each and ensure that the recommended solution best meets your business requirements. Design "walk-thru" meetings are a key activity during the design phase. You'll be asked to formally sign off on the detailed design documents indicating that you agree with the proposed technical solution.

DEVELOPMENT

IT specialists complete many of the activities in the development phase. Your role during this phase is to confirm any changes to business requirements and track the progress of tasks on the project plan to ensure timely delivery of the system. Constantly reevaluating the project plan during this phase helps you to determine if you be able to meet the final system delivery due date.

TEST

IT specialists also perform many of the activities during the testing phase. Your involvement is still critical, as you are the quality assurance expert. You're directly involved with reviewing the test conditions to ensure the IT specialists have tested all of the system functionality and that every single test condition has passed.

You perform the **user acceptance testing (UAT)** to determine if the system satisfies the business requirements and enables the knowledge workers to perform their jobs correctly. UAT is usually the final test performed on the system and if you decide that the system doesn't meet your expectations this is your last chance to stop the system implementation. You must sign off on the UAT as this gives your final approval to place the system into production.

IMPLEMENT

During implementation, you might attend training or help to perform the training. The system may have passed all of the tests; but if the knowledge workers don't use the system properly, the system will fail. You must ensure that all the knowledge workers have the required training in order to use the system correctly. For example, assume you have built a system to calculate employee paycheques. The system is programmed to ask for two numbers, one indicating the amount of time the employee worked, and the other indicating the employee's pay rate. The system then calculates the employee's paycheque by multiplying the two numbers. What would happen if the end user did not understand the system and entered the amount in the "time worked" field in minutes instead of hours? For example, if the end user entered in a $10 pay

TEAM WORK

YOUR RESPONSIBILITIES DURING EACH STEP OF THE SDLC

As a knowledge worker, you're a business process expert, liaison to the customer, quality control analyst, and manager of other people. However, according to which step of the SDLC you're in, your responsibilities may increase or decrease. In the table below, determine the extent to which you participate in each SDLC step according to your four responsibilities. For each row, number the SDLC steps from 1 to 7, with 1 identifying the step in which your responsibility is greatest and 7 identifying the step in which your responsibility is the least.

	Plan	Analysis	Design	Develop	Test	Implement	Maintain
Business process expert							
Liaison to the customer							
Quality control analyst							
Manager of other people							

rate per hour and 320 as the amount of time worked, the system would calculate a paycheque for $3200 rather than $800.

MAINTAIN

During maintenance, your primary role is to ensure all the knowledge workers have the support they require to use the system. You might be responsible for setting up a help desk or developing change request forms for your users to fill out if they require a change to the system. Not only do you have to track the change requests, but also you must ensure that any changes requested for the system are worth performing. Changes cost money, especially once a system has reached the maintenance phase. You must carefully weigh every requested change for merit and monetary worth.

IT SPECIALISTS AND KNOWLEDGE WORKERS WORKING TOGETHER

It's important to build systems with both the knowledge workers and IT specialists working together, because the knowledge workers are the business process experts and quality control analysts, and the IT specialists are highly skilled in designing, implementing, and maintaining the systems. By having knowledge workers and IT specialists combine their unique skills when performing the activities during the SDLC you'll be sure to build a solid system that supports your organization's strategies and goals.

Why Systems Fail

Only 20 percent of systems built today are successful. That's correct: 80 percent of systems fail, or only two systems out of ten will be successful. If you wonder why so many systems development efforts fail, that is difficult to answer, as systems can fail for so many different reasons, of which the following are primary:

- Unclear or missing requirements
- Skipping SDLC phases
- Failure to manage scope
- Failure to manage the project plan
- Changing technology

UNCLEAR OR MISSING REQUIREMENTS

The most common reason why systems fail is because the business requirements are either missing or incorrectly gathered during the analysis phase. The business requirements drive the entire system; if they are not accurate or complete there is no way the system can be successful.

Let's look at an example of gathering an inaccurate requirement. Assume you're building a student registration system. What happens if you documented the business requirement as the "System must not allow students to add classes"? This requirement is incorrect; it should be stated "System must allow students to add classes." If you built a student registration system that didn't allow students to add classes, it would be a complete failure.

Let's take a look at an example of missing a requirement. What if you're in the development phase and suddenly realize that the system must also calculate a student's grade point average. This is a major requirement, and trying to add this functionality to the system at this late date would be extremely difficult and expensive.

SKIPPING SDLC PHASES

The first thing individuals tend to do when a project falls behind schedule is start skipping phases in the SDLC. For example, a project is three weeks behind in the development phase, so the project manager decides to cut testing down from six weeks to three. Obviously, you can't perform all of the testing in half of the time. Failing to test the system will lead to unfound errors and chances are high that the system will fail. It's critical that you perform all phases in the SDLC during every project. Skipping any of the phases is sure to lead to system failure.

FAILURE TO MANAGE SCOPE

As the project progresses the project manager must track the status of each activity and adjust the project plan if a activity is added or taking longer than expected. **Scope creep** occurs when the scope of the project increases. Let's return to the student registration system example mentioned above. Imagine how the scope of the project changes if the knowledge worker suddenly requests that the system track instructor evaluations. This scope increase would cause the system development efforts to more than double in order to add in the extra request.

Feature creep occurs when developers add features that were not part of the initial requirements. A great example of feature creep would be if the developer decided to add in an online help feature for the students. This feature is in itself a great idea, but the knowledge workers had not requested it and it's not planned for in the budget or the project plan. Building this feature in would take time and money and jeopardize the project's success. Feature creep is difficult to manage and can easily put a project behind schedule.

FAILURE TO MANAGE THE PROJECT PLAN

Managing the project plan is one of the biggest challenges during systems development. Figure 6.6 is an example of a sample project plan. What is the first thing you notice about the project plan and the SDLC? The project plan outlines the SDLC as the primary phases performed during system development. Under each phase, you'll notice a sample activity that you'll complete during the phase. Beside each activity, you'll notice the estimated duration, or the time you have to complete the activity. Each activity also has a resource name indicating who must work on the activity. Notice that some activities have only one individual assigned and some activities have two. The project plan is the road map you follow during the development of the system. Developing the initial project plan is the easiest part of the project manager's job. Managing and revising the project plan is the hard part.

There are many reasons why the project manager must continually review and revise the project plan. Imagine what happens to the plan if an individual is off sick or on vacation and can't complete his/her activities? What happens if you have to add some activities to the project plan? What happens if you have to delete some of the activities? What happens if some of the activities take significant longer to complete than expected? All of these questions indicate why the project manager must continuously review and revise the project plan. The project plan is a living document; it changes almost daily on any project. Failure to monitor, revise, and update the project plan is a primary reason why many projects fail.

Figure 6.6

Sample Project Plan

				May 26,'02	June 2, '02	June 9, '02	June 16, '02	June 23, '02
ID	**Task Name**	**Duration**	**Resource Names**	S M T W T F S	S M T W T F S	S M T W T F S	S M T W T F S	S M T W T F S
1	**Plan**	**3 days**						
2	Set Scope	3 days	Scott	Scott				
3	**Analysis**	**8 days**						
4	Gather Business Requirements	8 days	Anne, Martha		Anne, Martha			
5	**Design**	**3 days**						
6	Model GUI	3 days	David			David		
7	**Develop**	**2 days**						
8	Build Database	2 days	Logan			Logan		
9	**Test**	**3 days**						
10	Write Test Condition	3 days	Martha				Martha	
11	**Implement**	**1 day?**						
12	Install System	1 day?	Leigh				Leigh	
13	**Maintain**	**6 days**						
14	Set Up Help Desk	6 days	Naomi					

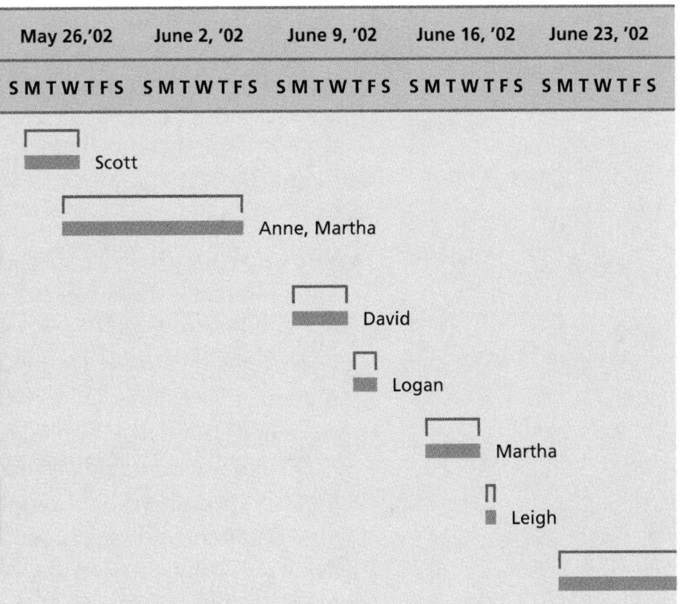

CHANGING TECHNOLOGY

Many of the system examples we have discussed in this chapter are small and easy to implement, such as a student registration system. They are great for discussion and initial understanding, but not indicative of real-world projects. Many actual projects have hundreds of business requirements, take years to complete, and cost millions of dollars.

Gordon Moore, co-founder of Intel Corporation, observed in 1965 that chip density (memory sizes, processor power, etc.) doubles every 18 months; this observation, known as Moore's law, is as true now as it was then. It's not unusual to have to revise your entire project plan in the middle of a project due to a change in technology. For example, imagine you're building a system that has a project time frame of three years to complete. What happens if one year into the project a new programming language is released that is far superior to the one you're currently using? If you decide to change to the new programming language, you will have to revise your entire project plan, and rewrite any code that has already been written. Technology changes so fast that it's almost impossible to deliver an information system without feeling the pain of changing technology.

Now that you understand the SDLC and your roles within it, let's turn our attention to who is going to actually build the system. When approaching systems development as a knowledge worker, you have three methods of dealing with this question:

- *Insourcing.* Using IT specialists within your organization
- *Selfsourcing.* Using knowledge workers such as yourself
- *Outsourcing.* Using another organization

Insourcing

Insourcing a project means using IT specialists within your organization to develop the system. It is one of the most common methods of system development, because it's typically the cheapest: the company doesn't have to hire contractors. Contractors, or external employees, are hired only temporarily. Insourcing is also popular because internal employees are already familiar with the operations of the company. This is a big advantage when you begin building systems that must support the business goals.

The above discussion introducing you to the SDLC and your roles within it assumed that you choose to insource. So you already understand the SDLC process through insourcing. Let's now turn our attention to selfsourcing and outsourcing.

Selfsourcing

What we want to look at now is how you, as a knowledge worker, can go about developing systems, which we call selfsourcing. **Selfsourcing** (also called **knowledge worker development** or **end user development**) is the development and support of IT systems by knowledge workers with little or no help from IT specialists. Selfsourcing is becoming quite common in most organizations and is part of the overall concept of knowledge worker development or end user computing.

It's important to understand that some selfsourcing projects still involve support from IT specialists. For example, Eaton Corp., a consulting firm, actively encourages the selfsourcing of systems development in Lotus Notes by providing training classes to knowledge workers. In these classes, knowledge workers learn how to set up a document database; use built-in templates to develop applications questions quickly; and create customized forms, views, and macros. And, when Eaton's knowledge workers actually begin creating their own systems, IT specialists are available to answer questions and handle more complicated technical issues, such as installing software on a client/server network or creating a local area network from scratch.[6]

THE SELFSOURCING PROCESS

Many of the smaller knowledge worker computing systems, such as customizing reports, creating macros, and interfacing a letter in a word processing package with a customer database to create individualized mailings, can be created in a matter of hours. More complicated systems, such as a student registration system or employee payroll system, require that you follow the formal SDLC process during development.

Figure 6.7 illustrates the selfsourcing process; the table entitled "Key Tasks in Selfsourcing" summarizes the main activities within some of the steps. As you can see, the

Figure 6.7

The Selfsourcing Process and Key Activities in Selfsourcing

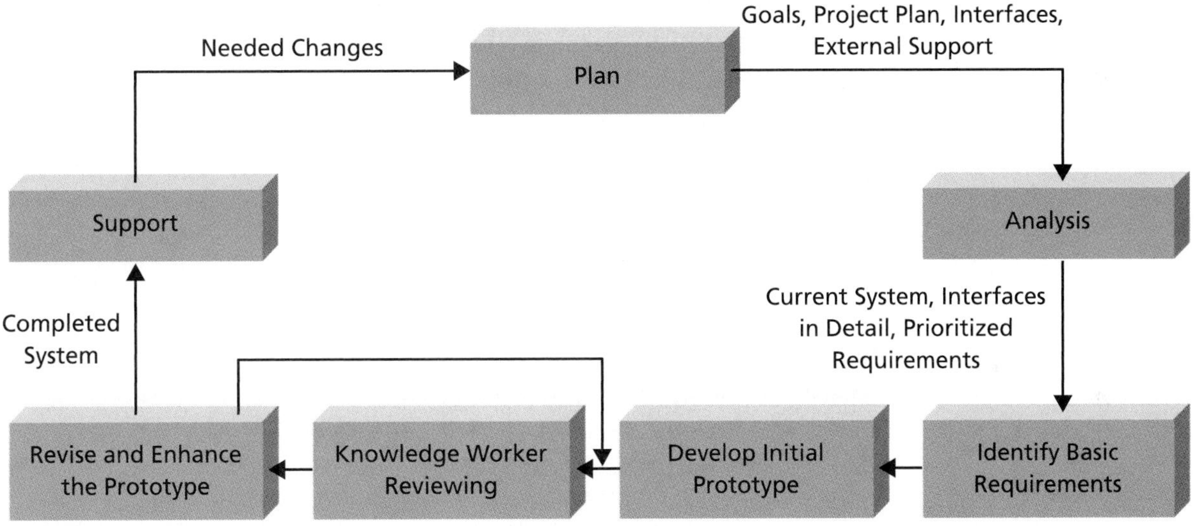

Key Tasks in Selfsourcing

Plan
• Define system goals in light of organizational goals. • Create a project plan. • Identify any systems that require an interface. • Determine what type of external support you will require.
Analysis
• Study and model the current system. • Understand the interfaces in detail. • Define and prioritize your requirements.
Maintain
• Completely document the system. • Provide ongoing maintenance.

selfsourcing process is similar to the steps in the SDLC. However, you should notice that the selfsourcing process does include prototyping (model building, which we'll discuss in detail in the a later section). This is key—when you develop a system for yourself, you will most often go through the process of prototyping.

As you study Figure 6.7, you should consider several important issues.

ALIGNING YOUR SELFSOURCING EFFORTS WITH ORGANIZATIONAL GOALS

When you first begin planning a system you want to develop, you must consider it in light of your organization's goals. If you're considering developing a system for yourself that runs counter to your organization's goals, you should abandon it immediately. Obviously, you don't want to build a system that reduces sales or decreases the number of customers. You have to consider how you spend your time building systems carefully as you are busy and your time is extremely valuable. It's important to remember that developing a system through selfsourcing takes time—your time.

Therefore, your first activity should always be to consider what you want to develop in conjunction with what your organization expects you to do.

DETERMINING WHAT EXTERNAL SUPPORT YOU WILL REQUIRE

As we've already stated, some selfsourcing projects will involve support from IT specialists within your organization. Your in-house IT specialists are a valuable resource during the selfsourcing process. Don't forget about them and be sure to include them in the planning phase. The chances of building a successful system increase greatly when you have both knowledge workers and IT specialists working together.

DOCUMENTING THE SYSTEM ONCE COMPLETE

Even if you're developing a system just for yourself, you still need to document how it works. When you get promoted, other people will come in behind you and probably use the system you developed and might even make changes to it. For this reason, you must document how your system works from a technical point of view as well as create an easy-to-use operating manual.

PROVIDING ONGOING SUPPORT

When you develop a system through selfsourcing, you must be prepared to provide your own support and maintenance. Since you are the primary owner and developer of the system, you're solely responsible for ensuring the system continues to function properly and continues to meet all of the changing business requirements. You must also be prepared to support other knowledge workers who use your system, as they will be counting on you to help them learn and understand the system you developed. For example, if you develop a customer relationship database using Microsoft Office XP, you must be prepared to convert it to Microsoft Office 2004 when that program becomes available and your organization adopts it. The systems development process doesn't end with implementation—it continues on a daily basis with support and maintenance.

THE ADVANTAGES OF SELFSOURCING

IMPROVES REQUIREMENTS DETERMINATION During insourcing, knowledge workers tell IT specialists what they want. In selfsourcing, knowledge workers essen-

ON YOUR OWN

HOW HAVE YOU SELFSOURCED?

You've probably performed the selfsourcing process many times. For example, if you've created a résumé, you probably prototyped it using a word processing package. And, if you've prepared a presentation for a class, you may have prototyped it using a presentation graphics software package.

Think about the many other instances when you've selfsourced and used personal productivity software. For each, identify your goal, what personal productivity software you used, and how you performed the prototyping process. Do some types of personal productivity software packages lend themselves better to prototyping than others? What are they? What types of personal productivity software packages do not lend themselves well to prototyping? Why is this true?

tially tell themselves what they want. This greatly improves the effectiveness of capturing requirements, which helps ensure the success of the new system.

INCREASES KNOWLEDGE WORKER PARTICIPATION AND SENSE OF OWNERSHIP No matter what you do, if you do it yourself, you always take more pride in the result. The same is true when developing an IT system through selfsourcing. If knowledge workers know that they own the system because they developed and now support it, they are more apt to actively participate in its development and have a greater sense of ownership.

INCREASES SPEED OF SYSTEMS DEVELOPMENT Many small systems do not lend themselves well to insourcing. These smaller systems may suffer from "analysis paralysis," because they don't require a structured step-by-step approach to their development. In fact, insourcing may be slower than selfsourcing for smaller projects.

PITFALLS AND RISKS OF SELFSOURCING

INADEQUATE KNOWLEDGE WORKER EXPERTISE LEADS TO INADEQUATELY DEVELOPED SYSTEMS Many selfsourcing systems never get completed because knowledge workers lack the real expertise with IT tools to develop a complete and fully working system. It may seem like no big deal—the system couldn't have been that important if the people who needed it never finished developing it. But that's not true. If knowledge workers choose to develop their systems, they must spend time away from their primary duties within the organization. This diverted time may mean lost revenue.

LACK OF ORGANIZATIONAL FOCUS CREATES "PRIVATIZED" IT SYSTEMS Many selfsourcing projects are done outside the IT systems plan of an organization. This simply means that there may be many "private" IT systems that do not interface with other systems and possess uncontrolled and duplicated information. These types of systems serve no meaningful purpose in an organization and can only lead to more problems.

INSUFFICIENT ANALYSIS OF DESIGN ALTERNATIVES LEADS TO SUB-PAR IT SYSTEMS Some knowledge workers jump to immediate conclusions about the hardware and software they should use without carefully analyzing all the possible alternatives. If this happens, knowledge workers may develop systems that are processing inefficiently.

LACK OF DOCUMENTATION AND EXTERNAL SUPPORT LEADS TO SHORT-LIVED SYSTEMS When knowledge workers develop systems, they often forgo documentation of how the system works and fail to realize that they can expect little or no support from IT specialists. All systems—no matter who develops them—must change over time. Knowledge workers must realize that those changes are their responsibility. They also need to realize that making those changes is easier if they document the system well.

Outsourcing

Your final choice is to outsource by choosing external employees from another organization, or contractors, to develop the system. Typically, large systems have both internal and external employees working on the development effort.

DEVELOPING STRATEGIC PARTNERSHIPS

The Outsourcing Research Council recently completed a study indicating that human resources (HR) is a top outsourcing area for many companies. Fifty percent of the companies surveyed said they were already outsourcing some or all of their payroll processing and another 38 percent said they were considering it.

Energizer, the world's largest manufacturer of batteries and flashlights, outsourced its HR operations to ADP, one of the top HR outsourcing companies. Energizer currently has over 3500 employees and 2000 retired employees who all require multiple HR services. ADP provides Energizer with centralized call centres, transaction processing services, and Web-based employee self-service systems. Energizer's vice-president of human resources, Peter Conrad, has stated, "ADP was clearly the most capable and offered the kind of one-stop shopping our company was looking for." For several of the systems provided by ADP employee usage has topped over 80 percent in the six months the systems have been active.[7]

Figure 6.8

Major Forms of Outsourcing Systems Development

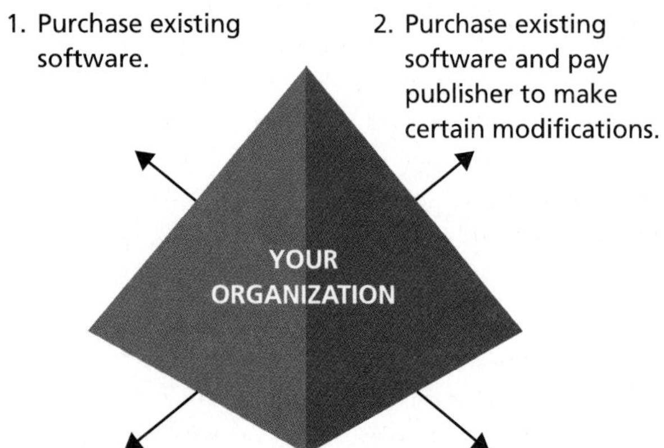

Energizer's choice of using ADP to develop its human resources system is an example of outsourcing. **Outsourcing** is the delegation of specific work to a third party for a specified length of time, at a specified cost, and at a specified level of service. IT outsourcing today represents a significant opportunity for your organization to capitalize on the intellectual resources of other organizations by having them take over and perform certain business functions in which they have more expertise than the knowledge workers in your company. IT outsourcing for software development can take on one of four forms (see Figure 6.8):

1. Purchasing existing software
2. Purchasing existing software and paying the publisher to make certain modifications

3. Purchasing existing software and paying the publisher for the right to make modifications yourself
4. Outsourcing the development of an entirely new and unique system for which no software exists

In these instances, we're not talking about personal productivity software you can buy at a local computer store. We're talking about large software packages that may cost millions of dollars.

For example, every organization has to track financial information, and there are several different systems they can purchase that help them perform this activity. For example, the Oracle Financials system tracks all an organization's financial information. Another good example of a pre-built system Arbor/BP, a telecommunications billing system developed by Kenan, a division of Lucent Technologies. Many telecommunications companies around the world have purchased it to track and bill customer phone calls and digital services.

A company could choose to build its own systems. However, this would take a significant amount of time, money, and expertise. Most companies find it cheaper, faster, and easier to buy a pre-built system and then customize it for the company's specific needs.

THE OUTSOURCING PROCESS

The outsourcing process is both similar to and quite different from the systems development life cycle. It's different in that you turn over much of the design, development, testing, implementation, and maintenance steps to another organization (see Figure 6.9). It's similar in that your organization begins with planning and defining the project scope. During one of these phases your organization may come to understand that it needs a particular system but cannot develop it in-house. If so, that proposed system can be outsourced. Below, we briefly describe the remaining steps of the outsourcing process.

Figure 6.9
The Outsourcing Process

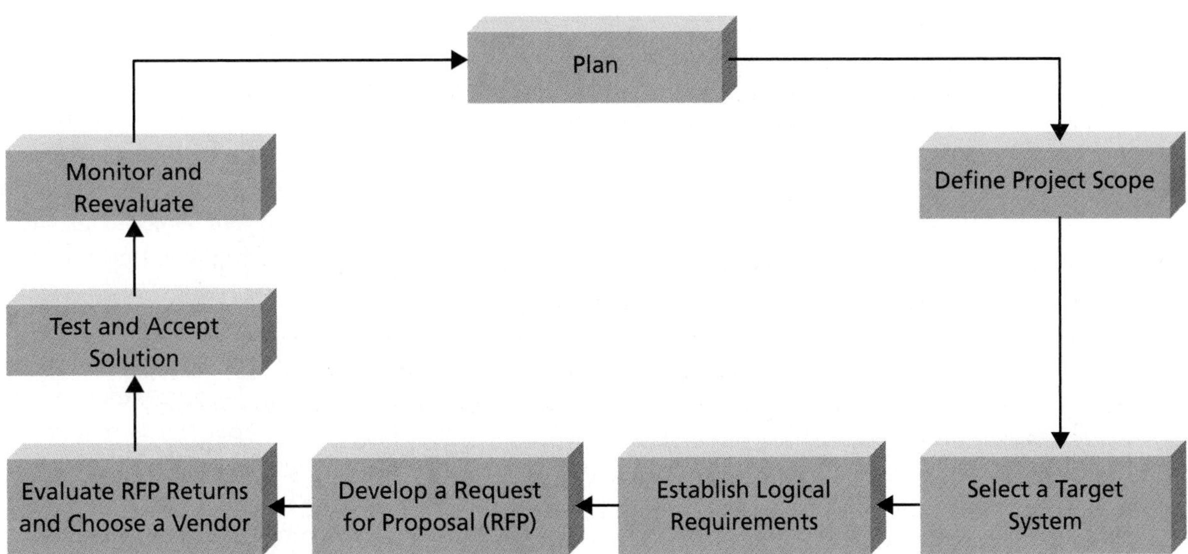

TEAM WORK

HOW MANY OUTSOURCING COMPANIES ARE THERE?

Assume your company is looking to outsource its payroll activities including calculating the payroll and generating the paycheques every month. Try searching the Internet for different companies that offer this outsourcing service. Fill in the following table comparing the advantages and disadvantages of the different companies you find. Discuss which one you would choose and why.

Company Name	Advantages	Disadvantages

SELECT A TARGET SYSTEM Once you've identified a potential system for outsourcing, you still have some important questions to answer. For example, will the proposed system manage strategic and sensitive information? If so, you probably wouldn't consider outsourcing it. That is, you don't want another organization seeing and having access to your most vital information. If you're building an ordering system you might not want people to view your product prices, as they may be a significant part of your strategic advantage.

You should also consider whether the system is small enough to be selfsourced. If so, let knowledge workers within your organization develop the system instead of outsourcing it. On the other hand, if the proposed system is fairly large and supports a routine, non-sensitive business function, then you should target it for outsourcing.

ESTABLISH LOGICAL REQUIREMENTS Regardless of your choice of insourcing or outsourcing, you must still perform the analysis phase including the primary activity of gathering the business requirements for the proposed system. Remember that the business requirements drive the entire system; if they are not accurate or complete there is no way the system will be successful. Regardless of your choice to insource or outsource you must still gather accurate and complete business requirements.

DEVELOP A REQUEST FOR PROPOSAL Outsourcing involves telling another organization what you want. What you want is essentially the logical requirements for a proposed system, and you convey that information by developing a **request for proposal (RFP)**—a formal document that describes in detail your logical requirements for a proposed system and invites outsourcing organizations (which we'll refer to as *vendors*) to submit bids for its development. An RFP is the most important document in the outsourcing process. For systems of great size, your organization may create an RFP that's literally hundreds of pages long and requires months of work to complete.

It's vitally important that you take all the time you need to create a complete and thorough RFP; eventually, it will become the foundation for a legal and binding contract into which your organization and the vendor will enter. At minimum, your RFP should contain the elements in Figure 6.10. Notice that an RFP includes key information such as an overview of your organization, underlying business processes that the proposed system will support, a request for a development time frame, and a request for a statement of detailed outsourcing costs.

All this information is vitally important to both your organization and the vendors. For your organization, the ability to develop a complete and thorough RFP means that you completely understand what you have and what you want. For the vendors, a complete and thorough RFP makes it easier to identify a proposed system that will meet most, if not all, your needs.

Figure 6.10

Outline of a Request for Proposal (RFP)

1. Organizational overview
2. Problem statement
3. Description of current system
    3.1 Underlying business processes
    3.2 Hardware
    3.3 Software (application and system)
    3.4 System processes
    3.5 Information
    3.6 System interfaces
4. Description of proposed system
    4.1 New processes
    4.2 New information
5. Request for new system design
    5.1 Hardware
    5.2 Software
    5.3 Underlying business processes
    5.4 System processes
    5.5 Information
    5.6 System interfaces
6. Request for implementation plan
    6.1 Training
    6.2 Conversion
7. Request for support plan
    7.1 Hardware
    7.2 Software
8. Request for development time frame
9. Request for statement of outsourcing costs
10. How RFP returns will be scored
11. Deadline for RFP returns
12. Primary contact person

EVALUATE REQUEST FOR PROPOSAL RETURNS AND CHOOSE A VENDOR Your next activity in outsourcing is to evaluate the RFP returns and choose a vendor. You perform this evaluation of the RFP returns according to the scoring method you identified in the RFP. This is not a simple process. No two vendors will ever provide RFP returns in the same format and the RFP returns you receive are usually longer than the RFP itself.

Once you've thoroughly analyzed the RFP returns, it's time to rank them and determine which vendor to use. Most often, you rank RFP returns according to cost, time, and the scoring mechanism you identified. Again, ranking RFP returns is not simple. One vendor may be the cheapest, but requires the longest time to develop the new system. Another vendor may be able to provide a system quickly, but without some of the features you have identified as critical.

Once you've chosen the vendor, a lengthy legal process follows. Outsourcing is serious business—and serious business between two organizations almost always requires a lot of negotiating and the use of lawyers. Eventually, your organization has to enter a legal and binding contract that very explicitly states the features of the proposed system, the exact costs, the time frame for development, acceptance criteria, and criteria for breaking the contract for nonperformance or noncompliance.

TEST AND ACCEPT SOLUTION As with all systems, testing and accepting the solution is crucial. Once a vendor installs the new system, it's up to you and your organization to test it before accepting it. You'll need to develop detailed test plans and test conditions for the entire system. This alone may involve months of running and testing the new system while continuing to operate the old one (the parallel conversion method).

When you "accept" a solution, you're saying that the system performs to your expectations and that the vendor has met its contract obligations so far. Accepting a solution involves granting your sign-off on the system, which releases the vendor from

OUTSOURCING FREES CANADIAN NATIONAL ARTS CENTRE TO FOCUS ON ITS CORE COMPETENCIES

Ottawa's National Arts Centre, founded in 1969 as a Crown corporation, boasts three concert stages and more than 111,400 square metres of space. This Canadian landmark is one of the world's largest live-performance centres, hosting several classical and pop music concerts, English and French theatre plays, and art festivals every year.

In 1997, the centre decided to outsource its IT to Compaq, including all network management, system administration, bilingual help desk support, and on-site service. "Before Compaq came in, the IT infrastructure was semi-dysfunctional. ... we had a very unstable network, inconsistent software on our desktops, outdated servers and PCs and no Internet access," says Richard Tremblay, director of administrative services. Over a period of 18 months, Compaq set up the Microsoft Windows NT Server network operating system, revamped the messaging system, provided access to the Internet, and installed nearly 200 new PCs running Microsoft Windows and the Office suite. Following a successful eight-month trial period, the centre signed on for a five-year outsourcing contract with Compaq covering support for all corporate applications and desktop software suites, and service for all desktops, servers, and communications devices.

Outsourcing simply made sense for the centre, because it allowed its people to focus on core competencies. "Our prime mission is to produce and stage live performances. We wanted to look at everything that was secondary to this mission and see if somebody else could do it better than we could," says Tremblay.[8]

any further development efforts or modifications to the system. Be careful when you do this because modifications to the system after sign-off can be extremely expensive. In 1996, the utility Duke Power Company continually tested but never accepted an outsourced system. Duke officially turned the lights out on a $23 million customer information system project after having invested over $12 million in its development. Duke Power had outsourced the project and had no choice but to terminate it when the vendor requested an additional two years to make necessary modifications.[9]

MONITOR AND REEVALUATE Just like systems you develop using the SDLC, systems you obtain through outsourcing need constant monitoring and reevaluation. You must continually evaluate and revise the project plan to ensure the system is going to meet its delivery schedule. In outsourcing, you also have to reassess your working relationship with the vendor. Is the vendor providing maintenance when you need it and according to the contract? Does the system really perform the stated functions? Do month-end and year-end processes work according to your desires? Does the vendor provide acceptable support if something goes wrong? These are all important questions that affect the success of your outsourcing efforts.

The most important question, though, is "Does the system still meet our needs and how much does it cost to update it?" In many outsourcing instances, if the system needs updating you must contract with the original vendor. This is one of the greatest drawbacks to outsourcing. When you outsource a system, you create a heavy dependency on that vendor to provide updates to the system, and updates are not inexpensive.

THE ADVANTAGES AND DISADVANTAGES OF OUTSOURCING

Making the decision to outsource is critical to your organization's success. Throughout our discussions of outsourcing, we've directly or indirectly described many of its

ON YOUR OWN

AN RFP AND THE SDLC

If you review Figure 6.10 closely, you'll notice that an RFP looks very similar to the steps of the SDLC. In the table below, identify which steps of the SDLC correspond to each element of an RFP.

Elements of a Request for Proposal	Step(s) of the SDLC
1. Organizational overview	
2. Problem statement	
3. Description of current system	
4. Description of proposed system	
5. Request for new system design	
6. Request for implementation plan	
7. Request for support plan	
8. Request for development time frame	
9. Request for statement of outsourcing costs	
10. How RFP returns will be scored	
11. Deadline for RFP returns	
12. Primary contact person	

advantages and disadvantages. We will now summarize the major advantages and disadvantages of outsourcing the systems development process in order to help you make this important decision.

ADVANTAGES OF OUTSOURCING A company's decision to outsource its system development, functions, and other needs can have a number of advantageous effects. Outsourcing allows an organization to:

- *Focus on unique core competencies.* By outsourcing systems development efforts that support noncritical business functions, your organization can focus on developing systems that support important, unique core competencies.
- *Exploit the intellect of another organization.* Outsourcing allows your organization to obtain intellectual capital by purchasing it from another organization. Often you won't be able to find individuals with all of the expertise required to develop a system. Outsourcing allows you to find those individuals with the expertise you need to get your system developed and implemented.
- *Better predict future costs.* When you outsource a function, whether systems development or some other business function, you know the exact costs. Zale Corp., a discount jewelry store, outsourced some of its IT systems and tied payments to the vendor according to how well Zale's stores perform. After all, the new IT systems will affect a store's performance, so why not tie a vendor's payment to it?[10]

INDUSTRY PERSPECTIVE

SHOULD YOU OUTSOURCE YOUR COMPANY'S LOGISTICS TO UPS?

In February 2002, UPS (www.ups.com) established a new business unit, UPS Supply Chain Solutions. The new organization makes it easier for customers to access UPS's expanding range of logistics, freight, financial, and consulting services in order to improve the performance of their global supply chains.

UPS Supply Chain Solutions offers customers the combined services of UPS Logistics Group, UPS Freight Services, UPS Capital, UPS Consulting, and UPS Mail Innovations. Together, these companies provide supply chain design and management, freight forwarding, customs brokerage, mail services, multimodal transportation, and consulting and financial services.

The company's supply chain services also leverage UPS' expertise in building and operating global IT and physical infrastructures and managing complex networks. Companies who do not possess world-class competence in supply chain management systems could let UPS run their systems for them (for a fee, of course).[11]

- *Acquire leading-edge technology.* Outsourcing allows your organization to acquire leading-edge technology without technical expertise and the inherent risks of choosing the wrong technology.
- *Reduce costs.* Outsourcing is often seen as a money saver for most organizations. And, indeed, reducing costs is one of the important reasons organizations outsource.
- *Improve performance accountability.* Outsourcing involves delegating work to another organization at a specified level of service. Your organization can use this specified level of service as leverage to guarantee that it gets exactly what it wants from the vendor.

DISADVANTAGES OF OUTSOURCING Outsourcing is not, however, without its potential problems. A company's decision to outsource its needs may cause it to suffer because it:

- *Reduces technical know-how for future innovation.* Outsourcing is a way of exploiting the intellect of another organization. It may also mean that your organization will no longer possess that expertise internally. If you outsource because you don't have the necessary technical expertise today, you'll probably have to outsource for the same reason tomorrow.
- *Reduces degree of control.* Outsourcing means giving up control. No matter what you choose to outsource, you are in some way giving up control over that function.
- *Increases vulnerability of strategic information.* Outsourcing systems development involves telling another organization what information you use and how you use that information. In doing so, you could be giving away strategic information and secrets.
- *Increases dependency on other organizations.* As soon as you start outsourcing, you immediately begin depending on another organization to perform many of your business functions. For example, GE was once all set to introduce a new washing machine—but it didn't happen on time. It seems that GE had outsourced some of its parts development and the vendor was late, resulting in a delayed product introduction that cost GE money.[12]

Now that you have a solid understanding of the selfsourcing, insourcing, and outsourcing processes, let's take a look at creating prototypes—another key decision you'll make during the design and development phases. When approaching systems development as a knowledge worker the decision to prototype has many significant advantages, which we'll discuss in detail in the next section.

Prototyping

Prototyping is the process of building a model that demonstrates the features of a proposed product, service, or system. A **prototype**, then, is simply a model of a proposed product, service, or system. If you think about it, people prototype all the time. Automobile manufacturers build prototypes of cars to demonstrate safety features, aerodynamics, and comfort. Building contractors construct models of homes and other structures to show layout and fire exits. Your instructor may give you sample test questions for an upcoming exam that are a model of what you can expect on the exam.

Building a small prototype during the design phase allows other knowledge workers to review the prototype and suggest changes, and further refine and enhance the prototype to include suggestions. Most notably, prototyping is a dynamic process that allows knowledge workers to see, work with, and evaluate a model and suggest changes to that model to increase the likelihood of success of the proposed system.

You can use prototyping to perform a variety of functions in the systems development process. Some of these are:

- *Gathering requirements.* Prototyping is a great requirements-gathering tool. You start by simply prototyping the basic systems requirements. Then you allow knowledge workers to add more requirements (information and processes) as you revise the prototype. Most people use prototyping for this purpose.
- *Helping determine requirements.* In many systems development processes, knowledge workers aren't sure what they really want—they simply know that the current system doesn't meet their needs. In this instance, you can use prototyping to help knowledge workers determine their exact requirements.
- *Proving that a system is technically feasible.* Let's face it, there are some things to which you cannot apply technology. And knowing whether you can is often unclear while defining the scope of the proposed system. If you're uncertain about whether something can be done, prototype it first. A prototype you use to prove the technical feasibility of a proposed system is a **proof-of-concept prototype**.
- *Selling the idea of a proposed system.* Many people resist changes in IT. The current system seems to work fine and they see no reason to go through the process of developing and learning to use a new system. In this case, you have to convince them that the proposed system will be better than the current one. Because prototyping is relatively fast, you won't have to invest a lot of time to develop a prototype that can convince people of the worth of the proposed system. A prototype you use to convince people of the worth of a proposed system is a **selling prototype**.

THE PROTOTYPING PROCESS

Prototyping is an excellent tool in systems development. However, who uses it and for what purpose determines how the process occurs. Most often, IT specialists use prototyping in the SDLC to form a technical system blueprint. In selfsourcing, however, you can often continue to refine the prototype until it becomes the final system. The prototyping process in either case is almost the same; only the result differs.

MICROSOFT UNVEILS LATEST MIRA PROTOTYPE

Imagine walking around your home with a computer monitor—just the monitor—and being able to do everything as though you were carrying the entire computer. You have merely ripped the display off your laptop and continue browsing the Web, checking e-mail, looking at photos, and listening to music.

This is the idea behind the Mira mobile monitor, the latest prototype developed by Microsoft. A new set of Windows-based technologies, collectively called Mira, enable wireless WebPAD devices for your home. A wireless link between the monitor and the computer keeps the connection alive. The full power of the computer is available, along with access to all its files and data. For more information, visit www.msn.com, keyword: "mira."

Figure 6.11 illustrates the difference between insourcing and selfsourcing prototyping. Regardless of who does it, the prototyping process involves four steps:

1. *Identify basic requirements.* During the first step, you gather the basic requirements for a proposed system. These include input and output information and, perhaps, some simple processes. At this point, however, you're typically unconcerned with editing rules, security issues, or end-of-period processing (e.g., producing W-2s for a payroll system at the end of the year).
2. *Develop initial prototype.* On the basis of the basic requirements, you then set out to develop an initial prototype. Most often, your initial prototype will include only user interfaces, such as data entry screens and reports.
3. *Knowledge worker reviewing.* Step 3 starts the truly iterative process of prototyping. When knowledge workers first enter this step, they evaluate the prototype and suggest changes or additions. In subsequent returns to step 3 (after step 4), they evaluate new versions of the prototype. It's important to involve as many knowledge workers as possible during this step. This will help resolve any discrepancies in such areas as terminology and operational processes.
4. *Revise and enhance the prototype.* The final step is to revise and enhance the prototype according to any knowledge worker suggestions. In this step, you make changes to the current prototype and add any new requirements. Next, you return to step 3 and have the knowledge workers review the new prototype.

For either insourcing or selfsourcing, you continue the iterative processes of steps 3 and 4 until knowledge workers are happy with the prototype. What happens to the prototype after that, however, differs.

During selfsourcing, you're most likely to use the targeted application software package or application development tool to develop the prototype. This simply means that you can continually refine the prototype until it becomes the final working system. For example, if you choose to develop a customer service application using Lotus Notes, you can prototype many of the operational features using Lotus Notes development tools. Because you develop these prototypes using the targeted application development environment, your prototype can eventually become the final system.

That process is not necessarily the same when insourcing. Most often, IT specialists develop prototypes using special prototyping development tools. Many of these tools don't support the creation of a final system—you simply use them to build prototypes. Therefore, the finished prototype becomes a blueprint or technical design for the final system. In the appropriate stages of the SDLC, IT specialists will implement

Figure 6.11

Prototyping Steps for Insourcing and Selfsourcing

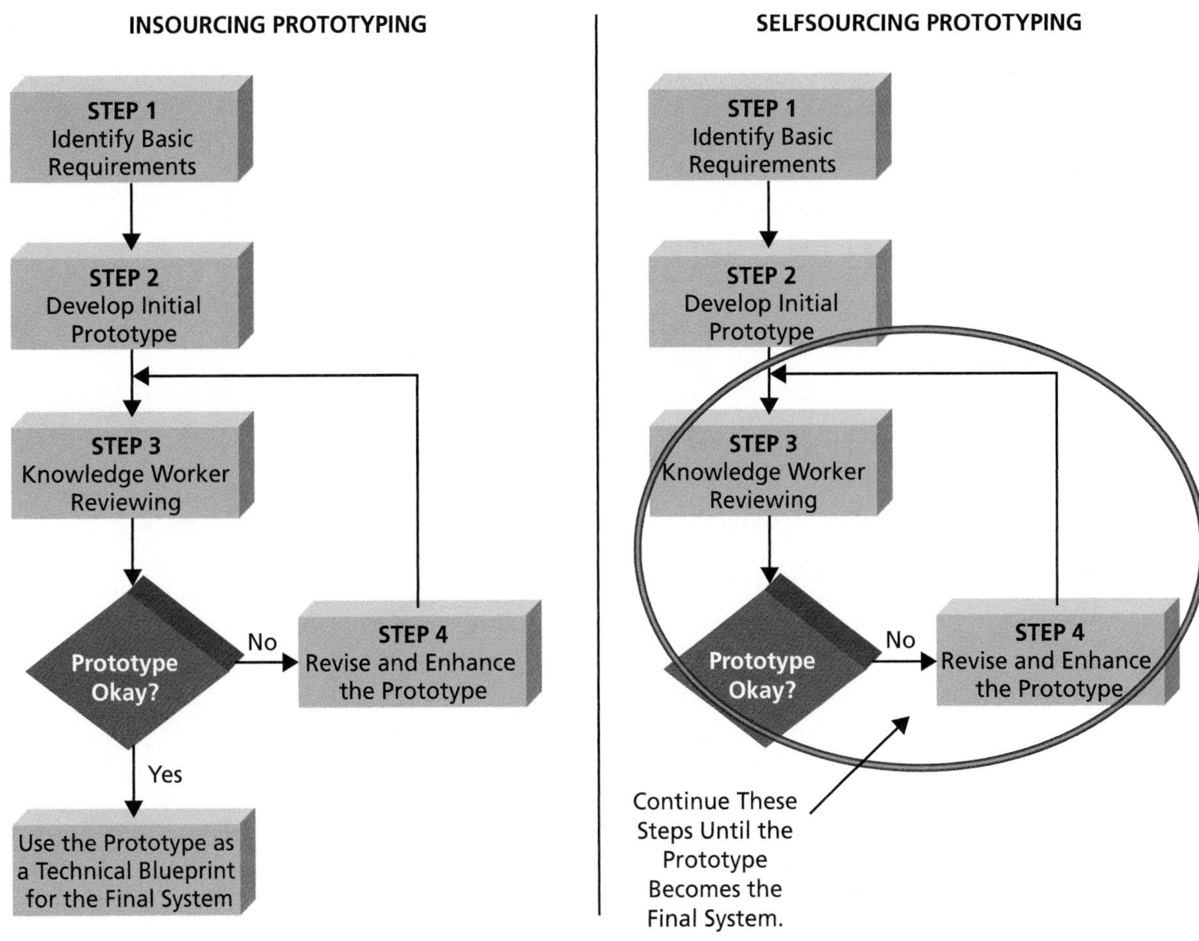

the prototypes in another application development environment better suited to the development of production systems.

THE ADVANTAGES OF PROTOTYPING

ENCOURAGES ACTIVE KNOWLEDGE WORKER PARTICIPATION First and foremost, prototyping encourages knowledge workers to actively participate in the development process. As opposed to interviewing and the reviewing of documentation, prototyping allows knowledge workers to see and work with working models of the proposed system.

HELPS RESOLVE DISCREPANCIES AMONG KNOWLEDGE WORKERS During the prototyping process, many knowledge workers participate in defining the requirements for and reviewing the prototype. The "many" is key. If several knowledge workers participate in prototyping, you'll find it's much easier to resolve any discrepancies the knowledge workers may encounter.

GIVES KNOWLEDGE WORKERS A FEEL FOR THE FINAL SYSTEM Prototyping, especially for user interfaces, provides a feel for how the final system will look, feel,

THE GLOBAL PERSPECTIVE

CUSTOMIZING YOUR PROTOTYPE FOR A GLOBAL MARKET

Thousands of prototypes are available for all different kinds of systems. System prototypes can be viewed on the Web, at conferences, or through individual meetings. If you place the prototype on the Web, anyone from anywhere in the world will be able to view it. If you attend a conference, people from all over your country, and perhaps other countries, will be able to view it. If you're going to a meeting, you'll know exactly who the individuals are that are going to view it.

One way to ensure your customers will be happy with what you have to show them is to customize your prototype for the intended audience. For example, if you build a calculator prototype for the Web you may want to incorporate into it the ability to change the number display to the customer's language if it is Chinese or Japanese. If you build a billing system, you might want the currency to change depending on the customer's origin.

and work. When knowledge workers understand the look, feel, and working of the final system, they are more apt to determine its potential for success.

HELPS DETERMINE TECHNICAL FEASIBILITY Proof-of-concept prototypes are great for determining the technical feasibility of a proposed system.

HELPS SELL THE IDEA OF A PROPOSED SYSTEM Finally, selling prototypes can help break down resistance barriers. Many people don't want new systems because the old one seems to work just fine, and they're afraid the new system won't meet their expectations and work properly. If you provide them with a working prototype that proves the new system will be successful, they will be more inclined to buy into it.

THE DISADVANTAGES OF PROTOTYPING

LEADS PEOPLE TO BELIEVE THE FINAL SYSTEM WILL FOLLOW SHORTLY When a prototype is complete, many people believe that the final system will follow shortly. After all, they've seen the system at work in the form of a prototype, so how long can it take to bring the system into production? Unfortunately, it may take months or years. You need to be sure that people understand that the prototype is only a model—not the final system missing only a few simple bells and whistles.

GIVES NO INDICATION OF PERFORMANCE UNDER OPERATIONAL CONDITIONS Prototypes very seldom take all operational conditions into consideration. This problem surfaced for the Department of Motor Vehicles in a U.S. state on the East Coast. During prototyping, the system—which handled motor vehicle and driver registration for the entire state—worked fine for 20 workstations at two locations. When the system was finally installed for all locations (which included over 1200 workstations), the system spent all its time just managing communications traffic—it had absolutely no time to complete any transactions. This is potentially the most significant drawback to prototyping. You must prototype operational conditions as well as interfaces and processes.[13]

LEADS THE PROJECT TEAM TO FORGO PROPER TESTING AND DOCUMENTATION You must thoroughly test and document all new systems. Unfortunately, many people believe they can forgo testing and documentation when using prototyping. After all, they've tested the prototype, and why not use the prototype as the documentation for the system? Don't make this mistake.

Prototyping is most probably a tool that you will use to develop many knowledge worker information systems. If you stick to the steps of the SDLC, have the correct resources, and learn how to make the most of your prototypes, you will be much more successful in your career as a knowledge worker.

Summary: Student Learning Outcomes Revisited

1. **List the seven steps in the systems development life cycle (SDLC) and an associated activity for each step.** The **systems development life cycle (SDLC)** is a structured step-by-step approach for developing information systems. The seven steps and activities are as follows:
   1. *Plan.* Set project scope, develop project plan
   2. *Analysis.* Gather business requirements
   3. *Design.* Design technical architecture, design system models
   4. *Develop.* Build technical architecture, build database and programs
   5. *Test.* Write test conditions, perform testing
   6. *Implement.* Perform user training, write user documentation
   7. *Maintain.* Provide a help desk, support system changes
2. **List four reasons why your participation during the systems development life cycle is critical.** Your participation during every step of the SDLC is critical because you are (or will be):
   - *A business process expert.* You know and understand how the business works better than anyone else does.
   - *A liaison to the customer.* You know what a certain customer segment wants, and you can relay that information to the project team.
   - *A quality control analyst.* You must review alternative solutions to assure that the chosen alternative meets your needs.
   - *A manager of other people.* You have ultimate responsibility for the work and productivity of others.
3. **Describe three reasons why projects fail.** Projects fail for many reasons and, throughout this chapter, we've discussed several of them. One of the primary reasons is missing or unclear business requirements. Since the entire project is based on the business requirements, if you fail to capture them correctly there is no way you will be able to build a successful system. Another common reason projects fail is that phases are skipped in the systems development life cycle. It's critical that you perform all phases in the SDLC during every project. Skipping any of them is sure to lead to system failure. Another reason system failure occurs is because you fail to manage the project plan and scope. Allowing **scope creep** or **feature creep** to occur will drastically increase the project's development effort. Finally, changing technology can be a big reason why projects fail. Technology changes so fast that it is almost impossible to deliver a system without having to deal with a change in technology, be it an operating system upgrade or the release of a new programming language.
4. **Define the three different ways you can staff a system development project.** Insourcing, selfsourcing, and outsourcing are the three different ways you can staff a system development project. **Insourcing** uses IT specialists within your organization, **selfsourcing** uses knowledge workers, and **outsourcing** uses another organization. It is important to note that most large projects typically use insourcing, selfsourcing, and outsourcing all at the same time.
5. **List two advantages of selfsourcing.** When you self-source a project you improve requirements determination, increase knowledge worker participation and sense of ownership, and increase the speed of systems development.
6. **Describe prototyping and profile an example of a prototype. Prototyping** is the process of building a model that demonstrates the features of a proposed product, service, or system. A **prototype**, then, is simply a model of a proposed

product, service, or system. If you think about it, people prototype all the time. Automobile manufacturers build prototypes of cars to demonstrate safety features, aerodynamics, and comfort. Building contractors construct models of homes and other structures to show layout and fire exits.

7. **Describe two advantages of prototyping.** First, prototyping encourages knowledge workers to actively participate in the development process. It allows them to see and work with working models of the proposed system, as opposed to just interviewing and reviewing documentation. Second, prototyping helps resolve discrepancies among knowledge workers. During the prototyping process, many knowledge workers participate in defining the requirements for and reviewing the prototype. The "many" is key. If several knowledge workers participate in prototyping, you'll find it's much easier to resolve any discrepancies the knowledge workers may encounter.

CLOSING CASE STUDY ONE

SOME PROTOTYPES HIT, SOME MISS, AND SOME WE ARE JUST NOT SURE ABOUT

Pick up any copy of a technology magazine and you'll see loads of new prototypes anxious to hit the consumer market. Would you like to buy new mountain bike that is built without using any chains for only $5593?

How about some Smart Trading Cards? This alternative to cardboard baseball cards comes with a CPU where you can review highlights and listen to important personal statistics such as the leading skateboarder's number of broken bones. Unfortunately, these Smart Cards don't come with a stick of chewing gum, which was the big perk with the traditional baseball trading cards. A stick of chewing gum can no longer compare to a CPU. Especially considering the price for traditional baseball cards was 10 cents and the Smart Cards sell for $8 plus $20 for the card reader. With those kind of prices who cares about a stick of chewing gum?

How would you like a pair of snorkelling flippers that can change shape on the fly to help you adapt easily to your changing underworld environment?

The list of new prototypes goes on and on ranging from wristwatches with a digital compass to Wave Boxes, the first portable hydraulic whirlpool perfect for those city dwelling kayak fans.

But what do you think happens after you make a prototype? Chances are it will take one of two paths. On the first path, the prototype is a big hit and the product goes into mass production and is found in every Wal-Mart and Kmart in the country. On the second path, the prototype is unsuccessful and goes into storage for eternity. Only about 10 percent of product prototypes make it to the consumer market.

Every year, the online magazine *Wired News* presents the Vaporware Awards to the top ten most eagerly awaited technology products that never made it to consumers. As the technology industry continues to generate products that promise to revolutionize consumers work and personal lives, *Wired News* follows them from planning to delivery. For more information, visit www.wired.com.

In Ithaca, New York you can visit Robert McMath's museum of failed products, which he has been maintaining for over 30 years. Are you interested in purchasing edible deodorant, a nice can of aerosol toothpaste for kids, toaster eggs, a garlic cake? The list is endless, and for many of them you have to wonder what the inventor was thinking. (If anyone can tell us when or why you would eat garlic cake, we would be grateful.)

Building prototypes is the only way to determine if your product is going to be a hit or a miss. Understanding the prototyping process and the advantages and disadvantages covered in this chapter is important to your career as a knowledge worker, as you'll be working with information system prototypes and perhaps building some yourself.[14,15]

Questions

1. Some products hit, some products miss, and some we are still not sure what the inventor was think-

ing. Many products end up sitting on a shelf or in a failed-products museum. There are thousands of them out there and some of these failed ideas are extremely entertaining. Research the Web to find three examples of failed products that never reached the consumer market.

2. Prototyping is an invaluable tool for systems development. Building a prototype allows knowledge workers to see, work with, and evaluate a model and suggest changes to the model. Refer back to the discussion on the cost of fixing errors or Figure 6.5. What do prototyping and this figure have in common? How can prototyping help you control your project budget and the cost of fixing errors?

3. Prototyping can be used in the analysis phase to help you gather business requirements. Throughout this chapter we discussed the importance of gathering solid business requirements. How can building a prototype help you gather solid business requirements on an information systems development project?

4. Listed above are many examples of prototypes. Use your creativity and business knowledge to generate an idea for a new product for a business or consumers. Or it can be a service that would help consumers perform their daily activities and activities. Write a brief paragraph describing your idea along with a picture of the product.

5. One of the disadvantages to building a prototype is that people tend to believe the final system will follow shortly. Why do you think this is so? If you were delivering a system prototype, how would you communicate to the system users that the real system would not be ready for another three years?

6. It is important to remember that communication is the primary key to deploying a successful prototype. When Planters Peanuts first started to market fresh-roasted peanuts, the product was a complete failure. Consumers continually confused the product with coffee beans and kept taking it home to grind it. The words "fresh-roasted" are probably what caused the product to initially fail. If you had been in charge, what could you have done to help consumers understand the product contained peanuts and not coffee beans?

CLOSING CASE STUDY TWO

THE STAMPEDE BARBEQUE RESTAURANT

The Stampede Barbeque Restaurant, located in Calgary, Alberta, has successfully been in business for 20 years. The restaurant specializes in barbeque chicken and beef and includes scrumptious side dishes of potato salad, coleslaw, and baked beans. Customers come from all around for a good old-fashioned barbeque dinner. On a Friday night you can expect the line to be out the door and the wait to be close to an hour. It is estimated that Shawn, the owner, serves over 500 barbeque dinners every day.

The restaurant is filled with 20 picnic tables with red-and-white tablecloths. There are a total of twelve wait-staff workers, five of whom have been working at the restaurant since it opened. Shawn cooks and prepares all of the special barbeque sauce himself along with three other cooks. The restaurant runs today just as it did 20 years ago. Shawn knows many of his customers by name. This is definitely part of the charm of the restaurant, but it is also one of its biggest problems. Everything in the restaurant is done manually, from taking orders to ordering inventory.

Shawn's daughter, Carmen, has just graduated from college and has come home to help run the family-owned business. She is amazed at how long it takes to perform all of the manual processes required to run the business. Every night she must manually count all of the money in the cash register and compare it to the paper sales tickets that the wait staff fills out representing the customer orders. She also manually counts the inventory, from cans of beans to slices of cheese. Deciding what to order each day is a complete mystery to Carmen. Some days the restaurant sells tons of chicken dinners, and other days tons of beef dinners; there doesn't seem to be any pattern. She continually finds herself ordering too much of one item and not enough of the other. Every week she has to calculate the employee paycheques by reviewing each employee's cardboard handwritten time card. At the end of each month she calculates the sales tax reports. This is incredibly difficult, since the reports must match all of the monthly paper tickets, of which there are close to 15,000.

Carmen quickly comes to the conclusion that the restaurant must be automated. Building an information system to support all of these manual processes will not only help the restaurant operate more efficiently, but also give Carmen more time to spend talking and dealing with her customers. Carmen and Shawn decide to visit a local restaurant trade show to see what types of information systems are available. The show displays all types of different restaurant systems. One uses microwave frequencies that allow the wait staff to send orders to a terminal in the kitchen using a type of PDA. Some systems can track sales for up to 20 years and generate sales forecasts based on anything from the day of the week to the weather. All of the systems produce daily sales reports and monthly tax reports. This feature alone would be a dream come true for Carmen, as this activity typically takes her from two to three hours a day.

Carmen and Shawn are overwhelmed by the number of restaurant information systems available. Having no formal training with the SDLC or systems development, they are confused and frustrated with so many choices.

Questions

1. Shawn is not a believer in technology and he thinks the business works just fine the way it is. How would you convince him that an information system will help his business become even more successful? How can you explain to him that using the SDLC will help him successfully implement a new system?

2. Carmen realizes that she does not have the expertise required to choose a restaurant information system. She decides to ask you for help, since you have studied this type of information in college. How would you describe to Carmen the steps in the SDLC and how she can use them to choose and implement a system?

3. At the beginning of the project you develop a project plan to help guide you through the systems development effort. Carmen does not understand the plan or why you continually keep changing it. How can you explain to Carmen the benefits of developing a project plan and why it must be continually revised and updated?

4. Shawn has hired you to help choose and implement the system for the restaurant. From the information you already have about the restaurant, write five of the business requirements. Remember, writing clear and accurate business requirements is critical to the success of a project.

5. Some members of the wait staff have worked at the restaurant since it began. You're worried that they won't be receptive to using an automated system. How would you convince the wait staff that the new system will help them perform their jobs? Why is including them in the requirements-gathering activity critical to the systems development effort?

6. Thanks to your help, Shawn has successfully implemented a new restaurant system. The system is up and running and Shawn is extremely pleased with your work. You offer to spend an extra week writing user manuals and system documentation. Shawn declines your offer, as he does not see any benefit in these tools. How would you convince Shawn that documentation is critical to the continued success of his system?

7. At the restaurant show, Shawn and Carmen saw many different restaurant information systems that they could purchase. Research the Web to find two restaurant information systems that might have been at the trade show. Of the systems you found, which one do you think you would choose and why?

Key Terms and Concepts

analysis phase, 220
business requirement, 220
critical success factor (CSF), 219
design phase, 221
development phase, 222
feature creep, 230
graphical user interface (GUI), 222
GUI screen design, 222
help desk, 225
implementation phase, 223
insourcing, 232
joint application development (JAD), 221
maintenance phase, 224
modelling, 222
online training, 224
outsourcing, 236
planning phase, 219
project manager, 220
project milestone, 220
project plan, 220
project scope, 220
project scope document, 220
proof-of-concept prototype, 243
prototype, 243
prototyping, 243
request for proposal (RFP), 238
requirements definition document, 221
scope creep, 230
selfsourcing (knowledge worker development, end user development), 232
selling prototype, 243
sign-off, 221
systems development life cycle (SDLC), 218
technical architecture, 221
test condition, 223
testing phase, 223
user acceptance testing (UAT), 228
user documentation, 224
workshop training, 224

Short-Answer Questions

1. What is the systems development life cycle (SDLC)?
2. What are the seven steps in the SDLC?
3. What is a critical success factor?
4. What is feature creep?
5. How does a project plan help the project manager do his/her job?
6. In what step in the SDLC do you define business requirements?
7. Why would a company outsource?
8. In what step in the SDLC do you build the technical architecture?
9. What is an activity performed in the design phase?
10. What is an activity performed in the testing phase?
11. How do online training and workshop training differ?
12. Why must you provide sign-off on the business requirements?
13. Will a project be successful if you miss business requirements?
14. What is selfsourcing?
15. What is a contractor?
16. Why would you build a prototype?
17. What is a selling prototype?

Assignments and Exercises

1. **SDLC AND THE REAL WORLD.** Think of the seven steps in the SDLC and try to apply them to one of your daily activities. For example, getting dressed in the morning would involve the following. First, you plan what you are going to wear. This will vary depending on what you are going to do that day and could include shorts, pants, jeans, etc. Second, you analyze what you have in your closet compared to what you planned to wear. Third, you design the outfit. Fourth, you get the clothes out of the closet and assemble them on your bed. Fifth, you test the outfit to ensure it matches. Sixth, you put on the outfit. Seventh, you wear the outfit throughout the day adjusting it as needed.

2. **HOW CREATIVE ARE YOU?** Congratulations! You've been appointed manager of the design team for Sneakers-R-Us. Your first activity is to design the GUI for the main system. The only requirements you are given is that the colours must be bold and the following buttons must appear in the screen.

   - Order Inventory
   - Enter Sales
   - Schedule Employees
   - Tax Reports
   - Sales Reports
   - Employee Vacation and Sick Time
   - Administrative Activities

   Create two different potential GUI screen designs for the main system. Provide a brief explanation of the advantages and disadvantages of each.

3. **REQUEST FOR PROPOSAL.** A request for proposal (RFP) is a formal document that describes in detail your logical requirements for a proposed system and invites outsourcing organizations (or *vendors*) to submit bids for its development. Research the Web and find three RFP examples. Briefly explain in a one-page document what the RFPs have in common and how each is different.

4. **UNDERSTANDING INSOURCING.** The advantages and disadvantages of selfsourcing and outsourcing are covered throughout this chapter. Compile a list of the different advantages and disadvantages of insourcing compared to selfsourcing and outsourcing.

5. **MANAGING THE PROJECT PLAN.** You are in the middle of an interview for your first job. The manager performing the interview asks you to explain why managing a project plan is critical to a project's success. The manager also wants to know what scope creep and feature creep are, and how you would manage them during a project. Write a one-page document stating how you would answer these questions during the interview.

6. **PROJECT MANAGEMENT.** Congratulations! You've been assigned the role of project manager for WakeUp Company. Your first project is to build an alarm clock. The project starts today and lasts for three months. You have the following resources available to work on the project.

   - Project manager (1)
   - Knowledge workers (3)
   - IT specialists (4)
   - Documentation experts (2)
   - Testing expert (3)
   - Extra experts (4)

   Your first activity is to develop an initial project plan with the above information. You must list the SDLC phases and associated activities, assign time frames to perform each activity, and finally assign a resource(s) to work on the activity.

7. **WHY PROTOTYPE?** You are in the middle of the design phase for a new system. Your manager does not understand why it's important to develop a prototype of a proposed system before building the actual system. In a one-page document explain what problems might arise if you went straight to developing the system.

8. **BUSINESS REQUIREMENTS.** Gathering accurate and complete business requirements is critical to the successful development of any system. Review the following requirements and explain any problems they might have.

   - The GUI must be red.
   - There should be three buttons labelled Start and Stop.
   - Buttons 1 through 8 are required for the calculator function.
   - There should be a text field for the user name and a button for the user password.

9. **WHY PROJECTS FAIL.** We've discussed five of the primary reasons why projects fail, but there are many more possible reasons. In order to be prepared for your role as a knowledge worker, research the Web to find

three additional reasons why projects fail. Prepare a document explaining them and how you could prevent these issues from occurring.

Discussion Questions

1. Why is it important to develop a logical model of a proposed system before generating a technical architecture? What problems might arise if you didn't develop a logical model and went straight to developing the technical design?

2. If you view systems development as a question-and-answer session, another question you could ask is "Why do organizations develop IT systems?" Consider what you believe to be the five most important reasons organizations develop IT systems. How do these reasons relate to topics in the first five chapters of this book?

3. When deciding how to staff a systems development project what are some of the primary questions you must be able to answer in order to determine if you will insource, selfsource, or outsource? What are some of the advantages and disadvantages of each?

4. Your company has just decided to implement a new financial system. Your company's financial needs are almost the same as those of all of the other companies in your industry. Would you recommend that your company purchase an existing system or build a custom system? Would you recommend your company insource, selfsource, or outsource the new system?

5. Why do you think system documentation is important? If you had to write system documentation for a word processing application what would be a few of the main sections? Do you think it would be useful to test the documentation to ensure it's accurate? What do you think happens if you provide system documentation that is inaccurate? What do you think happens if you implement a new system without documentation?

6. What would happen to an organization that refused to follow the systems development life cycle when building systems? If you worked for this organization what would you do to convince your manager to follow the systems development life cycle?

7. Imagine your friends are about to start their own business and have asked you for planning and development advice with respect to IT systems. What would you tell them? What if their business idea was completely Internet-based? What if their business idea didn't include using the Internet at all? Would your answers differ? Why or why not?

8. What would happen to a systems development effort that decided to skip the testing phase? If you were working on this project what would you do to convince your team members to perform the activities in the testing phase?

9. Imaging you are working on a project and are getting ready to enter the development phase. Your boss suddenly decides to outsource the rest of the project and move you into another area. What are the advantages and disadvantages of this situation?

10. You are talking with another student who is complaining about having to learn about the systems development life cycle because he/she is not going to work an IT department. Would you agree with this student? What would you say to try to convince this person that learning about the systems development life cycle is relevant no matter where he/she works.

11. A company typically has many systems it wants to build, but unfortunately it doesn't usually have the resources to build all of them. How does a company decide which ones to build?

12. When you start working on a new system one of your first activities is to define the project scope. Do you think this is an easy activity to perform? Why is the project scope so important? Do you think everyone on the project should know the project's scope? What could happen when people on the project are not familiar with it?

REAL HOT Electronic Commerce

Finding Freeware and Shareware on the Internet

Real HOT Links

When you buy your first computer, software seems a secondary decision, since most computers come preloaded with software. But after a while you begin to feel a need for other software. However, even simply upgrading to the latest version of your existing software can make a real dent in your pocketbook. And after installing new software, you may find it simply doesn't meet your needs. That's when you notice that you can't return opened software, you can only exchange it for a new copy. So if it doesn't meet your needs you're out of luck with commercial consumer software.

An alternative to commercial software that you might consider is shareware or freeware. Shareware is "try before you buy" software: users are permitted to try the software on their own computer system (generally for a limited time) without any cost or obligation; they then make a payment if they decide they want to keep using the software beyond the evaluation period. Freeware is software available at no charge to users for as long as they choose to use it.

USING YOUR COMPUTER FOR MORE THAN WORK

By far the most popular freeware/shareware applications are games. The quality of these titles is truly amazing for software that is free to download and begin playing immediately whenever you want. Shareware/freeware games are so numerous on the Internet that you'll often find games grouped by category: action/adventure, board, card, casino, educational, role-playing, simulation, sports, strategy and war, and word games.

When you're looking over the games available, remember that you should first ascertain whether the software is shareware or freeware. In some cases the Web site is not really clear on this issue. For example, some game descriptions make no mention of money, yet after you've downloaded the game it talks about registering your game for a price. At the other end of the spectrum you'll encounter traditional software that lists a price next to the description and requires a credit card to download and purchase, and often these games will describe themselves as shareware. Remember, though, true shareware permits you to download the software and try it for free; so in this case "shareware" is a bit of a misnomer.

Connect to the Internet and several sites that offer freeware and shareware games. Pick at least two games and download them. For each, answer the following questions:

A. Is a description of the game provided?

B. Are system requirements listed?

C. Can you tell if the game is freeware or shareware without downloading it?

D. Are any of the games you selected really commercial software that requires a purchase before you download the game?

E. If the game is shareware, how long may you use it before registration is required?

F. If the game is shareware, does the game cease to function after the free period? How can you tell without waiting that long?

G. How long does it take to download the game? Is it worth it?

ANIMATING YOUR COMPUTER SCREEN

Wander through most any office or even your school computer lab, and you'll see a variety of "screen savers" in action. Screen savers—the software that occupies your screen when the computer is unused for a period of time—are very common utilities. Sometimes they provide a beautiful scene with a recurring action. Others provide a different look every time they activate. Microsoft Windows includes several standard screen savers. In Windows 95 and beyond you'll also find **desktop themes** that do include a screen saver but go much further than that. In addition to providing software that activates when your computer is inactive, themes alter the look of the basic screen you see when you are working. Borders, standard application icons, and even the cursor are changed with desktop themes.

Connect to a couple of different sites that offer screen savers. Download at least two screen savers and answer the following questions:

A. Is a description of the screen saver provided?

B. Is the screen saver available for other operating systems?

C. Can you tell if the screen saver is freeware or shareware without downloading it?

D. Do any of the screen savers include desktop themes for Windows?

E. Are any other screen savers or desktop themes available at the site?

F. Does the screen saver work as advertised?

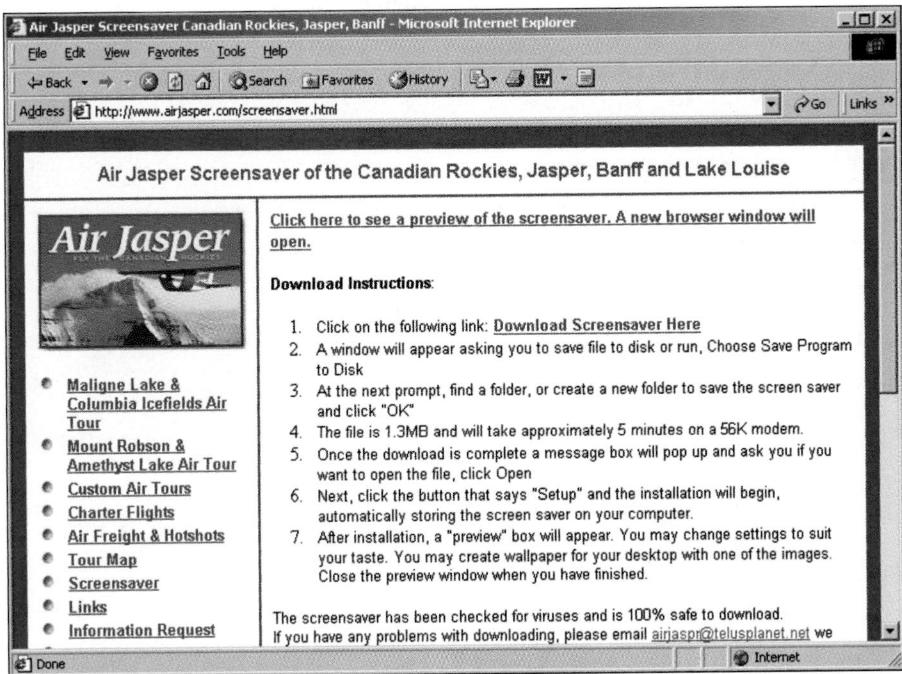

PROTECTING YOUR COMPUTER INVESTMENT

Have you ever been frantically typing away, desperately trying to make an assignment deadline, when all of a sudden something goes wrong with your computer? If you're lucky the problem is easy to identify, so you correct it and go on with your work. Other times the solution eludes you. Most of the time these problems have nice logical explanations such as hardware or software conflicts or failures of some kind. In a few rare instances, the problem may have been caused intentionally—by a computer virus—a program which someone develops with malicious intent to harm an IT system.

So how does a computer virus get into your system? Anytime you download software, open a file attachment to an e-mail, or read a file off a diskette from another computer, you stand the chance of contracting a computer virus. And access to the Internet increases your opportunity to download files from many different sources. So on every computer it owns virtually every company installs antivirus protection software that scans new files for known viruses and purges them from the system. The catch is that traditional antivirus software can find only viruses it knows about. As new viruses come along, the software must be updated. The deviant minds that develop viruses seem to find more and better ways to infiltrate your system every day.

Connect to a site that allows you to download antivirus software, download it, and answer the following questions:

A. Is the antivirus software shareware, freeware, or traditional retail software?

B. What viruses does it detect?

C. Does the software remove the virus as well as detect it?

D. Are updates for the software available to detect new viruses? How often are they available? At what cost?

E. Does the software detect viruses not yet created? How does it do that?

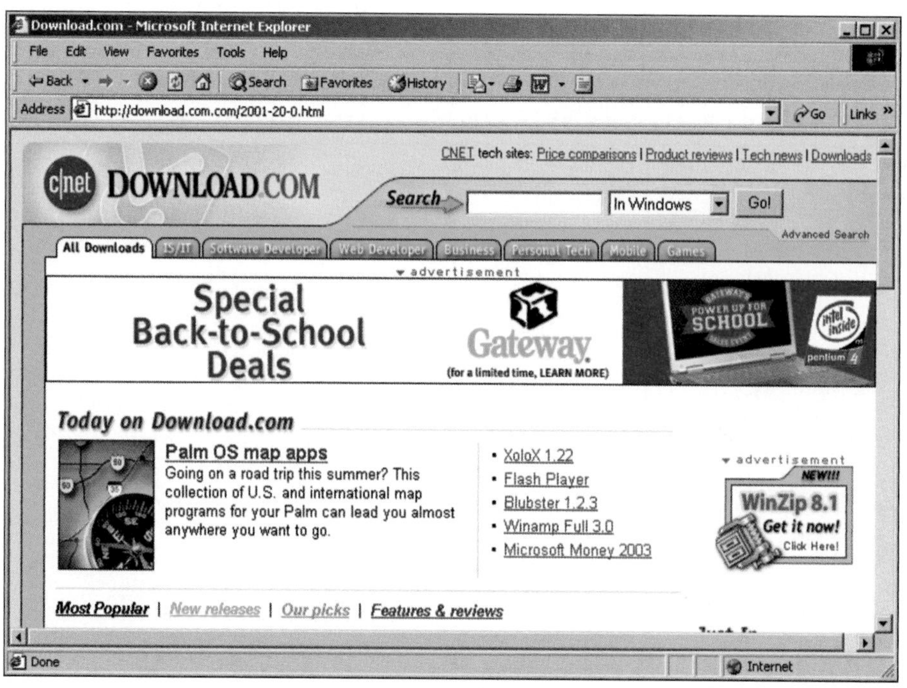

F. Does the software site offer recommendations to reduce your chance of contracting a virus?

G. Does the site tell you what to do if you have already contracted a virus?

SEARCHING FOR FREEWARE AND SHAREWARE

So maybe the shareware/freeware software concept appeals to you. You'd like to be able to try the software before you buy. If you want software such as screen savers or antivirus software, you're in luck. Just look through the Web links on the Online Learning Centre (www.mcgrawhill.ca/college/haag).

But what if you want some shareware to help you compose music or keep track of your soccer team's schedule? Well, then you'll have to go searching. You could use a general-purpose search engine such as Yahoo! and type in "shareware" and "music" or "soccer." If you do this you will find a few shareware software titles to download.

But suppose those few titles don't meet your needs. Finding shareware/freeware titles can be daunting, for two reasons. First, currently there are over a million shareware and freeware titles available to you. Unless a search engine is designed specifically for this type of software, you'll probably miss many of these titles using a general-purpose search engine. Second, most shareware/freeware developers don't have their own Web sites. Since many don't develop their software as a business, they can't justify the cost of a site. To address both these challenges, Web sites have been created that maintain databases of thousands of shareware/freeware software titles. Most also include a search engine to help you navigate through these titles.

Find a site that maintains a database of freeware and shareware software. As you peruse it, answer the following questions:

A. How does the site group the software?

B. Can you search by operating system or platform?

C. Does the site provide descriptions of the software?

D. Can you search by file size?

E. Are screen captures from the software provided?

F. Are reviews and/or ratings of the software provided?

G. When was the last update of the site?

Go to the Online Learning Centre at www.mcgrawhill.ca/college/haag for quizzes, extra content, a searchable glossary, and more! Click on "Electronic Commerce Projects" for links to hundreds of Web sites.

Go to the text CD-ROM for data files, extra content, and Skills Modules on Microsoft Excel, Microsoft Access, HTML, and e-portfolios.

CHAPTER SEVEN

STUDENT LEARNING OUTCOMES

1. Explain the relationship between the organization's roles and goals and the IT infrastructure.
2. List and describe four factors that help increase employee productivity.
3. Explain system integration and how it enhances decision making.
4. List and describe two different types of workflow systems.
5. List and describe two IT infrastructure components that create business partnerships and alliances.
6. List and describe two IT infrastructure components that enable global reach.

INDUSTRY PERSPECTIVES

FEATURES

WEB SUPPORT LINKS

- Online Magazines
- Online Movie Listings and Reviews
- Cooking from the Internet

Visit www.mcgrawhill.ca/college/haag

IT INFRASTRUCTURES
Business-Driven Technology

CASE STUDY:
WHAT'S THE DIFFERENCE BETWEEN NAPSTER AND GNUTELLA?

Many of you have probably heard of Napster, software that allows people to share music over the Internet. Originally, all a person had to do to listen to music for free was download Napster from the Internet, check the Napster directory to see a list of available songs, download the songs in MP3 format, and play them using the Napster software. Unfortunately for Napster, the Recording Industry Association of America (RIAA) filed a lawsuit claiming copyright infringement and tried to have Napster shutdown.

Napster attempted to avoid the RIAA lawsuit by changing its IT infrastructure. MP3s were no longer saved on the company's servers. Instead, Napster kept a directory of MP3s stored on individuals' computers, and users could share the MP3 files between each other. All Napster did was provide the software to play the MP3 files along with a list of places a user could find MP3 files. This attempt of Napster's to avoid legal problems didn't work, and the company was shutdown in December of 2001.

Today, there is a new product called Gnutella. Like Napster, it is a product that directly exchanges MP3 files between users. However, in a sense there is no Gnutella. It doesn't have a Web site, doesn't have an address or office building, and doesn't have any employees. The Gnutella software is designed to allow a network to grow without any single person or particular company's involvement. Basically, once you install and launch Gnutella, your computer becomes both a client and a server in the network, called GnutellaNet, and you can now share files other Gnutella users have made available. Each user makes as many, or as few, of their files available for other users connected to the network to search through and download. The Gnutella network literally changes every time a user logs on and off.

Do you think the RIAA should file a lawsuit against Gnutella for copyright infringement? If it did file a lawsuit, who would it sue?

This is a good demonstration of how a similar product using a different IT infrastructure can change the situation significantly. Designing and building the correct IT infrastructure is critical to the success of any business. Do you think Napster would still be around today if it had implemented a different IT infrastructure?

The term "IT infrastructure" includes all the hardware, software, and telecommunications equipment that your organization employs to support its goals, processes, and strategies. An IT infrastructure can easily make or break a company. What do you think happens to a company that can't provide its knowledge workers with Internet access, or only extremely slow access? A company must build a solid IT infrastructure that can handle all the current and future IT needs that will play a major role in helping the company achieve its organizational goals.[1]

Introduction

Because "IT infrastructure" means different things to different organizations at different times, it is difficult to formulate a definition that will encompass every possible meaning and satisfy everyone. For this reason, we have chosen the most basic and generic definition. An **IT infrastructure** includes the hardware, software, and telecommunications equipment that, when combined, provide the underlying technological foundation to support the organization's goals.

Organizations today can choose from literally thousands of different components to build their IT infrastructure. The components can include anything from software to strategic functions. Figure 7.1 provides a model of how the various components of an IT infrastructure support an organization's goals.

Just as your organization's goals dictate its structure, so they influence its IT infrastructure. For example, a flat structure has only a couple of managerial layers while a hierarchical one has many. If your organization has a flat structure, it might be attempting to support the goal of information sharing. If your organization has a hierarchical structure, it might be attempting to support the goal of information privacy and security.

As a knowledge worker, you may be faced with questions regarding how the IT infrastructure can best support your organizational goals. You may be asked to make decisions regarding which type of IT infrastructure components you want to pur-

Figure 7.1

How IT Infrastructure Supports the Organizational Goals

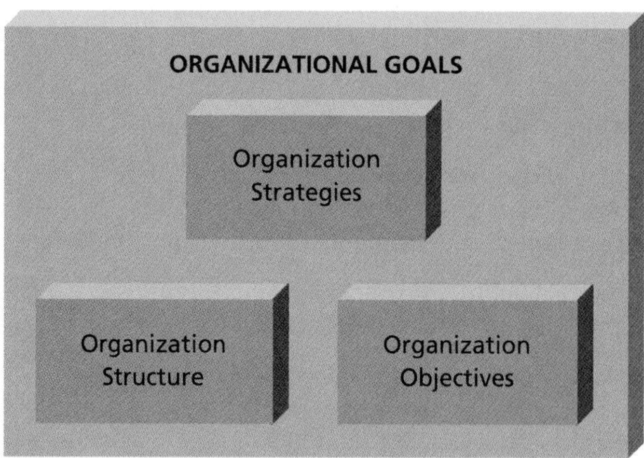

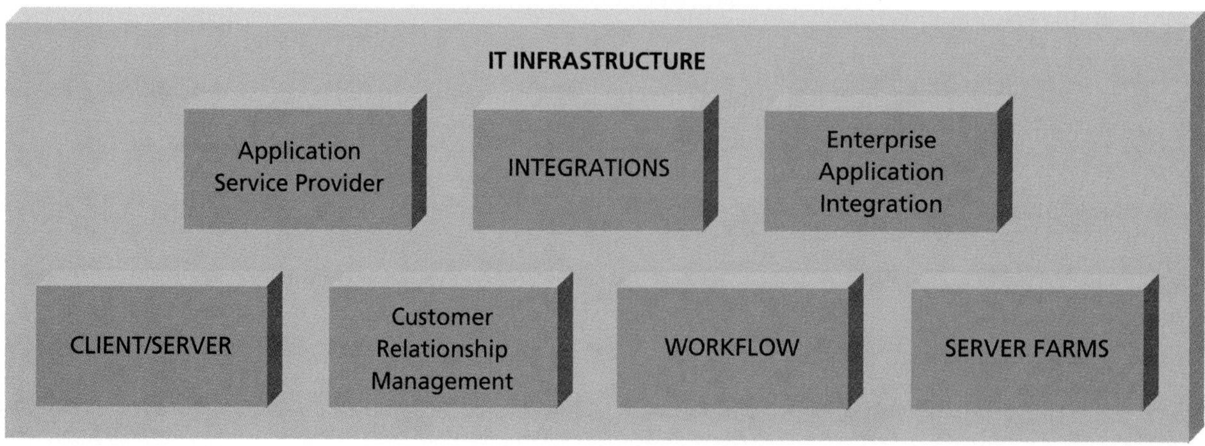

chase, and how you want to implement them. Of the many technologies available, how might you choose the ones that best meet your organizational needs?

This chapter discusses a few of the primary IT infrastructure components your organization can use to build a solid foundation that supports your organization. Enterprise application integration (EAI), customer relationship management (CRM), and enterprise resource planning (ERP) are just a few of the components we're going to discuss in the following pages. These components may not mean much to you now but, after reading this chapter, you'll have enough basic knowledge to understand how each works.

Organizational Goals and Strategies

Organizations spend a great deal of time determining primary goals, objectives, structures, and strategies. These critical components help your organization determine how it will operate in the marketplace, what its strategic directions or competitive advantages will be, and how it will achieve great success. A good IT infrastructure will support all of your organization's business and information needs.

Figure 7.2 lists the six primary roles and goals of information technology as we presented them in Chapter 1. It also provides a list of IT infrastructure components in support of each of the six. The remainder of this chapter walks you through each goal and related IT infrastructure components.

Figure 7.2

Roles and Goals of Information Technology and IT Infrastructure Components

Roles and Goals of IT	IT Infrastructure Components
Increase employee productivity	• Client/server network • Internet • Intranet • Extranet • Backup/recovery • Disaster recovery plan
Enhance decision making	• Integration • Enterprise application integration (EAI) • Enterprise application integration middleware (EAI middleware) • Storage devices
Improve team collaboration	• Documentation management systems • Enterprise information portals (EIPs) • Workflow systems
Create business partnerships and alliances	• Customer relationship management systems (CRM) • Sales force automation systems (SFA) • Electronic catalogue • Supply chain management systems (SCM)
Enable global reach	• Internet service provider (ISP) • Application service provider (ASP) • Collocation facilities • Server farms
Facilitate organizational transformation	• Enterprise resource planning (ERP) and enterprise software • Data warehouse • Infrastructure documentation

Increase Employee Productivity

Employees are the heart and soul of any organization. Without employees there simply wouldn't be an organization. Building an IT infrastructure that supports employee and customer needs should be one of the primary goals for any business. For example, every time a system crashes or fails, employees can't perform their jobs. Every time employees can't perform their jobs, the organization loses money. Employees are often sent home during system crashes, since there is no reason for them to sit around for hours without being able to work. For this reason alone, millions of dollars are lost each year due to system failures.

Building a solid IT infrastructure will reduce system failures, which increases employee productivity. The following IT infrastructure components support increasing employee productivity.

1. Client/server network
2. Internet
3. Intranet
4. Extranet
5. Backup/recovery
6. Disaster recovery plan

1. CLIENT/SERVER NETWORK

Building a client/server network is one of the best ways to ensure that the IT infrastructure supports employee productivity. In a **client/server network**, one or more computers are *servers* and provide services to the other computers which are called *clients*. The server or servers have hardware, software, and/or information that the client computers can access. Figure 7.3 is an example of a client/server network. You can see that several clients access a single server and a single printer. Almost all of the computer processing is performed on the server, which allows your organization to purchase **thin clients**—workstations that have only a small amount of processing power and cost less than a full-powered workstation. Purchasing thin clients can save your organization a tremendous amount of money when you consider that every single knowledge worker in the company needs a client station. A client/server network also allows your company to save money by purchasing a single printer that serves many individuals.

Prior to client/server networks, it was difficult for individuals to share information, applications, and hardware. For example, if a knowledge worker wanted to send a report out to several other knowledge workers he or she had to either manually copy the report several times or create several floppy disks containing the report. Using a client/server network, he or she can simply save the report on the server and other employees can directly access it or distribute it by e-mail. A client/server network also allows employees to share applications such as personal productivity software and hardware such as printers.

Review Extended Learning Module D for a detailed discussion of the many different types of client/server networks.

2. INTERNET

It's impossible to count the many number of ways the Internet makes an organization successful (or unsuccessful). Today, in the information age, most employees require an

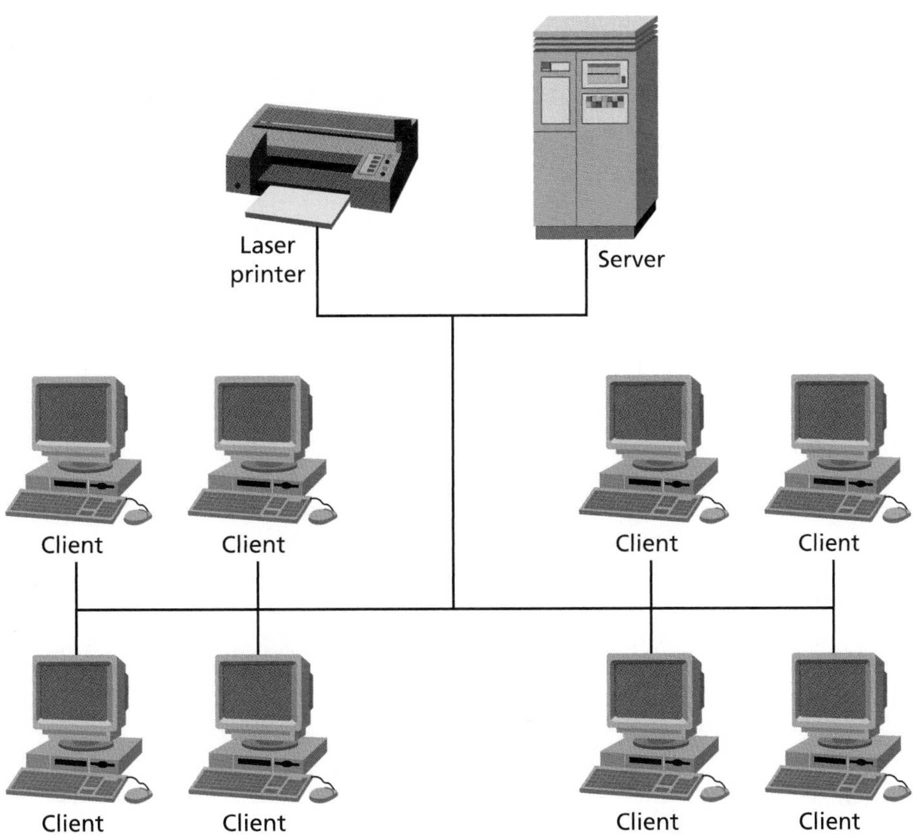

Figure 7.3
A Typical Client/Server Network

Internet connection in order to perform their jobs. The Internet allows employees to send e-mail to customers, suppliers, and other employees all over the world for a fraction of the cost of a telephone call or surface mail. This advantage is referred to as **global reach**, the ability to extend a company's reach to customers anywhere there is an Internet connection, and at a much lower cost. Employees also receive the benefit of being able to search through volumes of information from organizations and libraries all over the world.

One of the biggest benefits of the Internet is the ability to place orders and receive information electronically. This method of ordering saves a company time and money, because customers no longer have to call the company to place an order.

Placing the ordering responsibility in the hands of the customer helps to decrease the number of incorrect orders. An order can be incorrect for several reasons, including a wrong address, size, or quantity. Every incorrect order costs the company money and hurts the company's relationship with the customer. The Internet can help alleviate some of the problems with incorrect orders, since the customer has taken on the majority of the ordering responsibility.

One thing to mention about the Internet is that it does not always increase employee productivity. Sometimes it can actually decrease employee productivity. The Computer Security Institute/FBI recently reported that 78 percent of companies have detected employee abuse of their Internet access privileges. The abuse included playing games, downloading movies, listening to music, gambling, trading stocks, e-mailing jokes, and even distributing critical company information. Employees also abuse the Internet by spending significant time sending personal e-mails to friends and family members. This sounds like a tiny problem but studies indicate that the amount of time employees spend abusing the Internet directly affects employee productivity.[2]

One of the decisions you'll make regarding your IT infrastructure is how you're going to design your Internet connections. Some companies implement full Internet access to all employees, while other companies provide full Internet access for only certain employees. Deciding which Internet infrastructure to develop will depend on employee needs and how much control the organization wants to have over how employees use the Internet.

3. INTRANET

An **intranet** is an internal organizational Internet that is guarded against outside access by a special security feature called a *firewall* (which can be software, hardware, or a combination of the two). The primary characteristic of an intranet is that people outside the organization can't access it. Employees must have a username and password in order to log on to an intranet.

The intranet is an invaluable tool for supporting the dissemination of information throughout the organization. Thus, an intranet increases employee productivity by promoting information sharing and providing a central location where employees can go to look for information. An intranet hosts all kinds of company-related information such as benefits, schedules, strategic directions, and employee directories. At many companies, each department has its own Web page on the intranet for department information sharing. The advantages of an intranet are tremendous and one should be a major piece of your IT infrastructure.

4. EXTRANET

An **extranet** is an intranet restricted to an organization and certain outsiders, such as customers and suppliers. Where an intranet is entirely restricted to internal members of an organization, employees and outsiders alike can access an extranet by using a username and password. In this way, the extranet falls between the Internet and intranets: it is open to outside access, but at the same time that access is strictly controlled.

An extranet facilitates communication with customers, partners, suppliers, and vendors. These select parties outside of the company can look up current information (from calendars to expense reports), access needed files, provide constant input on ongoing projects, and more. In the case of a company that is outsourcing some of its operations, an extranet can allow for increased productivity between the company and the outside parties through a systematic relaying of information and materials. Outsiders and insiders alike are subject to the permissions setting of their particular username, allowing the extranet administrator to determine which outside parties are privy to what information and materials.

5. BACKUP/RECOVERY

How many times have you lost a document on your computer because it crashed or lost electricity and you hadn't saved or backed up your work? How many times have you accidentally deleted a file you needed? **Backup** is the process of making a copy of the information stored on a computer. **Recovery** is the process of reinstalling the backup information after the information was lost. You can use many different media to do a backup of your organization's information, including tapes, disks, and even CD-ROMs. The importance of backups cannot be overemphasized.

How often should knowledge workers back up their files? The answer depends on your organizational goals. If your organization deals with large volumes of critical information, it might require daily backups. If your organization deals with small

EMPLOYEE ABUSE OF THE INTERNET

The Internet doesn't necessarily increase productivity; in fact, employee abuse of the Internet can significantly decrease productivity. By some estimates, employees spend as much as six hours a day on the Internet playing games, gambling, buying stock, and sending personal e-mails.

Shawn Vidmar, IT director of an automotive dealership, has voiced concern over the problem at his company: "Employees obviously weren't doing their jobs and if they're trying to trade online and they're not doing their job, that's a problem. Productivity was being compromised and I was worried about corporate liability. If somebody gets offended by an e-mail, they could go after the company."

Vidmar implemented new policies and employee education, and also decided to install Vericept Corporation's VIEW, a network abuse management system that tracks and analyzes network traffic. "Sending out an e-mail from here is like sending it out on Vidmar letterhead. I would hate to lose the business my grandfather started 60 years ago over a bad Internet joke," says Vidmar.[3]

amounts of non-critical information, it only might require weekly backups. Deciding how often to back up is a critical decision for any organization.

6. DISASTER RECOVERY PLAN

Unfortunately, disasters—such as power outages, fires, floods, and even harmful hacking—occur all the time. Given that, your organization needs to develop a **disaster recovery plan**.

A good plan takes into consideration the location of the backup information. Many organizations choose to store backup information in an off-site storage facility, or a place separately located from the company and often owned by another company.

A good plan also considers the actual facility where knowledge workers will work. A **hot site** is a separate and fully equipped facility where the company can move immediately after the disaster and resume business. A **cold site** is a separate facility where the knowledge workers can move after the disaster but which does not have any computer equipment.

Your recovery plan should include a **disaster recovery cost curve** (see Figure 7.4), which charts (1) the cost to your organization of unavailability of information and technology and (2) the cost to your organization of recovering over time from a disaster. Where the two cost curves intersect is in fact the best recovery plan in terms of cost and time. Being able to quickly restore information and IT systems in the event of a disaster is a great way to provide a support structure that helps to continually increase employee productivity.

Figure 7.4

Deciding How Much to Spend on Disaster Recovery

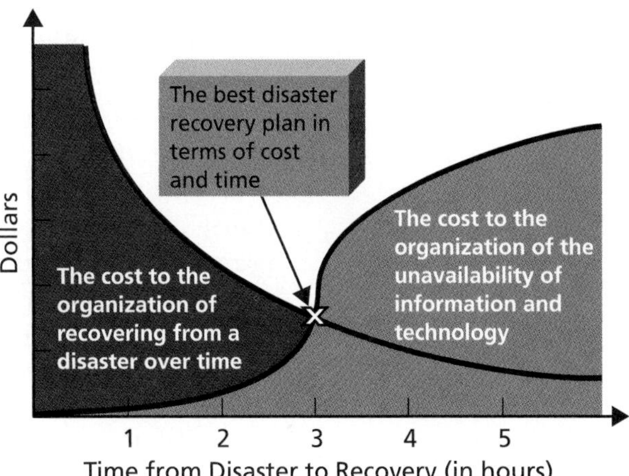

FACTORS THAT INCREASE EMPLOYEE PRODUCTIVITY

AVAILABILITY Not all knowledge workers work from 9 to 5. It's not uncommon for a knowledge worker to arrive at work early, stay late, or work on the weekend to meet a deadline. For this reason, it's crucial that the IT infrastructure support the knowledge workers' varied schedules.

Availability is determining when your IT system will be available for knowledge workers to access. Some companies have IT systems available 24 hours a day, seven days a week. What happens if your employees need to work late, or during the weekend, and they can't because the information systems are unavailable? This would certainly lead to a decrease in employee productivity.

Another reason a company might support 24/7 system availability has to do with time zones. Imagine you work for a company based in Vancouver, B.C., and the company also has an office in London, England. When the London employees are finishing work, the Vancouver employees are just starting; since the same IT systems are worked on by the two sets of employees, they must be available round the clock. What happens if the company has global customers? Its system has to be available 24/7 in order to support the customers in different time zones.

ACCESSIBILITY Accessibility is determining who has the right to access different types of IT systems and information. What do you think might happen if all employees have access to payroll information or bonus information? Payroll and bonus information is typically confidential, and at some companies you can be fired for having knowledge of or sharing this type of information.

Accessibility not only includes who can access information, but also how they can use it. "How" includes create, read, update, and delete, or what is often referred to as *CRUD* in the technology world. It's important that you define how each person can access information.

RELIABILITY Reliability ensures your IT systems are functioning correctly and providing accurate information. You might be surprised at how many times IT systems generate inaccurate or unreliable information. This can occurs for many reasons, including the information being entered incorrectly and the information becoming corrupted. Whatever the reason, if employees can't receive reliable information, then they can't perform their jobs.

Ensuring information is reliable is a critical and difficult task for all organizations. **Data cleansing** is the process of ensuring that all information is accurate. The more an organization can do to ensure its IT infrastructure promotes reliable information, the more money it will save by catching errors before they occur.

SCALABILITY Estimating how much growth your organization is expected to experience over the next few years is an almost impossible task. **Scalability** is the process of building information systems that can grow, or scale, as the organization and information needs grow. A number of factors can effect organizational growth, including market, industry, and the economy. If your organization grows faster than anticipated, you might find your systems experiencing all types of issues, such as running out of disk space or a slowing-down of transaction performance speed. To keep employees working and productive, your organization must try to anticipate growth and ensure that the IT infrastructure supports it.

FLEXIBILITY A single system can be designed in a number of different ways to perform exactly the same function. When you choose which design you want to implement, you must think about the system's flexibility, or the system's ability to change quickly. An inflexible system will cost your company money because it won't be able to handle market, business, or economic changes.

TEAM WORK

IT COMPONENTS AND FACTORS

Supporting and increasing employee productivity is a primary goal for many organizations. In a group, review the list of IT infrastructure components and factors and rank them by their ability to increase employee productivity, 1 indicating the biggest impact and 12 the least impact.

IT Infrastructure Component/Factor	Ability to Increase Employee Productivity
Client/server network	
Internet	
Intranet	
Backup/recovery	
Disaster recovery	
Availability	
Accessibility	
Reliability	
Scalability	
Flexibility	
Performance	
Capacity planning	

For example, say a company decides to expand its business into different countries and must add new languages and currencies to its IT system. The significant amount of time these modifications will take will cause the company to lose customers and sales. If the company had initially designed the system for this type of flexibility, it could have easily expanded the system to handle multiple languages and currencies.

PERFORMANCE Have you ever tried to connect to a Web site and it seemed to take forever? After waiting a minute or two, you probably gave up and headed for a different site. **Performance** measures how quickly an IT system performs a certain process. A **benchmark** is a set of conditions used to measure how well a product or system functions. Many factors affect the performance of an IT system, ranging from the design of the system to the hardware that supports it, and performance directly effects knowledge worker productivity. If a system is slow, it will take knowledge workers twice as long to perform their jobs.

One of the most common performance issues you'll find occurs because of uncontrolled growth. For example, if business is booming and your company doubles the size of its order entry department, it must ensure the system functions exactly the same with twice as many users. If you used to have 50 order entry specialists and you now have 100, your IT systems might not function correctly due to the increased number of users.

ON YOUR OWN

INCREASE STUDENT PRODUCTIVITY

Congratulations! You've been appointed Student IT Infrastructure Leader, and your primary responsibility is to approve all designs for any new information systems. The school is planning to build six new information systems next year, in order to increase student productivity.

Your first assignment is to compile a list of three IT infrastructure components and factors that must be incorporated into any information system design. Along with the components/factors, provide a brief description of how each will increase student productivity. You can choose only three components for all six projects, so choose wisely.

CAPACITY PLANNING **Capacity planning** determines the future IT infrastructure requirements for new equipment and additional network capacity. It's cheaper for an organization to implement an IT infrastructure that considers capacity growth at the beginning than to try to upgrade equipment and networks after the system has already been implemented. Not having enough capacity leads to performance issues and hinders the ability of knowledge workers to perform their jobs. For example, if you have 100 workers using the Internet, and you purchase modems that are too slow and the network capacity is too small, your workers will spend a great deal of time just waiting to get information off the Internet. Waiting for a site to return information is not the most productive way for workers to spend their time.

Enhance Decision Making

Employees make decisions every day that effect the operations and ultimately the success of the business, as you saw in Chapter 4. To make smart decisions, employees must be completely informed of everything happening in and around your business. This is an incredibly difficult task, and it becomes more and more difficult as your business and its information requirements grow. The following IT infrastructure components can help:

- Integration
- Enterprise application integration (EAI)
- Enterprise application integration middleware (EAI middleware)
- Storage architecture

INTEGRATION

Typically, a business maintains separate systems for every department in the organization. Marketing might have its own pricing and market forecasting systems, sales might have its own sales and customer tracking systems, and accounting might have its own financial systems. Some organizations have hundreds of different systems operating across all departments. What types of problems do you think occur when an organization has so many separate systems?

What do you think might happen if your professor assigned 50 different textbooks for this course and based each lecture on information from all of them? It would be almost impossible for you to read all those books every time you prepared for class. You might even run into the problem of the different textbooks contradicting each other on certain topics or key terms. This is exactly what happens to an organization that has separate systems. Employees have a hard time making informed decisions because the information they need is stored across several different systems and sometimes conflicts.

Let's take a look at a customer address change example to demonstrate the problems that arise from having separate systems. If a customer moves and sends a change-of-address form to your company, this information must be entered into every single system where the customer address information is stored. Chances are some of the systems will be missed, and the customer now has different address information in different systems, or conflicting address information. How would an employee know which address is correct when trying to send a letter to the customer?

To alleviate this problem organizations build integrations. An **integration** allows separate systems to communicate directly with each other by automatically exporting data files from one system and importing them into another. Building integrations between systems helps your organization maintain better control of its information and helps quickly gather information across multiple systems.

Figure 7.5 shows an example of how your organization can integrate customer information systems. Every time new entries or changes occur, the information is integrated, or automatically passed, to all of the other systems that maintain customer information. This eliminates the problem of having to enter the same customer information into multiple systems.

Integrations enhance employee's decision making by ensuring they have accurate and timely information. However, they are extremely hard and expensive to build and maintain, because you must find a way for systems that use different technologies to communicate. Integration issues also tend to increase exponentially as the number of systems in your company grows.

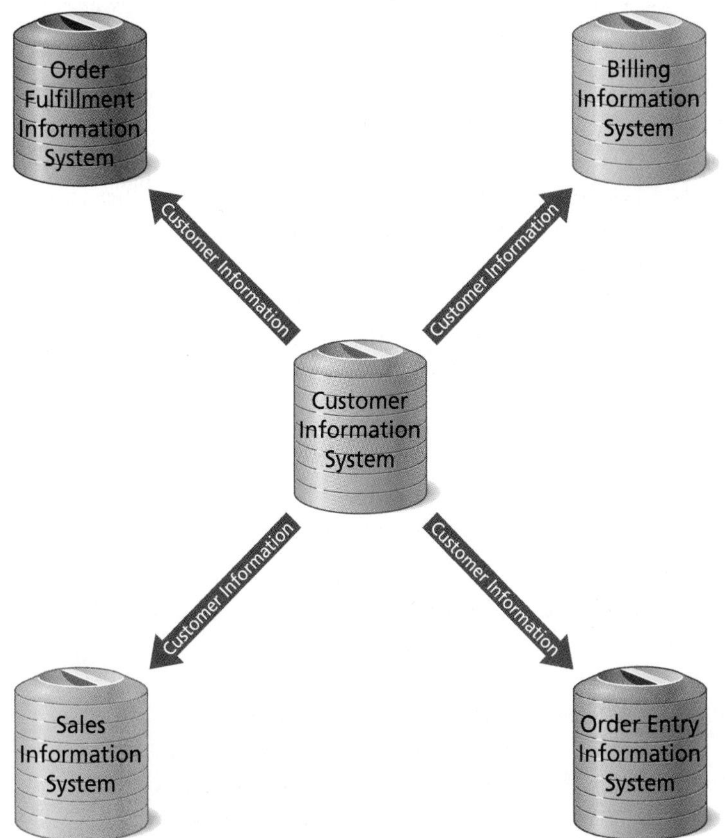

Figure 7.5
Integrating Customer Information into All Business Systems

ENTERPRISE APPLICATION INTEGRATION (EAI)

Enterprise application integration (EAI) is the process of developing an IT infrastructure that enables employees to quickly implement new or changing business processes. EAI is a way of increasing business value by integrating not only business information but also business processes. Companies are investing in EAI to streamline business processes while keeping all organizational information integrated. It's important to understand that EAI is not something you can buy like a product or a development tool—it's something organizations try to accomplish. Most businesses are successful at accomplishing certain types of EAI—database EAI (sharing and copying information across databases) and system EAI (sharing information across multiple systems. The ultimate goal—*common virtual system EAI*, in which every business aspect comes together and they appear as a single unified system—is something almost every organization will attempt for many years to come. A few organizations will succeed, but most won't.[4]

ENTERPRISE APPLICATION INTEGRATION MIDDLEWARE

Enterprise application integration middleware (EAI middleware) allows organizations to develop different levels of integration from the information level to the business process level. EAI middleware simplifies integrations by eliminating the need for custom-built software. An organization can purchase an EAI package from a vendor that supplies a pre-built connector that translates and transfers information from one system to another. An EAI package saves your organization time and money, because system developers don't have to spend time custom-building interfaces between systems.

ActiveWorks, an integration product that focuses on business process integration of front-office customer and back-end business systems, is one of the primary EAI middleware packages available today. It was built by Active Software, founded in 1995.[5]

STORAGE ARCHITECTURE

Informed decisions sometimes require reviewing past information as well as current information. Viewing historical information, or archived information, allows a company to perform detailed analysis on sales trends, customer trends, product trends, employee trends, etc. There is a wealth of knowledge in historical information.

So your IT infrastructure must define a *storage architecture*. A storage architecture describes in detail where and how information is stored and it usually includes the types and sizes of devices as well. Typically, historical information is stored on the same server as the current information. After a certain amount of time, it is *archived*—moved to a storage server—and in order to view it you must request that it be restored.

You also have to determine an appropriate cut-off date for archiving information. For example, if Bell Canada saved all billing information for every single customer throughout its history, it would need an incredible amount of space and most of the information would be outdated. You have to determine a cut-off date that makes business sense. If you make the cut-off date too soon, chances are you'll need frequent access to the archived information to answer questions and make decisions.

Improve Team Collaboration

Almost everything you do in your organization will be performed in a team environment. Very few tasks and assignments are performed individually in the working

THE GLOBAL PERSPECTIVE

1900 GAP STORES COMMUNICATING

The Gap Inc. has 1900 stores around the world, employing over 3000 people who generated $5.3 billion in revenue in 2001. The company's primary goal is to achieve and maintain a 20 percent growth rate each year. To maintain this goal, The Gap needed to keep all of the employees connected with immediate access to real-time information by sharing information between several different legacy systems and new applications. The Gap chose to implement CORBA middleware to build the integrations between the different systems.

CORBA stands for "common object request broker architecture." The software allows programs at different locations developed by different vendors to communicate. Building an IT infrastructure based on CORBA integrations and the Internet allowed The Gap to exchange real-time sales, inventory, and shipping information among all of its information systems and employees. The new infrastructure allowed the company to send information to and from any IT system in the world, which increased employee and company performance.[6]

world. So improving team collaboration greatly increase your organization's productivity and should be a primary goal of your organization's IT infrastructure. **Collaboration software** allows people to work together. In Chapter 4, we introduced you to many different types of collaboration software such as basic e-mail and group scheduling systems. Here we cover three additional collaboration software components including:

- Documentation management systems
- Enterprise information portals (EIPs)
- Workflow systems

DOCUMENTATION MANAGEMENT SYSTEMS

What do you think of when you hear the term "document"? The term can mean many different things to different people. A document can refer to any file that can be created and stored electronically including text, tables, forms, graphics, images, sound, video, etc.

It's not uncommon to find 15 or 20 knowledge workers editing the same document. Large companies produce thousands of documents every month and they need to be organized and categorized. A **documentation management system** manages a document through its life cycle. The following are the primary functions of such a system:

- *Creation.* Allows knowledge workers to create different document types.
- *Modification.* Manages the integrity of a document as it's edited or modified by knowledge workers; otherwise known as *version control.*
- *Security.* Controls access to a document and only allows knowledge workers with appropriate access to view and edit the document.
- *Approval.* A document is sent to a particular knowledge worker for approval, similarly to a workflow system discussed in detail below.
- *Distribution.* Knowledge workers distribute documents via e-mail or the Web.
- *Archiving.* Saving a document in a storage facility with the ability to extract the document in the future.

A typical documentation management system contains a relational database management system where the texts of all documents are stored, and provides knowledge workers with the ability to perform full-text searches. Most systems allow businesses

MANAGING MULTIPLE WEB SITES

Dow Corning Corporation develops and manufactures over 7000 products and services to customers all over the world. Every department in Dow Corning Corporation manages its own Web content.

When the company had a concern that the rush to publish information to the Web could cause the overall look and feel of the Web sites to suffer from a lack of consistency, it quickly realized it needed a documentation management system to ensure the consistency of its sites and company documentation while allowing experts in each department to contribute to the content.

Dow Corning decided to implement Documentum 4i eBusiness Platform, an e-business documentation management solution for creating, publishing, and managing Web site documentation. With Documentum, Dow Corning increased customer satisfaction and employee productivity, and improved partner relationships.[7]

to capture data about paper documents, with one of the attributes being the document's location. If a knowledge worker requires a certain document to perform his/her job he or she can simply search the system for it.

ENTERPRISE INFORMATION PORTALS (EIPs)

Enterprise information portals (EIPs) allow knowledge workers to access company information via a Web interface. An EIP is similar to an Internet search engine such as Google, Yahoo!, or AltaVista, except the only information stored on an EIP is company information. Using an EIP, a knowledge worker can find and view enterprise-wide business information by performing a simple search.

An EIP is different from an intranet. Intranets are more like a corporate newsletter or static database of corporate information; an EIP is dynamic and serves as an electronic workspace for knowledge workers. EIPs provide personalized access to key information and applications and real-time notification of important new information via e-mail. Critical information can also be presented in the form of graphics and charts that are continuously updated.

There are two primary categories of EIPs, collaborative processing and decision-processing. A **collaborative processing enterprise information portal** provides knowledge workers with access to workgroup information such as e-mails, reports, meeting minutes, and memos. A **decision-processing enterprise information portal** provides knowledge workers with corporate information for making key business decisions. EIPs are becoming increasingly popular in the workforce because of the amount of information sharing they provide for knowledge workers.

WORKFLOW SYSTEMS

Workflow defines all of the steps or business rules, from beginning to end, required for a process to run correctly. **Workflow systems** help automate business processes. Workflow systems help manage the flow of information through the organization whenever a process is executed. As a process is executed, a workflow system tracks where the information is and its status.

Let's take a look at how you could use a workflow system to help you complete a group project. The following are four steps you usually take when completing a group project:

ON YOUR OWN

WORKING AS A TEAM

Documentation management systems, enterprise information portals, and workflow systems are all great infrastructure components for improving team collaboration. Assume you have been assigned to work on a group project with ten other students. The project requires you to develop a detailed business plan for a business of your choice. How could you use a documentation management system to manage all of the documents required to create the business plan? Documentation might include market analysis, industry analysis, growth opportunities, the Porter Five Forces model, financial forecasts, competitive advantage information, etc. How could you use the enterprise information portals to share and post information with group members? How could you use a workflow system to manage the tasks for the group members to perform?

1. Find out what information and deliverables are required for the project and when they are due.
2. Divide up the work among the group members.
3. Determine due dates for the different pieces of work.
4. Compile all the work into a single project.

One of the hardest parts of a team project is getting information passed around among the various team members. Often one group member can't perform his/her work until another group member has finished. Group members waste a lot of time waiting to receive information from another group member. This exact same situation happens in the real world. You'll find the actual work is sitting idle waiting for an employee to pick it up to either fix it or continue working on it. Workflow systems help to automate the process of passing work around the organization.

A workflow system can automatically pass documents around to different team members in the required order. There are two primary types of workflow systems, messaging-based and database-based. **Messaging-based workflow systems** send work assignments through an e-mail system. The workflow system automatically tracks the order for the work to be assigned and each time it's completed it automatically sends the work to the next individual in line. If you used this type of workflow system to complete your group project it would automatically distribute the work to each group member via e-mail. Each time you finished a part of the project that needed to be sent to another group member the system would take care of this for you.

Database-based workflow systems store the document in a central location and automatically ask the knowledge workers to access the document when it's their turn to edit it. If you used this type of workflow system to perform your group project, the project documentation would be stored in a central location and you would be notified by the system when it was your turn to log in and work on your portion of the project.

Either type of workflow system will help improve teamwork by providing automated process support allowing knowledge workers to communicate and collaborate within a unified environment.

Create Business Partnerships and Alliances

With the growing popularity of performing business over the Internet, your IT infrastructure must support electronic business partnerships or your organization will not survive long in today's e-centric world. Creating business partnerships and alliances is a key strategy for any company that intends to be a serious player in the information age. There are four critical components to building a strong IT infrastructure to supporting these goals:

- Customer relationship management systems (CRM)
- Sales force automation systems (SFA)
- Electronic catalogue
- Supply chain management systems (SCM)

CUSTOMER RELATIONSHIP MANAGEMENT (CRM) SYSTEMS

Without customers a business couldn't exist. In fact, one important goal of any business is to increase customer satisfaction.

Keeping and retaining current and potential customers is one of the primary goals of any organization and customer relationship management has become one of the hottest buzzwords in businesses today. **Customer relationship management (CRM) systems** use information about customers to gain insights into their needs, wants, and behaviours in order to serve them better. Customers interact with companies in many ways and each interaction or experience should be enjoyable, easy, and error-free. Have you ever had an experience with a company that made you so angry you changed companies or returned the product? It's not uncommon for a customer to change companies after having a negative business experience. The goal of CRM is to limit these types of negative interactions and provide customers with positive business experiences.

It's important to note that CRM is not just software but also a business objective and encompasses many different aspects of a business including software, hardware, services, support, and strategic business goals. The IT infrastructure you create should support all of these aspects and must be designed to provide the organization with detailed customer information. Figure 7.6 is an example of a potential CRM system infrastructure. The **front office systems** are the primary interface to customers and sales channels; they send all of the customer information to the data warehouse. The **back office systems** are used to fulfill and support customer orders; they send all of the customer information to the data warehouse. The CRM system analyzes and distributes the customer information and provides the organization with a complete view of each customer's business experiences.

Many systems are available today that a company can purchase that offer CRM functionality; some of the big providers are Clarify, Oracle, SAP, and Siebel. Ensuring that your organization's IT infrastructure supports CRM is critical to your businesses success.

SALES FORCE AUTOMATION (SFA) SYSTEMS

The sales process includes many factors such as contact management, sales lead tracking, sales forecasting, order management, and product knowledge. **Sales force automation systems (SFA)** automatically track all the steps in the sales process. There are many SFA vendors, including Clairy, Siebel, Vantive, and Salesforce. Some basic SFA systems perform sales lead tracking or listing potential customers for the sales team to contact. They also perform contact management which tracks all of the times a sales person contacts a potential customer, what they discussed, and what are the next steps. More sophisticated SFA systems perform detailed analysis on market

Figure 7.6

A Sample Customer Relationship Management (CRM) System Infrastructure

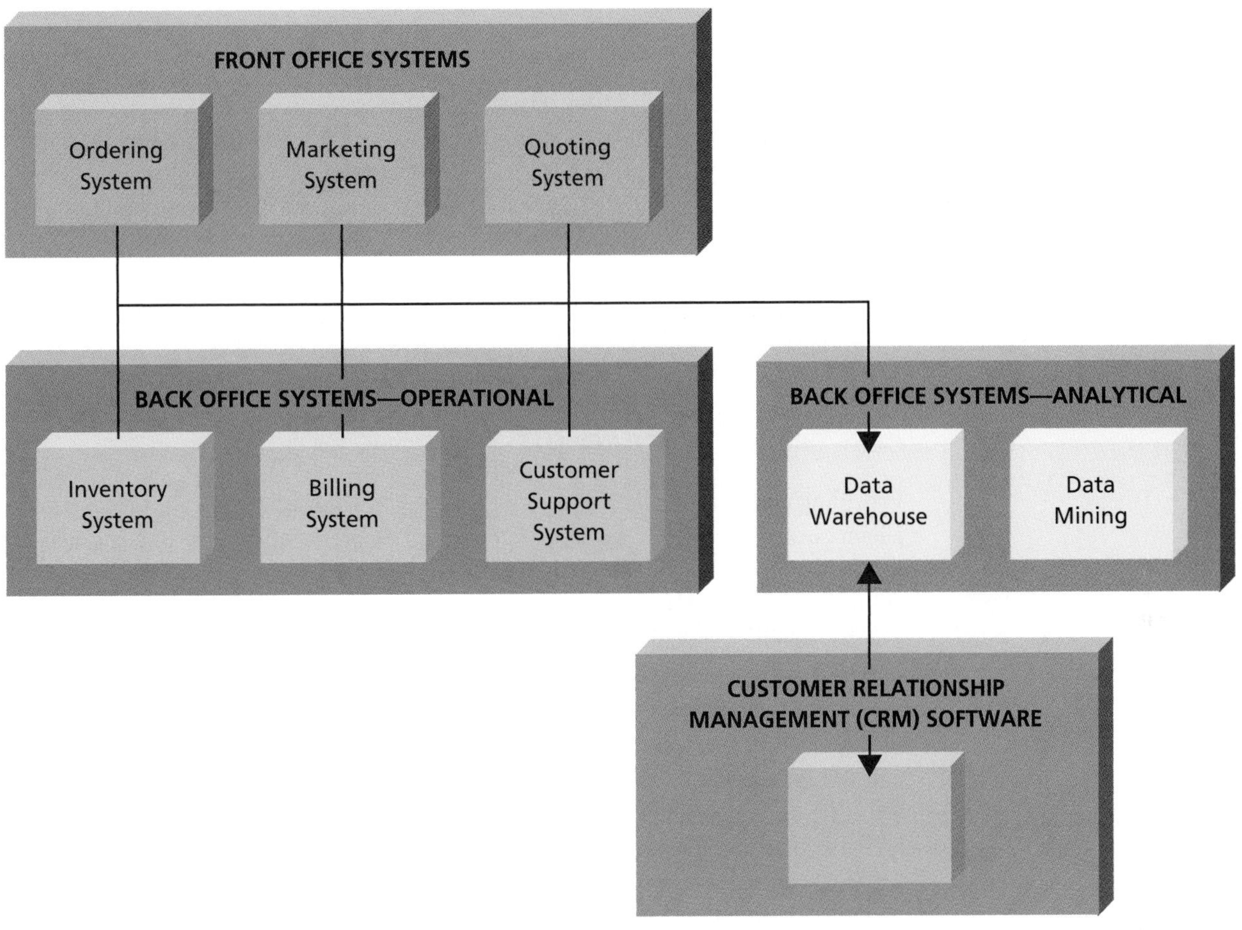

and customers and even offer product configuration tools where the customer can configure their own products.

One of the biggest problems organizations have when implementing SFA systems is developing the integrations. Sales, marketing, customer service centres, and customer billing are typically separate departments with separate systems. Often, these separate departments have communication problems that can hurt customer relationships. For example, a salesperson might talk to a customer and try to sell them a new product without realizing the customer has been on the phone all day with another department in the company trying to resolve an issue with a current product. This is probably not the best day for the salesperson to approach the customer about additional products.

Getting separate departments to talk to each other electronically is a big challenge. An SFA system attempts to provide electronic communication between the sales systems alleviating such problems, as mentioned above. If the company had implemented an SFA system, the salesperson in the above example would already know that the customer had been talking to the company all day and even known exactly what problems the customer is experiencing. The salesperson could then approach the customer, help with the problems, and then try to sell additional products. SFA is an invaluable tool for increasing customer sales.

FEDEX STREAMLINES SHIPPING

FedEx has become a master at supply chain management, using it to focus on building strong customer partnerships. FedEx has developed a tool, FedEx Ship Manager API, that can be downloaded for free off the Internet. The software allows customers to directly connect into FedEx's information systems when placing shipping orders and scheduling pickups.

This move gives FedEx an incredible competitive advantage. Customers now have complete control over shipping preparation, which helps to eliminate shipping errors since they enter the information directly. Customers can also monitor real-time shipping status right from their desk, which helps to increase employee productivity. FedEx has become a leader in the industry for its brilliant use of supply chain management.[8]

ELECTRONIC CATALOGUE

Providing an electronic catalogue is a great way to enable business partnerships and alliances. An **electronic catalogue** is designed to present products to customers or partners all over the world via the Web; it provides much more detailed information about products than paper catalogues, including real-time inventory status, photographs, product specifications, product instructions and safety procedures, video demonstrations, etc. Electronic catalogues even provide links to product reviews and industry information.

One of the biggest advantages of using an electronic catalogue is the search functionality. A customer can search the catalogue using a keyword, full text, line items, inventory levels, unit prices, etc. Giving customers such powerful search capabilities makes it easier for them to find a product especially if they know exactly what they want. Sometimes, however, the search functionality can make finding a product more difficult.

Let's assume you need to order new wastebaskets for your office. You simply open up a supplier electronic catalogue and type in the word "wastebasket." Unfortunately, your search returns 0 results. You then type in "trash bucket," "waste bucket," "trash bin," "garbage bin," and still nothing returns from your search results. You start to get a bit frustrated because you know this company sells office supplies and a wastebasket is a common office supply item. Finally you type in "garbage can," and several different types of wastebaskets appear on your screen.

This is one of the biggest issues with electronic catalogues, finding and associating all of the potential names for a given product. Everyone could potentially have a different name for a garbage can. If the company sells global products then it must also deal with offering the product in multiple languages. Trying to find all of the names and associating them with a given product is a critical and vital task to perform if the electronic catalogue is going to be successful.

Electronic catalogue software is available from many vendors, including Actinic, Harbinger, Mercado, and Requisite Technology. The software package already has the functionality of the catalogue aspects, and all a company has to do is input its own product information. Implementing an electronic catalogue is a huge advantage for any business, but of course it must be supported by the IT infrastructure.

SUPPLY CHAIN MANAGEMENT (SCM) SYSTEM

Managing the supply chain is fundamental to the success of any business and controlling inventory is one of the largest problems facing businesses today. **Supply chain**

management (SCM) systems track inventory and information among business processes and across companies. The primary goal of SCM is to reduce the amount of inventory a company must keep on hand by providing the company with a complete view into its suppliers to understand inventory levels and production capacity. SCM helps a company improve its operations and inventory tracking.

The solution for a successful supply chain management system includes either purchasing sophisticated software with Web interfaces or hiring a third-party Web-based application service provider that promises to provide part or all of the SCM service. Figure 7.7 provides an overview of how an organization's IT infrastructure can support SCM. The knowledge workers query the SCM software for information for ordering of inventory. The SCM software connects to potential suppliers, distributors, and transporting companies to determine where to purchase the inventory and the best way to have the inventory delivered. The SCM system also performs such functions as order validation, message validation to potential suppliers and distributors, inventory routing and validation, and electronic payments.

The two largest vendors of SCM systems include i2 and Manugistics. Dell Computer Corporation, one of the largest computer system companies in the world, recently implemented an i2 supply chain solution. Dell is a leader and innovator in Web-based sales and operation and is continually looking to set the industry standards for customer service, sales, and distribution. The company, undergoing enormous growth, decided to implement a SCM solution to help it manage its suppliers, distributors, transportation companies, and inventory. Dick Hunter, vice-president of

Figure 7.7

A Sample Supply Chain Management System (SCM) Infrastructure

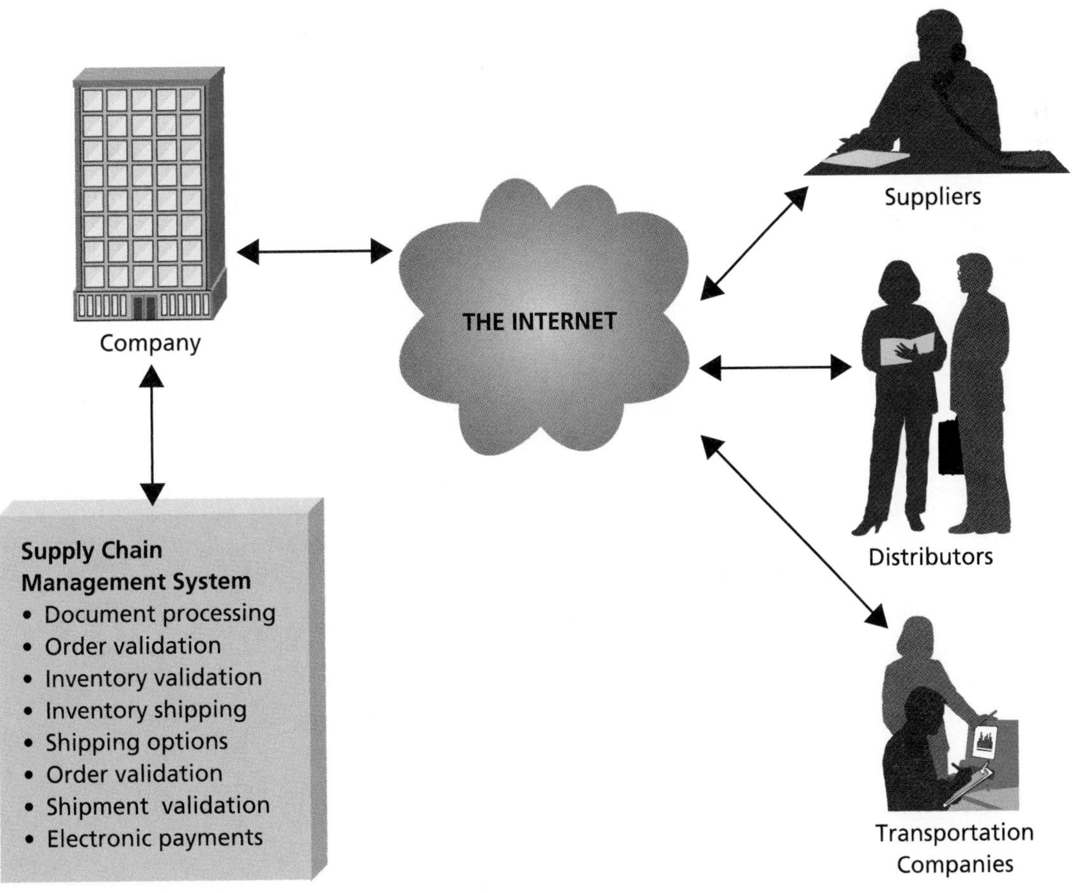

manufacturing operations, has stated, "the supply chain solution from i2—and the processes we put around i2—is allowing us to move materials so fast around our supply chain that we're able to take advantage of lower-cost materials quicker and pass those lower-cost materials on to our suppliers. And that's allowing us to fuel our growth."[9]

Enable Global Reach

The IT infrastructure of your organization must be able to support global employees, suppliers, distributors, and most importantly customers. The primary tool used to help all of these individuals communicate globally is the Internet. The following are four of the primary global IT infrastructure components your organization must consider:

- Internet service provider (ISP)
- Application service provider (ASP)
- Collocation facilities
- Server farms

INTERNET SERVICE PROVIDER (ISP)

An **Internet service provider (ISP)** is a company that provides individuals, organizations, and businesses access to the Internet. There are hundreds of ISPs. Usually, ISPs have permanent and continuous connection to the Internet and sell temporary connection time to subscribers. This can be done either on a variable-price basis (e.g., the price depends on the number of hours you connect to the Internet) or on a fixed rate (e.g., a given cost per month, with unlimited connection time). How many of you use an ISP to connect to the Internet from your home computer?

APPLICATION SERVICE PROVIDER (ASP)

Outsourcing is the delegation of specific work to a third party for a specified length of time, at a specified cost, and at a specified level of service (the guarantee of perfect delivery). An **application service provider (ASP)** is a company that provides an outsourcing service for businesses software applications. Hiring an ASP to manage your organizations software allows you to hand over the storage, operation, maintenance, and upgrade responsibilities for a system to an ASP.

Companies can outsource application and infrastructure services. Application services include business functions such as payroll, accounting, intranets, and e-mail. Infrastructure services include large systems such as customer relationship management systems, enterprise resource planning systems, and customer service call centres.

Figure 7.8 represents how your IT infrastructure might support using an ASP. Your company gets access to the software through the Internet. The company knowledge workers can log on to the software from their offices, laptops, and sometimes cellular equipment depending on how the software works. The ASP stores, maintains, and upgrades the software ensuring security and backups of the data.

One of the most important agreements between the customer and the ASP is the **service level agreement (SLA)**, which defines the specific responsibilities of the service provider and sets the customer expectations. SLAs include such items as availability, accessibility, performance, maintenance, backup/recovery, upgrades, equipment ownership, software ownership, security, and confidentiality. For example, an SLA might state that the ASP must have the software available and accessible from 7 a.m. to

Figure 7.8
A Sample Application Service Provider (ASP) Infrastructure

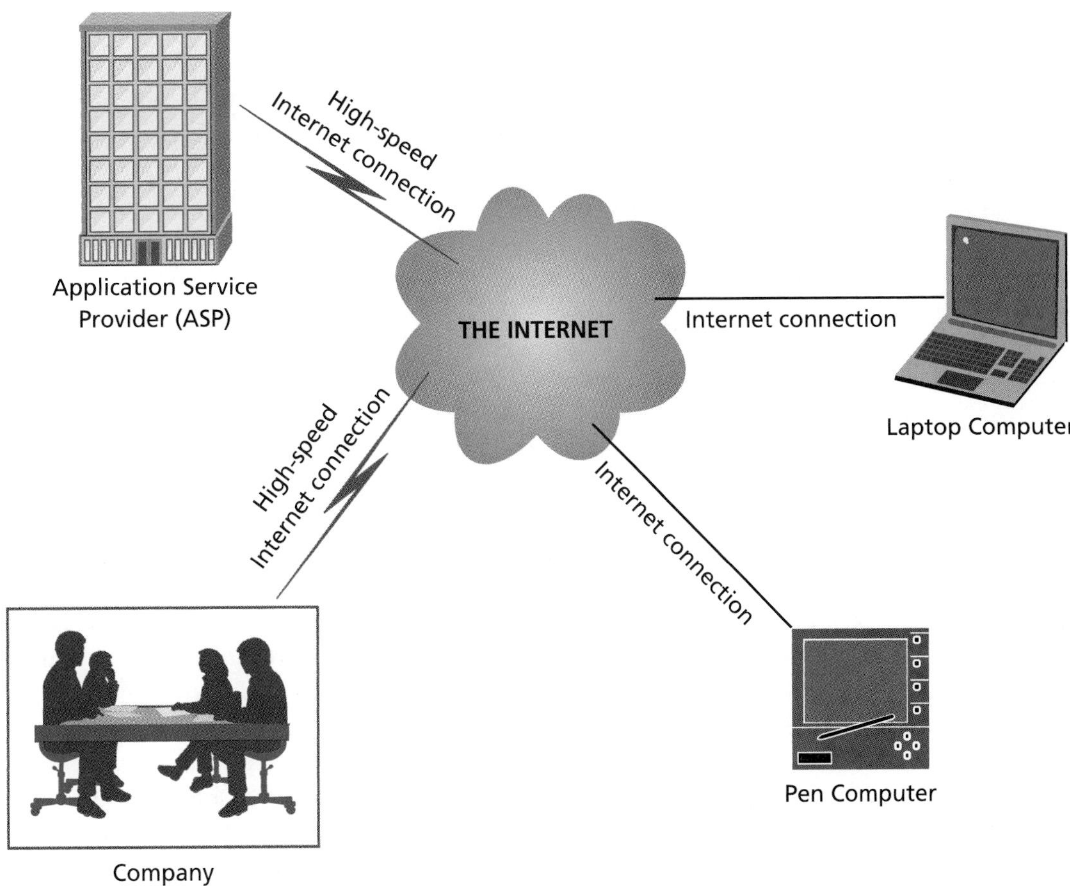

7 p.m. Monday through Friday. It might also state that if the system is down for more than 60 minutes the charge for that day of service will be waived.

Most industry analysts agree that the ASP market is growing rapidly. International Data Corp. estimates the worldwide ASP market will grow from around US$693.5 million in 2000 to US$13 billion by 2005. Zona Research (now the Sageza Group) reported in 2001 that 63 percent of the companies it surveyed are already using an ASP to access an average of two to six applications. As a knowledge worker, you'll find yourself working with ASPs and outsourced applications. You might even find yourself in the position of having to make the decision to outsource one of your business applications.[10]

COLLOCATION

Collocation (the word is variously spelled) is what happens when a company rents space and telecommunications equipment from another company, known as the *collocation vendor*. For example, if a company places a server that contains the company's Web site in a building owned by another company, the company has "collocated" its server with another company. Collocation facilities are typically warehouse-type buildings where hundreds of different companies can store computer hardware and software. If a company has a central office in Chicago and sales personnel in Chicago, Quebec City, and Hong Kong, the IT infrastructure must support all of the employees

THE GLOBAL PERSPECTIVE

EURORESINS' UNIQUE STRATEGY

Euroresins is a leader in the European chemical products market. When it decided to outsource its IT department to IBM Global Services, the company wanted to minimize the costs and still be able to support the organization's IT infrastructure. The ASP model offered a perfect solution, and the company choose to partner with Multrix, one of the first ASPs in the Netherlands. Multrix provides applications along with a complete range of other services such as management, maintenance, security, and support.

Since outsourcing with Multrix, Euroresins has experienced significantly lower costs, better and more sophisticated services, and greater flexibility for adding services in different locations, something critical to doing business globally. The overall service is far better than the company could ever have built themselves.[11]

even if there is no central office in the town where they work. If a server is located in a collocation facility in Quebec City and Hong Kong, the sales personnel in these places can dial in to the server and be connected to the Chicago office's intranet and information systems. This saves the company a lot of time and energy because the alternative to this model would be to have the employees dial a long-distance number to the Chicago office or rent an office in each location to maintain the server. Renting space from a collocation facility is cheap and easy compared to setting up an entire office.

SERVER FARM

A **server farm** or **server cluster** is a location that stores a group of servers in a single place. A server farm provides centralized access and control to files and printers, and backups for each server. The advantage of a server farm is that if one server fails there are others that can perform the work and the knowledge workers don't experience any downtime. Server farms are often located in collocation facilities.

A **Web farm** is either a Web site with multiple servers or an ISP that provides Web site outsourcing services using multiple servers. For the most part you can use a single server to handle user requests for files on a Web site. For large Web sites you might require multiple servers.

Facilitate Organizational Transformation

Everything changes, and your organization must be ready to change whenever the economy, industry, technology, etc. changes. Being able to change quickly and easily is a huge advantage. The IT infrastructure has several critical components to help organizations change, including:

- Enterprise resource planning (ERP) and enterprise software
- Data warehouse
- Infrastructure documentation

ENTERPRISE RESOURCE PLANNING (ERP) AND ENTERPRISE SOFTWARE

Today, many organizations have come to realize that the development of a particular system without regard to the organization as a whole has serious disadvantages. To move toward a more holistic view, organizations are adopting the concept of enterprise resource planning and using enterprise software to develop all systems in a coordinated fashion. We first introduced enterprise resource planning systems in Chapter 4; we'll dive deeper into the topic here.

Enterprise resource planning (ERP) is the method of getting and keeping an overview of every part of the business (a bird's-eye view, so to speak), so that production, development, selling, and servicing of goods and services will all be coordinated to contribute to the company's goals and objectives. ERP may sound like a solid concept that all organizations should follow, but it just isn't that easy. In organizations of any size, seeing and understanding the whole corporate picture is difficult. To plan for all the resources needed for any initiative is even more difficult.

Further complicating the problem is that processes and IT systems are already in place supporting a particular business function, but perhaps not the organization as a whole. So just adopting ERP requires that most organizations undertake numerous reengineering efforts to ensure that the entire organization is operating as a single entity.

Enterprise software directly supports the concept of ERP. **Enterprise software** is a suite of software that includes (1) a set of common business applications, (2) tools for modelling how the entire organization works, and (3) development tools for building applications unique to your organization. Leading enterprise software vendors include SAP, Oracle, PeopleSoft, J. D. Edwards, Computer Associates, and Baan.

Figure 7.9 gives an example of how an organization could implement enterprise software. All of the information from the different departments is sent to the software, which maintains the data and can provide a holistic view of the organization. Once you use enterprise software to see the big picture, you can also use it to make changes to your organizational model and processes.

To use enterprise software effectively in support of ERP, your organization must first model its existing structure, divisions and departments, and processes, such as inventory procurement, accounts receivable, customer service, and so on. In parallel, it must also develop a model of all IT systems, how they work together, and perhaps how they conflict with each other. Armed with that information, your organization can then undertake the process of ERP to determine how best to streamline processes and develop the appropriate underlying IT systems that will support those processes through decentralized computing and shared information.

In the future, it looks as though enterprise software suites will replace **computer-aided software engineering (CASE) tools**—software suites that automate systems development. CASE tools were originally developed to support systems development, which focuses only on the development of a single system. Later, planning capabilities were added to some CASE tools, but it seemed to be more an afterthought than a well-defined plan. So CASE tools do not really require your organization to take a holistic view.

THE REALITY OF ENTERPRISE RESOURCE PLANNING AND ENTERPRISE SOFTWARE Although ERP and enterprise software sound almost too good to be true, many organizations are exploiting them. In spite of their tremendous advantages, however, many other organizations are either not using ERP and enterprise software or only partially implementing them. Some reasons for this are:

- *The existence of legacy systems.* **Legacy systems** are IT systems previously built using older technologies such as mainframe computers and programming languages such as COBOL. Legacy systems may work well in isolation but they tend to be very difficult to interface with when your organization develops new

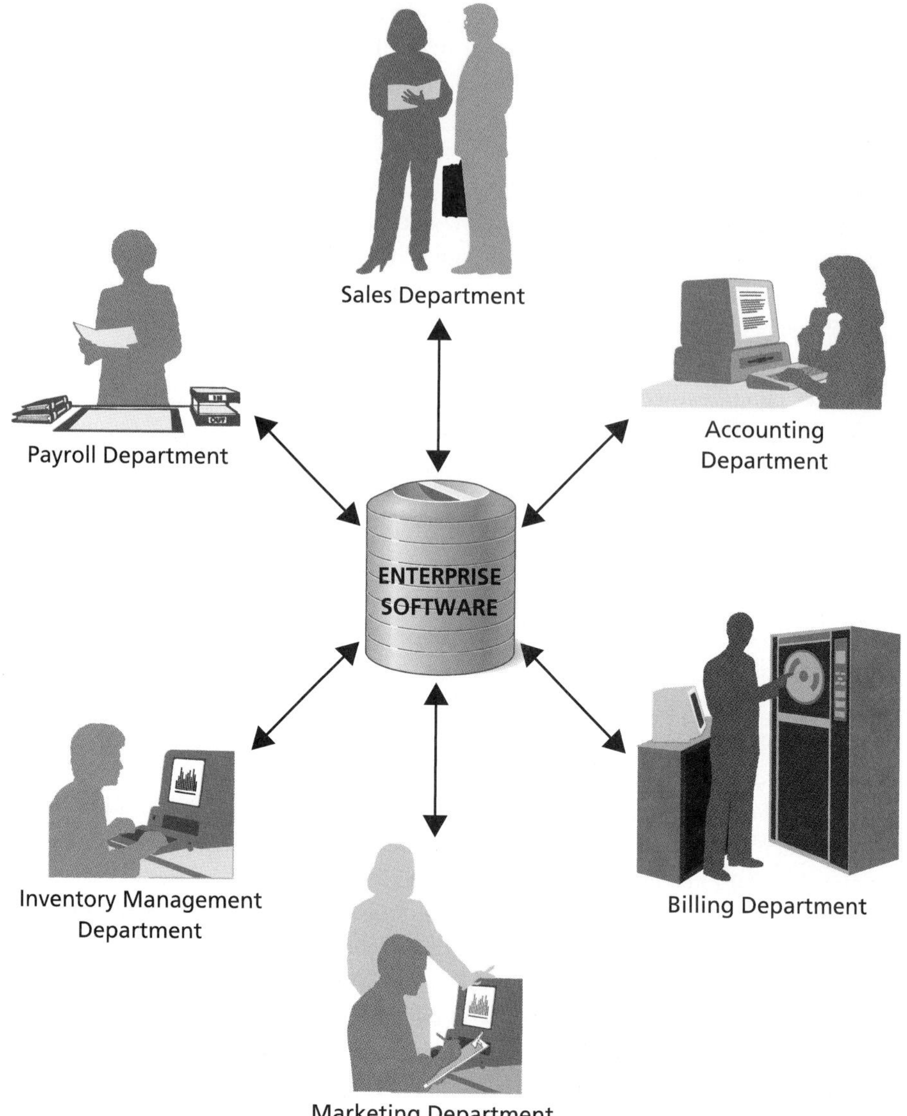

Figure 7.9
A Sample Enterprise Software Infrastructure

systems based on state-of-the-art technologies. Some organizations have invested literally billions of dollars in developing and maintaining legacy systems and they are not prepared to throw them away and switch to an ERP system.

- *The cost of ownership.* Enterprise software is among the most expensive software your organization can purchase, costing millions of dollars for a complete system. And after you purchase it, you have to customize it, which can easily cost millions of dollars more.
- *The cost of reengineering.* Fundamental to the concept of ERP is business process reengineering. Let's face it—organizations that have evolved over time have inefficient, redundant, and incompatible processes. To rectify this, they must undergo numerous reengineering efforts. **Business process reengineering (BPR)** is the reinventing of processes within a business. Many people today characterize BPR as a "knee-breaking" initiative in which you completely disregard what you're doing in favour of processes that are streamlined and completely integrated. This, again, represents a huge expense, which some organizations are not willing to undertake.

HOW ORLANDO SAVED 10,000 HOURS A YEAR

The Orlando, Florida city government has drastically improved its performance by implementing enterprise software. The city government has been using the J. D. Edwards ERP system since 1998. Today, over 400 Orlando government knowledge workers use it.

Rob Garner, comptroller, says, "All managers can view their budgets, drill down through multiple levels of financial information to individual transactions, and extract information and format it into any kind of report right from their desktops.

"Before implementing the system, we produced batch reports every month and shipped them to managers throughout city government. Now they don't have to rely on our IT department to generate financial information—they can get it themselves at any time, without having to ask anyone for it. We have redirected as much as 10,000 developer hours a year to supporting the needs of the user community."[12]

- *The expertise needed.* Finally, to use enterprise software, your organization must provide extensive training to its IT staff. And each software suite requires expertise unique to that particular suite. Enterprise software vendors such as SAP and J. D. Edwards provide months and even years of training to your organization if you choose to purchase one of their suites. This expertise is in such high demand that you can actually become a certified developer using different enterprise software suites. If you do, your career will be long, prosperous, and full of money.

DATA WAREHOUSE

The promise of an ERP system is that one system could solve all of the information needs of the organization. ERP systems are great at capturing and storing data but they lack the ability to understand and analyze the data. Knowledge workers find themselves frustrated with ERP systems because they can't get the information they need from the system.

For this reason many businesses have implemented data warehouses along with ERP systems. The data warehouse consolidates the ERP information along with other sources of information in order to perform and support analysis. A data warehouse can help knowledge workers organize, understand, and analyze the information collected by the organization. This information is the true competitive advantage in the information age.

For detailed information on data warehouses, see Chapter 3.

INFRASTRUCTURE DOCUMENTATION

One of the keys to building a solid IT infrastructure is to ensure every component is well documented and the documentation is available to all company employees. A major issue for organizations today is the lack of system documentation. For example, assume you are building a data warehouse that must integrate with all of the ERP systems in the organization, but there isn't any documentation on how the ERP systems are designed and implemented. It'd be impossible for you to successfully integrate two systems.

TEAM WORK

CHOOSING AN ERP VENDOR

Choose two of the leading enterprise software vendors (SAP, Oracle, PeopleSoft, J. D. Edwards, Computer Associates, and Baan) and, using the Internet, determine the primary differences between the two vendor's systems. Remember to think about the different IT infrastructure components mentioned in this chapter when you are performing your analysis.

IT Infrastructures and the Real World

Components of a solid IT infrastructure can include anything from documentation to business concepts to software and hardware. Throughout this chapter we have discussed many of these, including flexibility, scalability, client/server networks, supply chain management, and enterprise resource planning. It might seem like we have covered a great deal of material, but there are actually thousands of additional components that'll be important to building a solid IT infrastructure. Deciding which pieces to implement and how to implement them is becoming an almost impossible task as new products become available daily and businesses continually change. An IT infrastructure that meets your organizational needs today may not meet them tomorrow. Building an IT infrastructure that is scalable, flexible, available, accessible, and reliable is key to your organization's success.

As a knowledge worker you'll be responsible for approving the designs for the IT infrastructure for your systems. Remember to ask yourself the following questions before approving the designs:

- How big is your department going to grow? Will the system be able to handle additional users?
- How are your customers going to grow? How much additional information do you expect to store each year?
- How long will you maintain information in the systems? How much history do you want to keep on each customer?
- When do the people in your department work? What are the hours you need the system to be available?
- How often do you need the information backed up?
- What will happen to your system if there is a disaster? What is the recovery plan for your system?
- How easy is it to change the system? How flexible is it?

Ensuring your system designs answers each of these questions will put you on the path to building an IT infrastructure that will support your organization today and tomorrow.

Summary: Student Learning Outcomes Revisited

1. **Explain the relationship between the organization's roles and goals and the IT infrastructure.** An **IT infrastructure** includes the hardware, software, and telecommunications equipment that combined provide the foundation for the organizational goals, processes, and strategies. Organizational goals drive everything the organization does ranging from how it's structured to how it designs its IT infrastructure. For example, an organization can have many structures including flat or hierarchical. A flat organizational structure has only a couple of managerial layers while a hierarchical organizational structure has many. If an organization has a flat structure it might be attempting to support the goal of information dissemination. If an organization has a hierarchical structure is might be attempting to support the goal of information secrecy and security.
2. **List and describe four factors that help increase employee productivity.**
   - Availability is determining when your IT system will be available for knowledge workers to access.
   - Accessibility is determining who has the right to access different types of IT systems and information.
   - Reliability ensures your IT systems are functioning correctly and providing accurate information.
   - Scalability is the process of building information systems that can grow, or scale, as the organization and information needs grow.
   - Flexibility ensures the system is designed with the ability to quickly change.
   - Performance measures how quickly an IT system performs a certain process.
   - Capacity planning determines the future IT infrastructure requirements for new equipment and additional network capacity.
3. **Explain system integration and how it enhances decision making.** Many times an organization will have a separate and distinct system for each department. Some organizations end up with hundreds of different systems that do not communicate with each other. In order to help alleviate the problem of so many separate systems containing separate information, organizations build integrations. An integration allows separate systems to communication directly with each other by automatically exporting data files from one system and importing them into another system. Building integrations between systems helps the organization to maintain better control of its information and helps quickly gather information across multiple systems.
4. **List and describe two different types of workflow systems.**
   - **Messaging-based workflow infrastructures** send work assignments through an e-mail system. The workflow system automatically tracks the order for the work to be assigned and each time it's completed it automatically sends the work to the next individual in line.
   - A **database-based workflow** infrastructure stores the document in a central location and automatically asks the knowledge workers to access the document when it's their turn to edit it.
5. **List and describe two IT infrastructure components that create business partnerships and alliances.**
   - **Customer relationship management (CRM) systems** use information about customers to gain insights into their needs, wants, and behaviours in order to serve them better.
   - **Sales force automation (SFA)** is the process of automatically tracking all of the steps in the sales process.
   - **Electronic catalogues** are designed to present products to customers or partners all over the world via the Web.
   - **Supply chain management (SCM)** tracks inventory and information among business processes and across companies.
6. **List and describe two IT infrastructure components that enable global reach.**
   - An **Internet service provider (ISP)** is a company that provides individuals, organizations, and businesses access to the Internet.
   - **Collocation** simply means that a company rents space and telecommunications equipment from another company, or a collocation vendor.

- An **application service provider (ASP)** is a company that provides an outsourcing service for businesses software applications ranging from personal productivity programs to large enterprise-wide systems that would otherwise be located on the company's computers in the company's office building.
- A **server farm** or **server cluster** is the name of a location that stores a group of servers in a single place.

CLOSING CASE STUDY ONE

UNIVERSITY INFRASTRUCTURES

The year is 1982. Universities around the country are filled with students pursuing business degrees in accounting, marketing, management, and finance. The life of a student in 1982 is drastically different from the life a student in 2002. In 1982 only a couple of students had access to e-mail, none of the students had laptops, many of the students have never used a computer, and the idea of surfing the Internet was a concept students couldn't even understand. It's hard to believe that technology has come so far so fast.

Cheryl O'Connell graduated from university with a marketing degree in 1983. O'Connell says, "I remember all of my papers were either handwritten or typed on a typewriter; nobody had a computer. There were about 15 computers in the business school for all 3500 business students. The computers were in high demand and were primarily used for running statistical or spreadsheet programs, not word processing programs. I never dreamed that one day I would own a computer. The thought just never even crossed my mind."

In 1982 students didn't have access to e-mail, they weren't instant-messaging their friends, they had to use a dictionary to check their spelling, and they had to go to the library if they wanted to research a subject. If you had a conversation with one of these students and told them that in 20 years most students would own their own computers, they could automatically spell-check a 100-page paper in about ten minutes, and they could research libraries all over the world from their dorm rooms they would have told you that you were crazy.

In 1982 Apple Computer offered the Lisa computer, featuring 5-MHz 68000 microprocessor, 1 MB of RAM, 2 MB of ROM, a 12-inch black-and-white monitor, dual 5.25-inch 860-KB floppy drives, and a 5-MB hard drive. Its initial price was $10,000. In the same year IBM introduced the IBM PC-XT Model 370, with 8088 CPU, 768 K of RAM, a 360-K drive, and a 10-MB hard drive for $9000. Can you even imagine a 10-MB hard drive nowadays? A hard drive this small wouldn't even be able to handle one software package today.

In the 20 years since 1982 everything has changed. Over 90 percent of first-year students arrive on campus already owning or having personal access to a computer.

Today, one of the biggest selling features of a university is its IT Infrastructure. Offering Internet access to dorm rooms and supporting campus-wide wireless networks is quickly becoming a requirement for universities to offer its students.

Universities in general estimate that 30 percent of their network traffic is for e-mail, 40 percent is used to transfer files and downloads from the Internet, and 30 percent is everything else including games, instant messaging, and Web surfing.

A university's IT infrastructures are a strong factor students look at where they want to study. For this reason alone, it is critical that a university implement a solid IT infrastructure that meets the students' needs.[13,14]

Questions

1. Walking around your university, you probably see all kinds of technological gadgets that didn't even exist 20 years ago, including PDA's, cell phones, and wireless networks. How have these gadgets increased student productivity? How have they decreased it?

2. Does your university have a client/server network? If so, where are the clients located? Where is the server located? What kind of access do you have to the Internet? What type of activity do you think takes up the most capacity on the network?

   If your university does not have a client/server network, determine a design for the infrastructure to support one. Be sure to think about the factors that increase student productivity along with the IT infrastructure components. How big is your department going to grow? Will the system be able to handle additional users?

3. Imagine it's 2004 and your university has grown by 50 percent since 2002. How many students are now attending? Would the support departments such as accounting and human resources need to grow also as the number of students increases? What would happen to the university's IT infrastructure with the increased growth? What issues will the university encounter with its information systems due to this unexpected growth? What could your university have done to help prepare for this kind of unexpected growth?

4. Many different departments work at your university. Can you name them or are they listed on your school's Web site? What types of systems do they use? Do you see any reason for these systems to be integrated?

5. Your university has decided to implement an electronic catalogue for potential students to view when considering attending your school. What types of information would be saved in it? What would be three advantages of using an electronic catalogue instead of a paper brochure? What would be one of the primary problems people would encounter?

6. Try to imagine what a university will be like 20 years from now. What types of new technological gadgets will drastically change the lives of students in the year 2022? How will student productivity be affected by the new gadgets? Use the Internet to see if you can find any articles on where universities are headed in the future.

CLOSING CASE STUDY TWO

DOCUMENTATION MANAGEMENT SOLUTIONS IN THE AUTOMOTIVE INDUSTRY

Ford Motor Company is one of the oldest and largest automobile manufacturers in the world, with 114 manufacturing plants in over 40 countries. Ford has over 350,000 employees worldwide. Steven Scheerhorn, manager of knowledge workplace infrastructure, states "At Ford, customer satisfaction is our number one goal. How and what we communicate internally and externally is inextricably linked to that goal. We believe that the Internet is one of our most important means of exchanging information between employees, customers, dealers, suppliers, and trading partners. Trusted content is at the heart of every such e-interaction. Effective enterprise content management is imperative in order to provide accurate, consistent, and up-to-date content via our hundreds of intranet Web sites, intranet business portals, and business-to-consumer and business-to-consumer sites."

Ford has to communicate with customers, suppliers, and distributors all over the world. In order to help disseminate information Ford has implemented hundreds of internal and external Web sites. One of the problems that has stemmed from so many internal and external Web sites is managing the information posted on them. All the information needs to be current, accurate, consistent, accessible, reliable, etc. Imagine what a difficult task it is for Ford. Not only are thousands of documents posted, but they are also in multiple languages and currencies. How would you ensure that a document written in English is translated correctly into Spanish, French, Japanese, and Chinese? Ford also has the extra pressure of having to ensure its documentation is in compliance with all regulations.

To gain greater control, Ford implemented Documentum 4i eBusiness Platform. Documentum, which provides enterprise documentation management solutions, is currently installed in 1500 of the largest businesses in the world, helping intelligently create and manage all types of documents.

Documentum helped Ford to automate its document lifecycle processes while ensuring compliance with strict corporate records, management policies, and industry procedures. One example of Ford's success is its implementation of an engineering system. Documentum enables Ford's engineering department to submit designs online that are automatically routed to marketing to be placed in product information documentation.

Ford is also going to integrate its new employee information portal, producing a new search engine allowing any of Ford's employees with intranet access to search the company's and employees' documentation. Every department and process within Ford will have the ability to create and publish documents to the employee information portal. This new system will centralize document management and support the high-availability environment Ford requires.

It's also critical that Ford meet the legal automotive industry requirements and industry standards for automotive documentation. The new infrastructure also offers a workflow management system that has provided a way for Ford to ensure its documentation complies with current laws. After a document is completed, it's automatically transferred to Ford's legal department for final approval before being posted to the information portal.

The new systems also enable suppliers and dealers to access and add content to parts of the portal. Creating part of the site that is available in the business-to-business environment provides Ford's business partners with the same information that the company maintains. Documentum ensures that the content received by the suppliers and dealers is consistent and can be trusted.

By implementing a documentation management system and employee information portal Ford has helped to improve product quality and customer satisfaction by ensuring that content published by widely dispersed contributors to the hundreds of Ford internal and external Web sites is current and accurate. Ford has also improved its relationships with customers, suppliers, and partners by providing easy access to consistent, accurate information.

The most important benefit of Ford's new infrastructure is that it has captured the company's intellectual capital and business processes to maximize reuse and encourage best practices. The system provides a common infrastructure, which complies with the company's legal and security requirements, for easier capture, searching, retrieving, and exchanging of information throughout the enterprise.[15]

Questions

1. Almost anything you do in an organization is performed in teams. Very few tasks and assignments are performed individually in the working world. Improving knowledge workers' ability to collaborate can be a huge benefit for companies. Do you think Ford would benefit from improving team collaboration? If so, how could it use Documentum to perform team or group tasks?

2. There are several alternatives to Documentum for documentation management systems. Research on the Internet to find a competitor to Documentum. What are the differences between the competitor and Documentum? If you had to choose one of the two systems, which would you choose and why? Do you think Documentum was the best choice for Ford?

3. What is workflow? What is a workflow system? How has Ford used a workflow system to help improve its employee productivity and team collaboration?

4. What are the two primary types of workflow infrastructures? Explain the difference between them, including an example of how Ford might use each. What type has Ford implemented? What type would you recommend for Ford?

5. Enterprise information portals (EIPs) allow knowledge workers to access company information via a Web interface. How did Ford implement its EIP? Was the EIP successful? What was one of the major issues with Ford's EIP? How did Ford resolve the issue?

6. There are two primary types of EIPs, collaborative processing and decision-processing. Explain the main difference between them. Which type did Ford implement? Did Ford make the right decision?

7. Congratulations! You have been hired as Ford's IT infrastructure expert. Ford would like you to explain how a solid IT infrastructure can help the company support its primary goals. Ford also wants to know what the best IT infrastructure components are for increasing employee productivity and enhancing decision making.

Key Terms and Concepts

application service provider (ASP), 276
back office system, 274
backup, 264
benchmark, 267
business process reengineering (BPR), 282
capacity planning, 268
client/server network, 262
cold site, 265
collaboration software, 271
collaborative processing enterprise information portal, 272
collocation, 279
computer-aided software engineering (CASE) tools, 281
customer relationship management system (CRM), 274
data cleansing, 266
database-based workflow system, 273
decision-processing enterprise information portal, 272
disaster recovery cost curve, 265
disaster recovery plan, 265
documentation management system, 271
electronic catalogue, 276
enterprise application integration (EAI), 270
enterprise application integration middleware (EAI middleware), 270
enterprise information portal (EIP), 272
enterprise resource planning (ERP), 281
enterprise software, 281
extranet, 264
front office system, 274
global reach, 263
hot site, 265
integration, 269
Internet service provider (ISP), 278
intranet, 264
IT infrastructure, 260
legacy system, 281
messaging-based workflow system, 273
performance, 267
recovery, 264
sales force automation system (SFA), 274
scalability, 266
server farm (server cluster), 280
service level agreement (SLA), 278
supply chain management (SCM) system, 276
thin client, 262
Web farm, 280
workflow, 272
workflow system, 272

Short-Answer Questions

1. What is an IT infrastructure?
2. What is a client/server network?
3. What is an intranet?
4. Why do you need a backup of information?
5. Why would you need to recover information?
6. What are two organizational roles/goals?
7. What are two IT infrastructure components that increase employee productivity?
8. What is enterprise application integration middleware?
9. What are integrations and how are they used to enhance decision making?
10. Why does a business need a disaster recovery plan?
11. What is customer relationship management?
12. What is sales force automation?
13. What is one advantage of using an electronic catalogue over using a paper catalogue?
14. What is supply chain management?
15. How can you use supply chain management to create business partnerships and alliances?
16. Why would a company implement documentation management software?
17. What is an ISP and how is it different from an ASP?
18. How can enterprise resource planning facilitate organizational transformation?

Assignments and Exercises

1. **AN EIP FOR YOUR COURSE.** Enterprise information portals (EIPs) allow knowledge workers to access company information via a Web interface. You have been asked to create an EIP for this course. Please answer the following questions in order to determine how the EIP should be developed:
   - What type of information would be contained on the EIP?
   - Who would have access to the EIP?
   - How long would information remain on the EIP?

- What is the difference between a collaborative processing EIP and a decision processing EIP?
- Which type of EIP would you implement and why?

2. **SPONSOR OF THE IT INFRASTRUCTURE.** In order to build a solid IT infrastructure you must have executive sponsorship. Your current boss doesn't understand the importance of building a solid IT infrastructure. In fact, your boss doesn't even understand what an IT infrastructure. First, explain to your boss what an IT infrastructure is and why it is critical for any organization. Second, explain each of the following organizational goals to your boss along with two related IT infrastructure components.
   - Increase employee productivity
   - Enhance decision making
   - Improve team collaboration
   - Create business partnerships and alliances
   - Enable global reach
   - Facilitate organizational transformation
3. **ARABIAN NIGHTS VIDEO.** Mackenzie Spencer is the director of IT infrastructure at Arabian Nights Video, a $100M video manufacturing plant. Internally, the company manages video manufacturing systems and a client/server network that serves more than 1000 knowledge workers. Mackenzie is reflecting on her decision to hire a third-party vendor (ASP) to implement the new inventory tracking system. Mackenzie has hired you as an ASP expert. On the basis of your vast knowledge of IT infrastructure components, what would be your advice to Mackenzie regarding the advantages and disadvantages of working with an ASP? What would you tell Mackenzie to include in the service level agreement with the ASP?
4. **IT INFRASTRUCTURE COMPONENTS AND THE REAL WORLD.** Throughout this chapter we have discussed several IT infrastructure components including client/server, reliability, integrations, electronic catalogues, etc. Pick two of the components discussed in this chapter and try to find business examples of how companies are using these components in the real world. We have also mentioned that there are thousands of additional components you can use to build an IT infrastructure. Try to research the Internet to see if you can find two additional IT infrastructure components that were not discussed in this chapter along with business examples of how businesses are using the components in the real world.
5. **CREATING THE IDEAL INFRASTRUCTURE.** As a knowledge worker you'll be responsible for approving IT system designs which ultimately affect your company's IT infrastructure and its abilities to achieve its goals. This chapter has focused on many different IT infrastructure components including ERP, SCM, client/server, integrations, etc. Choose three of the different components discussed in this chapter and explain how you could use them to improve the IT infrastructure at your university. Be sure to think of current requirements as well as future requirements for the systems.
6. **THE COMPLETE IT INFRASTRUCTURE.** A document management system manages a document through its life cycle. The following table lists the document lifecycle phases in the first column. Explain what tasks a documentation management system would perform during each phase. Explain how you could use a documentation management system to help you work on a group project.

Document Lifecycle Phase	Tasks Performed	Group Project Tasks Performed
Creation		
Modification		
Security		
Approval		
Distribution		
Archiving		

7. Congratulations! You have been appointed Student Infrastructure Manager. Your first assignment is to approve the designs for the new on-campus Internet infrastructure. You're having a meeting at 9 a.m. tomorrow to review the designs with the student IT employees. In order to prepare for the meeting, you must understand the student requirements and their current use of the Internet, along with future requirements. The following is a list of questions you must answer before attending the meeting. Please provide your answer to each.

   - Do you need to have a disaster recovery plan, if so what might it include?
   - Does the system require backup equipment?
   - When will the system need to be available to the students?
   - What types of access levels will the students need?
   - How will you ensure the system is reliable?
   - How will you build scalability into the system?
   - How will you build flexibility into the system?
   - What are the minimum performance requirements for the system?
   - How will the system handle future growth?

Discussion Questions

1. IT infrastructures often mimic organizational hierarchies. Define two different types of organizational hierarchies and how the IT infrastructure would be built in order to support them.

2. IT infrastructure components can include anything from software to strategic functions. After reading this chapter and learning about a few of the primary IT infrastructure components, explain why a company's IT infrastructure can include so many different components.

3. Organizations tend to spend a great deal of time determining their primary goals, objectives, structure, and strategies. Define your university's goals, and define the objectives, structure, and strategies that support these goals. Explain how your university's IT infrastructure supports its goals.

4. What is a client/server network? Does your university have a client/server network? How does its client/server network increase student productivity? How does its client/server network decrease student productivity?

5. Providing Internet access to employees is a great way to increase employee productivity. It's also a great way to decrease employee productivity, if the employees abuse their Internet privileges. What does it mean to have employees abuse the Internet? What can you do as a manager to prevent this? What would happen if all students in your university spent ten hours a day surfing the Net? Using the Internet, find two different types of network monitoring software that you would recommend your university purchase to deter abuse.

6. Imagine you are working for a large cookie manufacturing company. The company is 75 years old and just starting to implement technology to improve operations. Your direct manager has asked you to put together a presentation discussing integrations. In your presentation you must include definitions of integration, EAI, and EAI middleware. You must also explain each concept in depth along with a real-world example of how the concept will help your company become more successful.

7. What are the four major categories of EAI? Discuss each, along with an example of how the EAI could be used in your university. Also discuss two EAI middleware vendors. You can use the Internet to find more detailed information about EAI middleware vendors.

8. Customer relationship management (CRM) is the objective of managing the customer's relationship with the company through all the different customer business experiences. Supply chain management (SCM) tracks inventory and information among business processes and across companies. What is the difference between these two IT infrastructure components? What do they have in common? Would a company implement both? If

they did, why, and what would be the advantage of having both components?

9. Informed decisions sometimes require reviewing past information as well as current information. Research different types of storage devices and explain which type you would choose and why.

10. With the growing popularity of doing business over the Internet, creating business partnerships and alliances should become a primary goal for any organization's IT infrastructure. List two IT infrastructure components you could use to help a business create business partnerships and alliances.

11. A fellow student is trying to write a paper on third-party vendors for IT infrastructure components. Throughout this chapter we have discussed several different third-party vendors including ISPs, ASPs, collocation facilities, and server farms. Explain each one of these components to your fellow student along with a real-world example of each.

12. Enterprise resource planning (ERP) is the coordinated planning of all an organization's resources involved in the production, development, selling, and servicing of goods and services. Describe ERP and how an organization might benefit from implementing an ERP system.

13. IT infrastructures should support the creation of flexible and scalable IT systems that can quickly adapt to support new business requirements. Give an example of an IT infrastructure that is inflexible and not scalable and a barrier to supporting a changing business. Give an example of an IT infrastructure that is flexible and scalable and supports expanding a business.

REAL HOT Electronic Commerce

Living Life on the Internet

Real HOT Links

The personal computer is quickly becoming a household necessity similar to a stove or a fridge. The primary reason the personal computer has become such an important part of our lives is the Internet. There are literally thousands of ways people use the Internet to perform tasks.

Do you have a personal computer with Internet connectivity in your home? How often do you use it and why? We bet you use it all the time to perform tasks ranging from sending e-mails to finding driving directions. There are so many great Web sites available, and all of them can help you accomplish things such as finding movie times, cooking a delicious meal, and seeking medical advice.

In this section we'll provide you with a few key Web sites you can use to help you live your life, and you can find many more sites on the Web site that supports this text (www.mcgrawhill.ca/college/haag).

ONLINE MAGAZINES

Every year, people spend an incredible amount of money buying magazines. Many of these magazines are received through the mail and never read, ending up in a giant pile a giant recycling plant. Do you receive magazines through the mail or buy them while doing your grocery shopping? How much are you paying for them, and do you actually find the time to read them? Did you know that many magazines are available online for free? That's right, free. Save yourself some money by using the Internet to

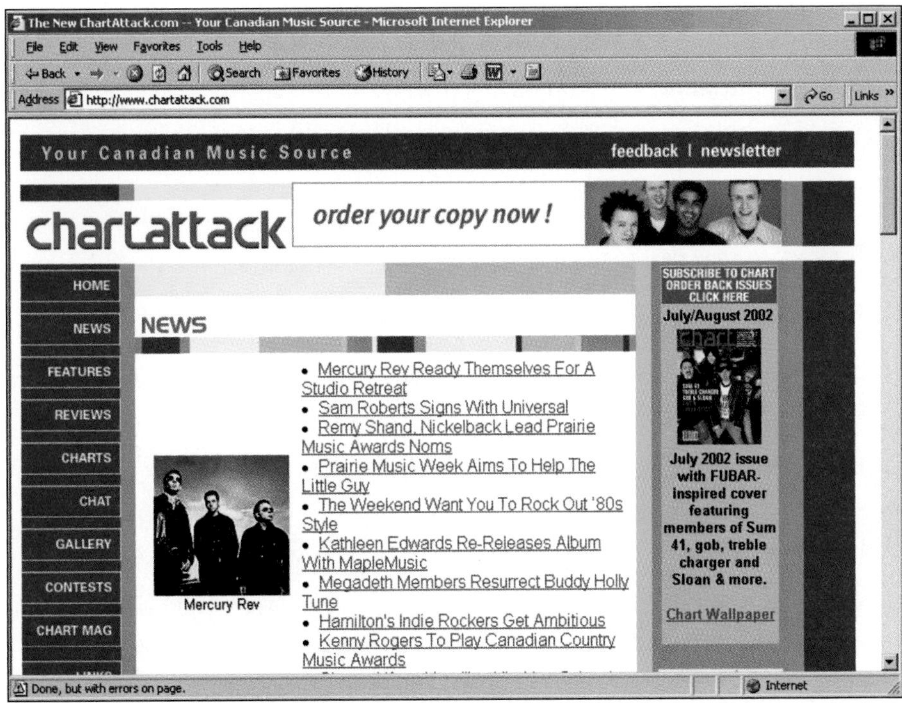

get the latest news and fashion tips instead of buying those costly magazines. Here are just a few of the many hundreds available:

- *Canadian Geographic* (www.canadiangeographic.com)
- *ChartAttack* (www.chartattack.com)
- *Sports Illustrated* (sportsillustrated.cnn.com)
- *Chatelaine* (www.chatelaine.com)
- *Maclean's* (www.macleans.ca)

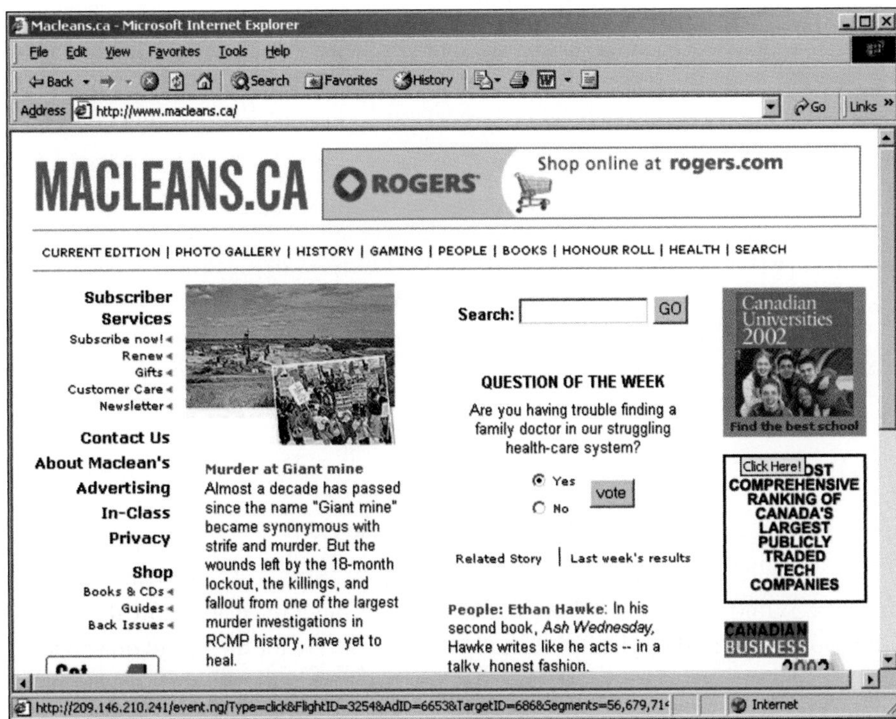

- *PC Magazine* (www.pcmagazine.com)
- *TV Guide* (www.tvguide.ca)
- *Popular Mechanics* (www.popularmechanics.com)

Connect to a few of these magazines and try answering the following questions:

A. Does the site contain the most recent issue?

B. Is it easy to view past issues or search for articles on a particular topic?

C. Can you find three additional magazines you enjoy that are not listed above?

D. Are there any additional features in the online version of the magazine that are not available in the paper version?

E. Do you enjoy reading the magazine online better than in print? Why or why not?

ONLINE MOVIE LISTINGS AND REVIEWS

How often do you get to go to the movies? How many times do you head out to the movies without knowing the theatre location, movie time, or movie rating? How often do you rent movies? Do you wander around the store unable to decide which to rent?

Wasting time and money on a bad movie happens to us all, but there is a way to eliminate this problem: the Internet.

The Internet has a wealth of information regarding movies, including theatre locations, movie times, and movie ratings and reviews. You can also check out detailed movie reviews at the Movie Review Query Engine site (www.mrqe.com). If you want a quick overview of a movie from tons of critics visit Check the Grid (www.checkthegrid.com). If you are interested in what movies are coming out over the next few months, try the Coming Attractions site (corona.bc.ca/films/main.html). You can search for movie times at your local theatres by visiting the Moviefone site (www.moviefone.com). Lastly, you must visit the Internet Movie Database (www.imdb.com), for tons of information on any movie ever made.

A. Can you find the movies that are currently playing at a theatre near you?

B. Try to research a classic movie such as *Grease* or *Animal House* to find out the movie's rating and the year it was released.

C. Try to locate three new movies that are coming out over the next year.

D. Log on to the Internet Movie Database and search for all the movies made by your favourite actor or actress. Were any movies listed that you had not watched?

E. Log on to the Internet Movie Database and try to research the top ten movies of all time.

COOKING FROM THE INTERNET

Does making a box of Kraft Macaroni and Cheese challenge your cooking skills? Don't worry, help is only a few clicks away. There are hundreds of Web sites that can provide you with recipes, detailed cooking instructions, and nutritional information.

The first stop you should make is the Nutrition Analysis Tool (NAT) site (www.nat.uiuc.edu). NAT analyzes the foods you eat for various different nutrients and gives you recommendations on the types of food that are missing from your diet.

Next, visit Cooking.com (www.cooking.com) for information on everything from cookbooks and cookware to recipes and cooking tips. For those of you interested in healthy meals try Cooking Light (www.cookinglight.com) and those of you interested in gourmet cooking try Good Cooking (www.goodcooking.com).

A. Try to find a recipe for barbequed chicken and mashed potatoes on one of the above sites.

B. Try logging on to the Nutritional Analysis Tool and find out the nutritional value of your last meal.

C. Try to find a Web site that will help you plan a menu for a dinner party of six people.

D. Log on to the gourmet site and see how many different recipes you can find for your favourite food.

E. Log on to Cooking Light and find a few tips on how you can decrease cholesterol in your diet.

Go to the Online Learning Centre at www.mcgrawhill.ca/college/haag for quizzes, extra content, a searchable glossary, and more! Click on "Electronic Commerce Projects" for links to hundreds of Web sites.

Go to the text CD-ROM for data files, extra content, and Skills Modules on Microsoft Excel, Microsoft Access, HTML, and e-portfolios.

CHAPTER EIGHT

STUDENT LEARNING OUTCOMES

1. Define ethics and describe the two factors that affect how you make a decision concerning an ethical issue.
2. Define and describe intellectual property, copyright, the Fair Use Doctrine, and pirated and counterfeit software.
3. Define privacy and describe ways in which it can be threatened.
4. Describe the two ways that information is valuable to business.
5. Describe the ways in which companies are vulnerable to computer attacks.
6. Define risk management and risk assessment and describe the seven security measures that companies can take to protect their information.
7. Define what a disaster recovery plan is and list the six components it should cover.

INDUSTRY PERSPECTIVES

FEATURES

WEB SUPPORT LINKS

- Transportation
- Air Travel
- Trains and Buses
- Rental Cars
- Road Conditions and Maps
- Lodging
- One-Stop Travel Sites
- Destination Information

Visit www.mcgrawhill.ca/college/haag

PROTECTING PEOPLE AND INFORMATION
Threats and Safeguards

CASE STUDY:
DIGITAL DESTRUCTION BEYOND ALL IMAGINATION

While it pales in comparison to the tragic loss of life, the extensive damage to computer and communications systems in New York on September 11, 2001 was considerable. The fact that most of the businesses located in the World Trade Center (WTC) were back up and running within days was amazing. Some of the fallout was so catastrophic that it should have taken years for companies to recover. Take Verizon Communications, for example.

Verizon Communications' main regional switching centre was located next to World Trade Center 7, which collapsed. The collapse of the twin towers sent a huge steel beam crashing through a bundle of optical fibre cables that had been buried about 2.4 metres below ground level. With the slicing of the optical fibre, more than 4 million high-speed-access lines and bursting water lines resulting in about 38 million litres of water flooding underground switching vaults. With primary power lost, backup power, running on diesel fuel generators, didn't last long. Lucent Technologies, one of Verizon's main system providers, quickly sent a 100,000-line switch to the site to replace the one that crashed through the window of the Verizon building. The company also made its entire inventory available to rescue operations. In addition to Verizon's damaged telecommunications system, at least 139 other fibre rings failed. In all, 1.5 million circuits serving the financial district went down.

Morgan Stanley estimates that about $500 million in computer equipment was lost when the twin towers went down. Other experts believe that it will cost up to $3.2 billion to replace technology lost—everything from servers to PCs and phone lines. And that's only the hardware. The most important part of a computer system is not the physical equipment—it's the information stored there. It's almost impossible to calculate the value of paper records, and the value of information on hard drivers, servers, tape drives, and other storage media that was lost. Given the nature of the businesses located in the WTC—many financial and consulting organizations—there was a huge concentration of stored information in that spot.

Even businesses not actually located in the WTC were strongly affected. American Express of New York City had offices opposite the twin towers and had to evacuate indefinitely. Lufthansa lost phone service for several days when AT&T, its provider, lost equipment in the Center.

TV and radio stations in New York City were hit hard, too. Most of the large broadcasters had crucial equipment in the WTC. Only WCBS-TV New York and Univision's Spanish-language station WXTV were able to stay on the air because they had backup facilities in the Empire State Building.

Despite all the mayhem, most financial institutions in or near the WTC were back in business within a few days. These companies were well prepared for disasters, although they probably didn't expect anything quite so sensational. Because of their foresight, fully 95 percent of the companies affected are expected to fully recover all their applications and information. This is pretty spectacular, given that one study found that only 6 percent of companies survive for five years after a catastrophic loss.

One of the lessons learned after 9/11 is that with careful and thorough protection of important information, not even a calamity like the one New York experienced can put you out of business. Of course, most companies don't face such severe tests of their information protection systems, but smaller and less sensational attacks can do damage too. And you need protection from these dangers.[1,2,3,4,5]

Introduction

As you've already learned, the three components of an IT system are information technology, information, and knowledge workers. Most of what you've seen in previous chapters has dealt with IT and how it stores and processes information.

In this chapter we're going to concentrate on information—its use, ownership, role, and protection. The best environment for handling information is one that has stability without stagnation and change without chaos.

To handle information in a responsible way, you must understand (see Figure 8.1):

- The importance of ethics in the ownership and use of information
- People's need for privacy
- The value of information to the organization
- Threats to information and how to protect against them (security)
- The need to plan for the worst-case scenario (disaster recovery)

The most important part of any IT system is the people who use it and are affected by it. How people treat each other has always been important, but in an electronic age, with huge computer power at our fingertips, we can affect more people's lives in more ways than ever before. How we act toward each other, and this includes how we view and handle information, is largely determined by our ethics.

You don't have to look far to see examples of questionable computer use:

- Employees search organizational databases for information they want on celebrities and friends.
- Organizations collect, buy, and use information and don't check the validity or accuracy of that information.
- Information system developers build systems that are hard to test completely and put them on the market before they work properly. A few years ago, the developers of an incubator thermostat control program didn't test it fully, and two infants died as a result.[6]
- People copy, use, and distribute software they have no right to.
- People create and spread viruses that cause a lot of trouble for people using and maintaining IT systems.
- People break into computer systems and steal passwords, information, and proprietary information.
- Employees destroy or steal proprietary schematics, sketches, customer lists, and reports from their employers.

Figure 8.1
Chapter Overview

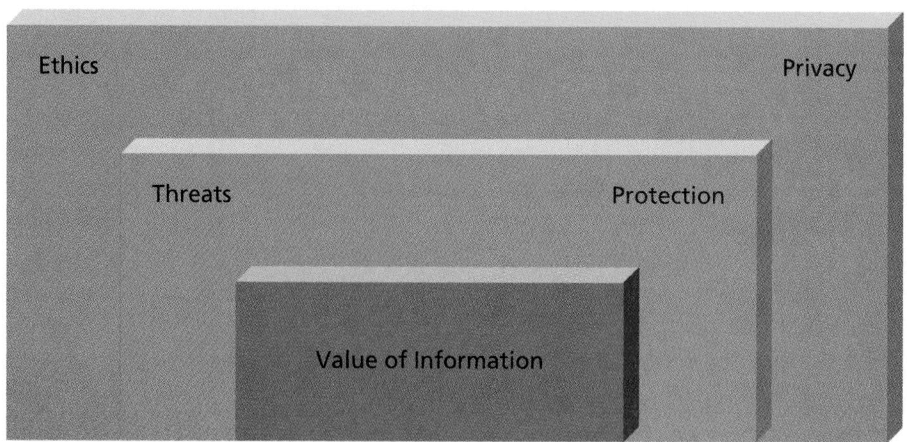

- People snoop on each other and read each other's e-mail and other private documents.

Ethics

Ethical people have integrity. They're people you can definitely trust. They're people who are just as enthusiastic about the rights of others as they are about their own rights. They have a strong sense of what's fair and right and what isn't. But even the most ethical people sometimes face difficult choices.

Ethics are the principles and standards that guide our behaviour toward other people. Acting ethically means behaving in a principled fashion and treating other people with respect and dignity. It's simple to say, but not so simple to do since some situations are complex or ambiguous. The important role of ethics in our lives has long been recognized. As far back as 44 B.C., Cicero said that ethics are indispensable to anyone who wants to have a good career. Having said that, Cicero, along with some of the greatest minds over the centuries, struggled with what the rules of ethics should be.

Our ethics, rooted in our history, culture, and religions, remain the same over time at important levels, but our sense of ethics shifts over time and from culture to culture. In this electronic age there's a new dimension in the ethics debate—the amount of information that we can collect and store, and the speed with which we can access and process that information.

TWO FACTORS THAT DETERMINE HOW YOU DECIDE ETHICAL ISSUES

How you collect, store, access, and distribute information depends to a large extent on your sense of ethics—what you perceive as right and wrong. Two factors affect how you make your decision when you're faced with an ethical dilemma (see Figure 8.2). The first is your basic ethical structure, which you developed as you grew up. The

Figure 8.2

Your Ethical Structure

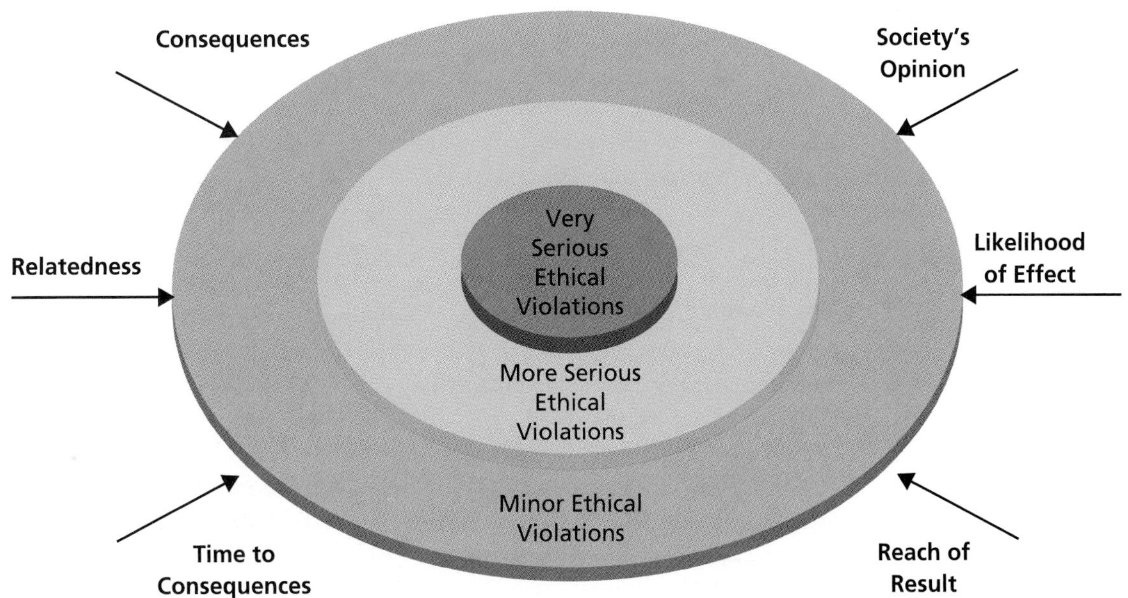

second is the set of practical circumstances involved in the decision that you're trying to make—that is, all the shades of grey in what are rarely black-or-white decisions.

Your ethical structure and the ethical challenges you'll face exist at several levels.[7] At the outside level are things that most people wouldn't consider bad, taking a couple of paper clips or sending an occasional personal e-mail on company time. Do these things really matter? At the middle level are more significant ethical challenges. One example might be accessing personnel records for personal reasons. Could there ever be personal reasons so compelling that you would not feel ethical discomfort doing this? Reading someone else's e-mail might be another "middle" example. At the innermost ethical level are ethical violations that you'd surely consider very serious: embezzling funds or selling company records to a competitor. And yet, over time, your ethical structure can change so that even such acts as these seem less unethical. For example, if everyone around you is accessing confidential records for their own purposes, in time you might come to think it's no big deal. And this might spell big trouble for you.

The practical circumstances surrounding your decision always influence you in an ethical dilemma.[8] It would be nice if every decision were crystal-clear and considerations such as these needn't be taken into account, but decisions are seldom so easy.

1. *Consequences.* How much or how little benefit or harm will come from a particular decision?
2. *Society's opinion.* What is your perception of what society really thinks of your intended action?
3. *Likelihood of effect.* What is the probability of the harm or benefit that will occur if you take the action?
4. *Time to consequences.* What length of time will it take for the benefit or harm to take effect?
5. *Relatedness.* How much do you identify with the person or persons who will receive the benefit or suffer the harm?
6. *Reach of result.* How many people will be affected by your action?

Let's hope your basic sense of right and wrong will steer you in the right direction, but no matter what your sense of ethics is or how strong it is, such practical aspects of the situation may affect you as you make your decision, perhaps unduly, perhaps quite justifiably. Ethical dilemmas usually arise, not out of simple situations, but from a clash between competing goals, responsibilities, and loyalties. Ethical decisions are complex judgments that balance rewards for yourself and others against responsibilities to yourself and others. Inevitably, your decision process is influenced by uncertainty about the magnitude of the outcome, by your estimate of the importance of the situation, sometimes by your perception of conflicting "right reactions," and more than one socially acceptable "correct" decision.

GUIDELINES FOR ETHICAL COMPUTER SYSTEM USE

Central to the ethical use of computers and information are the issues of ownership, responsibility, personal privacy, and access (see Figure 8.3).[9] And just to make it all more complicated, different countries have different views on personal privacy, copyrights, pornography, and so on.

Ownership embodies the rights to information and intellectual property. *Responsibility* deals with who is accountable for the accuracy and completeness of information. *Personal privacy*, which we will examine in more detail shortly, addresses the question of who owns personal information (the people who collect it or the people about

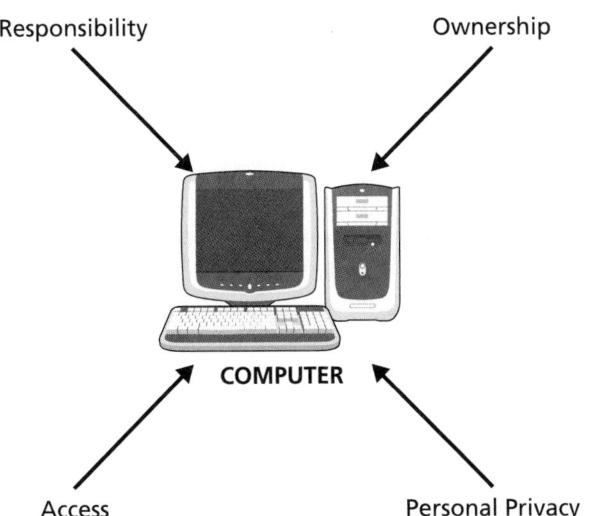

Figure 8.3
Ethical Dimensions of Information

whom it's collected)? *Access* deals with who can use, view, store, and process what information.

It's sometimes tough to decide what to do since there are few hard-and-fast rules. Knowing the law doesn't even help because what's legal is not always ethical and vice versa. In Figure 8.4 you see the four quadrants of ethical and legal behaviour. You're pretty safe if you can manage to stay in quadrant I.

So what do you do then if you're faced with a choice that is not perfectly ethically clear? If you feel you are in an ethical quandary—you probably are. If you find you're giving the situation a whole lot of thought, the situation very likely deserves it. You may wish to talk to a friend, a teacher, a supervisor, or a mentor. Know that we're all faced with such dilemmas, they are real, and they have consequences. And there *is* a line that you shouldn't cross.

Let's look at an example. Say your organization is developing a decision support system (DSS) to help formulate treatments for an infectious disease. Other companies in the industry are working on similar projects. The first system on the market will most likely reap huge profits. You may know that your DSS doesn't yet work properly—it's good, but not yet totally reliable. But you're feeling extreme pressure from your boss to get the system onto the market immediately. You're worried about the harm that might come to a patient because of your DSS; but, on the other hand, it does work well most of the time. Is it up to you or not? You have a family to support and student loans to repay. And you like being employed. Can you hold out and get more information on the system's reliability? What do you do? Where can you get help?

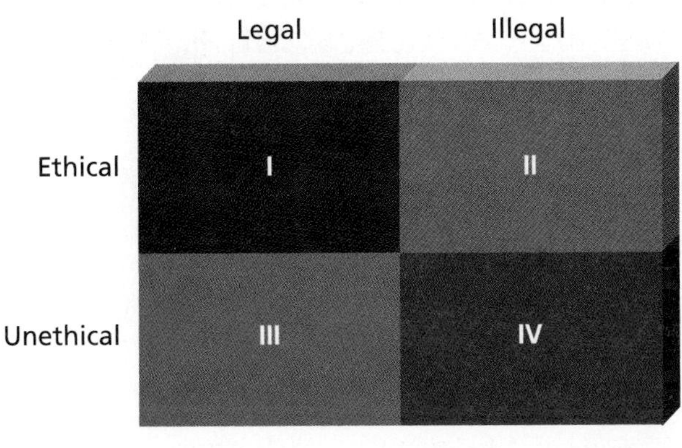

Figure 8.4
Acting Ethically and Legally Are Not Necessarily the Same Thing

You can certainly ask questions about what you're being asked to do—and you should. Sometimes legitimate actions look unethical, but if you find out more about the situation, you might find that it's perfectly all right. For instance, in the case above, management may be planning to leave out the dubious part of the system or warn customers that it has a problem. But, you must keep digging until you're very sure and comfortable with what you're being asked to do. If you really believe that what you're expected to do is wrong, you'll have to say so to your boss and be prepared to quit if you have to. But first, explain what you think is so bad and couch it in terms of the company's future and reputation if at all possible. Be sure and think also of your own future and reputation, many Enron employees wish they had taken a firm stand when they had the chance.[10]

Your company may well have an office or person (sometimes called an "ombudsman") whose job it is to give advice on work-related ethical dilemmas. Many companies do. Failing that, you could look up your company's code of ethics. If you can't find that or don't think it's taken seriously in your place of work, you can check your profession's ethical code. The ACM, for example, has a code of ethics for IT employees.

Another source of help is the Computer Ethics Institute (www.brook.edu/its/cei/cei_hp.htm). This organization has developed the "Ten Commandments of Computer Ethics" to help guide you in the general direction of ethical computer use (see Figure 8.5).

1. *Don't use a computer to harm other people.* This one is the bedrock for all the others.
2. *Don't interfere with other people's computer work.* This includes the small sins like sending frivolous e-mail, to the big ones, like spreading viruses, and the really big ones like electronic stalking.

Figure 8.5
Computer Ethics Institute

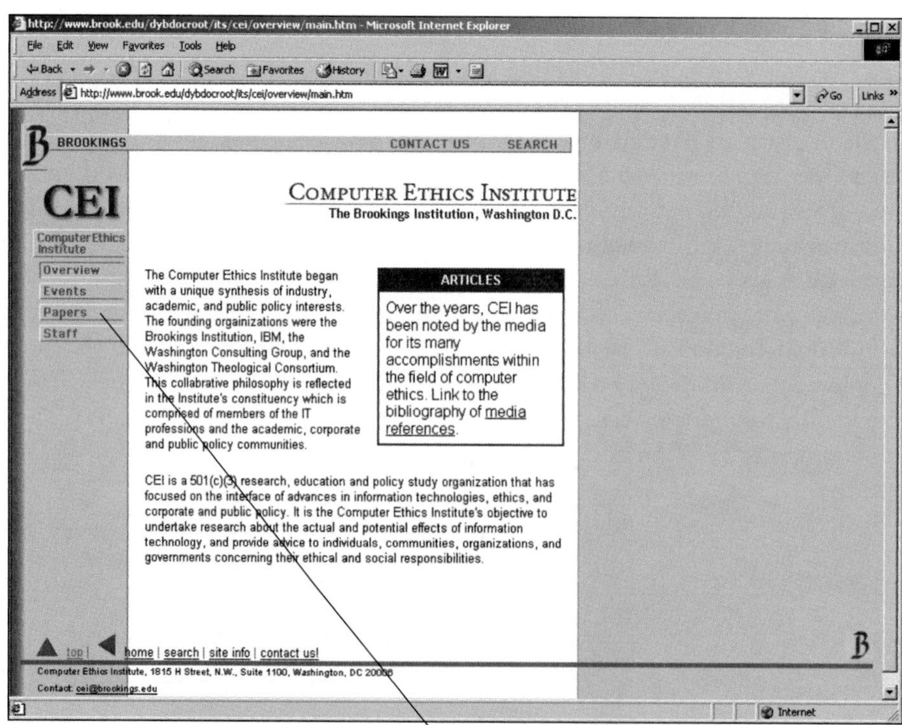

You can find many resources on computer ethics at the Computer Ethics Institute site.

3. *Don't snoop around in other people's computer files.* This means you shouldn't access another person's computer files unless expressly authorized to do so.
4. *Don't use a computer to steal.* This one's pretty obvious.
5. *Don't use a computer to bear false witness.* This means you shouldn't spread rumors and spoof your address (change the sender portion of the e-mail to make it look like it came from someone other than you). It's much easier to lie and cause trouble when you're not using your real name.
6. *Don't copy or use proprietary software for which you have not paid.* Buying one copy of a game and copying it for all your friends is both illegal and unethical. This also applies to shareware (software you can try before you buy).
7. *Don't use other people's computer resources without authorization or proper compensation.* This includes using company time and resources to surf the Web, send e-mail, print large volumes of material, and work on your own private projects.
8. *Don't appropriate other people's intellectual output.* This includes taking and using images, text, music off the Web without permission and it certainly includes claiming material as your own that came from someone else.
9. *Always think about the social consequences of the IT system you're involved in.* Even if you're not a programmer or a systems analyst, you may be supervising a project that involves a computer system.
10. *Always use a computer in ways that ensure consideration and respect for your fellow humans.* People are entitled to the same respect and consideration whether your contact with them is in the "brick" or the "click" world.

INTELLECTUAL PROPERTY

An ethical issue you will almost certainly encounter is one related to the use or copying of proprietary software. Will you take care to do the right thing? Software is a type of intellectual property. **Intellectual property** is intangible creative work that is embodied in physical form.[11] Music, novels, paintings, and sculptures are all examples of intellectual property. So also are your company's product sketches and schematics and other proprietary documents. These documents, along with music, novels, and so on, are worth much more than the physical form in which they are delivered. For example, a single Sarah McLachlan song is worth far more than the CD it's purchased on. It's also an example of intellectual property that is covered by copyright law.

Copyright law protects authorship of literary and dramatic works, musical and theatrical compositions, and works of art. **Copyright** is the legal protection afforded an expression of an idea, such as a song, video game, and some types of proprietary documents. Having a copyright means that no one can use your song or video game without your permission. As a form of intellectual property, software is usually protected by copyright law, although sometimes it falls under patent law, which protects an idea, such as the design of a sewing machine or an industrial pump valve.

Copyright law doesn't forbid the use of intellectual property completely. It has some notable exceptions. For example, a TV program could show your video game without your permission. This would be an example of the use of copyrighted material for the creation of new material, that is, the TV program. And that's legal; it falls under the Fair Use Doctrine. The **Fair Use Doctrine** says that you may use copyrighted material in certain situations—for example, in the creation of new work or, within certain limits, for teaching purposes. One limit is on the amount of the copyrighted material you may use. Generally, the determining factor in copyright disputes is whether the copyright holder has been or is likely to be denied income because of

ON YOUR OWN

ARE YOU CAREFUL ABOUT YOUR POSTURE?

Health experts have developed guidelines for the safe use of computers. Figure 8.6 shows the upright, right-angled posture of a person using a computer correctly. You should look straight at, or a little down at the monitor.

Choose three computers that you have access to and answer the following questions for each.

Question	Answer
1. Do you sit with your thighs parallel to the floor?	
2. Is your back straight when you type?	
3. How far is the monitor from your eyes?	
4. Do you feel discomfort when you work at a keyboard for an extended period? If so, where?	
5. Do you rest periodically, at least once an hour?	

Figure 8.6
Sitting at a Computer

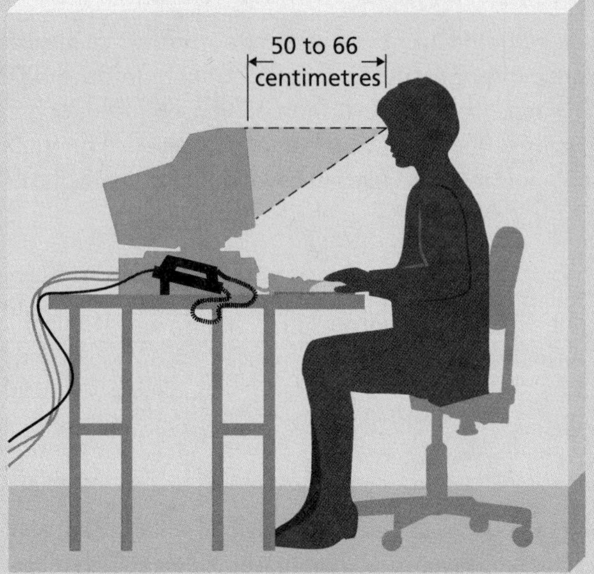

the infringement. Courts will consider factors such as how much of the work was used and how, and when and on what basis the decision was made to use it.

Remember that copyright infringement is *illegal*. That means it's illegal, outside of a fair use situation, to simply copy a copyrighted picture, text, or anything else without permission, whether the copyrighted material is on the Internet or not. In particular, it's illegal to copy copyrighted software. But there's one exception to that rule. You may always make one copy of copyrighted software to keep for backup purposes. When you buy copyrighted software, what you're paying for is the right to use it—and that's all.

How many other copies you may make depends on the copyright agreement that comes with the software package. Some software companies say emphatically that you may not even put the software on more than one computer—even if they're both yours and no one else uses either one. Other companies are a little less strict, and agree to let you put a copy of software on multiple machines—as long as only one person is using that software package at any given time. In this instance, the company considers software to be like a book in that you can have it in different places and you can loan it out, but only one person at a time may use it.

If you copy copyrighted software and give it to another person or persons, you're pirating the software. **Pirated software** is the unauthorized use, duplication, distribution or sale of copyrighted software.[12] Software piracy costs businesses an estimated $12 billion a year in lost revenue. Microsoft gets more than 25,000 reports of software piracy every year, and the company follows up on every one. The biggest losers (in rank order) are the United States, Japan, United Kingdom, Germany, China, France, Canada, Italy, Brazil, and the Netherlands. One in four business applications in the United States is thought to be pirated.[13] In some parts of the world more than 90 percent of business software is pirated. The Software and Information Industry Association (SIIA) and the Business Software Alliance (BSA) say that this means lost jobs, wages, tax revenues, and a potential barrier to success for software startups around the globe.[14]

With the crackdown by software manufacturers and the growing awareness of corporations, illegally copied software is actually declining in businesses. But a new threat is emerging in the form of counterfeit software. **Counterfeit software** is software that is manufactured to look like the real thing and sold as such. Counterfeit software is being sold by sophisticated crime organizations, and sometimes the counterfeit is so perfect that the software even includes a valid certificate of authenticity.[15] The results of counterfeit software are greater than just lost revenue, which in itself is considerable. Many resellers unwittingly buy counterfeit software and then find that they've sold buggy or infected software to their customers. The legitimate manufacturers have to deal with irate customers who believe that their software and its problems came directly from the software company. It's a public-relations nightmare.

Beware when buying software off the Internet. The BSA estimates that there are close to 950,000 Internet sites selling software illegally. If you buy from a shady site you might never receive your software at all. Or you might get counterfeit software that has a virus. You need to be careful when buying software off the Internet. Following are some guidelines.[16]

- Buy only from trustworthy sources. Official manufacturers' sites can often tell you where you can buy the software.
- Make sure to get full details about the company you're buying from (such as name, address, and telephone number). It's a bad sign if the seller is reluctant to divulge this information.
- Find out, before you buy, the site's policy on return, service, and warranty policies. Again, avoid a site that doesn't want to provide you with this information.
- Make sure to print out all pertinent information, such as order numbers, order confirmations, invoices, and receipts, and keep it until after the software proves to be satisfactory.
- An extraordinarily low price is a good tipoff that something is not right.
- Sellers know about consumer's suspicions about very low prices, so be on the watch for ads like "special deals with the manufacturer" and "liquidated inventories." These phrases are designed to make you believe you're getting a good deal and not an illegal one.
- As usual, knowledge is power, so know something about the product you're buying. If you do, it will be easier to recognize a counterfeit.
- The manufacturer will usually be glad to tell you what the package should have in it and may even be able to tell you about the site you're buying from.

Privacy

Privacy is the right to be left alone when you want to be, to have control over your own personal possessions, and not to be observed without your consent. It's the right to be free of unwanted intrusion into your private life. Privacy has several dimensions. Psychologically it's a need for personal space. All of us to a greater or lesser extent need to feel in control of our most personal possessions, and personal information belongs on

THE GLOBAL PERSPECTIVE

AMERICANS ALREADY PREPARING FOR NEW CANADIAN PRIVACY LAW

The Canadian Personal Information Protection and Electronic Documents Act was enacted in January 2001. The new law stipulates that businesses must give guarantees to Canadian citizens regarding the collection and use of their personal information. Companies will now have to get the customer's consent before sharing any customer information with its affiliates or commercial partners. By 2004, all businesses operating in Canada will be affected.

According to Murray Long, a privacy consultant in Ottawa, this law promises to create "some interesting nightmares" particularly for Canadian affiliates that store their customer information on servers south of the border. After 2004, American firms with information on Canadian citizens will have to enter into contractual agreements which will commit them to following Canada's privacy law. This means that multinational companies operating in Canada will have to have contracts with anybody who supplies them with any personal information, including their own subsidiaries. Of particular concern to many U.S. companies is the lack of a grandfather clause, which would have exempted customer information collected before the law's enactment. Many companies have already started asking for their customers' consent before they are legally required to do so. Without this consent, companies will not be legally allowed to use any customer information after 2004 even if the data was collected years before.[17]

the list of those possessions. Legally, privacy is necessary for self-protection.[18] If you put the key to your house in a special hiding place in your yard, you want to keep that information private. This information could be abused and cause you grief.

In this section we'll examine some specific areas of privacy—individuals snooping on each other, employers' collection of information about employees, businesses' collection of information about consumers, government collection of personal information, and the issue of privacy in international trade.

PRIVACY AND OTHER INDIVIDUALS

Other individuals, like family members, associates, fellow employees, and "hackers" could be electronically invading your privacy. Their motives might be simple curiosity, an attempt to get your password, or to access something they have no right to. Obviously, there are situations in which you're well within your rights to snoop—for example, if you suspect that your child is in electronic contact with someone or something undesirable, or if you think that someone may be using your computer without permission. Hundreds of Web sites are offering programs, collectively referred to as "snoopware," to help you find out.

For general snooping, you can get **key logger**, or **key trapper**, **software**, which records keystrokes and mouse clicks performed at the computer, thus capturing all e-mail, instant messages, chat room exchanges, Web sites visited, applications run, and passwords typed in. Spector Pro is an example of key logger software; from the same software company you can also get eBlaster, which will actually e-mail you activity reports—every 30 minutes, if you'd like. A word of caution: be careful that you're not breaking the law; family members and friends don't have carte blanche to monitor each other.

If you want to disable activity-monitoring programs like Spector Pro, you can get a free program from www.idcide.com called Privacy Companion, or one called Who's Watching Me from www.trapware.com.

TEAM WORK

WHAT WOULD YOU DO?

Analyze the following situation. You have access to the sales and customer information in a flower shop. You discover that the boyfriend of a woman you know is sending roses to three other women on a regular basis. The woman you know is on the flower list, but she believes that she's the only woman in his romantic life. You really think you should tell the woman. Your dilemma is that you have a professional responsibility to keep the company's information private. However, you also believe that you have a responsibility to the woman. Do you tell her?

Are there factors that would change your decision? Each team member should individually consider the additional information below, then indicate whether any one or more of these factors would change his or her decision. Form a consensus with your team.

Additional Facts	Yes	No	Why?
1. The woman is your sister.			
2. The man is your brother.			
3. The woman is about to give the man her life savings as a down payment on a house in the belief that they will soon be married.			
4. The woman is already married.			

You can at least make sure that your social insurance number, bank account number, passwords, mother's maiden name, and credit card numbers are not stored on your computer for someone to find. Make sure you clear the "Use inline AutoComplete" or similar option in your browser, a feature that starts suggesting the rest of the entry when you type in the first few letters while filling out a form. You can disable it in Internet Explorer from the menu: go Tools/Internet Options/Advanced and clear the check box for "Use inline AutoComplete." Don't forget to click OK when you're done.

Also available for monitoring computer use are screen capture programs that periodically record what's on the screen (they get the information straight from the video card). These don't trap every single screen, just whatever is on the screen when the capturing program activates, but they still give whoever is doing the monitoring a pretty good idea of what the computer user is up to. Other tools for monitoring include packet sniffers (that examine the information passing by) on switches, hubs, or routers (the devices on networks that connect computers to each other), and log analysis tools that keep track of logons, deletions, and so forth.

As you're probably already aware, e-mail is completely insecure. It might as well be written on a postcard for all the privacy it has. Not only that, but every e-mail you send results in at least three or four copies being stored on different computers (see Figure 8.7). If you write an e-mail, it's stored first in the e-mail program in the computer you're using. Second, it's stored on the e-mail server—the computer through which it gets onto the Internet. Third, it's stored on the recipient's computer and may also be archived on the recipient's e-mail server.

Some people like to "encrypt" their e-mail (see fuller discussion below). Lots of products on the market will do this for you, such as ZixMail, CertifiedMail, PrivacyX, and SafeMessage. Disappearing Email gives you a slightly different type of e-mail protection. This software is free and sends a self-destructing message with the e-mail so that the e-mail deletes itself after the period of time you specify. Before the recipient opens the e-mail the Disappearing Email software checks with the Disappearing server that the e-mail hasn't passed its expiration date. However, you can defeat this feature by copying the text and pasting it somewhere else.

PRIVACY AND EMPLOYEES

Companies need information about their employees and customers to be effective in the marketplace. But people often object to having so many details about their lives available to others. If you're applying for a job, you'll most likely fill out a job application, but that's not the only information a potential employer can get about you. For a small fee, employers, or anyone else, can find out about your credit standing, your telephone usage, your insurance coverage, and many other interesting things. An employer can also get information on what you said on the Internet from companies who collect and collate chat room exchanges. An employer can also ask a job applicant to take drug and psychological tests, the results of which are the property of the company.

After you're hired, your employer can monitor where you go, what you do, what you say, and what you write in e-mails—at least during working hours. One reason that companies monitor employees' e-mail is that they can be sued for what their employees send to each other and to people outside the company. Chevron Corporation and Microsoft have had to settle sexual harassment lawsuits for $2.2 million each because employees sent offensive e-mail. Other companies, such as Dow Chemical Company, Xerox, and Edward Jones, have chosen to take preemptive action by firing people who send or store pornographic or violent e-mail messages.[19]

Another reason employers monitor their workers' use of IT resources is to avoid wasting resources, or "cyberslacking": visiting pornographic sites and news sites, chatting, gaming, trading stocks, participating in auctions, shopping, checking sports scores, or doing anything else not in one's job description. In May 2000, Victoria's Secret had an online fashion show at three o'clock in the afternoon on a weekday. About two million people watched the show, presumably many of them on their companies' computers. One employee watching the show used as much bandwidth as it would take to download the entire *Encyclopaedia Britannica.*[20] So, not only is the employee wasting company time, the employee is also slowing down the work of others.

That about 70 percent of Web traffic occurs during work hours is reason enough for companies to monitor what, and for how long, employees are looking at. Again,

Figure 8.7

The E-Mail You Send Is Stored on Many Computers

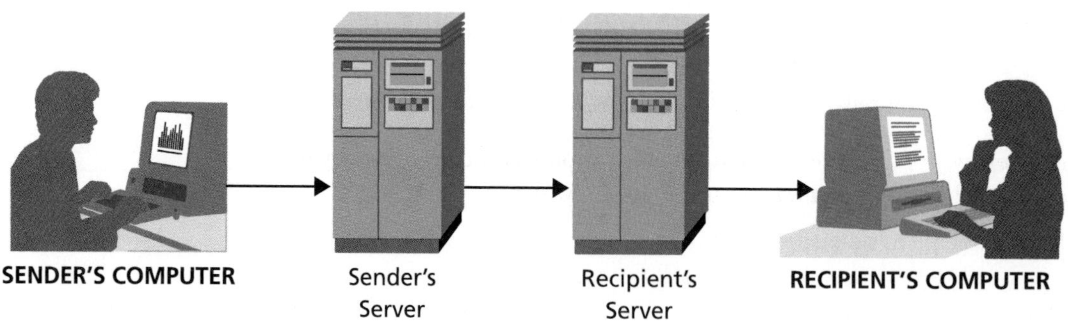

various software packages are available to keep track of people's surfing. Some software actually blocks access to certain sites.

To sum up, businesses have good reasons for seeking and storing personal information on employees:

1. They want to hire the best people possible and to avoid being sued for failing to adequately investigate the backgrounds of employees.
2. They want to ensure that staff members are conducting themselves appropriately and not wasting or misusing company resources.
3. They can be held liable for the actions of employees.
4. Financial institutions are even required by law to monitor all communications including e-mail and telephone conversations.

MONITORING TECHNOLOGY Numerous vendors offer software that scans both incoming and outgoing e-mail, looking for specific words or phrases in the subject lines or in the message, and flagging unsolicited ads and newsletters. You can sneak this software onto someone's computer using the "Trojan horse" approach (see below); that is, you can hide it in an innocent-looking e-mail.

Some companies use an approach less invasive than actually reading employees' e-mail. Their e-mail inspection programs just check for a certain level of e-mail to and from the same address. This indicates that there may be a problem and the employee is informed of the situation and asked to remedy it. Then, no intrusive supervisory snooping is necessary.[21]

An employer can track your keyboard activity with a software key logger, just as another individual can (see above). A harder-to-detect alternative is a *hardware* key logger, which captures keystrokes on their journey from the keyboard to the motherboard. These devices can be in the form of a connector on the system-unit end of the cable between the keyboard and the system unit. There's another type you can install into the keyboard that "bugs" it. Both types have enough memory to store about a year's worth of typing. But you have to have access to the bugged computer to be able to see the log of activity. And these devices can't capture anything that's not typed. To defeat them a person can copy the password (or whatever) and paste it into its new location. Although the key logger can tell a copy-and-paste operation was performed, it cannot tell what was copied and pasted.[22]

There is little sympathy in the legal system for private-sector employees who are being monitored. Employers have the legal right to monitor the use of their resources and that includes the time they're paying you for. In contrast to your home, you can have no expectation of privacy when using a company's resources.

PRIVACY AND CONSUMERS

Businesses face a dilemma:

- Customers want businesses to know who they are, but at the same time they want them to leave them alone.
- Customers want businesses to provide what they want, but at the same time they don't want businesses knowing too much about their habits and preferences.
- Customers want businesses to tell them about products and services they might like to have, but they don't want to be inundated with ads.

Like it or not, massive amounts of information are available to businesses. A relatively large Web site may get about 100 million hits per day. The site gets about 200 bytes of information for each hit. That's about 20 gigabytes per day.[23] This level of information load has made electronic customer relationship (eCRM) systems the fastest-growing area of software development. Part of managing customer relationships is personalization. Web sites greeting you by name, and Amazon.com's famous feature telling you that "People who bought this also bought . . ." are examples of personalization, which is made possible by the Web site knowing about you.[24]

Apart from being able to collect its own information about you, a company can readily access consumer information elsewhere. Credit card companies sell information, and so do mailing list companies. Web traffic tracking companies such as DoubleClick follow you (and every other surfer) around the Web and then sell the information about where you went and for how long. DoubleClick can get to know you over time and provide their customers with a profile on you that is highly refined. DoubleClick is also a middleman for companies that want to advertise to surfers. When hired by a company wanting to sell something, DoubleClick identifies people who might be receptive and sends the ad to them as a banner or pop-up ad. Proponents of this practice claim that it's good for the surfer because they get targeted advertising and less unwanted advertising. DoubleClick at first undertook to track consumers without attaching their identity to the information. Then, in 1999, DoubleClick changed its policy and announced that it would henceforth attach consumer names, personal information, and e-mail addresses. Responding to negative consumer reaction, DoubleClick withdrew its proposed change. Interestingly, DoubleClick didn't undertake never to resume the abandoned policy, but only agreed to wait until standards for such activity are in place.[25]

COOKIES: THE ROOT OF ALL EVIL The basic tool of consumer Web monitoring is the **cookie**—a small file a Web site places on your computer that contains information about you and your Web activities. It can be used for many purposes. For example, it's used to keep ID and password information so that you don't have to go through the whole rigmarole every time you log onto a site. It's also used to store the contents of electronic shopping carts, so that the next time you log on, the Web site will be able to see your wish list—and they don't have to store all that information themselves.

A cookie can also be used to track your Web activity. It can monitor and record what sites you visit, how long you stay there, what Web pages you visited, and the sites you came from and go to. This type of cookie is called a *unique* cookie. Some cookies are very temporary and some stay there recording indefinitely.

Apart from the unique cookies above, there are also third-party or *common* cookies that have many privacy advocates disturbed. A common cookie is one that started out as a unique cookie, but the original site sold access to it to a third party such as DoubleClick, that can then change the cookie so that the third party can track the surfer's activity across many sites. The third party collects information about surfers without names or other identifiable personal information. What they usually collect is an IP address and they then link it to a random identifying ID so that the surfer can be identified at other sites. Surveys have shown that the vast majority of people (91 percent) don't like unknown companies gathering the information about them that they provide to the site they interact with.[26]

You have two options if you want to block cookies. First, you can set your browser to reject all cookies, or get your browser to warn you when a site wants to put a cookie on your computer. Second, you can get cookie management software with additional options not available on your browser. For example, CookieCop 2, from *PC Magazine*, will let you accept or reject cookies on a per-site basis. It also allows you to replace banner ads with the image of your choice and to block ads for sites you find offensive. With this or other cookie-stopper software, you can disable pop-up windows,

THE JUDGE SAYS "GET PERSONAL" WITH CUSTOMERS

SonicBlue Inc.'s ReplayTV system enables you to record TV shows without the commercials; send programs to other ReplayTV owners over the Internet; and find all the times and stations a particular show is playing and record them without commercials.

When the system was offered, several movie studios and television networks filed suit, claiming that the commercial skipping and the sharing of programming violated copyright law. Before a court case is heard, there is usually a process called "discovery" in which each side must share information with the other. As part of this process, the plaintiff wanted to know exactly how SonicBlue's customers were using ReplayTV. SonicBlue said that the company doesn't collect that information.

Unbelievably, the judge told SonicBlue to write software to monitor all shows that customers watch, every skipped commercial, and all programs they send over the Internet. The order was based on the published privacy policy of SonicBlue, which said that the company may collect audience data. SonicBlue said that it originally planned to collect such information, but decided not to on the basis of the negative reaction from customers that Tivo, ReplayTV's competitor, got when it proposed the same idea.

So SonicBlue found itself in the strange situation of having to go to court to avoid having to collect personal information on its customers—in effect to protect the privacy of its customers. The company filed an appeal and the new judge overturned the previous ruling. However, the original ruling sent shock waves throughout the privacy advocate community.[27]

and stipulate that certain cookies can stay on your hard drive for the duration of one session only.

SPYWARE Some companies are really sneaky about getting information from you. For example, the first release of RealNetworks' RealJukebox sent information back to the company about what CDs the people who downloaded the software were playing on that computer. This information collection was going on when the customer wasn't even on the Web.[28]

If you've downloaded a game or other software from the Web for free, you may have noticed that it came with banner ads. These ads are created by **adware**—software to generate ads that installs itself when you install some other (usually free) program. This is a type of **Trojan-horse software**, meaning that it's software you don't want hidden inside software you do want. At installation there's usually a disclaimer saying that by installing the software you are agreeing to accept the adware also. Very few people read the whole agreement, and advertisers count on that. This technique is sometimes called *click-wrap* because it's like the agreement you accept by breaking the shrink wrap on a software box.

Most people don't get upset about pure adware, since they feel it's worth having to view a few ads to get software for free. However, a more insidious extra called **spyware** (also called **sneakware** or **stealthware**) is now being bundled into free downloadable software. Spyware is software that tracks your online movements, mines the information stored on your computer, or uses your computer's processor and storage for some task you know nothing about. For example, unknown to you, your computer may become part of peer-to-peer network operation (called *grid computing*) to solve complicated computer problems—you're paying for the "free" software in CPU cycles. Spyware is fast becoming the hidden cost of free software. Software such as Kazaa Media Desktop and Audiogalaxy, which are the successors to Napster for sharing music and other files online, include spyware. If you download free software and it has banner ads, it's quite possible that it has spyware too. There's usually something in the "I agree" screens about the spyware, but it can be hard to find.[29] Spyware can stay on your computer long after you've uninstalled the original software.

You can detect all kinds of Trojan-horse software with The Cleaner from www.moosoft.com. Also check out www.wilders.org for Trojan First Aid Kit (TFAK). The best-known stealthware blockers are Ad-aware (free from www.lavasoftusa.com) and PestPatrol. These scan your whole computer and offer to any delete spyware programs.

If you want to check out free software for spyware *before* you download it, go to www.spychecker.com, a site that will tell you if a particular free software includes adware or spyware.

For preventing your computer from automatically communicating over the Internet without your approval, a firewall is good. A very popular software firewall is ZoneAlarm (www.zonelabs.com). It also offers protection from ads and cookies.

Even without spyware, a site can still find out a lot about its visitors from its *Web log*.[30] This is a record consisting of one line of data for every visitor to the site, it is usually stored on the company's server. At the very least, a log file can tell the Web site company:

- What company or ISP you come from
- The amount of time you spent on the site
- The number of pages you viewed
- How you clicked in to the site, that is, from a search engine or some other site, or from your e-mail advertising

The latter three bits of information are collectively called the **clickstream**, which can also include what Web sites you visited, what ads you looked at, and what you bought.

If, as a consumer, you want to protect information about your surfing habits, you can use various software packages to do so. Apart from cookie management software you can avail yourself of **anonymous Web browsing (AWB)** services, which in effect hide your identity. Anonymizer (www.anonymizer.com), and other programs like it, route your browsing data through their server and remove all identifying information. AWB services available include disabling pop-up promotions, defeating tracking programs, and erasing your Internet history files. If you don't want to go through an outside server, you can download software like SurfSecret (www.surfsecret.com), a shareware anti-tracking package.

Finally, remember that even if a company promises, and fully intends, to protect its customer information, this may not be possible. Faced with a subpoena, a company will have to relinquish customer records.

PRIVACY AND GOVERNMENT AGENCIES

Government agencies have about 2000 databases containing personal information on individuals.[31] The various branches of government need information to administer entitlement programs, such as social security, welfare, student loans, law enforcement, and so on.

LAW ENFORCEMENT You've often heard about someone's being apprehended for a grievous crime after a routine traffic stop for something like a broken taillight. The arrest most likely ensued because the arresting officer ran a check on the licence plate and driver's licence. The officer probably checked the police database and found the

YOU CAN INSURE AGAINST IDENTITY THEFT

Insurance companies are beginning to cover one of the fastest-growing white-collar crimes—identity theft. Chubb Personal Insurance is one of the first to offer such coverage. Since 1999, Chubb has included $25,000 of coverage for expenses related to identity theft on all its homeowner policies. Travelers Property Casualty was the first in the industry to offer this type of coverage and later added a freestanding policy.

In 2001, almost 12,000 Canadians were victims of identity theft. Take, for example, Dan and Sharon Millar from Hamilton, Ontario. The couple first noticed that their *TV Guide* did not arrive when it should have, the first Tuesday of the month. Over the next few weeks, all mail had simply stopped coming. After contacting Canada Post, the stunned couple discovered that someone had applied for a change of address, diverting all their mail to another address. By the time the whole plot was uncovered, the fraud artist had applied for, received, and used a credit card in the Millars' name. The Millars were not alone. In 2001, Canada Post caught 400 cases of fake address changes, ten times more than in the previous year. Inspector John Sliter of the economic crimes branch of the RCMP says that once someone has acquired your identity, it is actually quite easy to take over financial accounts, transfer bank balances, apply for loans and credit cards, and purchase items. Often, a social insurance number and a date of birth are all that is needed to assume someone's identity. According to Canada's social insurance registry, there are currently about 1.4 million more social insurance cards in circulation than there are Canadians. According to the Council of Better Business Bureaus in Canada, identity theft accounts for a loss of $2.5 billion a year to Canadian consumers, banks, credit card firms, stores, and other businesses.

Identity theft is the fastest-growing fraud in North America. Consequently, the U.S. Congress has passed the Identity Theft and Assumption Deterrence Act in 1998 making identity theft a federal crime. Convictions carry maximum penalties of 30 years' imprisonment, a fine, and confiscation of any personal property used to perpetrate the crime. In Canada, the penalties are much less severe. Under the Criminal Code of Canada, impersonation *with intent* results in a jail term of up to ten years. The RCMP would like the law to be toughened and unified across Canada. For instance, Inspector Sliter says that one such revision could include passing a law declaring that carrying multiple identities is a prosecutable offence.[32]

outstanding warrant there. This is how the culprits responsible for the Oklahoma City bombing were caught.

The database of the Canadian Police Information Centre (CPIC), available to police agencies across Canada, holds information on outstanding warrants, missing children, gang members, juvenile delinquents, stolen guns and cars, and so on. CPIC, located in the RCMP headquarters complex in Ottawa, Ontario and in operation since 1972, serves over 60,000 Canadian law enforcement agents. Officers access it from a terminal located in their office or vehicle. CPIC is also linked to more than 400 criminal justice national and international agencies across the planet. One of these is the U.S. National Crime Information Center (NCIC), which has a huge database with information on the criminal records of more than 20 million people. This Canada-U.S. crime fighting partnership has become ever more prevalent with the North American Free Trade agreement (NAFTA). Today, information sharing between Canada and the United States has been routinized by the Automated Canadian/US Police Information Exchange System (ACUPIES) and officers on either side of the border have access to each other's national criminal databases on a 24-hour basis.

It is not surprising that these databases have been abused. Several police departments have found that a significant number of employees illegally snooped for criminal records on people they knew or wanted to know.

WHAT DOES THE LAW SAY ABOUT PRIVACY?

Although the Canadian Privacy Act, implemented on July 1, 1983, was aimed at regulating government record keeping practices as a result of computerization, at the time data mining, direct marketing, and online retailing did not exist. The Act was aimed specifically at making government more accountable for the personal information it held in its databanks. Today, however, countries have recognized that companies can also collect massive amounts of personal information about customers. Hence, protecting citizens from misuse of information in commercial contexts has become important. However, Canada, the United States, and the European Community have not developed a consistent set of laws. Europe's standards are considered the most stringent, followed closely by those of Canada. In effect since 2001, the Canadian privacy law (better known as the Personal Information Protection and Electronic Documents Act, or simply "PIPEDA") mandates as law ten principles adopted in 1996 as voluntary industry standards:

- *Accountability.* Organizations are responsible for the uses of the information they collect. They must ensure its proper handling by third parties with whom they share it.
- *Identifying purposes.* The purposes for which the data is being collected must be identified to Canadian citizens at or before the time the information is collected.
- *Consent.* Consent from Canadian citizens is required for the collection, use, or disclosure of personal information. Exceptions include emergencies, law enforcement, and debt collection.
- *Limiting collection.* It is prohibited to indiscriminately collect information. Only the information necessary to fulfill the purposes that have been identified may be collected.
- *Use, disclosure, and retention limited to what is necessary.* After the personal information collected is no longer required to fulfill the identified purposes, it should be destroyed, erased, or made anonymous.
- *Accuracy.* Collected personal information must be accurate, complete, and up to date.
- *Safeguards.* Collected personal information must be securely protected against unauthorized access, disclosure, copying, use, or modification.
- *Openness.* Organizations' management of personal information must be made open.
- *Individual access.* Canadian citizens must be granted access to their personal information, and be given the ability to correct this information.
- *Compliance challenges.* Canadian citizens will be entitled to challenge organizations on the principles listed above if organizations are noncompliant.

Like the EU's Directive on Protection of Personal Data, the Canadian law applies to its citizens regardless of whether they are inside or outside of Canada. However, although Canada's legislation is similar in many aspects to that of the EU, important differences do exist. Unlike the Directive, which applies to all entities collecting and processing information that could identify a person, Canada's law applies only to personal information collected and disclosed while conducting commercial activities. It does permit the collection and dissemination of personal information without personal consent "for personal and domestic purposes" or for "journalistic, artistic, and literary purposes." Moreover, unlike the EU legislation, the Canadian law exempts names, titles, business addresses, and telephone numbers from its definition of "personal information." Such information can be collected and disseminated freely by companies operating in Canada. Conversely, the U.S. government has traditionally preferred a more hands-off approach to privacy, arguing that private industry should be left alone to self-regulate in this regard. The United States eventually succumbed to EU pressure concerning privacy protection (i.e., the "Safe Harbor" principles—see below). By law, the EU interdicts member countries from conducting transactions involving the transfer of personal information with foreign companies that do not safeguard it in accordance to EU law. Originally, the United States would not offer such guarantees. Through ongoing negotiations, however, the United States has accepted to ensure that EU laws will be respected. Yet, by 2004, U.S. companies will also have to adapt to the Canadian law as well if they want to continue conducting business in Canada—their largest trading partner. Several differences between the Canadian and the European privacy law means that compliance will be difficult not only for U.S. companies but also for Canadian and European companies that decide to operate in all three markets.[33]

PRIVACY AND INTERNATIONAL TRADE

If a customer in Europe buys books from Amazon.com's United Kingdom division, you'd probably be surprised to find out that Amazon may not transfer the customer's credit card information to Amazon in the United States without making sure it is in compliance with **Safe Harbor principles**, a set of rules to which U.S. businesses that want to trade with the EU must adhere. You probably wouldn't think twice about sending customer information, such as a name and address, via e-mail from one part of the company to another. But if you're in a subsidiary in an EU country and the recipient is in the United States you might have a problem.

Canadians do not have this problem when it comes to trading with the EU. The Personal Information Protection and Electronic Documents Act (PIPEDA) received Royal Assent in April 2000 and was adopted into law. Its provisions are being phased in from January 1, 2001 to January 1, 2004. Provinces are being given a three-year grace period to pass their own equivalent privacy laws; afterwards, any province that does not have its own, equivalent privacy law will be subject to Canada's federal law, PIPEDA. The European Commission has ruled that PIPEDA meets the rigorous standards for data protection.

The EU has very stringent rules about the collection of personal information and has implemented a Directive on Protection of Personal Data, mentioned above. In 1998, the EU set privacy goals and each country had to make laws to achieve those goals according to its own culture and customs. So there are still differences in privacy laws among European countries. In general, the rights granted EU citizens include the consumer's right to:

- Know the marketer's source of information
- Check personal identifiable information for accuracy
- Correct any incorrect information
- Specify that information can't be transferred to a third party without the consumer's consent
- Know the purpose for which the information is being collected

If information can be linked to you—either directly or indirectly—it's personal identifiable information. The list of identifying tags includes names, ID numbers, and unique physical characteristics.[34]

The United States and the European Union began negotiations on the heels of the EU Directive to create Safe Harbor principles for U.S.-based companies to be able to transfer personal information out of European countries. The rules cover every indus-

ON YOUR OWN

WHAT'S YOUR OPINION?

A nationwide survey was conducted by the journal *Marketing Management* on consumer attitudes toward online privacy.[35] It investigated what impact privacy policies have on consumer purchasing behaviour and what consumers considered to be acceptable levels of information gathering.

The questions and responses are listed below. State whether you agree or disagree with the answers and why.

Question	Survey Response	Your Response	
		Yes	*No*
1. Does your perception of a site's Web privacy affect your willingness to purchase from it?	Depends on the site: 49%		
2. Should a Web site be able to analyze Web traffic on an anonymous aggregate level?	Yes: 75%		
3. Is lack of control over who gets your personal information a strong privacy concern for you?	Yes: 39%		
4. Is spam a strong privacy concern for you?	Yes: 37%		
5. Is it very important to you to be able to access a site's information about you?	Yes: 22%		
6. Would it be acceptable to you if the site protected your privacy, but didn't let you see information about you any time you wished?	Yes: 80%		

try and almost all types of personal information. After extensive negotiations, in June 2000 the United States became the first country outside the EU to be recognized as meeting information privacy requirements of EU states.[36] Without this agreement, disruption of the $350 billion in trade between the United States and Europe would have been a distinct possibility.

So for your company, or Amazon.com, to be able to transfer personal information out of EU countries, you'd have to first register with the U.S. Department of Commerce and agree to adhere to the Safe Harbor principles. Although participation is theoretically voluntary, if you transfer personal information without having registered, you're risking punitive action from the U.S. Federal Trade Commission as well as from the European country from which you transferred the information.[37]

See Closing Case Two for more on the European Directive on Protection of Personal Data and the Safe Harbor Agreement.

LAWS ON PRIVACY

Unlike the EU and Canada, the United States doesn't have a comprehensive or consistent set of laws on the use or misuse of information. However, some laws are in place. Two newer examples are the Health Insurance Portability and Accountability Act (HIPAA) and the Financial Service Modernization Act.

The **Health Insurance Portability and Accountability Act** gives the U.S. health care industry until April 14, 2003 to formulate and implement the first set of compliance regulations that require all members of the industry to install policies and procedures to keep patient information confidential. The Act seeks to:

- Limit the release and use of your health information without your consent
- Give you the right to access your medical records and find out who has accessed them
- Overhaul the circumstances under which researchers and others can review medical records
- Release health information on a need-to-know basis
- Allow the disclosure of protected health information for business reasons as long as the recipient undertakes, in writing, to protect the information

Many critics in Canada and the EU consider the U.S. approach to privacy protection still too piecemeal and far behind the curve, often putting the interests of businesses ahead of those of their own citizens. For instance, although HIPAA is a move in the right direction in terms of privacy protection in the U.S. health care industry, by comparison Canada's Personal Information Protection and Electronic Documents Act (PIPEDA) is all-encompassing. It covers all personal data that enters the commercial sphere in all sectors of the economy (see www.privcom.gc.ca for details). In sum, because the Canadian law applies to all industries, it underscores the belief that all Canadians have a fundamental right when it comes to their privacy and that they are not obligated to provide information about themselves. It gives Canadians the right to ask why information requested from them is needed and how it is to be used.

Information

In this section we'll consider the dual roles of information in an organization. Nothing is as universal or versatile as information. What else can you sell or lease to someone else—and simultaneously retain for yourself? This unique resource called "information" has two functions in an organization: as raw material and as capital (see Figure 8.8).

INFORMATION AS RAW MATERIAL

Raw materials are the components from which a product is made. For example, the raw materials for a chair might be wood, glue, and screws. But almost everything you buy has information as part of the product. If you doubt this, wander through a store and see how many products incorporate absolutely no information. Even bananas have stickers telling you something about their distributor. Of course, the amount of information varies. You get a lot more information if you buy a jet airplane than if you buy a cake mix. Sometimes it's the information that makes a product particularly valuable. Take the example of two identical pairs of sports shoes that were originally made by the same company but sold under different logos. It's very likely that the shoes with the more widely known or prestigious logo will sell for a higher price than those with the lesser logo. The more desirable logo doesn't increase the functional value of the shoes. They're the same shoes! But the information (in this case the logo) proclaims something to the world that the wearer wants to be associated with. For that statement, whatever it is, the customer is prepared to pay extra.

The most successful companies put the highest value on information. United Parcel Service (UPS) is an example. The company's IT budget is second only to

Figure 8.8

Information as Raw Material and Capital

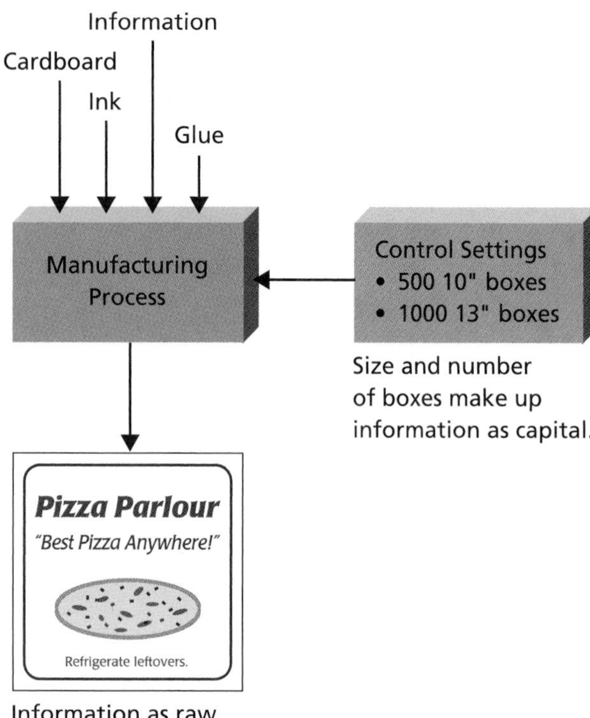

its expenditures on aircraft.[38] This is because UPS is selling not only a shipping service, but also information. You can connect to the UPS Web site and track your package. As UPS Chief Information Officer (CIO) Frank Ergbrick puts it, "A package without information has no value."

General Motors doesn't just sell vehicles. As we've described elsewhere in this text, its Cadillacs feature an option called OnStar that combines a global positioning system (GPS)—which identifies your position anywhere on earth—with networked sensors, a cell phone, and a link to customer support centres. With the OnStar system you can get directions to any destination and even advice on where to dine. OnStar also contributes to your safety. If the car's airbag inflates, the sensor sends a signal to the customer support centre, which tries to contact you on the car phone. If there's no response, the centre uses the GPS component to locate your car, then alerts the nearest emergency service. The OnStar system can help track your car if it's stolen. So a Cadillac is not just a car—it's an IT system on wheels.

INFORMATION AS CAPITAL

Capital is the asset you use to produce a product or service. Buildings, trucks, and machinery are examples of capital. For our chair manufacturer, the capital would be the factory building, the saw, the glue dispenser, screwdrivers, and so on. These items are not part of the chair, but they're necessary to build it. You incur a cost in acquiring capital, and you expect a return on your investment. Additionally, you can sell or lease capital assets.

You can think of information as capital. It's used by companies to provide products and services. Organizations need information to provide what their target market wants. They need information in the form of manufacturing schedules, sales reports, marketing plans, accounting information, and so on.

Information capital is one of the most important and universal types of capital in an organization. Not every company has a building or a truck, but every single one has information. We cannot state the case too strongly; an organization cannot exist without information any more than you can survive without oxygen.

Security

It is estimated that computer sabotage costs businesses somewhere close to $10 billion every year. Companies are increasing their spending on Internet security software, already having spent more than $4 billion in 2000; this figure is expected to double by 2003.[39] Hard disks can crash, computer parts can fail, hackers and crackers can gain access and do mischief, thieves engaged in industrial espionage can steal your information, and disgruntled employees or associates can cause damage.

SECURITY AND EMPLOYEES

Most of the press reports are about outside attacks on computer systems, but actually companies are in far more danger of losing money from employee misconduct than they are from that of outsiders. It's a problem that predates computers. A 300-restaurant chain with 30 employees in each location loses, on average, $218 per employee. And then there's the customers. The Cracker Barrel chain is constantly replacing the signature rocking chairs that sit on the porch outside each store, and other restaurants report the taking of salt shakers and silverware as "souvenirs."

But white-collar crime is where the big bucks are lost (see Figure 8.9). White-collar crime in general, from Fortune 100 firms to video stores to construction companies, accounts for about $400 billion every year—and information technology makes it much easier to accomplish and conceal. (Compare that to the $292 billion in the federal defence budget.) In white-collar fraud, the biggest losses are those incurred by management misconduct. Losses caused by managers are quadruple those of other employees, and the median losses are 16 times greater. Take embezzlement, for example. The average cost of a nonmanagerial employee's theft is $60,000, while that for managerial employees is $250,000. The most astonishing aspect of this is that most inside fraud (up to two-thirds) is never reported to the legal authorities, according to the Association of Certified Fraud Examiners (ACFE). A survey by Ernst & Young disclosed that two out of five businesses suffered more than five fraud losses, and fully one-quarter of those resulted in over a loss of over $1 million. The reason most often cited for lack of legal action was fear of damaging the company's reputation or brand name.[40]

Computer-aided fraud includes the old standby crimes like vendor fraud (taking payment for a nonexistent vendor or being paid for goods not delivered), writing payroll cheques to fictitious employees, claiming expense reimbursements for false claims, and so on. In addition, there are newer crimes such as stealing security codes, credit card numbers, and proprietary files. Intellectual property is one of the favourite targets of theft by insiders. In fact, the companies that make surveillance software say that employers are buying and installing the software not so much to monitor employees as to track how intellectual property, like product design sketches, schematics, and so on, are moving around the network.

Fraud examiners have a rule of thumb that in any group of employees, 10 percent are completely honest, 10 percent will steal, and for the remaining 80 percent, it will depend on circumstances. Most theft is committed by people who are strapped for cash, have access to funds that are poorly protected, and perceive a low risk of getting caught.

- White-collar crime costs an estimated $400 billion per year.
- Average nonmanagerial embezzlement is $60,000.
- Average managerial embezzlement is $250,000.
- Two-thirds of insider fraud is not reported.
- Of the known losses, one-quarter cost more than $1 million.

Figure 8.9
Statistics on White-Collar Crime

SECURITY AND COLLABORATION PARTNERS

Computer security used to be an internal matter. It concerned only the company and those who actually used the computers. With the advent of collaboration systems, however, company representatives are gaining access to each other's computer systems. It's very important to be sure that the computer system of the company you're giving access to is as least as secure as yours; otherwise, you'll create a back door into your own system. So now you need to worry about your partners', suppliers', and customers' computer security as well as your own.

Not surprisingly, not having good computer security in place can sour a deal. A large bank was about to close a multimillion-dollar deal with a cheque processing company when the bank's security chief asked the cheque processing company's chief information officer about its security policy. The cheque processing company didn't have one. In fact, it didn't even have the most basic security like firewalls. The deal was put on hold until the security met the bank's standards.[41]

The bank wasn't the only organization worried about the security of its associate companies. Many companies are checking out their suppliers' and other business partners' security before allowing them access to online company information. Goodrich Corporation, an aerospace company, uses collaboration systems so that suppliers can view design drawings. A large portion of Goodrich's $4 billion in annual sales comes from the department of defence. So espionage is a real threat. Goodrich has cut costs dramatically by using collaboration systems with file-sharing capabilities. But, before a supplier can be part of the team, Goodrich checks out the newcomer's security measures. The Goodrich people examine firewalls and encryption, and even how physically secure the information on the system is. Then if everything meets their tough standards, the Goodrich team sets up a detailed procedure to be followed in case there's a security breach. The moral of the story is: if you want to do business with Goodrich, or many other companies, you'd better have a secure computer system.[42]

GRID COMPUTING A new kind of computer infrastructure is beginning to take hold in the business world. **Grid computing** is a way of linking far-flung computers to share CPU power, databases, and database storage via the Internet or a virtual private network. The government is already engaged in grid computing, as evidenced by the National Science Foundation's National Technology Grid and NASA's Information Power Grid. Grid computing software is in development by IBM, Compaq, Sun, and HP. Grid computing includes peer-to-peer file sharing, but it's much more. The core of grid software is its common interface that allows any computer on the grid to tap into the CPU power or storage of other available computers. Companies as diverse as Pratt & Whitney, Bristol-Myers Squibb Co., and American Express are using grid computing. Analysts say that it will turn computing power into a utility—the provider will simply send you as much or as little power or storage as you happen to need at that moment.[43]

The issues still to be resolved before grid computing becomes widespread are many and complex, and not least among them is security. Security issues involving computers from multiple locations spans cultural and technical issues ranging from rights of access to data sharing to legal and departmental policies.

SECURITY AND OUTSIDE THREATS

A Computer Security Institute survey found that the computer systems of 85 percent of large companies and governmental agencies were broken into during 2001. Of

THE GLOBAL PERSPECTIVE

TOP TEN DOT-CONS

According to a study published in 2000 following a yearlong investigation with the collaboration of five U.S. agencies and consumer groups from various countries including Canada, the top ten dot-cons are:

- Internet auction fraud
- Internet service provider scams
- Internet Web site design/promotions—Web cramming
- Internet information and adult services—credit card cramming
- Multi-level marketing/pyramid scams
- Business opportunities and work-at-home scams
- Investment schemes and get-rich-quick scams
- Travel/vacation fraud
- Telephone/pay-per-call solicitation frauds (including modem diallers)
- Health care frauds

The most popular scams are advertising computer software and electronic consumer goods at various e-auction sites and taking cashier's cheques or money orders in payment but never delivering the goods. Internet service provider scams consist of sending consumers "rebate" cheques. When the consumer cashes these, he or she is unwittingly agreeing to allow the scammer to be his Internet service provider. Monthly charges on the consumer's telephone bill soon follow. Web cramming involves billing consumers for a Web page they didn't even know they had. Con artists usually target small businesses and not-for-profit organizations with this scam by calling and offering these organizations a "free" Web page. Similarly, credit card cramming includes Web sites which offer visitors to view adult-oriented content for free after leaving their credit card numbers to prove they are over 18. Pyramid schemes promise customers to get rich by recruiting other people to sell particular products and services. Shams also include work-at-home scams that make exaggerated earning claims on the Internet and in print ads to sell "how to" packages over the Internet. Still other deceptions pertain to Web site operators' misleading use of testimonials promising quick riches with little or no risk to consumers. Many consumers have been tricked in this manner into signing up for day trading programs following misrepresentations about their high-risk nature. Some scams also include offering free access to adult material after downloading dialler software which disconnects your modem and then reconnects your computer through international long-distance numbers without your knowledge. The study also warns consumers about Web sites offering luxury trips at very low prices then hitting you with hidden charges after you pay, and unlicensed online pharmacies operating as "cyber-drugstores" but that do not meet regulatory standards, some offering bogus miracle cures for all ills.

As part of this ongoing Internet law enforcement initiative, more than 700 law enforcement and consumer protection officials are being trained in online investigation and law enforcement techniques across 20 different countries including 14 Canadian consumer protection offices. According to Jodie Bernstein, director of the FTC's Bureau of Consumer Protection, "the Internet is revolutionizing the way we gather information, shop and do business. ... This collaboration with law enforcement agencies, industry and consumers will create a climate where e-commerce can be conducted with confidence. We want the dot con artists to know that we're building a consumer protection coalition that spans the globe. We aim to make the Net safe for consumers."[44]

those, 64 percent said they had suffered financial loss, but only 35 percent wanted to put a figure on the loss. Despite such a small proportion of victims reporting an amount, the total came to more than $375 million. "There's no Fortune 500 company that hasn't been hacked, I don't care what they tell you," says one hacker.[45] "Hacking" means achieving unauthorized access to computers and computer information. 3Com gets "thousands of attacks a week. From kids to criminals to foreign governments," says David Starr, senior VP.[46] Even Microsoft's computers have been hacked.

The threats from outside are many and varied. Competitors might try to get your customer lists or the prototype for your new project. Kids might be joyriding in cyber-

THE GLOBAL PERSPECTIVE

SETI

One of the first large-scale experiments in grid computing is Project Phoenix from the SETI Institute, an organization whose mission it is "to explore, understand and explain the origin, nature, prevalence and distribution of life in the universe." You can download a screensaver from www.seti-inst.edu to make your computer part of a huge worldwide network of private computers that analyze telescope data for this project.

space looking for something interesting to see, steal, or destroy. You might become the victim of a generalized attack such as a virus or worm or a targeted attack such as "denial of service" (see later). If you have something worth stealing or manipulating on your system, there could be people after that too. For example, the online gambling industry is plagued by attacks in which hackers have illicitly gained access to the servers that control the gambling, corrupting games to win millions of dollars.[47] Exploiting well-known system weaknesses accounts for 95 percent of hacker damage; only 5 percent results from breaking into systems in new ways.[48]

People who break into the systems of others are known as **hackers**. They are generally very knowledgeable computer users. They have varying motives. Some just do it for the fun of it. Others (called "hacktivists") have a philosophical or political message they want to share, and still others (called "crackers") are hired guns who break in for a fee. The latter can be a very lucrative undertaking. Some highly skilled crackers charge up to $1 million per job. (See Figure 8.10 for the terminology of hacker types.)

TYPES OF CYBER-CRIME Cyber-crimes range from electronically breaking and entering to cyberstalking and murder. In October 1999, 21-year-old Amy Boyer was shot and killed outside the building where she worked. Her killer, Liam Youens, had been electronically stalking her for two years. Youens became obsessed with Amy and had even posted a Web site dedicated to her on which he announced his intention to kill her. He got her social security number online, found out where she worked, tracked her down, and shot her, after which he shot himself.

Most cyber-crimes are not as bad as murder, but they can be serious nonetheless. Computer viruses and worms and denial-of-service attacks are the most common types of cyber-crime that companies need to protect themselves against.

Figure 8.10
Hacker Types

- *White-hat hackers* find vulnerabilities in systems and plug the holes. They work at the request of the owners of the computer systems.
- *Black-hat hackers* break into other people's computer systems and may just look around, but they may steal credit card numbers or destroy information.
- *Hacktivists* have philosophical and political reasons for breaking into systems. They often deface a Web site as a protest.
- *Script bunnies*, or *script kiddies*, find hacking code on the Internet point-and-click and their way into systems, causing damage or spreading viruses.

A **computer virus** (or simply **virus**) is maliciously created software that spreads from file to file causing annoyance or damage. A virus can be benign or malicious. The benign ones just display a message on the screen or slow the computer down, but don't do any damage. The malicious kind targets a specific application or set of file types and corrupts or destroys them.

Viruses first came on the scene in the 1980s. Today, **worms** are the most prevalent type (see Figure 8.11 for the genealogy of viruses). Worms are viruses that spread themselves, not just from file to file, but from computer to computer via e-mail and other Internet traffic. They don't need your help to spread. They find your e-mail address book, grab the addresses, and send themselves to your contacts, using your e-mail address as the return address.

The "Love Bug" was the first worm to catch the attention of the popular press. It did a lot of damage. Ford Motor Co, H.J. Heinz, Merrill Lynch, AT&T, Capitol Hill, and the British Parliament all fell victim. It's estimated that the Love Bug and its variants affected 300,000 Internet host computers and millions of individual PC users, causing file damage, lost time, and high-cost emergency repairs costing about $8.7 billion.[49,50] Newer versions of worms include Klez, a very rapidly spreading worm, Nimda, and Sircam.

For more information about viruses see Extended Learning Module B, "Computer Crime and Forensics."

A **denial-of-service attack (DoS)** floods a Web site with so many requests for service that it slows down or crashes. The objective is to prevent legitimate customers from accessing the target site. E*TRADE, Yahoo!, and Amazon.com have all been victims of this type of attack.

Code Red, first discovered in July 2001, was the first virus to combine the worm's ability to propagate and the denial-of-service attack's ability to bring down a Web site. It broke into servers and used e-mail address lists to send itself to other servers. Then it lay dormant, ready for a signal. The idea was to send the signal to all of the infected servers (millions of them) and make them all try to access the White House Web site at the same time and bring it down. The White House Webmaster foiled the plot by changing the IP address of the site so that the attacks would go to a defunct address.

There are even virus hoaxes, perpetrated by sending out an e-mail about a nonexistent virus threat, and sometimes recommending a protective action that will, in fact, damage one's system. People who get such an alert will usually tell others, who react in the same way. Within companies, the losses from such a prank can be very severe, not least because computer professionals are forced to spend precious time and effort looking for a nonexistent problem.

- *1980s.* The first viruses were boot-sector viruses that attacked the operating system and spread when people traded floppy disks.
- *1990s.* Macro viruses were all the rage. They spread when people traded e-mail with Word or Excel attachments. The virus was part of the attachment and corrupted the Word or Excel application. Macro viruses needed humans to swap disks or attachments to find new places to infect.
- *2000s.* Polymorphic worms that change their form and are hard to detect started to appear. Viruses such as Klez spoof the return address, making it very difficult to track down the source.

Figure 8.11
The Genealogy of Viruses

As well as knowing what viruses can do, you need to know what they can't do. Computer viruses:

- Can't hurt your hardware, such as your monitor or processor
- Can't hurt any files they weren't designed to attack; a virus designed for Microsoft's Outlook generally doesn't infect Qualcomm's Eudora, or any other e-mail application
- Can't infect files on write-protected disks

SECURITY PRECAUTIONS

It has been said that while in years past managers had nightmares about takeover bids, they now have nightmares about teenagers with computers and Internet access. Lloyd's of London says that 70 percent of risk managers see the Internet and e-commerce as the biggest emerging risks in the new century.[51] Worldwide security software revenue is expected to grow from $6.3 billion in 2001 to $11.9 billion by 2004. Since the 9/11 terrorist attacks, which left people and companies feeling more vulnerable than before, most experts expect that number to rise sharply.[52]

The only really safe computer system is one that is never connected to any other computer and locked away so that almost no one can get to it. In today's business world that's just not practical. Computers are like motor vehicles; they can be used to cause harm unintentionally and maliciously, and just driving one puts you at risk, especially when you're on the road with other cars. However, we still use motor vehicles, but we build in safety features and take precautions to lessen the risk. So it is with computers. The big difference is that security threats in cyberspace are always changing.

Given the extraordinary importance of information in an organization, it's imperative that companies make their best efforts to protect that information; that is, they should practice risk management. **Risk management** consists of the identification of risks or threats, the implementation of security measures, and the monitoring of those measures for effectiveness. The first step in the process is establishing what the threats are and what parts of the system are vulnerable. This is **risk assessment**: the process of evaluating IT assets, their importance to the organization, and their susceptibility to threats, to measure the risk exposure of these assets. In simple terms, risk assessment asks: (1) What can go wrong? (2) How likely is it to go wrong? and (3) What are the possible consequences if it does go wrong?[53]

Implementing the correct amount and type of security is not an easy matter. Too much security can hamper employees' ability to do their jobs, resulting in decreased revenue. Too little security leaves your organization vulnerable. You need strong enough security to protect your IT systems but not so much that the right people can't access the information they need in a timely fashion. Generally, security consists of a combination of measures such as backup procedures, antivirus software, firewalls, access authorization, encryption, intrusion-detection software, and system auditing.

BACKUPS As always, an ounce of prevention is worth a pound of cure. The easiest and most basic way to prevent loss of information is to make backups of all your information. There's no action you can take that's more rudimentary or essential than making copies of important information methodically and regularly (at least once a week). Employee carelessness and ignorance cause about two-thirds of the financial cost of loss or damaged information.[54] Take the example of one company whose accounting server went down the day that paycheques should have been distributed. The crisis arose during an administration transition. The people who had been temporarily run-

THE GLOBAL PERSPECTIVE

GIVE YOUR COMPUTER THE FINGER

If you're an elementary school student in Stockholm, Sweden, and you want to access your course materials, you don't need a password, instead you just need your fingerprints—and it's hard to forget those. The 85,000 students who attend elementary school in Stockholm often forgot their passwords, like lots of people do. And teachers had to issue new passwords every 100 days in keeping with city policy. It was becoming a real burden.

In October of 2001, 25,000 fingerprint scanners were ordered from Bellevue Washington's Saflink Corp. Shortly thereafter, all of the other 120,000 government computers used by city workers were activated by biometrics, smart cards, tokens, or biometrics. The days of the password were over in Stockholm.

Samir Hamouni, manager of the fingerprint project for the city, said that the installation of the fingerprint scanners and software went very fast. The part of the project that took the most time was getting all the fingerprints into the system.[55]

ning the system thought that backup occurred automatically. It didn't, so all payroll information was lost. To get the system up and running again, the company had to pay thousands of dollars to consultants to restore the network application, and had to pay four people for 300 hours of overtime to re-enter information. In addition, it cost $48,000 for a disk-recovery company to retrieve the information from the damaged disk drive. And all this trouble and expense could have been avoided if backup procedures had been followed.

Make sure you back up *all* information. It's easy to forget about the information that's not stored in the main computer system or network, such as correspondence and customer information kept only by administrative assistants and receptionists, and private information not kept in the main organizational databases or data warehouses. Your backup schedule should include not only your information, but also your software.

You have several options when backing up information. You can use removable hard disks, a hard disk on another computer, or CD-Rs, CD-RWs, and tapes. Also you should consider where the backups are to be stored:

- *In a safe.* Should you choose to store your backups in a safe, make sure that the safe is not only fireproof, but also heatproof. Mylar disks (like those in zip disks) and CDs suffer damage at temperatures above 125 degrees Fahrenheit. Also remember that water causes damage too, so get a safe that's waterproof.
- *At a different location.* Most experts recommend that you store your backups in a separate building in case the whole building is threatened. Many accounting firms, banks, and other financial institutions send information off the premises at the end of every work day.
- *In a televault.* You can store a copy of your information with a security company that specializes in encrypting and storing backups. This is known as *televaulting*. Several Internet sites offer this service. Many will store backups for individuals too. Sometimes you get a certain amount of space free, perhaps about 20 megabytes, and then you have to pay for any more you need.

ANTIVIRUS SOFTWARE Antivirus software is an absolute must. **Antivirus software** detects and removes or quarantines computer viruses. New viruses are created every day and each new generation is more deadly (or potentially deadly) than the previous ones. When you're looking for virus protection, *PC World* magazine[56] has the following advice. Look for virus protection that finds:

- Viruses on removable media like floppies, CDs, and zip disks, as well as on the hard disk
- Trojan-horse viruses (viruses hiding inside good software) and backdoor programs (viruses that open a way into the network for future attacks)
- Polymorphic viruses and worms, which are sometimes hard for antivirus programs to find because they change their form as they propagate
- Viruses in .zip or compressed files, and even .zip files inside other .zip files.
- Viruses in e-mail attachments

Two final points. First, your antivirus program should be able to get rid of the virus without destroying the software or information it came with. Second, you must update your antivirus software frequently, since new viruses come along every day. Some antivirus sites will automatically send updates to their software.

FIREWALLS A **firewall** is hardware and/or software that protects computers from intruders. The firewall examines every message as it seeks entrance to the network, like a border guard checking passports. Unless the message has the "right" markings, the firewall blocks the way and prevents it from entering. Any competent network administrator will have at least one firewall on the network to keep out unwelcome guests.

ACCESS AUTHORIZATION While firewalls keep outsiders out, they don't necessarily keep insiders out. In other words, unauthorized employees may try to access computers or files. One of the ways companies try to protect computer systems is with authentication systems that check who you are before they let you have access.

There are three basic ways of showing your identification: (1) what you know, like a password; (2) what you have, like an ATM card; (3) what you look like (or rather what your fingerprint or your hand's bone structure looks like).

Passwords are very popular and have been used since there were computers. You can password-protect the whole network, a single computer, a folder, or a file. But passwords are not by any means a perfect way to protect a computer system. People forget their passwords, so someone has to get them new passwords or find the old one. Banks spend $15 per call to help customers who forget their passwords. Then if a hacker breaks into the system and steals a password list, everyone has to get a new password. Another bank had to change 5000 passwords in the course of a single month at a cost of $12.50 each.[57]

Which brings us to biometrics, or what you look like. **Biometrics** is the use of some distinguishing physical personal characteristic to authenticate a person's identity. Roughly a dozen different types of biometric devices are available at the moment, fingerprint readers being the most popular. About 44 percent of the biometric systems sold are fingerprint systems. It works just like the law enforcement system where your fingerprint is stored in the database and when you come along, your finger is scanned, and the scan is compared to the entry in the database. If they match, you're in.

Another promising type of biometric system is facial recognition. Wells Fargo is testing a system which uses facial recognition instead of PINs at ATM machines. Many airports are proposing biometric systems to check that passengers are who they say they are. Most envision that the recording of passengers' biological characteristics will be voluntary, so that frequent flyers could sign up, have their physical characteristic scanned, and then forever bypass the long manual clearing process. Chicago's

THE GLOBAL PERSPECTIVE

CHASING THE BAD GUYS ALL OVER THE WORLD

In Chapter 4 you saw how banks are using artificial intelligence systems to catch fraudulent credit card and cheque transactions. Worldwide a problem just as large is sending large banks back to technology for solutions. Money laundering is always a concern when dealing with wealthy clients and large sums of foreign currency. The International Monetary Fund estimates that $590 billion from criminal and terrorist activities is sent through banks to be "cleaned." And a big bank can spend $15 million a year to meet legal requirements governing antilaundering activities.

Deutsche Bank, the German bank which is the largest in Europe, has developed its own screening system to ferret out money laundering schemes. It creates risk scores for people opening new accounts similar to those that banks assign people applying for loans. The scores are based on past business transactions and other pertinent factors. The information Deutsche Bank uses has been gathered on customers in its 107-country banking system. Since implementation of its system, Deutsche Bank needs only four full-time employees to watch for money laundering instead of the 50 previously required.

The first antilaundering systems simply flagged deposits over a certain amount. But the people doing the laundering figured this out and adjusted their transactions accordingly. The Bank Secrecy Act first obliged banks to report cash transaction of $10,000 or more, but during the 1990s money laundering crimes rose sharply and the U.S. Treasury was getting more reports than agents could read. So the agency created the Financial Crimes Enforcement Network (FinCEN) to counter the increasingly complex transactions. Internationally, FinCEN shares information with other countries and has joined forces with 28 other countries to track money laundering worldwide. In fact, this coalition has threatened to impose sanctions on nations such as Egypt, Nigeria, the Philippines, and Russia for their banking practices.[58]

O'Hare airport, the busiest in the world, has been using biometrics for years to authenticate employees' identity.[59]

Besides fingerprint and iris scanners, there are also retinal scanners, which check the back of the eye rather than the coloured circular part on the front. Signature checkers activate as you sign your name and check the rhythm, pressure, speed and acceleration of the signature. One system being tested checks the rhythm of your typing, another checks your voice pattern scanners, and still another scans the veins in your hand. Each of these would compare the scan with the stored pattern to see if they match.

ENCRYPTION If you want to protect your messages and files and hide them from prying eyes, you can encrypt them. **Encryption** is the process of scrambling a message so that it can't be read until unscrambled. There are various ways of encrypting. You can switch the order of the characters, replace characters with other characters, or insert or remove characters. All of these methods alter the look of the message, but used alone, each is fairly simple to figure out. So most encryption methods use a combination of methods.

Companies that get sensitive information from customers, such as credit card numbers, need some way of allowing all their customers to use encryption to send the information. But they don't want everyone to be able to decrypt the message, so they might use **public key encryption (PKE)**, an system that uses two keys: a public key that everyone can have and a private key for only the recipient. So if you do online banking, the bank will give you the public key to encrypt the information you send them, but only the bank has the key to decrypt your information. It works rather like wall safe: anyone can lock it (just shut the door and twirl the knob), but only someone with the combination can open it.

KEEPING TRACK OF SHOE SALES IS VERY IMPORTANT

Payless ShoeSource, Inc., is North America's largest family footwear retailer. In 2000, Payless sold about $3 billion worth of shoes (average price about $12) at its 4900 stores in Canada, the United States, Puerto Rico, Central America, and Guam.

Shoes are shipped automatically to all stores. The entire system relies on a data centre in Topeka, Kansas. All the data analysis, decision making, and control are based on the information the Topeka data centre collects and stores daily. Payless has a mainframe, several minicomputers, and thousands of PCs. The entire corporate network is controlled from the Topeka data centre. Even if there is a network problem in Taiwan, the people in Topeka handle it. Since Kansas is located in "Tornado Alley," the data centre is underground—all 16,000 square feet of it.

Every night, the data centre polls all the stores, domestic and overseas, for information about their sales for that day. The company has a data warehouse with two years' worth of information on every shoe type and size sold in every store that's available for online analytical processing (OLAP). Since losing this information would be disastrous, Payless has lots of safeguards in place:

- In the event of a problem with AT&T, the phone system will automatically switch to Sprint.
- An array of 120 heavy-duty batteries take over if the power goes down, then a backup generator takes over. There's even a backup generator to the backup generator.
- The data centre also has two backup air conditioning systems in case the original one goes out.
- If fire breaks out, firefighting gas (FM 2000) sprays from the ceiling to suffocate the flames within seconds. If that doesn't work, water sprinklers kick in. But only as a last resort—water isn't good for computer equipment.
- All information is backed up on high-capacity cassette tapes. The company has about 30,000 of these. Every day the tapes are sent off-site by truck.
- Every year all the IT staff practise a disaster drill.

INTRUSION-DETECTION AND SECURITY-AUDITING SOFTWARE Two other types of security software are:

- **Intrusion-detection software**, which looks for people on the network who shouldn't be there or who are acting suspiciously. For example, someone might be trying lots of passwords to gain access. "Honey pots" are a type of intrusion-detection software that create attractive, but nonexistent, targets for hackers. What actually happens is that hackers' keystrokes are recorded instead.
- **Security auditing software**, which checks out your computer or network for weaknesses. The idea is to find out where hackers could get in and to plug up the hole. Many third parties, such as accounting firms or computer security companies, also provide this service.

Disaster Recovery

So far you've seen some of the threats that are out there and the security measures you can take to protect your information and IT system. But what if something catastrophic happens? Annually about 250 natural disasters occur worldwide. This is merely an interesting statistic unless you're bang in the middle of such a disaster—then it's much more than interesting. But natural disasters aren't the only danger on the IT system horizon. Fires, burst water pipes, gas leaks, power outages, and other infrastructure breakdowns can all cause serious damage to your IT system and information. Of the companies hit with a catastrophic loss of computerized records, 43

DISASTER RECOVERY PLANS: CAN YOU EVER BE PREPARED ENOUGH?

In 1998, a severe ice storm hit parts of Quebec, Ontario, New York, and New England, causing power outages and forcing many businesses to scramble as it affected many computer operations. In some regions, the power failures lasted up to two weeks and forced many businesses to operate with skeleton staffs while relying on generators, move to remote disaster sites, or in many cases shut down completely. Estimated losses were nearly $1 billion in Canada alone.

The storm made many companies realize that IT disasters did not necessarily entail direct physical damage to their computer equipment. Many companies had disaster recovery plans in place and were relying on electricity provided by generators. However, because a majority of roads were closed by fallen trees, broken power lines, and utility poles, many people could not even get to work. The shortage of information technology staff to keep systems running became an unexpected but serious problem. "Most of our problem was just getting people in ..., our technical support came to a screeching halt for a solid week," said Richard Cox, a project manager at Air Canada in Montreal.

Moreover, many businesses were prepared for power outages of no more than a couple of days. Several relied on uninterruptible power supplies (UPS) and diesel generators, sometimes in combination, to keep their computers running. This strategy had worked well for the Kennebec Valley Health Hospital in Augusta, Maine, where medical staff were able to continue providing normal care. Others were not so lucky. Diesel generators began to break down after a couple of days. At Domco, Inc., located in Farnham, Quebec, generators failed after running for only three days. The company had to quickly switch their IT operations to SunGard Data Systems, Inc.'s disaster recovery site in Philadelphia. However, because all order and shipping applications were centrally managed by the Farnham site, the ice storm had repercussions for Domco's U.S.-based plants, forcing them to shut down computer operations for three days until the hot site became active. Prior to the storm, like many other companies across the region, Domco felt confident that it had a good disaster recovery plan in place. "You can plan for a disaster when a building is destroyed, but we never figured on a disaster where we couldn't communicate with our Farnham offices," said Guy Chamberland, Domco's IT director.[60]

percent never reopen, 51 percent close within two years, and only 6 percent survive long-term.[61] Since September 11, the prospect of a major disaster has been seen as much more of a real threat than ever before.

To make sure your organization is in that slim 6 percent, you need to be prepared. Banks are required by law to have a **disaster recovery plan**—a detailed plan of what is to be done in the event of a disaster to minimize downtime. General Motors demands that all of its dealers have one.

A good disaster recovery plan will take the following into consideration: customers, facilities, knowledge workers, business information, computer equipment, and communications infrastructure (see Figure 8.12, over).

- *Customers.* You're more likely to retain the business of people who know what's going on. Customers will be reassured if you inform them what's happening so that they can plan accordingly.
- *Facilities.* You'll most likely need to move operations to another facility if disaster strikes. One option is a **hot site**, a separate and fully equipped facility to which you can move immediately after the disaster and resume business. Hot sites are popular with financial firms, who spend about $300 a year to rent them. The Chubb Contingency Trading Facility, near Wall Street, is one such site. The

Figure 8.12
Disaster Recovery Plan

facility has ten trading rooms with faxes, copy machines, printers, backup generators, 1000 phone lines, a local area network with PCs, and so on.[62] Another alternative is a **cold site**, which doesn't have computer equipment installed, but is ready for the refugee company to move in.

- *Knowledge workers.* Disaster recovery usually involves long working days. Before your employees can concentrate on your business, they may have to make arrangements for the care of family members. You may have to make sleeping and eating arrangements for your employees too.
- *Business information.* You've already seen how important it is to back up your business information. Actually, this should be a regular part of daily operations. You'll see its value very clearly during times of disaster.
- *Computer equipment.* Most companies have complex networks with a mixture of software and hardware from various vendors. This makes the networks hard to duplicate for third-party recovery services. So some companies develop their own recovery plan. NationsBank did just that, with 118 software applications running on 77 platforms, with equipment from Digital Equipment, Hewlett-Packard, IBM, Stratus, and Tandem. Although being disaster-ready costs the bank millions of dollars a year, it's still the lesser of two evils.[63]
- *Telecommunications infrastructure.* As the September 11 attacks dramatically demonstrated, communication is one of the most critical factors in dealing with an emergency. Having a backup carrier and enough cell phones for everyone is very important. The most important next step is to be able to move non-voice information around. To do that you need either backup equipment or a hot site.

As the quality of telecommunications improves, with more bandwidth at a lower cost, disaster recovery plans will most likely change, says Bob Roth, disaster recovery coordinator at Payless ShoeSource. In the future, companies will most likely simply mirror all of their information at a second site so that if one goes down, the other can carry on business as usual. Some companies already do this.

Summary: Student Learning Outcomes Revisited

1. **Define ethics and describe the two factors that affect how you make a decision concerning an ethical issue. Ethics** are the principles and standards that guide our behaviour toward other people. How you will decide ethical issues depends on your basic ethical structure and the practical circumstances surrounding your decision.
2. **Define and describe intellectual property, copyright, the Fair Use Doctrine, and pirated and counterfeit software. Intellectual property** is intangible creative work that is embodied in physical form. **Copyright** is the legal protection afforded an expression of an idea, such as a song or a video game. The **Fair Use Doctrine** says that you may use copyrighted material in certain situations. **Pirated software** is illegal copies of copyrighted software made for unauthorized use, duplication, distribution. **Counterfeit software** is software manufactured to look like the real thing and sold as such.
3. **Define privacy and describe ways in which it can be threatened. Privacy** is the right to be left alone when you want to be, to have control over your own personal information, and not to be observed without your consent. Your privacy can be compromised by other individuals snooping on you, by employers monitoring your actions, by businesses who collect information on your needs and preferences and surfing practices, and by various government agencies that collect information on citizens.
4. **Describe the two ways that information is valuable to business.** Information is valuable as raw material, which uses information as part of the product, and as capital, which is something that goes into the production of goods and services, but which is not actually part of the product.
5. **Describe the ways in which companies are vulnerable to computer attacks.**
   - **A.** Most of the financial loss due to crimes where a computer played a large part is due to employee fraud of various kinds.
   - **B.** You give a access to your computer information to collaboration partners who could do damage.
   - **C.** Grid computing will mean many computers working together with the potential for information to move between computers when it shouldn't.
   - **D.** Hackers and crackers may try to break into computers and steal, destroy, or compromise information.
   - **E.** Hackers can spread **computer viruses** or launch **denial-of-service attacks (DoS)** that can cost millions to prevention and cleanup.
6. **Define risk management and risk assessment and describe the seven security measures that companies can take to protect their information. Risk management** consists of the identification of risks or threats, the implementation of security measures, and the monitoring of those measures for effectiveness. **Risk assessment** is the process of evaluation IT assets, their importance to the organization, and their susceptibility to threats, to measure the risk exposure of these assets.

   Seven security measures companies can take are:
   - **A.** Backups—make sure there is more than one copy of everything.
   - **B.** **Antivirus software** detects and removes or quarantines computer viruses. However, to be effective it must be updated regularly and often.
   - **C.** A **firewall** is hardware and/or software that protects computers from intruders.
   - **D.** Access authorization makes sure that those who have access to information have the authorization to do so with password or biometrics.

E. **Encryption** is the process of scrambling a message so that it can't be read until it's unscrambled again.
F. **Intrusion-detection software** looks for people on the network who shouldn't be there.
G. **Security-auditing software** checks out your computer or network for weaknesses that could be exploited.

7. **Define what a disaster recovery plan is and list the six components it should cover.** A **disaster security plan** is a detailed plan of what is to be done in the event of a disaster to minimize downtime. A disaster security plan should cover customers, facilities, knowledge workers, business information, computer equipment, and the telecommunications infrastructure.

CLOSING CASE STUDY ONE

PROTECTING MORE THAN HEALTH

When you go for medical care, do you assume that your information is safe and that it will be protected along with your health?

Health care institutions do their best to hire ethical people who will protect patients' personal information as well as their health, and who won't steal. But now and then employees act in a way that breaches the trust placed in them. While many companies are concerned about their customers' privacy, the health industry may shortly be bound by law to protect their patients' personal information from unauthorized parties.

Even without laws, medical institutions operate in large part on trust and therefore must be particularly careful with personal information. To protect patient information from browsing or worse by staff members, many hospitals will soon be using biometrics to protect computer files. Biometrics involves using a personal characteristic like a fingerprint or retinal scan to make sure that the person trying to access information has the right to do so. Biometrics is easier to use than passwords, since, with the former, staff don't have to memorize anything. It's also safer, since you can't give someone else your fingerprint. And in the end it is probably less costly, since organizations often spend a lot of time and money replacing passwords that become compromised in some way.

Clinics must also protect their computer system from viruses, worms, and other *malware*, software designed to cause trouble for computer users. Clinics also have to protect against intrusion by those who want to use their computers to launch attacks on other computers in DoS attacks. Malware is often spread by e-mail, although that's not the only propagation method, and can cause trouble like destroying files, filling up memory so that the computer system crashes, and compromising applications like Word so that they don't work properly. Particularly malevolent malware can even reformat a hard disk, making the files that were stored there hard to retrieve.

To prevent computer viruses getting into their system, clinics have installed software that scans all e-mail coming in and out. They have also installed firewalls on the network, which prevent intruders, and intrusion-detection software to catch those who get by the firewall.

Questions

1. What steps could clinics take to ensure as much honesty as possible in their organization? Some studies show that the corporate culture employees work in exerts a strong influence on their behaviour. What actions of management would encourage or discourage such a culture?

2. What could hospital staff steal that would be valuable? Describe three situations in which a hospital employee, otherwise an honest person, might be motivated to do something unethical.

3. What sort of biometric system would work well in a hospital? What would be best—facial recognition, fingerprint checks, retinal scans, bone structure comparisons, or something else?

4. Apart from antivirus and anti-intrusion software, what protective software could clinics install to protect the organization's information? Can you think of damage other than the theft of personal

information that the hospital or its inhabitants could suffer if someone from the outside broke into a hospital's computer system?

5. Would it be practical for the hospital to keep all databases internal and not be connected to the Web or have any electronic paths to the outside world at all? What would the advantages of such a move be? What would the disadvantages be? Apart from a presence on the Web, which is almost required for any company in today's business world, what other entities would a hospital need to be able to transfer information to and from?

CLOSING CASE STUDY TWO

IS THE SAFE HARBOR SAFE FOR U.S. BUSINESSES?

European countries and Australia have passed laws protecting the privacy of name-linked information of consumers. In Europe it's the European Union Directive 95/46/EC, which was adopted in 1998, and in Australia it's the Privacy Amendment Act of 2000. The Australian law says that personal information can be collected only with the consent of the person it's being collected about. The law goes further and forbids transfer of personal information to any other country that does not have privacy protection. The result is that U.S. companies with an Australian subsidiary cannot transfer personal information they have collected to the United States since the country has no privacy protection of this type.

In Europe, the 15 countries that belong to the European Union are supposed to have passed laws by now requiring that personal information can only be collected with the express and unambiguous consent of the person to whom the information applies. And this rule applies to invisible information collection such as the information collected in cookies and details on a person's Web surfing activities.

An individual's information can only be collected without consent under the following circumstances:

1. It's necessary to fulfill a contract.
2. It's necessary to save a life, as when a procedure is necessary on an unconscious person.
3. It's necessary for greater good, such as tax collection.
4. The processing of the information is required by a legal contract.
5. The third party to the information has a lawful right to do so as in an arbitration situation.

Even within these guidelines there is certain "sensitive information" that cannot be asked for. This type of information cannot be processed without specific consent. Such information includes a person's racial or ethnic origin, political and religious affiliations, trade union membership, and sexual preferences. This exception of sensitive information was deemed necessary in the light of hundreds of years of persecution in Europe of one ethnic or religious group or other.

The EU Directive also says that people must be informed when information about them is to be used for direct mailings, and the rules apply any time the information is being processed within the European Union, even if the those who are providing the information are located elsewhere. So why does it matter to U.S. businesses what privacy laws the Europeans choose to have? It matters because it threatens the annual $350 billion trade between the United States and the EU, so the U.S. Department of Commerce and the European Commission has agreed to voluntary, so-called Safe Harbor provisions, which represent a compromise between the strict consumer privacy requirements of Europe and the more relaxed attitude of American law. At its inception, the Safe Harbor agreement was hailed as a great breakthrough and a guarantee that business would indeed continue to thrive.

However, the Safe Harbor agreement no longer seems quite so wonderful, for several reasons. First, it's a voluntary program, and very few companies had signed up for it by the middle of 2001. Second, not all European countries have actually passed laws yet to comply with the Directive. (An EU directive is simply a statement of intent and each member country must enact its own laws to ensure the outcome of the directive.) France, Ireland, and Luxembourg had not passed any such laws by the middle of 2001. Third, some European countries think that the Safe Harbor agreement is much too weak, and is not in keeping with the intent of the Directive. The worry for U.S. companies is that countries such as Sweden might refuse to allow information transfer to countries they deem to be deficient. Fourth, the Safe Harbor agreement may not be enforceable by law, since the FTC doesn't have the authority to protect European consumers' rights within the United States. And finally, EU authorities have the power to intervene in cases of serious violation and suspend the transfer of information to a country until the matter has been resolved.

Questions

1. Imagine, for a moment, that a federal law very similar to the EU Directive were to take effect in Canada at the beginning of next year. What would the implications be for companies that collect huge amounts of personal information on their customers and clients?

2. Would you like to have stronger privacy laws in this country? If so, what form should they take? If not, do you have any reservations about your personal information being bought and sold like any other commodity? Should there be limits on who can buy what information and for what purposes? If so, what should they be? If not, provide some examples of the advantages of having all personal information available to anyone with the means to acquire it.

3. Strangely enough, the European Union is considering a law that flies squarely in the face of the privacy directive. The proposal is to give border police access to e-mail and Internet use by citizens. The law would mean that police would be able to access any and all e-mail and Internet usage information from ISPs simply by requesting it. No court order would be needed. There would be no restrictions on the amount or type of information that the police could access on people's personal and business lives. What do you think of this law? What do the privacy directive and the proposed law imply about the European attitude toward access to personal information? Who do the European Union see as the abusers of personal information and who are the good guys? Is it the same in the United States? How do the European and American philosophies differ?

4. Do you think Canada should have stricter border laws? At airports the focus tends to be on luggage. Should there be more emphasis on who is travelling? For instance, should everyone, citizens included, be fingerprinted and checked out before they enter or leave the country? If so, would you be prepared to have a special ID card with your fingerprints or some other biometric feature on it to allow you to pass through the checkpoints at ports of entry faster?

Key Terms and Concepts

Short-Answer Questions

1. What are ethics and how do ethics apply to business?
2. What are the two factors that determine how you decide ethical issues?
3. Six practical circumstances affect how you decide ethical issues. What are they?
4. Describe one exception to the copyright rules.
5. If you buy a CD with software on it, what did you buy?
6. What is pirated software?
7. Are counterfeit software and pirated software the same thing? If not, what is the difference?
8. What does a key logger do?
9. What is spyware?
10. What is grid computing?
11. Is a worm the same as a virus?
12. What is a denial-of-service attack?
13. What does risk management consist of?
14. Why is your security measures important to a partner company?

Assignments and Exercises

1. **HELPING A FRIEND.** Suppose you fully intend to spend the evening working on an Excel assignment due the next day. Then a friend calls. Your friend is stranded miles from home and desperately needs your help. It will take most of the evening to pick up your friend, bring him home, and return to your studying. Not only that, but you're very tired when you get home and just fall into bed.

   The next day your friend, who completed his assignment earlier, suggests you just make a copy of his, put your own name on the cover, and hand it in as your own work. Should you do it? Isn't it only fair that since you helped your friend, your friend should do something about making sure you don't lose points because of your generosity? What if your friend promises not to hand in his or her own work so that you can't be accused of copying? Your friend wrote the assignment and gave it to you so there's no question of copyright infringement.

2. **FIND ANTIVIRUS SOFTWARE.** You've read how important it is to have antivirus software on your computer. Find out what choices are available and what their features and cost are at the following sites:

   - Norton Antivirus (www.symantec.com)
   - McAfee (www.mcafee.com)
   - PC-cillin (www.trend.com.tw/pc-cillin/index.htm)
   - Dr. Solomon Antivirus Toolkit (www.drsolomon.com)
   - Kaspersky Lab Antivirus (www.kaspersky.com)
   - Panda Antivirus (www.pandasoftware.com)

3. **FIND OUT WHAT HAPPENED IN CANADA.** In Canada, in March 2001, the government opened up a 90-day comment period so that citizens could voice their opinions on a proposed law concerning cellular phones. The new law would silence cell phones in places where they are a public nuisance, such as restaurants, concert halls, and movie theatres. Essentially, if the law were to pass, it would allowing the jamming of phone signals in such places. This would be a departure from the traditional view on signal jamming. Most countries, including the United States but excluding Israel, prohibit jamming except when public safety would be endangered or when law enforcement or other government agencies find it appropriate. With all this in mind, answer the following questions:

   A. Find out how the citizens of Canada reacted this proposal and whether the law passed.

   B. Would you like to have such a law passed in this country? Why? Or why not?

C. What rights do you have to talk when and where you want to as opposed to the rights of others to be free of noise pollution?

D. What other noisy, intrusive pollution (noise or otherwise) would you like to have outlawed?

4. **FIND OUT ABOUT MONITORING SYSTEMS.** The text lists several monitoring systems, other systems that defeat them, and e-mail encryption programs. Find two more of each of these items:

   A. Programs that monitor keyboard activity

   B. Programs that detect the keyboard monitoring programs

   C. E-mail encryption programs

Discussion Questions

1. When selling antiques, you can usually obtain a higher price for those that have a "provenance," that is, information detailing the origin and history of the object. For example, the property owned by Mrs. Jacqueline Kennedy Onassis and Princess Diana sold for much more than face value. What kinds of products have value over and above a comparable product because of such information? What kind of information makes products valuable? Consider both tangible (resale value) and intangible value (sentimental appeal).

2. Personal cheques that you use to buy merchandise have a standard format. They have only a very few different sizes, and almost no variation in format. Consider what would happen if everyone could create his or her own size, shape, and layout of personal cheque. What would the costs and benefits be to business and the consumer in terms of buying cheques, exchanging them for merchandise, and bank cheque processing?

3. Consider society as a business that takes steps to protect itself from the harm of illegal acts. Discuss the mechanisms and costs that are involved. Examine ways in which our society would be different if no one ever broke a law. Are there ever benefits to our society when people break the law—for example, when they claim that the law itself is unethical or unjust?

4. Many European countries have very strict laws about what you can and can't do with name-linked information. In France, for example, the law stipulates that no information may be saved, electronically or on paper, about a person's religious or political affiliation. Discuss the implications of such laws for an open-information society such as the United States. What kind of information might be appropriate for such laws here, and how would they affect the management of IT systems?

5. Can you access all the IT systems at your college or university? What about payroll or grade information on yourself or others? What kinds of controls has your college or university implemented to prevent the misuse of information?

6. You know that you can't use a Macintosh to access information stored on a disk using a PC (unless you have a PowerPC or special software). What other instances of the lack of interoperability have you experienced personally or heard of? For example, have you used different versions of PowerPoint or MS Access that won't work on all the PCs that you have access to?

7. If a major disaster such as a tornado or flood were to strike your college or university in the middle of the semester, who would be impacted and how? Consider all stakeholders.

8. Say you had a small business and you were considering buying expensive ergonomically designed office furniture such as chairs and desks for your knowledge workers. What would the intangible benefits be to your company of having employees who are comfortable?

REAL HOT Electronic Commerce

Making Travel Arrangements on the Internet

It's very likely that in the course of business you'll be expected to travel either within the United States or abroad. You can use the Internet to check out all aspects of your journey, from mode of travel to the shopping opportunities that are available. The Internet can also give you pointers and direction about aspects of the trip you might not even have thought about.

Real HOT Links

In this section, we've included a number of Web sites related to making travel arrangements on the Internet. On the Web site that supports this text (www.mcgrawhill.ca/college/haag), click on "Electronic Commerce Support," select "Real HOT Electronic Commerce Project Support," and then select "Making Travel Arrangements on the Internet"). We've provided direct links to all these Web sites as well as many, many more. This is a great starting point for completing this section. We would also encourage you to search the Internet for other sites.

TRANSPORTATION

If you're not taking your own transportation—your private jet or your car—you'll have to find flights, buses, trains, and/or rental cars to suit your needs. Let's look at sites where you can get this kind of information.

AIR TRAVEL Some people are happy to travel with whatever airline provides the flight that fits into their schedule. Others insist on certain airlines, or won't travel on certain airlines. No matter how you feel, the Internet can help you find a flight. On the Internet, you can even get maps of the airports you'll be using. Many airports have sites on the Internet, such as Dallas/Ft. Worth International Airport at Aéroports de Montréal (www.admtl.com). These sites can help you with provisions at the airport for disabled people, among other available services.

The Federal Aviation Authority site (www.faa.gov) has a comprehensive list of airlines all over the world. Find five appropriate Web sites and answer the following questions.

A. Can you make a flight reservation online at this site?

B. If you can book flights, does the site ask you to type in your departure and destination cities, or can you choose from a menu?

C. Again, if you can book flights at this site, rate on a scale of 1 to 10 how difficult it is to get to the flight schedule. That is, how many questions do you have to answer, how many clicks does it take, how much do you have to type in?

D. Is there information on when the lowest fares apply (e.g., three-week advance booking, staying over Saturday night, etc.)?

E. Does the site offer to send you information on special deals via e-mail?

F. Does the site offer information on frequent flier mileage? Can you check your frequent flier account online?

G. Does the site offer you a map of the airports you will be using?

TRAINS AND BUSES If you want to travel by rail or long-distance bus, you can find many helpful sites. Here is a taste of what's available:

- VIA Rail Canada (www.viarail.ca) has a site that lets you look up train travel times and fares and buy tickets online for train travel in Canada.

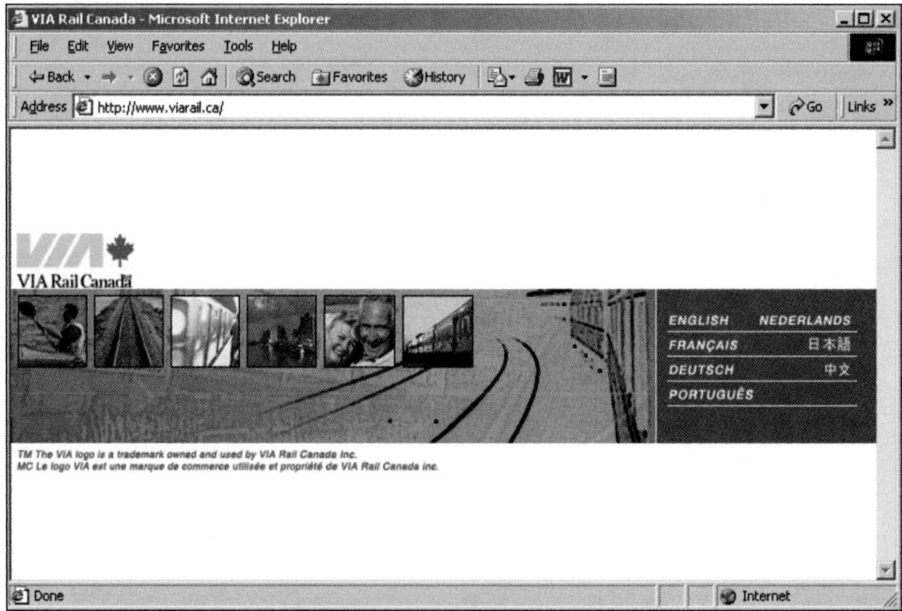

- Rail Europe (www.raileurope.com) offers comprehensive coverage of all modes of travel in Europe, including, of course, rail travel.
- The Orient Express site (www.orient-expresstrains.com) is a great help if you're interested in travelling by rail in Asia or Australia.

Look at two of these sites and see whether you can book tickets online. Do you need a password to see schedules? Incidentally, when you're looking up sites outside the United States, remember that the date is often expressed with the day first, then the month, then the year, so that September 10, 1998, would be 10.9.98 or 10-9-98. Also, most of Europe uses 24-hour time, so that 2:15 p.m. would be 14:15.

RENTAL CARS When you arrive at your destination, you may need a car. Some sites such as RentalCarGuide's site (www.bnm.com) have information on multiple companies, and all the large car rental companies have sites on the Internet. Find six Web sites that rent cars and answer the following questions.

A. Can you reserve a car at the Web site?

B. Can you search by city?

C. Is there a cancellation penalty? If so, how much?

D. Can you get a list of car types? Does this company rent sports utility vehicles?

E. Are there special weekend rates?

F. What does the site say about collision insurance purchased from that company in addition to your own insurance?

G. Can you get maps from the site?

H. Are special corporate rates specified on the site?

ROAD CONDITIONS AND MAPS

You can generate maps online at several sites. MapQuest (www.mapquest.com) is one of the most popular. Its TripQuest section has city-to-city and turn-by-turn directions, and its Map Shortcuts module gives you a list of cities and countries for which you can get maps. Examine three map sites and answer the following questions.

A. Do these sites all give turn-by-turn driving directions?

B. Will they provide a map of an area without start and end points?

C. Do they have zoom-in and zoom-out capabilities?

D. Can you customize the map, perhaps by inserting a landmark or circling an area?

E. Are hotels, restaurants, etc. marked on the map?

F. If the site offers driving directions, can you specify whether you want the scenic route or the main highways?

LODGING

Hotels, especially the larger chains, usually have Web sites. Here you have access to a wealth of information about rates, amenities, and sometimes even information about the hotel's surroundings. The National Hotel Directory (www.evmedia.com) has lists of a variety of hotels and also trade shows. The Hotel Guide site (www.hotelguide.com) has information on 60,000 hotels all over the world, and The Trip.com (www.trip.com) has hotel reviews and promises discounted prices for certain hotels. Choose four Web sites and answer the questions below.

A. Can you search for a specific city?

B. Can you book a room online?

C. Can you see a picture of the room on the Internet?

D. Does the site tell you about special deals or promotions?

E. Is there information about perks you can get by staying there frequently?

F. Do you get a discount for booking online?

ONE-STOP TRAVEL SITES

Some travel sites on the Internet allow you to book your entire trip from start to finish, offering a combination of airline, hotel, and other helpful information. Two of

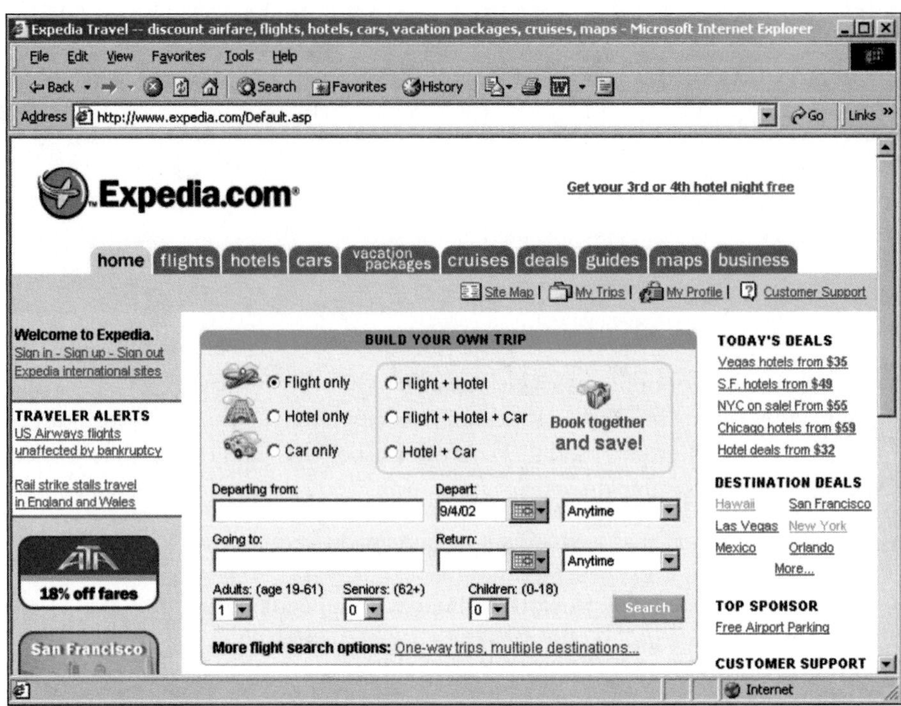

the most widely used are Microsoft's Expedia (expedia.msn.com) and Preview (www.travelocity.com). Choose five Web sites and answer the following questions.

A. How many different booking services are offered from this site (airlines, hotels, rental cars, rail travel, etc.)?

B. If the site offers flight booking, how many flight alternatives does it offer? 3? 10? 20? 30? More than 30?

C. Does the site have information on low-cost specials for airlines, hotels, and/or rental cars?

D. Is there a traveller's assistance section?

E. Will the site answer your specific questions?

F. Can you search by destination or company for flights and lodging?

DESTINATION INFORMATION

You might like to know before you get to your destination what restaurants, museums, shows, shopping, and special attractions are available. Many of the sites previously mentioned have this kind of information. MapQuest (www.mapquest.com) is an excellent example of such a site, as are many of the one-stop travel sites.

No matter what your interest or hobby, the Internet has a site for you. You can find sites dedicated to birdwatching, bungee jumping, golf, or anything else that takes your fancy. Many others cater to entertainment events such as concerts. You can find destination information sites on the Web at the following sites:

- Excite's Travel site (city.net), which has destination information from Fodor's Travel.

- The Trip (www.trip.com) includes restaurant reviews among its services.
- Restaurant Row (www.restaurantrow.com) has a list of 100,000 restaurants in 25 countries. You can search by country, city, and cuisine.
- The Open World site (www.openworld.co.uk) has information on 100 of the most popular cities to visit.

Go to the Online Learning Centre at www.mcgrawhill.ca/college/haag for quizzes, extra content, a searchable glossary, and more! Click on "Electronic Commerce Projects" for links to hundreds of Web sites.

Go to the text CD-ROM for data files, extra content, and Skills Modules on Microsoft Excel, Microsoft Access, HTML, and e-portfolios.

EXTENDED LEARNING MODULE B

COMPUTER CRIME AND FORENSICS

Student Learning Outcomes

1. Define computer crime and list three types of computer crime that can be perpetrated from inside and three from outside the organization.
2. Define hackers. Also identify the seven types of hackers and what motivates each group.
3. Define computer forensics and describe the two phases of a forensic investigation.
4. Identify and describe three places on a storage medium where you can find stray information.
5. Identify and describe seven ways of hiding information.

Introduction

Computers play a big part in crime—they're used to commit and to solve crime. This should come as no surprise, since they're such a big part of almost every other part of our lives. Computers are primarily used two ways in the commission of a crime or misdeed: as targets and as weapons. A computer is the target when someone wants to bring it down or make it malfunction, as in a denial-of-service attack or a computer virus infection. Crimes that use a computer as a weapon would include acts like changing computer records to commit embezzlement, breaking into a computer system to steal information, and intentionally spreading a virus. See Figure B.1 for examples of computer-related offences that use computers as weapons and targets.

Some crimes are clearly what we'd call computer crimes, like Web defacing, denial-of-service attacks, and so on. But, as is the case in so many parts of our modern lives, computers are so integrated into crime that it's sometimes hard to separate them out. Here's an example from the case files of Walt Manning, an expert in computer investigation.

A member of a crime syndicate was sprayed with driveby gunfire and severely wounded. Believing his services were no longer wanted by his crime gang, he switched sides, agreeing to become a witness. The police secured an isolated intensive care unit room for him and guarded it heavily, only allowing access to medical staff and those on a very short list of visitors. Because the man was so badly wounded, there was a distinct danger of infection, and since he was allergic to penicillin, the doctor prescribed a synthetic alternative.

One evening, a nurse wheeling a medicine cart went through the police cordon and into the man's room. He injected the patient with penicillin, and the patient died shortly thereafter. An investigation started immediately and the nurse was potentially in big trouble. He insisted that when he looked at the patient's chart on the computer, there was an order there for penicillin. Subsequent examination of the computer records showed no such order. Eventually, it occurred to someone that perhaps a computer forensics expert should look at the computer angle more closely. Having retrieved the backup tapes (nightly backups are standard operating procedure in most places), the expert found that the record was changed from the synthetic to penicillin,

Figure B.1

Examples of Computer Crimes That Organizations Need to Defend Against

	Inside the Organization	Outside the Organization
Computers as Weapons	• Intellectual property theft • Accessing information on others for personal reasons • Spite or revenge activities • Extortion • Reading the e-mail of others	• Murder • Theft of information • Embezzlement • Harassment • Extortion • Credit card theft • Cargo theft by diverting shipments
Computers as Targets	• Information destruction • Planting destructive code • Stealing customer information • Stealing product information • Altering information	• Virus attacks • Denial-of-service attacks • Web defacing • Rerouting network traffic • Crashing servers

and then changed back. The examination revealed the point and time of access, and indicated that the medical record was changed by someone outside the hospital. So, in fact, a hacker had electronically slipped into the hospital's network unnoticed, made the change, and slipped out again—twice.

Most crimes involving a computer are not as lethal as this, but that doesn't mean they're insignificant, and organizations want to make sure their networks' defences are strong, and can prevent their computers from being used as part of unlawful or unethical acts. That's why so much time, money, and effort goes into security, as discussed in Chapter 8.

This Module focuses on the sort of threats that computer systems are susceptible to and the examination of electronic evidence.

Computer Crime

For our purposes, a **computer crime** is one in which a computer, or computers, play a significant part. Figure B.2 gives a list of crimes in which computers, although perhaps not essential, usually play a large part.

In this section we'll focus on crime from the organization's viewpoint. First, we'll examine some of the more high-profile types of computer crime that are perpetrated against organizations from the outside. Then we'll discuss the varying motivations of people who commit these acts. Lastly, we'll briefly discuss computer crime within the organization.

OUTSIDE THE ORGANIZATION

Businesses are very concerned about the threat of people breaking into their computers and causing damage. In 2001, 90 percent of U.S. companies discovered online security breaches, according to the Computer Security Institute, and only 34 percent of those companies reported the attack. The cost to business was $455 million, as against $377 million in 2000. The losses that are reported, and experts say that most are not, average about $1.8 billion per year.[1] Ninety-four percent of companies detected computer viruses in 2001 and that figure is up from 85 percent in 2000. To combat these and other attacks, businesses spent about $7.5 billion in 2000 on security software.[2] That market is expected to triple to $21 billion by 2005.

VIRUSES **Computer virus** or **virus** is a generic term for lots of different types of destructive software written with the intent to cause annoyance or damage. Two hundred new viruses are developed every day.[3] There are two categories.

The first comprises *benign* viruses that display a message or slow down the computer, but don't destroy any information. The second comprises *malignant* viruses

Figure B.2

Crimes in Which Computers Usually Play a Large Part

• Illegal gambling	• Racketeering
• Forgery	• Fencing stolen goods
• Money laundering	• Loan sharking
• Child pornography	• Drug trafficking
• Hate message propagation	• Union infiltration
• Electronic stalking	

that scramble or delete your files, shut your computer down, make your software act funny, or damage flash memory in your digital camera so that it won't store pictures any more. Obviously, these are the viruses that cause IT staff (and everyone else) the most headaches.

Macro viruses, one very common type, spread by binding themselves to software such as Word or Excel. When they infect a computer, they *replicate* (make copies of themselves) and spread from file to file, destroying or changing them in some way. Some leave markers behind to mark that computer as "done."

This type of virus needs human help to move to another computer. If you have a macro virus on your system and you e-mail an infected document as an attachment, the person who gets the e-mail gets the virus as soon as the infected attachment is opened. When you click on the attachment, Word (or the appropriate program) also loads, thereby setting the executable statements in motion.

A **worm**, the most prevalent type of replicating virus, replicates and spreads itself, not only from file to file, but from computer to computer via e-mail and other Internet traffic. Worms don't need your help to spread. They find your e-mail address book and help themselves to the addresses, sending themselves to your contacts. The first worm to catch the attention of the popular press was the Love Bug, and permutations of it are still out there.

Released on an unsuspecting world in 2000, the Love Bug caused the Massachusetts state government to shut down its e-mail, affecting 20,000 workers. It also shut down e-mail at the British Parliament. Companies as diverse as Ford Motor Co., H. J. Heinz, Merrill Lynch & Co., and AT&T were infected.[4] All in all, the Love Bug and its variants affected 300,000 Internet host computers and millions of individual PC users, causing file damage, lost time, and high-cost emergency repairs totalling about $8.7 billion.[5,6]

A closer look at the Love Bug will give you a general idea of what worms do. It arrives in your e-mail as an attachment to an e-mail message. The subject of the e-mail is "I LOVE YOU"—a very alluring message to be sure. The text says to open the attached love letter, the name of which is, appropriately, LOVE LETTER. However, what's attached is anything but love. It's a mean piece of software that is set loose in your computer system as soon as you open the attachment.

The Love Bug has three objectives—to spread itself as far and as fast as it can, to destroy your files, and to gather passwords and other information (see Figure B.3). First, it spreads by mailing itself to everyone in your Outlook address book (a previous worm of the same type named Melissa sent itself only to the first 50 people listed in the address book). And, as if that weren't enough, it also uses your Internet chat software to spread itself to chat rooms.

Second, it locates files on your computer that have certain extensions—.mp3 (music files), .jpg (picture files), .doc (Word files), .xls (Excel files), .wav (sound files), .html (Web page files), and many others—then wipes them out and puts itself in their place, appending .vbs to the filename. For example, if you had a file called MySong.wav on your hard disk drive, the Love Bug would change the name to MySong.wav.vbs after it had done its dirty work.

Before it's done, the Love Bug worm changes your Internet Explorer start page and downloads a program that looks for passwords and network information, sending this information off by e-mail to the virus originator.[7]

There are at least 29 versions of the Love Bug. After people were warned not to open the LOVE LETTER attachment, the originators of the virus changed the name. For example, one version is "MOTHER'S DAY," and the body of the text says that the receiver has been charged hundreds of dollars for a Mother's Day "diamond special." You have to open the attachment to print the invoice—and then the virus goes into action.

Figure B.3

The Love Bug Worm

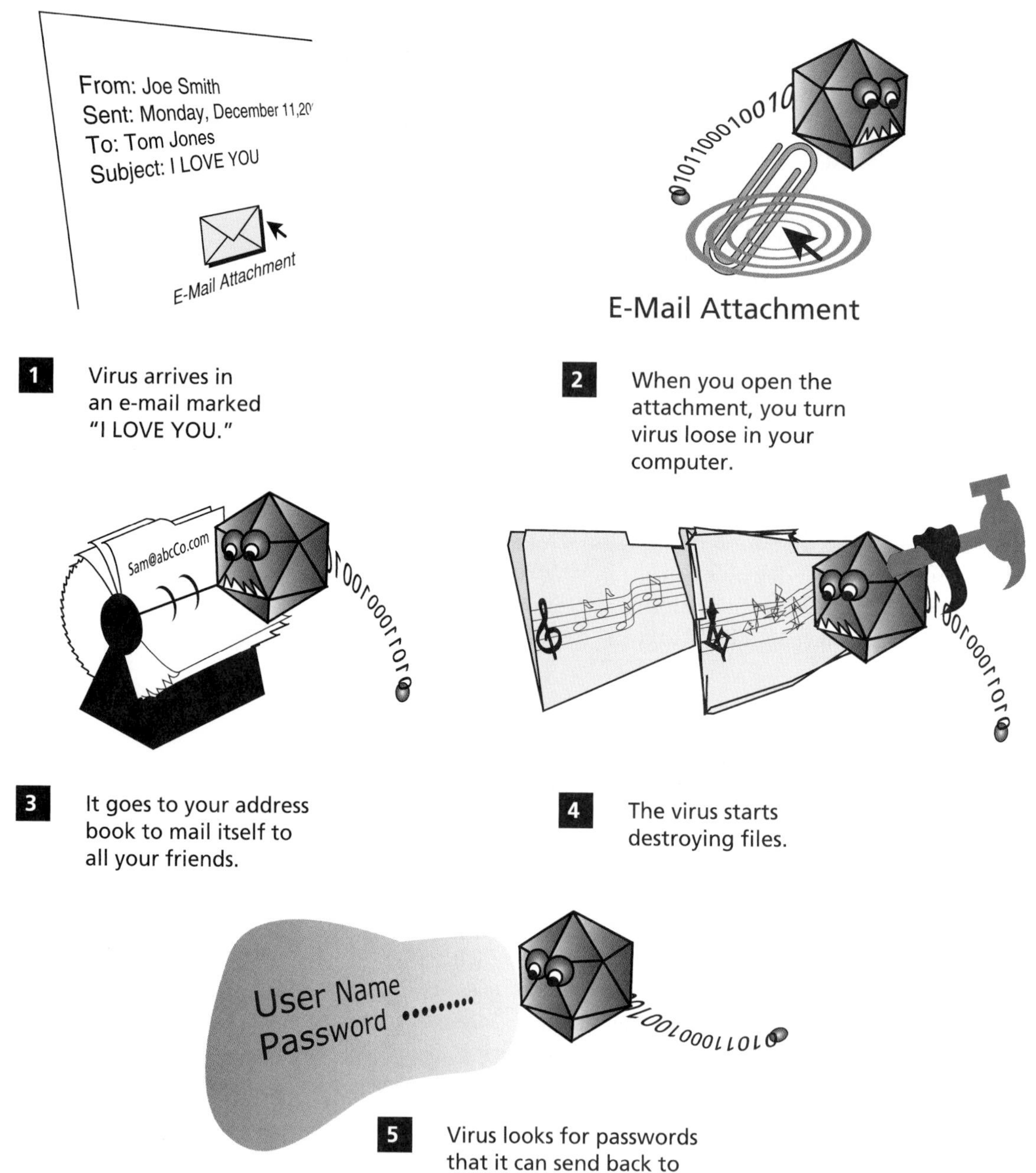

The moral of the story is that you should be very careful about opening an attachment if you're not sure what it is and where it came from. That won't necessarily save you from all virus attacks, but it will certainly help.

If you buy new shrink-wrapped software, you may feel secure thinking that it can't have a virus if it came from the manufacturer. However, the counterfeit software business is growing rapidly (see Chapter 8), and although the store might think that it bought software for resale from a reliable source, it might be counterfeit and carry a virus. So, as a precautionary measure, always check new software with a virus checker before you install it.

DENIAL-OF-SERVICE ATTACKS Many organizations have been hit with **denial-of-service (DoS) attacks**, which flood a Web site with so many requests for service that it slows down or crashes. The objective is to prevent legitimate customers from getting into the site to do business. There are several types of DoS attack, of which the most devastating is the **distributed denial-of-service attack (DDoS)**—an attack from multiple computers that floods a Web site with so many requests for service that it slows down or crashes. A common type of DDoS attack is the "Ping of Death," in which thousands of computers try to access a Web site at the same time, overloading the target site and shutting it down. A ping attack can also bring down the firewall server (the computer that protects the network), giving free access to the intruders. E*TRADE, Amazon.com, and Yahoo!, among others, have been victims of this nasty little game. The process is actually very simple (see Figure B.4).

The plan starts with the hackers planting a program in networks that aren't protected well enough. Then, on a signal sent to the networks from the attackers, the program activates and "pings" every computer on its network. A ping is a standard operation networks use to check that all computers are functioning properly. It's a sort of roll call for the network computers. The server asks "Are you there?" and each computer in turn answers "Yes, I'm here." But the hacker ping is different in that the return address of the "Are you there?" message is not the originating server, but the intended victim's server. So on a signal from the hackers, thousands of computers repetitively try to access E*TRADE or Amazon.com, saying "Yes, I'm here." The flood of calls overloads the online companies' computers and they can't conduct business.

Figure B.4

Distributed Denial-of-Service Attack

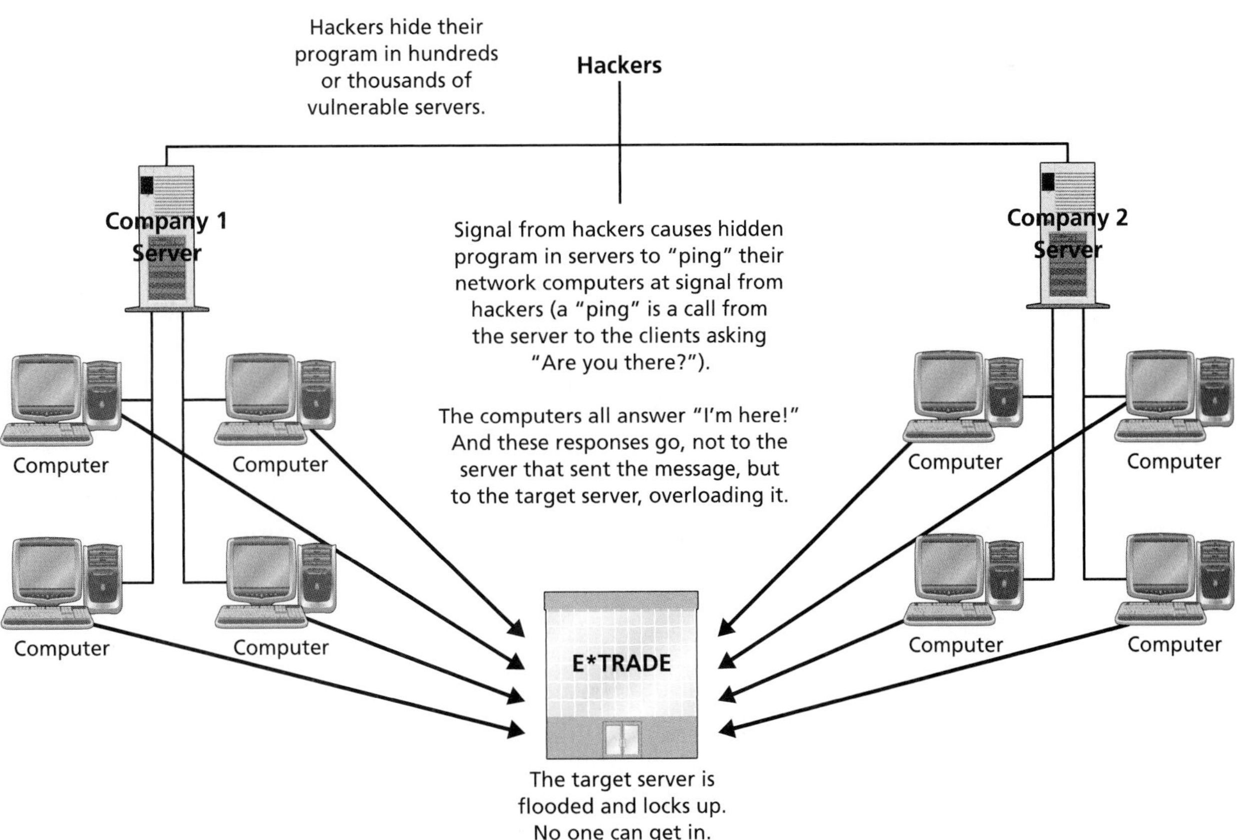

ON YOUR OWN

WHAT POLYMORPHIC VIRUSES ARE FLOATING AROUND CYBERSPACE?

In the wake of the Love Bug, a new and deadly worm called NewLove popped up. It disabled Windows and made other files unusable. This worm had two new features: first, it buried its destructive logic somewhere that make it much harder to find; second, it changed its code every time it succeeded in infecting a computer, adding some code randomly and growing with each infection. It didn't spread very far, but it caused a stir within the IT community because of its ability to change its own code; they called this new kind of virus "polymorphic." Essentially a **polymorphic virus** encrypts itself to evade detection by antivirus software, but changes the way it does it each time.

Visit the Web and look up five currently active polymorphic viruses. For each find out:

A. The name of the virus
B. What it does
C. The name of antivirus software that finds it
D. The symptoms of infection by it

For an online stockbroker, DoS attacks can be disastrous. It may make a huge difference whether you buy shares of stock today or tomorrow. And since stockbrokers need a high level of trust from customers to do business, the effect of having been seen to be so vulnerable is very bad for business.

COMBINATION WORM/DoS Code Red was the first virus that combined a worm and a DoS attack. It was discovered in July 2001. Code Red attacked servers running a specific type of system software. It used e-mail address books to send itself to lots of computers, and it was very efficient, with the ability to infect as many as 500,000 other servers per day. Its first action was to deface the Web site it infected. Then it went about finding other servers to infect. The last part of the plan was for all the infected servers to attack the White House site and shut it down. But, having been warned of the impending attack, the White House changed its IP address.

Even though Code Red had cost an estimated $2.4 billion in prevention, detection, and cleanup, in the end it didn't destroy files or otherwise do much damage; however, this type of attack power is very dangerous.

VIRUS HOAXES As discussed in Chapter 8, virus hoaxes are usually in the form of e-mail sent intending to frighten people about a virus threat that is, in fact, bogus, and sometimes recommending a protective action that will actually damage one's system.

Following are some general guidelines for identifying a virus hoax.[8] The e-mail:

- Says to forward it to everyone you know, immediately
- Describes the awful consequences of not acting immediately
- Quotes a well-known authority in the computer industry

These are signs that the e-mail is not meant to help but to cause harm. If you get an e-mail like this, delete it immediately.

STAND-ALONE VIRUSES In any given month, between 200 and 300 viruses are travelling from system to system around the world, seeking a way in to spread mayhem.[9] And they're getting more deadly. Whereas the Love Bug was a Visual Basic virus (i.e., it used Visual Basic script to run), the latest worms can stand alone and run on any computer that can run Win32 programs (Windows 98 or later versions).

Examples are SirCam, Nimda, and Klez. Nimda adds JavaScript to every home page on the server it infects, then passes it on to visitors to the site. Viruses of this independent type are very numerous.

The Klez virus is actually a family of worms that introduced a new kind of confusion into the virus business. They spoof e-mail addresses. **Spoofing** is the forging of the return address on an e-mail so that the e-mail message appears to come from someone other than the actual sender. Previous worms went to the recipient from the infected sender's computer and contained the infected person's return e-mail address. The worm found recipient addresses in the infected computer's address book.

Klez goes a step further and uses the address book to randomly find a return address as well as recipient addresses. The result is that people who are not infected with the virus get e-mail from the irate recipients and spend time looking for a virus they may not have. Even worse, some of virus-laden e-mails look as though they came from a technical support person, leading an unsuspecting victim to open them, believing them to be safe.

TROJAN-HORSE VIRUSES A type of virus that doesn't replicate is a **Trojan-horse virus**, which hides inside other software, usually an attachment or download. It's software you don't want hidden inside software you do. For example, Trojan-horse software can carry the "Ping of Death," which hides in a server until the originators are ready to launch a DoS attack.

Key logger or **key trapper** software is usually available in Trojan-horse form. Key-logger software is used to find out what people are doing on a particular computer; once installed, it records every keystroke and mouse click. You can find out more in Chapter 8.

WEB DEFACING

Web defacing is a favourite sport of the people who break into computer systems. They replace a Web site with a substitute that's unattractive, uncomplimentary, or otherwise reflects badly on the owners. They might convert the Web site to a mostly blank screen with an abusive or obscene message, or a message that reads "So-and-so was here." In essence, Web site defacing is electronic graffiti, where a computer keyboard takes the place of a paint spray can.

Web site defacing is becoming increasingly popular, and sites accessed by many people worldwide are favourite targets. The *USA Today* site was attacked in July 2002, causing the newspaper to shut down the whole site for three hours to fix the problem. The hackers replaced several news stories on the site with bogus stories full of spelling errors. One story said that the Pope had called Christianity "a sham." The phony stories were only up for 15 minutes before they were spotted and the site was taken offline.[10]

THE PLAYERS

Who's spreading all this havoc? The answer is **hackers**—knowledgeable computer users who invade other people's computers. There are several categories of hackers, and their labels change over time. The important thing to note in the following discussion is that the motivation and reasons for hacking are as many and varied as the people who engage in it.

THRILL-SEEKER HACKERS **Thrill-seeker hackers** break into computer systems for entertainment. Sometimes, they consider themselves to be the "good guys," since they expose vulnerabilities and some even follow a "hackers' code." While they break into computers they have no right to access, they may report the security leaks to the victims. Their thrill is in being able to get into someone else's computer. Their reward is usually the admiration of their fellow hackers. There's plenty of information on the Web for those who want to know how to hack into a system—about 2000 sites offer free hacking tools, according to security experts.[11]

WHITE-HAT HACKERS The thrill-seeker hackers used to be called **white-hat hackers**. But, lately, the term "white-hat" is being increasingly used to describe the hackers who legitimately, with the knowledge of the owners of the IT system, try to break in to find where the vulnerable areas are and to fix them. These ethical hackers are computer security professionals hired by a company to do what they do. Ethical hackers are sometimes called counter-hackers, or penetration testers.

BLACK-HAT HACKERS **Black-hat hackers** are cyber vandals. They exploit or destroy the information they find, steal passwords, or otherwise cause harm. They deliberately cause trouble for people just for the fun of it. They create viruses, bring down computer systems, and so on, often for no reason other than the dubious satisfaction of having wasted the time and money of people they've probably never met and never will.

One 16-year-old black-hat hacker was sentenced to six months' detention after he hacked into military and NASA networks and caused the systems to shut down for three weeks. He intercepted more than 3000 e-mails and stole the names and passwords of 19 defence agency employees. He also downloaded temperature and humidity control software worth $1.7 billion that helps control the environment in the international space station's living quarters.[12]

CRACKERS **Crackers** are hackers for hire who engage in electronic corporate espionage. This can be a pretty lucrative undertaking, paying up to $1 million per gig. Typically an espionage job will take about three weeks and may involve unpleasant tasks like dumpster digging to find passwords and other useful information and "social engineering." **Social engineering** is conning your way into acquiring information that you have no right to. Social engineering methods include calling someone in a company and pretending to be a technical support person and getting that person to type in a login and password, sweet-talking an employee to get information, and for difficult jobs perhaps even setting up a fake office and identity. Often when crackers have accumulated about a half a billion dollars, they retire to some country that doesn't have extradition agreements with this country.[13]

HACKTIVISTS **Hacktivists** are politically motivated hackers who use the Internet to send a political message of some kind. The message can be a call to end world hunger, or it can involve an alteration of a political party's Web site so that it touts another party's candidate. It can be a slogan for a particular cause or some sort of diatribe inserted into a Web site against a particular religious or national group.

CYBERTERRORISTS Since September 11, the threat from cyberterrorists has had officials worried. A **cyberterrorist** is one who seeks to cause harm to people or destroy critical systems or information for political reasons. Targets of such attacks would be air traffic control systems and nuclear power plants, and anything else that could harm the infrastructure of a nation. At a less lethal level, a cyberterrorist might try shutting down e-mail or even part of the Internet itself, or destroying government records on, say, social security benefits or criminal records.

TEAM WORK

MAKE UP A GOOD PASSWORD

One way to protect files, folders, and the privacy of your stock trading, banking, and other online accounts is to have a good password. That's the theory anyway. The problem is that most people choose passwords that are easy to remember, and consequently they're easy for others, who perhaps have malevolent intentions, to crack. Others write passwords down, which makes them very accessible to anyone who comes near their desk. Often hackers can get access to a server by way of a legitimate user's ID and password.

Another problem companies face is that people seem unaware of how important it is to keep passwords secret. In a London underground (subway) station, an experiment was conducted in which commuters were offered a cheap pen if they would disclose the password to their company's system. A very large number of people took the deal. Of course, there's no way to know whether they actually gave the real passwords or not, but judging from other studies, it's not unlikely that they did.

ZDNet offers some good advice on picking passwords. You should never pick a password that has a word from any dictionary, or one that is a pet's name or a person's. Instead, you should pick a phrase and put in capitalization, punctuation characters, and digits.

For example, the saying "Just hang loose, just have fun, you only live once" might become JhL?H6+oLo. If you could remember the mnemonic and your substitutions, you'd certainly have a password that would be hard to break.

To find out about breaking passwords, look on the Web for information about "John the Ripper," which is a famous password-cracking program. Find three more such programs, and note whether they're public domain, freeware, or shareware, or whether you have to pay for them. At ElcomSoft Co. Ltd. (www.elcomsoft.com) you'll find all sorts of password crackers for Microsoft and other popular products. The stated purpose of this site is to help you recover lost corporate files. What other "helpful" products does this or similar sites have, and what do they do?

However, government agencies in Canada, the United States, and other countries are very much aware of the threats they face from computer-based attacks, and have taken steps to protect the infrastructure. They can enjoy a reasonable expectation of success, since a computer system is a lot easier to protect than public structures like buildings and bridges.

SCRIPT KIDDIES **Script kiddies** or **script bunnies** are people who would like to be hackers but don't have much technical expertise. They download click-and-point software that automatically does the hacking for them. An example of this was the young man in Holland who found a virus toolkit on the Web and started the Kournikova worm. It was very similar to the Love Bug in that it sent itself to all the people in the Outlook address book. Tens of millions of people got the virus after opening the attachment hoping to see a picture of Anna Kournikova.[14]

The worrying thing about script kiddies, according to the experts, apart from the fact that they can unleash viruses and DoS attacks, is that they can be used by more sinister hackers. These people manipulate the script kiddies, egging them on in chat rooms, encouraging and helping them to be more destructive.

INSIDE THE COMPANY

There are plenty of attacks visited on an organization's computer system from outside the organization but the insider fraud and embezzlement is where the big bucks are lost. You can find more information on insider crime in Chapter 8.

ON YOUR OWN

DIGITAL SIGNATURES AND CERTIFICATES

Digital signatures are a way of protecting electronic messages, like e-mails, on their journey through cyberspace. It's an anti-tampering device. The basis of a digital signature is that a set of characters in the message is used in arithmetic operations to generate a unique "key" for that message. When the message arrives, the recipient redoes the same operations in the exact order, the result should be the original key. If it's not, then the message has been tampered with.

Digital signatures are often used in conjunction with digital certificates. What are digital certificates? Do some research and write a one-page report on digital certificates and how they're used.

But companies have learned to be careful when investigating harassment complaints, as the following example shows. One company had a complaint from a woman who claimed a male colleague was sending her offensive e-mail. The colleague denied it, but when his computer was checked, the pornographic pictures that the woman claimed she had received in e-mails were found. This could have meant his dismissal. But, fortunately for the man, a computer forensics expert was called in to find the truth. The expert looked beyond the pictures and discovered that the times and dates of the downloading and sending of the e-mails corresponded with times the man was out of town. Later, the woman admitted that she had downloaded the pictures and e-mailed them to herself from the man's computer. If the company hadn't been as thorough in its investigation, it could have escaped a harassment lawsuit only to find itself facing a wrongful termination lawsuit. So what exactly did the computer forensics expert do? In the next two sections we'll discuss that.

Computer Forensics

We're used to the idea of computers being used in the analysis of crime-scene evidence for matching DNA, tracing credit card purchases, and so on. We see examples of this all the time in mystery novels, on TV shows like *CSI* and *Law and Order*, and of course in real life. But computers themselves are often where the clues and evidence are, so instead of just helping to solve crimes computers are sometimes the actual crime scene.

Many computer forensics investigations involve intellectual property cases, where a company believes that an employee is secretly copying, and perhaps selling, proprietary information such as schematics, customer lists, financial statements, product designs, or notes on private meetings. Other investigations involve child endangerment, domestic disputes, labour relations, and employee misconduct cases. In all such cases, the appropriate response strategy is usually **computer forensics**, which is the gathering, authentication, examination, and analysis of electronic information stored on any type of computer media, such as hard drives, floppy disks, or CDs. Computer forensics experts are trained in finding and interpreting electronic evidence to discover or reconstruct computer-related misconduct of various kinds.

There are basically two motivations for engaging in computer forensics. The first is to gather evidence to present in court. The second is to establish what one or more people are doing on a computer, usually for the purposes of dispute settlement. You probably know that if you're going to court, you must meet different evidentiary standards for legal and for civil cases. In criminal cases the standard is "beyond a reasonable doubt"; in civil cases it's the "preponderance of evidence." If you don't have to, and don't want to, involve the legal system, your standard can be lower, perhaps just enough to fire someone without worrying about a wrongful termination lawsuit.

In a well-conducted computer forensics investigation, there are two major phases: (1) collecting and authenticating electronic evidence and (2) analyzing the findings.

THE COLLECTION PHASE

Step one of the collection phase is to get physical access to the computer and related items. Thus, the computer forensics team collects computers, disks, printouts, Post-it notes, and so on. This process is similar to what police do when investigating crime: collecting hair, clothing fibres, bloodstained articles, papers, and anything else that they think might be useful. Police investigators usually take these potential clue carriers with them and secure them under lock and key, where only authorized personnel may have access, and even they must sign in and out.

Computer forensics experts use the same kind of protocol. To conduct a thorough investigation, you have to look in all the places information might be stored. The hard disk is an obvious place to look, but computer forensics investigators also collect *all* floppy disks, CDs, Zip disks, and backup tapes. If they can't take a clue source with them, they secure it and examine it in place.

As well as the electronic media, investigators collect any other potentially helpful items, especially passwords, for use in case any of the files they come across are encrypted or can't otherwise be accessed. Apparently, a favourite hiding place for passwords that people write down (which you should *not* do) is under the keyboard, so that's the first place investigators look. Then they look in desk drawers and anywhere elsewhere passwords might be, such as on Post-it notes or slips of paper. Other helpful items might be printouts and business cards of associates or contacts of the person being investigated.

Step two of the collection process is to make a forensic image copy of all the information. A **forensic image copy** is an exact copy or snapshot of the contents of an electronic medium. To get a forensic image copy, the forensic software copies every fragment of information, bit by bit, on every storage medium—every hard disk (if there's more than one), every floppy disk, every CD, every Zip disk. That's usually a lot of stuff. Remember that a CD holds about a half a gigabyte of information, and you can build a hard disk array (several hard disks tied together into one unit) that holds a terabyte (one trillion bytes) or more. It can take a long, long time to copy it all. Also you must be able to swear in court that you, as the investigator, supervised the entire copying process, and that no one and nothing interfered with the evidence. This could mean sitting in the lab literally for days just copying files. And, many experts advise that you make two copies of everything in case there's a problem later with the first copy.

To get a forensic image copy of hard disk and other media contents, investigators physically remove the hard disk from the computer—they never turn the suspect computer on. Believe it or not, when you turn your PC on, Windows accesses over 400 files, changing access dates, temporary files, and so on. So, once turned on, the hard drive is no longer exactly the same as it was when it was shut down.[15] Thus opposing counsel could argue that this is not the same hard disk that the suspect used.

Having removed the hard disk, investigators connect it to a special forensics computer that can only read files, but can't write or rewrite any medium. Then they use forensics software such as EnCase that starts up the forensics computer without changing any data on the confiscated media in any way.

THE AUTHENTICATION PROCESS "How do we know that nothing changed on any disk during the entire investigation, from the time the computer was seized up to the present time?" That's the question that opposing counsel will ask the computer forensics expert on the witness stand. So, during the collection phase and later, the analysis phase, the investigators have to make absolutely sure that nothing that might be used as evidence in a trial could have been planted, contaminated, or altered in any way. This is a basic evidentiary rule for all court proceedings. You have to be able to document a "chain of custody" and be able to account for the whereabouts and protection of evidence.

In a computer forensics investigation, investigators use an authentication process so that they can show sometime in the future—perhaps in two years' time—that nothing changed on the hard drive or other storage medium since seizure. They can do this with an **MD5 hash value**—a mathematically generated number that is unique for each individual storage medium at a specific point in time, because it's based on the contents of that medium.

The term "hash" refers to a mathematical method of assigning numbers to an event. Here's a very simplified example of the hashing process. Count the number of bits in each file on the disk. Then multiply that by "23857493202747," add that to a 24-digit number, take the middle 22 digits out of the result, do some more arithmetic, and so on—you get the idea. Thus you arrive at a number that can be generated using the exact same procedure at a later date that will match the original hash value. It's proof that the medium hasn't been altered, since adding so much as one space in one tiny Word document on the disk will change the MD5 hash value. See Figure B.5 for an example of an MD5 hash value generated by EnCase forensic software.

MD5 hash values are considered very reliable and have become an industry standard accepted by the FBI, the CIA, and most other law enforcement authorities as a way of uniquely identifying a set of contents on a particular storage medium. This confidence in MD5 hash values is based on the fact that the probability of two sets of hard disk contents having the same MD5 hash value is one in 10 to the 38th power—that's 1 with 38 zeros after it. This makes the MD5 hash value a sort of DNA or fingerprint for computer media contents. Actually, it's more reliable than those physiological identifiers, since the probability of two sets of hard disk contents resulting in the same MD5 hash value are less than the odds of the DNA or the fingerprints of two people being identical.

FORENSIC HARDWARE AND SOFTWARE TOOLS As we've already mentioned, computer forensics experts use special hardware and software to conduct investigations. Usually the computer system has more power than the standard computer on a desktop and much more RAM, as well as a much larger hard disk. This is to speed up the copying and analysis process. Computer forensics experts are also very careful not to let static electricity cause any information to change on magnetic media (like hard disks, Zips, and floppies). Therefore they use non-conductive mats under all computer parts, and wear wristbands that connect by wire to the ground of an electrical outlet. And just in case they need tools, like screwdrivers, they have a special non-conductive set of these nearby too.

There are many kinds of software that can help in forensic investigations. Quick View Plus, used by many forensic experts, will load Word, Excel, image, and many other file formats. So that if they come across a file with an .xls extension, but it's actually an image and not a spreadsheet file, when it appears on the screen, it will, in fact, show up as an image file. That saves the investigator having to try it in multiple programs after loading fails in Excel.

Figure B.5

MD5 Hash Value

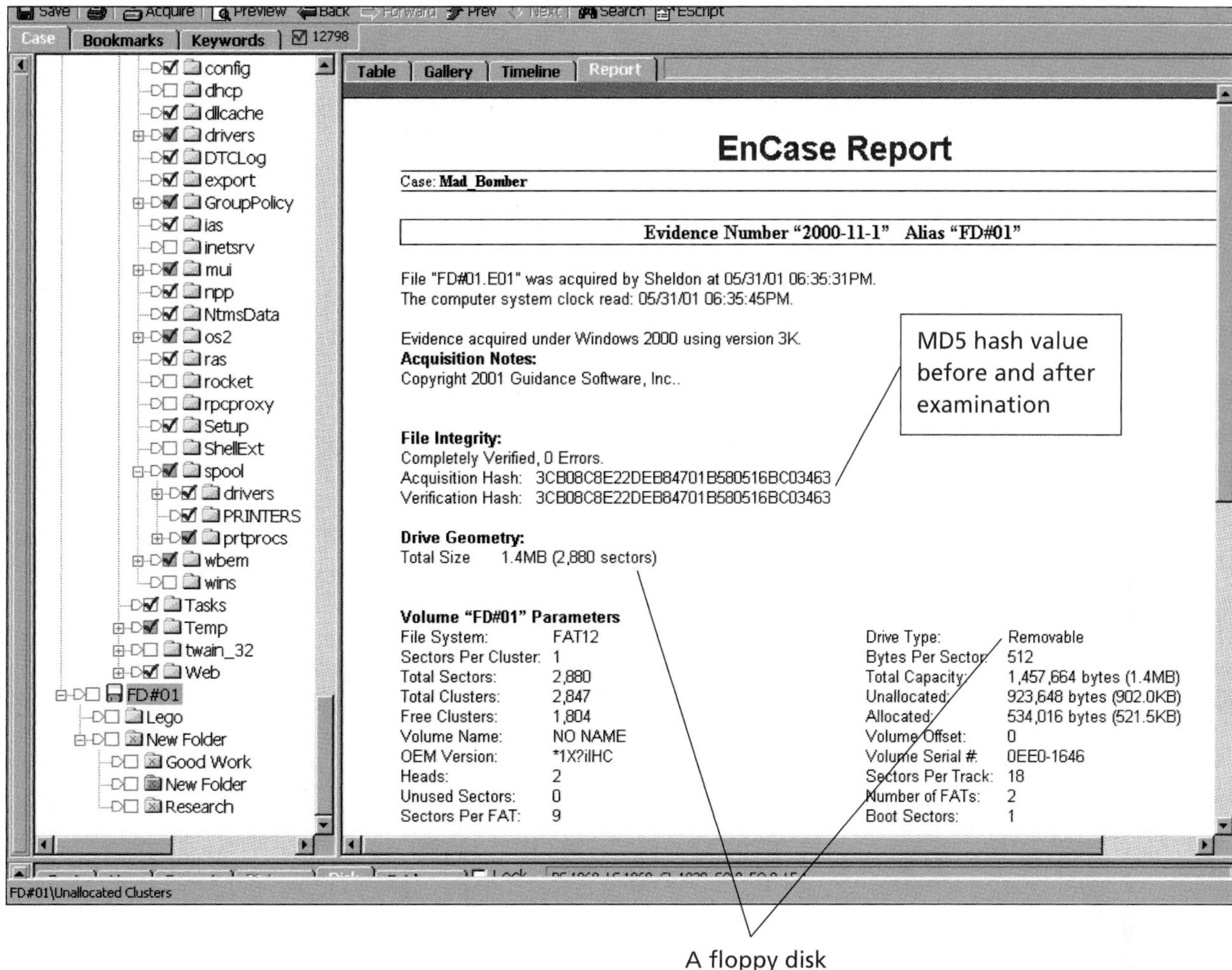

THE ANALYSIS PHASE

The analysis phase of the investigation is when the investigator follows the trail of clues and builds the evidence into a crime story. This is the phase that really tests the skill and experience of the investigators. The analysis phase consists of the recovery and interpretation of the information that's been collected and authenticated. If all the necessary files were there in plain sight with names and extensions indicating their contents, life would be much easier for the forensic investigator, but that's seldom the case. Usually, particularly if those involved know that they're doing something wrong, the damning files will have been deleted or hidden.

You can recover all of a deleted file pretty easily as long as no new information has been written to the space where the file was. But you can also recover fragments—perhaps rather large fragments—of files in parts of a disk where new files have been written, but have not completely filled the space where the old file was. With the appropriate software you can recover files or fragments of files from virtually any part of any storage medium (see Figure B.6).

Computer forensic programs can pinpoint a file's location on the disk, its creator, the date it was created, the date of last access, the date it was deleted, as well as file formatting, and notes embedded or hidden in a document (see Figure B.7).

Figure B.6

Some of the Files Recoverable from Storage Media

E-Mail Files	Program Files and Data Files
• E-mail messages • Deleted e-mail messages	• Word (.doc) and backup (.wbk) files • Excel files • Deleted files of all kinds • Files hidden in image and music files • Encrypted files • Compressed files
Web Activity Files	**Network Server Files**
• Web history • Cache files • Cookies	• Backup e-mail files • Other backup and archived files • System history files • Web log files

Figure B.7

History of File Activity

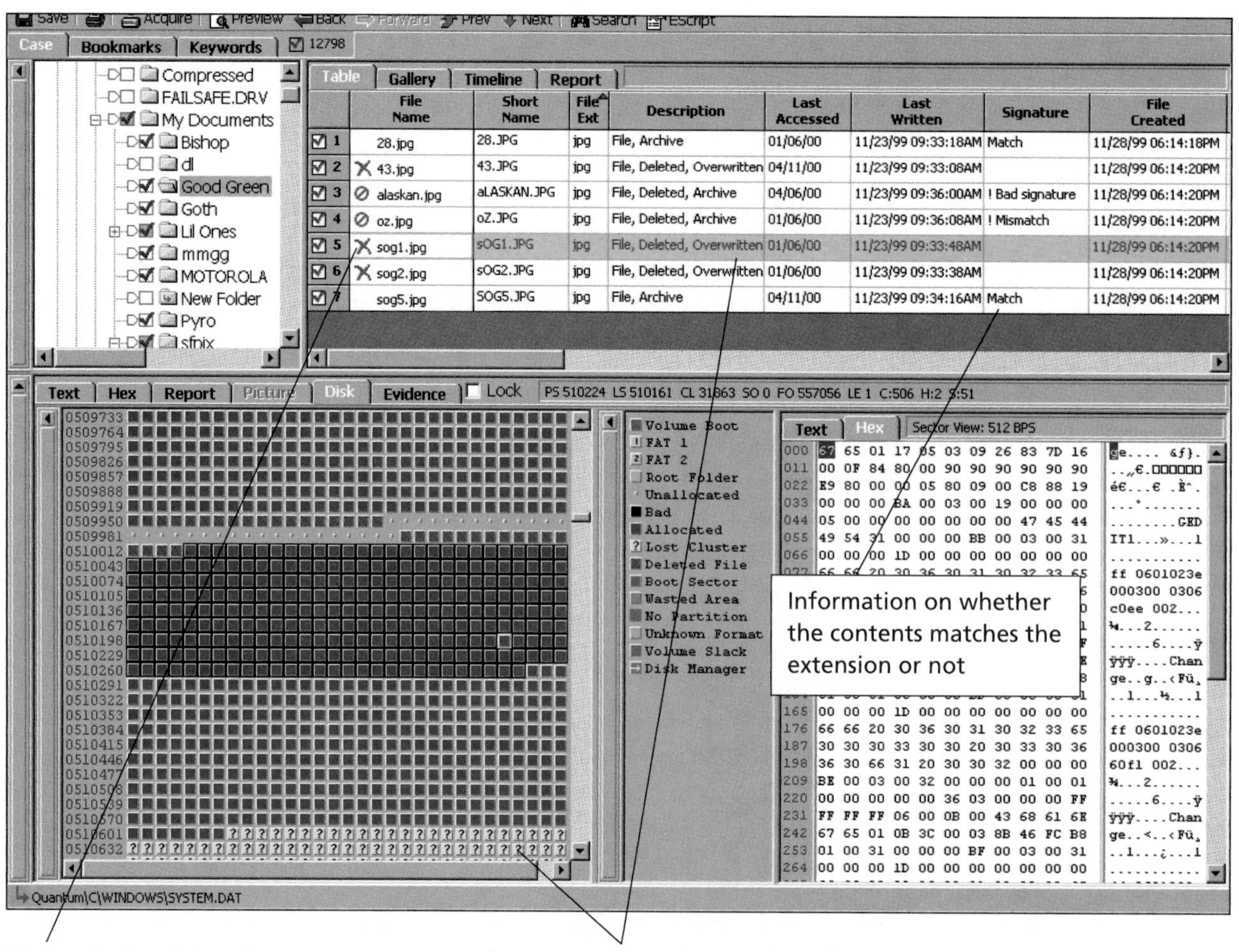

File marked as deleted

Details of where files are located on the disk— whether they've been deleted, overwritten, or archived

Also stored on the hard disk is information about where the computer user went on the Web. In addition, Web servers have information on which computer connected to the Web and when. The same server can also tell you the sites visited by the user of that computer, the date and time of the visits, and the actions of the user at the site. This is useful if the suspect claims to have reached an inappropriate site by accident, since delving deeper into the site implies a deliberate action. And, of course, if a password was required to reach the material in question, you can rest your case.

Recovery and Interpretation

As with all evidence, the analysis of the electronic clues and the assembling of the pieces into a credible and likely scenario of what happened are very important. Much of the information may come from recovered deleted files, currently unused disk space, and deliberately hidden information or files.

Following is a discussion, not necessarily exhaustive, of places from where computer forensics experts can recover information.

PLACES TO LOOK FOR STRAY INFORMATION

Information is written all over a disk, not only when you save a file, but also when you create folders, repartition the disk, and so on. System and application software alike continually create temporary files resulting in space and file locations being rearranged. Leftover information stays on the disk until another file is written over it, and is often recoverable with forensic software. Next, we'll examine three places where files or file remnants could be: areas of the disk with deleted files, slack space, and unused disk space.

DELETED FILES AND SLACK SPACE It's actually not very easy to get rid of electronically stored information completely. A surprising number of people think that if you delete a file it's gone. It's not—at least not immediately, and perhaps never. When you delete a file, all you're actually doing is marking it as deleted in the disk's directory. The actual file contents are not affected *at all* by a delete action.

If you delete a file from a hard disk, you usually get a message asking you if you want it in the Recycle Bin and then you can recover it simply by using the Undelete option. On a removable medium, such as a Zip or floppy disk, it's a little harder, but not much. The message you get asks whether you're sure you want to delete the file because it may not be recoverable. Actually that should read "*not as easily recoverable as files in the Recycle Bin*," since you can get it back with utility programs such as Norton, and of course, forensic software.

When you mark a file as deleted, the space is freed up for use by some other file. So another file may shortly be written to that space. However, it's not quite that straightforward. The operating system divides storage space into sectors of bytes or characters. The sectors are grouped into clusters. A file is assigned a whole number of clusters for storage, whether it completely fills the last cluster or not. This storage allocation method usually leaves unused portions of clusters. If the previously stored file (the deleted one) was bigger and used that last part of the space, then the remnants of the deleted file remain and can be recovered using the appropriate software. The space left over when a file doesn't completely fill the last cluster of sectors is called **slack space**, and leftover information there can be recovered by forensic software (see Figure B.8).

Figure B.8

Fragment of E-Mail Found in Slack Space by EnCase

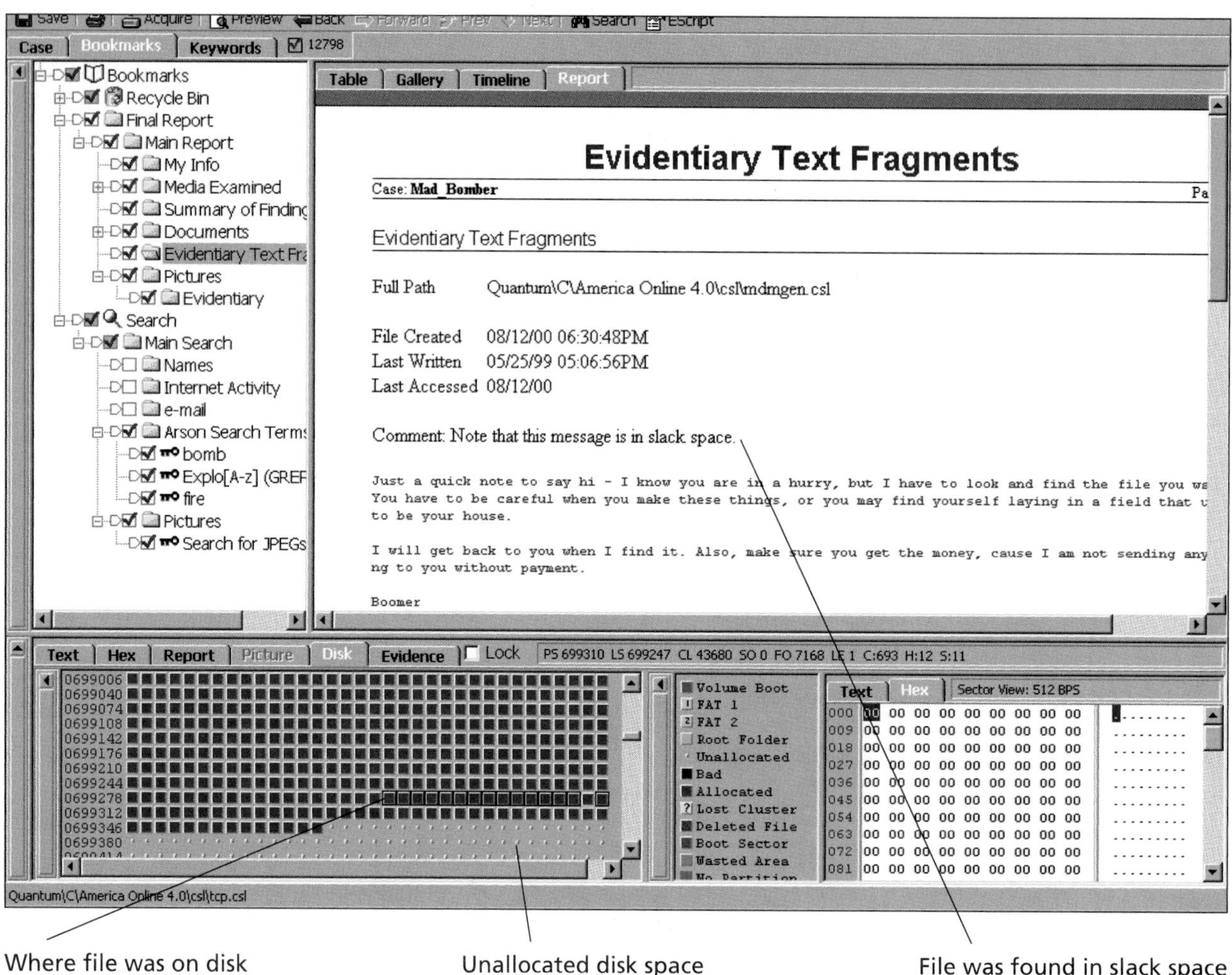

Can you never completely erase information from a storage medium, then? The answer is "Yes, you can," but you have to know what you're doing. You can get "wiper" programs that erase information from a disk drive by writing nonsense information over all the previous contents, and utilities like Norton have this feature. However, erasing a disk takes a lot of time. A 10-gigabyte hard disk (not that big) would take two hours to clean. Even then you're not necessarily safe, for three reasons. First, a single overwrite may not get everything. Many government agencies write over old information seven (*seven!*) times to be sure it's gone completely. Second, many programs keep track of what was deleted when and by whom. Third, Windows has an internal log mechanism that records what or who deleted files. This log file is not easy to erase. You'd have to be a pretty skilled Windows operating system specialist to manage it.

UNUSED DISK SPACE If your hard disk gets a lot of use, it's probable that each sector has had information put into it many times. The operating system is always moving files around, and if you changed a Word file and resaved it, the previous version is marked as "deleted" and the space becomes unallocated. **Unallocated space** is the set of clusters that have been set aside to store information, but have not yet received a file, or still contain some or all of a file marked as deleted. Until the new information takes up residence, the old information remains. The bigger the hard disk is, the longer it usually takes for old space to be used.

When a hard drive is repartitioned, the new partitioning may not use all the space on the hard disk. So, again, those unused portions are not overwritten. The partition table and other operating system information are stored on their own tracks and are not visible under normal circumstances, but may have once stored a Word document. To be able to see the fragments of files tucked away in these tracks you need forensics software.

WAYS OF HIDING INFORMATION

There are many ways of deliberately hiding information (other than deleting the file) and some are easy to defeat and others not so easy. Following is a sampling of methods that people use to try to hide files.

RENAME THE FILE The simplest, and most easily detected, way of deliberating hiding a file in Windows would be to change the extension of the file. Say you had an Excel file that had calculations you didn't want anyone to know about, you could change the extension name to Space Needle.jpg. Then it would appear in Explorer in the list of files as a .jpeg image file, with the name implying that it's just a vacation photo or something else innocuous.

However, if you try to click on that file, Windows will try to load it with the default .jpg viewer. And, of course, it won't load. What computer forensic experts usually do is load the file into a program that accommodates many file formats. This way, you save a lot of time trying to load the renamed file into lots of different types of software. Even more helpful is a forensic tool like EnCase that actually flags files with extensions that don't match the contents, and also show files in their true formats.

MAKE THE INFORMATION INVISIBLE They always say that the best hiding place is in plain sight. A very simple way to hide information inside a file, say a Word document, is to make the information the same colour as the background. This works in Excel and other types of files too. So if you suspect that something interesting is hidden this way, you could check the size of the file to see if it looks consistent with the contents. You may have to laboriously go through each Excel sheet and Word document and change the colour of all the text. With Excel, start by moving the cursor around and watching the top toolbar to see if any text, numbers or formulas show up in the upper toolbar. Also, watch where the scroll bars are located. That will give you an indication of how much of that sheet was used. Holding down the Ctrl key and hitting the End key will send you to the bottommost corner of the spreadsheet.

USE WINDOWS TO HIDE FILES Windows has a utility to hide files of a specific type. You simply open up that drive or folder, choose View, then Options, and hide the files by indicating what extensions you want hidden. If you go through this process, you'll probably see that there's a list of hidden files already on your computer. These are files that have to do with the correct functioning of your computer and to list them would just clutter up Windows Explorer and risk their being changed or deleted by accident.

PROTECT THE FILE WITH A PASSWORD Word lets you password-protect files so that when someone tries to open the file a pop-up window asks for the password. Unless you know the password, you won't be able to read the file. However, many people set Word to automatically make backup copies (that have the extension .wbk) so that if they lose the original, they'll still have a backup. So the investigator can look to see if any of those files exist, if the password for the .doc files is unavailable.

ENCRYPT THE FILE **Encryption** scrambles the contents of a file so that you can't read it without having the right decryption key. Often you can find that in a password file or on bits of paper somewhere around the keyboard. There are also password-cracking programs that will find many passwords very easily (alarmingly easily, in fact). They have dictionaries of words from multiple languages, so whole words from any language are not hard to crack. Some people put a digit or two on the front or back of a word. That doesn't fool the password-cracking programs at all.

Sometimes investigators can figure out passwords from knowing something about the person. That's why birthdays, anniversaries, children's or pet's names are not good passwords. Also, since you usually need passwords for lots of reasons, and it's hard to remember lots of different random ones, many people used just two or three different passwords, so if investigators find one password, they can try that. Also having one password often offers a clue as to what the other passwords might be. For example, if the one an investigator knows is a little piece of a nursery rhyme, then the others might be too.

USE STEGANOGRAPHY **Steganography** is the hiding of information inside other information. Paper money is a good example of steganography. If you hold a dollar bill up to the light you'll see a watermark. The watermark image is hidden inside the other markings on the bill, but it can be viewed if you know what to do to see it.

You can electronically hide information using this method. For example, if you want to hide a text file inside an image file, you can use a program called Steganos that does the work for you. Steganos takes nonessential parts of the image and replaces them with the hidden file. "Non-essential" means that these are parts of the picture that you can't see anyway, so changing those to the hidden message makes the message invisible (see Figure B.9). Steganography is a process is similar to file compression, where nonessential information is removed, but to save space rather than hide anything.

Law enforcement agencies believe that worldwide terrorist networks communicate using steganography. They set up a Web site and find pictures that they can hide messages in. When the message is hidden, the innocent-looking picture goes back up on the Web site. Fellow terrorists can download the picture, click on it and get a pop-up window asking for a password. With the correct password the hidden message appears.

COMPRESS THE FILE Compressing a file makes it invisible to keyword searches. To find out what's in it you'll have to decompress it with the right software. This may be on the hard disk on another disk somewhere around the suspect's desk. That's why investigators take all media for examination.

A DAY IN THE LIFE OF A COMPUTER FORENSICS EXPERT

Being a computer forensics expert is a profession that's very demanding. You have to know a lot about computers, and you have to keep learning, since things change fast in the computer world. You have to be infinitely careful and patient. You also have to be good at explaining to juries how computers work, and must be cool under pressure, since some of the situations you face will be quite adversarial. Lanny Morrow is a young man who has these qualities—and an interesting job.

Figure B.9

Steganography Hides a File in an Image

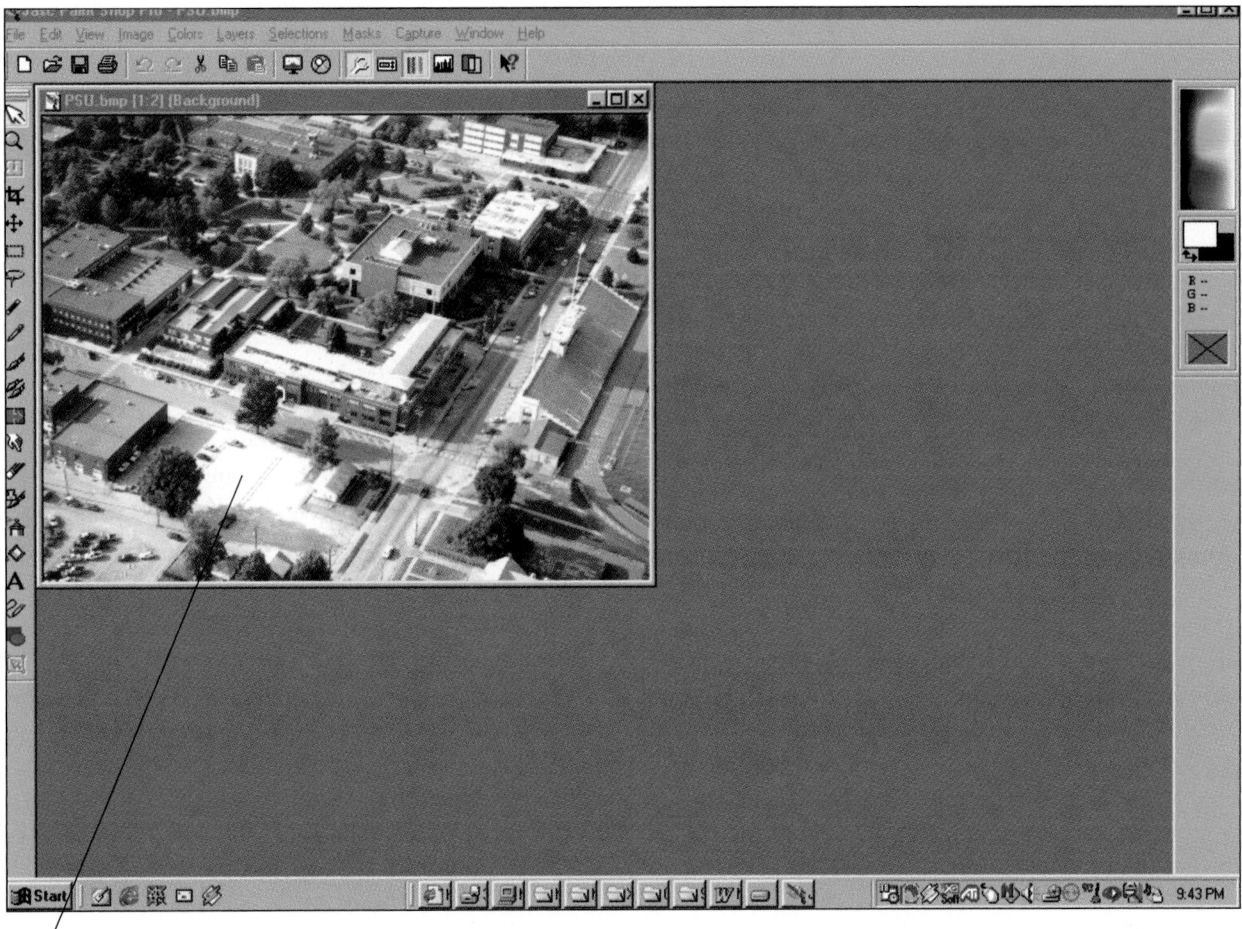

You can't see the parts of the picture that were changed to encode the hidden message. You'll only be able to access the hidden file when you put the right password into a pop-up window.

Lanny is a computer forensics expert for DataProbe, the Forensics and Dispute Consulting division of Baird, Kurtz, and Dobson, one of the largest accounting firms in North America. Organizations, both for-profit and not-for-profit, who need some detective work done, as well as legal firms, hire DataProbe to get the goods.

Lanny's cases are many and varied. His life is certainly not boring. Some cases take a long time and some are resolved pretty fast like the divorce case where the wife believed that her husband was hiding assets, and that the records were on their home computer. No one (wife, lawyers, friends) could find anything incriminating on the hard drive or on any floppies or Zip disks. But the wife was adamant that the records were there. Lanny was called in. His first step as always was to open up the computer and have a look inside to see if anything in there looked unusual. And there it was—a second hard drive that wasn't plugged in, and was just sitting inside the system unit. When the husband wanted to do his secret accounting, he just opened up the box and swapped hard disk connections, reversing the process when he was done.

A more complex case involved a grade-school teacher whom the principal suspected of being involved in child pornography using school computers. The teacher (now ex-teacher) argued that anything found on school computers could have been put there by anyone since the computers were available to lots of people.

Lanny established dates and times, some of which turned out to be weekends, when the Web activity was taking place. He also assessed the duration and intent of the activity by inspecting entries that showed the amount of time spent on each Web site. He demonstrated that downloads couldn't have been made by accident since there were warnings in pop-up boxes between Web pages about the nature of the material and, to continue, the surfer would have had to click OK multiple times.

Next, he talked to a custodian who saw this teacher working on that computer at times during the weekend when the two of them were the only ones in the building. In the face of the mounting evidence, the teacher admitted his wrongdoing.

Some cases are solved in a manner similar to the way a knitted sweater unravels, by pulling on one stray strand. One instance of stolen design drawings was like that. A supervisor suspected that an employee who was leaving for a more prestigious position with a competing company, had bought his way in by stealing schematics for that company. The IT staff at the company couldn't find any smoking gun. Again, the job was handed off to Lanny.

While collecting the computer and other items, he picked up a floppy disk and was told that it had been checked in Windows Explorer and had been found to be blank. He took it with him anyway. Later, he ran EnCase on the disk and found a deleted file called "Sales Quotes.txt," but when he tried to open it in Notepad, it wouldn't load, indicating that, despite its extension, it wasn't a text file. Next he tried Quick View Plus, which opens many different formats, and found that the file contained a schematic. Further investigation revealed that this file had originated on the hard drive and had been renamed to hide its true contents. Not only that, but the file had been copied to the hard disk from the company's intranet. Interesting!

But could Lanny prove that the employee had done anything more than download a company file to his computer? He went looking for a list of the employee's contacts to see if anything turned up. He found the name and e-mail address of an officer of the competing company in a business contact database—and this record had been deleted.

He then used the keyword search feature of EnCase to search all storage media for the competitor company's name. He found outgoing e-mail to this competitor officer from the suspect employee, complete with an attachment called "Sales Quotes.txt." After that, it was just a matter of tying up loose ends. Lanny documented the sequence of events using the time and date stamps on all the files involved, and criminal proceedings were initiated against the ex-employee. Civil litigation is ongoing against the competitor that accepted the stolen goods.

Summary: Student Learning Outcomes Revisited

1. **Define computer crime and list three types of computer crime that can be perpetrated from inside and three from outside the organization.** Computer crime is crime in which a computer, or computers, plays a significant part. Crimes perpetrated outside the organization include:
   - **Computer viruses**
   - **Worms**
   - **Denial-of-service (DoS) attacks**
   - Combination worm/DoS
   - Virus hoax
   - Stand-alone viruses
   - **Trojan-horse virus**

   Crimes perpetrated inside the organization include:
   - Fraud
   - Embezzlement
   - Harassment
2. **Define hackers, and identify the seven types of hackers and what motivates each group.** **Hackers** are knowledgeable computer users who use their knowledge to invade other people's computers. The seven types are:
   - **Thrill-seeker hackers**, who are motivated by the entertainment value of breaking into computers
   - **White-hat hackers**, who are hired by a company to find the vulnerabilities in its network
   - **Black-hat hackers**, who are cyber vandals
   - **Crackers**, who are hackers for hire and are the people who engage in electronic corporate espionage
   - **Hacktivists**, who are politically motivated hackers who use the Internet to send a political message of some kind
   - **Cyberterrorists**, who seek to cause harm to people or destroy critical systems or information
   - **Script kiddies** or **script bunnies**, who would like to be hackers but don't have much technical expertise
3. **Define computer forensics and describe the two phases of a forensic investigation. Computer forensics** is the gathering, authentication, examination, and analysis of electronic information stored on any type of computer media, such as hard drives, floppy disks, or CDs. A computer forensics investigation has two phases: (1) collecting and authenticating electronic evidence and (2) analyzing the findings. The collection phase consists of:
   - Getting physical access to the computer and any other items that might be helpful
   - Creating a **forensic image copy** of all storage media
   - Authenticating the forensic image copy of all storage media by generating an **MD5 hash value** for it, that will be altered if the contents have changed in any way
   - Using forensic hardware that can read storage media but cannot write to them
   - Using forensic software that can find deleted, hidden, and otherwise hard-to-access information

   The analysis phase consists of:
   - Finding all the information and figuring out what it means
   - Assembling a crime story that fits the information that has been discovered
4. **Identify and describe three places on a storage medium where you can find stray information.** The three places are:
   - **Slack space**, where part of an old file was stored and has not been overwritten by a new file because the new file doesn't take up all the space
   - **Unallocated space**, which is the set of clusters that have been set aside to store information
   - Unused space that results from repartition of the disk
5. **Identify and describe seven ways of hiding information.** Seven ways of hiding information are:
   - Rename the file to make it look like a different type of file
   - Make information invisible, for example by making text the same colour as its background
   - Use the Windows operating system's hidden-file utility to hide all files that have a certain extension
   - Protect the file with a password
   - Encrypt the file, that is, scramble its contents
   - Use steganography, that is, hide a file inside another file
   - Compress the file so that a keyword search can't find it

Key Terms and Concepts

Short-Answer Questions

1. In what two ways are computers used in the commission of crimes or misdeeds?
2. What constitutes a computer crime?
3. What kind of software is a computer virus?
4. What differentiates a worm from a macro virus?
5. How does a denial of service attack work?
6. What is the effect of a virus hoax?
7. What is the difference between the Klez family of viruses and previous worms?
8. What is a Trojan-horse virus?
9. One type of cyber vandalism destroys Web sites. What type is it?
10. What differentiates different types of hackers?
11. What is a white-hat hacker?
12. What do crackers do?
13. Is there a difference between a cyberterrorist and a hacktivist? If so, what is it?
14. What are the two phases of a computer forensics investigation?
15. What feature does a forensic computer have that other computer systems don't usually have?

Assignments and Exercises

1. **FIND COMPUTER FORENSICS SOFTWARE.** On the Web there are many sites that offer computer forensics software. Find five such software packages, and for each answer the following questions:
   - What does the software do? List five features it advertises.
   - Is the software free? If not, how much does it cost?
   - Is there any indication of the software's target market? If so, what market is it (law enforcement, home use, or something else)?
2. **IS YOUR FINANCIAL IDENTITY AT RISK FOR THEFT?** Identity theft is one of the fastest-growing crimes. It uses a computer as a weapon to steal the financial identity of someone with good credit. The thief runs up a huge credit card debt, takes out loans, writes bad cheques, travels to exotic destinations, all the while pretending to be you, financially speaking. After that, your financial reputation is ruined. You can't cash a cheque, your credit cards are refused, and you can't get a bank loan. You probably won't have to cover the bad debts, but that doesn't mean you're not seriously affected. You'll have to create a new financial identity, getting new bank accounts, credit cards, social security number, and driver's licence. That's not easy, since the latter two were intended to stay with you for life.

3. **THE INTERNATIONAL ANTI-CYBERCRIME TREATY.** The Web is, by definition, worldwide. This causes headaches and disputes between countries as to how to enforce their own laws on cyberspace. There are also issues of jurisdiction and extradition. To try and solve some of these problems, the Council of Europe, Canada, Japan, South Africa, and the United States has been working since 1997 on a treaty that all could agree to. In May 2001, the 27th draft of the Convention on Cybercrime was approved by all participants. But the treaty is not yet in force, since it has to be ratified by each country individually. The countries in the European Union were represented at the negotiations by the Council of Europe. So the treaty is not likely to be in force for at least several months.

   Find out what the provisions of the treaty are and how they will affect the United States. One of the concerns that will have to be addressed is the issue of whether laws of one country should apply to all. For example, if certain sites are illegal in Saudi Arabia, should they be illegal for all surfers? Or if Germany has a law about hate language, should a German or a U.S. citizen be extradited to stand trial for building a neo-Nazi site? What do you think?

4. **WHAT IS THE GOVERNMENT DOING ABOUT CYBERTERRORISM?** Cyberterrorism can take many forms: manipulation of banking records to generate funds, spreading misinformation to create panic, altering the software instructions that run the drug manufacturing systems, or any one of many other chaos-causing or harmful acts. Write a report on cyberterrorism.

CHAPTER NINE

STUDENT LEARNING OUTCOMES

1. Describe why information filtering is becoming important and the two trends that will support information filtering.
2. Describe the movement toward intellectual computing including automatic speech understanding and the role of people in decision making.
3. Define biometrics, automatic speech recognition, virtual reality, and CAVEs as they relate to changes in physiological interaction.
4. Describe the various technology innovations and trends that will increase portability and mobility.
5. Discuss the challenges of and technological innovations for the coming digital frontier.
6. Describe the broadening of e-government and the coming C2C explosion as they relate to the rebirth of e-commerce.

INDUSTRY PERSPECTIVES

FEATURES

WEB SUPPORT LINKS

- Master's Programs
- Graduate School Information and Tips
- Tele-Education (Distance Learning)

Visit
www.mcgrawhill.ca/college/haag

EMERGING TRENDS AND TECHNOLOGIES
Business, People, and Technology Tomorrow

CASE STUDY:
WOULD YOU USE AN INTERNET-ENABLED TOILET?

We hope the question in the title doesn't sound too strange or far-fetched. Matsushita recently announced its plan to make Internet-enabled toilets widely available to the public. The toilets are electronic and can be connected to the Internet.

Sensors within the toilet take readings of your biological output. That information can then be sent to your doctor's computer for immediate analysis. Your doctor's office could then notify you, perhaps, that your blood sugar is low or that you have the beginning symptoms of the flu. The toilet seat may even be able to take your pulse, which would provide more information for your doctor to use.

Aside from personal use in your home, many assisted-living care facilities are already planning to install Internet-enabled toilets. This will enable the nursing staff to constantly monitor the health of its patients. Many people in assisted-living care facilities need around-the-clock attention, especially with respect to the early diagnosis of seemingly simple health problems such as a cold or the flu.

Internet-enabled toilets are an example of the coming future of technology and how technological innovations will forever change your life. These types of toilets are also an example of how your physiological interactions with technology will change. In the case of these types of toilets, a computer will essentially measure your biometrics and use that information according to some purpose (e.g., checking your health status). Biometrics is certainly growing in importance, and we'll discuss it in this chapter.

Internet-enabled toilets are also an example of the growing importance of carefully considering every technological innovation within the context of ethics and privacy. For example, what if your employer began using Internet-enabled toilets for random drug testing? Is that an invasion of your privacy? Depends on how you look at it. What if you used an Internet-enabled toilet at your house to test a nanny for drug and alcohol use? Is that an invasion of the nanny's privacy? Considering that you're trusting a nanny to keep your children safe and treat them well, do you have the right to test a nanny for drug and alcohol use? Again, it depends on how you look at it.

As we move into this exciting future, all eyes will be on numerous technological innovations such as this one. But we would encourage you to think, and determine how it will impact your life. Even more importantly, you need to consider how it will impact your privacy. Most technological innovations will in fact affect your privacy. They will allow organizations and other people to gather and use significant information about you. It's your responsibility—to yourself and society at large—to ensure that any new technological innovation is used in the best possible way while minimizing any negative impact on privacy.

Introduction

Technology is changing every day. But even more important than simply keeping up with changes in technology is thinking about how they will affect your personal and business life. It's interesting to read and learn about leading- and bleeding-edge technologies; and in fact this is something we would encourage you to do. However, the consequences of the changes are far greater than you might imagine.

In this final chapter, we want to take a look at several new technologies, including speech recognition, implant chips, and digital cash, and more importantly how they can and will impact your personal and business life. Technology for its own sake is never a good thing; using technology to enhance your personal life and to move your organization toward its strategic initiatives, on the other hand, are.

To introduce you to just a few of the many new technologies on the horizon, we've chosen those we feel will have the greatest impact. And we present those horizon technologies within the context of six important trends, including (see Figure 9.1):

1. The need for information filtering
2. The movement toward intellectual computing
3. The changing of physiological interaction
4. Increasing portability and mobility
5. The digital frontier
6. The rebirth of e-commerce

Figure 9.1
Emerging Trends and Technologies

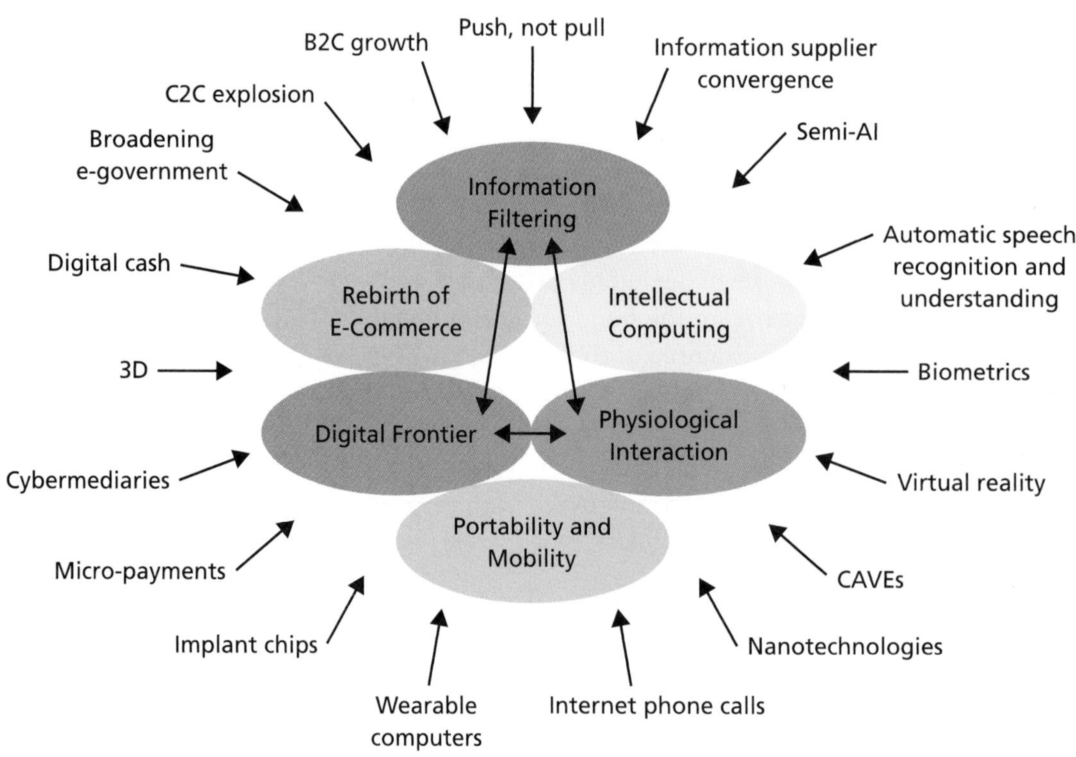

The Need for Information Filtering

In the information age, "information" is certainly not at a premium. Quite the opposite: we seem to have an abundance of it. And too much of a good thing is not a good thing. Every day, you probably receive unsolicited e-mail (spam). Much of it probably comes from viral marketing, in which one of your friends or a family member has provided your information to a Web site. You may receive other spam just because you've visited a Web site.

In business, people are constantly given access to vast amounts of information. The real problem lies in sifting through it and deciding what is and is not important. Decision makers can suffer from "analysis paralysis," because they simply have too much information to consider. That's why many people use intelligent agents, called data mining agents (refer to Chapters 3 and 4) to find important relationships in information stored in a data warehouse.

Information filtering, then, is a must. We see two advances here—(1) push, not pull technologies and (2) information supplier convergence.

PUSH, NOT PULL TECHNOLOGIES

Right now, we live in a "pull" technology environment. That is, you see an ad for something you want, and then you go somewhere and request it. On the Internet, for example, you get spam or see an interesting banner ad, visit the site, and request information, services, and products. So you're figuratively being "pulled in" by the advertiser. But in the future **push technology** environment, businesses and organizations will more often be "pushing" their product at you, coming at you with information, services, and product offerings based on your profile (see Figure 9.2).

For example, in some parts of the country you can subscribe to a cell service that pushes information to you in the form of video rental information. Whenever you pass

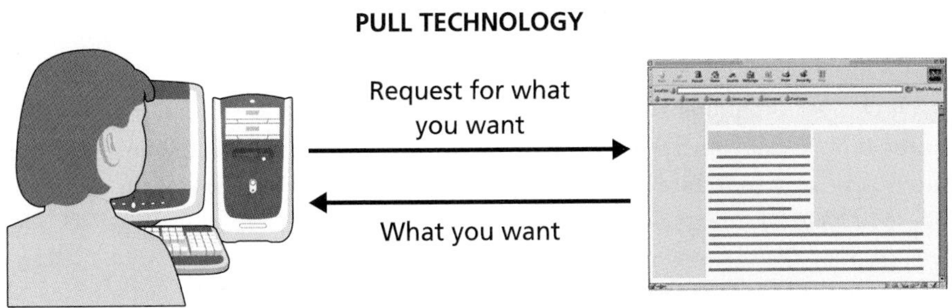

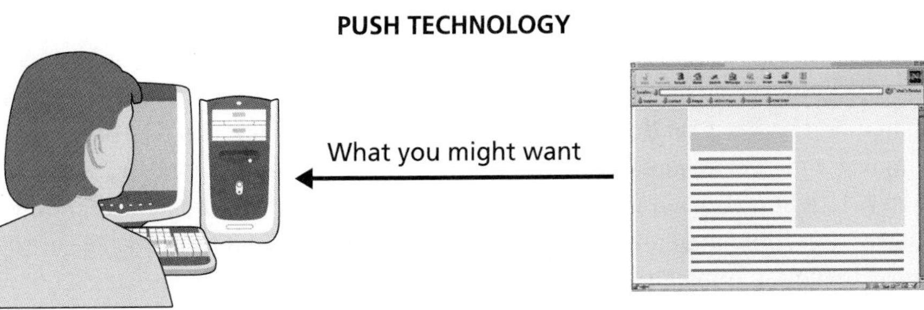

Figure 9.2
Pull Versus Push Technology

RESEARCH IN MOTION'S BLACKBERRY DEVICE SUCCESS STORY

Research in Motion (www.rim.net), founded in 1984 and headquartered in Waterloo, Ontario, has been one of the most successful Canadian companies in the Internet appliance market. In 1999, RIM received the "Product of the Year Award" in the Mobile Computing category from *InfoWorld* magazine for the simple setup and deployment, ease of use, and superior product functionality of its two-way e-mail pager called BlackBerry.

This cigarette-pack-sized wireless device was the first to offer users both e-mail and organizer capabilities. The initial popularity of the device lay in its ability to check e-mail anywhere anytime. In 2002, the company introduced its newest gizmo in the BlackBerry line, the 5810. Although almost identical to the previous generation of BlackBerry, not only does this newest device include a tiny QWERTY-style keyboard on which you type using your thumbs, "always on" e-mail, organizer functions (calendar and address book), a Web browser, and Short Messaging Service capabilities, it is now combined with cell-phone capabilities. "Our customers told us they wanted voice in the BlackBerry when they need it, and that is what we did," says Mike Lazaridis, cofounder and co-CEO of Research in Motion.

It is because of this close attention to what customers wanted and continuous innovation that the BlackBerry user base has grown to 289,000 people in 13,200 companies and the little device now accounts for 80 percent of the company's quarterly sales revenue. RIM has also more than doubled its employee base and has more than 200 students as co-ops and interns working for them.[1]

near a video store, your cell phone (which is GPS-enabled) triggers a computer within the video store that evaluates your purchasing history to see if any new videos have arrived that you might be interested in viewing. If so, the video store computer will call your cell phone with a message concerning a new release. It will also give you street-by-street directions to the video store and hold the video for you. If the video store doesn't have any new releases that might interest you, you won't receive a phone call.

You might also someday receive a personalized pizza delivery message on your television as you start to watch a ball game. The message may say, "We'll deliver your favourite sausage and mushroom pizza to your doorstep before the game begins. On your remote control, press the ORDER NOW button."

Of course, situations such as these rely on IT's ability to store vast amounts of information about you. Technologies such as databases and data warehouses will definitely play an important role in the development of technologies that do more than just send spam and mass e-mail. In the case of the pizza delivery message on your television, a local pizzeria would have determined that you like sausage and mushroom pizza and that you order it most often while watching a ball game.

INFORMATION SUPPLIER CONVERGENCE

You'll notice a greater ability to filter information when you start to enjoy **information supplier convergence**—the merging of all types of organizations that provide information and access to it. Information suppliers include businesses that provide you with magazines, newspapers, Internet access, telephone service, cable TV, books, and the like. Right now, you probably receive many of these information-based products and services from numerous suppliers. In that case, it's difficult for any single organization to filter information for you because it's coming from so many sources.

In the future, for example, you could receive your newspaper from the same organization that provides you with Internet access. In doing so, that organization could determine your likes and dislikes and provide you with an electronic newspaper tailored to what you want. That same organization could own and operate a worldwide news source arm that would search international news and provide it to you, if its content meets with your desires.

You may already be seeing this happen. Perhaps your cable TV provider is also your telephone service provider. Perhaps you use an information service on the Web that delivers daily articles to you based on your reading preferences. That information service is probably gathering daily information from numerous other news services, filtering it, and providing only what you want.

The Movement Toward Intellectual Computing

The key term in "artificial intelligence" (AI) is most certainly *artificial.* The many AI tools you studied in Chapter 4, including expert systems, neural networks, and genetic algorithms, are designed to mimic human thinking, but they still have to be programmed concerning what to do. Expert systems, for example, must be supplied specific rules and outcomes for every rule. They then follow those rules exactly; they are not capable of changing the rules or adding new ones with new outcomes.

There is much debate on whether we'll ever be able to create truly intelligent software. And there's just as much debate concerning whether we should do so even if we have the capability. We'll not take sides on those arguments here. But, if we can and do create intelligent software, we see two important future impacts—automatic speech understanding and the realization that people will still make the decisions.

AUTOMATIC SPEECH UNDERSTANDING

Automatic speech recognition (which we'll discuss in more detail in the next section) has come a long way in the past several years. But it still has a ways to go with simple tasks such as determining your words when you have a cold, determining the words of another person using your system, and even distinguishing between content and commands. We do, however, expect speech recognition to become standard within the next decade.

If we someday create intelligent software, speech recognition will become speech understanding. Consider the phrase "The glory that was Greece." In written form, you know exactly what it means. In spoken form, however, a computer may decide that "Greece" is actually "grease." If the computer could grasp that you were dictating a term paper on Greek and Roman mythical figures, it would not make this error. However, speech recognition systems can't do that. An intelligent system capable of understanding what you're saying would make far fewer errors. Who knows—if this happens, your computer may become your friend. Food for thought.

PEOPLE WILL STILL MAKE THE DECISIONS

It is important to keep in mind that, regardless of how intelligent a computer system may become, it will never completely replace people in all aspects of decision making. Some systems may make good, solid recommendations on the basis of certain conditions, but people must consider those recommendations before taking any important action.

Why? Because most decisions do not have a absolute right or wrong answer. Even if they did, you might come across a set of circumstances that would change your

ON YOUR OWN

WHERE SHOULD THE DECISION REST?

The degree to which you allow a computer to take over a decision-making task is often a function of the decision being made. For example, most inventory management systems are very good at determining what quantities of a given product line to reorder. If the system orders too many, no real harm is done, because excess inventory just sits on the shelf; if not enough is ordered, the business will simply experience a stock-out for a given period of time.

On the other hand, you should never let a computer system tell you how much of a dose of medicine to give a patient without first verifying the recommendation. The wrong dose—whether too much or too little—can have catastrophic effects, leading to serious illness and even death.

List three decisions in the business world that can be largely left to a computer and list three that should definitely not be left to a computer. (Do not use our previously mentioned examples.)

mind. People in general are unique because they possess intuition, insight, and feelings. That uniqueness gives us the ability to live and work together, and often make decisions that are not necessarily in the best interest of the bottom line. A computer will never be able to do that.

The Changing of Physiological Interaction

Right now, your primary physical interfaces to your computer include a keyboard, mouse, monitor, and printer. These are physical interfaces, not physiological. Physiological interfaces capture and utilize your real body characteristics, such as your breath, your voice, your height and weight, and even the retina in your eye. These all fall within the realm of **biometrics**, the use of your physical characteristics—such as your fingerprint, the blood vessels in the retina, the sound of your voice, or perhaps even your breath—to provide identification. That's the strict definition of biometrics, but it is beginning to encompass more than just identification.

Technological advances are appearing that allow you to physiologically interact with a computer system. In the strictest definition of biometrics for the purpose of identification, high-security environments require fingerprints or palm prints for entry into restricted areas. The military uses biometrics extensively in this way. Many banks now use a retina scan to determine your identification for using an ATM machine. Essentially, you have no ATM card—you allow the ATM to scan your eye.

When biometrics is broadened beyond using your physiological characteristics for identification, we will see a whole new generation of computing applications. Technologies to watch in this area include automatic speech recognition, virtual reality, and CAVEs.

AUTOMATIC SPEECH RECOGNITION

The most common and well-known example of the broader consideration of biometrics is automatic speech recognition (ASR). One of the Canadian leaders in biometrics is Diaphonics Incorporated of Halifax, Nova Scotia (www.diaphonics.com), a devel-

GETTING SMALL WITH NANOTECHNOLOGIES

One of the single greatest drawbacks to technological advances is size. The best chip manufacturers can do is make circuit elements with a width of 130 nanometres. A nanometre is one-100,000th the width of a human hair. That may seem very, very small, but current manufacturing technologies are beginning to limit the size of computer chips, and thus their speed and capacity.

Nanotechnologies aim to change all that. In nanotechnology, everything is simply atoms. Nanotechnology researchers are attempting to move atoms and encourage them to "self-assemble" into new forms. Consider this: "Change the molecular structure of the materials used to make computer chips, for instance, and electronics could become as cheap and plentiful as bar codes on packaging. Lightweight vests enmeshed with sensors could measure a person's vital signs. Analysis of a patient's DNA could be done so quickly and precisely that designer drugs would be fabricated on the fly. A computer the size of your library card could store everything you ever saw or read."

Nanotechnology—it's a bleeding-edge technology worth watching. The changes it will bring about are unimaginable.[2]

oper of speech recognition and voice security technologies. Diaphonics enables companies to automate and improve interaction with customers over the telephone. With voice biometrics that verify the identity of callers, companies using this software can enable customers to conduct secure, automated self-service transactions over any phone by giving simple, natural voice commands. An **automatic speech recognition (ASR)** system not only captures spoken words but also distinguishes word groupings to form sentences. To do this, an ASR system follows three steps:

1. **Feature analysis**. The system captures your words as your speak into a microphone, eliminates any background noise, and converts the digital signals of your speech into phonemes (syllables).
2. **Pattern classification**. The system matches your spoken phonemes to a phoneme sequence stored in an acoustic model database. For example, if your phoneme was "dü," the system would match it to the words "do" and "due."
3. **Language processing**. The system attempts to make sense of what you're saying by comparing the word phonemes generated in step 2 with a language model database. For example, if you were asking a question and started with the phoneme "dü," the system would determine that the appropriate word is "do" and not "due."

ASR is certainly now taking its place in computing environments. Manulife Canada, for instance, has adopted speech recognition to address the problem of an increasing number of "dropouts"—customers who hang up because they'd rather speak to a live operator than push a sequence of buttons on a touchtone telephone. "We knew we were either going to have to hire more service reps so people could speak to a live operator or change the way that customers obtained their information," says chief strategy officer Kendall Kay. After "speech-enabling" high-service transaction areas including fund rebalance and interaccount transfers, "we've received positive feedback from our customers. ... We feel that this system is a business driver because it deals with a customer satisfaction level. People want access to know what their money is doing," says Kay.[3] Visit the Web site that supports this text (www.mcgrawhill.ca/college/haag) to learn more about ASR systems.

VIRTUAL REALITY

On the horizon (and in some instances here today) is a new technology that will virtually place you in any experience you desire. That new technology is **virtual reality**—a three-dimensional computer simulation in which you actively and physically participate.

NASA, for instance, used virtual reality to train its astronauts to operate the Canadarm (developed by Spar Aerospace Limited) to catch and repair the Hubble Space Telescope. Rather than being one of NASA's great and most ambitious accomplishments, deployment of the telescope initially turned out to be of its most embarrassing moments. The main mirror was too flat by 1/50th the width of a human hair. This is all it took to create a huge defect in terms of optics. To correct the problem, astronauts had to use the Canadarm, a remotely operated appendage that can be used on board any space shuttle and designed to perform a variety of missions, to grab the 12.7 tonne satellite and place it on a rotating service platform at the rear of space shuttle *Endeavour*'s cargo bay in order to repair it. Before the mission, the crew extensively trained for over 400 hours, a procedure that included space walks in deep-water tanks and the use of virtual reality simulators to make sure they would perform all the necessary repairs quickly and thoroughly.[4]

In a virtual reality system, you make use of special input and output devices that capture your physiological movements and send physiological responses back to you. These include a:

- **Glove.** An input device that captures and records the shape and movement of your hand and fingers and the strength of the movements
- **Headset.** A combined input and output device that (1) captures and records the movement of your head and (2) contains a screen that covers your entire field of vision and displays various views of an environment on the basis of your movements
- **Walker.** An input device that captures and records the movement of your feet as you walk or turn in different directions

APPLICATIONS OF VIRTUAL REALITY Virtual reality applications are popping up everywhere, sometimes in odd places. The most common application is found in the entertainment industry. There are a number of virtual reality games on the market, including downhill Olympic skiing, racecar driving, golfing, air combat, and marksmanship. Other applications include:

- *Matsushita Electric Works.* You design your kitchen in virtual reality and then choose the appliances you want and even request colour changes
- *Volvo.* For demonstrating the safety features of its cars
- *Airlines.* To train pilots how to handle adverse weather conditions
- *Motorola.* To train assembly-line workers in the steps of manufacturing a new product[5]
- *Health care.* To train doctors in surgery on virtual humans[6]

Let's consider the potential ramifications of virtual reality and how you might someday interact with your computer. New virtual reality systems include aroma-producing devices and devices that secrete fluid through a mouthpiece that you have in your mouth. So you could conceivably experience a Hawaiian luau: the aroma-producing device would generate various smells and the mouthpiece would secrete a fluid that tastes like pineapple or roasted pig. If were using virtual reality to surf big waves, the mouthpiece would secrete a fluid that tastes like salt water.

TEAM WORK

FINDING APPLICATIONS OF VIRTUAL REALITY

Virtual reality is quickly taking its place in the technology world. In our discussion of it, we listed several well-known applications.

Your task is twofold in this project. First, search the Web for more applications of virtual reality. Find at least three and provide a brief description of each. Only one of these applications can be in the area of entertainment, that is, game-oriented.

Second, identify five potential applications for virtual reality. For each, describe how virtual reality would be used and why it would be beneficial. Each application must relate to the use of virtual reality by an organization. As you describe each application, also list the types of organizations or industries that would use it.

Those examples are the "fun" uses of virtual reality. In business, building contractors would use virtual reality to show a new building and the location of fire exits. Managers may be able to experience how a proposed downsizing effort would affect productivity. The possibilities are virtually limitless.

CAVEs

A **CAVE (cave automatic virtual environment)** is a special 3D virtual reality room that can display images of other people and objects located in other CAVEs all over the world. CAVEs are **holographic devices**—devices that create, capture, and/or display images in true three-dimensional form. (If you watch any of the *Star Trek* movies, you'll see an example of a holographic device called the *holodeck*.)

It works like this: You would enter a CAVE. At the same time, someone else would enter another CAVE (see Figure 9.3). Numerous digital video cameras in each CAVE would capture likenesses of both of you and the images of each room would be sent to the other. Then you and the other person could see and carry on a normal conversation with each other, and you would feel as if that other person were in the same room with you.

Current CAVE research is also working on the challenges of having other physical objects in the room. For example, if you sat on a couch in your CAVE, the couch would capture the indentation you made in it and pass it to the couch in the other CAVE. That couch would respond by constricting a mesh of rubber inside it so that your indentation would also appear there. And what about playing catch? Each of you would have a virtual ball. When you threw it, the CAVE would capture your arm movement to determine the speed, arc, and direction of the ball. That information would be transmitted to the other CAVE and it would use that information to make the virtual ball fly through the air accordingly.

Unlike virtual reality, you don't need any special gear. Let your imagination run wild and think about the potential applications. If an unhappy customer calls a business to complain, within seconds a customer service representative would appear in the room. Now that's great customer service! Your teacher might never show up in your classroom; instead he or she would enter a CAVE. Of course, you might not really be in class either, but rather a holographic likeness of you.

Are CAVEs a realistic possibility? The answer is definitely yes. They may be the successor to virtual reality. So virtual reality may not be a long-term technological innovation, but rather a stepping stone to the more advanced CAVEs. In any case,

Figure 9.3
CAVEs (Cave Automatic Virtual Environments)

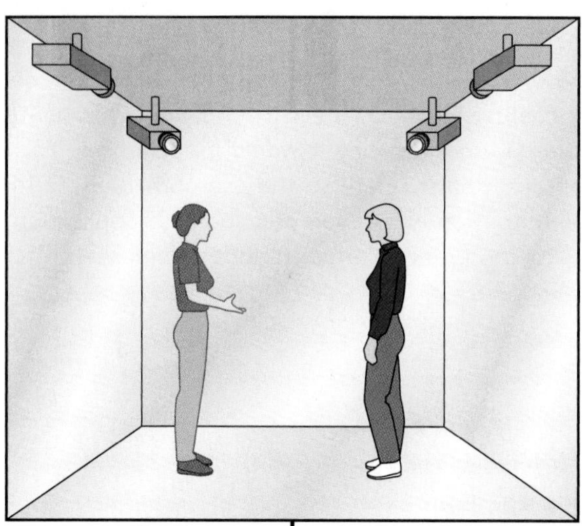
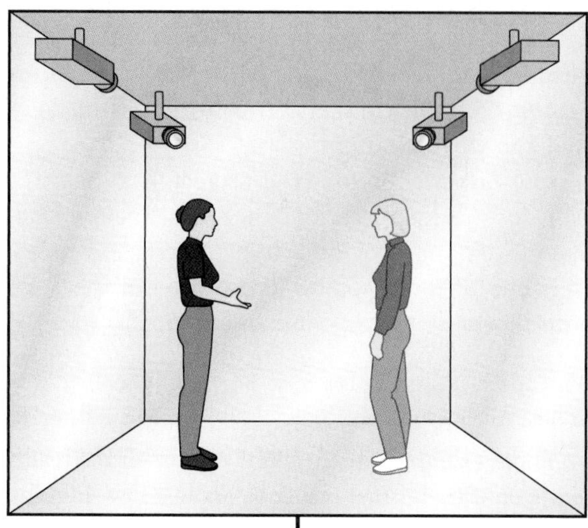

The Web

CAVEs will not only significantly alter how you interact with your computer (can you imagine the thrill of video games in a CAVE?), they will even more significantly alter how you interact with people. With CAVE technologies, you can visit your friends and relatives daily no matter where they live. You might even have television shows and movies piped into your home CAVE.

Increasing Portability and Mobility

Portability and mobility go hand in hand. Portability, in this instance, refers to how easy it is for you to carry around your technology. Mobility is much broader and encompasses what you have the ability to do with your technology while carrying it around. For example, personal digital assistants (PDAs) are very portable—they weigh less than half a kilogram and fit easily in your pocket or purse. However, your mobility may be limited with a PDA. That is, while you can manage your schedule, take some notes, and even use e-mail, you certainly can't generate spreadsheets with elaborate graphs. You want technology that is no more intrusive than your wallet or purse.

Clearly, to achieve maximum portability and mobility, we would need completely wireless communications. We won't delve into this vast and dynamic field here. However, you shouldn't have to sit at a desk to generate a spreadsheet with elaborate graphs. You shouldn't have to find your credit card every time you want to make a purchase on the Internet. You should be able to work on your computer as you walk down the street. In that context, let's discuss free Internet phone calls, micro-payments and financial cybermediaries, wearable computers, and implant chips.

FREE INTERNET PHONE CALLS

The Internet offers worldwide communication. Today, that already includes making phone calls through your computer while you're connected to the Internet. Many services offer this type of long-distance phone calling capability for just a few pennies per minute. Others, such as Net2Phone, offer this service completely free if you're using your computer to call another person using his or her computer. Standard computers today include speakers and microphones, so you really have all the technology you need to make the call.

To use Net2Phone, you connect first to its Web site (web.net2phone.com) and download and install some simple software (see Figure 9.4). You also pick a user name and password. Later, when you connect to the Internet again, you go to Net2Phone's Web site and place yourself on the "Active Contact List." You'll also be able to see everyone else on the Internet who also has Net2Phone service. All you have to do is pick someone to call and click on a few buttons. You then use your computer's microphone and speakers as if they were an actual telephone.

Internet phone calling will certainly increase your mobility, not to mention reduce your phone bill. And, as we discussed in Chapter 5, this type of Internet telephony will increase customer service on the Internet by providing integrated call centres with Web sites.

Figure 9.4
Making an Internet Phone Call

THE BASICS

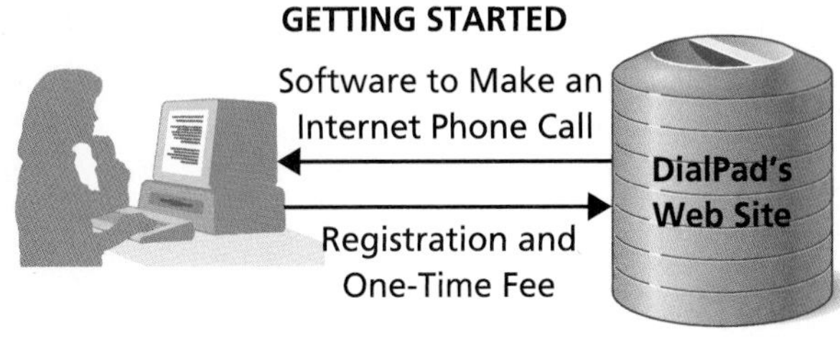

GETTING STARTED

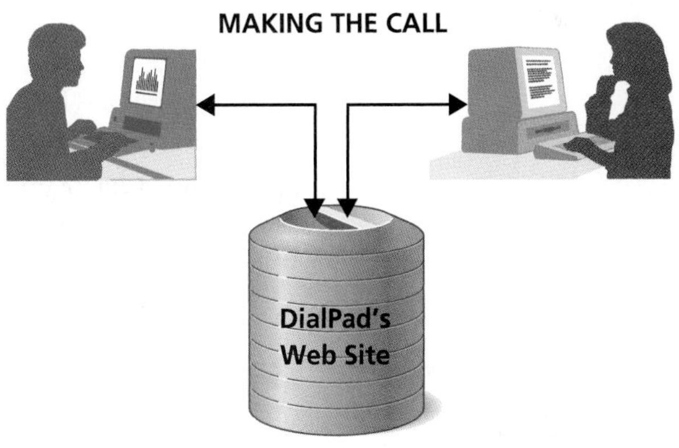

MAKING THE CALL

DialPad's
Web Site

MICRO-PAYMENTS AND FINANCIAL CYBERMEDIARIES

In Chapter 5, we also discussed micro-payments and cybermediaries. **Micro-payments** are techniques to facilitate the exchange of small amounts of money for an Internet transaction. Micro-payments enable you to make purchases for very small amounts (say 25 cents) on the Internet. You certainly can't do that with a credit card. **Financial cybermediaries** are Internet-based companies that make it easy for one person to pay another over the Internet. Think of a financial cybermediary as a "Western Union in cyberspace" that allows you to wire money.

Micro-payments and financial cybermediaries will enhance your mobility. That is, they will allow you to make payments, wire money, and even pay your utility bills no matter where you are. Of course, you'll need your technology to perform such transactions, so portability is a necessity for this mobility.

WEARABLE COMPUTERS

Focusing on portability now, let's turn our attention to wearable computers. A **wearable computer** is a fully-equipped computer that you wear as a piece of clothing or attached to a piece of clothing similarly to how you would carry your cell phone on your belt. Wearable computers are not some far-off dream. Today, Levi Strauss, Charmed Technology, and Xybernaut are already manufacturing and selling them (see Figure 9.5). Levi Strauss makes a jacket that contains a fully functional computer in it, with various parts located in the lapel, pockets, and waistline.

Xybernaut makes a computer that you wear like a cell phone by attaching it to your clothing. At the time of writing, their Poma wearable computer retailed for about

Figure 9.5
Wearable Computers

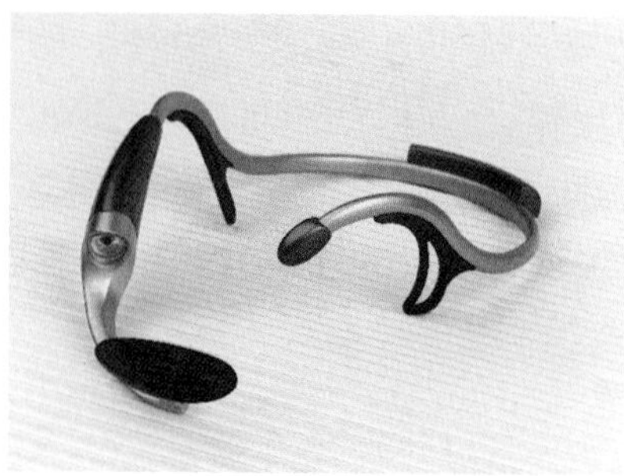

$1500. It included a 128 MHz processor, 32 MB of RAM, an optical pointing device, and a 640 × 480 VGA full-colour headset. Its software primarily supports e-mail, Internet access, music, and games. You can't use it for word processing and spreadsheet applications, but new releases will undoubtedly include those features. You can purchase a Poma directly from Xybernaut (www.xybernaut.com).

Again, the focus of wearable computers is portability first and mobility second. Right now, wearable computers are very unobtrusive (portability). But they do have limited processing capabilities, so your mobility is limited. You can certainly expect that to change very soon. As technology increases in capability and decreases in price and size, wearable computers will offer you as much processing capability (mobility) as a standard desktop or notebook computer.

Let your imagination run wild again. Imagine carrying and using your wearable computer as if it were a cell phone. You would have high-speed, wireless access to the Internet. You could use one eye to view your headset and work on a spreadsheet application while using your other eye to watch a baseball game. No matter where you were or what you were doing, you could still use your wearable computer to write term papers, send and receive e-mail, buy products on the Internet (m-commerce using micro-payments or digital cash, which we'll discuss in a moment), or just having fun surfing the Web.

IMPLANT CHIPS

Finally, in the areas of portability and mobility let's discuss a widely-debated use of technology—implant chips. An **implant chip** is a technology-enabled microchip implanted into the human body. These chips serve two functions. First, they contain memory that stores important information about you—your identification, medical history, medications to which you're allergic, contact information in case of an emergency, and so on. Second, many of these chips are GPS-enabled. The **global positioning system (GPS)** is a collection of 24 earth-orbiting satellites that continuously transmit radio signals to determine your current longitude, latitude, speed, and direction of movement.

If you consider the advantages of the first function, you could be vacationing in Newfoundland and have some sort of water skiing accident. The hospital could quickly

TEAM WORK

SELLING THE IDEA OF IMPLANT CHIPS AT YOUR SCHOOL

Let's assume for a moment that your team is in favour of using implant chips that contain vitally important information such as identification and medical information. Your task is to put together a sales presentation to your school that would require that all students obtain implant chips. Within your presentation, including the following:

- The school-related information each chip would contain
- The non-school-related information each chip would contain
- The processes within your school that would use the information on the chips
- The benefits your school would realize by requiring implant chips
- The benefits students would realize by having implant chips

Your presentation should be no more than five minutes long, so it must be a powerful pitch. Good luck.

scan your implant chip to view your medical history and determine what medications you might be allergic to. Many people are in favour of implant chips that serve this purpose. However, the "tracking" function of implant chips has raised heated debate.

If your implant chip is GPS-enabled, then the government could conceivably track your every move. Many people are not in favour of that use. But think a little more. Would we ever have lost or kidnapped children? Couldn't the police determine who broke into your home? So there are advantages.

Already, in parts of Europe, people are using them. Certain European countries tend to accept leading-edge uses of technology more easily than North America. But it was recently reported that a family of four in Florida was the first North American family to receive implant chips. And those chips are GPS-enabled. There is other evidence that implant chips are becoming more acceptable. Most zoos put chips into rare animals to track them if they are ever stolen. Many veterinarians now recommend that chips be implanted into household pets. The famed dogsled race across Alaska, the Iditarod, uses chips in the dogs. When the race is over, the organizers can scan them to ensure they are the same dogs that started.

The GPS is not used exclusively with implant chips. For a couple hundred dollars you can buy a GPS system complete with city and road maps. Airline pilots and fishermen commonly use a GPS system to fly around no-fly zones and return to places in an ocean or sea where the fishing was particularly good the day before. GPS is an invaluable technology in many instances. You may not agree with its use in implant chips for tracking people, but it does have beneficial uses.

So what's your take on GPS-enabled implant chips. Do you want Big Brother looking over your shoulder as you shop on the weekend? Should parents be able to use GPS-enabled implant chips to find their children if they're late in coming home for dinner? If children receive GPS-enabled implant chips at birth, at what age should they have the right to have them removed? Should the implant chips ever be removed? Think long and hard about these types of questions. You'll have to answer them in your lifetime.

The Digital Frontier

In Chapter 1, we alluded to the coming **digital economy**, marked by the electronic movement of all types of information—not only numbers, words, graphs, and photos but also physiological information such as voice recognition and synthesization, biometrics (your retina scan and breath for example), and 3D holograms. And in this chapter we've already introduced you to a variety of leading-edge technologies that will enable the arrival of the digital economy.

Are we there yet? Absolutely not. The full-fledged digital economy will not arrive for about ten or more years. In many parts of the world, the digital economy may not be realized for as many as 50 years. What seems to be the most major challenges—the technology or the willingness of people to embrace these new technologies? The answer is both. People are certainly resistant to change, no matter how good it may be. And, in spite of major strides and innovations in technology, it cannot yet fully support a digital economy.

You may have noticed this while working at home on the Internet. Your connection is really fast at school or work, but seems to slow to a crawl while at home. If so, you're experiencing the **last-mile bottleneck problem**, which occurs when information is travelling on the Internet over a very fast line for a certain distance and then comes near your home where it must travel over a slower line. For example, if you're using a 56 kbps modem to dial into the Internet, the information you request moves much slower from your telephone company to your home than it does from a Web site to your telephone company. Even if CAVEs, virtual reality, and other information-intensive applications were cheap and widespread, you probably still couldn't use them because of the last-mile bottleneck problem.

Again, just about everything we've introduced you to in this chapter—speech recognition, virtual reality, biometrics, CAVEs, Internet phone calls, micro-payments, and GPS-enabled implant chips—centres around enabling the upcoming digital economy. Let's now look specifically at two more technology innovations that will support a digital economy and the digital frontier—3D and digital cash.

THREE-DIMENSIONAL (3D) TECHNOLOGY

Real **three-dimensional (3D)** presentations of information give you the illusion that the object you're viewing is actually in the room with you. You can see the depth of the image, turn it to reflect different angles to see its various perspectives, and in some ways understand the density of the object. 3D is a fundamental technology for other technologies such as virtual reality and CAVEs. In fact, it is essential for them. However, widespread use of 3D is not here yet. For example, most spreadsheet software offer you pseudo-3D graphs by incorporating shades and shadows to simulate depth and angles. But you're not seeing those graphs in true 3D form.

The only real obstacle to widespread 3D use is speed. It takes a lot of computing horsepower to manipulate and display 3D images. And it takes significant throughput across the Internet to pipe 3D Web sites into your home. But 3D is a just a matter of time—perhaps a couple of years.

DIGITAL CASH

When the digital economy arrives, so must digital money. Coins and folding cash have no real value—they are simply surrogate representations of value. They have become the standard on which the worldwide economy works because it's much easier to pay for products and services with them than it is to use gold and silver. It makes sense then that, in a digital economy, money will also be digital.

In Chapter 5, and earlier in this chapter, we discussed micro-payments, a technique for making a purchase for a small amount of money over the Internet. Micro-

FACIAL RECOGNITION SOFTWARE AT THE AIRPORT

Airport security is now a must. And most airports and airlines are no longer relying on government-issued forms of identification for determining who should and who should not be allowed on planes. Instead, they're relying on facial recognition software such as FaceIt, a joint-venture product of ARINC and Visionics Corporation. FaceIt creates a digital map of a person's face and compares it to a database that contains the facial images of unwanted flyers and known terrorists.

Facial recognition software plays an important role in the use of biometrics for providing and authenticating identification. FaceIt's ARGUS system can handle an unlimited number of video cameras capturing facial images and comparing them to a database that is also unlimited in size. To learn more about FaceIt, visit ARINC (www.arinc.com) and Identix (www.identix.com).[7]

payments are a small (no pun intended) part of the much larger picture called digital cash. **Digital cash** (also called **electronic cash** or **e-cash**) is an electronic representation of cash.

To use digital cash, you must first purchase it from an electronic bank (see Figure 9.6). You can do this by sending real cash in the mail, using a debit or credit card, or actually opening an account with the electronic bank and requesting that an amount of digital cash be deducted from your balance and sent to you. Whatever the case, the electronic bank will electronically send you your digital cash files. For example, you could request $100 in digital cash in $20 increments. What you would end up with is five digital cash files, each representing $20 on your hard disk.

Figure 9.6

How Digital Cash Will Work on the Internet

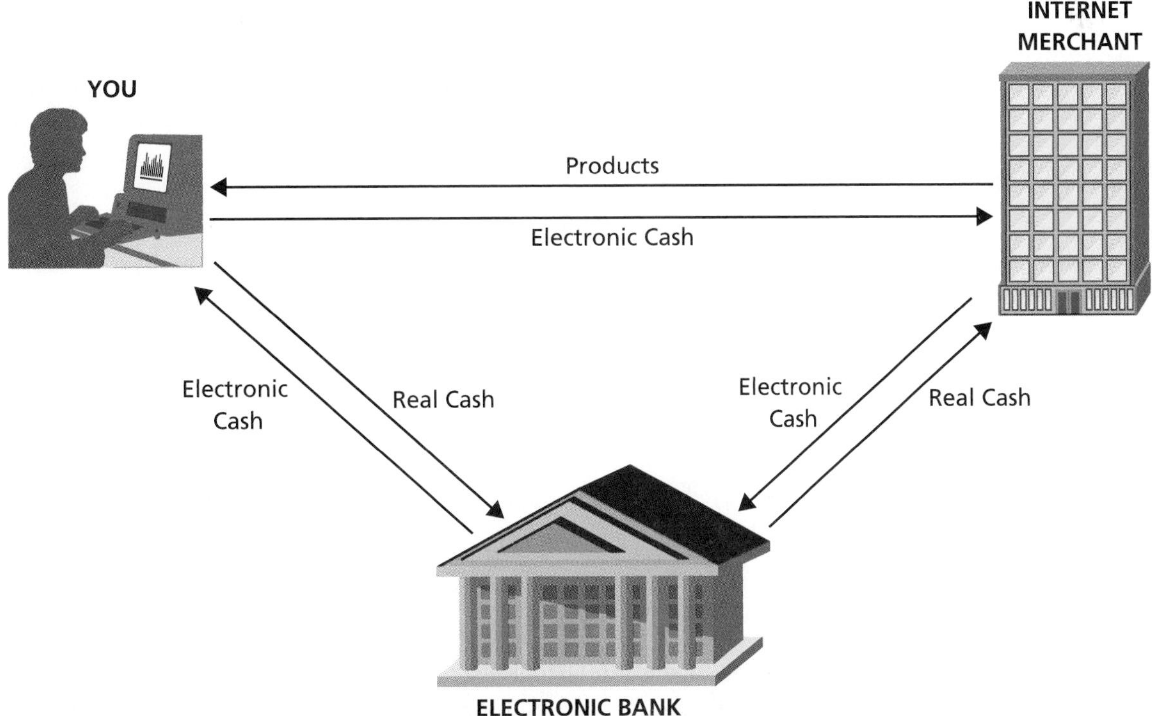

Of course, in the case of micro-payments, you may have hundreds of digital cash files, ranging in value from a nickel to 50 cents. Now all you have to do is find a product or service on the Internet you want to buy. You would send the merchant the appropriate number of digital cash files to equal the purchase amount. The merchant could then use those digital cash files to buy other merchandise or return it to the electronic bank for real money.

The concept is actually quite simple when you think about it. The implementation, however, has turned out to be extremely difficult, for many reasons including the following:

- If your system crashes and your digital cash files are wiped clean, you've lost your money. It's rather like losing your wallet. The electronic bank will not replace the files.
- There are no standards for how digital cash should look. So a digital cash file from one electronic bank may not look like digital cash from another electronic bank. That makes many merchants very hesitant to accept digital cash.
- Digital cash makes money laundering easy. Because none of your personal information travels with the digital cash when you use it to make a purchase, it's extremely difficult to tell where it came from. So illegally obtained cash can be easily exchanged for digital cash.
- Digital cash travels across the vast Internet and is susceptible to being stolen. Digital information (which includes digital cash) is easy to steal and hard to trace. This may be the single biggest obstacle to the widespread use of digital cash.

In spite of the above challenges and many others, digital cash is destined to take its place as a standard technology. The real question is how soon.

The Rebirth of E-Commerce

In the late 20th century and the early part of the 21st century (which seems almost odd to say), e-commerce was touted as the next big business frontier. Venture capitalists and individuals alike poured literally trillions of dollars into dot-com businesses. Most of those dot-coms had no idea what they were doing and could very seldom show a clear and reasonable "path to profitability" ("P2P"). Of course, the e-commerce balloon popped in the middle of the year 2000. As a result, many "millionaires on paper" became "paupers on paper" ("POP") overnight.

But e-commerce as a business principle survived—the dot-coms who failed to implement it correctly did not and became "dot-bombs." Over the next ten years or so we will see a strong resurgence in the e-commerce area, this time led by companies backed by sound business principles and clear paths to profitability. As you witness this, you'll see some interesting trends, including the broadening of e-government and the explosion of consumer-to-consumer (C2C) e-commerce.

BROADENING OF E-GOVERNMENT

In Chapter 5, we briefly introduced you to the role of government in e-commerce, known as e-government. Within the e-government arena, there are four primary focuses (see Figure 9.7):

- **Government-to-government (G2G)**. Limited to performing electronic commerce activities within a single nation's government focusing on vertical integration (local, municipal, provincial, and federal) and horizontal integration (within and among the various branches and agencies)

- **Government-to-business (G2B).** The electronic commerce activities performed between a government and its business partners for such purposes as purchasing direct and indirect materials, soliciting bids for work, and accepting bids for work
- **Government-to-consumer (G2C).** The electronic commerce activities performed between a government and its citizens or consumers, including paying taxes, registering vehicles, and providing information and services
- **International government-to-government (IG2G).** The electronic commerce activities performed between two or more governments, including providing foreign aid

You should take an interest in e-government for two reasons. First, many e-government applications will have a direct impact on your personal and business life. In the not-too-distant future, the Canada Customs and Revenue Agency will no longer accept paper-based income tax returns. That is, you'll be using G2C to submit your tax forms electronically. Many governmental agencies are also using G2B to send out and accept bids for work. They simply refuse to work with businesses that cannot perform this electronic commerce activity. If your organization can't, don't count on getting government contracts.

Most importantly, there are substantial career opportunities in the e-government arena. Governments of all types desperately need motivated knowledge workers skilled in the creation and execution of all types of e-commerce initiatives. It's a business segment worth looking into.

EXPLOSION OF C2C E-COMMERCE

Of all the types of private-sector e-commerce activities—B2B, B2C, C2C, and C2B—the least revenue to be made right now is in the C2C (consumer-to-consumer) space.

Figure 9.7

The Primary Focuses of E-Government

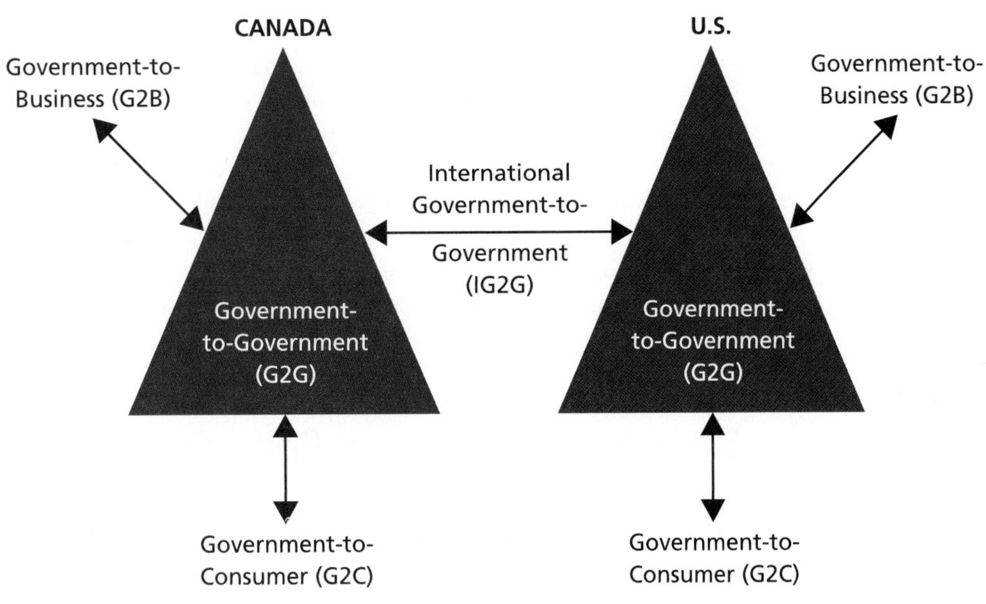

THE GLOBAL PERSPECTIVE

BUYING SODA WITH A CELL PHONE

In many European, especially Scandinavian, countries, you won't find a coin slot on soda vending machines. No, it's not because the sodas are free or because there's an extremely high criminal and vandalism rate. It's just that you have to buy the soda with your cell phone.

On the machine is a telephone number you call. When you do, the the soda machine is automatically triggered so you can make a selection. The best part is that the cost of the soda is charged to your cell phone bill. No more trying to find the right change. No more trying to get the creases out of a dollar bill. Of course, at the end of every month you still have to pay, but it is indeed convenient.

This is an example of how B2C (business-to-consumer) e-commerce is beginning to incorporate non-traditional computing technologies. Within the context of C2C (consumer-to-consumer) e-commerce, it should help you expand your mind and think of endless and wild possibilities for selling products and services to other consumers.

C2C e-commerce will require that everyone "think outside the box," or "beyond your ears" as we like to put it. Don't rule out any idea, no matter how strange or far-fetched. Thomas Watson, CEO and chairman of IBM in 1943, stated, "I think there is a world market for maybe five computers." He was definitely wrong and, to some extent, narrow-minded in his futuristic views. Don't make the same mistake.

But we expect that to change rather dramatically in the next several years. eBay is a good example. It's really just a cyber market in which consumers buy and sell products from and to each other. eBay doesn't guarantee the quality or authenticity of any products or services sold in its auction format. It simply provides a convenient mechanism for allowing consumers to gather and buy and sell products and services.

But consider the impacts of push technologies, m-commerce, digital cash and micro-payments, wearable computers, and even GPS-enabled implant chips. You could, for example, drive around your neighbourhood in search of garage sales. As you neared one, your GPS-enabled implant chip would trigger someone's personal computer that would call you on your cell phone and notify you what they have for sale and even provide you with driving directions. Once you arrive at the garage sale and find something to buy, you could make a digital cash or micro-payment transfer.

Of course, garage sales aren't the only possibility. You may someday be able to create and store a C2C Web site on a personal digital assistant (PDA). People would access your PDA, view the products you have to sell, and then make digital cash payments. Throughout the day, your PDA would constantly update your inventory records and notify you instantly of any stockouts. At the end of the day, your PDA would display to whom you need to send what products and where to send them.

These are not far-fetched ideas. Right now, we think in terms of setting up e-commerce Web sites and hosting them on Web server computers. That will change someday and your home computer, wearable computer, or even PDA will become a server that hosts your site and includes all the necessary e-commerce software. When that happens, expect C2C e-commerce to explode.

The Most Important Considerations

Throughout this chapter, we've been discussing some key emerging trends and technologies. They are certainly exciting and hold great promise that the future will be dynamic and changing, to say the least.

THE GLOBAL PERSPECTIVE

CREATING A WIRELESS INTELLIGENT HOME

Zensys, a bleeding-edge technology developer, recently announced its plan to create a wireless digital control system, called Z-Wave, for the typical homeowner. As Michael Dodge, Zensys' vice-president of marketing, explained it, "Z-Wave will truly make the 'intelligent home' available to everyone, by allowing the average consumer to effectively control his lighting, appliances, heating, air conditioning, and other home systems at a reasonable cost."

Z-Wave will allow a homeowner to connect each home appliance to a central device such as a computer or even a PDA. He or she then uses the latter device to control the appliances. This could include turning on water sprinklers, setting a freezer to defrost, and starting a VCR, all while perhaps driving down the road several hundred miles away.

Your home of the future may be more than you can ever imagine.[8]

As we close this chapter and potentially your studies in this course, let's take a close look at five key topics. Each is a culmination in some way of the material you've learned in this course. Each is inescapable and you will have to deal with them sooner or later. Finally, each is vitally important and reaches far beyond the technologies that either necessitate or support them. For you, these last few pages are a chance to reflect on what you've learned and place that knowledge within the bigger picture.

The five important considerations are:

- The necessity of information technology
- Closing the great digital divide
- Technology for the betterment of people and society
- Exchanging privacy for convenience
- Ethics, ethics, ethics

THE NECESSITY OF INFORMATION TECHNOLOGY

Like it or not, information technology is a necessity today. It's hard to imagine a world without it. Just as we need electricity to function on an everyday basis, we need IT.

Of course, that doesn't mean you should adopt IT for the its own sake. Rather, you need to carefully evaluate each technology and determine if it will help you become more productive, enhance your personal life, enrich your learning, or move your organization in the direction of its strategic goals and initiatives.

Information technology is no panacea. If you throw technology at a business process that doesn't work correctly, the result is that you'll simply perform that process incorrectly millions of times faster per second. At the same time, you can ill afford to ignore technology when it will help you and your organization become more efficient, effective, and innovative.

CLOSING THE GREAT DIGITAL DIVIDE

We must, as a human race, completely eliminate the great digital divide. The power of technology needs to be realized on a worldwide scale. We cannot afford to have any technology-challenged nation or culture (within reason). If you live and work in a technology-rich country, don't keep it to yourself. When possible, take it to other countries by creating international business partnerships and strategic alliances. The world will benefit greatly from your efforts.

ON YOUR OWN

NECESSITY, CONVENIENCE, AND PRIVACY

As you consider your own use of technology, it's important that you consider that use within the context of necessity, convenience, and your own privacy. You really have two questions to answer. They are:

1. *Necessity.* If you truly need technology to perform a personal task, how much of your personal privacy are you willing to forgo?
2. *Convenience.* If you can use technology to make your life more convenient (but your use of it isn't an absolute necessity), how much of your personal privacy are you willing to forgo?

Regarding question 1, provide your answer on a scale of 1 to 5. A 1 represents the fact that you would relinquish all your privacy to use technology that is a necessity. A 5 represents the fact that you would not relinquish any privacy even if it meant not being able to use a technology that was a necessity.

Regarding question 2, provide your answer on a scale of 1 to 5. A 1 represents the fact that you would relinquish all your privacy in exchange for using technologies that would make your life more convenient. A 5 represents the fact that you would not relinquish any of your privacy even if it meant not being able to use a technology that made your life more convenient.

Compare your answers with those of several classmates. How do you compare to everyone else?

TECHNOLOGY FOR THE BETTERMENT OF PEOPLE AND SOCIETY

The business world isn't just about making money. As you approach the development and use of technological innovations (or even standard technologies), think in terms of the betterment of people and society in general.

Medical research is performing marvellous work in the use of technology to treat ailments and cure diseases. But, if we are only profit-driven, we may never realize the benefits. For example, people are using virtual reality to teach autistic people to cope with increasingly complex situations. We know for a fact that this use of technology isn't making anyone any money. But sometimes it isn't about making money, but about helping people who face daily challenges far greater than ours. You're fortunate to be in an environment of learning. Give back when you have the chance.

EXCHANGING PRIVACY FOR CONVENIENCE

On a personal level, you need to consider how much of your personal privacy you're giving up in exchange for convenience. The extreme example is GPS-enabled implant chips. The convenience is knowing where you are and being able to get directions to your destination. But you're obviously giving up some privacy. And convenience can take many forms. When you use a discount card at a grocery store to take advantage of sales, that store then tracks your purchasing history in great detail. You can bet the store will use that information to sell you more tailored products.

It really is a tradeoff. In today's technology-based world, you give up privacy when you register for sweepstakes on certain Web sites. You give up privacy just surfing the Web because tracking software monitors your activities. Even when you click on a banner ad, the Web site you go to knows where you came from. Some such tradeoffs may seem insignificant, but small ones add up to a big one over time.

Because you are very much a part of this, it's often hard to see the big picture and understand that every day you're giving up just a little more privacy in exchange for a little more convenience. Don't ever think that organizations won't use the information they're capturing about you. They're capturing it so they can use it. Of course, much of it will be used to better serve you as a customer, but some of it may not.

ETHICS, ETHICS, ETHICS

And, as our final note to you, we cannot overstress the importance of ethics. Ethics guide your behaviour that affects other people. And the ethics of others guide their behavior that affects you. We realize that business is business and that businesses need to make money to survive. But they shouldn't do it to the personal detriment of people. It's quite possible to be very ethical and very successful. That's our challenge to you.

Summary: Student Learning Outcomes Revisited

1. **Describe why information filtering is becoming important and the two trends that will support information filtering.** Information filtering is becoming important because the information age has created a glut of information. Two trends that will support information filtering include:
   - **Push technology.** An environment in which businesses and organizations come to you with information, services, and product offerings based on your profile
   - **Information supplier convergence.** A merging of all types of organizations that provide information and access to information
2. **Describe the movement toward intellectual computing, including automatic speech understanding and the role of people in decision making.** Right now, the key term in artificial intelligence is "artificial." But much research is under way to create truly intelligent computer systems. If these systems are created, you'll be able to carry on a normal conversation with your computer through automatic speech understanding. Everyone must realize, however, that computers—no matter how smart they may be—will never be able to grasp and use human intuition, insight, and feeling. So the final decision must always rest with a person, not a computer.
3. **Define biometrics, automatic speech recognition, virtual reality, and CAVEs as they relate to changes in physiological interaction.** Most people use a keyboard, mouse, and monitor to work with a computer on a physical level. This is rapidly changing to an environment that will include purely physiological interactions. Key technologies here include:
   - **Biometrics.** The use of your physical characteristics—such as your fingerprint, the blood vessels in the retina of your eye, the sound of your voice, or perhaps even your breath—to provide identification
   - **Automatic speech recognition (ASR).** A system that not only captures spoken words but also distinguishes word groupings to form sentences
   - **Virtual reality.** A three-dimensional computer simulation in which you actively and physically participate
   - **CAVEs (cave automatic virtual environments).** Special 3D virtual reality rooms that can display images of other people and objects located in other CAVEs all over the world
4. **Describe the various technology innovations and trends that will increase portability and mobility.** To further increase portability (the ability to easily carry around technology) and mobility (what you can do with your technology as you carry it around), you can look toward the following technologies:
   - *Free Internet phone calls.* Using your computer and the Internet to make free long-distance phone calls
   - **Micro-payments.** Techniques to facilitate the exchange of small amounts of money for an Internet transaction
   - **Financial cybermediaries.** Internet-based companies that make it easy for one person to pay another over the Internet

- **Wearable computers.** Fully equipped computers that you wear as a piece of clothing similar to the way you would carry your cell phone on your belt
- **Implant chips.** Technology-enabled microchips implanted into the human body
- **Global positioning system (GPS).** A collection of 24 earth-orbiting satellites that continuously transmit radio signals to determine your current longitude, latitude, speed, and direction of movement

5. **Discuss the challenges of and technological innovations for the coming digital frontier.** The coming digital frontier, also called the **digital economy**, will the marked by the electronic movement of all types of information. One challenge of the digital frontier is to overcome the **last-mile bottleneck problem**, which occurs when information is travelling over the Internet over a very fast line for a certain distance and then comes near your home where it must travel over a slower line. Technological innovations for the digital frontier include:
   - **3D.** Technology presentations of information that give you the illusion that the object you're viewing is actually in the room with you
   - **Digital cash.** Electronic representations of cash
6. **Describe the broadening of e-government and the coming C2C explosion as they relate to the rebirth of e-commerce.** The broadening of e-government will come in four forms:
   - **Government-to-government (G2G).** Within a country's government focusing on vertical and horizontal integration
   - **Government-to-business (G2B).** Between government and its business partners
   - **Government-to-consumer (G2C).** Between government and its citizens or consumers
   - **International government-to-government (IG2G)**—between two or more governments

   You can also expect to see an explosion of C2C (consumer-to-consumer) e-commerce as part of the rebirth of e-commerce. This will enable individuals to easily buy and sell products from and to each other.

CLOSING CASE STUDY ONE

AIRTEXTING—WAVE YOUR CELL PHONE MESSAGE IN THE AIR

North American manufacturers of cell phones and providers of cell phone service are heavily targeting one select group of customers—teenagers. In North America, only about 38 percent of all teenagers have cell phones, compared to over 80 percent in most European countries and some Asian countries. Cell phone providers and manufacturers know that there is plenty of room to grow in the teenage market, not only because 62 percent don't currently have cell phones but also because teenagers are very quick to embrace and use new technologies. Those same companies know that teenagers aren't as frugal with money and tend to spend much more time talking on a cell phone than adults.

Of course, cell phones aren't really new technologies, but what you can do with them is. Motorola, for example, manufacturers a cell phone with FM radio capability (XM radio may not be far behind). Samsung offers a cell phone service that includes AOL Instant Messenger (with audio and limited video). Sony Ericsson offers cell phones with cameras and multimedia messaging.

One of the future leaders in this dynamic and changing industry is Wildseed. It regularly holds cell phone focus groups just for teenagers. Wildseed has determined that teenagers have three cell phone concerns:

1. *Visual appeal.* A cell phone should make a fashion statement. Teenagers also believe that cell phones should be a statement of individuality ("I want a cell phone that doesn't look like anyone else's").
2. *Functionality.* A cell phone should do more than just support phone-calling capabilities.
3. *Price.* Long-term calling plans are not the way to go.

VISUAL APPEAL

Wildseed has tested numerous cell phone designs on teenagers. One cell phone holder was designed to be worn like a garter belt, and it flopped in a big way. According to one young man in the focus group, "Is a guy supposed to wear that?" And a young girl in the focus group commented, "It looks like something for a prostitute." But Wildseed did hit upon a good idea. It now manufactures "smart skins," cell phone covers that have an embedded computer chip. According to what the teenager is wearing, he or she can quickly change the design of the cell phone face plate. While skateboarding one day, for example, a young man could change his cell phone face plate to a splashy rendition of hard colours such as red, yellow, and green.

FUNCTIONALITY

Cell phones are certainly no longer devices just for talking. Most have e-mail capabilities and support surfing the Web. Those are no longer a competitive advantage for any cell phone manufacturer. Wildseed tried a couple of new ideas on its teenage focus groups—the first failed and the second met with great success. The first additional functionality was a cell phone that supported Morse code. No one liked that, because no one knew how to send and interpret Morse code. Additionally, teenage girls stated they would have problem sending Morse code, because their long fingernails made it difficult to type. The second was "airtexting." Using an airtexting-enabled cell phone, you type in a brief message (e.g., "Call me") and then wave your cell phone back and forth in the air. Blinking red lights on the cell phone are synchronized to display the message in the air. That way, someone across the room can receive your message without having to use a cell phone. You may have seen airtexting clocks that have an arm that moves back and forth through the air and seems to suspend the time and day in the air. As one young lady put it, "That's tight."

PRICE

Price is a major drawback for most teenagers, not necessarily the per-minute charge but rather the long-term contract that must be signed. In the United States, as opposed to most other countries, you must typically sign a six-month or one-year contract for cell phone service. That precludes many teenagers getting a cell phone because they have to get their parents to co-sign. Unfortunately, Wildseed is a manufacturer of cell phones and not a cell phone service provider.[9]

Questions

1. The role and the purpose of cell phones have certainly changed over the past few years. Not too long ago, business professionals were the only ones to use them. Now, over one in every three teenagers have a cell phone and about 99 percent of them don't use them for business. Are cell phones becoming a technology of convenience and not necessity? If people use them just for the convenience of communicating anywhere anytime, are they really a necessity? On the other hand, if you use a cell phone as your primary mode of communications, is it no longer just a convenience?

2. Airtexting sounds like a good idea. From across a room, you'll be able to easily send someone a short message without using your minutes or having the other person's phone ring. But you are giving up some privacy. If you airtext your message, everyone in the room will be able to see it. Are you willing to give up some amount of privacy to use an airtexting feature? Why or why not? What about while being in a classroom? Should you be able to airtext a message in the middle of class? Does your school have a policy requiring you to turn off your cell phone when entering a classroom? If so, should this policy apply to airtexting? Why or why not?

3. Functionality is very important for cell phones. What types of functionality does your cell phone support beyond making and receiving phone calls? If you could design the "perfect" cell phone, what additional functionality would you include?

4. Do you foresee a day when cell phones will be the standard "phone" and we'll simply do away with land-based phone lines? It's probably going to happen. How easy will it then be to move? If you have a cell phone, will you need to change your phone number? Your area code? If cell phones do become the standard, how will you access the Internet at home?

CLOSING CASE STUDY TWO

STADIUMS OF THE FUTURE

Several industries always seem to be leaders in using technological innovations. The movie industry, for example, quickly embraced 3D technologies and animation to create such movies as *Shrek*, *Terminator*, and *The Matrix*, all blockbusters in part because of their use of technological innovations. The movie industry is even exploring how to create and use virtual actors and actresses. Real people may no longer be used in movies—instead, likenesses of them will be computer-generated and -controlled.

Another, related industry always on the forefront of the use of new technologies is professional sports. It may not be an industry that immediately popped into your mind, but it must strive daily to attract and retain large audiences (just check out the salaries many professional athletes make and you'll understand why). The professional sports industry wants your business in one of two ways—by having you either watch a sporting event on television or attend a sporting event. For the latter, sports franchises are building some unbelievable arenas and stadiums that make use of technological innovations. Consider these technology-based activities that you'll be able to perform in the stadium of the future.

ORDER AND PAY FOR FOOD AND BEVERAGES AT YOUR SEAT

In future stadiums, you won't have to catch the attention of a stadium vendor selling popcorn, beverages, and hot dogs. Instead, you'll use a small keypad at your seat to view a menu and order exactly what you want. You'll use the same keypad to pay for your order by swiping your credit card. Your order will be transmitted to a kitchen where it's made and then given to a runner who will deliver it to you.

WATCH REPLAYS ON A PRIVATE SCREEN

Your seat will also have a private screen that folds down and within your armrest. At any point during the game, you can unfold the screen and view replays. You'll be able to choose from a variety of camera angles, and you'll be able to zoom in and out.

VIEW HOLOGRAPHIC REPLAYS SUSPENDED IN THE AIR

Ideally, you'll be able to watch replays not on a flat two-dimensional screen but rather suspended in the air in front of you as a holographic image. These holographic images will be completely three-dimensional, allowing you to view them at different angles. Many believe that much of the audience will opt to watch an entire game in this fashion in preference to using binoculars.

PARTICIPATE IN REAL-TIME INTERVIEWS WITH PLAYERS

Almost all player interviews occur after the game is over and are primarily viewed by people watching a game on television. In a future stadium, you'll be able to request and participate in a real-time interview with a player during the game. For example, after a player makes a great catch in a baseball game to end the inning, you'll be able to interview that player and ask him or her how the catch was made.

VIEW STATISTICS ON ANY PLAYER

You'll also be able to use your screen and keypad to pull up any sort of statistics you might want to view. These could include career statistics for a specific player, season statistics for a specific team, current game statistics for a specific player, and even records within a particular sport. You'll even be able to request that this type of information be presented in graphical form, perhaps accompanied by an audio analysis provided by sport or statistics expert.

VIEW SCORES AND HIGHLIGHTS OF OTHER GAMES

And you certainly won't have to wait for a stadium to display scores and highlights of other games on a hanging big-screen monitor. You'll be able to view scores and highlights of other games at the press of a button. You'll even be able to attend one game and watch another completely on your screen.

SEND MESSAGES TO PEOPLE IN THE STADIUM

If you buy tickets the day before a sporting event, it's often difficult to get your group all seated together, and you miss out on some of the fun associated with attending a sporting event with friends. That won't be a problem in future stadiums. You'll soon be able to use videoconferencing software to communicate with any other person in the stadium.

Questions

1. Will this type of stadium of the future further widen the digital divide? It makes sense that people who don't have enough money to buy personal technologies will also not have enough money to attend sporting events. Will that group of people fall further behind because they can't take advantage of technological innovations in the stadium of the future? Or is this use of technology one of convenience and not necessity?
2. How do you think players will react to being interviewed during the middle of a game? Can you think of some professional athletes who would not want to do this? Can you think of some professional athletes who would want to do this? Many governing bodies of professional sports such as the NHL and NBA require that athletes be available before and after the game for interviews. Should those same governing bodies require that athletes be available during games for interviews? Why or why not?
3. Do you believe that stadiums of the future will encourage more people to attend sporting events? Why or why not? Right now, you can sit at home, watch picture-in-picture to see multiple games, and change channels to see yet other games. And let's not forget that these stadiums of the future will be extremely expensive to build and maintain, so you can expect ticket prices to go up as well.
4. In this chapter, we introduced you to several leading-edge and bleeding-edge technologies. Of those that we didn't highlight in this Case Study, which do you believe could be used to enhance the experience of attending a sporting event? How would you use them? Would the use of those technologies further encourage you to attend a sporting event? Why or why not?

Key Terms and Concepts

automatic speech recognition (ASR), 373
biometrics, 372
CAVE (cave automatic virtual environment), 375
digital cash (electronic cash, e-cash), 381
digital economy, 379
feature analysis, 373
financial cybermediary, 377
global positioning system (GPS), 378
glove, 374
government-to-business (G2B), 383
government-to-consumer (G2C), 383
government-to-government (G2G), 382
headset, 374
holographic device, 375
implant chip, 378
information supplier convergence, 370
international government-to-government (IG2G), 383
language processing, 373
last-mile bottleneck problem, 380
micro-payment, 377
pattern classification, 373
push technology, 369
three-dimensional (3D), 380
virtual reality, 374
walker, 374
wearable computer, 377

Short-Answer Questions

1. Why is it becoming important to filter information?
2. How will push technologies work?
3. How does automatic speech understanding differ from automatic speech recognition?
4. Why are currently popular input and output technologies such as keyboards, mice, and

monitors physical interfaces and not physiological interfaces?

5. What are the three steps in automatic speech recognition?
6. What are the three types of input and output devices commonly used in virtual reality?
7. What are three known applications of virtual reality?
8. How is a CAVE a form of holographic device?
9. How can you make a free long-distance phone call using the Internet?
10. Why are micro-payments important for increasing portability and mobility?
11. What companies are currently manufacturing wearable computers?
12. What two purposes do implant chips serve?
13. What is the last-mile bottleneck problem?
14. In what ways will C2C e-commerce explode?

Assignments and Exercises

1. **RESEARCHING WEARABLE COMPUTERS.** One of the leading-edge manufacturers of wearable computers is Xybernaut. Connect to its Web site (www.xybernaut.com) and research its Poma wearable computer. What is its CPU speed? How much RAM does it include? What functions can you perform with a Poma? What sort of technology devices can you add to a Poma? Is the Poma advanced enough and cheap enough that you would consider buying one? Why or why not?
2. **INFORMATION SUPPLIER CONVERGENCE IN YOUR AREA.** Do a little research of the various organizations in your area that either provide information to you (such as a cable TV company) or provide you with access to information (such as an ISP). Which of those organizations can provide you with more than one type of information? Which of those organizations can provide you with information and also the access to information?
3. **FINDING A GOOD AUTOMATIC SPEECH RECOGNITION SYSTEM.** Research the Web for automatic speech recognition (ASR) systems. Make a list of the ones you find. What are the prices of each? Are they speaker-independent or speaker-dependent? Do they support continuous speech recognition or discrete speech recognition? What sort of add-on vocabularies can you purchase? How comfortable would you feel speaking the contents of a term paper as opposed to typing it? Would have to be more or less organized to use speech recognition as opposed to typing? Why?
4. **UNDERSTANDING THE RELATIONSHIPS BETWEEN TRENDS AND TECHNOLOGICAL INNOVATIONS.** In this chapter, we presented you with numerous key technologies and how they relate to six important trends. (See Figure 9.1 for the list of technologies and trends.) For each trend, identify all the technologies presented in this chapter that can have an impact. For each technology that you do identify, provide a short discussion of how it might have an impact.
5. **UNDERSTANDING CYBERSICKNESS IN VIRTUAL REALITY.** Virtual reality systems do have downsides to them, most notably eye strain, flashbacks, and simulator sickness. Do some research and provide a description of each of these. As you describe each, also provide a recommendation on how to overcome it.
6. **MAKING A PHONE CALL ON THE INTERNET.** Visit the Internet and find a Web site that provides free long-distance phone calling. Net2Phone is one such Web site but there are many others. Download and install the necessary software and subscribe as a user. Now make a phone call to someone you know. What was your overall experience? What was the quality of the call? How did you go about scheduling the call with the other person? Did you ever notice a "crackle" in the communications? Should organizations be using these types of Web sites for long-distance phone calls to cut down on their expenses?
7. **RESEARCHING INTELLIGENT HOME APPLIANCES.** Visit a local store and find three home appliances that contain some sort of intelligence. For each appliance, prepare a short report that includes the following information:

- A description and price for the intelligent home appliance
- The "intelligent" features of the appliance
- How those features make the appliance better than the non-intelligent version

8. **RESEARCHING E-GOVERNMENT SERVICES.** Visit the Web sites for your local, municipal, and provincial governments. As you do, find electronic services that you would commonly use. What are they? Can you really sign up for these services electronically or can you simply download forms that you must fill out and send via regular mail? Why is it so important that various government agencies get into the "e" game?

9. **FINDING TECHNOLOGICAL INNOVATIONS.** Do some research on the Internet and in various technology-oriented magazines. Find at least three technological innovations that we did not specifically discuss in this chapter. For each, prepare a one-minute presentation. Your presentation should include:

   - A brief description of the innovation
   - References that other people can use to learn more about the innovation
   - Your own thoughts concerning how the innovation might change our lives

Discussion Questions

1. Right now there is much pending legislation in many states that would make it illegal for people to use a cell phone while driving a car. The reason is that society has already noticed a significant increase in the number of traffic accidents in which one of the people in the accident was using a cell phone. Think beyond that for a moment and include wearable computers. As this new technology becomes more widely available, isn't it possible for someone to be driving a car while using a computer? Should the government enact legislation to prevent it? Why or why not?

2. In a push technology environment, businesses and organizations will come to you with information, services, and product offerings based on your profile. How is a push technology environment different from mass mailings and spam? Is it an invasion of your privacy to have organizations calling you on your cell phone every time you come near a store? Why or why not? Should you be able to opt in or out of these offerings? Is this really any different from someone leaving a flyer at your house or on your car while it's parked in a parking lot?

3. What's your take on intellectual computing? Do you believe that it's really possible to create computer systems that are capable of true human-like thinking? Why or why not? Refer back to Chapter 4 and our discussion of artificial intelligence systems including expert systems, neural networks, and genetic algorithms. Which, in its current form, most closely mimics human thinking and behaviour? What advances will have to be made in that AI technology to make it truly intelligent?

4. There are three steps in automatic speech recognition (ASR)—feature analysis, pattern classification, and language processing. Which is most challenging for a computer to perform? Why? Which is least challenging? Why? If ASR systems are to become automatic speech understanding systems, which step must see the greatest improvement in its capabilities? Why?

5. Micro-payments, financial cybermediaries, and digital cash are destined to greatly impact the use of coins and folding cash. What sort of future do you foresee if we do away completely with traditional forms of currency and just use electronic forms? Will this help eliminate the digital divide or will the digital divide prove a barrier to the widespread use of electronic forms of payment? Justify your answer.

6. What's your take on GPS-enabled implant chips? Should we all have them? Why or why not? Some U.S. states are now releasing criminals on parole and making them wear GPS-enabled bracelets so their every movement can be tracked? In your view, is this appropriate? Why or why not? Should any groups of people be required to wear some type of GPS-enabled tracking technology? If not, why not? If so, who are those groups and why should they have to wear such devices?

7. Overcoming the last-mile bottleneck problem is definitely key as we move toward a complete digital frontier and digital economy. Contact two local Internet service providers in your area. Which offer technical solutions, such as DSL and cable modems, that will help you reduce the time it takes to send and receive information over the Internet? What is the monthly charge of the various options? Is it worth it to you to have high-speed Internet access? Why or why not?

8. What are the ethical dilemmas associated with using facial recognition software? Is the use of this type of software really any different from a store asking to see your driver's licence when you use your credit card? Why or why not? Should the government be able to place digital video cameras on every street corner and use facial recognition software to monitor your movements? Why or why not?

REAL HOT Electronic Commerce

Continuing Your Education Through the Internet

Real HOT Links

For many of you, this course may mark the end of your endeavours in higher education. Indeed, you may be preparing right now to enter the business world by sending out résumés, participating in job interviews, and building an e-portfolio (see Skills Module 4). If so, we certainly hope you're letting the Internet help (see the Real HOT Electronic Commerce section in Chapter 1, "Using the Internet as a Tool to Find a Job"). For others of you, you may still have another year or two before completing your education. Whatever the case, you need to consider the current landscape of the business world and what it's going to take for you to compete now and in the future.

To be perfectly honest, it's a dog-eat-dog world out there. The competitive landscape of business is more intense than ever. And that competitiveness spills over into your personal life. Many of you are in school right now to get an education to better compete in the job market. But many knowledge workers are finding out that an undergraduate degree is simply not enough to compete in the business world.

So it is that many people are turning once again to higher education to obtain a master's degree, professional certification such as CA or CFP (certified financial planner), or perhaps even a Ph.D. in business. You may also be considering the same, either immediately upon graduation or sometime in the near future.

And, just like businesses, graduate schools (and schools in general) are using the Internet as a way to communicate information to you. Many are even offering online courses you can complete through the Internet to further your education.

On the Web site that supports this text (www.mcgrawhill.ca/college/haag), we've provided many links related to continuing your education through the Internet. These are a great starting point for completing this Real HOT section.

MASTER'S PROGRAMS

Many of you will undoubtedly choose to continue your education by obtaining a master's degree. The market for the best business positions is extremely competitive, with hiring organizations seeking individuals who can speak more than one language, have job experience, and have extended their educational endeavours beyond just getting an undergraduate degree.

Choose a couple of different graduate schools, visit their Web sites, and answer the following questions for each:

A. What school did you choose?

B. Does that school offer a graduate program in your area of interest?

C. Does the graduate program Web site contain biographical sketches of faculty?

D. Can you apply online?

E. Is there a major benefactor for the school? If so, who is it?

F. Does the site list tuition and fee costs?

G. Does the site contain a list of the graduate courses offered in your area of interest?

GRADUATE SCHOOL INFORMATION AND TIPS

Before you begin your decision-making process concerning which graduate school to attend, you should gather a variety of material. For example, obtaining a directory of universities (both domestic and international) would be helpful. Perhaps even more importantly, you should ask yourself several questions. Are you ready for graduate school? Why are you considering going to graduate school? How do you determine which school is best for you on the basis of such issues as price, location, and area of specialization?

Many of these questions are very personal to you. For example, we can't help you determine if you're really ready for graduate school or answer why you're considering going to graduate school. But what we can do is point you toward some valuable resources on the Internet to help you answer some of your questions and find a wealth of information relating to universities. On the Web site that supports this text (www.mcgrawhill.ca/college/haag), we've included many links to those types of sites.

At your leisure, we recommend that you connect to several of these sites and see what they have to offer. Some simply provide a list of universities, whereas others may be particularly useful as you make that all-important decision.

TELE-EDUCATION (DISTANCE LEARNING)

Throughout this text, you've explored the concept of 24-hour connectivity through information technology. Using IT (part of which is the Internet), organizations today are sending out telecommuting employees, and medical and health facilities are establishing telemedicine practices. And your school may be doing the same—using IT to develop the environment of tele-education.

Tele-education—variously referred to as *e-education*, *distance learning*, *distributed learning*, and *online learning*—enables you to get an education without "going" to school. Quite literally, you can enroll in a school on the East Coast and live in Brandon, Manitoba, enjoying great winter skiing. Using various forms of IT (videoconferencing, e-mail, chat rooms, and the Internet), you can take courses from schools all over the world. Some of those schools even offer complete degree programs via IT.

As well, many for-profit organizations offer courses on the Internet that range from preparing for the CA exam to IT-focused courses such as Windows NT and COBOL programming. You should definitely connect to the Web site that supports this text (www.mcgrawhill.ca/college/haag) and view the list of sites related to tele-education. And if you're interested in taking online courses from a specific school, we recommend you connect to its Web site to determine if it offers courses over the Internet.

Connect to at least five sites and explore the possibilities of tele-education. As you do, consider the issues below.

A. Can you just take courses or must you enroll in a complete degree program?

B. What is the cost?

C. What process do you go through to enroll in a tele-education program?

D. How would you feel about staying at home instead of going to class?

E. How do tele-education programs foster interactivity between students and teachers?

F. How much do you think you would learn in a tele-education program compared to what you would learn in a traditional in-class program?

G. For what type of individual is a tele-education program best suited?

Go to the Online Learning Centre at www.mcgrawhill.ca/college/haag for quizzes, extra content, a searchable glossary, and more! Click on "Electronic Commerce Projects" for links to hundreds of Web sites.

Go to the text CD-ROM for data files, extra content, and Skills Modules on Microsoft Excel, Microsoft Access, HTML, and e-portfolios.

EXTENDED LEARNING MODULE C

COMPUTER HARDWARE AND SOFTWARE

Student Learning Outcomes

1. Define information technology (IT) and its two basic categories —hardware and software.
2. Describe categories of computers by size.
3. Compare the roles of personal productivity, vertical market, and horizontal market software.
4. Describe the roles of operating system and utility software as components of system software.
5. Define the purposes of the six major categories of hardware.

Introduction

In this Module, we cover the basics of computer hardware and software, including terminology, characteristics of various devices, and how everything works together to create a complete and usable computer system. If you've had a previous computing concepts course, this material will be a quick, solid review for you. If this is your first real exposure to hardware and software technologies, you'll definitely learn a great deal from this Module.

Information technology (IT) is any computer-based tool that people use to work with information and support the information and information-processing needs of an organization. So information technology (IT) is the Internet, a personal computer, a cell phone that can access the Web, a personal digital assistant you use for note-taking and appointment scheduling, presentation software you use to create a slideshow, a printer, a joystick or game pad for playing video games ... the list is almost endless.

All of these technologies help you perform specific information processing tasks. For example, a printer allows you to create a paper version of a document, the Internet connects you to people all over the world, a floppy disk allows you to store information for use a later time, and word processing software helps you create letters, memos, and term papers.

So do you need all of these various technologies? Yes and no. As you'll read throughout this Module, there are categories of both hardware and software. More than likely, you'll need some sort of technology within each category. But you certainly won't need every single piece of available technology.

A Quick Tour of Technology

There are two basic categories of technology. **Hardware** is the physical devices that make up a computer (often referred to as a *computer system*). **Software** is the set of instructions that your hardware executes to carry out a specific task for you. If you create a graph, you would use various hardware devices such as a keyboard to enter information and a monitor to see the graph, and you would use software such Microsoft Excel, the most popular spreadsheet software.

All hardware falls into one of six categories—here's a quick summary (see Figure C.1):

- An *input device* is a tool you use to capture information and commands.
- An *output device* is a tool you use to see, hear, or otherwise receive the results of your information processing requests.
- A **storage device** is a tool you use to store information for use at a later time.
- The *central processing unit (CPU)* is the actual hardware that interprets and executes the software instructions and coordinates how all the other hardware devices work together. *RAM*, or *random access memory*, is temporary storage that holds the information you're working with, the application software you're using, and the operating system software you're using.
- A **telecommunications device** is a tool you use to send information to and receive it from another person or location.
- *Connecting devices* include such things as parallel ports into which you would connect a printer and connector cords to connect your printer to the parallel port.

There are two main types of software—application and system. **Application software** is the software that enables you to solve specific problems or perform specific

Figure C.1

Six Categories of Computer Hardware

Mice and keyboards are the most popular input devices.

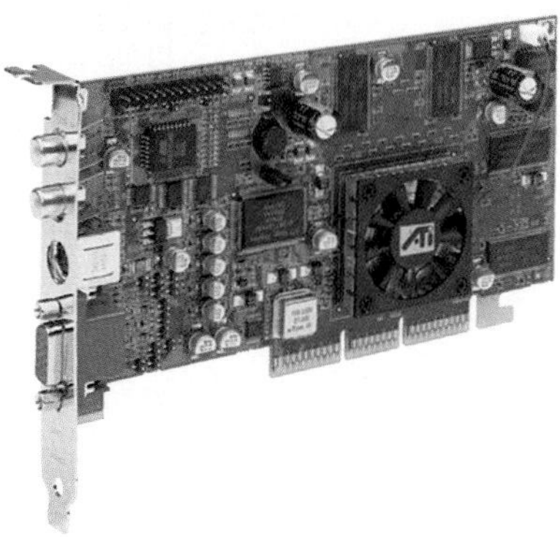

Video cards connect a monitor to the rest of the hardware.

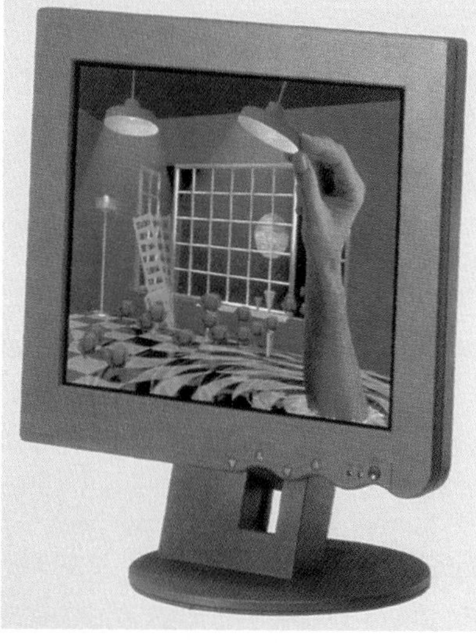

Monitors are the most common output devices.

Floppy disks are common storage devices.

The Intel Pentium 4 is a CPU.

tasks (see Figure C.2). Microsoft PowerPoint, for example, can help you create slides for a presentation, so it's application software. From an organizational perspective, payroll software, collaborative software such as videoconferencing (within groupware), and inventory management software are all examples of application software.

System software handles tasks specific to technology management and coordinates the interaction of all technology devices. System software includes both operating system software and utility software. **Operating system software** is system software that controls your application software and manages how your hardware devices work together. Popular personal operating system software includes Microsoft Windows XP, Microsoft Windows 2000 Me, Mac OS (for Apple computers), and Linux (an open source operating system). There are also operating systems for networks (Microsoft Windows NT is an example), operating systems for personal digital assistants (Windows CE is an example), and operating systems for just about every other type of technology configuration.

Utility software is software that provides additional functionality to your operating system. Utility software includes antivirus software, screensavers, disk optimization software, uninstaller software (for properly removing unwanted software), and a host of others. Just because utility software provides "additional" functionality doesn't mean that this type of software is optional. For example, antivirus software protects you from deadly computer viruses that can be very bad for your computer. You definitely need antivirus software.

So ends of our quick tour of technology. In the remainder of this Module we'll explore categories of computers by size, software in more detail, hardware in more

Figure C.2

Quicken and Excel Are Application Software Tools

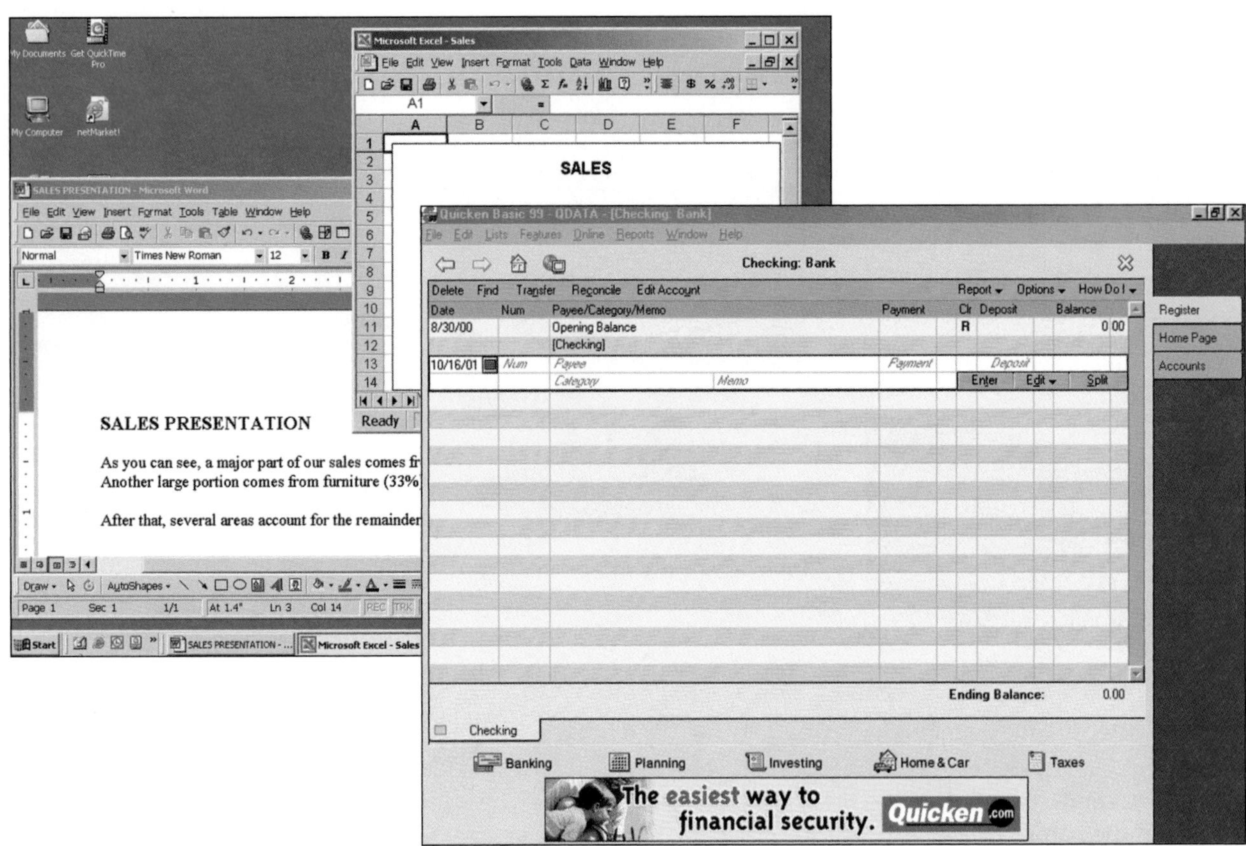

detail, and finally how all technology components work together to perform a specific task for you.

Categories of Computers by Size

Computers come in different shapes, sizes, and colours. Some are small enough that you can carry them around with you, while others are the size of a telephone booth. Size in some way equates to power and speed, and thus price.

PERSONAL DIGITAL ASSISTANTS (PDAs)

A **personal digital assistant (PDA)** is a small, handheld computer that helps you surf the Web and perform simple tasks such as note-taking, calendaring, appointment scheduling, and maintaining an address book (see Figure C.3). The PDA screen is touch-sensitive, allowing you to directly write on the screen with the screen capturing what you're writing. PDAs today cost from $200 to $500.

NOTEBOOK COMPUTERS

A **notebook computer** is a fully functional computer designed for you to carry around and run on battery power. Notebooks come equipped with all the technology to meet your personal needs and weigh as little as four pounds. If you need a fully functional computer in a variety of places—home, work, school, and/or on the road—then a notebook may be just the answer. Notebook computers range in price from about $800 to several thousand dollars.

DESKTOP COMPUTERS

A **desktop computer** is the most popular choice for personal computing needs. You can choose a desktop with a horizontal system box (the box is where the CPU, RAM, and storage devices are held) and place a monitor on top of it or choose one with a vertical system box (called a tower) that you usually place on the floor near your work area. Desktops range in price from a little less than $500 to several thousand dollars. Dollar for dollar, a desktop is faster and more powerful than a notebook with comparable characteristics.

Which you need—a PDA, notebook, or desktop computer—is a function of your needs. PDAs offer great portability and allow you to keep a calendar, send and receive e-mail, take short notes, and even access the Web. But they certainly can't help you write a term paper, build a Web site, or create a complex graph with statistical software. For any of those tasks, you would need either a notebook or desktop computer.

So there's another question. Say you need a computer that supports full word processing, spreadsheet, presentation, Web site development, and some other capabilities. Should you buy a notebook or a desktop? In short, you need to decide *where* you'll need your computer. If you need to use your computer at home and at school (or perhaps at work), then you should buy a notebook computer because it is in fact portable. But, if you think you might want a notebook because it would be nice to take it with you on vacation, think again. Do you really want to sit in your hotel room and work on your computer instead of having fun on the beach? Probably not.

Figure C.3

PDAs, Notebooks, and Desktops

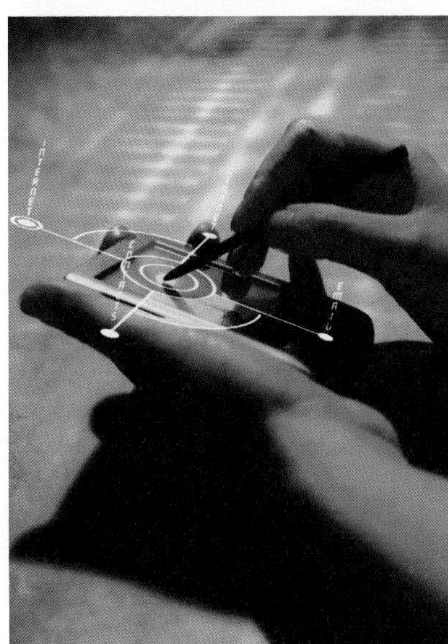

PDAs are small handheld computers.

Notebooks are fully functional portable personal computers.

Some desktops have vertical system boxes called "towers."

MINICOMPUTERS, MAINFRAME COMPUTERS, AND SUPERCOMPUTERS

PDAs, notebooks, and desktop computers are designed to meet your personal information processing needs. In business, however, many people often need to access and use the same computer simultaneously. In this case, businesses need computing technologies that multiple people can access and use at the same time. Computers of this type include minicomputers, mainframe computers, and supercomputers (see Figure C.4).

A **minicomputer** (sometimes called a **mid-range computer**) is designed to meet the computing needs of several people simultaneously in a small to medium-size business environment. Minicomputers are more powerful than desktop computers but also cost more, ranging in price from $5000 to several hundred thousand dollars. Businesses often use minicomputers as servers, either for creating a Web presence or as an internal computer on which shared information and software is placed. For this reason, minicomputers are well suited for business environments in which people need to share information, processing power, and/or certain peripheral devices such as high-quality, fast laser printers.

A **mainframe computer** (sometimes just called a **mainframe**) is designed to meet the computing needs of hundreds of people in a large business environment. They are a step up from minicomputers in size, power, capability, and cost. Mainframes can easily cost in excess of $1 million. With processing speeds greater than a trillion instructions per second (as against a typical desktop which can process only about 2.5 billion instructions per second), mainframes can easily handle the processing requests of hundreds of people simultaneously.

The fastest, most powerful, and most expensive type of computer is the **supercomputer**. Organizations such as NASA that are heavily involved in research and "number crunching" employ supercomputers because of the speed with which they can process information. Other large, customer-oriented businesses such as General Motors and Bell Canada employ supercomputers just to handle customer information and transaction processing.

How much do you really need to know about the technical specifics (CPU speed, storage disk capacity, and so on), prices, and capabilities of minicomputers, mainframe computers, and supercomputers? Not much, unless you plan to major in information technology. As a typical and well-informed knowledge worker you really only

Figure C.4

Minicomputers, Mainframes, and Supercomputers

Minicomputers are well suited for small to medium-size businesses.

Mainframe computers support the information processing tasks of large businesses.

Supercomputers are very expensive and fast "number crunchers."

need to know what we've stated above. What you should definitely concentrate on, though, is the technical specifics, prices, and capabilities of PDAs, notebooks, and desktop computers. These will be your companions for your entire business career. Learn and know them well.

Software—Your Intellectual Interface

The most important tool in your technology tool set is software. Software contains the instructions that your hardware executes to perform an information processing task for you. Software is really your *intellectual interface*, designed to automate processing tasks that you would undertake with your mind. Without software, your computer is just a very expensive doorstop. As we've stated before, there are two categories of software—application and system.

APPLICATION SOFTWARE

Application software is the software you use to meet your specific information processing needs, including payroll, customer relationship management, project management, training, word processing, and many, many others.

PERSONAL PRODUCTIVITY SOFTWARE **Personal productivity software** helps you perform personal tasks—such as writing a memo, creating a graph, and creating a slide presentation—that you might do even if you didn't use a computer. You're probably already familiar with some personal productivity software tools, including Microsoft Word and Excel, Netscape Communicator or Internet Explorer, and Quicken (personal finance software).

Skills Module 1 Decision Analysis—Excel

Skills Module 2 Database Design—Access

In fact, we have Modules in this text that help you learn how to use two of these tools—Skills Module 1 (for Microsoft Excel, spreadsheet software) and Skills Module 2 (for Microsoft Access, database management system software). Figure C.5 describes the ten major categories of personal productivity software and includes some of the more popular packages within each.

VERTICAL AND HORIZONTAL MARKET SOFTWARE While performing organizational processes in your career, you'll also frequently use two other categories of application software—vertical market software and horizontal market software.

Vertical market software is application software that is unique to a particular industry. For example, the health care industry has a variety of application software unique to it, including radiology software, patient-scheduling software, nursing allocation software, and pharmaceutical software. This type of software is written with a specific industry in mind; health care industry patient-scheduling software, for example, wouldn't work for scheduling hair and manicure appointments in a beauty salon.

Horizontal market software is application software general enough to be suitable for use in a variety of industries. Examples are software used for the following purposes:

- Inventory management
- Payroll
- Accounts receivable
- Billing
- Invoice processing
- Human resources management

Figure C.5

Categories of Personal Productivity Software

Category	Examples*
Word processing. Helps you create papers, letter, memos, and other basic documents.	• Microsoft Word • Corel WordPerfect
Spreadsheet. Helps you work primarily with numbers, including performing calculations and creating graphs.	• Microsoft Excel • LotusIBM Lotus 1-2-3
Presentation. Helps you create and edit information that will appear in electronic slides.	• Corel Presentations • LotusIBM Freelance Graphics
Desktop publishing. Extends word processing software by including design and formatting techniques to enhance the layout and appearance of a document.	• Microsoft Publisher • Quark QuarkXPress
Personal information management (PIM). Helps you create and maintain (1) to-do lists, (2) appointments and calenders, and (3) points of contact.	• Corel Central • LotusIBM Organizer
Personal finance. Helps you maintain your chequebook, prepare a budget, track investments, monitor your credit card balances, and pay bills electronically.	• Quicken Quicken • Microsoft Money
Web authoring. Helps you design and develop Web sites and pages that you publish on the web.	• Microsoft FrontPage • LotusIBM FastSite
Graphics. Helps you create and edit photos and art.	• Microsoft PhotoDraw • Kodak Imaging for Windows
Communications. Helps you communicate with other people.	• Microsoft Outlook • Internet Explorer
Database management system (DBMS). Helps you specify the logical organization for a database and access and use the information within a database.	• Microsoft Access • FileMaker FileMaker Pro

*Publisher name given first.

The above functions (and many others) are very similar, if not identical, in many different industries.

If you think about it, personal productivity software is actually a type of horizontal market software in that it is general enough to be suitable for use in a variety of industries. For example, no matter in which industry you work, you need basic word processing software for creating memos, business plans, and other basic documents. There are, however, some key differences between personal productivity software and horizontal and vertical market software. First is the issue of price. You can buy a full suite of personal productivity software for less than $400. In contrast, some individual horizontal and vertical market software packages may cost as much as $500,000 or more. Second is the issue of customizability. When you purchase personal productivity software, you cannot change the way it works. That is, you're buying the right to use it but not to change how it operates. With horizontal and vertical market software you may in fact also be able to purchase the right to change the way the software works. So, if you find a payroll software package that fits most of your organizational needs, you can buy the software and the right to change the operation of the software

TEAM WORK

BUYING PERSONAL PRODUCTIVITY SOFTWARE SUITES

When you buy personal productivity software, we recommend that you do so in the form of a suite. A **software suite (suite)** is a group of various applications that comes from the same software publisher and costs less than buying all the software individually.

In this project, your team has two tasks. First, research the most popular personal productivity software suites. These include Microsoft Office, Corel WordPerfect Office, and Lotus SmartSuite. For each, identify which specific software pieces falls into the ten categories of personal productivity software listed earlier. Then try to find information that describes the market share of each suite.

Second, choose one suite and determine the price for each individual application in it. Now do a price comparison. How much cheaper is the entire suite? Can you think of a situation in which someone would buy the individual pieces as opposed to the entire suite? If so, please describe it.

so that it meets 100 percent of your needs. This is a very common business practice when purchasing and using horizontal and vertical market software.

In Chapter 6 we discussed how organizations go about developing software unique to their particular needs, including how organizations can and do purchase vertical and horizontal market software and then customize that software.

SYSTEM SOFTWARE

System software is software that controls how your various technology tools work together as you use your application software to perform specific information processing tasks. It includes two basic categories—operating system and utility.

OPERATING SYSTEM SOFTWARE As mentioned above, operating system software is system software that controls your application software and manages how your hardware devices work together. For example, while using Excel to create a graph, if you choose to print the graph, your operating system software would take over, ensuring that you have a printer attached and that the printer has paper (and notifying you if it doesn't), and sending your graph to the printer along with instructions about how to print it.

Your operating system software also supports a variety of useful features, one of which is multitasking. **Multitasking** allows you to work with more than one piece of software at a time. Suppose you wanted to create a graph in Excel and insert it into a word processing document (see Figure C.6). With multitasking, you can have both pieces of application software open at the same time, and even see both on the screen. So, when you complete the creation of your graph, you can easily copy and paste it into your word processing document without having to go through a series of steps to exit the spreadsheet software and start your word processor.

Within operating system software, there are different types for personal environments and for organizational environments that support many simultaneous users (these are called *network operating systems* or *NOSs*, and we explore some of these in greater detail in Extended Learning Module D). Popular personal operating systems include:

- **Microsoft Windows 2000 Professional (Windows 2000 Pro)**. For people who have a personal computer connected to a network of other computers at work or at school

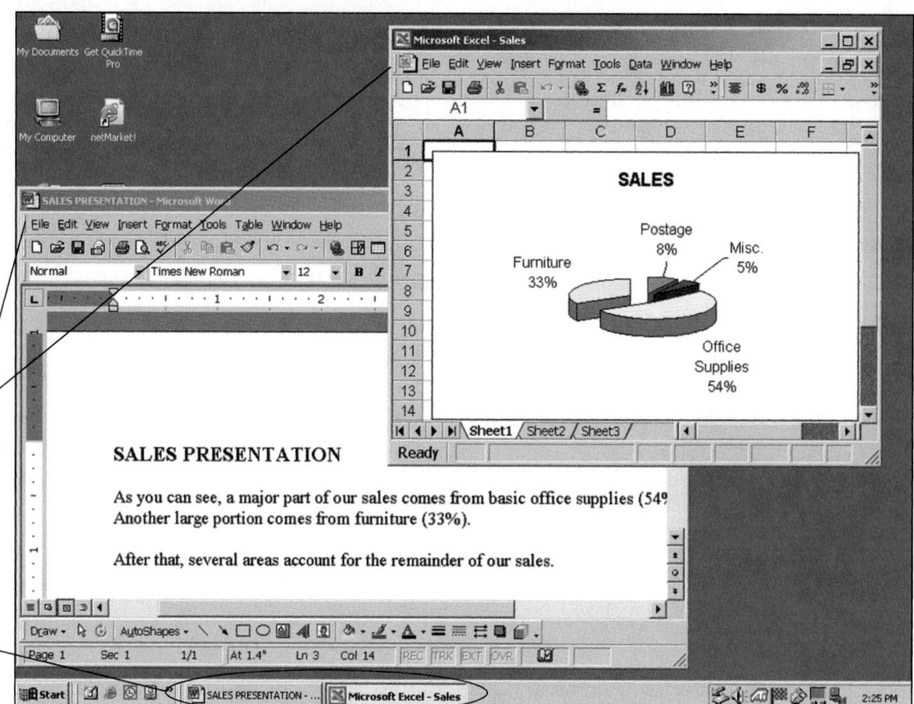

Figure C.6

Most Operating Systems Support Multitasking

Multitasking allows you to work with more than one piece of software at a time.

The task bar area tells you what software you're currently working with.

- **Microsoft Windows 2000 Millennium (Windows 2000 Me).** For a home computer user with utilities for setting up a home network and performing video, photo, and music editing and cataloguing
- **Microsoft Windows XP Home.** Microsoft's latest upgrade to Windows 2000 Me, with enhanced features for allowing multiple people to use the same computer
- **Microsoft Windows XP Professional (Windows XP Pro).** Microsoft's latest upgrade to Windows 2000 Pro
- **Mac OS.** The operating system for today's Apple computers
- **Linux.** An open source operating system that provides a rich operating environment for high-end workstations and network servers

If you're considering purchasing a notebook computer that you'll use extensively at school connected to a network there, we recommend that you contact your school's technology support department to determine which operating system is best for you.

UTILITY SOFTWARE Utility software adds additional functionality to your operating system. A simple example is that of screensaver software (which is probably also a part of your operating system). Most importantly, utility software includes **antivirus software**—utility software that scans for and can destroy viruses in your RAM and on your storage devices. Viruses are everywhere today, with 200 to 300 new ones surfacing each month. Some are benign—they might merely cause your screen to go blank (or something on that order) but do not corrupt your information. Others are deadly, often reformatting your hard disk or altering the contents of your files. You definitely need antivirus software to combat them. We talk much more about this vitally important topic, including denial-of-service attacks, in Chapter 8.

Other types of utility software include:

- **Crash-proof software.** Utility software that helps you save information if your system crashes and you're forced to turn it off and then back on again

TEAM WORK

EVALUATING UTILITY SOFTWARE SUITES

Just as you can purchase personal productivity software suites that contain many pieces of software, you can also purchase utility software suites. In the table below, we've included the three most popular utility software suites—McAfee Office Pro, Norton SystemWorks, and Ontrack SystemSuite.

As a team, do some research and determine what major pieces of software are included in each. As you do, fill in the table.

Now, pick a particular utility suite and visit its Web site. What is the process for updating your software? Is it free? How often does the site recommend that you update your utility software?

Utility Software Piece	McAfee Office Pro	Norton SystemWorks	Ontrack SystemSuite

- **Uninstaller software**. Utility software you can use to remove software from your hard disk that you no longer want
- **Disk optimization software**. Utility software that organizes your information on your hard disk in the most efficient way

We would once again state that utility software is not optional just because it is meant to add functionality to your computer. You definitely need utility software. The four specific pieces we described above are just a few of the many you'll find in a utility software suite.

Hardware—Your Physical Interface

To properly understand the significant role of your hardware (the physical components of your computer), it helps to know something about how your computer works differently from you. You work with information in the form of characters (A–Z, a–z, and special ones such as an asterisk) and numbers (0–9). Computers, on the other hand, work in terms of bits and bytes. Basically, computers use electricity to function, and electrical pulses have two states: on and off.

A **binary digit (bit)** is the smallest unit of information that your computer can process. A bit can either be a 1 (on) or a 0 (off). The challenge from a technological point of view is to be able to represent all our characters, special symbols, and numbers in binary form. Using ASCII is one way to do this. **ASCII (American Standard Code for Information Interchange)** is the coding system most personal computers use to represent, process, and store information. In ASCII, a group of eight bits represents one natural language character and is called a **byte**.

For example, if you were to type the word "COOL" on the keyboard, your keyboard (a hardware device) would change it into four bytes—one for each character—that would look like the following used by other parts of your computer (see also Figure C.7):

01000011	01001111	01001111	01001100
C	O	O	L

This grouping of 1s and 0s is then used throughout the rest of your computer, as it travels from one device to another, is stored on a storage device, and is processed by your CPU.

There are three important conclusions that you should draw from the previous discussion. First, your hardware works with information in a different form (although with the same meaning) than you do. You work with characters, special symbols, and the numbers 0–9. Your computer, on the other hand, represents all these in binary form, a collection of unique 1s and 0s. Second, the term "byte" is the bridge between people and a computer. A computer can store one character, special symbol, or number in the form of a byte. One byte is essentially one character. So a floppy disk with a storage capacity of 1.44 megabytes can hold approximately 1.44 million characters of information.

Finally, a primary role of your input and output devices (such as a keyboard and monitor) is to convert information from one form to another, either from how you understand information to bits and bytes (the role of input devices) or from computer-stored bits and bytes to a form you understand (the role of output devices). All other hardware internally works with information in the form of bits and bytes.

Figure C.7

Representations of Information As It Moves Through Your Computer

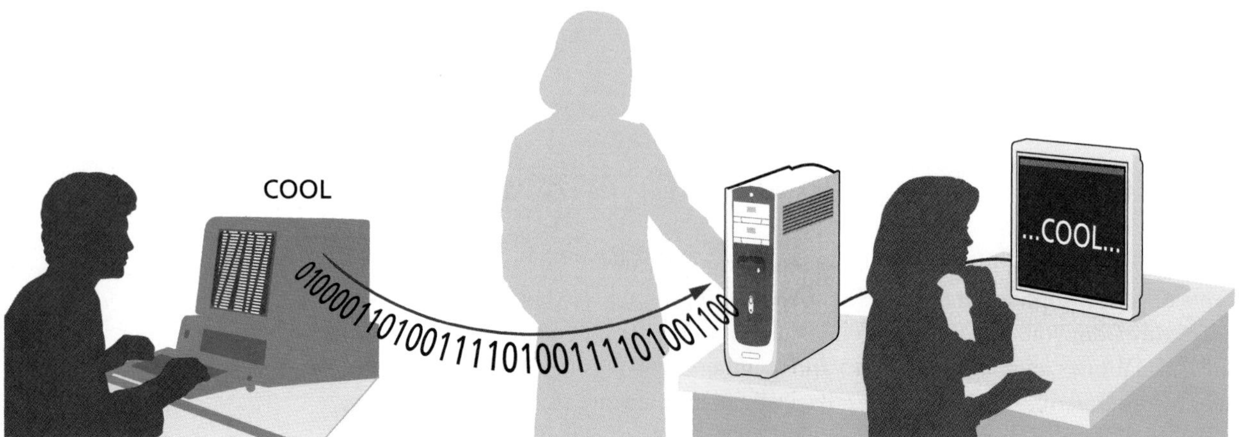

COMMON INPUT DEVICES

An **input device** is a tool you use to capture information and commands. You can, for example, use a keyboard to type in information and use a mouse to point and click on buttons and icons. And, as we have just stated, input devices are responsible for converting your representation of information (the letter "C" for example) into a form that the rest of your computer can work with (01000011).

Within almost any complete technology environment, you'll find numerous input devices, some of which have more suitable applications in a business setting than in a personal setting. Some common input devices include (see Figure C.8):

- **Keyboard**. Today's most popular input technology
- **Point-of-sale (POS)**. For capturing information at the point of a transaction, typically in a retail environment
- **Microphone**. For capturing live sounds such as a dog barking or your voice (for automatic speech recognition)
- **Mouse**. Today's most popular "pointing" input device
- **Trackball**. An upside-down, stationary mouse in which you move the ball instead of the device (mainly for notebooks)
- **Pointing stick**. Small rubberlike pointing device that causes the pointer to move on the screen as you apply directional pressure (popular on notebooks)
- **Touch pad**. Another form of a stationary mouse on which you move your finger to cause the pointer on the screen to move (also popular on notebooks)

Figure C.8
Popular Input Devices

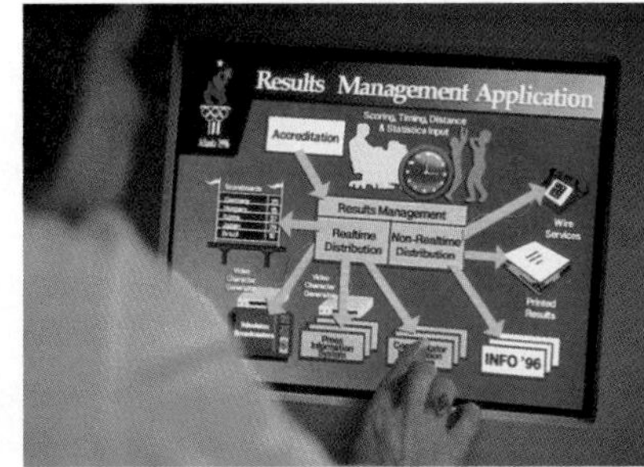

- **Touch screen**. Special screen that lets you use your finger to point at and touch a particular function you want to perform
- **Barcode reader**. Captures information that exists in the form of vertical bars whose width and distance apart determine a number
- **Optical mark recognition (OMR)**. Detects the presence or absence of a mark in a predetermined place (popular for multiple-choice exams)
- **Scanner**. Captures images, photos, and artwork that already exist on paper

COMMON OUTPUT DEVICES

An **output device** is a tool you use to see, hear, or otherwise accept the results of your information processing requests. Among output devices, printers and monitors are the most common, but you'll also usually find speakers and even plotters (special printers that draw output on a page) being used. And output devices are responsible for converting computer-stored information into a form that you can understand.

MONITORS Monitors come in two varieties—CRT or flat-panel display (see Figure C.9). **CRTs** are monitors that look like television sets, while **flat-panel displays** are thin, lightweight monitors and take up much less space than CRTs. When considering monitors as an output device, you need to think about monitor size, viewable screen size, resolution, monitor type, and dot pitch.

Monitor size determines how large your entire monitor is, measured diagonally from corner to corner. Monitor size, especially for CRTs, gives you some idea of the amount of space your monitor will require. However, the size that really is of interest to you is viewable screen size, often expressed as *VIS* or *viewable inch screen*. Viewable screen size tells you the size of your screen, which is measured diagonally from corner to corner and always smaller than monitor size. Viewable screen size tells you the size of the screen on which you will see things. So a monitor with a 17" VIS has a screen on which you will see things that measures 17 inches diagonally (1 inch = 2.54 centimetres).

The **resolution of a screen** is the number of *pixels* it has. Pixels (picture elements) are the dots that make up an image on your screen. For example, a monitor with a resolution given as 1024 × 768 has 1024 pixels horizontally and 768 vertically. The number of dots varies with the type of monitor you have, but larger numbers (of pixels) provide more clear and crisp screen images than smaller ones. Monitor types range from basic VGA (with a resolution of 640 × 480) to QXGA (with a resolution of 2048 × 1536). QXGA monitors obviously cost the most and provide the clearest images.

Dot pitch is the distance between the centres of a pair of like-coloured pixels. So a monitor with a 0.24 millimetre dot pitch (0.24 millimetres between pair of like-

Figure C.9
Monitors Are Common Output Devices

ON YOUR OWN

FINDING A PRINTER TO MEET YOUR NEEDS

A printer for a personal environment is definitely a "personal choice." Some people care only about print quality for mainly words and numbers. Others may want a personal printer that creates high-quality colour images. Whatever the case, you need to choose a printer carefully.

As you think about buying a printer, do so first in terms of quality and speed. Once you've considered those two aspects, find one inkjet, one laser, and one multifunction printer that will meet your needs. Compare them now on price and capability. Which would you choose and why?

Finally, check out some complete computer systems that you can buy at a local computer store. Do they include a printer for free? If so, would getting this printer for free encourage you to purchase the system? Why or why not?

coloured pixels) is better than one with a 0.28 millimetre dot pitch because the dots are smaller and closer together, giving you a better-quality image.

PRINTERS Printers are another common type of output device, creating output on paper. A printer's sharpness and clarity depends on its resolution. The **resolution of a printer** is the number of dots per inch (dpi) it produces, which is the same principle as resolution in monitors. The more dots per inch, the better the image, and usually the more costly the printer.

Most high-end personal printers have a resolution of 1200 × 1200 dpi or better. Multiplying these numbers gives you 1,440,000 dots per square inch. Also, printers that have the same number of dots per inch both vertically and horizontally give you a better-quality image.

Common types of printers are:

- **Inkjet printers**. Make images by forcing ink droplets through nozzles (see Figure C.10). Standard inkjet printers use four colours—black, cyan (blue), magenta (purplish pink), and yellow. Some inkjet printers produce high-quality images and are often advertised as photo printers. These have six colours (a second shade of magenta and of cyan).
- **Laser printers**. Form images using an electrostatic process, the same way a photocopier works. Laser printers are more expensive than inkjet printers but do provide higher-quality images. Most common personal laser printers only print in black and white. You can buy high-end colour laser printers, but be ready to spend a lot more money.
- **Multifunction printers**. Scan, copy, and fax, as well as print. These are becoming quite popular in the personal technology arena, mainly because they cost less than if you bought separate tools (printer, scanner, copier, and fax machine). Multifunction printers can be either inkjet or laser, the latter being more expensive and providing better quality.

Figure C.10

Printers Are Also Common Output Devices

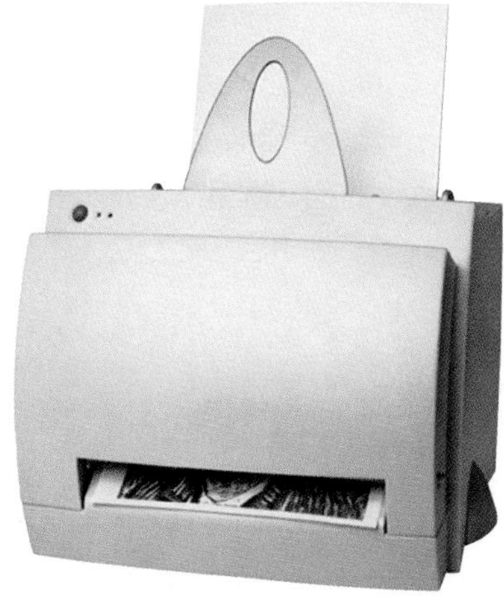

CHARACTERISTICS OF CPUs AND RAM

Together, your CPU and RAM make up the real brains of your computer. As well, your CPU will largely determine the price of your system. The **central processing unit (CPU)** is the actual hardware that interprets and executes the software instructions and coordinates how all the other hardware devices work together. **RAM**, or **random access memory**, is temporary storage that holds the information you're working with, the application software you're using, and the operating system software you're using.

The CPU is often referred to as a microprocessor or a CPU chip. The dominant manufacturers of CPUs today include Intel (with its Celeron and Pentium lines for personal computers) and AMD (with its Athlon series). The most helpful information when comparing CPUs is their relative speeds.

CPU speed is usually quoted in **megahertz (MHz)**, which is millions of CPU cycles per second, and **gigahertz (GHz)**, which is billions of CPU cycles per second. The number of CPU cycles per second determines how fast a CPU carries out the software instructions—more cycles per second means faster processing. And, as you might expect, faster CPUs cost more than their slower counterparts.

A CPU contains two primary parts—the control unit and the arithmetic/logic unit (see Figure C.11). The **control unit** interprets software instructions and tells the other hardware devices what to do, on the basis of the software instructions. The **arithmetic/logic unit (A/L unit)** performs all arithmetic operations (e.g., addition and subtraction) and all logical operations (such as sorting and comparing numbers).

These two units perform very different functions. The control unit actually gets another instruction from RAM which contains your software (this is called a *retrieve*). It then interprets the instruction, decides what each other device must do, and finally tells each device what to do (this is called *decoding*). The A/L unit, on the other hand, responds to the control unit and does whatever it dictates, performing either an arithmetic or a logic operation (this called an *execution*). At the end of this Module, we'll take you through a small program that demonstrates all these steps at work.

RAM is a sort of chalkboard your CPU uses while it processes information and software instructions. That is why we refer to RAM as "temporary." When you turn off your computer, everything in RAM is wiped clean. That's also why people (and your operating system) will always tell you to save your work before shutting down your computer. So, while you type in a term paper using word processing software, the contents of your term paper (that appear on your screen) are actually stored in RAM. When you perform a save function, the contents are copied from RAM to your designated storage device.

Figure C.11

Your CPU and RAM at Work

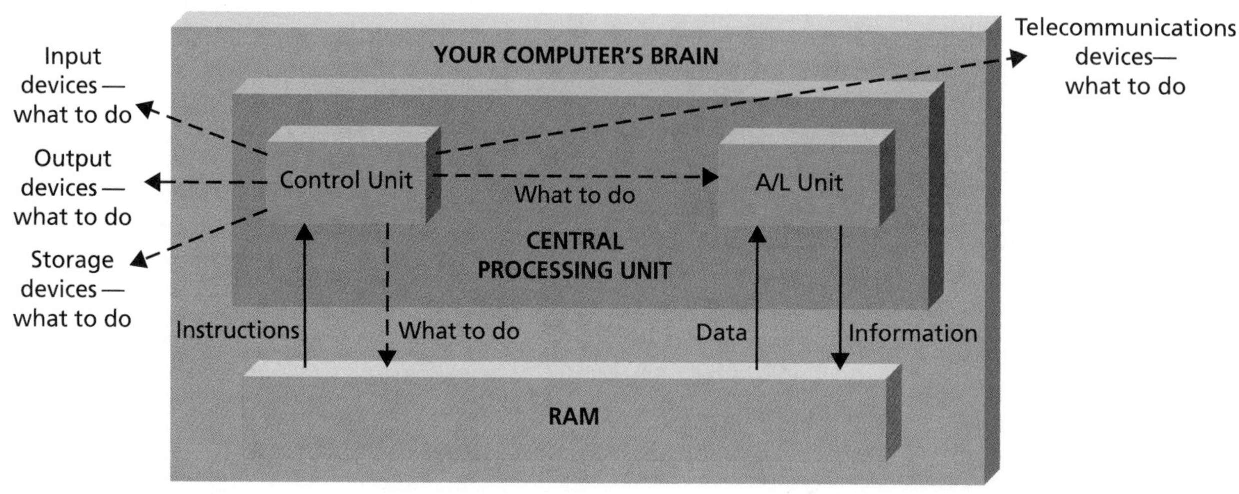

RAM capacity is expressed in bytes, megabytes being the most common unit of measurement. A **megabyte (MB** or **M** or **meg)** is roughly one million bytes. So, if your computer has 256 MB of RAM, your RAM can hold roughly 256 million characters of information and software instructions. RAM is cheap compared to most other parts of your computer, so don't hesitate to buy as much as you need.

COMMON STORAGE DEVICES

As opposed to RAM, which is temporary, storage devices don't lose their contents when you turn off your computer. Although we use the term "permanent" for storage devices, most do give you the ability to change your information or erase it altogether. When considering which storage device(s) are best, you should ask (1) whether you need to be able to update the information on the storage device and (2) how much information you have to store.

Some storage devices, such as a hard disk, offer you easy update capabilities and a large storage capacity. Others, such as floppy disks, offer you easy update capabilities but with limited storage capacities. Still others, such as CD-ROM, offer no update capabilities but do posses large storage capacities. When we talk about storage device capacities, we still measure it in terms of bytes, megabytes, gigabytes, and terabytes. A **gigabyte (GB** or **gig)** is roughly one billion characters. A **terabyte (TB)** is roughly one trillion bytes. Most standard desktops today have a hard disk with storage capacity in excess of 20 GB. And hard disks (sometimes called *hard disk packs*) for large organizational computer systems can hold in excess of 100 TB of information. To give you some idea of these capacities, consider that a typical double-spaced page of pure text is roughly 2000 characters. So a 20 GB (20 gigabyte or 20-billion-character) hard disk can hold approximately 10,000,000 pages of text.

Common storage devices include (see Figure C.12):

- **Floppy disk**. Great for portability of information and ease of updating but holds only 1.44 MB of information.
- **High-capacity floppy disk**. Great for portability and ease of updating and hold between 100 MB and 250 MB of information; examples are Superdisks and Zip disks are examples.
- **Hard disk**. Rests within your system box and offer both ease of updating and great storage capacity.

Figure C.12

Common Storage Devices

- **CD-ROM**. Optical or laser disc that offers no updating capabilities with about 800 MB of storage capacity. Most software today comes on CD-ROM.
- **CD-R (compact disc—recordable)**. Optical or laser disc that offers one-time writing capability with about 800 MB of storage capacity.
- **CD-RW (compact disc—rewritable)**. Offers unlimited writing and updating capabilities on the CD.
- **DVD-ROM**. Optical or laser disc that offers no updating capabilities with upwards of 17 GB of storage capacity. The trend is now for rental movies to be on DVD.
- **DVD-R**. Optical or laser disc that offers one-time writing capability with upwards of 17 GB of storage capacity.
- **DVD-RW**, **DVD-RAM**, or **DVD+RW** (all different names by different manufacturers). Optical or laser disc that offers unlimited writing and updating capabilities on the DVD.

TELECOMMUNICATIONS DEVICES

Telecommunications is the most dynamic, changing, exciting, and technically complicated aspect of MIS and IT today. Telecommunications basically describes our ability to be *connected*, to almost anyone, anywhere, and at any time. Because this topic is so vast, we've devoted all of Extended Learning Module D to it. Here, we want to just introduce you to the basics of telecommunications and its associated technologies, by focusing on your personal needs while at home.

Telecommunications enables the concept of a network. A **network** is two or more computers connected so that they can communicate with each other and possibly share information, software, peripheral devices, and/or processing power. A simple example of a network is two computers connected to the same printer. The most well-known (and complicated) example of a network is the millions of computers connected all over the world that make up the Internet.

Let's talk about how you would connect to the Internet from home. First, you need some sort of modem that will serve as a connection from your home computer to another network, that is, the Internet. There are many types of modems, including:

Figure C.13
The Role of a Telephone Modem

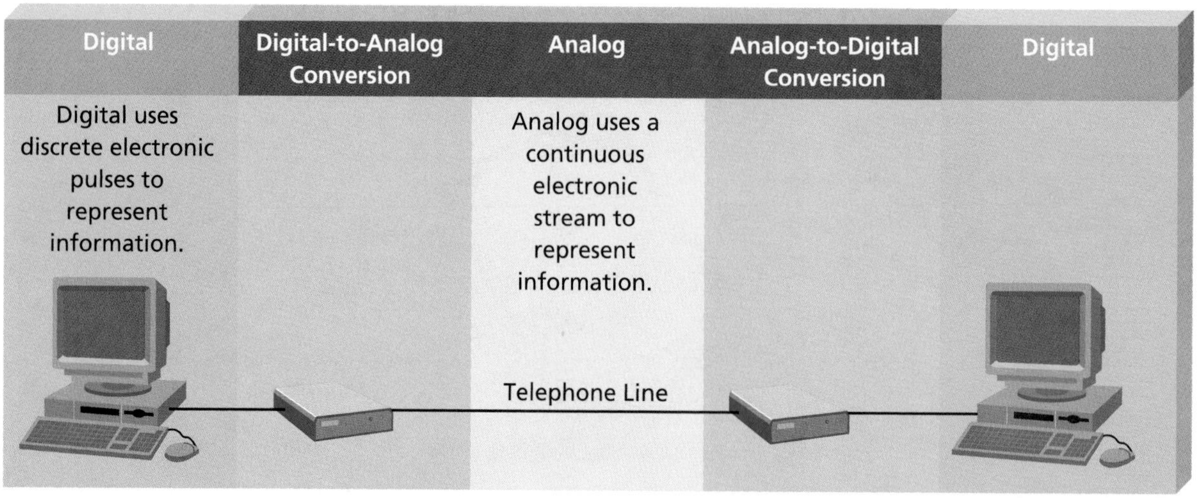

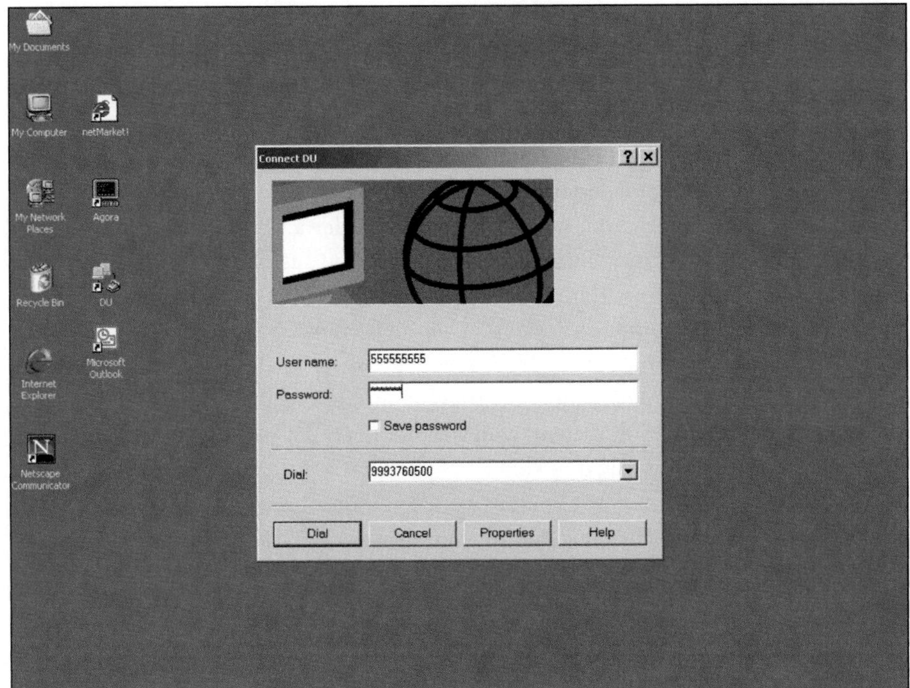

Figure C.14
Connecting with Connectivity Software

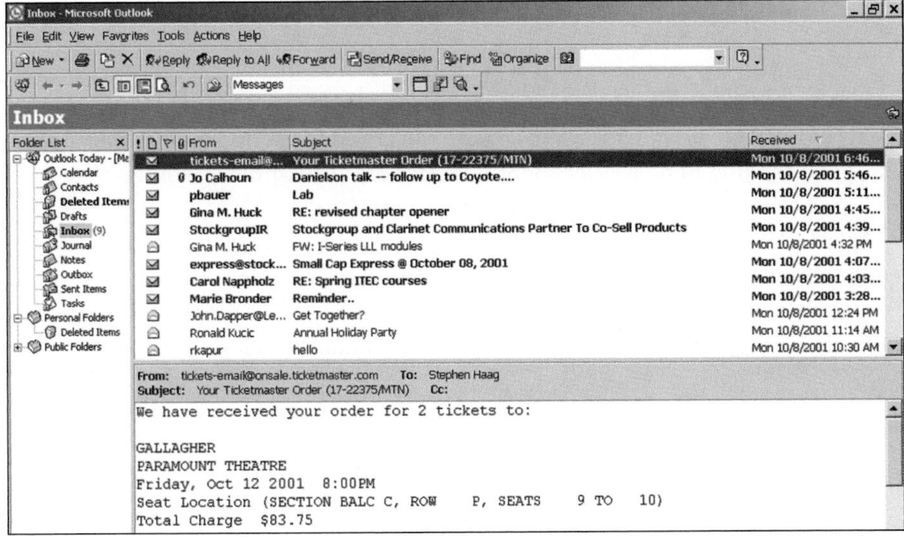

Figure C.15
Microsoft Outlook Is E-Mail Software

- A telephone modem
- Digital subscriber line (DSL) modem
- A cable modem
- A satellite modem

In Extended Learning Module D, we cover DSL, cable, and satellite modems in more detail. Here, we focus on the **telephone modem**—a device that connects your computer to your phone line so that you can access another computer or network (see Figure C.13). If you use your standard telephone line for connecting to a network, a telephone modem is necessary because it acts as a converter of sorts. Your computer (and the network you're connecting to) work in terms of digital signals, while a standard telephone line works in terms of analog signals. Digital signals are discrete with each signal representing a bit (either 0 or 1). Think of analog signals as being "wavy." So your modem must convert the digital signals of your computer into analog signals that can be sent across the telephone line (this conversion process is called *modulation*). At the other end, another modem (similar to yours) translates the analog signals into digital signals which can then be used by the other computer or network (this conversion process is called *demodulation*). So, modems *mo*dulate and *dem*odulate signals, hence the term.

When you type information on a Web form to order a product, that information starts in digital form within your computer. When you hit the Submit button, your modem converts that information to analog form and sends it on its way through your telephone line. At the other end, another modem converts it back to digital form, which allows a server computer to process your request. Then the server prepares its response in digital form and sends it through a modem which converts it to analog form. When the information reaches you, your modem first converts it to digital form so your computer can display it to you.

As you may recall, whenever you use your computer for any task, you need both hardware and software. For telecommunications, your hardware—in our example of connecting to the Internet—is a modem. You also need communications software, specifically:

- **Connectivity software**, which enables you to use your computer to "dial up" or connect to another computer
- **Web browser software**, which enables you to surf the Web
- Probably **e-mail software** (short for **electronic mail software**), which enables you to electronically communicate with other people by sending and receiving e-mail

For example, if you want to connect to your school so that you could surf the Web and send and receive e-mail, you would first use connectivity software to dial up your school's computer (see Figure C.14). Once you are connected to your school's computer, you can use Web browser software to surf the Web or e-mail software (such as Microsoft Outlook in Figure C.15) to send and receive e-mail.

Again, this is a very brief introduction to telecommunications and focuses on only using your home computer and a telephone modem to connect to your school so you can get to the Internet. We encourage you to read Extended Learning Module D for a more complete discussion of networks and telecommunications devices.

CONNECTING DEVICES

Connecting devices enable all your hardware to communicate with each other. For example, you use a connector, called a parallel connector, to plug your printer into your system box. When you do, you're plugging it into a parallel port connected to an expansion card. That card is connected to the expansion bus (via an expansion slot) which moves information between various devices and RAM. The expansion bus is a part of the larger system bus, which moves information between the RAM and CPU and to and from various other devices. That may seem like an awful lot of technical jargon, so let's break it down a bit.

BUSES, EXPANSION SLOTS, AND EXPANSION CARDS The **system bus** consists of the electronic pathways which move information between basic components on the motherboard, including between your CPU and RAM (see Figure C.16). A part of the system bus is called the **expansion bus**, which moves information from your CPU and RAM to all of your other hardware devices such as your microphone and printer. So, there's actually only one common "highway" that connects all of your hardware.

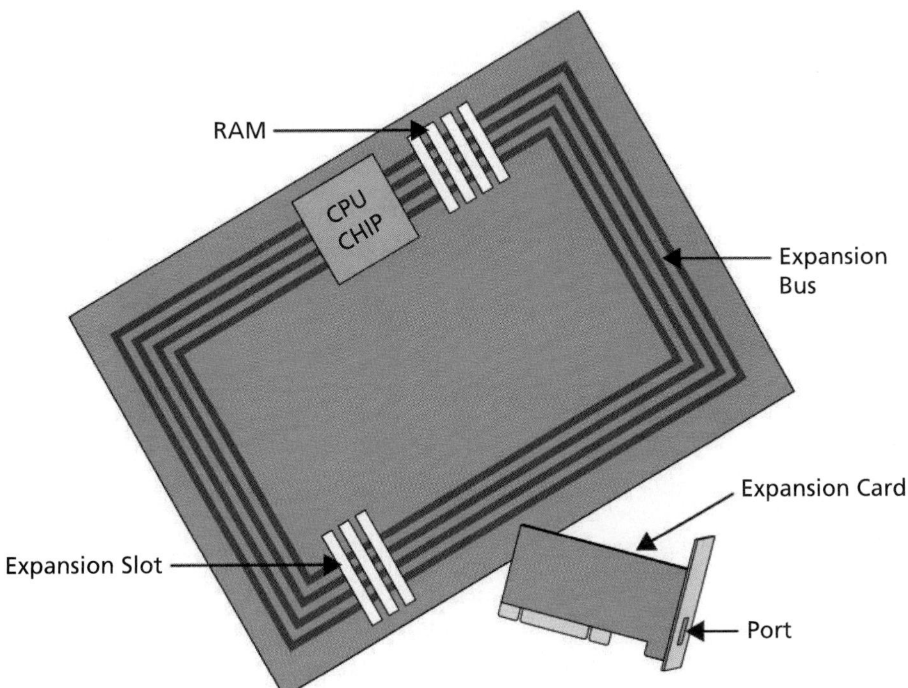

Figure C.16

Buses, Expansion Slots, and Expansion Cards

Along the expansion bus, you'll find expansion slots. An **expansion slot** is a long, skinny socket on the motherboard into which you insert an expansion card. An **expansion card** is a circuit board that you insert into an expansion slot. Expansion cards include such things as video cards (for your monitor), sound cards (for your speakers and microphone), and modem cards (obviously for your modem). Each expansion card contains one or more ports (which we'll soon discuss further) into which you plug a connector (which we'll also discuss soon) connected to some other hardware device such as a printer.

When you buy a complete computer system, it comes already equipped with the expansion cards inserted into the expansion slots. All you have to do is plug the appropriate connectors into the right ports. If, however, you decide to buy a new monitor and want increased video capacity, you may have to remove your old expansion card and insert a new one.

PORTS AND CONNECTORS Different hardware devices require different kinds of ports and connectors. **Ports** are simply the plug-ins found on the outside of your system box (usually in the back) into which you plug a connector (see Figure C.17). Popular connectors include:

- **USB (universal serial bus)**. These are becoming the most popular means of connecting devices to a computer. Most standard desktops today have at least two USB ports, and most standard notebooks have at least one.
- **Serial connector**. Usually has 9 holes but may have 25, which fit into the corresponding number of pins in the port. Serial connectors are often most used for monitors and certain types of modems.
- **Parallel connector**. Has 25 pins, which fit into the corresponding holes in the port. Most printers use parallel connectors.

You can also have a special type of port called an IrDA, which has no physical corresponding connector. **IrDA (Infrared Data Association) ports** are for wireless

Figure C.17

Ports and Connectors

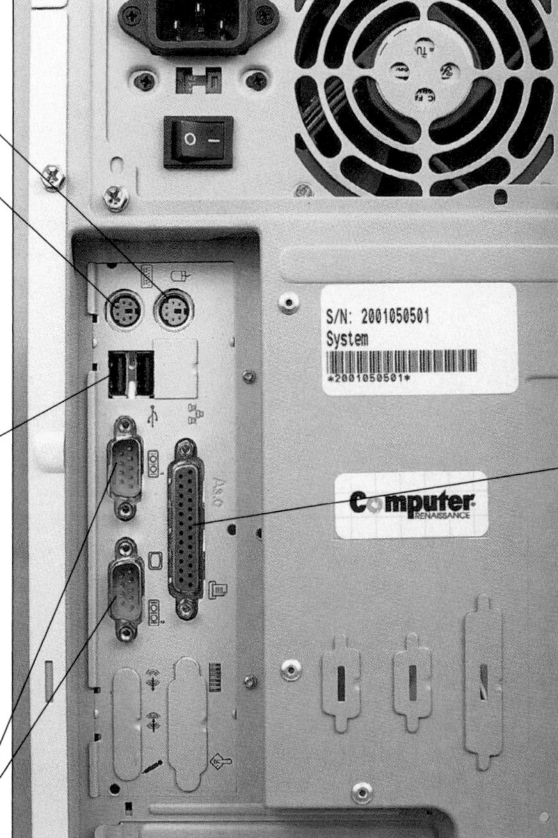

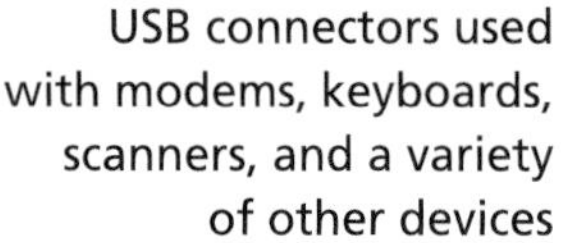

devices that work in essentially the same way as the remote control on your TV does. To use IrDA, both your computer and the wireless device (such as a mouse) must have an IrDA port, which is why we say that IrDA ports have no physical corresponding connectors. We discuss the technical specifics of wireless communication in Extended Learning Module D.

Now that you've seen what's under the hood and what it takes to connect everything together, let's see how your computer processes a piece of application software.

The Complete Computer at Work

As we explore a simple example of how your computer processes a piece of application software, remember first that no matter what you want to do with your computer, you need both hardware and software. For our example, let's suppose that you have an icon on your Windows desktop for a special program that you use frequently. That program allows you to enter two numbers and then it displays the result of adding the two numbers together. Of course, we realize that you would never use such a piece of software, but it suits our illustration just fine.

When you double-click on that icon, your mouse sends that command to your CPU. Using the operating system instructions which reside in your internal memory (RAM), your control unit (inside your CPU) determines that you want to launch and use a program. So your control unit determines the path to that program and sends a message to your hard disk. That message includes where the program is located on your hard disk and instructions that tell your hard disk to get it and transfer it to your RAM. Then your control unit tells your RAM to hold the program for processing.

With that stage set, let's look at the software as well as what happens on your screen. The software is shown in Figure C.18 and what appears on your screen is shown in Figure C.19. Looking at Figure C.18, you can see the program contains six lines of code. The first is line 10, the last is line 60. Below, we list each line of code and the corresponding series of internal instructions that your computer must perform.

10 CLS

10.1 Your control unit must first send a message to your RAM telling it to pass the first line of code (fetch).

10.2 Your control unit interprets the line of code and determines what each hardware device needs to do (decode).

10.3 Your control unit sends a message to your screen, telling your screen to build a small window with no contents (execution).

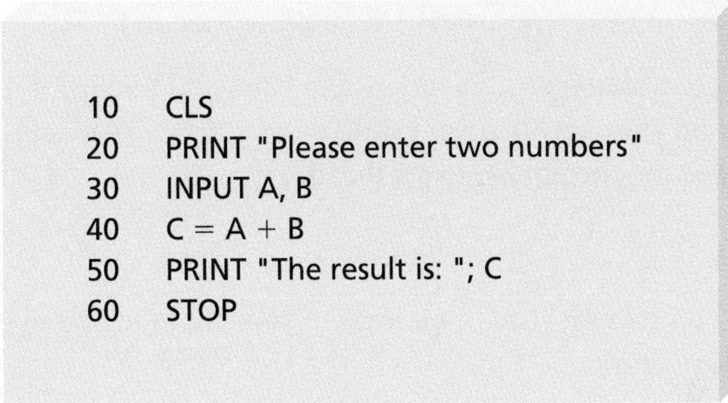

```
10    CLS
20    PRINT "Please enter two numbers"
30    INPUT A, B
40    C = A + B
50    PRINT "The result is: "; C
60    STOP
```

Figure C.18

Software Program for Adding Two Numbers

Figure C.19

What Appears on Your Screen

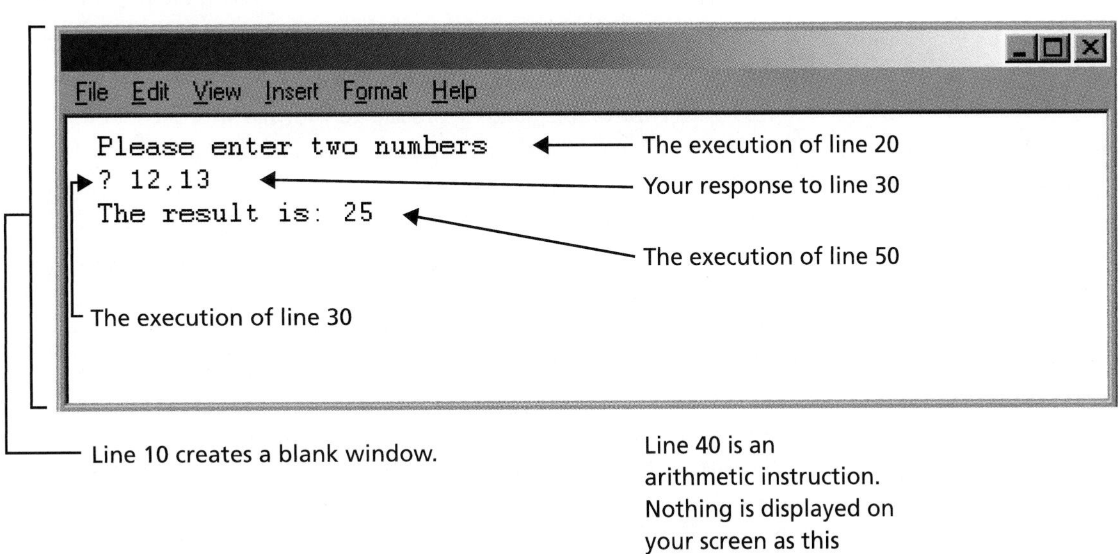

20 PRINT "Please enter two numbers"

20.1 Your control unit sends a message to your RAM telling it to pass the next line of code (fetch).

20.2 Your control unit interprets the line of code (which is a display function) and determines what each hardware device needs to do (decode).

20.3 Your control unit takes what is between quotes (*Please enter two numbers*), passes it to your screen, and tells your screen to display it (execute).

30 INPUT A, B

30.1 Your control unit sends a message to your RAM telling it to pass the next line of code (fetch).

30.2 Your control unit interprets the line of code (which is a data entry function) and determines what each hardware device needs to do (decode).

30.3 Your control unit sends a message to your screen telling it to display a question mark (execute).

30.4 Your control unit sends a message to your keyboard telling it to accept two numbers and pass those to RAM (another execute).

30.5 Your control unit sends a message to your RAM telling it to accept two numbers from your keyboard and store them in memory positions A and B (another execute—beginning to get the idea?).

40 C = A + B

40.1 Your control unit sends a message to your RAM telling to pass the next line of code (fetch).

40.2 Your control unit interprets the line of code (which is an arithmetic function) and determines what each hardware device needs to do (decode).

40.3 Your control unit sends a message to RAM telling it to pass the contents of A and B to your A/L unit (execute).

40.4 Your control unit sends a message to your A/L unit telling it to accept the two numbers from RAM, add the two numbers, and pass the result back to RAM (another execute).

40.5 Your control unit sends a message to your RAM to accept the result from the A/L unit, and store the result in memory position C.

50 PRINT "The result is: "; C

50.1 Your control unit sends a message to your RAM telling it to pass the next line of code (fetch).

50.2 Your control unit interprets the line of code (which is another display function) and determines what each hardware device needs to do (decode).

50.3 Your control units sends a message to your RAM telling it to pass the contents of memory position C to your screen.

50.4 Your control units sends a message to your screen telling it to display the text between the quotes (*The result is:*) and the content of memory position C that was passed to it by RAM (execute).

60 STOP

60.1 Your control unit sends a message to your RAM telling it to pass the next line of code (fetch).

60.2 Your control unit interprets the line of code (which is a termination function) and determines what each hardware device needs to do (decode).

60.3 Your control unit sends out a broadcast message telling each hardware device to "stand down" and await further instructions (execute).

That is a very realistic example of what goes on inside your computer while you use software. What is amazing is that most software packages include millions of lines of code and require that buttons, images, and icons appear on the screen.

Summary: Student Learning Outcomes Revisited

1. **Define information technology (IT) and its two basic categories—hardware and software.** **Information technology (IT)** is any computer-based tool that people use to work with information and support the information and information processing needs of an organization. IT includes cell phones, PDAs, software such as spreadsheet software, and a printer. **Hardware** is the physical devices that make up a computer (often referred to as a computer system). **Software** is the set of instructions that your hardware executes to carry out a specific task for you.
2. **Describe categories of computers by size.** Categories of computers by size include personal digital assistants, notebook computers, desktop computers, minicomputers, mainframe computers, and supercomputers. A **personal digital assistant (PDA)** is a small handheld computer that helps you surf the Web and perform simple tasks such as note-taking, calendaring, appointment scheduling, and maintaining an address book. A notebook computer is a fully functional computer designed for you to carry around and run on battery power. A **desktop computer** is the most popular choice for personal computing needs. These three are all computers designed to for use by one person. A **minicomputer (mid-range computer)** is designed to meet the computing needs of several people simultaneously in a small to medium-size business environment. A **mainframe computer (mainframe)** is a computer designed to meet the computing needs of hundreds of people in a large business environment. A **supercomputer** is the fastest, most powerful, and most expensive type of computer. In the order given, PDAs are the smallest, least powerful, and least expensive while supercomputers are the largest, most powerful, and most expensive.
3. **Compare the roles of personal productivity, vertical market, and horizontal market software.** **Personal productivity software** helps you perform personal tasks—such as writing a memo, creating a graph, and creating a slide presentation—that you can usually do even if you don't own a computer. **Vertical market software** is application software that is unique to a particular industry. **Horizontal market software** is application software that is general enough to be suitable for use in a variety of industries. Personal productivity software is very inexpensive when compared to both vertical market and horizontal market software. With personal productivity software, you do not obtain the right to change the way the software works. If you buy vertical market or horizontal market software, you can often buy the right to change the way the software works.
   - **Describe the roles of operating system and utility software as components of system software.** **System software** handles tasks specific to technology management and coordinates the interaction of all technology devices. Within system software, you will find operating system software and utility software. **Operating system software** is system software that controls your

application software and manages how your hardware devices work together. So operating system software really enables you to use your computer to run application software. **Utility software** is software that adds additional functionality to your operating system. It includes such utilities as antivirus software, screensavers, crash-proof software, uninstaller software, and disk optimization. Although these would be considered "additional" functionality, you need utility software, especially antivirus software.

- **Define the purposes of the six major categories of hardware.** The six major categories of hardware include:
  - **Input devices.** Help you capture information and commands and convert information in a form you understand into a form your computer can understand
  - **Output devices.** Help you see, hear, or otherwise accept the results of your information processing requests and convert information in a form your computer understands into a form that you can understand
  - **CPU** and **RAM.** The real brains of your computer that execute software instructions (CPU) and hold the information, application software, and operating system software you're working with (RAM)
  - **Storage devices.** Help you store information for use at a later time
  - **Telecommunications devices.** Help you send information to and receive it from another person or location
  - *Connecting devices.* Help you connect all your hardware devices to each other

Key Terms and Concepts

antivirus software, 406
application software, 398
arithmetic/logic unit (A/L unit), 412
ASCII (American Standard Code for Information Interchange), 408
barcode reader, 410
binary digit (bit), 408
byte, 408
CD-R (compact disc—recordable), 414
CD-ROM, 414
CD-RW (compact disc—rewritable), 414
central processing unit (CPU), 411
connectivity software, 416
control unit, 412
crash-proof software, 406
CRT, 410
desktop computer, 401
disk optimization software, 407
dot pitch, 410
DVD-R, 414
DVD-ROM, 414
DVD-RW, DVD-RAM, DVD+RW, 414
e-mail (electronic mail) software, 416
expansion bus, 416
expansion card, 417
expansion slot, 417
flat-panel display, 410
floppy disk, 413
gigabyte (GB or gig), 413
gigahertz (GHz), 412
hard disk, 413
hardware, 398
high-capacity floppy disk, 413
horizontal market software, 403
information technology, 398
inkjet printer, 411
input device, 409
IrDA (Infrared Data Association) port, 417
keyboard, 409
laser printer, 411
Linux, 406
Mac OS, 406
mainframe computer (mainframe), 402
megabyte (MB or M or meg), 413
megahertz (MHz), 412
microphone, 409
Microsoft Windows 2000 Millennium (Windows 2000 Me), 406
Microsoft Windows 2000 Professional (Windows 2000 Pro), 405
Microsoft Windows XP Home, 406
Microsoft Windows XP Professional (Windows XP Pro), 406
minicomputer (mid-range computer), 402
mouse, 409
multifunction printer, 411
multitasking, 405
network, 414
notebook computer, 400
operating system software, 399
optical mark recognition (OMR), 410
output device, 410
parallel connector, 417
personal digital assistant (PDA), 400
personal productivity software, 403
point-of-sale (POS), 409
pointing stick, 409
port, 417
RAM (random access memory), 412
resolution of a printer, 411
resolution of a screen, 410
scanner, 410
serial connector, 417
software, 398
software suite (suite), 405
storage device, 398
supercomputer, 402
system bus, 416

system software, 399
telecommunications device, 398
telephone modem, 415
terabyte (TB), 413
touch pad, 409
touch screen, 410
trackball, 409
uninstaller software, 407
USB (universal serial bus), 417
utility software, 399
vertical market software, 403
Web browser software, 416

Short-Answer Questions

1. What are the two categories of information technology (IT)?
2. What are the six categories of hardware?
3. What is the difference between application and system software?
4. What are the four categories of computers by size? Which is the least expensive? Which is the most powerful?
5. Dollar for dollar with comparable characteristics, which is faster and more powerful—a desktop computer or notebook computer?
6. What are the major categories of personal productivity software?
7. What is the difference between vertical market and horizontal market software?
8. How is personal productivity software a type of horizontal market software? How is personal productivity software not a type of horizontal market software?
9. What are some of the personal operating systems on the market today?
10. Why is antivirus software important today?
11. What do the terms *bits* and *bytes* mean?
12. What are some popular pointing input devices for notebook computers?
13. How are resolution of a screen and resolution of a printer different and how are they similar?
14. What is the relationship between a megabyte, a gigabyte, and a terabyte?
15. What are the major types of storage devices? How do they compare in terms of updating capabilities and amount of storage?
16. What communications software do you typically need to use the Internet?
17. What is the role of expansion slots, expansion cards, ports, and connectors?

Assignments and Exercises

1. **CUSTOMIZING A COMPUTER PURCHASE.** One of the great things about the Web is the number of e-tailers that are now online offering you a variety of products and services. One such e-tailer is Dell, which allows you to customize and buy a computer. Connect to Dell's site (www.dell.ca). Go to the portion of Dell's site that allows you to customize either a notebook or a desktop computer. First, choose an already-prepared system and note its price and capability in terms of CPU speed, RAM size, monitor quality, and storage capacity. Now, customize that system to increase CPU speed, add more RAM, increase monitor size and quality, and add more storage capacity. What's the difference in price between the two? Which system is more in your price range? Which system has the speed and capacity you need?
2. **UNDERSTANDING THE COMPLEXITY OF SOFTWARE.** Software instructions, such as those in Figure C.18, must be provided to a computer in great detail and with excruciating accuracy. For example, you can easily change line 40 to read C = A + B + 1. If you did, your computer would follow it exactly and always arrive at the wrong result. To understand how detailed you must be, pick a partner for this project and imagine you are standing in a kitchen. The task for one of you is to write down all the instructions necessary to make a

peanut butter and jelly sandwich. When complete, have the other person follow those instructions exactly. How successful was the second person in making the sandwich? Did your instructions include every single step? What did you leave out?

3. **WEB-ENABLED CELL PHONES AND WEB COMPUTERS.** When categorizing computers by size for personal needs, we focused on PDAs, notebook computers, and desktop computers. There are several other variations, including Web-enabled cell phones that include instant text messaging and Web computers. For this project, you'll need a group of four people, split into two groups of two. Have the first group research Web-enabled cell phones, their capabilities, and their costs. Have that group make a purchase recommendation based on price and capability. Have the second group do the same for Web computers. What's your vision of the future? Will we ever get rid of clunky notebooks and desktops in favour of more portable and cheaper devices such as Web-enabled cell phones and Web computers? Why or why not?

4. **ADDING MEDIA TO A PRESENTATION.** We certainly live in a "multimedia" society, in which it's often easy to present and receive information using a variety of media. Presentation tools such as Microsoft's PowerPoint can help you easily build presentations that include audio, animation, and video. And this may help you get a better grade. Using your preferred presentation software, document the steps necessary to add a short audio or video clip to a presentation. How does the representation of the clip appear on a slide? How can you initiate it? Does your presentation software include any clips that you can insert or do you have to record your own? Now, try recording a short audio clip. What steps must you perform?

5. **OPERATING SYSTEM SOFTWARE FOR PDAS.** The personal digital assistant (PDA) market is a ferocious, dynamic, and uncertain one. One of the uncertainties is what operating system for PDAs will become the dominant one. For notebooks and desktops right now, you're pretty well limited to the Microsoft family unless you buy an Apple computer (in which case your operating system is Mac OS) or you want to venture into using Linux (which we wouldn't recommend for most people). Do some research on the more popular PDAs available today. What are the different operating systems? What different functionality do they offer? Are they compatible with each other? Take a guess—which one will come out on top?

6. **TYPES OF MONITORS AND THEIR QUALITY.** The monitor you buy will greatly affect your productivity. If you get a high-resolution, large-screen monitor, you'll see the screen content better than if you get a low-resolution, small-screen monitor. One factor in this is the monitor type. Seven major types are available today—HDTV, QXGA, SVGA, SXGA, UXGA, VGA, and XGA. Do a little research on them. Rank them from best to worst in terms of resolution. Also, determine a price for each.

EXTENDED LEARNING MODULE D

NETWORK BASICS

Student Learning Outcomes

1. Identify and describe the four basic concepts on which networks are built.
2. Describe how to set up a small peer-to-peer network at home.
3. Compare and contrast the various Internet connection possibilities.
4. Describe client/server business networks from a business and physical point of view.
5. Define and compare local area networks (LANs), municipal area networks (MANs), and wide area networks (WANs).
6. Compare and contrast the types of communications media.

Introduction

When you're surfing the Web, accessing software on your school's server, sending e-mail, or letting your roommate use his/her computer to access the files on yours, your computer is part of a network. A **computer network** (which we simply refer to as a *network*) is two or more computers connected so that they can communicate with each other and share information, software, peripheral devices, and/or processing power. Many networks have dozens, hundreds, or even thousands of computers.

BASIC PRINCIPLES OF NETWORKS

Networks come in all sizes, from two computers sharing a printer to the Internet. The Internet is the largest network on the planet, joining millions of computers of all kinds all over the world. In between are business networks, which vary in size from a dozen or fewer computers to many thousands.

Some basic principles apply to all networks, large or small.

1. Each computer on a network must have a network card (either as an expansion card or integrated into the motherboard) that provides the entrance or doorway in that computer for information traffic to and from other computers. An expansion card allows you to add a device to a computer. For example, a sound card is one type of expansion card. It makes the physical connection between the speakers/microphone and the motherboard, and is hence connected to the CPU, thereby allowing you to input and output sound. Similarly, a network connects the rest of the network to your motherboard, allowing you to send and receive messages to and from other computers on that network. Therefore, it's the doorway into for network traffic in and out of your computer.
2. A network usually has at least one connecting device (such as a hub or a router) that ties the computers on the network together and acts as a switchboard for passing messages.
3. There must be communications media like cables or radio waves connecting network hardware devices. The communications media transport information around the network between computers and the connecting device(s).
4. Each computer must have software that supports the movement of information in and out of the computer. This might be modem software and/or a network operating system.

First, we'll examine the smallest networks—a few computers connected in a home or dorm room—and then discuss ways to connect a single computer or home network to the largest network of them all, the Internet. Finally, we'll move on to large business networks, LANs, MANs, WANs, and communications media.

Peer-to-Peer Home Network

The simplest kind of network is a peer-to-peer network. If you have two computers and you'd like both to be able to print to a single printer, you can connect all three devices to create a **peer-to-peer network**—a network in which a small number of computers share hardware (such as a printer), software, and/or information. Each computer independently stores its own software and information, but can access the information on the other computers.

You can set up a small peer-to-peer network one of two ways—either with Ethernet cards and dedicated network cabling or by using your existing phone wiring.

HOME NETWORK COMPONENTS

You can set up a peer-to-peer network at home with a few computers—say between two and ten—to share a printer or an Internet connection relatively easily. You'll need:

- Ethernet network cards in each computer
- A home router as a connecting device to tie the computers together and pass messages between computers
- Cables as the transmission medium
- Software that allows information to flow between computers (Windows will do nicely)

NETWORK CARDS IN EACH COMPUTER First, the network cards—you'll need a network interface card in each computer. A **network interface card (NIC)** is an expansion card or a PC card (for a notebook computer) that connects your computer to a network and provides the doorway for information to flow in and out.

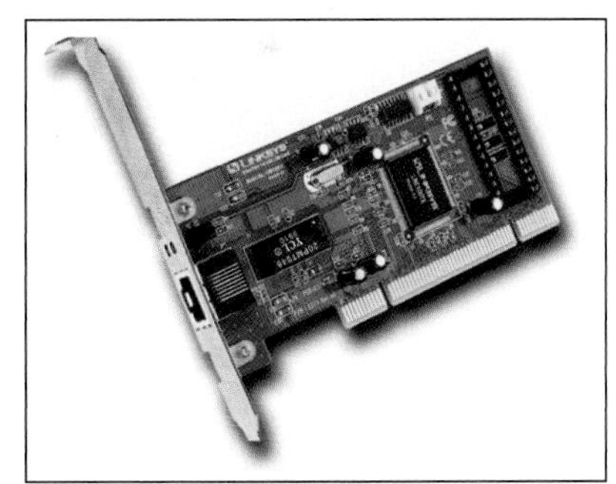

An **Ethernet card** is the most common type of network interface card. You plug the card into an ISA or PCI expansion slot in your desktop computer. An Ethernet card has a connector, usually an RJ-45 type that looks very like a telephone connector, except that it's a little larger. Ethernet cards are also sold as PC cards that plug into the side of notebook computers.

NETWORK CONNECTING DEVICES Second, the connecting device—you'll need a way to pass information and messages to the correct destination computers. To do that you use a connecting device that ties the computers together and lets information pass from one to the other. Network connecting devices come in various types. The ones we'll consider here are basic hubs, switches, and routers.

A **network hub** is a device that connects multiple computers into a network. A basic hub allows only one communication link at a time, in the same way that only one car at a time can proceed at an intersection that has four-way stop signs. Now imagine that, instead of just a junction of four roads, the intersection has hundreds of roads coming together. It might take a while for each car to move forward. In cities, where there's heavy traffic at road junctions, there are cloverleaf intersections so that no car has to stop and let others pass. In networking, a switch does the cloverleaf thing. A

Figure D.1
Hub, Switch, and Router as Roadway Intersections

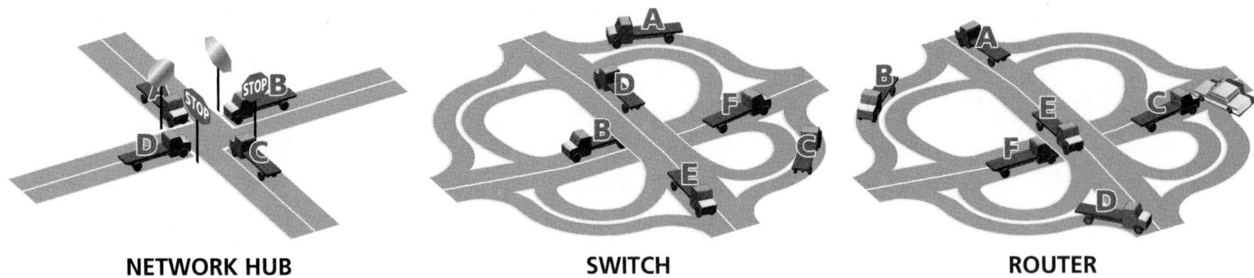

switch is a device that connects multiple computers into a network in which multiple communications links can be in operation simultaneously (see Figure D.1).

Four-way stop and cloverleaf intersections let all vehicles go wherever they want. This is fine for highways, but not so good for information on networks. Back in the metropolis, let's say one road runs between two large intersections, one of which is in Internet City and other in Home Network City. If Home Network City were to be quarantined, police would set up a roadblock just outside Home Network City, and every vehicle is checked to see that it's actually going to a destination in Home Network City. If it's not, the vehicle is turned back. Also, the police won't let vehicles through whose origin and destination are both in Home Network City.

The roadblock separates the two cities and their traffic. In networking, the police roadblock is a router, but the router does more—it's also the cloverleaf. A **router** is a device that acts as a smart hub connecting computers into a network, and it also separates your network from any other network it's connected to. In fact, this isolating feature of routers is precisely the reason that network administrators install routers on larger networks, and it's related to how an Ethernet network works.

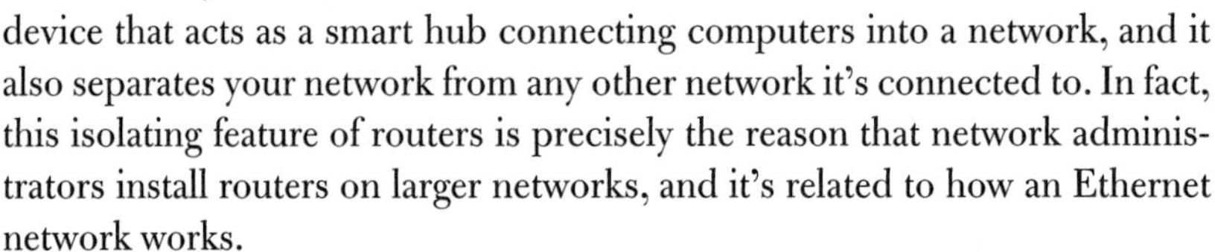

On an Ethernet network, each message sent out goes to all the computers on the network and each computer looks at the address on the message to see if it's meant for that computer or not. This makes the network relatively simple to design and operate, but it means that a large file can slow the network down since every computer looks at every message that every other computer sends. A way around this problem is to divide the large network into smaller networks and connect them with a router. A router is a device you can use to connect two networks, passing information from one to the other. A router makes sure that messages get to the right destination computer without going to everyone else, but makes also sure that the messages go outside the network only when necessary.

In a home network, the isolating feature of a router is a very good reason to use it, since the network you're separating yours from is the Internet (see Figure D.2). You want to be able to send and receive information and messages to and from the Internet, but you don't want unauthorized access from intruders. A home router protects your home network by making it more or less invisible to the Internet. It therefore acts as a hardware firewall, giving you much better security for your home computers. A **firewall** is software or hardware that protects your network from intruders.

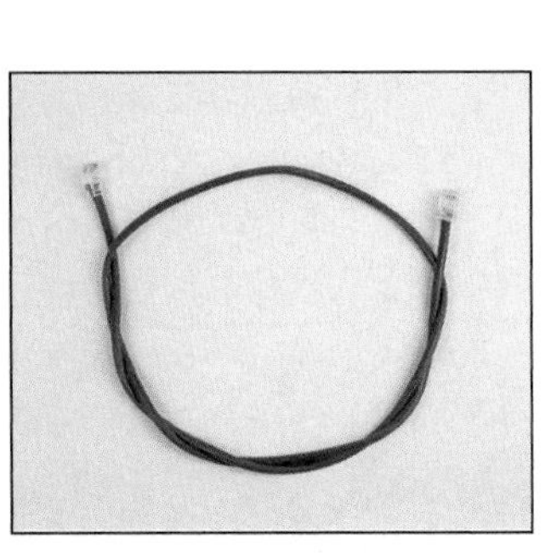

WIRED AND WIRELESS TRANSMISSION MEDIA The most common transmission medium for a home network is Cat 5 cable, which is similar to phone cable (ordinary twisted-pair cable). **Cat 5**, or Category 5, cable is a better-constructed version of

Figure D.2
Typical Home Network

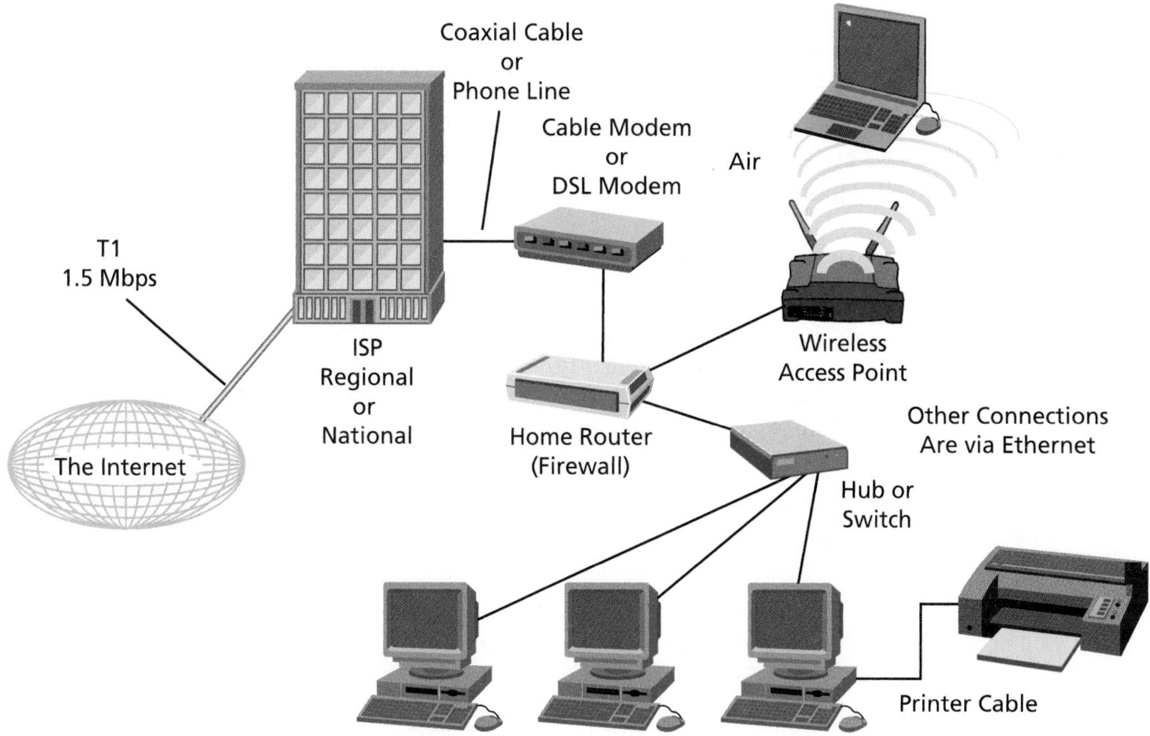

the phone twisted-pair cable. Each end of the Cat 5 cable has an RJ-45 connector. One plugs into the Ethernet card in your computer and the other end into the home router.

WIRELESS ACCESS TO YOUR HOME NETWORK

If you'd like to wirelessly access your home network with your notebook computer, you'll need another device on the network called a wireless network access point. A **wireless network access point** or **wireless access point** is a device that allows computers to access a wired network using radio waves. A wireless access point has a transmitter and a receiver for the bi-directional flow of information. It also has an antenna to capture the radio waves out of the air.

Your wireless access point connects with a cable to the hub or switch in the same way wired computers do (see Figure D.2). Your notebook and any other device that wirelessly accesses the network must have a wireless adapter, which would be a PC card in the case of the notebook computer, which incorporates a transmitter, a receiver, and an antenna. A wireless access point is usually itself a router, so you could have a completely wireless network using the wireless access point as the connecting device.

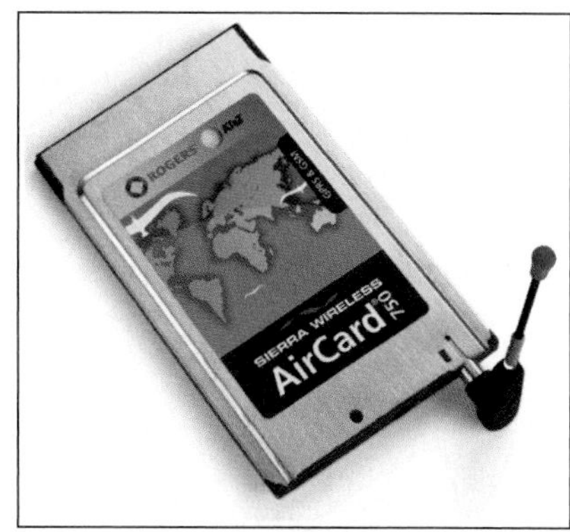

The type of wave transmission often used in home networks is **WiFi**—which stands for **wireless fidelity** (also known as **IEEE 802.11b**), a way of transmitting information in wave form that is reasonably fast and is often used for notebooks. Currently, two million people use it and that number is expected to double within a year. Apart from home networks, WiFi is used by companies to allow their employees to go wireless, and is also available in various public places like airports, hotels and even restaurants such as Happy Donuts and Starbucks. Pretty soon we'll have WiFi-capable airplanes.[1]

A relatively new and competing wireless technology for short-range wireless connections, also using radio waves, is called Bluetooth. Named for a Viking king, **Bluetooth** technology provides entirely wireless connections for all kinds of communication devices. For example, Bluetooth could replace the cable connecting a notebook to a cellular telephone. Virtually all digital devices, such as keyboards, joysticks, printers, etc., can be part of a Bluetooth system. Bluetooth is also adaptable to home appliances like refrigerators and microwaves.

NETWORK SOFTWARE As always, when you have hardware, you need software to make it work. For a small home network, Windows will do fine (use version Windows 98 SE or newer) and must be installed on each network computer. To make the files on your computer available to the other computers on the network, you have to turn on the filesharing option in Windows and indicate which drives, directories, or files to share. When you do this the files on one computer will appear as additional folders on the other computer.

HOME NETWORK WITH EXISTING PHONE WIRING

A relatively new technology called **Home PNA**, which stands for Home Phoneline Networking Alliance, allows you to network your home computers using telephone wiring. You'll need:

- PNA adapter cards for each computer
- Ordinary phone wire with phone jacks for each computer

First, you must install a PNA adapter card in each computer. A **PNA adapter card** is an expansion card you put into your computer to act as a doorway for information flowing in and out. The PNA adapter card has a connector for a telephone jack (RJ-11 connector) into which you plug one end of the phone cable. You plug the other end into an extra phone jack in the wall (see Figure D.3). And that's pretty much all you have to do, assuming you have a late version of Windows on all the computers.

Note that in this case you don't need a router. You also don't need special cable or connectors. It's simpler than the previous home network configuration, but it's also slower.

Figure D.3
Home PNA Network

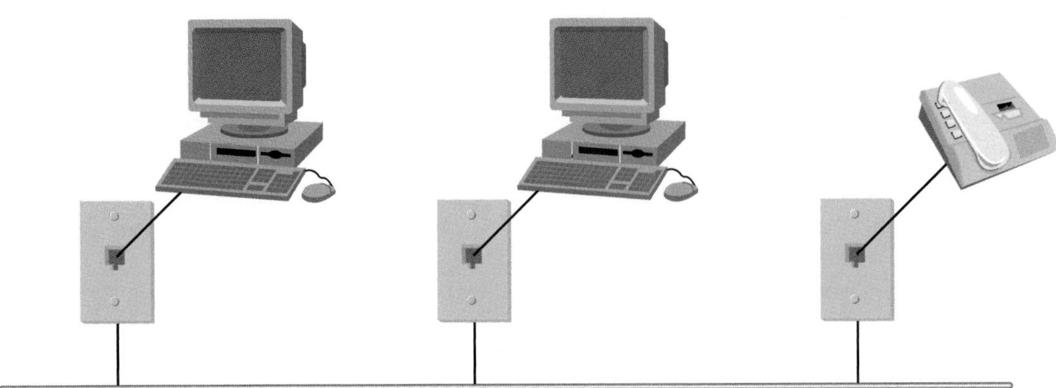

Internet Access

Whether or not you have a network at home, if you have a computer you are probably already connected to the Internet, or want to be. There are five possible ways of accessing the Internet from home. These include using:

- A telephone line and a telephone or dial-up modem
- A telephone line and a digital subscriber line (DSL) modem
- A cable TV line and a cable modem
- A satellite dish and a satellite modem
- A provider that offers wireless connection for your notebook computer or one that offers wireless connection for handheld devices (some cellular phone companies do this)

DSL, cable, satellite, and metropolitan wireless systems are broadband connections. **Broadband** is a high-capacity telecommunications pipeline capable of providing high-speed Internet service. There is some disagreement in the industry as to what "high-speed" means exactly. The U.S. Federal Communications Commission defines it as a capacity of 200 kBps (or 200 kilobytes per second) both upstream and downstream. At the other end of the spectrum are experts who believe that the telecommunications speed must be at least 750 kBps.

TELEPHONE OR DIAL-UP CONNECTION

A telephone or dial-up connection requires that you have a computer, a phone line, a modem, and, of course, an Internet service provider or ISP. Simply put, a telephone modem is a telephone for your computer. People use a phone apparatus to talk to each other using the phone lines. Similarly, computers can use telephone or dial-up modems to swap information. A **telephone modem** (usually referred to as simply a **modem**) is a device that connects your computer to your phone line so that you can access another computer or network. If you want to connect to the Internet, you use your modem to first access your ISP. Your ISP then connects you to the Internet. A modem is a device that converts the digital signals from your computer into analog form (by modulating the signal) that can be transmitted over a phone line, and then converts the analog signal back to digital signals (by demodulating the signal) for the computer at the receiving end of the transmission (see Figure D.4). In short, a modem *mo*dulates and then *dem*odulates transmissions.

Nowadays, telephone modems are often integrated into the motherboard of new computers. If your computer doesn't have this feature, you can buy a modem board or card to plug into a PCI expansion slot in your desktop or a PC card for your notebook computer.

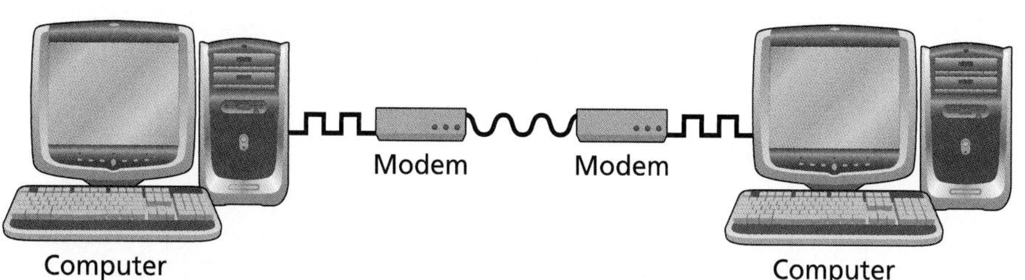

Figure D.4

The Role of a Telephone Modem

A telephone modem provides the slowest Internet connection you can get. The fastest transmission possible with a telephone modem is 56 kbps (or about 56,000 bits per second).

DIGITAL SUBSCRIBER LINE (DSL)

A **digital subscriber line (DSL)** is a high-speed Internet connection using phone lines, which allows you to use your phone for voice communications at the same time. There are many kinds of DSL systems (ADSL or asymmetric DSL, SDSL or symmetric DSL, HDSL or high-bit-rate DSL, to name a few). DSL divides your phone line into channels which separate the information and voice traffic on the line so you can still make and take phone calls while you're connected to the Web.

In order to get a DSL Internet connection at all, you need to live close within about 4.8 kilometres of the phone company offering the service, called the CO or central office. In larger cities, remote COs are located throughout the metropolitan area. The speed of your DSL line depends on the distance between you and the CO. Speeds vary from 144 kbps (144,000 bits per second) to 1.54 Mbps (1,540,000 bits per second) and can even go as high as 6.0 Mbps. A phone company provides the DSL connection. However, you can buy the Internet service directly from the phone company, in which case it becomes your ISP too, or from an independent ISP that buys the service from the phone company and sells it to you.

Once you're within range of a DSL provider, you'll need a DSL modem that connects on one side to the splitter at your house and on the other to your computer (see Figure D.5). The cable from the DSL modem connects to your computer in one of two ways, either to an Ethernet card in your computer or to a USB port. A DSL Internet connection has three big advantages over a dial-up connection:

1. DSL is much faster—up to 25 times faster than a telephone modem.
2. DSL is an "always on" connection giving you Web access without having to dial into your ISP first.
3. You can still use the same phone line for voice communications.

CABLE MODEM

If you have cable television, you know it comes into your home on a coaxial cable that connects to your television set. This same cable can connect you to the Internet too. Both cable TV signals and your Internet connection travel from the cable company on one wire.

Figure D.5
DSL Internet Access

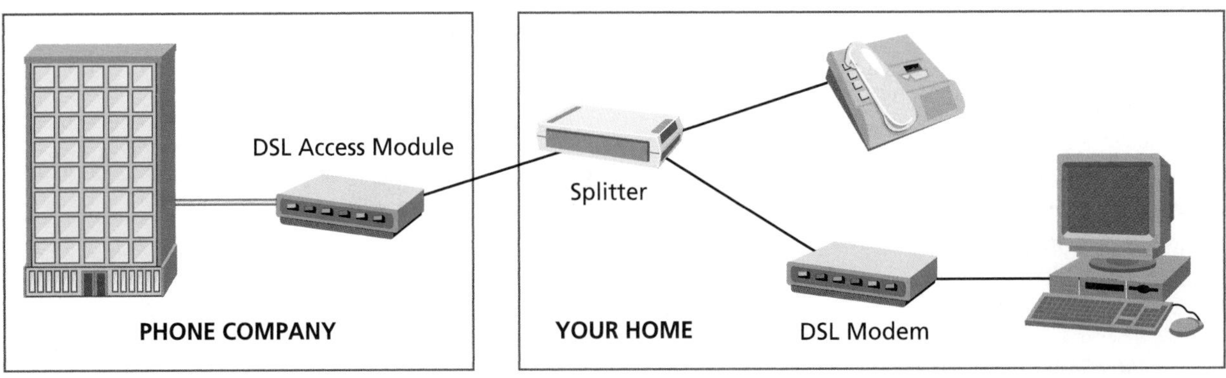

Figure D.6
Cable Internet Access

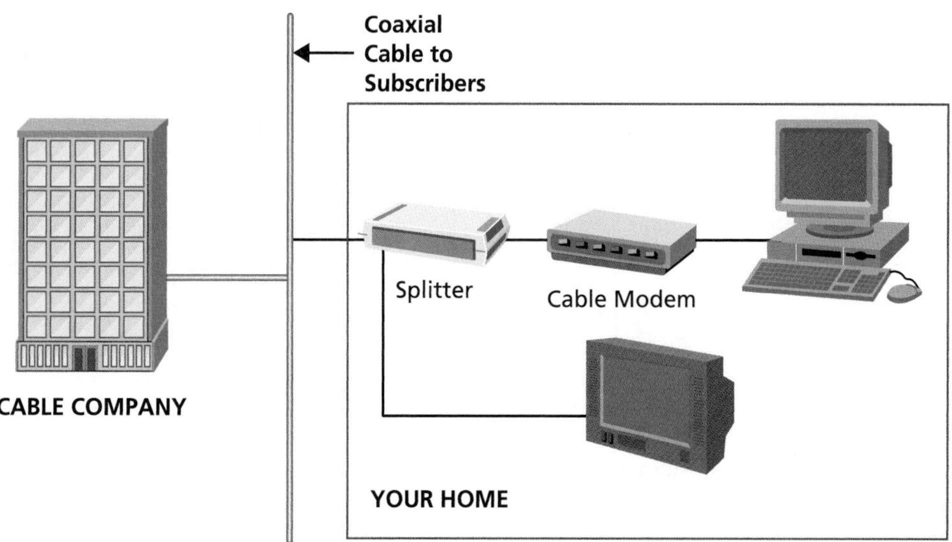

A splitter at your home splits the incoming cable sending one part to the TV and the other to your cable modem. A **cable modem** is a device that uses your TV cable to deliver an Internet connection (see Figure D.6). The cable from the cable modem attaches to either an Ethernet card (an expansion card that connects your computer to a network) or to a USB port in your computer. The speed of transmission with a cable modem is much faster than with a phone modem. It's also an "always on" connection and doesn't use a phone line at all.

While the speed of a DSL connection is guaranteed, the speed of a cable Internet connection depends on how many users are online. If all your neighbours are surfing the Web with a cable connection at the same time you are, you'll notice a reduction in your access speed.

INTERNET OVER SATELLITE

You can also get to the Internet using a satellite dish and a satellite modem. This is called *Internet over satellite (IoS)*. Satellite Internet uses a satellite dish that looks very like your TV satellite dish (or antenna). A **satellite modem** is a modem that allows you to get Internet access from a satellite dish (see Figure D.7). You'll need the right type of satellite dish (i.e., antenna).

The big difference between a TV satellite dish and an Internet satellite disk is that a satellite Internet antenna is two-way—you can send as well as receive transmissions. You can get a system for Internet access alone or one that gives you both Internet access and satellite TV. Internet over satellite is relatively new and is an ideal way of bringing the power of the Internet to isolated locations.

The speed of information coming to you is called download speed. The download speed of an Internet satellite is about 10 times faster than that of a phone modem.

For satellite Internet you'll need:

- An appropriate satellite dish
- A satellite modem
- A cable between the satellite modem and the dish

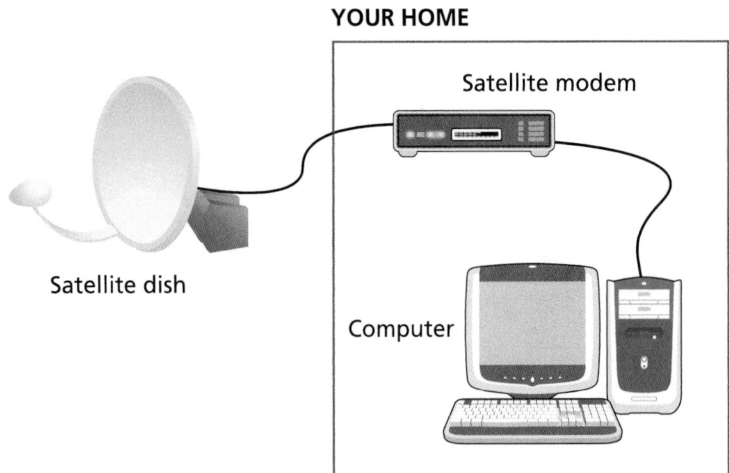

Figure D.7
Satellite Internet Access

- An unobstructed view in the direction of the equator, above which the telecommunications satellites orbit (your dish will point south if you're in the northern hemisphere and north if you're in the southern hemisphere)

INTERNET ACCESS ON MULTIPLE COMPUTERS

If you'd like to have one Internet connection for your whole home network, you can do it with DSL, a cable Internet connection, or an Internet over satellite. You'll be able to use the same home router because routers have IP addresses of their own, which they assign to each computer on the network.

Say you have a cable modem, then the cable provider assigns you one IP address. The router also has something called a *network address translator (NAT)*, which swaps messages between the computer IP addresses and the modem IP address.

A word of caution. Before you hook up a network to a single Internet connection, make sure that it's not a violation of the contract you signed with your ISP.

WIRELESS INTERNET CONNECTION

If your notebook, or desktop for that matter, has a wireless port and the network you're accessing has a wireless access point within range, you can wirelessly join that network. And if the network has Web access, you can get to it too. But what if you don't have access to such a network?

In that case, you'll need a **wireless Internet service provider (wireless ISP)**, who does the same job as standard Internet service providers except that you don't need a wired connection for access. In fact, some ISPs provide both wired and wireless connections. If you travel a lot, you'll need a wireless ISP with a wide geographic reach, just as you do with a cellular phone.

If you want to reach the Web with something smaller than a notebook, you can use handheld wireless devices such as a PDA, Web phone, or pager. A **personal digital assistant (PDA)** is a small handheld computer that helps you surf the Web and perform simple tasks such as note-taking, calendaring, appointment scheduling, and maintaining an address book.

Probably, PDAs will be the dominant handheld wireless devices of the future for Internet access. Distinctions between handheld devices, however, are already blurring. Some manufacturers are already combining cellular phones and PDAs. Some are mostly phones with PDA capabilities, and others are PDAs with phone capabilities.

There are two major types of PDAs, (1) Palms and Handspring and (2) PocketPCs. The difference between Palms/Handspring and PocketPCs is similar to the difference between PCs and Macs in that they use different operating systems. The Palm/Handspring-type PDAs run on the **Palm Operating System (Palm OS)**, while PocketPCs run on **Pocket PC OS** (which used to be called **Windows CE**).

Wireless ISPs support one or the other or both, so if you plan on buying a wireless PDA for Internet access, be sure to check it out. In general, don't expect to surf the Web with a handheld wireless device the way you would with a notebook or desktop. The various wireless service providers use one of several other standards that were designed for cell phones and, while they're fine for talking, they're too slow for good Web access. The drawbacks of using handheld devices for Web access are that access is very slow and not particularly reliable. Also, the screen is too small to be able to see it well.

Business Networks

In the peer-to-peer home networks described above the computers were all equal. Each one had its own files and devices, which it can share with the other computers. But, unless you're a business with very few computers, you'd probably use a client/server network instead of a peer-to-peer network.

A **client/server network** is one in which one or more computers are *servers* and provide services to the other computers which are called *clients*. The server or servers have hardware, software, and/or information that the client computers can access. Servers are usually powerful computers with large storage systems. Depending on the network, the server could be a high-end PC or a minicomputer and large companies often have several servers, each of which may provide services to different parts of the company. It's usually cheaper and more efficient to have software on a server where everyone can access it:

- A network licence allowing a fixed number of people or everyone on the network to use a software package is usually cheaper than buying separate copies of software for each computer.
- It's easier to update one server copy of software than to update hundreds or even thousands of separate copies.
- Control and security of software and information is easier if they're on the server.

CLIENT/SERVER: A BUSINESS VIEW

The term *client/server network* can mean a network structure, that is, one or more computers providing services to other computers. However, the term also describes a business model. As a business model, "client/server" describes distributed processing. That is, it describes where processing takes place. Different companies have different processing needs. For example, if your school has an online system on which you can check your grades, you'll probably find that you can't change grades at your end—access to that kind of processing is severely restricted. On the other hand, a bank employee would need to be able to process a loan at his or her computer.

You can use one of five basic client/server implementation models. Which you use depends on your business environment and where you want processing implemented. Client/server networks differ according to three factors:

1. Where the processing for the presentation of information occurs, that is, where the information that you see on the screen or printout is formatted, and the editing of information as you enter it.

TEAM WORK

WHAT SORT OF COMPUTER NETWORK DOES YOUR SCHOOL HAVE?

Find out what kind of network your school has. Ask the technical people the following questions:

- How many computers are on the network?
- How many people use the computers?
- What is the computer to student ratio?
- How many servers, the computers that provide services to other computers, are there? (For example, there's probably an e-mail server.)

Here's an example of the concept. Say you have a data warehouse with information on sales over the past five years. Your client workstation gets its information from your company's OLTP (online transaction processing) server or servers. Software on the servers extract the information you need and transfer it to your client workstation. Your client workstation then builds the data warehouse according to your requirements and you can use your data warehouse for the OLAP (online analytical processing) you need.

In this example, you see a separation of duties to suit particular business needs. The servers process company-wide OLTP software on transaction information, and copy to your workstation the information you want to have. Your client computer has, and processes, only the information that you need. This is in fact called a distributed data management model where the server's only duty is to help with data management; the client does everything else (see Figure D.8). This is one way of assigning the processing, logic, and data management. In the set of models that you'll see next, this is Model 5.

Figure D.8

Model 5: A Personal Data Warehouse in a Client/Server Implementation

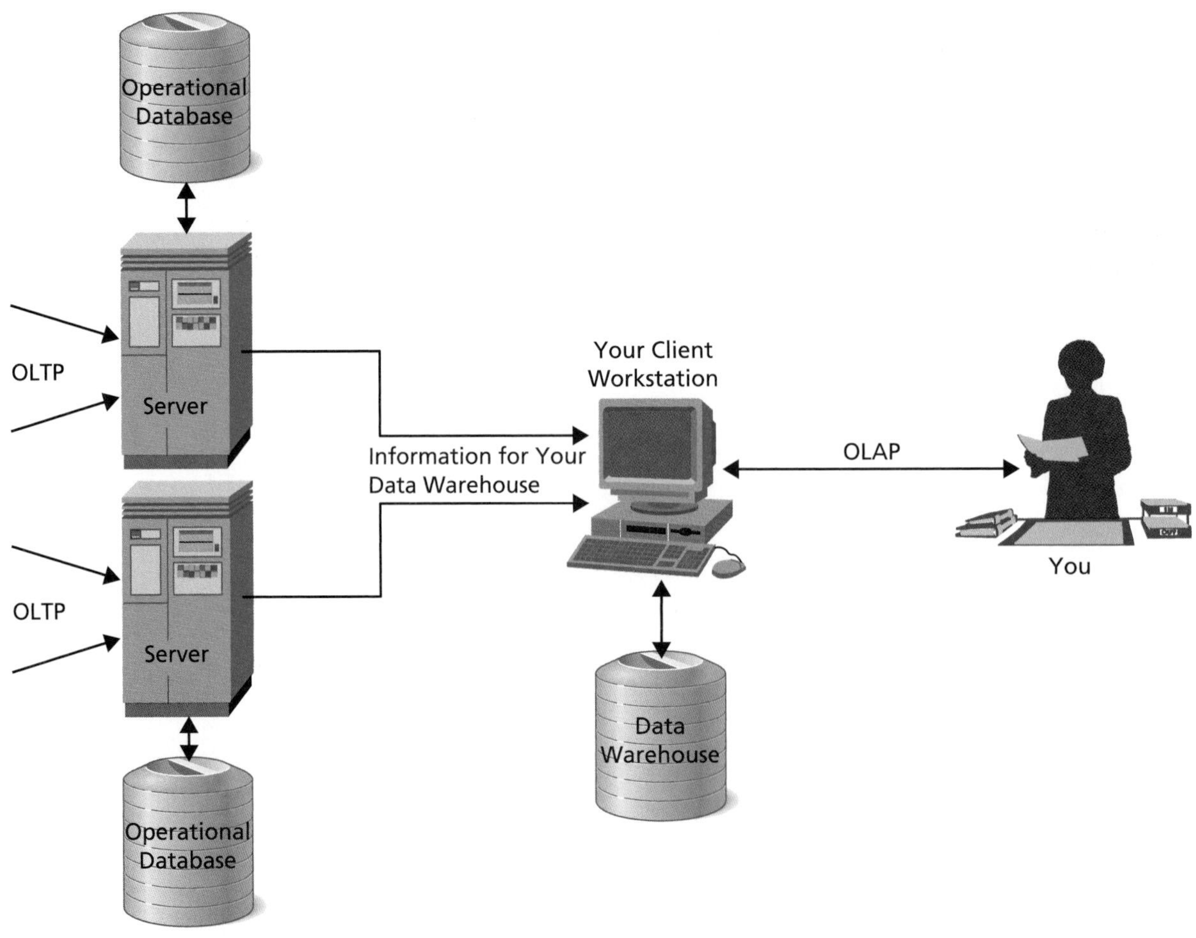

2. Where the processing of logic or business rules occurs. *Logic* deals with the processing the software implements. For example, in a payroll application, the logic would dictate how to handle overtime, sick leave, and vacation time.
3. Where the data management component (DBMS) and information (database) are located. Or, to put it another way, how the information in the database is stored and retrieved.

Each of the five business client/server models that follow has a different way of parcelling out the three tasks of presentation processing, logic processing, and data management. See Figure D.9 for a graphical representation of the five models.

CLIENT/SERVER MODEL 1: DISTRIBUTED PRESENTATION In this first model, the server handles almost all functions, including a major portion of the presentation. The only processing that the client does is to help with formatting of the information you see on the screen or printout.

CLIENT/SERVER MODEL 2: REMOTE PRESENTATION In the second model, the client handles all presentation functions. The processing of business rules happens on the server as does data management.

CLIENT/SERVER MODEL 3: DISTRIBUTED LOGIC In this model, the server handles all data management and the client handles all presentation formatting, but the logic processing is shared between the server and the client.

CLIENT/SERVER MODEL 4: REMOTE DATA MANAGEMENT In the fourth model, duties are fully separated again. The server handles data management only, and the client processes business rules and formats the presentation of results. (In the name of this model, the word "remote" is apparently from the client's viewpoint, unlike for Model 2.)

CLIENT/SERVER MODEL 5: DISTRIBUTED DATA MANAGEMENT In this final model, the client handles all presentation formatting and business rule processing, and both the server and client share data management duties.

Which model you choose depends on the organization of your business and where you want processing to occur. We have already looked at Model 5, so now let's examine a more complicated case—Model 3, distributed logic.

CLIENT/SERVER IMPLEMENTATION: MODEL 3 In Model 3 (distributed logic), the server handles the entire data management function, the client handles the entire presentation function, and server and client share in the processing or application of business rules (see Figure D.10).

Suppose you're the manager of the manufacturing division of an organization and need to give pay raises to each of your employees. You use the following divisional and organizational rules for determining pay raises.

Divisional Rules

1. Each manufacturing employee begins with a base raise of $2500.
2. No manufacturing employee can receive less than a $2000 raise.
3. If loss of time because of injury is longer than three days, deduct $500 from the pay raise.
4. If the employee worked less than five days of overtime, deduct $500 from the pay raise.

Figure D.9
Five Models for Client/Server Implementation[2]

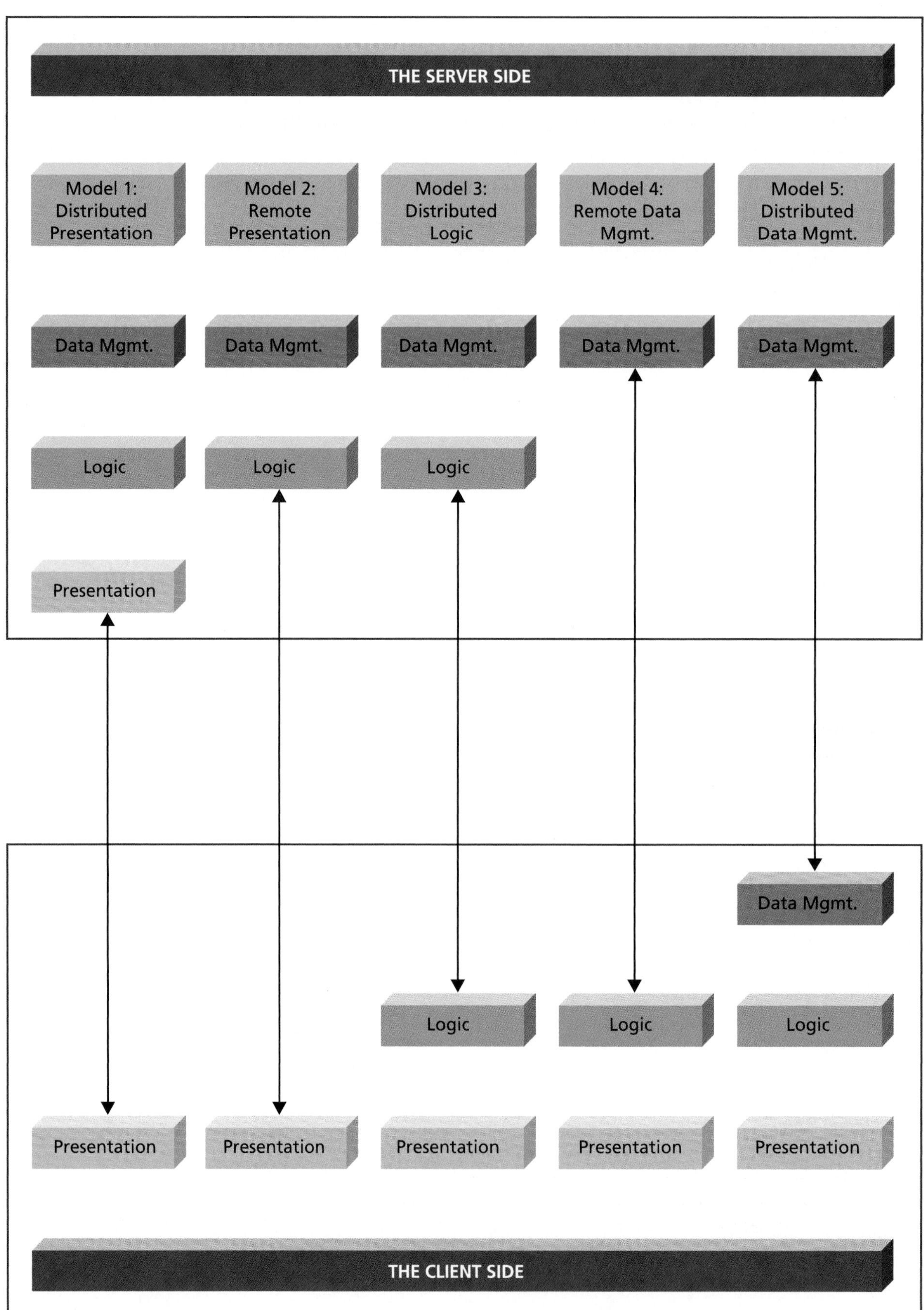

Organizational Rules

1. No employee with less than five years of experience can receive a pay raise that exceeds $2500.
2. Each employee's pay raise must be within 20 percent of last year's raise.
3. Each employee who has taken three or more business-related trips in the last year gets an extra $500 raise.

The following process would then determine the exact pay raise for each employee:

1. You would request information for the employee.
2. Your client workstation would send that request to the server.
3. The server would retrieve the employee information from the employee database.
4. The server would return the employee information to your client workstation.
5. Your client workstation would execute the divisional manufacturing business rules (or logic) that apply to pay raises for manufacturing employees.
6. Your client workstation would format and present the information pertaining to the employee and the appropriate pay raise.
7. You would submit the proposed pay raise for processing.
8. Your client workstation would send that information to the server.
9. The server would execute the organizational business rules or logic relating to pay raises for all employees.
10. The server would return the employee's pay raise (modified according to the organizational business rules) to your work station.
11. Your client workstation would format and present the modified pay raise.
12. You would submit the finalized pay raise for final processing.
13. Your client workstation would send that information to the server.
14. The server would update the employee database to reflect the employee's pay raise.

In this example the server was responsible for data management (retrieving and updating employee information) and executing the business rules or logic that apply to all employees for pay raises. Your client workstation is responsible for editing your entry of information, formatting the presentation of information to you, and executing the business rules or logic that apply to pay raises for manufacturing employees.

When you take the process of distributed logic apart as we did in this example, it seems very complex and tedious. And if you're writing the software to do it, it is. However, as a knowledge worker, the process is completely transparent, meaning that you don't know (or care) how data management, logic, and presentation are handled.

From a management point of view, client/server is a very tidy, organized, and flexible way to make information that all managers need available to them, while keeping information and processing that individual departments need local to the appropriate office.

CLIENT/SERVER: A PHYSICAL VIEW

There are more physical implementations of client/server networks than cars on the road. However, conceptually, large networks work on the same principle as little ones. You still need network cards, hubs, switches, and/or routers, communications media, and network operating systems on all the computers in the network. However, this is not to say that large networks are simple to build and maintain—they most definitely are not. The number of considerations goes up exponentially with the size of the network. For a client/server network, you need a special operating system for the servers.

Figure D.10
Model 3: Client/Server Implementation for Employee Pay Raises

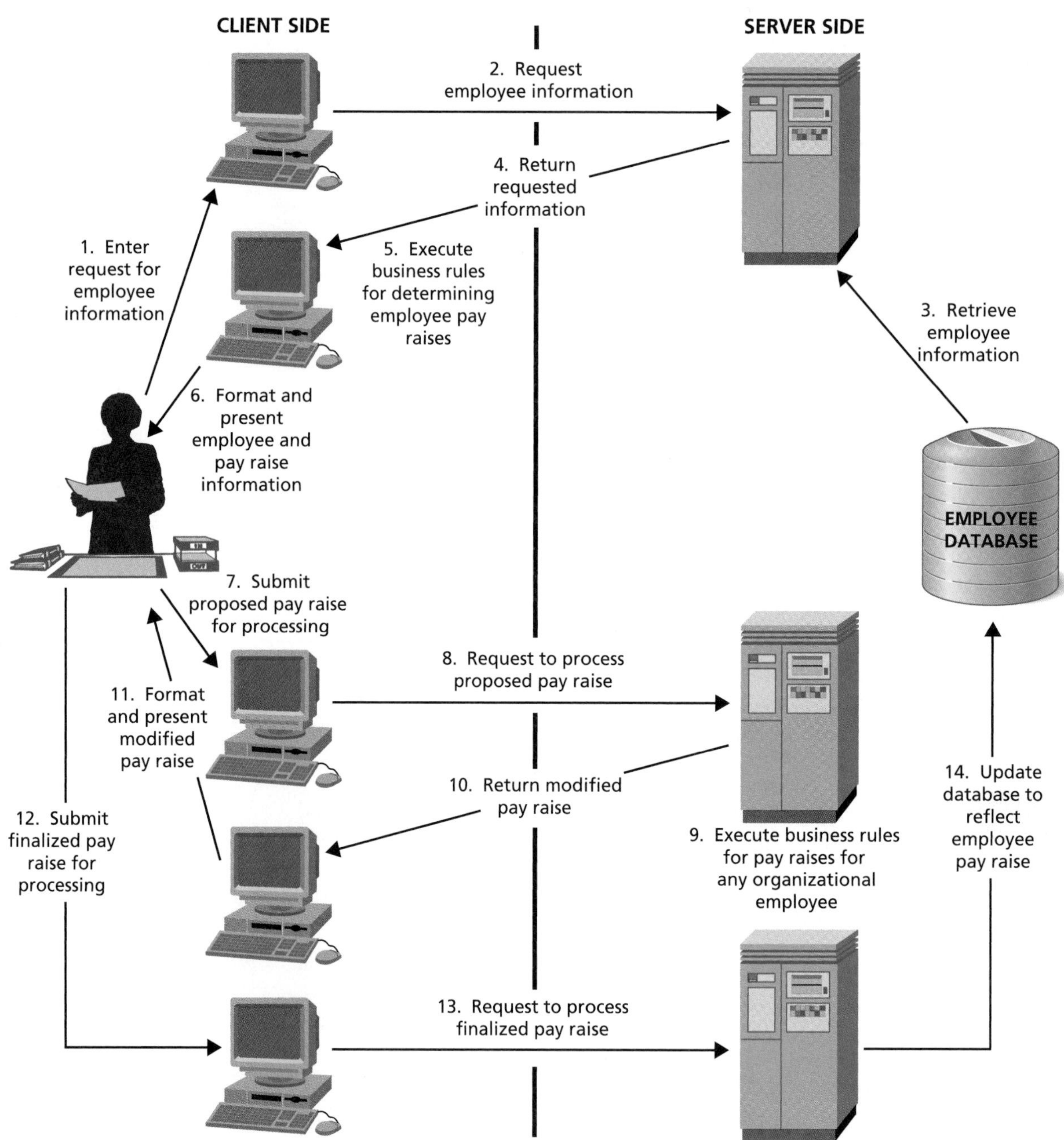

You may have to install special network processors, such as multiplexors, which collect transmissions from several communications media and send them over a single line that operates at a higher capacity. You also have to consider the type of topology (how the computers and servers are arranged in relation to each other) and what sort of protocol to use. A **communications protocol (protocol)** is a set of rules that every computer follows to transfer information. You may have heard of TCP/IP (transmission control protocol/Internet protocol) which is the protocol that computers connected to the Internet have to use to be able to talk to the other computers. It's quite a simple concept—if the computers don't all speak the same language they can't communicate. The electronic data interchange (EDI) of basic business documents that

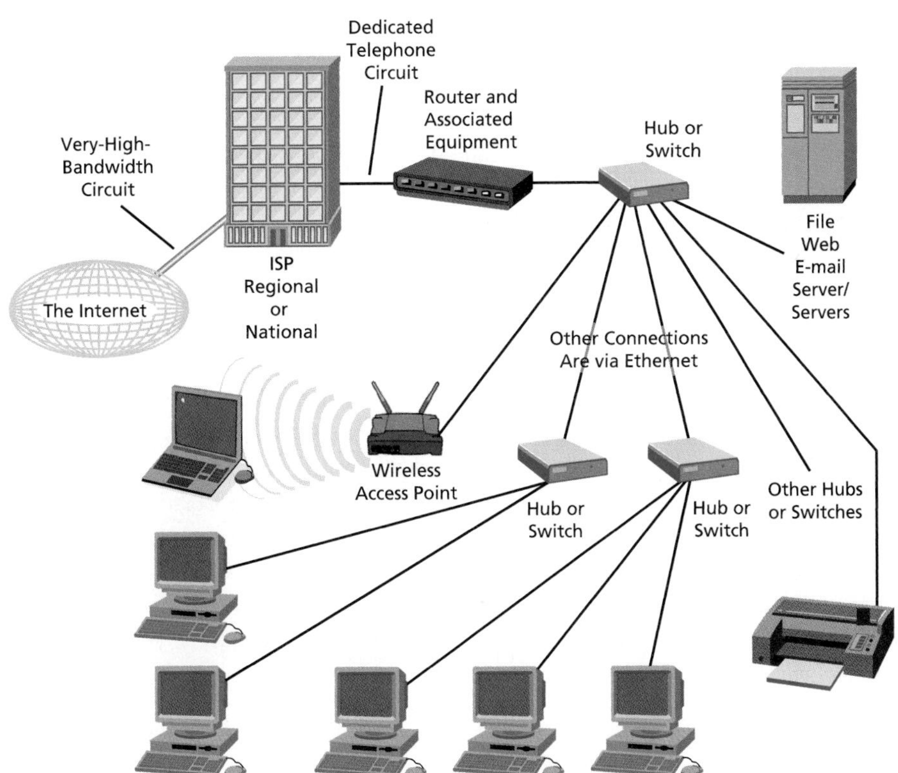

Figure D.11

A Typical Client/Server Network for a Medium-Sized Business

you learned about in Chapter 2 uses ANSI X.12 protocol. So a network wanting to access the Web and conduct EDI will need both protocols.

Figure D.11 shows a typical Ethernet configuration for a medium-sized business. You can see that, in this network, the company has a dedicated phone circuit (discussed later in this Module), which is necessary for the amount of traffic that a medium-sized business would have. A router connects the company's network to the ISP which provides Internet access. A hub or switch serves to connect the smaller company networks to the server or servers, which will have control over the organizational databases, and there might also be a wireless network connection for people with laptops. One or more servers are also available to all the computers in the network. One server would most likely provide Internet and e-mail services.

An enterprise-wide network might span many provinces or even be scattered all over the world. Such a network would most likely have mainframes and older, legacy networks that must be tied to the more modern network. Parts of the network would need high bandwidth or high-capacity communications media (which we'll discuss later). There would probably be multiple servers on such a large network, probably one for each of the smaller networks.

LANs, MANs, WANs, and Communications Media

Many, many types of networks exist today. Earlier in this Module we discussed peer-to-peer and client/server networks. A peer-to-peer network is one in which all the computers are equal and share information and hardware. A client/server network has one or more computers that provide services to the others. However, this isn't the only way you can classify computer networks. You can also classify networks by geographic distance.

CLASSIFICATION OF NETWORKS BY GEOGRAPHIC DISTANCE

There are three basic types of networks in this category: LANs, MANs, and WANs. A **local area network (LAN)** covers a limited geographic distance, such as an office, building, or a group of buildings close to each other. A **municipal area network (MAN)** covers a metropolitan area.

Wide area networks (WANs) cover large geographic distances, such as a province, a country, or even the entire world. A wide area network is essentially a network of smaller networks. The Internet is the biggest WAN on the planet. When a company's LAN is connected to the Internet, the LAN becomes part of a WAN.

An example of a company WAN is Metropolitan Life Insurance Co., which uses a WAN to connect its LANs.[3] At Met Life, a central server makes the organization's pension database available to employees who work all over the country. The database has information on all current and prospective clients, as well as information about competitors. Each LAN also has its own server with a database of client and product information for that particular area. As updates are made at each LAN site the LAN servers communicate those updates to the central WAN server. Likewise, the central server updates all appropriate information on the LAN site servers nightly. When Met Life sales associates are on the road, they can dial into the central server to receive whatever updates they need.

TELECOMMUNICATIONS MEDIA—THE PATHS THAT CARRY INFORMATION

The objective of networks and telecommunications is to move information from one place to another. This may be as simple as sending information to the office next door, or as far-reaching as sending a message to the other side of the world. Whatever the case, information must travel over some path from its source to its destination. **Communications media** are the paths, or physical channels, in a network over which information travels.

All communications are either wired or wireless. **Wired communications media** transmit information over a closed, connected path. **Wireless communications media** transmit information through the air. Forms of wired and wireless communications media include:

Wired	**Wireless**
Twisted-pair cable	Microwave
Coaxial cable	Satellite
Optical fibre	Infrared

BANDWIDTH

Before discussing the various types of communications media we should first address bandwidth. **Bandwidth**, or the capacity of the communications medium, refers to the amount of information that a communications medium can transfer in a given amount of time. You measure the capacity of a communications medium in bits per second (bps), thousands of bits per second (kbs), or millions of bits per second (Mbps). For example, if a particular communications medium has a maximum capacity of 16 megabits per second (Mbps), up to 16 million bits of information can be transferred in a single second. The bandwidth is comparable to the size of a drinking straw. The fatter the straw, the more liquid you can drink in a given period of time.

ON YOUR OWN

HOW IS A SERVER DIFFERENT FROM A CLIENT COMPUTER?

Compare a high-end desktop PC designed to be a network server and a typical PC designed for a single individual. What's the difference in the CPU chips? What's the difference in price? How many CPUs are there in the server? Is there a difference in the memory (the amount and type) in the two machines? How about the hard disk drives? Is there any sort of automatic backup on the server? Would you like such an automatic backup system on your computer? Why or why not? Dell (www.dell.ca) and Gateway (www.gateway.com) are places you could start, although they're only two of the many, many sites selling servers.

WIRED COMMUNICATIONS MEDIA

Wired communications media are those which tie devices together with cables of some kind. Twisted pair, coaxial cable, and optical fibre are the types of cabling you'd find in computer networks.

TWISTED-PAIR Twisted-pair cable comes in several varieties. The Cat 5, which you have already read about in connection with home networks earlier in this Module, is one type. Most of the world's phone system is twisted-pair, and since it's already in place it's an obvious choice for networks.

The simplest type of twisted-pair phone cabling (Cat 1) provides a slow, fairly reliable path for information at up to 64 kilobits per second (kbps), while a better type (Cat 3) provides up to 10 megabits per second (Mbps). However, distance, noise on the line, and interference tend to limit reliability most types of twisted-pair cabling. For example, a crackle that changes a credit card number from 5244 0811 2643 741 to 5244 0810 2643 741 is more than a nuisance; in business it means re-transmitting the information or applying a charge to the wrong person's credit card.

Cat 5 or Category 5 provides a much higher bandwidth than ordinary phone cable, meaning it carries more information in a given time period, at least for distances up to 91 metres. It's the most widely used cabling for data transfer in today's LANs. Cat 5 is relatively inexpensive and is fairly easy to install and maintain. Note, however, that twisted-pair of any kind is relatively easy to tap into and so it's not very secure. It's even possible to access the information by simply detecting the signals that "leak" out.

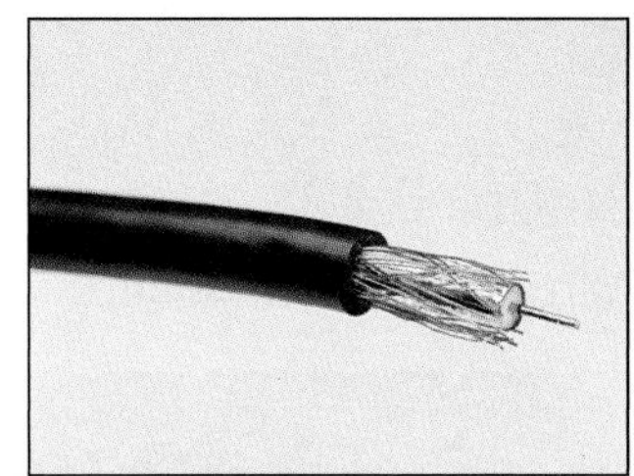

COAXIAL CABLE An alternative to twisted-pair cable is **coaxial cable (coax)**, which is one central wire surrounded by insulation, a metallic shield, and a final case of insulating material. (Coax is the kind of cable that delivers cable television transmissions and also carries satellite TV from the dish to your house.) While coaxial cable was once the cable of choice for internal LAN wiring, it has been almost completely replaced by twisted-pair cable. Coaxial cable is capable of carrying at least 500 Mbps, or the equivalent of 15,000 voice calls, simultaneously. Because of its shielded construction, coaxial cable is much less susceptible to outside interference and information damage than twisted-pair cable. However, coaxial cable is generally more expensive than twisted-pair and is more difficult to install and maintain. Security is about the same with coaxial cable as with twisted-pair, except that the radiation, or leaking, of information is much less. Coax is commonly used for leased-line private networks.

OPTICAL FIBRES The fastest and most efficient medium for wired communication is **optical fibre**, which uses a very thin glass or plastic fibre through which pulses of light travel. Information transmission through optical fibre works rather like flashing code with a light through a hollow tube. Optical cable's advantages are size (one fibre has the diameter of a human hair), capacity (exceeding 1400 Mbps), much greater security, and no leakage of information. It's very hard to tap into optical fibre. Attempts are pretty easy to detect, since installing a tap disrupts service on the line—and that's noticeable. However, optical fibre is very expensive and very difficult to install and maintain.

WIRELESS COMMUNICATIONS MEDIA

For many networks, wired communications media are simply not feasible, especially for telecommunication across rugged terrain or great distances, or when one or more parties may be in motion. For whatever reason, if wired communications media don't fit your needs, wireless may be the answer. Wireless communications radiate information into the air, either very narrowly beamed or in many directions like ripples from a pebble tossed into a pond. Since they radiate through the air, they don't require direct cable connections of any kind. Obviously, security is a big problem, since the information is available to anyone in the radiation's path. However, wireless encryption methods are good, and getting better.

INFRARED AND OMNIDIRECTIONAL MICROWAVE FOR SHORT DISTANCES

Infrared is the oldest type of wireless communication. **Infrared** is a wireless communications medium that uses radio waves to transmit signals or information. Your TV remote control uses infrared transmission. You can use infrared to connect handheld devices, such as pocket PCs, to peripheral devices such as printers. Wireless keyboards and mice are usually connected to your PC with an infrared link. Infrared communication is totally line-of-sight, meaning that you can't have anything blocking the path of the signal or it won't work. Infrared transmission has very limited bandwidth (typically 1 Mbps).

Another method of short-distance wireless communications is omnidirectional (all directions) microwave transmission. **Microwave** transmission is a type of radio transmission. You can choose one of two systems—Bluetooth, discussed earlier in this Module, and WiFi, which is a well-established industry standard. To add WiFi to your network, you'd connect a wireless access point to the wired network, which would then act as a receiver for messages coming into the network and a transmitter for messages going out to the wireless device. The wireless device has a companion receiver and transmitter, and can access the network as if it were cable-connected.

Figure D.12
Microwave Transmission

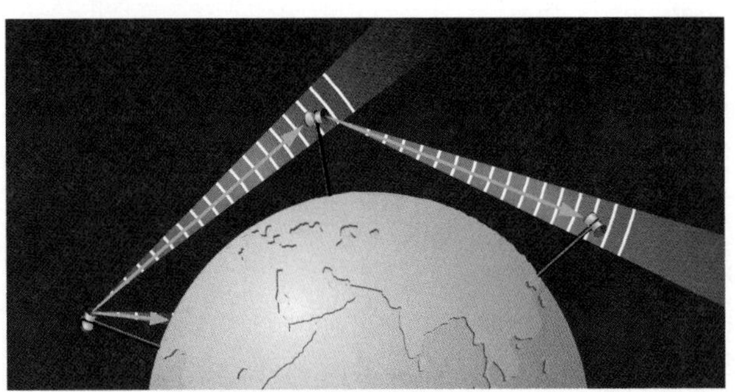

DIRECTIONAL MICROWAVE FOR MEDIUM DISTANCES

Microwaves may be transmitted very directionally with a parabolic dish antenna or can be radiated in a wide curved path for broader use. Microwave transmission is a line-of-sight medium: the signal cannot follow the curved surface of the earth. So to send the information over a distance of more than about 32 kilometres you'd have to use repeaters (see Figure D.12). A **repeater** is a device that receives a radio signal, strengthens it, and sends it on. (You've probably seen microwave towers—they're the tall towers with lots of little dishes on them that stand near an industrial complex.) Microwave signals have difficulty getting through walls or trees or other solid objects, so there must be a clear path from sender to receiver.

Figure D.13
Satellite Transmission

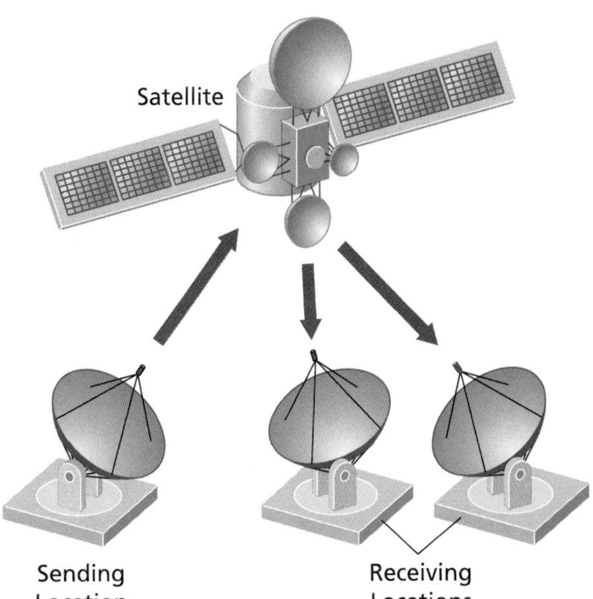

SATELLITES FOR LONG DISTANCE

Communications satellites are microwave repeaters in space. They solve the problem of line-of-sight since the transmission shoots up into the sky in a straight line, bounces off, and shoots back down to earth again (see Figure D.13). Since satellites are so high, an array of them can essentially cover the earth (as the two dozen or so GPS satellites do). As with land-based repeaters, satellites receive information from one location and relay it to another. You'd usually use satellite communications to connect land-based networks in far-flung locations or to connect moving vehicles to each other or to the organizational network.

Satellite communications are cost-effective for moving large amounts of information, especially given a large number of receiving sites. For example, Kmart and other retailers place *very small aperture terminal (VSAT)* satellite dishes on the roofs of their stores. The VSATs allow individual stores to transmit information to the home office, and the home office, in turn, can transmit information to all the stores simultaneously. Satellite radio is another example far-flung satellite transmission. If you have satellite radio in your car, you'll never be completely out of range of your favourite satellite radio station.

Communications Service Providers

You can set up your own cabling, routers, switches, multiplexors, protocols, and so on and have your own communications network, or you can get a third party to provide it for you. Which strategy you take determines network ownership. Network ownership determines:

- Rights to the network
- Cost
- Availability
- Services provided
- Speed
- Security

Small networks within an office building are almost always private. That means that the company buys, installs (or contracts out the installation), and maintains the network. Therefore that company has exclusive rights to the use of the network.

The following discussion deals with networks that cover a large geographic area and require **communications service providers**, third parties who furnish the conduit for information. You can support your network with a public network, a private network, a value-added network, or a virtual private network.

A **public network** is a one on which your organization competes for time with others (see Figure D.14). The telephone system is a public network. You're not guaranteed that you'll be able to get a line when you want to make a call—as you may have found out if you unsuccessfully tried to call your mother on Mother's Day. When all the lines are busy you get a recorded message to that effect. And when you dial into the Internet you're competing with others for access, and you'll find that the speed of getting to Web sites varies greatly.

A **private network** consists of the communications media that your organization owns or exclusively leases to connect networks or network components. You can lease dedicated lines from a communications service provider.

A **value-added network (VAN)** is a semipublic network that provides services beyond the movement of information from one place to another. The "value-added" part of this type of network is what makes it attractive. For example, if you need EDI (electronic data interchange) capabilities to automate the exchange of standard business documents between your organization, your suppliers, and customers, you might hire a communications service provider to set up a network and provide EDI capability. VAN providers also offer security, auditing, and translation services between different versions of EDI systems.

General Electric Information Services offers VAN services. If you buy their VAN, all you have to do is develop an interface between (1) your system and GE's VAN and (2) your customers' and suppliers' systems and GE's VAN. GE will do the rest.

Of course, you could do all this yourself. You could build a private network, and develop software to handle the conversions that you'll need for EDI. Most companies don't adopt this strategy, as it's too complex and expensive.

A **virtual private network (VPN)** is a public network that promises availability to your organization, but doesn't provide you with a dedicated line or communications

Figure D.14

Comparison of Types of Network Ownership

Cost	Availability	Services	Speed	Security
Public				
Pay-as-you-go	Compete for time and use	Moves information only	Slower than private network	Little or none guaranteed
Private				
Pay for all of it *or* Pay flat fee for leased line	No competition for use	Can have additional services	Faster than that of public networks	Higher than that of public networks
Value-Added Network				
Pay-as-you-go	Little or no competition for use	VAN provider offers additional services	Faster than that of public networks	Much better than that of public networks
Virtual Private Network				
Flat fee per month plus usage fee	Compete for use	VPN owner provides some additional services	Slower than that of equivalent public network	Better than that of public networks

TEAM WORK

WHAT'S THE BIG DEAL WITH FREQUENCIES?

A radio wave is an electromagnetic wave sent out by an antenna. Radio waves have different frequencies, and by tuning a radio receiver, a cell phone (which has a receiver), or a baby monitor (which also has a receiver) to a certain frequency you can pick up a specific signal. Frequencies are measured in KHz (kilohertz—thousands of cycles per second), MHz (megahertz—millions of cycles per second), and GHz (gigahertz—billions of cycles per second).

You may have heard that there are a fixed number of frequencies and competition for control of those available is fierce. All wireless gizmos require a radio frequency to transmit and receive, so communications companies spend billions of dollars for the rights to part of the spectrum that's for sale. Other parts are free (such as the WiFi part) and still others are set aside for government agencies such as the U.S. Department of Defense.

The figure below shows the part of the spectrum in common use for wireless information delivery all day every day.

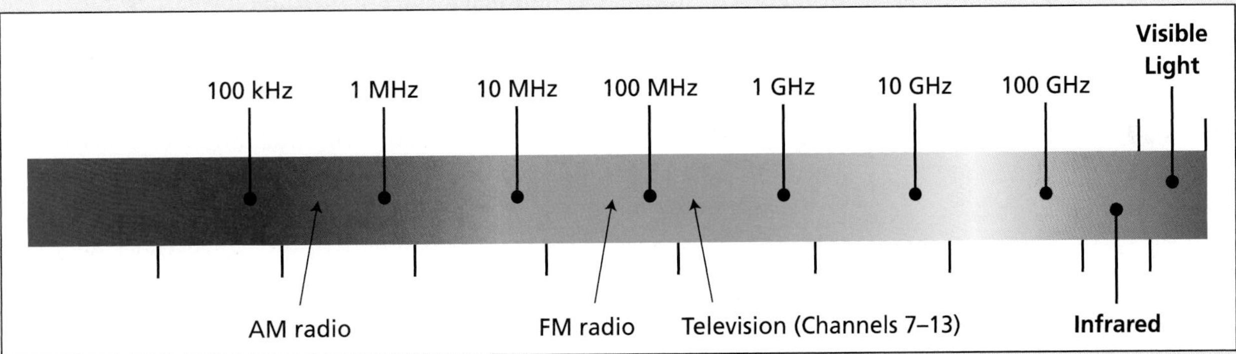

Here are some common frequency bands:

- FM radio: 88 megahertz to 108 megahertz
- AM radio: 535 kilohertz to 1.7 megahertz
- Television stations: 174 to 220 megahertz for Channels 7 through 13

Place on the spectrum each of the following wireless services:

A. WiFi
B. GPS devices
C. Microwave ovens
D. Police radar guns
E. TV channels 2–6
F. Wildlife tracking collars
G. CB radio
H. Aviation navigation
I. Cordless phones

media. Your information travels with information from other organizations. A VPN usually offers additional services such as data encryption.

VPNs are prevalent on the Internet as organizations move into electronic commerce functions across the Internet. An **Internet virtual private network** gives you a way to establish a *virtual* Internet network that consists of you, your customers, and suppliers. This arrangement is often called an *extranet*. Practically every national phone service provider (Baby Bells, AT&T, MCI, and so on) offers domestic VPN services.

If you need to transmit information further abroad, you can use an **international virtual private network (international VPN)**—virtual private networks that depend on services offered by phone companies of various nationalities. Two current examples are Phoenix and Worldpartners. Phoenix is an alliance between Deutsche Telekom AG (Germany), France Telecom, and Sprint. Worldpartners is the largest international VPN and consists of AT&T, Kokusai Denshim Denwa (Japan), Singapore Telecom, and Unisource, which is itself an alliance of telecommunications providers from Spain, the Netherlands, Sweden, and Switzerland.

KEY CONSIDERATIONS FOR COMMUNICATIONS MEDIA

Communications media technology is vitally important in a network. To determine the most appropriate communications medium, you must consider the capacity, reliability, cost, and distance that your network covers as well as the mobility of your network users.

- *Capacity* or *bandwidth* determines (1) how much information can travel over the communications medium at once and (2) how fast the information can travel. Twisted-pair has the lowest capacity, and optical fibre the highest.
- *Reliability* is a measure of how much you can depend on your network. If you need a network with the greatest reliability, you probably won't choose wireless communications because wireless networks are the most susceptible to outside interference.
- *Cost* is always a very important consideration in the building and maintenance of a network. Your choice of capacity and reliability will usually affect the cost.
- *Distance* is a consideration in what medium you choose. Infrared, for example, works only over small distances, whereas optical fibre and satellite work well over great distances.
- *Mobility* may be important to your organization. If so, you may want to investigate wireless communications so that connectivity becomes mobile within a building. For larger distances, you'll need cellular phones to give you an alternative to land phone lines for connecting to the network when out of the office.

Summary: Student Learning Outcomes Revisited

1. **Identify and describe the four basic concepts on which networks are built.** There are four basic concepts on which almost all networks are built:
   - **Network interface cards (NICs)** in each computer
   - A connecting device like a **hub**, **switch**, or **router**
   - At least one communications medium
   - Network operating system software
2. **Describe how to set up a small peer-to-peer network at home.** To set up a **peer-to-peer network** at home, you'd need:
   - **Ethernet cards** (as the NICs) in each computer
   - A home router
   - **Cat 5** cables
   - The Windows operating system
3. **Compare and contrast the various Internet connection possibilities.** There are five ways to connect a computer or network to the Internet:
   - Phone line and **modem**, which uses a phone line and prevents your using the same line for voice communications. It's the slowest type of connection.
   - Phone line and **DSL**, which, although it uses the phone line, does not prevent simultaneous voice communication. A DSL connection is a **broadband** connection.
   - Cable TV line and **cable modem**, which brings Internet access in with your cable modem and doesn't use the phone line at all. It's also broadband.

- Satellite antenna (dish) and **satellite modem**, which provides Internet access using a satellite dish. Satellite Internet access is also broadband.
- Wireless connection and a wireless device such as a notebook computer or a PDA. Access with a notebook is usually fast, but access with any handheld device that uses cell phone technology is slow.

4. **Describe client/server business networks from a business and physical point of view.** A **client/server network** is a network in which one or more computers are servers and provide services to the other computers, which are called clients.

   From the business point of view, there are five different configurations based on three factors:
   - Where the processing for the presentation of information occurs
   - Where the processing of logic or business rules occurs
   - Where the data management component (DBMS) and information (database) are located

   From the physical point of view, the concepts on which larger networks are based are the same as those on which small networks are built. However, there are many more considerations, such as network processors, communications media, protocols, and so on.
5. **Define and compare local area networks (LANs), municipal area networks (MANs), and wide area networks (WANs).** A **local area network (LAN)** covers a limited geographic distance, such as an office, office building, or group of buildings close to each other. A **municipal area network (MAN)** covers an entire city including suburbs. A **wide area network (WAN)** covers large geographic distances, such as a province, a country, or even the entire world.
6. **Compare and contrast the types of communications media. Communications media** are the paths, or physical channels, in a network over which information travels. There are two options: wired and wireless. Wired communications media include twisted-pair cable, coaxial cable, and optical fibre. Of these, optical fibre is the fastest and the most secure. Wireless communications media include satellite, microwave, and Infrared. Satellite is for long distances, microwave has short- and medium-distance versions, and infrared is for very short distances only.

Key Terms and Concepts

bandwidth, 442
Bluetooth, 430
broadband, 431
cable modem, 433
Cat 5 (Category 5), 428
client/server network, 435
coaxial cable (coax), 443
communications media, 442
communications protocol (protocol), 440
communications satellite, 445
communications service provider, 445
computer network, 426
digital subscriber line (DSL), 432
Ethernet card, 427
firewall, 428
Home PNA (Phoneline Networking Alliance), 430
infrared, 444
international virtual private network (international VPN), 447
Internet virtual private network, 447
local area network (LAN), 442
microwave, 444
municipal area network (MAN), 442
network hub, 427
network interface card (NIC) , 427
optical fibre, 443
Palm Operating System (Palm OS), 435
peer-to-peer network, 427
personal digital assistant (PDA), 434
PNA adapter card, 430
Pocket PC OS (Windows CE), 435
private network, 446
public network, 445
repeater, 444
router, 428
satellite modem, 433
switch, 428
telephone modem (modem), 431
value-added network (VAN), 446
virtual private network (VPN), 446
wide area network (WAN), 442
WiFi (wireless fidelity or IEEE 802.11b), 429
wired communications medium, 442
wireless network access point (wireless access point), 429
wireless communications media, 442
wireless Internet service provider (wireless ISP), 434

Short-Answer Questions

1. What is a computer network?
2. What is a peer-to-peer network?
3. How is a peer-to-peer different from a client/server network?
4. What is an Ethernet card?
5. What does a network hub do?
6. How does an Ethernet network work?
7. What is Cat 5 cable used for?
8. What is Bluetooth?
9. What do you need to have a dial-up connection to the Internet?
10. How is a DSL Internet connection different from a telephone modem connection?
11. What is a satellite modem?
12. How is client/server Model 1 different from client/server Model 2?
13. What does WiFi do?
14. What are communications service providers?

Assignments and Exercises

1. **INVESTIGATE CELL PHONE TECHNOLOGY.** A wireless device that you may have used, or perhaps use all the time, is a cell phone. A cell phone is actually a radio (with a transmitter and a receiver) and uses radio waves of certain frequencies. There are different systems (called *cellular access technologies*) for cell phones: TDMA, GSM, CDMA. Go to the Web and find the answers to the following questions. *Hint:* A good place to look is HowStuffWorks (www.howstuffworks.com).

   A. What do the letters TDMA, GSM, and CDMA stand for?
   B. What's the difference between them?
   C. Why are they called "cell" phones?
   D. Why was this "cellular" method used in the first place?

   Do some research (the Web can help) and find out the frequencies for:

Wireless System	Frequency
Baby monitors	
Air traffic control radar	
Global positioning systems	
Garage door openers	
Standard cordless phones	
900-megahertz cordless phones	
Bluetooth	

2. **FIND OUT ABOUT PERSONAL DIGITAL ASSISTANTS.** Many people have personal digital assistants (PDAs), which are handheld computers that allow you to perform many computer tasks wirelessly. Some of the features of PDAs are calendar management, appointment management, spreadsheet and word processing

capabilities, and Web access—and sometimes a PDA can even double as a cell phone. Do some research on PDAs and answer the following questions:

A. What are three other features common in PDAs that are not listed above?

B. What does the term "synching" mean?

C. What are the two types of handwriting recognition systems used on PDAs?

3. **WHAT ARE THE INTERNET ACCESS OPTIONS IN YOUR AREA?** Write a report on what sort of Internet connections are available close to you. How many ISPs offer telephone modem access? Is DSL available to you? Is it available to anyone in your area? Does your cable company offer a cable modem? Can you get wireless Internet access in your area? Compare each available service on price and extras like a help line, or people who will come out to your home and help you if you're having difficulties. What type of Internet connection do you currently use? Do you plan to upgrade in the future? If so, to what type of connection? If not, why not?

4. **INVESTIGATE BUILDING YOUR OWN HOME NETWORK.** Build your own home network on paper. Assume you have the computers already and just need to link them. Find prices for hubs and routers on the Web. Also research Ethernet cards and cables. If you were to get a high-speed Internet connection, such as a cable modem or DSL modem, how much would they cost? Can you buy your own, or would you have to rent the modems from the phone or cable company?

5. **INVESTIGATE SATELLITE RADIO.** At the time of writing, there were two satellite radio stations: Sirius and XM. Surf the Web to find out if there are any new ones. Also, determine what equipment you need to install each type. Find out what is the cost of the antenna, and how the system would work in your car. What is the monthly subscription?

6. **FIND OUT ABOUT FIREWALLS.** Go to the Web and find out about software and hardware that protects your computer and home network, respectively.

A. If you only have one computer connected to the Internet, then a software firewall such as ZoneAlarm will most likely be enough protection from intruders. Find three different firewall software packages on the Web. A good place to start looking would be the sites that sell antivirus software. Compare the firewall software on price and features.

Some sites to try are as follows:

- Symantec (www.sarc.com)
- Trend Micro (www.trendmicro.com)
- VirusList.com (a virus encyclopedia) (www.viruslist.com)
- McAfee (www.mcafee.com)

B. If you have a home network, you'd be well advised to check into a hardware firewall. One place to look is at Linksys (www.linksys.com) or any site that sells computer hardware.

EXTENDED LEARNING MODULE E

THE WORLD WIDE WEB AND THE INTERNET

Student Learning Outcomes

1. Define the relationships among Web site, Web site address, domain name, Web page, and uniform resource locator (URL).
2. Explain how to interpret the parts of an address on the Web.
3. Identify the major components and features of Web browser software.
4. Describe the differences between directory and true search engines.
5. Describe the various technologies that make up the Internet.
6. Identify key considerations in choosing an Internet service provider (ISP).
7. Describe the communications software and telecommunications hardware you need to connect to the Internet.

Introduction

Perhaps the most visible and explosive information technology tool is the Internet, and subsequently the World Wide Web. No matter where you look or what you read, someone always seems to be referring to one of the two. On television commercials, you find Web site addresses displayed (such as "www.iam.ca" for a Molson Canadian commercial or "www.toyota.com" for a Toyota commercial). In almost every magazine these days, you'll find articles about the Internet because of its growing significance in our society. Most major business publications, such as *Fortune*, *Forbes*, and *Business Week*, devote entire issues every year to the Internet and how to use it for electronic commerce. Of course, many such publications have been carrying articles detailing how and why so many dot-coms failed in recent years (now affectionately referred to as *dot-bombs*).

The Internet really is everywhere—and it's here to stay. What's really great about the Internet is that it takes only a couple of hours to learn. Once you've read the text for this Module, you should try your hand at the "Internet scavenger hunts" (just enter that phrase into a search engine to find out more about these). You'd be surprised to learn how easy it is find information on the Internet.

World Wide Web

The **World Wide Web**, or the **Web** as you probably know it, is a multimedia-based collection of information, services, and Web sites supported by the Internet. The **Internet** is a vast network of computers that connects millions of people all over the world. Schools, businesses, government agencies, and many others have all connected their internal networks to the Internet, making it truly a the ultimate network of computers. So the Internet and all its technological infrastructure are really what make the Web possible.

Most people consider "the Web" and "the Internet" to be synonymous, and—although there are both subtle and clear differences between the two—we'll momentarily accept that terminology for our purposes here.

WEB SITES, ADDRESSES, AND PAGES

As you use the Web, you'll most often be accessing Web sites. A **Web site** is a specific location on the Web where you visit, gather information, and perhaps even order products. Every site has its own Web site address. A **Web site address** is a unique name that identifies a specific site on the Web. Technically, this address is called a domain name. A **domain name** identifies a specific computer on the Web and the main page of the entire site; most people use the term "Web site address." For example, the Web site address for the *Globe and Mail* is "www.globeandmail.com" (see Figure E.1).

Most Web sites include several and perhaps hundreds of Web pages. A **Web page** is a specific portion of a Web site that deals with a certain topic. The address for a specific Web page is called a URL. A **URL (uniform resource locator)** is an address for a specific Web page or document within a Web site. Most people use the common term *Web page address* when referring to a URL. As you can see in Figure E.1, you can click on the link for "Sports" on the main page for the *Globe and Mail*. You will then be taken to a specific Web page within the *Globe and Mail* site. The URL or Web page

Figure E.1

The *Globe and Mail* Web Site and Its Sports Web Page

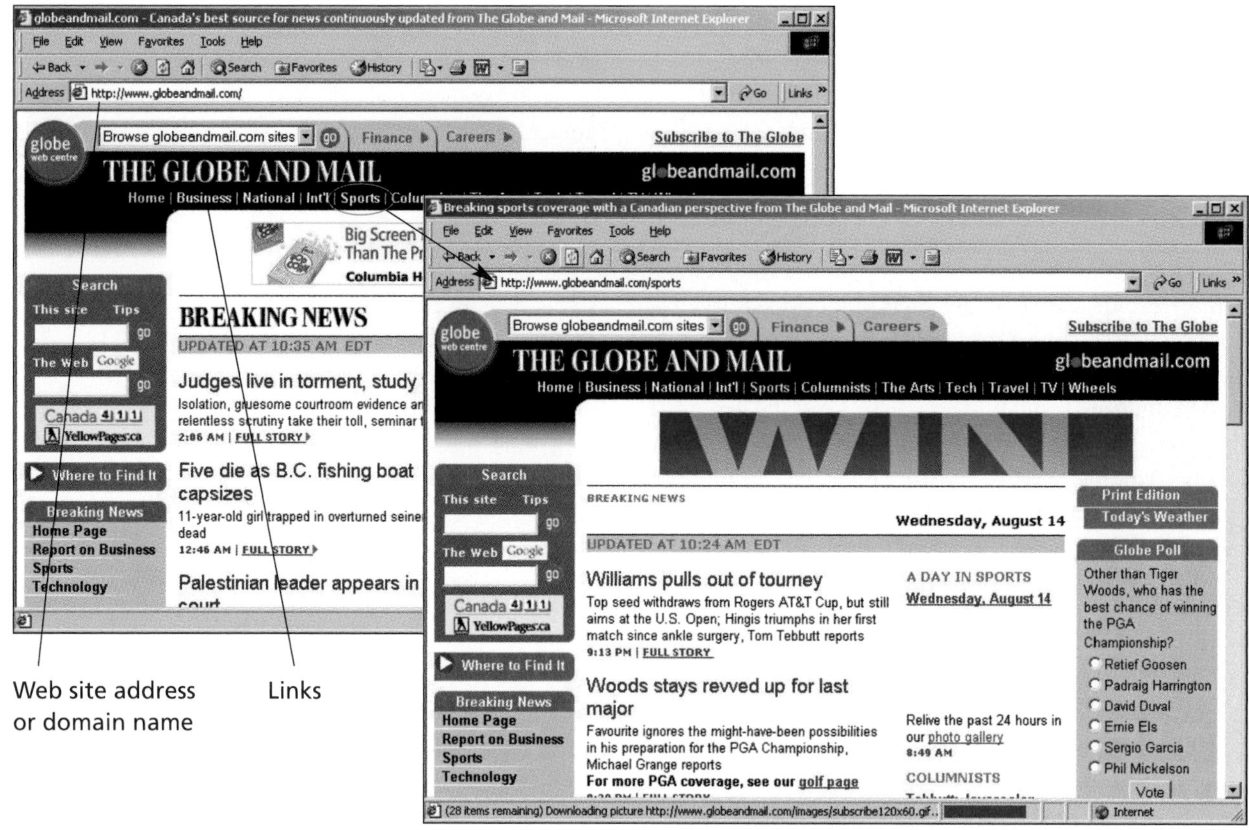

address for that page is "www.globeandmail.com/sports." A **link** (the technical name is **hyperlink**) is clickable text or an image that takes you to another site or page on the Web. Links are important on the Internet.

UNDERSTANDING ADDRESSES

When you access a certain Web site or page, you do so with its unique address, such as "www.globeandmail.com" (for our *Globe and Mail* example). Addresses, because they are unique, give you important information about the site or page. Let's consider two different examples (see Figure E.2)—Priceline (www.priceline.com) and the University of Technology in Sydney, Australia (www.uts.edu.au).

Most addresses start with "http://www," which stands for "hypertext transfer protocol" and "World Wide Web." The "http://" part is so common now that you don't even have to use it in most cases. The remaining portion of the address is unique for each site or page. Consider the URL "www.priceline.com." You might guess correctly that it's the address for an organization called Priceline. You can also discern that it's a commercial organization by the last three letters, "com." This three-letter extension can take many forms and is referred to as the **top-level domain**. Some of the most common top-level domains and their meanings are:

- com—commercial or for-profit business
- edu—educational institution
- gov—U.S. government agency

Figure E.2

Understanding Addresses

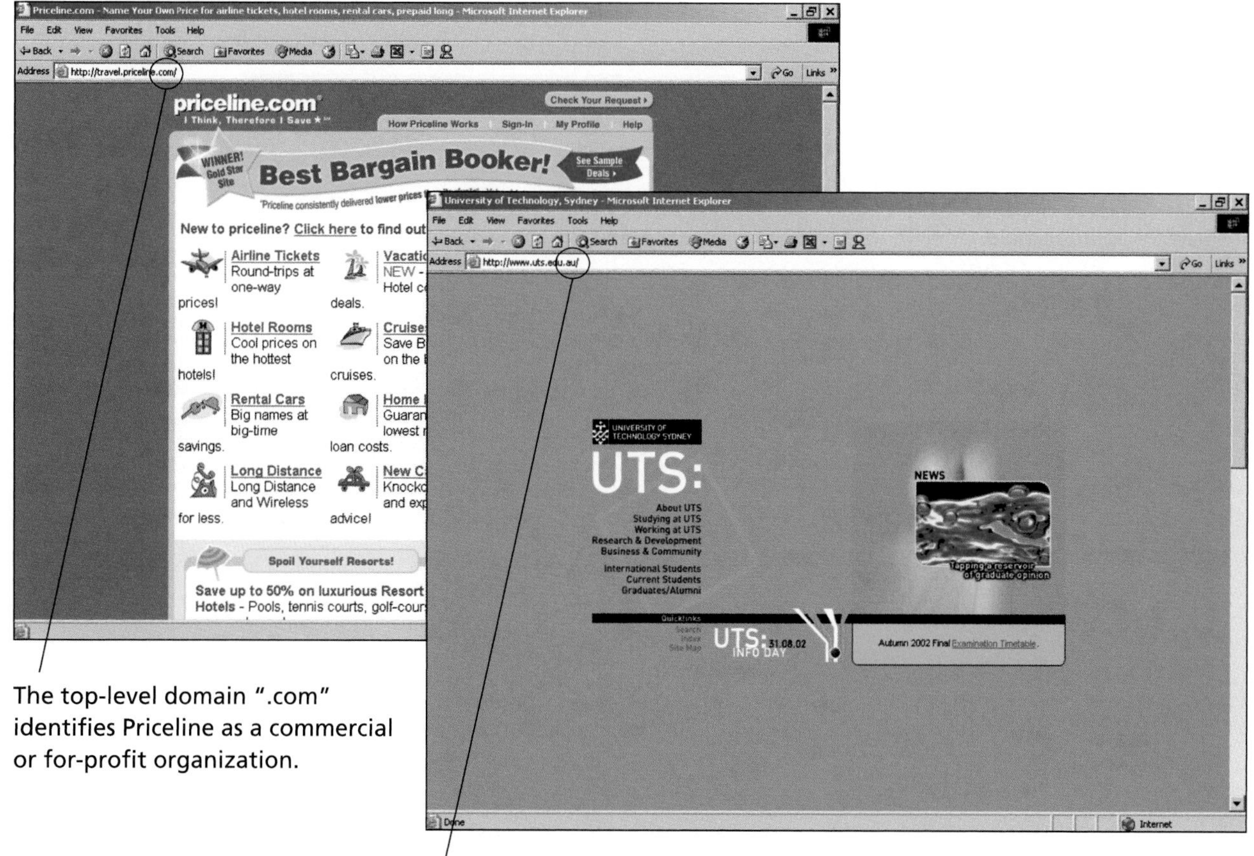

The top-level domain ".com" identifies Priceline as a commercial or for-profit organization.

The ".au" after the top-level domain identifies the country of origin (Australia in this case).

- mil—U.S. military organization
- net—Internet administrative organization
- org—professional or non-profit organization
- int—international treaties organization
- info—general information
- biz—business
- name—personal

Some addresses have a two-character extension that follows the top-level domain identifying the country location of the site. For example, the University of Technology in Sydney, Australia site address is www.uts.edu.au. From that address, you can tell it's for an educational institution (edu) located in Australia (au).

USING WEB BROWSER SOFTWARE

Web browser software enables you to surf the Web. It is in fact the software we used to view sites for the *Globe and Mail*, Priceline, and the University of Technology in Sydney, Australia. The most popular Web browsers today are Internet Explorer and Netscape Communicator. These are free for you to use, Internet Explorer being standard on most computers today.

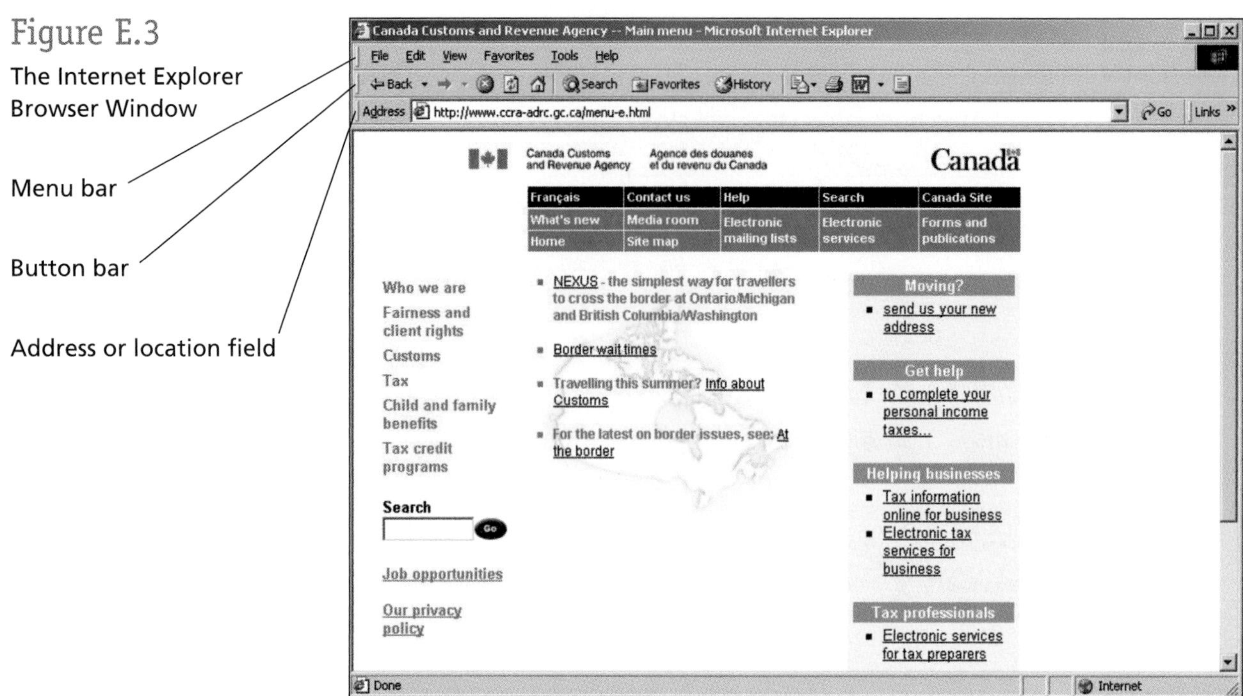

Figure E.3
The Internet Explorer Browser Window

To demonstrate how you use Web browser software, let's take a quick tour of Internet Explorer and Netscape Communicator. In Figures E.3 and E.4, you can see we are using Internet Explorer and Netscape Communicator, respectively, to view the Web sites for the Canada Customs and Revenue Agency (www.ccra-adrc.gc.ca) and for eBay (www.ebay.com). In Figure E.3, you can see the menu bar for Internet Explorer that includes the functions for File, Edit, View, Favorites, Tools, and Help. In Figure E.4, you can see the menu bar for Netscape Communicator that includes the functions of File, Edit, View, Go, Communicator, and Help. The two menu bars are very similar and support the same basic functions. For example, if you click on File in either Internet Explorer or Netscape Communicator, you'll then see a pull-down menu that allows you to initiate other actions such as printing out the Web page and sending it by e-mail to someone else.

Below the menu bar, you'll find a button bar on both browsers that support more functions. We won't go into any of these in detail here—you can simply play with them at your leisure. Below the button bar, you'll find the Address field for Internet Explorer and the Location field for Netscape Communicator. They are the same. If you know the address for where you want to go, click in either of these two fields, type in the address, and then hit Enter.

One of the most important features of any Web browser is that you can create and edit a list of your most commonly visited sites. In Internet Explorer it's called a Favorites list, in Netscape Communicator a Bookmarks list. So, if you frequently visit eBay, you can save the address in one of these lists while you're viewing it. In Internet Explorer, you would click on the Favorites button and then Add. In Netscape Communicator, you would click on the Bookmarks button and then Add Bookmark. Later, when you want to visit eBay, you would click on the appropriate button (Favorites for Internet Explorer or Bookmarks for Netscape Communicator) and then click on the eBay link. That's all there is to it.

Web browser software is the easiest personal productivity software to learn. Most people find that they need very little instruction and seldom need a book. Just connect to the Web, start the Web browser of your choice, play around for an hour or so, and you'll soon be a Web surfing expert.

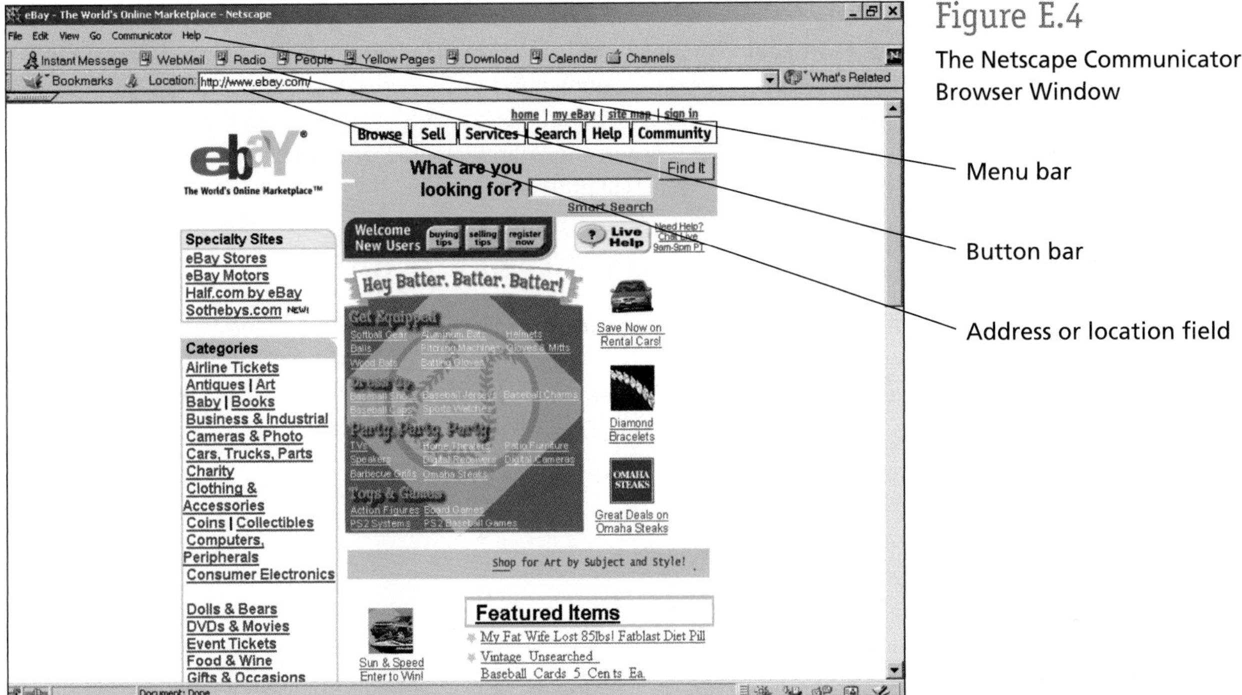

Figure E.4

The Netscape Communicator Browser Window

It really is quite simple. When you start your Web browser software, you'll first see what is called a *home page*—the Web site your Web browser automatically connects to and displays when you first start surfing. Once you're there, you can click on any of the links that interest you, or you can type in a new address and go to any other site.

If you're not sure of the exact Web site address, you begin to search for it in one of two ways. The first is to use a search engine, which we'll discuss in the next section. The second is to type in a logical name in the Address field (using Internet Explorer) or the Location field (using Netscape Communicator). For example, if you want to download tax forms from the Canada Customs and Revenue Agency Web site but don't know the address of the CCRA, you can simply type in "ccra" in the Address or Location field. Your Web browser will automatically begin a search for Web sites related to those terms and hopefully find the right one for you. In the instance of searching for the CCRA, both Internet Explorer and Netscape Communicator do in fact take you to the site you need.

Search Engines

There will be times when you want to find information and services on the Web but you don't know exactly which site you should be visiting. In this case, you can either type in a logical name as we have just explained, or you can use a search engine. A **search engine** is a facility on the Web that helps you find sites with the information and/or services you want. There are many types of search engines on the Web; the two most common are directory search engines and true search engines.

A **directory search engine** organizes the sites that make up the Internet into hierarchical lists. Yahoo! is the most popular and well-known of these. If you want to find information using a directory search engine, you start by selecting a specific category and continually choose subcategories until you arrive at a list of Web sites with the information you want.

A **true search engine** uses software agent technologies to search the Internet for key words and then puts them in indexes. True search engines thus allow you to ask questions, as opposed to continually choosing subcategories, to arrive at a list of Web sites. Ask Jeeves is the most popular and well-known true search engine.

To see how directory and true search engines differ, let's now try to find out who won the Academy Awards in 2002.

USING A DIRECTORY SEARCH ENGINE

As we have stated, Yahoo! is the most popular and well-known directory search engine. Figure E.5 shows the sequence of pages (categories) you would traverse through using Yahoo! to determine who won the Academy Awards in 2002. The sequence of categories appears as:

- Arts & Humanities
- Awards
- Movies and Films@
- Academy Awards
- Coverage of the 74th Academy Awards

In the final screen, a list of links headed "Site Listings" appears below "Categories"; one of these links is likely to contain the information you want.

There are some definite advantages to performing a search in this way. If you look at the next-to-last screen, for example, ("Academy Awards"), it also includes subcategories for the Academy Awards in each of the past six years (1996–2001). So you can easily find related information using a directory search engine.

You can also use directory search engines in a different fashion. For example, in the first screen, we could have entered *academy +awards +2002* in the field immediately to the left of the Search button and then clicked on the Search button. This particular search would yield a list of Web sites very similar to the list we received by choosing subcategories.

Notice that we included plus signs (+) in our key terms list. By doing so, we limited the search to finding just sites that included all three words. That is, the plus sign is interpreted as "and"; leaving it out would imply the word "or" between your key terms. Likewise, if you want to limit a search so that it won't show Web sites that contain certain key words, you would use a minus sign, represented by a hyphen (-); this is interpreted as "not." For example, if you wanted to find Web sites that contain information about the NFL Toronto Raptors, you could enter *Toronto +Raptors*. That would probably yield a list of suitable sites, but it might also include sites that include information about watching raptors (the extinct version) in Toronto. You can further refine your search by entering something like *Toronto +Raptors -dinosaur -jurassic*. That search will yield a list of Web sites that have the terms *Toronto* and *Raptors* but will eliminate any sites that have the term *dinosaur* or *jurassic*.

When you use a directory search engine and type in specific terms instead of traversing through subcategories, we definitely recommend that you make use of the plus sign and/or the minus sign. For example, if you want to find sites about wind tunnels, using *wind tunnel* will return a list of sites related to wind tunnels but also to wind (i.e., weather sites) and tunnels in general. Using the plus sign like this—*wind +tunnel*—will yield a more refined list of sites. We recommend that you complete the Team Work project "Finding and Using Search Engines" here. You'll find that some search engines support advanced and unique capabilities that can help you further refine your search criteria.

Figure E.5

Using a Directory Search Engine

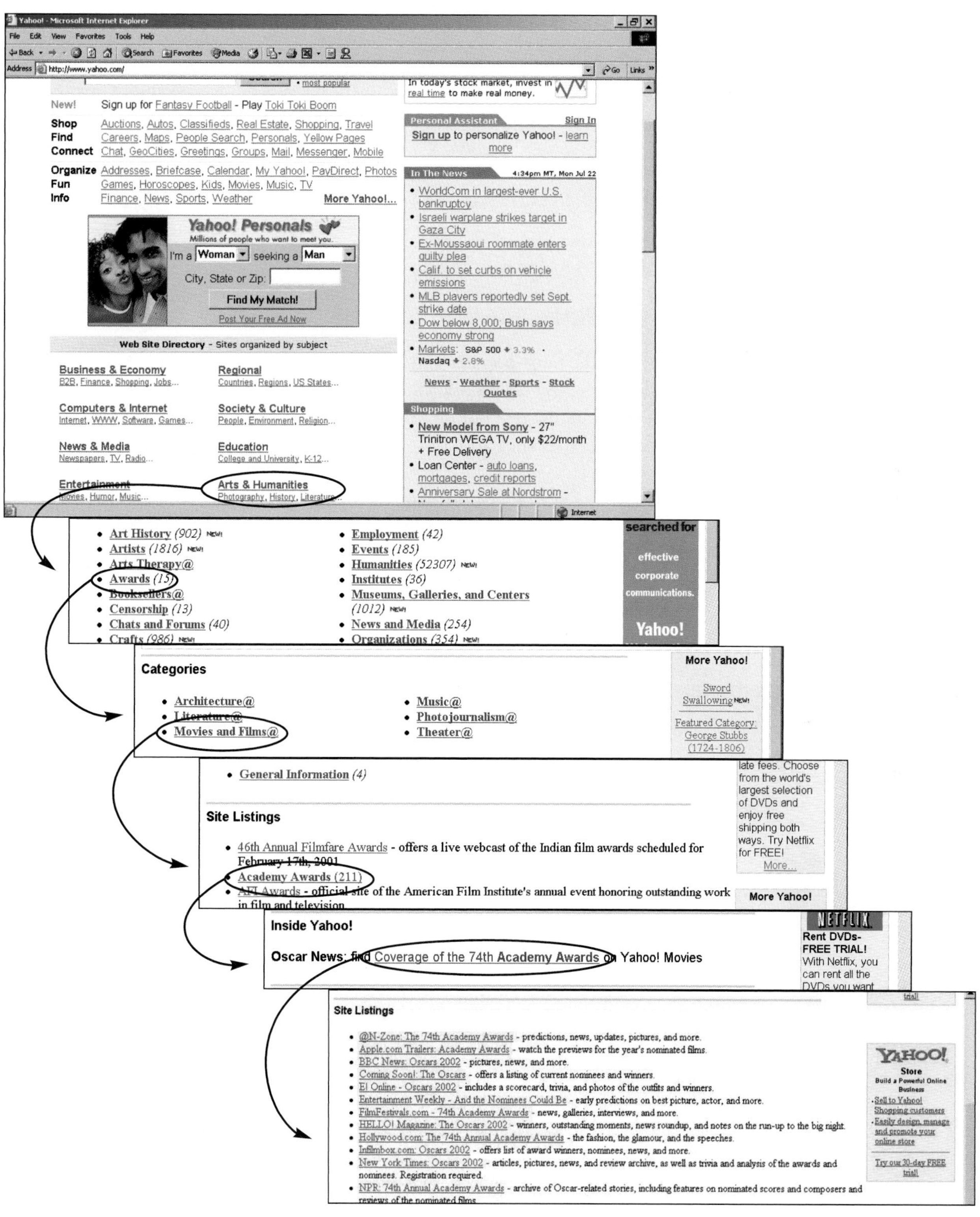

TEAM WORK

FINDING AND USING SEARCH ENGINES

Search engines are easy to find on the Web and even easier to use. In fact, there are about 100 search engines that you can use to find almost any information you need.

Your group's tasks include (1) creating a list of the ten most popular search engines on the Web and (2) performing a search on each for the same information. As you complete the second task, evaluate how easy or difficult it was to use each search engine. Also, evaluate the quality of the Web site list you received from each search engine.

USING A TRUE SEARCH ENGINE

Ask Jeeves is the most popular and well-known true search engine. Because it uses natural language, you simply ask a question such as "Who won the Academy Awards in 2002?" and hit the Ask button. As you can see in Figure E.6, Ask Jeeves returns a list of possible Web sites and a list of questions Jeeves can definitely answer from which you can choose the one closest to the one you asked.

Both types of search engines are very easy to use. Which you choose is really a function of how you think. Some people think in terms of hierarchical lists while

Figure E.6

Using a True Search Engine

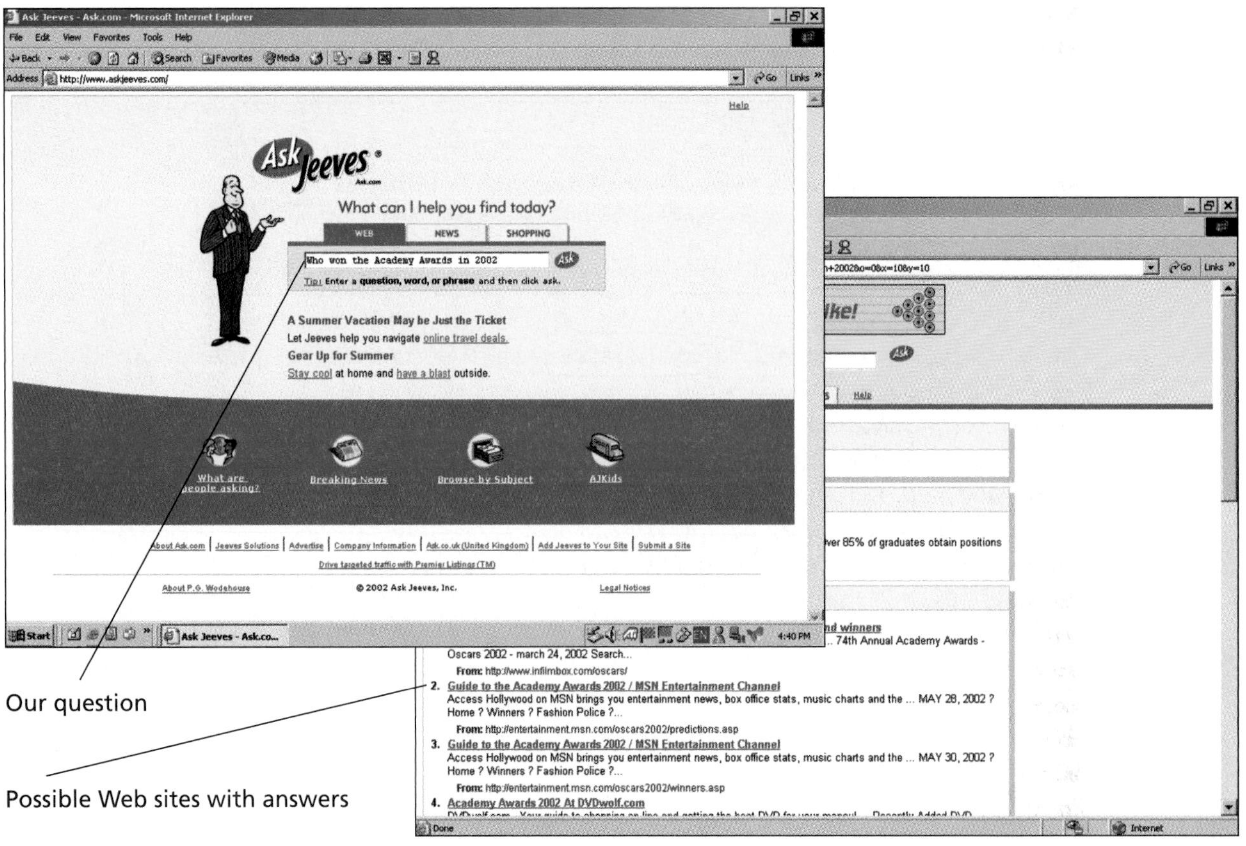

others think in terms of questions. What you'll undoubtedly find is that directory search engines are better in some cases while true search engines are better in others.

Internet Technologies

To best take advantage of everything the Web has to offer, it often helps to understand what's going on behind it. The Web is somewhat of a graphical user interface (GUI) that sits on top of the Internet, which is the set of underlying technologies that makes the Web possible. The Web allows you to click on links to go to other sites, and allows you to view information in multiple forms of media. The Internet would still exist and be usable even without this capability. The reverse is not true.

THE INTERNET BACKBONE

The **Internet backbone** is the major set of connections for computers on the Internet (see Figure E.7). A **network access point (NAP)** is a point on the Internet where several connections converge. At each NAP is at least one computer that simply routes Internet traffic from one place to another (much like an airport where you merely switch planes). These NAPs are owned and maintained by network service providers. A **network service provider (NSP)**, such as MCI or Bell Canada, owns and maintains routing computers at NAPs and even the lines that connect the NAPs to each other. In Figure E.7, you can see that Calgary is a NAP, with lines converging from Vancouver, Edmonton, Chicago, and Toronto.

At any given NAP, an Internet service provider may connect its computer or computers to the Internet. An **Internet service provider (ISP)** is a company that provides individuals, organizations, and businesses access to the Internet. ISPs include AOL, Juno (which is free), and perhaps even your school. In turn, you "dial up" and connect your computer to an ISP computer. So your ISP provides you access to the Internet (and thus the Web) by allowing you to connect your computer to its computer (which is already connected).

If you live in the Moncton area and send an e-mail to someone living near Saskatoon, your e-mail message might travel from Moncton to Montreal, then to Toronto, then to Calgary, then to Edmonton, and finally to Saskatoon. But, no matter—your message will get there. Can you imagine the route that your e-mail message would travel if you were in Moncton sending it to someone in Venice, Italy? One time, it might go west around the world through Australia. The next time, it might go east around the world through Halifax and then on to London, England.

INTERNET SERVERS

There are many types of computers on the Internet—namely, router (which we've already discussed), client, and server computers (see Figure E.8). Your computer that you use to access the Internet and surf the Web is called a *client*. Your client computer can be a traditional desktop or notebook computer, a Web or Internet appliance, a PDA, or perhaps even a cell phone.

Internet server computers are computers that provide information and services on the Internet. There are four main types of server computers on the Internet—Web, mail, ftp, and IRC servers. A **Web server** provides information and services to Web surfers. So, when you access eBay (www.ebay.com), you're accessing a Web server with your client. Most often, you'll be accessing and using the services of a Web server.

Figure E.7
The Internet Backbone in Canada

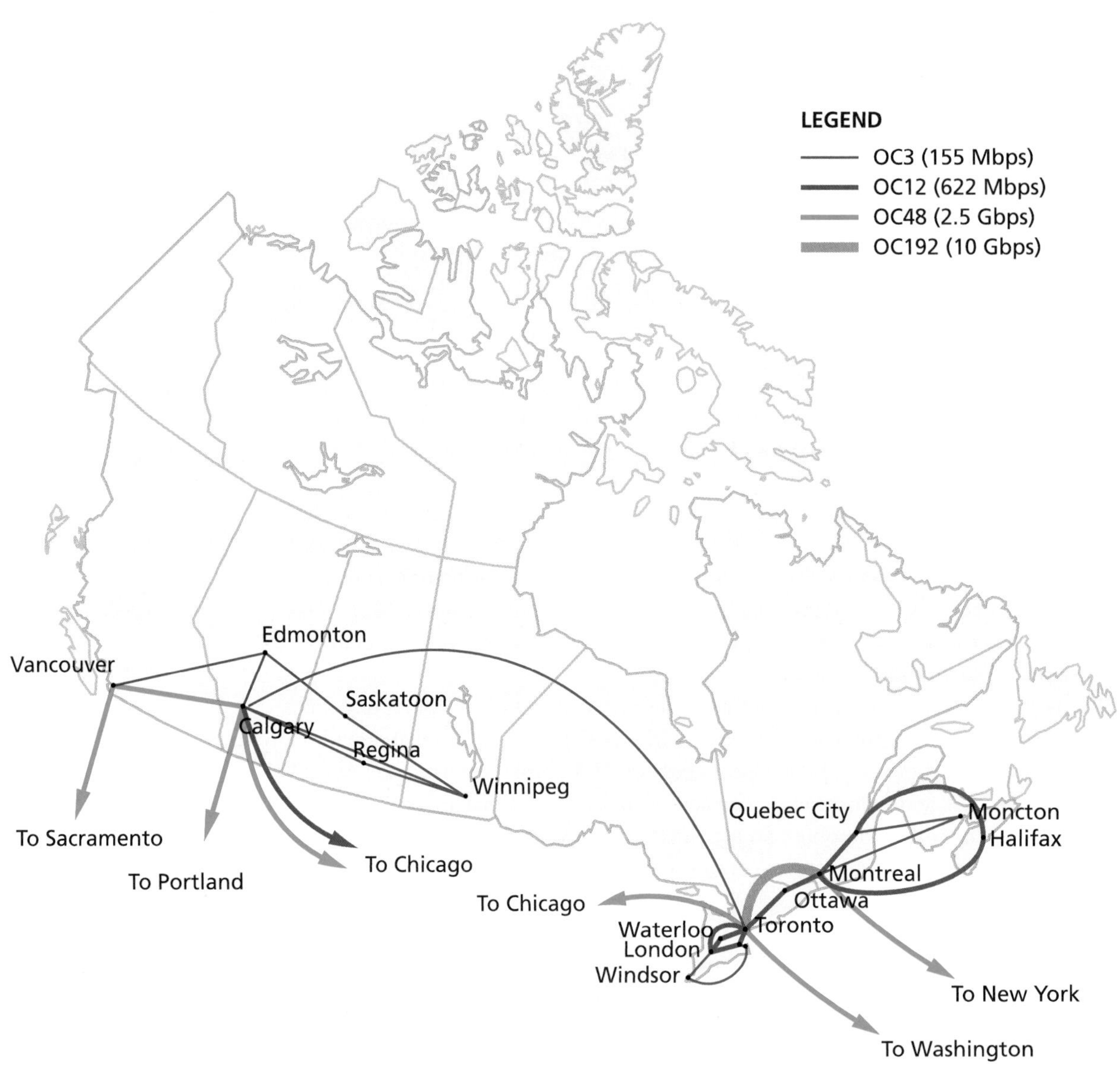

A **mail server** provides e-mail services and accounts. Many times, mail servers are presented to you as a part of a Web server. For example, Hotmail is a free e-mail server and service provided by MSN. An **ftp (file transfer protocol) server** maintains a collection of files that you can download. These files can include software, screen savers, music files (many in MP3 format), and games. An **IRC (internet relay chat) server** supports your use of discussion groups and chat rooms. IRC servers are popular hosting computers for sites such as Epinions (www.epinions.com). There, you can share your opinions about various products and services, and the site will even pay you (in the form of *eroyalties*) if people read the reviews you write.

COMMUNICATIONS PROTOCOLS

As information moves around the Internet, bouncing between network access points until it finally reaches you, it does so according to various communications protocols.

Figure E.8
Servers on the Internet

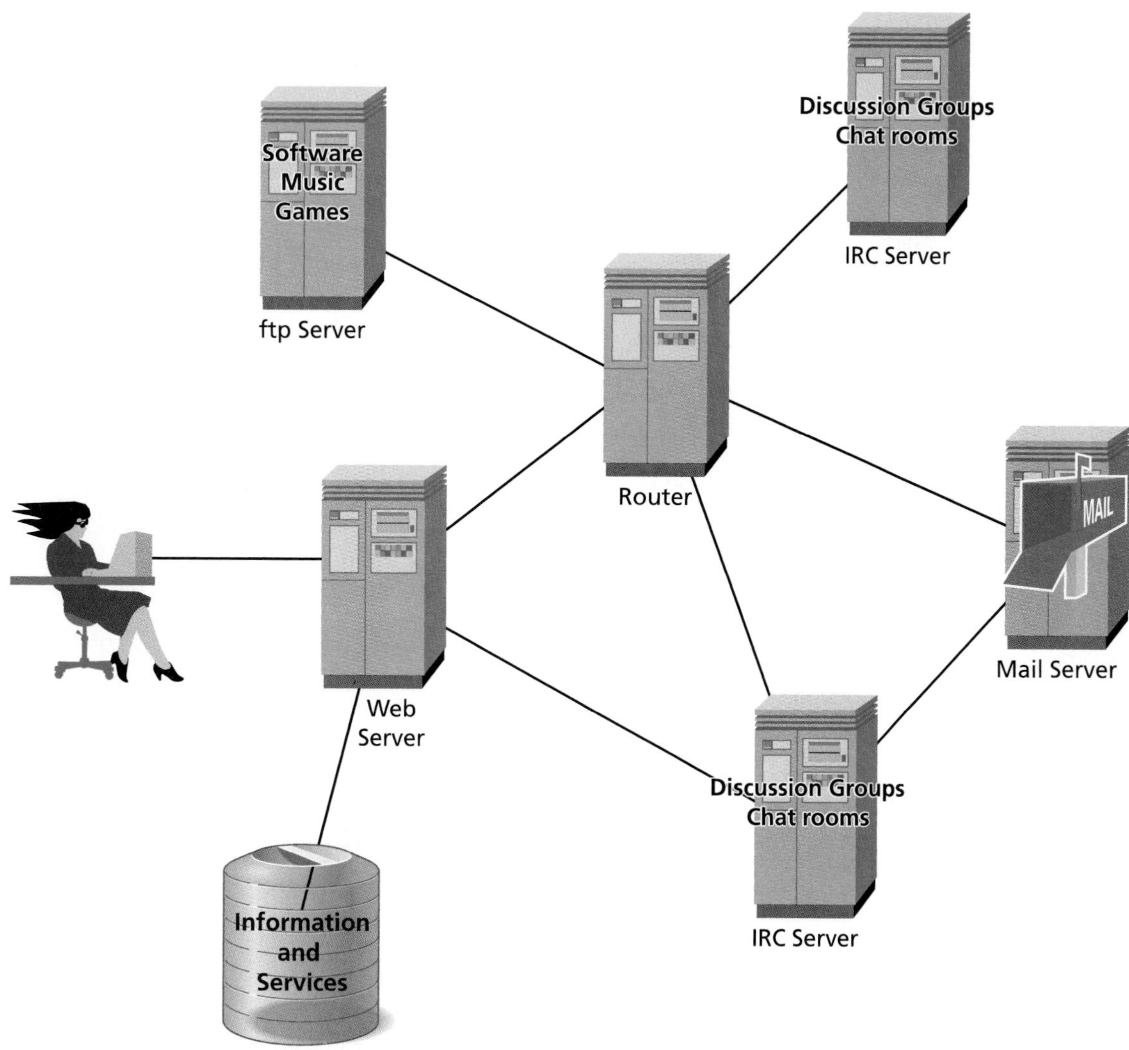

A **communications protocol (protocol)** is a set of rules that every computer follows to transfer information. The most widely used protocols on the Internet are TCP/IP, http, and ftp.

TCP/IP, or **transmission control protocol/Internet protocol**, is the primary protocol for transmitting information over the Internet. Whenever any type of information moves over the Internet, it does so according to TCP/IP. **Hypertext transfer protocol (http)** is the communications protocol that supports the movement of information over the Web, essentially from a Web server to you. That's why Web site addresses start with "http://." Most Web browser software today assumes that you want to access a Web site on the Internet, so you don't even have to type "http://" if you don't want to.

File transfer protocol (ftp) is the communications protocol that allows you to transfer files of information from one computer to another. When you download a file from an ftp server (using ftp), you're using both TCP/IP (the primary protocol for the Internet) and ftp (the protocol that allows you to download the file). Likewise, when you access a Web site, you're using both TCP/IP and http (because the information you want is Web-based).

ON YOUR OWN

USING A WEB PORTAL

Most Web browser software is already configured to take you to a certain Web site when you start surfing. For example, Internet Explorer usually starts at the Microsoft Network site (MSN at www.msn.com). Sites such as MSN, Yahoo!, and The Go Network (www.go.com) are often referred to as **Web portals**. A Web portal is a site that provides a wide range of services, including search engines, free e-mail, chat rooms, discussion boards, and links to hundreds of different sites.

The nice thing about Web portals is that they often let you customize the first page you see. You can request a ticker of your favourite stocks, the weather forecast for your area over the next three days, and a list of sites you commonly visit.

In this project, you are to create a customized and personal Web portal at two different places on the Web. We recommend that you do so at one of the sites below (although there are many others):

- www.msn.com
- www.go.com
- www.excite.com
- www.yahoo.com

As you build each portal, answer the following questions:

1. What is the registration process required to build a Web portal?
2. Can you receive a free e-mail account? If so, must you establish it?
3. Can you create categories of your most commonly visited sites?
4. Can you request customized local information for your area? If so, what type of information?
5. How do you adjust your Web browser settings so that it automatically takes you to your Web portal page?

Connecting to the Internet

To access the Web (via the Internet), you need an Internet service provider (ISP) as we discussed earlier. ISPs can include your school, your place of work, commercial ISPs such as AOL, and free ISPs such as Juno. Which you choose is a function of many things.

One of the nice things about going to school or being employed is that you often get free Web access. All you have to do is connect your home computer to your school's or work's computer (we'll talk about this process in a moment) and you're ready to surf. However, some schools and places of business may restrict where you can go on the Web. And they may even monitor your surfing.

Commercial ISPs charge you a monthly fee, just as your telephone company charges you a monthly fee for phone service. This fee usually ranges from a few dollars a month to about $20. Popular worldwide commercial ISPs include Microsoft (MSN), AOL, and CompuServe, to name just a few.

Free ISPs are absolutely free, as their names suggest—you don't pay a setup fee, you don't pay a monthly fee, and you usually have unlimited access to the Web. But there are some catches. Many free ISPs do not offer you **Web space**—a storage area for your Web site—as opposed to most commercial ISPs, which do. So, if you want to create and maintain a Web site, you may have to choose a commercial ISP over a free ISP (your school probably also offers you Web space). Also, when using a free ISP, you will often see banner ads that you can't rid of (see Figure E.9). You can move them around and from side to side, but you can't remove them completely from your screen. Finally, technical support is often limited with a free ISP. Some offer only e-mail support, while others do offer phone support but no toll-free number.

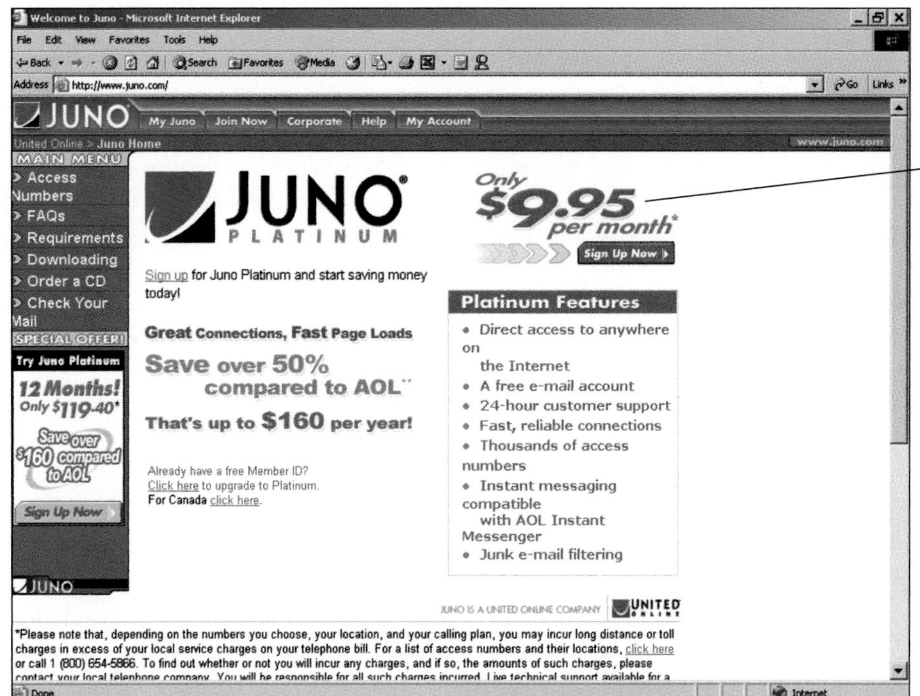

Figure E.9

Juno Is a Popular Free ISP

Juno's free ISP service will require that you see a lot of banner ads. If you want, you can subscribe to Juno's Platinum service (at a cost of $9.95 per month) which has fewer advertisements.

In spite of those drawbacks, many people do choose free ISPs over commercial ISPs, mainly because of cost (remember—$20 per month equals $240 per year). Popular free ISPs are Juno (www.juno.com; see Figure E.9) and NetZero (www.netzero.net).

To decide which type of ISP is best for you, ask these questions:

- Do you need Web space? If yes, a free ISP may not be the right choice.
- Is great technical support important? If yes, then a commercial ISP may be the right choice.
- Is money a serious consideration? If yes, then a commercial ISP may not be the right choice.
- Is privacy important to you? If yes, then your school or work may not be the right choice.

COMMUNICATIONS SOFTWARE

To access and use the Web, you need communications software, namely:

- **Connectivity software.** Enables you to use your computer to "dial up" or connect to another computer
- **Web browser software.** Enables you to surf the Web
- **E-mail software** *(short for* **electronic mail software***)***.** Enables you to electronically communicate with other people by sending and receiving e-mail

Connectivity software is the first and most important. With connectivity software, you essentially use your computer (and a phone line) to call up and connect to the server computer of your ISP. Connectivity software is standard on most personal computers today. To use connectivity software, you really only need to know the number to call. Then it's a relatively easy process—within Microsoft Windows, click on Start, Programs, Accessories, Communications, Network and Dial-up Connections, and then select Make New Connection (your exact menu choices may vary slightly according to which version of Windows you're using).

TEAM WORK

EVALUATING ISP OPTIONS

Choosing an Internet service provider (ISP) is an important, but not terribly complicated, task. In this project, your group is to evaluate three different ISPs—a well-recognized commercial ISP such as AOL or AT&T WorldNet, a free ISP such as Juno (there are many others), and a local or regional ISP in your area (you may to look in your phone book to find one of these).

Compare these ISPs in terms of (1) price per month, (2) amount of Web space provided, (3) monthly limit of hours you can be connected without paying an additional fee, (4) customer support, and (5) the ability to have e-mail.

Of the three, which would you choose and why?

Web browser software and e-mail software are also standard today. If your school or work is your ISP, then you'll most often be using commercially available Web browser software such as Internet Explorer or Netscape Communicator, and the e-mail software you use will vary according to your school's or work's preference. If you're using a commercial or free ISP, then your choice of Web browser software and e-mail software will depend on that particular organization.

Regardless of your choice of ISP, the unique Web browser software and e-mail software provided work in similar fashion. So, if you're used to using Internet Explorer and then choose AOL as your ISP, AOL has its own Web browser software—it will look different on the screen, but it supports the same functionality (a favourites list of some sort, moving forward and backward through your list of visited Web sites, and so on). All you have to do is get used to a new interface. Different e-mail software will also look different but support the same functionality.

TELECOMMUNICATIONS HARDWARE

In addition to communications software, you also need some telecommunications hardware to access the Web (again, via the Internet). If you're at school or work, you'll probably be able to connect your computer directly to a network that is then connected to the Internet. This often amounts to simply plugging a network line into your computer and starting your preferred Web browser or e-mail software. We discuss this type of connection to the Internet in more detail in Extended Learning Module D.

If you're connecting from home, you'll need some sort of modem. There are many types, including:

- **Telephone modem.** Connects your computer to your phone line so that you can access another computer or network
- **Digital subscriber line (DSL) modem.** A high-speed Internet connection using phone lines, which allows you to use your phone line for voice communication at the same time
- **Cable modem.** Uses your TV cable to deliver an Internet connection
- **Satellite modem.** Allows you to get Internet access from your satellite dish

DSL, cable, and satellite modems are among the newest, most expensive, and fastest. They also don't tie up your phone line. If, for example, you're using a basic telephone modem, you can't use your telephone line for voice communications at the same time. A DSL modem on the other hand, for example, basically splits your telephone line so that you can use it simultaneously for voice communications and for

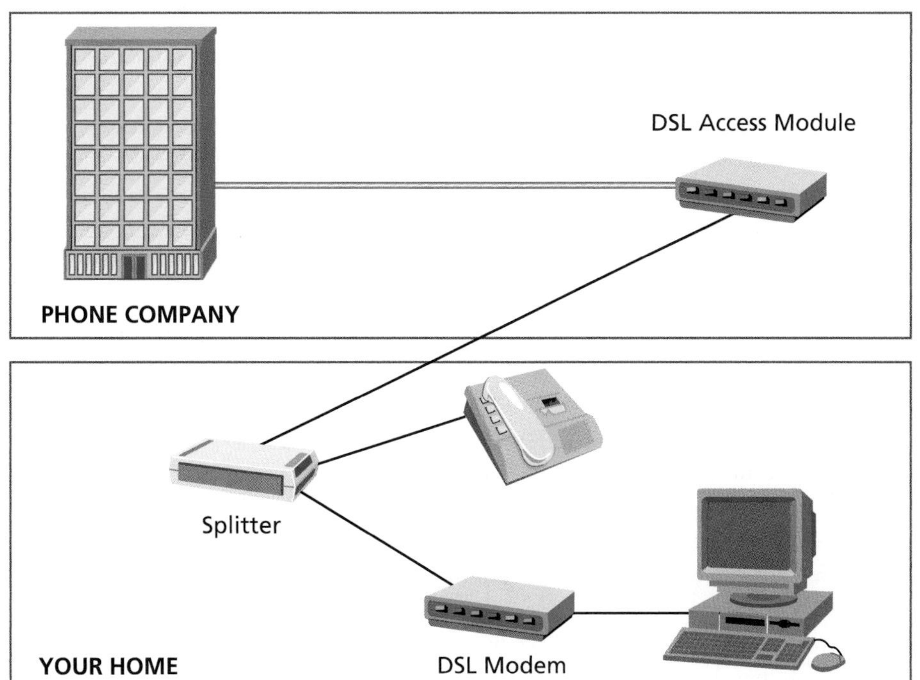

Figure E.10
DSL Modem Connection

connecting to the Internet (see Figure E.10). What's more, DSL, cable, and satellite modems offer you an "always on" Internet connection.

The biggest factor in determining your choice of telecommunications hardware (beyond price) may be that of availability. In many areas of the country, phone companies and cable TV service providers do not yet support the use of DSL, cable, and satellite modems. So, you may limited to just using a basic telephone modem. If some of the other options are available to you, we definitely recommend that you research them.

Summary: Student Learning Outcomes Revisited

1. **Define the relationships among Web site, Web site address, domain name, Web page, and uniform resource locator (URL).** A **Web site** (such as that for the *Globe and Mail*) is a specific location on the Web where you visit, gather information, and perhaps even order products. A **Web site address** ("www.globeandmail.com" for the *Globe and Mail*) is a unique name that identifies a site. Technically, a Web site address is called a **domain name**. A **Web page** is a specific portion of a Web site that deals with a certain topic. Technically, the address for a specific Web page is called a **URL (uniform resource locator)**.
2. **Explain how to interpret the parts of an address on the Web.** Most Web site addresses start with "http://www." Beyond that, the address is unique. The next part provides the name of the organization or Web site (using "www.uts.edu.au" as an example, the "uts" means the University of Technology in Sydney). Then comes the **top-level domain**, which gives the type of organization ("edu," describing it as an educational institution). If something follows after that, it usually provides a country of origin ("au," which identifies the country of origin as Australia).
3. **Identify the major components and features of Web browser software.** The two most popular Web browsers are Internet Explorer and Netscape Communicator. Each includes a menu bar (with functions such as File, Edit, and View), a button

bar (for commonly performed tasks such as printing), and an address or location field into which you can type a Web site address. Web browsers also allow you to maintain a list of commonly visited sites. In Internet Explorer, this is called a Favorites list, while Netscape Communicator refers to it as a Bookmarks list.

4. **Describe the differences between directory and true search engines. Search engines** are facilities on the Web that help you find sites with the information and/or services you want. A **directory search engine** organizes Web sites into hierarchical lists. With a directory search engine, you start by selecting a category and continually refine your search by choosing subcategories. A **true search engine** uses software agent technologies to search the Internet for key words and then places them into indexes. You use a true search engine by asking a question or typing search terms.
5. **Describe the various technologies that make up the Internet.** At the heart of the Internet is the **Internet backbone**, the major set of connections for computers on the Internet. A **network access point (NAP)** is a point on the Internet where several connections converge. **Network service providers (NSPs)**, such as MCI, own and maintain routing computers at NAPs and even the lines that connect the NAPs to each other. Besides your computer (called a *client*) which you use to access the Internet, there are also four types of **Internet server computers** that provide information and services on the Internet. These include **Web servers** (providing information and services to Web surfers), **mail servers** (providing e-mail services and accounts), **ftp servers** (maintaining a collection of files that you can download), and **IRC servers** (supporting your use of discussion groups and chat rooms). As information travels from these servers to you, it follows a set of **communications protocols**—rules every computer follows to transfer information. The most common protocols are **TCP/IP** (the primary protocol for transmitting information), **http** (for supporting the movement of information over the Web), and **ftp** (for allowing you to transfer files of information from one computer to another).
6. **Identify key considerations in choosing an Internet service provider (ISP).** When choosing an ISP—whether a commercial ISP, a free ISP, your school, or your employer—you need to consider the following:
   - *Web space.* If you want to publish a Web site, your ISP must provide you with Web space,
   - *Technical support.* This can be in the form of e-mail, 24-hour toll-free assistance, or perhaps none at all.
   - *Money.* Commercial ISPs are the most expensive, while free ISPs, your school, and your employer are free.
   - *Privacy.* Your school or employer may monitor your surfing activities.
7. **Describe the communications software and telecommunications hardware you need to connect to the Internet.** Communications software for connecting to the Internet includes **connectivity software** (for dialling up another computer), **Web browser software** (for actually surfing the Web), and **e-mail software** (for electronically communicating with other people. Telecommunications hardware includes devices called *modems* that you use to physically connect your computer to a network, which may through a phone line or a cable. Types of modems are a telephone modem, a DSL modem, a cable modem, and a satellite modem.

Key Terms and Concepts

telephone modem, 466
top-level domain, 454
true search engine, 458
URL (uniform resource locator), 453
Web browser software, 465
Web page, 453
Web portal, 464
Web server, 461
Web site, 453
Web site address, 453
Web space, 464
World Wide Web (Web), 453

Short-Answer Questions

1. How do the Web and the Internet differ?
2. What is the technical equivalent of a Web site address?
3. What is the relationship between a Web site and a Web page?
4. Why are links important on the Web?
5. What are the two most popular Web browsers?
6. What is the difference between a directory search engine and a true search engine?
7. How can you use plus signs and minus signs (represented by hyphens) to refine a search?
8. What is the relationship between the Internet backbone, a network access point, and a network service provider?
9. What are the four major types of servers on the Internet?
10. What is the primary protocol for transmitting information over the Internet?
11. What are the advantages and disadvantages of choosing a commercial ISP?
12. What communications software do you need to use the Web?
13. What are the four main types of modems you can use to access the Internet while at home?
14. Why is it important to consider the availability of Web space when choosing an ISP?

Assignments and Exercises

For each of the following questions, find the answer and URL on the Web. One restriction—you are not allowed to use encyclopedia sites such as *Encyclopaedia Britannica*.

1. What is the weight of the moon?
2. Who was the first Canadian billionaire?
3. Who is Olive Oyl's brother?
4. Who wrote "It was the best of times, it was the worst of times ..."?
5. What does the Seine river empty into?
6. What is a lacrosse ball made of?
7. Who lives at 39 Stone Canyon Drive?
8. What is the colour of Mr. Spock's blood?
9. At what did the S&P/TSX 300 stock market close yesterday?
10. What is the most frequently broken bone in the human body?
11. What is a pregnant goldfish called?
12. Who was the first pope to visit Africa?

13. How many tusks does an Indian rhinoceros have?
14. What does a pluviometer measure?
15. What is the fear of the number 13 called?
16. Which ear can most people hear best with?
17. Who is the patron saint of England?
18. What boxer's life story was titled *Raging Bull*?
19. What was the first domesticated bird?
20. What is the population of Canada right now?

EXTENDED LEARNING MODULE F

OBJECT-ORIENTED TECHNOLOGIES

Student Learning Outcomes

1. Explain the primary difference between the traditional technology approach and the object-oriented (OO) technology approach.
2. List and describe the five primary OO concepts.
3. Explain how classes and objects are related.
4. Describe the three fundamental principles of OO technologies.
5. List and describe two types of OO technologies.

Introduction

The explosion of object-oriented (OO) technologies is radically changing the way businesses view information and develop information systems. It's difficult to find a business or IT department that isn't using OO concepts; every single Fortune 500 company is using some type of this technology. Knowledge workers everywhere are quickly learning how to write software in OO programming languages, create databases using OO database management systems, and design new systems using OO analysis and design techniques. The race to learn and understand object-oriented concepts began many years ago and is still going strong.

"Object-oriented" is a revolutionary concept that has changed the way systems developers create computer programs. Historically, computer systems were viewed as logical procedures that took in information, processed it, and outputted resultant information. Object-oriented computer systems view information as sets of *objects* that are manipulated. Objects are anything you need to store and manipulate information on: people, animals, employees, students, courses, payroll, buildings, desks, etc. Basically, everything stored in the system is an object. It's easy to see that the OO computer system view is drastically different from the historical computer system view.

By reading this Module you'll be taking a giant leap toward understanding object-oriented concepts, which is a great asset for you as a knowledge worker. Even though you may not be planning to be a systems developer, it's important that you learn the fundamentals of OO, because you'll be involved in analyzing, designing, and using OO systems. Learning about object-oriented concepts and technologies will help prepare you for your future role as a knowledge working in the information age. This Module walks you through several important OO concepts including:

- The traditional technology approach
- The OO technology approach
- The five primary concepts of OO technologies including information, procedures, classes, objects, and messages
- The three fundamental principles of OO technologies including inheritance, encapsulation, and polymorphism
- A detailed business case example
- The three types of OO technologies, including OO programming languages, OO databases, and OO technologies and client/server environments

You might already be familiar with a few of the key terms and concepts related to object-oriented technologies: *information*, *procedures*, *classes*, *objects*, *messages*. If so, you've already been introduced to OO concepts. If you're unfamiliar with these concepts there's no need to worry, because you'll gain a solid understanding of each in the next few pages. We certainly don't claim that you'll become an object-oriented expert, but you'll get a great head start on understanding the whole OO environment.

It is important to note that one of the primary goals of this Module is to introduce you to the OO approach for developing information systems. The approach combines information and procedures into a single view. This statement probably seems a bit confusing but, after reading the next few sections, it will become crystal-clear. Just remember, the key to understanding the object-oriented approach is to recognize that combining information and procedures is quite different from the traditional technology approach where information is separated from procedures.

Traditional Technology Approach

Let's take a detailed look at the traditional technology approach in order to help you understand the object-oriented approach. The **traditional technology approach** has two primary views of any system—information and procedures—and it keeps these two views separate and distinct at all times.

INFORMATION VIEW

You're probably already familiar with many terms that describe information including *data*, *variables*, or *attributes*. All of these terms refer to the same thing, and in this text we refer to these things as *information*. You can think of *information* as a key characteristic stored within a system. For example, if we built a system to store student information, key characteristics could include *Student Last Name* or *Student Phone Number*. The **information view** includes all of the information stored within a system. To gain a better understanding of the information view, let's take a look at a sample Student Grading system.

In Figure F.1, you see all of the different types of information required to build the grading system such as *Student Last Name*, *Student ID*, and *Final Exam Grade*. The information view simply focuses on the information required to develop the system. The problem with the information view is that it gives no thought to how the information is used by the system. For example, it doesn't define the weights associated with each assignment or exam to derive the *Final Course Grade*.

PROCEDURE VIEW

You're probably also familiar with many terms that describe procedures including *formulas*, *functions*, and *methods*. All of these terms refer to the same thing and in this text we refer to these things as *procedures*. A *procedure* manipulates or changes information. For example, if a student moved, we would need to change his or her address in our Student Grading system. The way we do this is to run an *Update Student Address* procedure that changes the *Student Address* information. The **procedure view** contains all of the procedures within a system.

There are four primary procedures, or ways, a system can manipulate information; they include *create*, *read*, *update*, and *delete*—commonly referred to as **CRUD**. Can

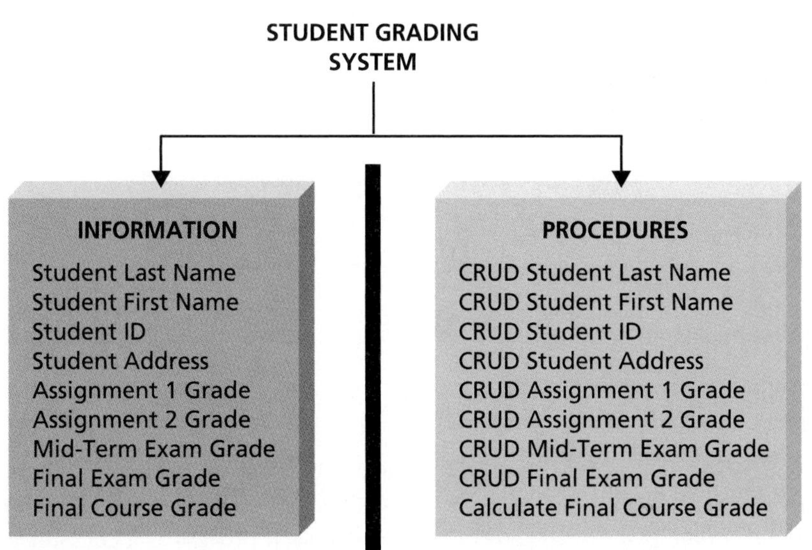

Figure F.1
Student Grading System: Separate Information and Procedure Views

you think of any other procedures you might use to manipulate information in a system? How about *calculate*, *run*, *save*, *cut*, *copy*, *spell check*, *select*, *overwrite*, etc.? These are all examples of procedures that manipulate or change information.

Can you identify the different procedures in Figure F.1? They include the basic *CRUD* on most of the information and a *Calculate Final Course Grade* procedure that calculates the average, on the basis of various weights, for all of a student's grades. These procedures define how the system uses the information. Do you see a problem with the procedure view? The problem is that it gives no thought as to what information is stored in the system. For example, there is a *CRUD Student Address* procedure but there is nothing that ensures there is a *Student Address* information field.

THE PROBLEM WITH THE TRADITIONAL TECHNOLOGY APPROACH

The primary problem with the traditional technology approach is that the separate views can lead to potential disconnects between the information and procedures. For example, it's possible to have the correct information but not be able to do anything with it because you don't have the corresponding procedures. Likewise, you could have the correct procedures but not be able to do anything with it because you don't have the corresponding information. In the first instance, it's rather like having a workbook but no spreadsheet software. In the second instance, it's like having the spreadsheet software but no information to work with.

Object-Oriented Technology Approach

The object-oriented approach bridges the gap between information and procedures by providing a holistic view of an information system. That is, an **object-oriented (OO) approach** combines information and procedures into a single view.

INFORMATION AND PROCEDURE VIEWS COMBINED

Let's take a look at the Student Grading system in Figure F.2. This diagram represents the same system as in Figure F.1, except that this diagram uses an OO approach. Notice that the diagram represents a holistic view of the entire system with the information in the middle and the procedures surrounding the information.

When you build an object-oriented system you think of the procedures and information as a single unit. Think how easy it would be for a knowledge worker to look at this diagram and instantly understand what types of information are in the system and what kinds of procedures can be performed on the information. Knowledge workers who use the OO approach, looking at both information and procedures combined, find it easier to perform the following three important tasks:

- Understand the system as a whole
- Determine if any key information is missing that would be required in order to perform all of the procedures
- Determine if any key procedures are missing required to manipulate the information

OBJECT-ORIENTED APPROACH AND THE REAL WORLD

The object-oriented approach not only makes a knowledge worker's job easier; it also improves overall systems development, because the system more closely models the real world. In the real world, you actually view a given process as a combination of

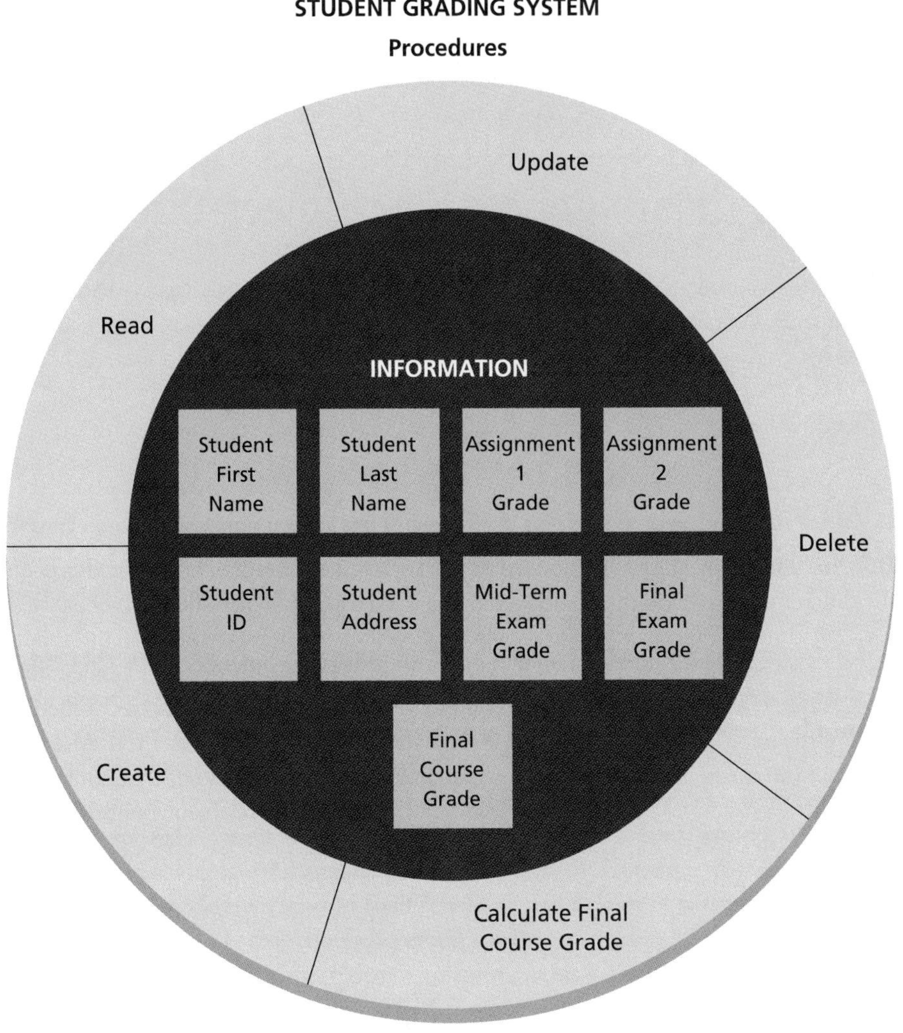

Figure F.2

Student Grading System: Combined Information and Procedures

information and the procedures you need to act on that information. Have you ever purchased a product that requires "some assembly," such as a mountain bike or gas grill? Upon opening the box and spreading out the contents you immediately reach for the instruction booklet. In the instructions you'll find a detailed set of steps concerning assembly along with a description of the various parts. Both the information and procedures are provided together which is similar to an OO approach. You won't find the set of instructions separate from the description of the parts—they are combined because this makes sense.

If you viewed only the procedures in the Student Grading system example, would they make any sense? Probably not, and it would be difficult for you to understand the procedures without understanding the information. For example, it would be impossible for you to understand the *Calculate Final Course Grade* procedure if you didn't know what type of information was used in this calculation.

Let's take a look at an inventory tracking process, another great example of how the object-oriented approach models the real world. If you consider a business process such as "track inventory," you can quickly identify several key characteristics required to perform this process such as *Part Number*, *Part Name*, *Part Manufacturer*, *Quantity on Hand*, *Reorder Point*, and *Cost*. These are all examples of information. At the same time, you can identify how the information needs to be manipulated to perform this process such as *Calculate Quantity to Order*, *Add a New Part*, *Change a Part Cost*, and so on. These are all examples of procedures. In short, you are considering both information and procedures to be an integrated part of the "track inventory" process. So object-oriented concepts basically provide a real-world view in which information and procedures are considered together.

Five Primary Concepts of Object-Oriented

There are five basic object-oriented concepts that you as a knowledge worker should understand. We have introduced you to two of these in the previous section. Can you guess which they are? If you said *information* and *procedures*, you're correct. Although we've already discussed these concepts, we'll briefly review them again in this section. The other three basic object-oriented concepts are *classes*, *objects*, and *messages*.

INFORMATION

Information is key characteristics stored within a system. You're already familiar with the different types of information stored in the Student Grading system such as *Student Last Name* and *Final Course Grade*, so let's take a look at information stored in a different sample system. Imagine you're building a Dog Tracking system for a kennel business. What types of information do you think the system needs in order to track different types of dogs? The answer to this question can be any key characteristic you can think of related to a dog including *Name*, *ID*, *Breed*, *Colour*, *Weight*, *Height*, *Owner*, etc. These are all examples of different types of information the system could store.

PROCEDURES

A **procedure** manipulates or changes information. Again, you're already familiar with the procedures in the Student Grading system including *CRUD Student Last Name* and *Calculate Final Course Grade*, so let's try to define the different procedures required to build the Dog Tracking system mentioned above. What types of procedures do you think the system needs? The answer to this question can once again be anything you think you'll need in order to manipulate the dog information including *CRUD Dog Name* and *CRUD Dog ID*. It's also important to understand that procedures are used not only for CRUD on information, but also to perform functions or operations. Can you think of any other procedures that a Dog Tracking system might perform besides the basic CRUD on information? How about calculating the cost for a dog to stay at the kennel or scheduling employees who work at the kennel? Both of these are great examples of procedures the system might need to perform.

CLASSES

A **class** contains information and procedures and acts as a template to create objects (instances of a class). Yes, classes are that simple. They are simply what we call the combination of information and procedures as displayed in Figure F.3. It sometimes helps to think of classes as similar to a definition in a dictionary. Let's return to our Dog Tracking sample system. If you looked up the definition of "dog" in a dictionary, it will give you an overview of what a dog is and explain what a dog can do. A class does exactly the same thing. If you look at the class Dog in Figure F.3, you can quickly understand all of the information required to describe a dog and many of the procedures the dog system can perform including *Calculate Cost for Dog Stay* and *Create Dog Name*.

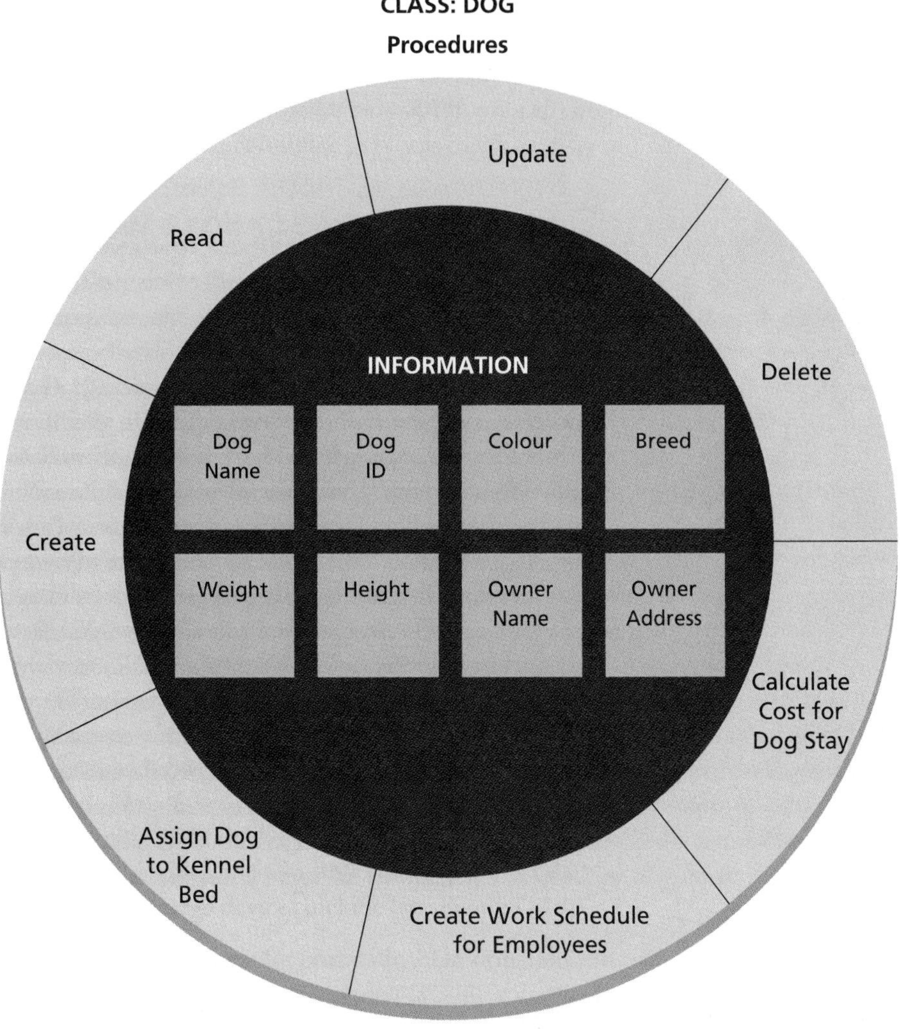

Figure F.3
Class Dog

MULTIPLE CLASSES For the Student Grading system and for the Dog Tracking system we've identified only a single class for each. Classes become a little more difficult when you start to think of having 50 or 500 different classes in a single system.

Can you guess why a single system might have so many classes? Imagine if you put all of the information for the Dog Tracking system into a single class. This class would be enormous. Just think of all the different types of information it might contain. There could be owner, diet, vaccine, accident, injury, training, and kennel inventory information to name just a few. If all of this information were in a single class, the class would quickly become unmanageable. Determining which types of information belonged to which procedures would be impossible. Breaking down the information and procedures into multiple classes for ease of use and understandability, or practising **information decomposition**, is a great way to structure your information system. Information decomposition makes IT specialists and knowledge worker's jobs easier, because the information is broken down into understandable pieces. It is certainly possible to put all the information and procedures for the system into a single class, but this is a bad system design and leads to multiple system problems.

OBJECTS

An **object** is an instance of a class. This definition probably seems a bit confusing, so an easier way to think of an object is the actual item represented by the class.

Figure F.4

Gus and Oreo: Two Instances (Objects) of Class Dog

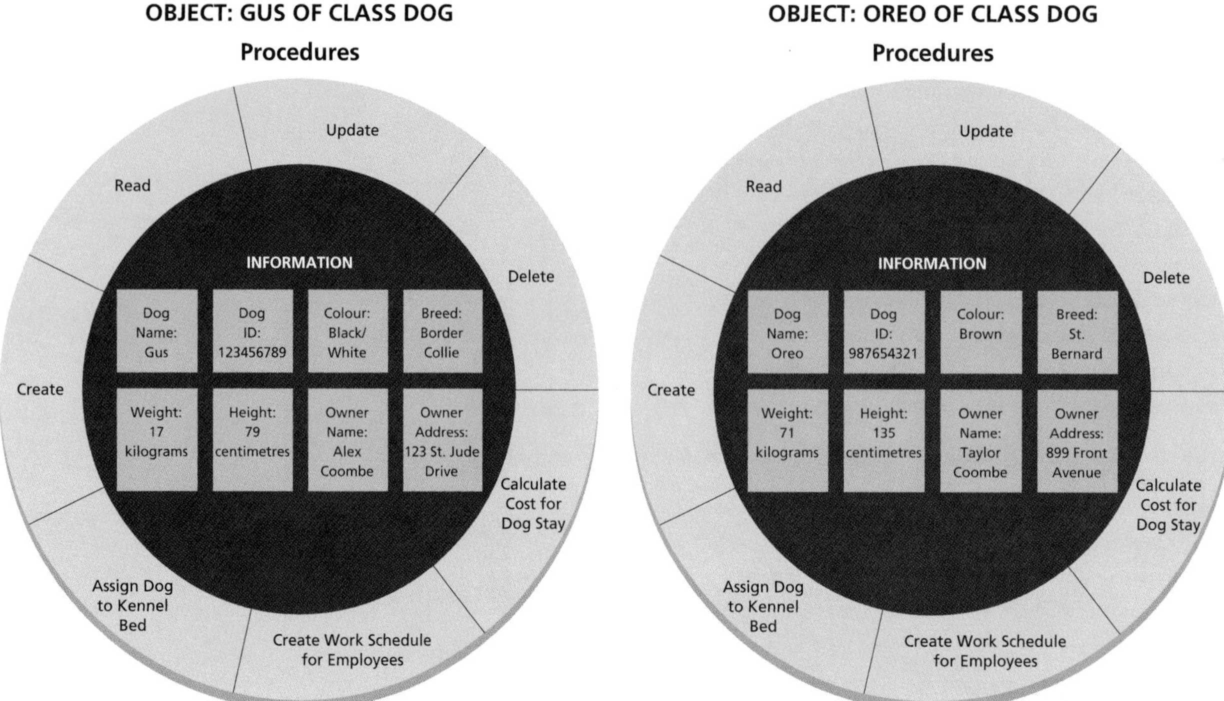

Let's take a look at the two objects (Gus and Oreo) of the class Dog represented in Figure F.4. Can you describe the primary difference between the Dog class diagram in Figure F.3 and the Dog object diagrams in Figure F.4? Sure, you noticed the Dog object diagram contains the information representing the actual dogs that the system tracks. Using Figure F.4, you can describe the first object, Gus. Gus is a black-and-white border collie owned by Alex Coombe. You can also describe the second object, Oreo. Oreo is a brown St. Bernard owned by Taylor Coombe. Every dog the system tracks is a separate object and every dog object is an instance of (or created from) the class Dog. Gus and Oreo are both examples of objects of that class.

HOW CLASSES AND OBJECTS INTERACT Do you remember the original definition of a class? Classes contain information and procedures and act as templates to create objects. Essentially, the class is a blank template which defines all the different types of information the system can store about an object. Once you create an object from the class, you can fill in the template with the actual information. For example, the Dog class can give you a high-level definition of a dog object, such as *Dog Name*, but it can't tell you the actual name of the dog. The class will only tell you that it can store information for the dog's name. The object stores the actual information and can tell you the dog's name is Gus.

MESSAGES

Now that you know something about objects, you may be asking: Do objects communicate with each other, and if so how? These are great questions, and the fact that you're asking them means you're quickly becoming an OO expert.

Messages are how objects communicate with each other. One object can send a message to another object asking it to perform a certain procedure. But why do objects need to communicate with each other? In general, systems are created by developing many dif-

ON YOUR OWN

IDENTIFYING OBJECT-ORIENTED CONCEPTS

Let's practise the five primary OO concepts by applying them to another sample system. Assume you're building a Music Tracking system for a store such as HMV or Virgin Records. Answer the following questions:

1. What different types of information do you need to track?
2. What different procedures are required to act on the information?
3. What are the classes you need to create?
4. How many objects are going to be created from each class?
5. How can you tell the difference between the classes and the objects?
6. How are the objects going to interact with each other?

ferent classes that work together to perform tasks. Let's refer back to our Student Grading system. If you build this system, you might have one class representing students, a second class representing courses, and a third class representing instructors. Objects from each of the classes communicate with each other in order to enter the student's course grades. The student object passes a request to enroll in courses to the course object. The instructor object passes a request to teach specific courses to the course object. The instructor object also passes the student's final course grades to the course object. Combining these three classes gives you a fully functioning Student Grading system.

HOW THE FIVE PRIMARY CONCEPTS INTERACT

Let's review information, procedures, classes, objects, and messages as important object-oriented concepts and how they relate to each other.

- Information and procedures create classes
- Classes create objects
- Objects communicate with other objects via messages

Let's take a look at the individuals who build the systems and the individuals who use the systems as another perspective on how the object-oriented concepts relate to each other.

Systems developers are the individuals who build the systems and are responsible for building the classes which contain information and procedures. *System users* are the individuals who use a system and are responsible for inputting the actual information or creating the objects. If you think about the Dog Tracking system, you can easily identify which individuals are responsible for the different tasks. The systems developer would be responsible for building the Dog class and the associated information and procedures. The kennel owner, or system user, would be responsible for creating the objects or inputting the actual dog information.

With these basic concepts—information, procedures, classes, objects, and messages—you are now in a position to understand the basics of object-oriented technologies. Next, let's take a close look at some real-world examples.

Real-World Object-Oriented Example

Can you think of something you use every day that is a good example of an object-oriented system? Here's a hint—a real-world OO system has several different components working together to create a single system. Does that help? We'll bet you can think of several different everyday items that are great examples of object-oriented systems.

How many of you thought of a car? The steering wheel, tires, and engine are different components that work together in order to accomplish the common goal of driving. How many of you thought of a computer? A computer is a great example of several different components working together and sending messages to each other in order to accomplish a common task. (See Extended Learning Module C for how computer components work together and send messages to each other.) The keyboard, monitor, mouse, and operating system all work together to run applications.

How many of you thought of a home stereo system? This is a perfect analogy for an OO system. If you created a class for each stereo component, the classes might include:

- Amplifier
- CD player
- Cassette deck
- Equalizer
- Speaker
- CD
- Cassettes

Can you name some of the information items stored within the CD class? *Title*, *Artist*, *Date Recorded*, and *Number of Songs* are a few. Can you determine how many objects would be created from this class? This number varies depending on how many CDs you own. Can you guess what the primary procedure is in the amplifier object? If you guessed *Set Volume*, you're correct. In fact, manipulating the volume of the music is a primary procedure of the amplifier object.

In order for the system to work, objects are created from each class and each of the objects works with specific information and procedures. The information for the CD player, for example, could include the *Manufacturer Name*, *Model Number*, *Play Speed*, etc. The procedures for the CD player could include *Play*, *Fast Forward*, *Rewind*, *Skip*, *Stop*, etc. If you called the *Play* procedure for the CD player object, do you think you would be able to hear music? No, you would not be able to hear anything. The CD player can play the CD, but it has to send a message to the amplifier object, which sends a message to the speaker object to play the music.

A home stereo system is a true example of a real-world object-oriented system. All components must work together for the system to function. Thus, each component in a home stereo system really is an object. As an object, each component works with only certain information and performs certain procedures. If one component needs another procedure performed, it must send a message to another object (or component) that can perform that procedure.

Three Fundamental Principles of Object-Oriented

A business can gain huge advantages by using object-oriented technologies. The three fundamental principles of OO technologies are:

1. Inheritance
2. Encapsulation
3. Polymorphism

These may sound difficult but they're actually rather simple to understand. Let's explore each in detail.

INHERITANCE

One of the most powerful features of object-oriented technologies is inheritance. **Inheritance** is the ability to define *superclass* and *subclass* relationships among classes. Generalization and specialization relationships are another way of thinking of superclass and subclass relationships. Take a minute and review Figure F.5, and try to determine which class is the superclass and which classes are the subclasses.

The Car class is the superclass and the Bronco and Porsche classes are the subclasses. Another way to state this relationship is that the Bronco and Porsche subclasses inherit all of the information and procedures from the Car superclass. For example, the *CRUD* procedures are not defined in the Bronco and Porsche subclasses because they are inherited from the Car superclass.

Defining inheritance is simply a matter of defining both *generic* and *specific* information and procedures. Generic information and procedures apply to all subclasses; specific information and procedures apply only to a particular subclass. For example, notice how the Car superclass in Figure F.5 contains generic information and procedures that are shared by both the Bronco and the Porsche subclass. Both the Bronco and the Porsche subclass have a *Model*, *Year*, *Price*, and *Colour* and both can *Honk Horn*, *Break*, and *Drive*.

The subclasses contain specific information and procedures unique to each subclass. The Bronco subclass contains information for *4-Wheel Drive* and the Porsche subclass contains a procedure to *Drive over 225 km/h*. These unique features are stored in the subclass because they are not generic enough to store in the Car superclass. If you stored the procedure for *Drive over 225 km/h* in the Car superclass, then every subclass of Car inherits this procedure. This is a rather big mistake, since there are many types of cars that can't drive over 225 kilometres per hour. Hence, we must store this unique feature at the subclass level.

Inheritance, or the ability to define superclass and subclass relationships, is a unique feature of OO technologies. Can you think of the benefits inheritance brings to an IT department or system?

BUSINESS BENEFITS OF INHERITANCE—REUSE The true business benefit gained from using inheritance is the ability to easily expand and maintain a system. Let's look at an example of how defining a superclass allows a system to be easily expanded. If you decided to add a piece of information called *Mileage* to the Car class, it's only developed in one place, the Car class, and it's automatically inherited by every subclass. The *Mileage* information is reused by all of the subclasses.

If you're using the traditional approach to develop this system, the *Mileage* information must be developed in each of the Car, Bronco, and Porsche classes, because the traditional approach does not support the concept of inheritance or reuse. Imagine if you had 50 subclasses of the Car class. Obviously, if you used the traditional approach it would take a great deal of time and energy to build *Mileage* information into all 50 subclasses. With the object-oriented approach, you only build it once and all 50 subclasses automatically inherit this valuable piece of information.

Another example of how inheritance makes it easy to expand a system would be if you decided to add a new class, Volkswagen Beetle, to the system. If you placed this class as a subclass of Car, it would automatically inherit the information and procedures already developed in the Car class. All you need to develop is any unique information

Figure F.5
Inheritance

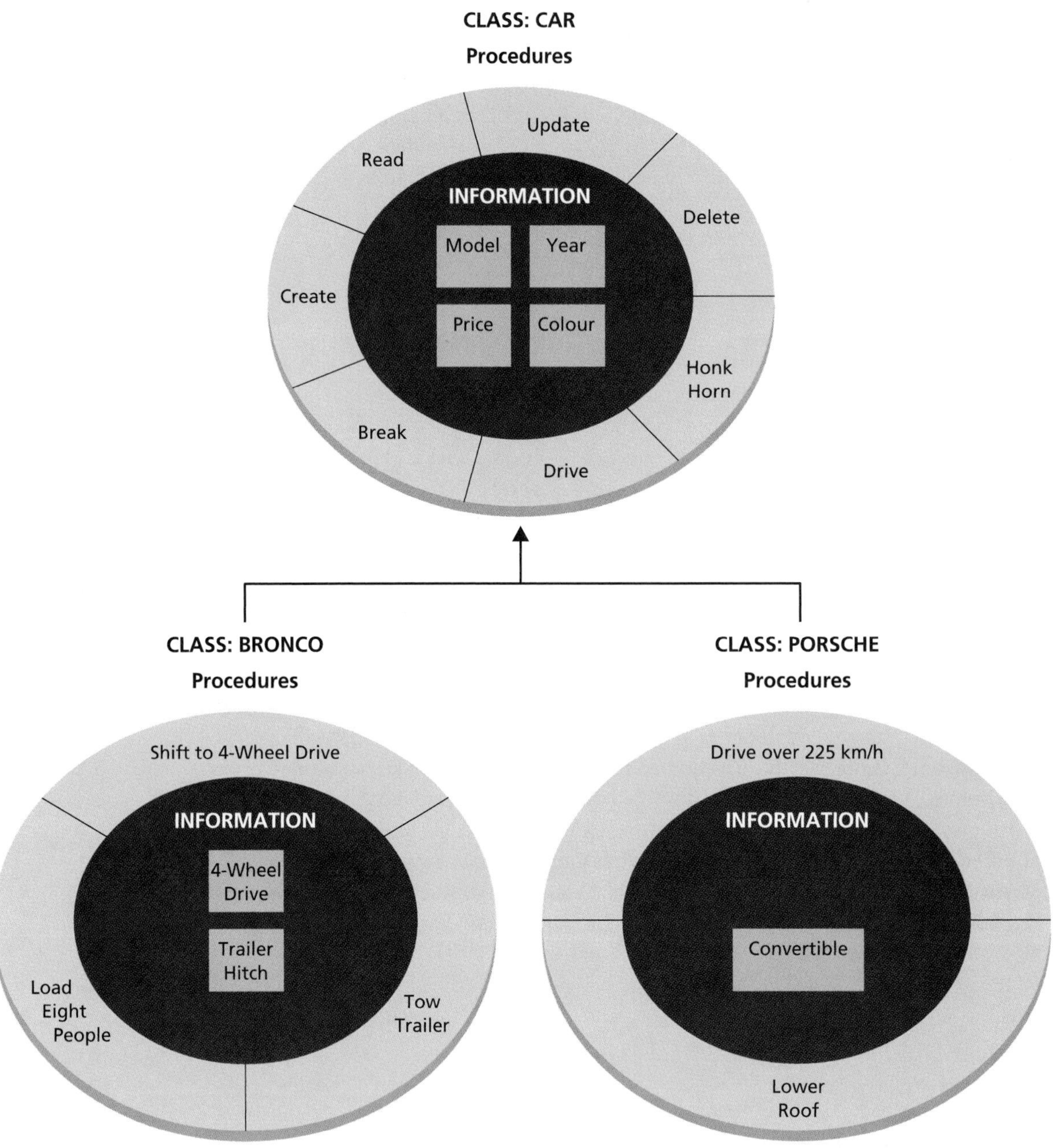

or procedures the Volkswagen Beetle class requires. If you added a Volkswagen Beetle class using the traditional approach, you must build every single piece of information and every procedure including *Model*, *Year*, *Price*, *Colour*, *CRUD*, *Honk Horn*, *Drive* and *Break*. Inheritance is obviously a valuable principle for businesses in terms of saving money, effort, and time when developing and maintaining information systems.

ENCAPSULATION

Encapsulation means information hiding. This concept has a simple definition and provides tremendous benefits when you're building an information system. Let's take a look at how object-oriented technologies encapsulate information.

TEAM WORK

CAN YOU FIND THE ERRORS IN THIS CLASS DIAGRAM?

Take a look at the Car class diagram and determine what errors exist. If you'd like a hint, think about information, procedures, and inheritance.

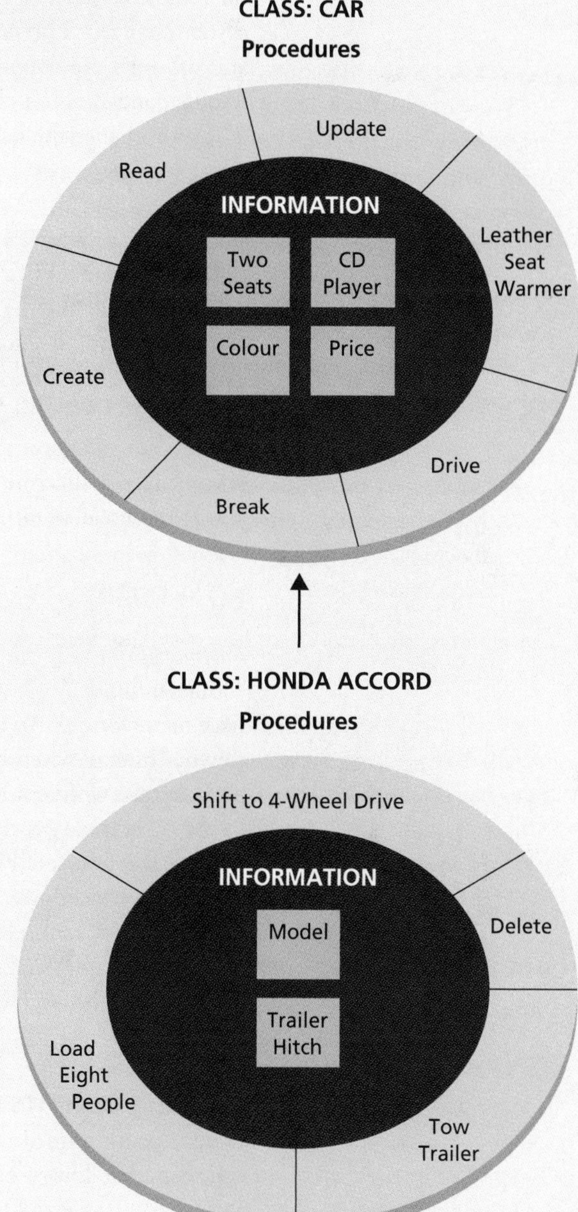

Objects are sometimes referred to as "black boxes," as the information inside them is hidden. Imagine you're in a park and you see an animal. In terms of OO, you can instantly determine that the animal is a member of the class Dog. However, you don't know all the information about the dog. You can't tell the dog's name, weight, height, etc. just by looking at it. Hence, the actual information stored in the object is hidden, or encapsulated, but this doesn't prevent you from seeing the dog and being able to communicate with it.

Let's take a look at an example of encapsulation. If you order AT&T digital cable, you receive a remote control used as the interface to the cable box. An **interface** is any device that calls procedures and can include such things as a keyboard, mouse, and touch screens. Recently, AT&T changed its entire digital cable system including the menu colours, item locations, and cable features. Suddenly, when a user turned on the television everything on the digital cable menu looked completely different. However, the remote control, or system interface, continued to work exactly as it did before the system changed. The same buttons on the remote control were used to turn the TV on and off, turn the volume up and down, and select different menu items. Since the remote control didn't change, the customers could use their system exactly as before. The only change the users had to deal with was getting used to the new look and feel of the system.

BUSINESS BENEFITS OF ENCAPSULATION—QUALITY Can you explain the business benefits AT&T received from its use of encapsulation? AT&T used encapsulation to hide the digital cable system changes from its users. The system changed significantly but, because the user's remote control, or interface, continued to work exactly the same, the users were unaffected. The users continued to receive the same high-quality service from AT&T. In other words, the changes were hidden from the users. This is a good example of the huge benefits a company can receive by using encapsulation. Imagine the millions of dollars AT&T would be required to spend if it had to retrain all of its customers every time it wanted to make a system change.

POLYMORPHISM

Polymorphism is an impressive word and, like so many technical words, it looks and sounds intimidating but has a very simple meaning. **Polymorphism** simply means "to have many forms." An example of polymorphism in daily life is the word *bark*. What do you think of when you hear the word? Many of you probably thought of a dog's bark, but the word could also refer to tree bark. This is true polymorphism, the ability to use exact same word to mean different things.

Let's take a look at Figure F.6. Notice how the Rectangle, Square, and Circle classes all contain procedures called *CalculateArea*. However, the *CalculateArea* procedure is different for each class. The formula to calculate the area of a rectangle (*Length* × *Width*) is completely different from the formula to calculate the area of a square (4 × *Side*). Thus, each class has an identically named procedure that calls for different calculations.

BUSINESS BENEFITS OF POLYMORPHISM—PRODUCTIVITY If you build a procedure using a traditional technology, you must ensure that the procedure has a unique name. Imagine how difficult this would be if there were 1000 procedures in the system. Using an OO approach removes the problem of defining complex naming structures and increases productivity.

Putting It All Together: A Business Example

Let's assume you're starting your own business, Ice Blue Snowboards Inc. Your business manufactures and sells snowboards, bindings, boots, and apparel. In order to prepare for the launch of the business, you researched similar businesses to discover any problems they've encountered so you can avoid making the same mistakes. The following is a list of common competitor problems:

Figure F.6
Polymorphism

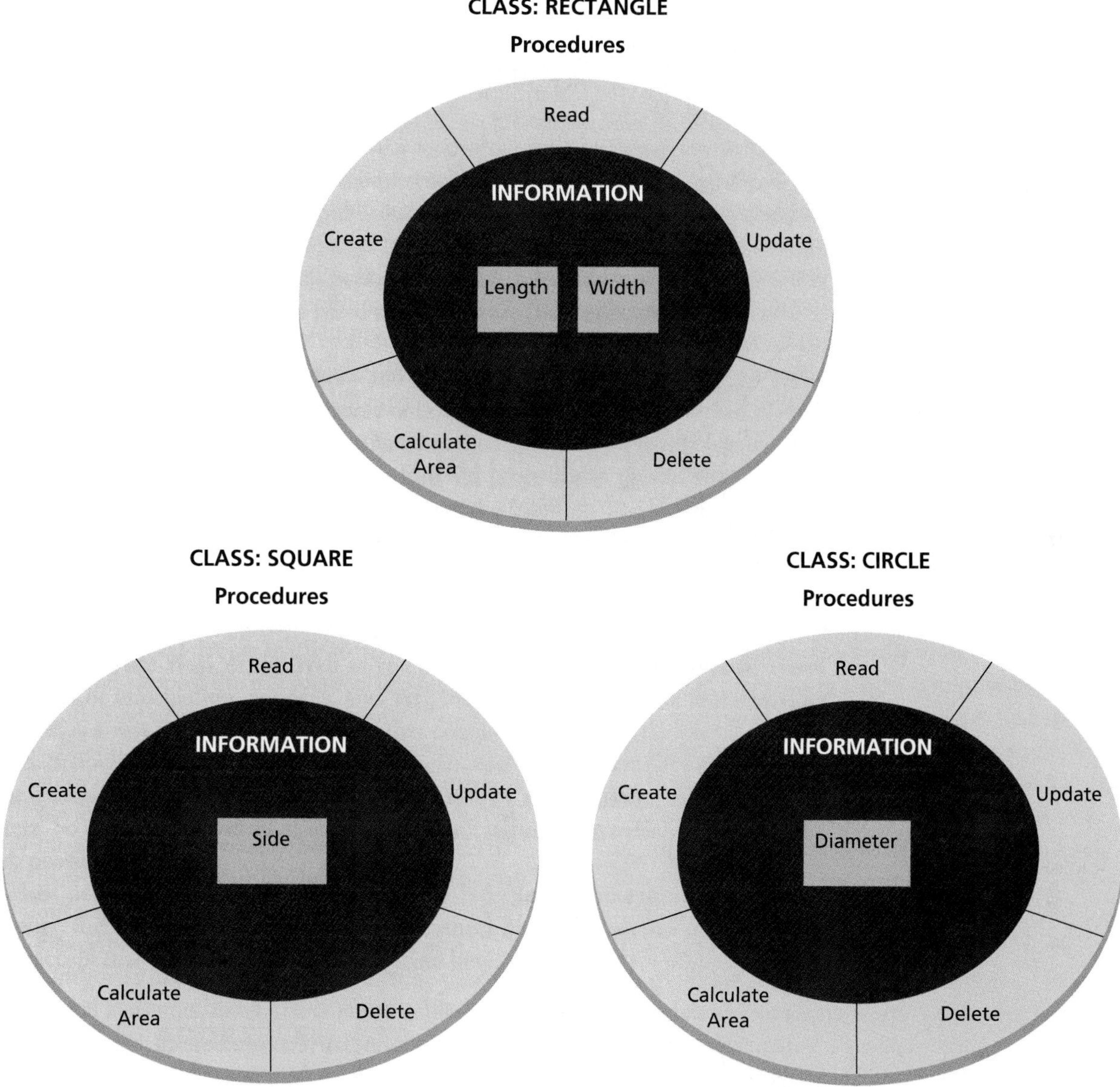

- Eighteen months to get a new product to market
- Inventory control
- Scalability and expandability

Let's take a detailed look at each problem and discuss how using an object-oriented approach will help you minimize or eliminate these problems.

EIGHTEEN MONTHS TO GET A NEW PRODUCT TO MARKET

In order for your business to be competitive you must be able to get your new products on the market as soon as they're finished. Having a fast time-to-market is critical for the success of your new business. Eighteen months is simply too long for you to wait to get a new product on the market. Using an object-oriented approach will help you reduce this critical time-to-market factor. The typical high-level processes for developing new products include the following:

- Generating and accepting the idea
- Manufacturing the product
- Updating all current systems to support the new product
- Implementing the new product

Every time a new product is developed it takes almost 18 months for your competitors to get it on the market. I'll bet you're asking how this process takes 18 months. The reason is primarily because several applications must be changed every time a new product is introduced. A typical business will have a different system for every business function including inventory, sales, orders, customer, marketing, billing, etc. Every system must be updated with the new product information before you can begin selling the product to your customers. Can you think of how using an OO approach could help you decrease the time and effort required to update every system?

The following is an example of how you could define an object-oriented snowboard selling system. First, a class called Snowboard would be created. The Snowboard class would be responsible for tracking all snowboard information including *Pricing*, *Model*, *Features*, *Discounts*, etc. The Snowboard class would also be responsible for establishing all of the procedures associated with marketing and selling snowboards including promoting in magazines and competitor pricing analysis. Second, an interface would be designed to perform all of these procedures. This would encapsulate the information and procedures in the Snowboard superclass and allow you the flexibility to change things without affecting the knowledge workers. Third, you would practise inheritance. A subclass would be created for each type of snowboard. Defining subclasses, or using inheritance, saves you a great deal of time and energy because each subclass inherits all of the information and procedures from the superclass. The only work required to create a subclass is defining the unique information or procedures associated with the subclass. After creating each class once, you can reuse the classes across all of your business applications. Finally, you would create one object that communicates with all of the other objects across every system in your business.

Defining a new snowboard product would now require no more than one hour. The following are the steps required to define a new product:

- Create a single subclass for the new product.
- Assign a subclass/superclass relationship between the new class and the Snowboard class.
- Define any unique pieces of information for the new product subclass.
- Define any unique procedures for the new product subclass.
- Reuse the new product subclass by copying it directly into every business application.
- Create an object from the new subclass.

By understanding and using OO technologies, you've decreased your product introduction time from 18 months to an hour. The key to reducing the time-to-market for your products is having business systems that use the same generic interfaces for dealing with products. Every time you introduce a new product, as long as it conforms to the generic interface, all the business applications are able to add it without any modification or interruption to the knowledge workers.

Figure F.7 is a good example of a snowboard business case class diagram. It assumes your business offers an electronic catalogue on the Internet listing all the snowboarding products you sell. By creating a catalogue object whose primary procedure is to update

Figure F.7
Snowboard Business Case Class Diagram

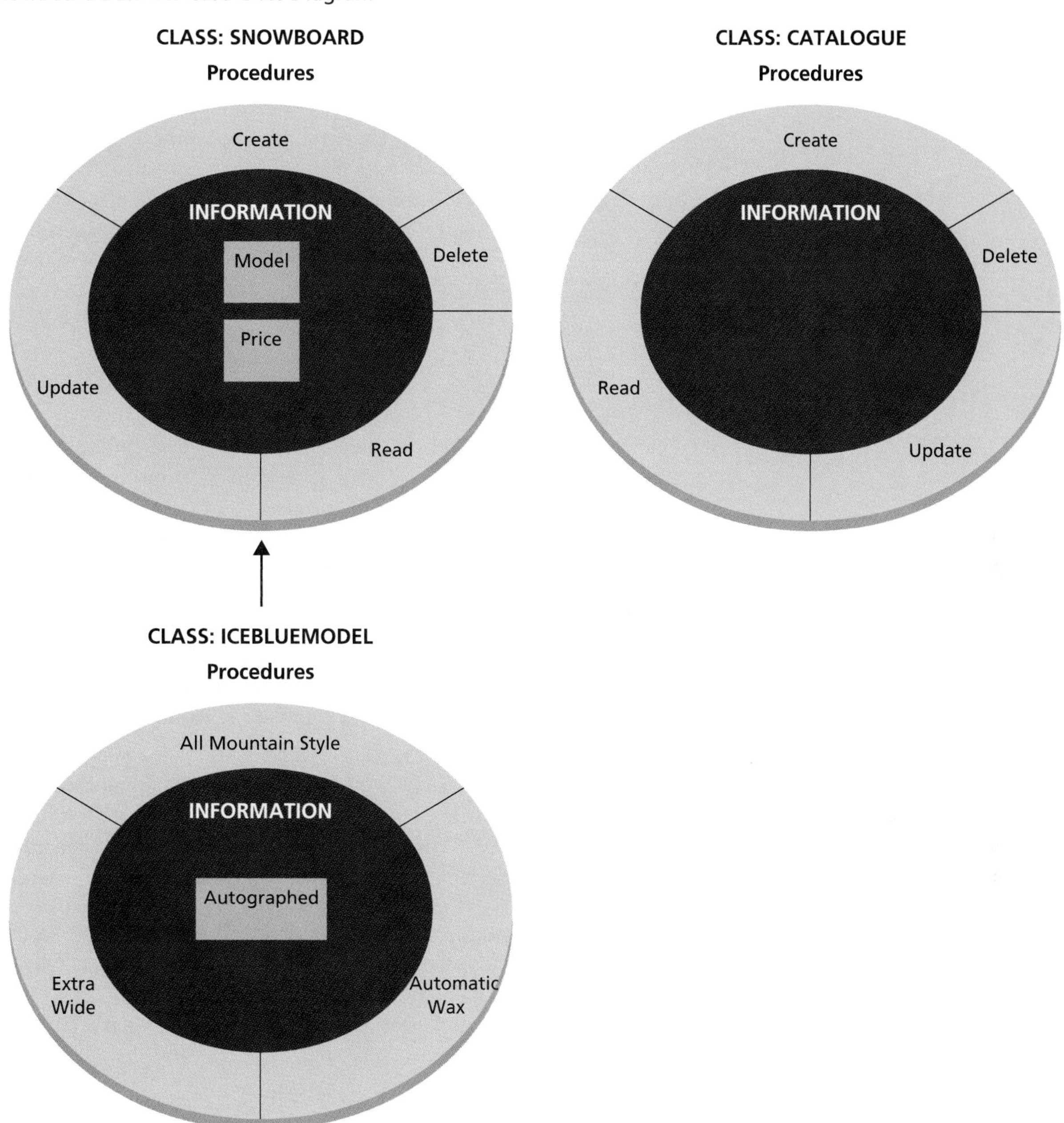

the electronic catalogue, you wouldn't be required to change anything when adding a new product to the catalogue. The catalogue object already understands how products are added and listed in the catalogue. The new product object simply sends a message to the catalogue object to execute the update catalogue procedure. The new product would be added to the catalogue without any need for system modification.

INVENTORY CONTROL

Controlling inventory is one of the largest problems facing businesses today. Businesses need to be able to have sufficient inventory on hand to meet current production needs while minimizing the associated expenses including storing the inventory, transporting it, and maintaining it. This problem is part of supply chain management and it hits all businesses small and large. Managing the supply chain is fundamental to the success of any business. If you neglect to manage your supply chain, then you'll find your business experiencing high storage costs, the inability to manufacture products due to low inventories, and lost inventory.

Can you guess how supply chain management can be implemented efficiently using object-oriented technologies? You can define Shipping, Distribution, and Vehicle classes. Creating shipping, distribution, and vehicles objects allow you to control your inventory. Shipping objects know their origin, destinations, and their primary goal of arriving at the destination on time at the lowest expense. Distribution objects designate which modes of transportation will be used to ship the inventory. Vehicle objects move the inventory. Using these three objects will help your business track and maintain correct inventory levels.

SCALABILITY AND EXPANDABILITY

Scalability refers to how well your system can adapt to increased demands. Increased demands can include such things as additional users, information, and processing speeds. When a system grows, the size of the database that stores the information grows. As the database grows, the system tends to perform procedures slower. **Expandability** refers to how easy it is to add features and functions to a system. If you design a system without thinking about expandability you'll run into major problems when your business starts to grow.

Take a look at Figure F.8. Do you notice a problem with the class diagram? Can you explain why the ExpertSnowModel class was unable to be placed in a superclass/subclass relationship with the Snowboard class? As we discussed, it's important to take advantage of inheritance, as it saves time and effort when developing a system. The reason the ExpertSnowModel class can't inherit the functionality from the Snowboard class is because of the procedure called *Deep Powder Specific*—a procedure that doesn't apply to all types of snowboards. Snowboards are designed for powder, ice, and all mountain terrain. For this reason, the ExpertSnowModel class can't be designated as a Snowboard subclass. If you did place the ExpertSnowModel class as a subclass of Snowboard, an ExpertSnowModel would be able to perform the *Deep Powder Specific* procedure. This is a rather large system error. Defining subclasses that are too specific and not being able to take advantage of inheritance is a common problem with OO systems.

Did you notice anything else wrong with the class diagram? The ExpertSnowModel class doesn't contain any information. This indicates a disconnect between the information and procedures. The ExpertSnowModel class contains the *Create*, *Read*, *Update*, and *Delete* procedures, but what are these procedures going to manipulate if there isn't any information? This is a typical error if you are using traditional technology because information and procedures are viewed separately. Using the object-oriented approach, you notice this disconnect right away.

Now that you are armed with the powerful knowledge associated with OO technologies you'll be able to build all of the systems needed to start Ice Blue Snowboards Inc. You'll even be able to avoid many of the common pitfalls your competitors have faced.

Types of Object-Oriented Technologies

Many technologies are in use today that support object-oriented concepts and techniques. Many more of these technologies are being developed every day as the

Figure F.8
Scalable Systems

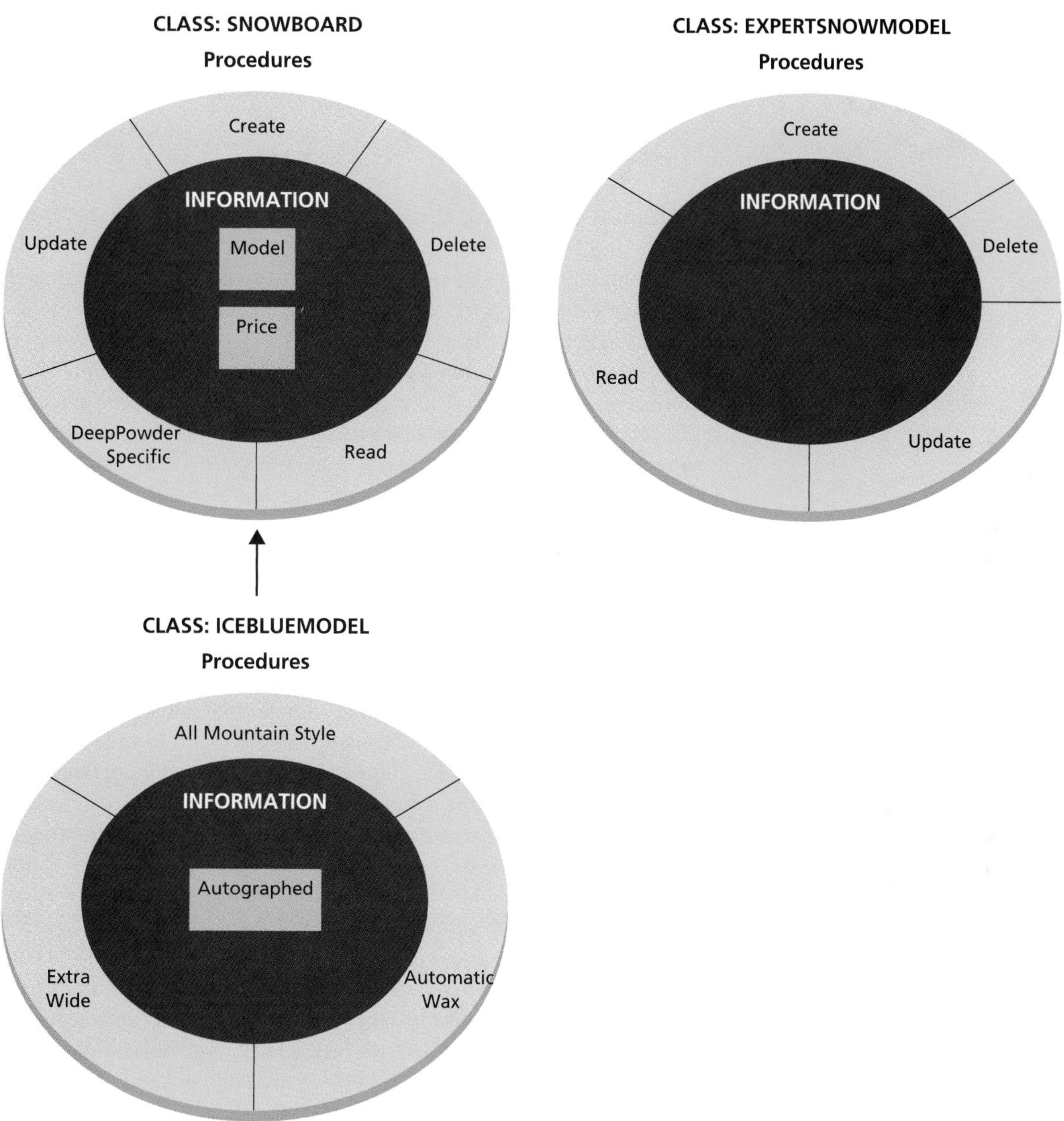

business world continues to rush toward OO. As a knowledge worker, it's important that you have some general knowledge of the different types of OO technologies available and used throughout IT departments.

OBJECT-ORIENTED PROGRAMMING LANGUAGES

In general, programs are what make computers work. A **program** is a set of instructions that, when executed, cause a computer to behave in a specific manner. A program is almost like a recipe. It contains ingredients and directions, or information and procedures that tell the computer how to perform different tasks. Microsoft Word and Excel are both examples of programs. Can you think of others?

A **programming language** is the tool developers use to write a program. An **object-oriented programming language** is a programming language used to develop OO systems. Programming languages that are not OO can't handle classes, objects, messages, inheritance, encapsulation, etc. Currently, there are close to 100 different object-oriented programming languages available. The three most popular today are Java, C++, and Smalltalk.

OBJECT-ORIENTED DATABASE SYSTEMS

Relational databases (the most popular, which you learned about in Chapter 3) organize information into fields, records, and files (or relations). **Object-oriented databases** work with traditional database information and also complex data types such as diagrams, schematic drawings, video, sound, and text documents.

The relational database model, although it may allow you to store and view such data types, does not include good mechanisms for allowing you to manipulate and change information within those data types. For example, you can include a CAD drawing of a part as a field in a relational database, but it's literally impossible to work with any specific information in the drawing (such as cuts, specific components, and the ordering of assembly) without having that information also stored in other fields.

Another feature of OO databases is that you are not restricted to two-dimensional tables. This gives you greater flexibility in storing and defining procedures that work with complex data types. In fact, most of today's multimedia applications rely on the use of objects and OO databases.

Most other database models also restrict you to working with specific data types—alphabetic, numeric, decimal, currency, date, and so on. In an object-oriented database environment, however, you can create and work with data types that may be unique to a specific business process. For example, if you had an object that included an address you could easily define that this field includes a street address and a unit number. You could then define a procedure that requires the entry of both pieces of information. This is an example of a unique data type that requires not only a street address, but also a unit number.

OBJECT-ORIENTED TECHNOLOGIES AND CLIENT/SERVER ENVIRONMENTS

Client/server is the emerging blueprint for organizational networks, and most organizations are choosing to develop client/server networks through object-oriented technologies. A *client/server network* is one in which one or more computers are servers and provide services to the other computers, called clients. Spreading objects across a client/server network makes sense: client workstations contain objects with local procedures for working with local information, and servers contain objects with global procedures for working with global information.

Figure F.9 shows how objects work in a client/server environment. The server handles the entire data management function, the client handles the entire presentation function, and the two share in processing the logic or business rules. So the server object contains procedures for retrieving and storing information (data management) and for processing some of the logic or business rules. Likewise, the client object contains procedures for some of the logic or business rules and for presenting information (the presentation function). To demonstrate, assume you are the manager of the manufacturing division in an organization and need to give pay raises to each of your employees. For assigning pay raises, you also have to follow several rules—some for just your division and some for all organizational employees.

Figure F.9

Object-Oriented Technologies and Client/Server—The Perfect Match

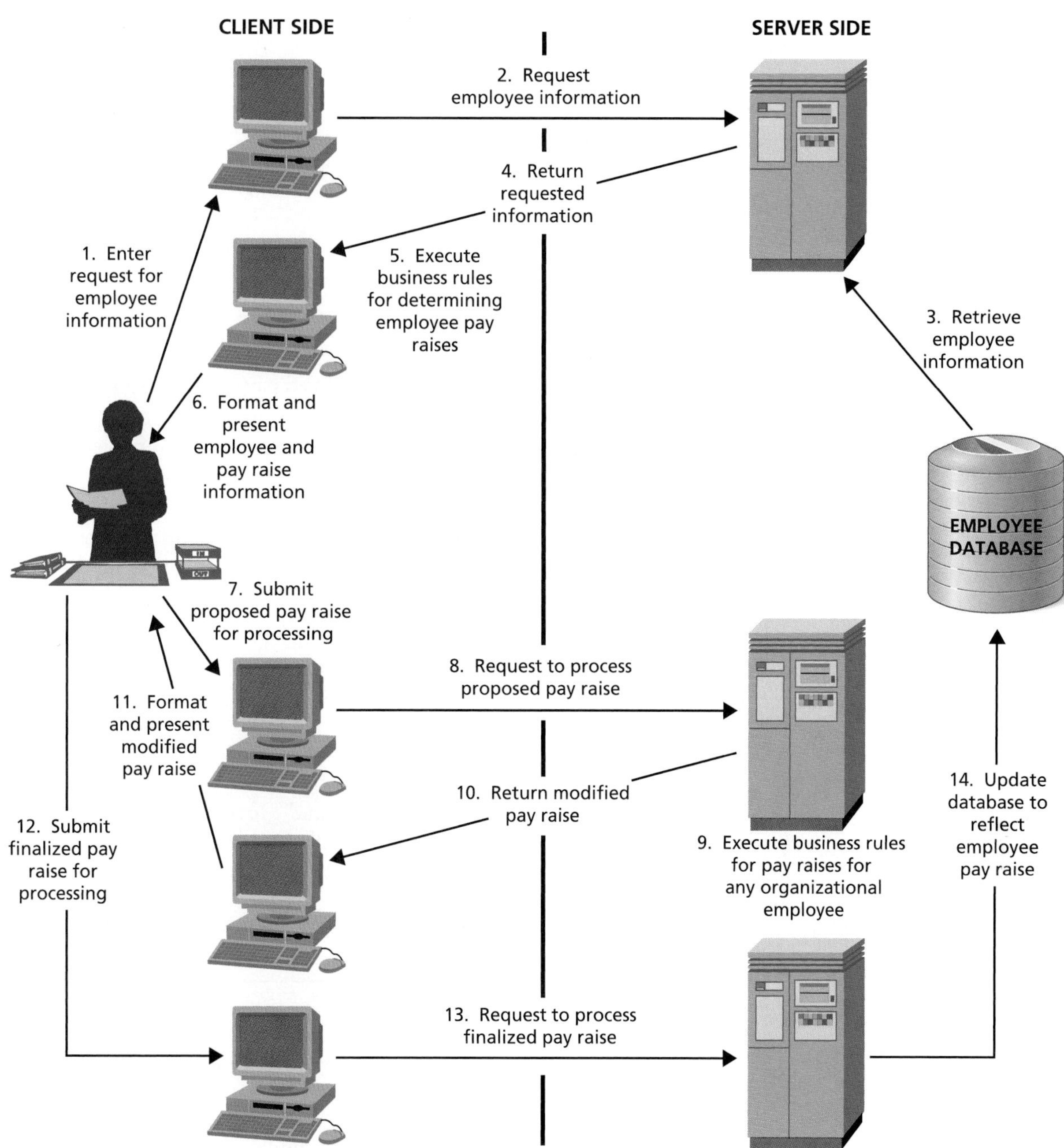

In an OO environment, your client workstation contains an object for assigning pay raises to manufacturing division employees according to manufacturing division rules. The server contains an object for assigning pay raises according to organizational rules and for retrieving information from and saving information to the database.

Let's review how this would actually work. First, your client object, or Manufacturing Employee object, asks you for an employee and sends a message to the server object, or Organizational Employee object, to retrieve that employee's information from the database. Your client object then executes the rules for determining pay raises for manufacturing employees, displays that information to you, and sends the proposed pay raise to the server object. The server object then executes the organizational

TEAM WORK

RESEARCHING POET

One of the most popular object-oriented databases is Poet. You can find information about Poet at its site (www.poet.com). Visit the site and do some research. As you do, answer the following questions:

1. How can you learn more about Poet? At a Web seminar? A face-to-face seminar? By some other means?
2. Who are some customers of Poet?
3. Who are some business partners of Poet?
4. To what extent do Poet solutions focus on "e" or electronic business initiatives?
5. What is a catalogue management solution?

rules for assigning pay raises and returns the modified pay raise to your client object. Your client object then displays that information to you and allows you to submit the finalized pay raise for processing to the server object. Finally, the server object updates the Employee database to reflect the employee's pay raise.

It's possible that while you're assigning pay raises to your manufacturing division employees, other managers of other departments could be assigning pay raises to their employees. In this instance, you and any other managers essentially share the server object—another excellent example of reuse.

THE FUTURE OF OBJECT-ORIENTED TECHNOLOGIES

Let's end this Module with a brief discussion of the future of object-oriented technologies. The number of OO development tools increases daily, and with this increase the importance of understanding OO concepts becomes even more critical. In the future, object-oriented tools will perform tasks and provide functionality that we haven't even thought of yet. We hope this Module has provided you with a solid understanding of OO technologies and concepts preparing you for your job as a knowledge worker.

Summary: Student Learning Outcomes Revisited

1. **Explain the primary difference between the traditional technology approach and the object-oriented technology approach.** The primary difference between the traditional technology approach and the object-oriented technology approach is the way information and procedures are viewed and developed. The **traditional technology approach** has two primary views of any system—information and procedures—and it keeps these two views separate and distinct at all times. The primary problem with this approach is that the separate views allow for information disconnects. For example, you might have all of the required information but not the correct procedures to manipulate the information. The **object-oriented (OO) approach** combines information and procedures into a single view.
2. **List and describe the five primary object-oriented concepts.** The five primary OO concepts are:
   - Information is any key characteristic stored within a system.
   - A **procedure** manipulates or changes information.

- A **class** contains information and procedures and acts as a template to create objects (instances of a class).
- An **object** is an instance of a class.
- **Messages** are how objects communicate with each other. One object can send a message to another object asking it to perform a certain procedure.

In general, the combination of information and procedures creates a class. A class creates objects and objects communicate with other objects via messages. A system usually contains many classes and many objects can be created from a single class.

3. **Explain how classes and objects are related.** Classes contain information and procedures and are used as a template to create objects. The class is basically a blank template which defines all of the different types of information the system can store about an object. An object can only be created from a class. Once you create an object from a class, you can fill in the template with the actual object information.

   One way to describe the interaction between classes and objects is to think of classes as a high-level definition and to think of an object as a real item. For example, the Dog class can give you a high-level definition of a dog object, such as *Dog Name*, but it can't tell you the actual name of the dog. The class will only tell you that it can store information for the dog's name. The actual name of the dog, Gus, is stored in the dog object.
4. **Describe the three fundamental principles of object-oriented technologies.** The three fundamental principles of OO technologies are:
   - **Inheritance**, which is the ability to define superclass and subclass relationships among classes. The subclass inherits all of the information and procedures from its superclass. Other names for superclass/subclass relationships include parent/child relationships and generalization/specification relationships.
   - **Encapsulation**, which means information hiding. A remote control is used to control AT&T's digital cable. The remote control hides the system information from the knowledge workers.
   - **Polymorphism**, which simply means to have many forms. Basically, polymorphism provides you with the ability to use the same word for a procedure and have it mean different things for different classes.
5. **List and describe two types of object-oriented technologies.** One type of object-oriented technology is an object-oriented programming language. An **object-oriented programming language** is one used to develop object-oriented systems. Just as English, French, and Italian are all different types of languages you can use to write a paper, so Java and C++ are two different types of languages you can use to write a program. An OO programming language must be used in order to develop an OO system.

   A second type of object-oriented technology is an object-oriented database system. **Object-oriented databases** work with traditional database information and also complex data types such as diagrams, schematic drawings, video, sound and text documents.

Key Terms and Concepts

class, 476
CRUD, 473
encapsulation, 482
expandability, 488
information, 476
information decomposition, 477
information view, 473
inheritance, 481
interface, 483
message, 478
object, 477
object-oriented (OO) approach, 474
object-oriented (OO) database, 490
object-oriented (OO) programming language, 490
polymorphism, 484
procedure, 476
procedure view, 473
program, 489
programming language, 490
scalability, 488
traditional technology approach, 473

Short-Answer Questions

1. What is the combination of information and procedures?
2. What is an example of a real-world object-oriented system?
3. What are classes?
4. How are messages used?
5. What is the information view?
6. What is an example of information?
7. What is information decomposition?
8. Why would you use information decomposition?
9. What is an instance of a class?
10. What is a procedure?
11. How do objects and classes relate?
12. How do superclasses and subclasses relate?
13. What is polymorphism?
14. What is an object?
15. Why is scalability important when building a system?
16. What is a benefit of using the OO approach?
17. What is an interface?
18. What is another term for a superclass/subclass relationship?
19. Why is expandability important when building a system?
20. What is another term used to describe information hiding?

Assignments and Exercises

1. **CLASSES IN THE CLASSROOM.** Take a look around your classroom and on a piece of paper list 20 different objects located in the classroom—desks, chairs, lights, students, etc. If you were going to build a classroom inventory tracking system, how many classes would you need to define in order to track all of the objects? What would be the name of each class? What information and procedures would be stored in each class? On a separate sheet of paper draw a class diagram displaying all of the classes along with the different types of information and procedures they contain. Be sure to try to take advantage of inheritance. Take both sheets of paper and match each object to an appropriate class. If all of the objects match a class, you have created a successful system. Chances are, every student's class diagram is going to be different, because there is no right or wrong answer to this exercise; so be creative and have fun defining your classes. Be sure to look at some of the other students' diagrams to see how they defined their classes.
2. **TREES-R-US.** Congratulations! You've been hired to build an inventory tracking system for the landscaping company Trees-R-Us. Trees-R-Us is excited about the use of inheritance in OO systems and wants to see how you're going to use it in the system. Trees-R-Us has already defined the Tree, Grass, Flowers, Fence, Equipment, and Plant classes. Your job is to define all of the information and procedures for each class and the inheritance structure of the classes, or the superclass and subclass relationships. Provide a class diagram that displays all the classes for the Tree-R-Us inventory tracking system, and be sure to include inheritance. Again, there is no right or wrong answer for this exercise; so be creative and look at some of the other students' class diagrams to see how they defined their classes.
3. **OO CONCEPTS AND A REAL-WORLD SYSTEM.** Create a list of a computer and all of its parts. Be sure to include the monitor, keyboard, mouse, hard drive, disk drive, memory, CD-ROM drive, software, and printer. Write a brief explanation describing each of the following:
   - What types of information are associated with the computer?
   - What types of procedures are associated with the computer?
   - What parts of the computer, if any, represent the classes?

- What parts of the computer, if any, represent the objects?
- How many classes are there?
- How many objects are there?
- How are messages used?
- How do all of the components work together to create a complete system?

4. **UNDERSTANDING OO CONCEPTS AND TERMINOLOGY.** Create a brief presentation explaining the primary differences between each of the following:

   - Traditional technology approach and OO technology approach
   - Information and procedures
   - Classes and objects
   - Messages and interfaces
   - Encapsulation and inheritance
   - Generalization and specialization

   Feel free to use any of the figures located in this Module. You can find them on the Web site that supports this text at www.mcgrawhill.ca/college/haag.

5. **EXPLAINING OO TO YOUR MANAGER.** Assume you're working for a large oil and gas company. Your current manager has very little experience with object-oriented technologies and has asked you to write a paper describing, in generic terms, each of the following OO concepts. Be sure to include explanations on how using these concepts will contribute to building and implementing successful information systems.

   - Encapsulation
   - Polymorphism
   - Inheritance

6. **CLASSES AT THE VIDEO STORE.** Consider your local video rental store. What would be three important classes? How many different objects do you think there are for each class? On a separate sheet of paper, draw a class diagram displaying all of the classes along with the different types of information and procedures they contain. Do you think video rental stores in general use OO systems? Why or why not?

7. **RESEARCHING JAVA.** Java is perhaps the most popular of all the OO programming languages. It was developed by Sun Microsystems in the early to mid-1990s. Connect to the case studies section of Sun's Web site for Java (industry.java.sun.com/casestudies) and click on the Case Studies link. Find a case study that interests you about a company that has used Java to implement an OO system. Prepare a short report for your class detailing that case study. Now, do some more research on the Web. Although Java is currently the dominant OO programming language, there are some new ones on the horizon that will compete with it. Find one. What is it? How is it designed to compete with Java? Who provides it?

NOTES

CHAPTER ONE

1. R. Hiebeler, Thomas Kelly, and C. Ketteman, *Best Practices: Building Your Business with Customer-Focused Solutions* (New York: Simon & Schuster, 1998).
2. Mortimer Zuckerman, "America's silent revolution," *U.S. News & World Report*, July 18, 1994, p. 90.
3. Rick Bionda, "Profile: Canberra-Packard Canada," *Laboratory Business*, Spring 1996, available at CPC site <www.cpcan.ca/spring96.pdf>, accessed August 10, 2002.
4. Martin Keohan, "The virtual office: impact and implementation," *Business Week*, September 11, 1995, pp. 95–98.
5. EKOS Research Associates Inc., press release, 2001, available <www.ekos.com/admin/press_releases/telework4.pdf>, accessed August 10, 2002; EKOS Research Associates Inc., press release, 1998; available <www.ekos.com/admin/press_releases/nov98.pdf>, accessed August 10, 2002.
6. *Fortune*: August 1975; August 11, 1980; August 19, 1985; July 30, 1995; August 7, 2000; Strategis: Canada's Business and Consumer site <strategis.ic.gc.ca>.
7. "SYSTRAN Enterprise," SYSTRAN site <www.systransoft.com/Corporate/Enterprise.html>, accessed November 14, 2002.
8. Brian Dumaine, "What Michael Dell knows that you don't," *Fortune Small Business*, June 3, 2002.
9. Thomas Stewart, "Intellectual capital: ten years later, how far we've come," *Fortune*, May 28, 2001, pp. 192–193.
10. Ernest Kallman and John Grillo, *Ethical Decision Making and Information Technology* (San Francisco: McGraw-Hill, 1993).
11. Marc Peyser and Steve Rhodes, "When e-mail is oops mail," *Newsweek*, October 16, 1995, p. 82.
12. T. Tripp and M. Gross, "The evolution of an Intranet at Spar Aerospace," *The Courier* (Special Libraries Association—Toronto Chapter), 35(2)(November/December 1997), available <www.sla.org/chapter/ctor/courier/v35/v35n2a8.htm>, accessed August 11, 2002; T. Tripp and M. Gross, "From static Web pages to interactive information delivery," *The Courier* (Special Libraries Association—Toronto Chapter), 35(3)(January/February 1998), available <www.sla.org/chapter/ctor/courier/v35/v35n3a1.htm>, accessed August 11, 2002.
13. "History," Nokia site <www.nokia.com/aboutnokia/inbrief/history.html>, accessed November 14, 2002.
14. Acxiom site <www.acxiom.com>.

CHAPTER TWO

1. Miguel Helft, "Fashion fast forward," *Business 2.0*, May 2002, available <www.business2.com/articles/mag/print/0,1643,39407,FF.html>.
2. "Scorecards," Gomez.com <www.gomez.com/benchmarks/scorecard.asp>, accessed November 14, 2002.
3. "The Dell Direct model," Dell site <www.dell.com/la/la/en/gen/corporate/vision_directmodel.htm>, accessed November 14, 2002.
4. "Overview: Ariba punchout," Cisco Systems site <www.cisco.com/commarch/html/eprocurement/ariba/punchout.html>, accessed November 14, 2002.
5. Peter Fingar and Ronald Aronica, "The death of e and the birth of the real new economy," *Tampa Bay* (Tampa, FL: Meghan-Kiffer Press, 2000), p. 25.
6. Michael E. Porter, "Strategy and the Internet," *Harvard Business Review*, March 2001, pp. 62–78.
7. "EMC, CISCO and ORACLE unveil new ecostructure blueprint for accelerated information access," ECOStructure, press release, May 22, 2001, available <www.eecostructure.com/052201.html>, accessed November 14, 2002.
8. Singapore Economic Development Board site <www.sedb.com/edbcorp/index.jsp>, accessed November 14, 2002.
9. Lynda M. Applegate, F. Warren McFarlan, and James L. McKenney, *Corporate Information Systems Management: Text and Cases*, 5th ed. (New York. Irwin/McGraw-Hill, 1999), p. 64.
10. David Orenstein, "Remote surgery," *Business 2.0*, December 2001 <www.business2.com/articles/mag/print/0,1643,35201,00.html>, accessed November 14, 2002.
11. Owen Edwards, "Bow Tech: ASAP case study," *Forbes ASAP*, June 3, 1996, pp. 54–58.
12. Egghead.com <www.egghead.com>, accessed November 14, 2002.
13. Irene M. Kunii, "How do you say 'cool' in Japanese? Tsutaya," *Business Week OnLine*, May 13, 2002 <www.businessweek.com/print/premium/content/02_19/b3782131.htm?mainwindow>, accessed November 14, 2002.
14. F. Warren McFarlan and Duncan G. Copeland, "Note on airline reservations systems (revised), part II," Harvard Business School, Product Number 9-189-099, October 31, 1988, available <harvardbusinessonline.hbsp.harvard.edu/b01/en/common/item_detail.jhtml?id=189099>, accessed November 13, 2002.
15. Michael Johnson, "Think channel collaboration, not conflict," Digitrends.net, July 12, 2001, <www.digitrends.net/ebiz/13643_14471.html>.
16. Peter Wayner, "i spy," Computerworld, February 5, 2001 <www.computerworld.com/securitytopics/security/story/0,10801,57280,00.html>, accessed November 13, 2002.
17. See the OnStar Corp. site <www.onstar.com>.
18. Speedpass site <www.speedpass.com>.

CHAPTER THREE

1. Meridith Levinson, "Slices of lives," *CIO Magazine*, August 15, 2000, available <www.cio.com/archive/081500_slices.html>, accessed August 19, 2002.
2. Shelley Zulman, "Dressing up data," *Oracle Magazine*, January/February 1995, pp. 46–49.
3. "The chain store age 100," *Chain Store Age*, August 1996, p. 3A.
4. James Cash, "Gaining customer loyalty," *InformationWeek*, April 10, 1995, p. 88.
5. Royal Caribbean International Cruise Vacations site <www.royalcaribbean.com>.
6. Sami Lais, "Satellite ho!," *Computerworld*, May 29, 2000, pp. 70–71.
7. Gary Anthes, "Car dealer takes the personal out of PCs," *Computerworld*, August 14, 1995, p. 48.
8. Michael O'Reilly, "Smile, your name may be on line," *eCMAJ* (online Canadian Medical Association Journal), May 4, 1999, accessed August 27, 2002 <www.cmaj.ca/content/vol160/issue9/index.shtml>.
9. Karen Watterson, "A data miner's tools," *BYTE*, October 1995, pp. 91–96.
10. Jennifer Maselli, "Insurers look to CRM for profits," *InformationWeek*, May 6, 2002 <www.informationweek.com/story/IWK20020502S0007>.
11. Nikhil Hutheesing, "Surfing with Sega," *Forbes*, November 4, 1996, pp. 350–351.
12. Julia Kling, "OLAP gains fans among data-hungry firms," *Computerworld*, January 8, 1996, pp. 43, 48.
13. Alice LaPlante, "Big things come in smaller packages," *Computerworld*, June 24, 1996, pp. DW/6–7.
14. "News and events," press release, Burntsand site, October 31, 2001, available <www.burntsand.com/news_events/2001/oct31_2001.asp>, accessed August 27, 2002.
15. Rosemary Cafasso, "OLAP: who needs it?," *Computerworld*, February 2, 1995, p. 12.
16. Tischelle George, "Big bucks dry up," *InformationWeek*, April 29, 2002 <www.informationweek.com/story/IWK20020426S0005>.
17. Ben Phillips, "Ice service's data warehouse goes with the flow," *PC Week*, January 22, 1996, pp. 45–46.
18. Rick Whiting, "Analysis gap," *InformationWeek*, April 22, 2002 <www.informationweek.com/story/IWK20020418S0007>.

CHAPTER FOUR

1. Robyn Tamlyn, Medical Office of the Twenty-First Century (MOXXI) Project, Faculty of Medicine, McGill University <www.moxxi.mcgill.ca>, accessed November 14, 2002.
2. Kristin Krause, "Airlines feel your pain," *Traffic World*, April 30, 2001, pp. 28–30.

3. Jill Gambon, "A database that 'ads' up," *InformationWeek*, August 7, 1995, pp. 68–69.
4. Roberta Maynard, "Leading the way to effective marketing," *Nation's Business*, October 1996, pp. 10–11.
5. Scott McCartney, "Airlines catch technology tailwind: computers discover ways to cut costs to offset higher fuel, labor expenses," *Star Tribune* (Minneapolis, MN), p. 1d.
6. Steven Kauderer and Amy Kuehl, "Adding value with technology," *Best's Review*, October 2001, p. 130.
7. "M/W planning: it's all in the data," *Railway Age*, January 2001, pp. 60–61.
8. Steven Marlin, Cristina McEachern, and Anthony O'Donnell, "Cross selling starts with CRM system," *Wall Street & Technology*, December 2001, pp. A8–A10.
9. D. K. Taft, "Arlington ships decision tool," *Computer Reseller News*, November 27, 1995, p. 165; M. Pass, "New software packages help you make up your mind, develop company policy, and devise the perfect name," 2002, available <www.inc.com/incmagazine/articles/2633.html>.
10. Paul Korzeniowski, "New ways to stay connected," *Utility Business*, January 2000, pp. 58–60.
11. Peter Fingar, "Don't just transact—collaborate," *CIO*, June 1, 2001.
12. Marianne Kolbasuk McGee and Chris Murphy, "Collaboration is about more than squeezing out supply-chain costs," *InformationWeek*, December 10, 2001 <www.informationweek.com/story/IWK20011207S0016>, accessed October 30, 2002.
13. Marianne Kolbasuk McGee and Chris Murphy, "Collaboration is about more than squeezing out supply-chain costs," *InformationWeek*, December 10, 2001 <www.informationweek.com/story/IWK20011207S0016>, accessed October 30, 2002.
14. "PictureTel now shipping SwiftSite II compact videoconferencing system," news releaese, Vantage Systems home page <www.vantagesystems.com.au/news/pr/1999/03/PCTL_SSIIFinalRelease.asp>, accessed October 30, 2002.
15. Marianne Kolbasuk McGee and Chris Murphy, "Collaboration is about more than squeezing out supply-chain costs," *InformationWeek*, December 10, 2001 <www.informationweek.com/story/IWK20011207S0016>, accessed October 30, 2002.
16. "Desktop collaboration software: solution scenarios," Groove Networks, Inc. site, 2002 <www.groove.net/solutions/scenarios>, accessed November 14, 2002.
17. Marianne Kolbasuk McGee and Chris Murphy, "Collaboration is about more than squeezing out supply-chain costs," *InformationWeek*, December 10, 2001 <www.informationweek.com/story/IWK20011207S0016>, accessed October 30, 2002.
18. J. B. Smelcer and E. Carmel, "The effectiveness of difference representations for managerial problem solving: comparing tables and maps," *Decision Sciences*, 1997, pp. 391–420.
19. Bob Brewin, "IT helps waste hauler handle anthrax safely," *Computerworld*, November 12, 2001, p. 8.
20. Amy Dunkin, "The quants may have your numbers," *Business Week*, September 25, 1995, pp. 146–147.
21. Otis Port, "Computers that think are almost here," *Business Week*, July 17, 1995, pp. 68–71.
22. Matthew Axvig, "Cool robot: Dante II: volcano explorer," National Robotics Engineering Consortium site, <www.rec.ri.cmu.edu/education/multimedia/l2p2.shtml>, accessed October 30, 2002.
23. Rob Grimes, "Consumer acceptance of robots could signal future use by foodservice," *Nation's Restaurant News*, August 20, 2001, available <www.findarticles.com/cf_0/m3190/34_35/77498093/p1/article.jhtml?term=grimes+%2Brobots>, accessed October 30, 2002.
24. Ann Stuart, "A dose of accuracy," *CIO*, May 15, 1996, pp. 22–24.
25. Alison Overholt, "True or false: you're hiring the right people," *Fast Company*, February 2002, pp. 110–114.
26. Alexx Kay, "Artificial neural networks," *Computerworld*, February 12, 2001, p. 60, available <www.computerworld.com/softwaretopics/software/appdev/story/0,10801,57545,00.html>, accessed October 30, 2002.
27. Alexx Kay, "Artificial neural networks," *Computerworld*, February 12, 2001, p. 60, available <www.computerworld.com/softwaretopics/software/appdev/story/0,10801,57545,00.html>, accessed October 30, 2002.
28. William Perry, "What is neural network software?," *Journal of Systems Management*, September 1994, pp. 12–15.
29. Otis Port, "Diagnoses that cast a wider net," *Business Week*, May 22, 1995, p. 130.
30. William G. Baxt and Joyce Skora, "Prospective validation of artificial neural network trained to identify acute myocardial infarction," *The Lancet*, January 6, 1997, pp. 12–15.
31. Laton McCartney, "Technology for a better bottom line," *InformationWeek*, February 26, 1996, p. 40.
32. Linda Punch and Jason Fargo. "The downside of convenience checks," *Credit Card Management*, November 2000, pp. 78–82.
33. Greg Michlig, "To catch a thief," *Credit Union Management*, January 2001, pp. 48–50.
34. Rick Whiting, "Companies boost sales efforts with predictive analysis," *InformationWeek*, February 25, 2002 <www.informationweek.com/story/IWK20020221S0018>, accessed October 30, 2002.
35. Rick Whiting, "Companies boost sales efforts with predictive analysis," *InformationWeek*, February 25, 2002 <www.informationweek.com/story/IWK20020221S0018>, accessed October 30, 2002.
36. Linda Punch, "Battling credit card fraud," *Bank Management*, March 1993, pp. 18–22.
37. "Cigna, IBM tech tool targets health care fraud," *National Underwriter Property & Casualty-Risk & Benefits*, October 1994, p. 5.
38. Gary H. Anthes, "Picking winners and losers," *Computerworld*, February 18, 2002, p. 34.
39. Patricia E. Moody, "What's next after lean manufacturing?," *Sloan Management Review*, Winter 2001, pp. 12–13.
40. Patrick, C. L. Hui, S. F. Ng Frency, and C. C. Chan Keith, "A study of the roll planning of fabric spreading using genetic algorithms," *International Journal of Clothing Science & Technology* 12(1)(2000): 50–62, available from Emerald Fulltext <operatix.emeraldinsight.com/vl=3595504/cl=36/nw=1/rpsv/cgi-bin/linker?ini=emerald&reqidx=/cw/mcb/09556222/v12n1/s4/p50>, accessed November 14, 2002.
41. S. Begley, "Software au naturel," *Newsweek*, May 8, 1995, pp. 70–71.
42. Bernard Baumohl, "Can you really trust those bots?," *Time*, December 11, 2000, p. 80.
43. Nikki Swartz, "App intelligence," *Wireless Review*, September 1, 2001, pp. 8A–10A, available <wirelessreview.com/ar/wireless_app_intelligence/index.htm>.
44. Mike O'Brien, "Virtually helpful," *Telephony*, February 11, 2002, p. 56. available <currentissue.telephonyonline.com/ar/telecom_virtually_helpful>.
45. Kevin Dobbs, Sarah Boehle, Donna Goldwasser, Jack Gordon, and David Stamps, "The return of artificial intelligence," *Training*, November 2000, p. 26.
46. Rick Whiting, "Companies boost sales efforts with predictive analysis," *InformationWeek*, February 25, 2002 <www.informationweek.com/story/IWK20020221S0018>, accessed October 30, 2002.
47. Jane Griffin, "OLAP vs. data mining: which one is right for your data warehouse?," dataWarehouse.com <www.datawarehouse.com/iknowledge/articles/article.cfm?ContentID=281>, accessed October 30, 2002.
48. Howard Wolinsky, "Advisa helps companies get more from their data: helps managers to understand market," *Chicago Sun-Times*, December 20, 2000, p. 81.
49. Maryellen Mott Allen, "The myth of intelligent agents, *Online*, November/December 2000, pp. 45–51.
50. "Weblining," *Business Week Online*, April 3, 2000 <www.BusinessWeek.com>.
51. A. Shaw, "From hospitals to home care, wireless improves data collection at point-of-care," *Canadian Healthcare Technology*, April 2002, available <www.canhealth.com/apr02.html>.
52. J. Zeidenberg, "Leading hospitals test new health-record software," *Canadian Healthcare Technology*, May 2001, available <www.canhealth.com/may01.html>.

CHAPTER FIVE

1. Ellen Neuborne, "Pepsi's aim is true: the cola giant's web strategy finds the new generation of customers," *BusinessWeek Online*, January 22, 2001 <www.business week.com/2001/01_04/b3716045.htm>, accessed November 14, 2002.
2. Jeffrey F. Rayport and Jaworski, Bernard J., *e-Commerce* (New York: McGraw-Hill/ Irwin MarketspaceU, 2001), p. 4.
3. Michael Pastore, "Canadian firms seeing benefits of B2B e-commerce," Cyber Atlas, February 6, 2001, available <cyberatlas.internet.com/markets/b2b/ article/0,1323,10091_581201,00.html>.
4. "B2B ecommerce sales set to increase," ElectricNews, May 9, 2002 <www.nua .com/surveys/?f=VS&art_id=905357936& rel=true>.
5. "B2B spending to exceed USD1 trillion in 2004," Nua.com, April 26, 2002 <www.nua.com/surveys/?f=VS&art_id= 905357891&rel=true>.
6. Mundo Acuatico site <mundoacuatico .com/eng/about/statistics.htm>. Original statistics from CIA World Fact Book <www.odci.gov/cia/publications/ factbook>, Purchasing Power Parity <pacific.commerce.ubc.ca/xr/PPP.html>, Global Reach <www.glreach.com>, Wired Magazine <www.wired.com/wired/ current.html>, e-Marketer, 2001 <www.emarketer.com>.
7. C. Wood, "A two-tier system," *Maclean's* 112(23)(June 7, 1999): 32–33.
8. Ian Wylie, "Who runs this team, any-way?," *Fast Company* 57(April 2002): 32, available <www.fastcompany.com/ online/57/finland.html>.
9. Peter G. W. Keen and Ron Mackintosh, *The Freedom Economy: Gaining the mCommerce Edge in the Era of the Wireless Internet* (Berkeley, CA: Osborne McGraw-Hill, 2001), p. 5.
10. "Canadians avid users of health related websites," National Speakers Bureau, 2001, available <www.nsb.com/whats new.asp?i_newsid=148> and <www.benefitsworld.com/AA/Survey/ Health_Websites.asp>.
11. Abstract of James R. Sheats, "Information technology, sustainable development and developing nations," *Greener Management International* 32(Winter 2001):33, available <www.greene commerce.com/news.html>.
12. "Innovation through e-commerce: profiles from Atlantic Canada," ACOA site, 2002, <www.acoa.ca/e/business/ innovation/ecommerce/ecommprofiles .shtml#6b>, accessed November 14, 2002.
13. Toni Will-Harris, "Top 10 dos and don'ts for web site building," eFuse.com <www.efuse.com/Design/top_10_do_s_ and_don_ts.html>, accessed November 14, 2002.
14. "Marketing strategy," Teknik Industri site, July 2000 <teknikindustri.com/ marketing/main.htm>, accessed October 31, 2002.
15. See Rex Briggs, Measuring Success series, Interactive Advertising Bureau site, <www.iab.net/resources/measuring_ suc.asp#>, accessed October 30, 2002.
16. Chana Schoenberger, "Web? What web?" *Forbes*, June 10, 2002, p. 132.
17. Peter Keen and Mark McDonald, *The eProcess Edge* (Berkeley, CA: Osborne, McGraw-Hill, 2000), p. 96.
18. Electronic Commerce Branch, Industry Canada, "Household Internet Use Survey," Electronic Commerce Release, available <e-com.ic.gc.ca/english/research/ rep/backgounder_oct23_01.pdf> (note typo in URL—do not correct it); "Electronic commerce and technology," *The Daily*, April 3, 2001, available <www.statcan.ca/Daily/English/010403/ d010403a.htm>; D. W. Conklin and M. Trudeau, "The e-tail evolution: challenges and limitations," *Ivey Business Journal* 64(4)(March/April 2000): 44.
19. "Enabling electronic business with ebXML," ebXML site, sponsored by UN/CEFACT and OASIS, December 2000 <www.ebxml.org/white_papers/white paper.htm>, accessed October 31, 2002.
20. Robin Cover, "OAGI supports ebXML," Cover Pages site, July 30, 2001, <xml.coverpages.org/OAGI-ebXML 200107.html>, accessed October 31, 2002.
21. Eric Knorr, "Make way for web services. They're inevitable. Just ask the big guys," *CIO Magazine*, October 15, 2001, available <www.cio.com/archive/101501/ et_article.html>.
22. J. Kirby, "Grand design," *Canadian Business* 74(6)(April 2, 2001): 19–20; S. Larson, "Making its point by creating a ruckus," *National Home Center News* 27(15)(August 6, 2001): 30–33; Rainforest Action Network site <www.ran.org>.
23. See Customer Relationship Management Research Center, CIO.com site <www.cio.com/research/crm/>, accessed October 31, 2002.
24. See "Press releases," eBags.com <www.ebags.com/info/aboutebags/ index.cfm?Fuseaction=press>, accessed November 14, 2002.
25. Steve Konicki, "Revving up," *Information Week*, March 29, 2002 <www.information week.com/story/IWK20020329S0043>, accessed October 31, 2002.

CHAPTER SIX

1. "Global electronics distributor implements Internet EDI, achieving first year cost savings of over $1,200,000: solution pays for itself in less than one month," available <www.adx.com/downloads/ files/2/Case_Study_-_Newark_ Electronics.pdf>.
2. Bruce Abbott, "Requirements set the mark," *Infoworld*, March 2, 2001 <www.inforworld.com>.
3. Microsoft site <www.microsoft.com>.
4. D. Shortt, "The search for schools in IT," 2001, available <www.globetechnology .com/woman/archive/20010510.html>; "IT and educational leaders team up for a new initiative in the quest for life-long learning working together to address Canada's skills gap," news release, 2000, Hewlett-Packard Company site <www.hp.ca/corporate/highlights/tli>, accessed November 14, 2002; Vancouver Labour Market Bulletin (2000/2001), available <www.bc.hrdc-drhc.gc.ca/ vancouver/common/lmb_octnov00.pdf>.
5. Prescott, Carter Anne, "Marriott redefines the shared service model," Accenture site <www.accenture.com/xd/ xd.asp?it=enWeb&xd=ideas\outlook\ 1.2002\marriott.xml>, accessed November 14, 2002.
6. Bronwyn Fryer, "When users take notes," *Computerworld*, August 8, 1994, p. 82, available <www.computerworld.com/ news/1994/story/0,11280,15767,00.html>, accessed October 31, 2002.
7. "ADP: delivering HR solutions every day for companies of every size," Firmbuilder.com, August 30, 2002 <www.firmbuilder.com/articles/1/103/ 758/>, accessed October 31, 2002.
8. "A long-running hit at Canada's National Arts Centre," Compaq Case Studies, January 2001 <www.compaq.com/case studies/stories/nationalarts/story.html>, accessed November 14, 2002.
9. Thomas Hoffman and Julia Kling, "Utility unplugs object project," *Computerworld*, February 26, 1996, pp. 1, 125.
10. Bruce Caldwell, "The new outsourcing partnership," *InformationWeek*, June 24, 1996.
11. "New UPS supply chain solutions links logistics, freight and financial services," press release, UPS Pressroom <www.pressroom.ups.com/pressreleases/ archives/archive/0,1363,3919,00.html>, accessed October 31, 2002.
12. John Byrne, "Has outsourcing gone too far?," *Business Week*, April 1, 1996, pp. 26–28.
13. Stephen Haag and Peter Keen, *Information Technology: Tomorrow's Advantage Today* (New York: McGraw-Hill, 1996).
14. Farhad Manjoo, "Vaporware 2001: empty promises," *Wired*, January 2002, available <www.wired.com>.
15. Carole Jerome, "Failed products," *Marketplace*, February 1, 2000, available <www.cbcnews.com>.

CHAPTER SEVEN

1. Joe Barr, "Napster, Gnutella, and Internet guerrillas," *CNN.com*, May 15, 2000 <www.cnn.com>.
2. Sharon Gaudin, "Employees' abuse of Internet rampant," *Internetnews.com*, April 24, 2002 <www.internetnews.com>.
3. Sharon Gaudin, "Employees' abuse of Internet rampant," *Internetnews.com*, April 24, 2002 <www.internetnews.com>.
4. "EAI," Webopedia <www.webopedia .com/TERM/E/EAI.html>, accessed October 31, 2002.
5. Jeff Sweat, "The integrated enterprise," *Information Week Online*, April 26, 1999 <www.informationweek.com>.
6. "The Gap Inc.," Object Management Group's CORBA site, September 17, 2001 <www.corba.org/industries/retail/ gap.html>, accessed November 14, 2002.

7. "Dow Corning: forging stronger relationships with customers and partners through content management" Documentum, Inc. site <www.documentum.com/customer_success/success/dow_corning.htm>, accessed November 14, 2002.
8. "Business tools," FedEx Canada site <www.fedex.com/ca_english/businesstools>, accessed October 31, 2002.
9. i2 Technologies site <www.i2.com>.
10. Michael Booth, "The ABCs of ASPs," ebizQ.net, January 28, 2002 <b2b.ebizq.net/asp/booth_1.html>, accessed October 31, 2002.
11. Lindy Dragstra, "Multrix wins ASPire award for management and operations," Multrix site, January 7, 2002 <www.multrix.com/index.asp?content=/company/company.asp&lang=en>, accessed October 31, 2002.
12. "City of Orlando gives managers immediate access to budget-critical financial information," April 2002 <www.jdedwards.com/content/enUS/Customer-Customers/orlando.pdf>, accessed October 31, 2002.
13. See also the Obsolete Computer Museum <www.obsoletecomputermuseum.org>, accessed October 31, 2002.
14. Eryn Brown, "33 days, 8 campuses, 127 kids and an infinity of gizmos," *Fortune*, June 24, 2002, pp. 126–138.
15. "Improving customer satisfaction through global content management," www.documentum.com/products/customer/ford.htm.

CHAPTER EIGHT

1. Martin Garvey, "Disaster recovery isn't just for big business," *InformationWeek*, April 1, 2002, p. 44.
2. Dan Verton, "Digital destruction was worst imaginable," *Computerworld*, March 4, 2002, p. 8.
3. Eric Savitz, "Read this, then go back up your data," *Time Incorporated*, Winter 2002, pp. 28–29.
4. Michael Grotticelli, "Planning for the worst," *Broadcast Engineering*, April 2002, pp. 82–86.
5. Juliana Gruenwald, "Communications that won't quit," *Fortune*, Winter 2002, pp. 88–92.
6. Linda Pliagas, "Learning IT right from wrong," *InfoWorld*, September 29, 2000 <www.infoworld.com/articles/ca/xml/00/10/02/001002caethics.xml>, accessed November 1, 2002.
7. Christine Fogliasso and Donald Baack, "The personal impact of ethical decisions: a social penetration theory model," Second Annual Conference on Business Ethics, New York, 1995, sponsored by Vincentian Universities in the United States.
8. T. M. Jones, "Ethical decision-making by individuals in organizations: an issue-contingent model," *Academy of Management Review*, 1991, pp. 366–395.
9. Ernest Kallman and John Grillo, *Ethical Decision-Making and Information Technology* (San Francisco: McGraw-Hill, 1993).
10. Kristin Zhivago, "Et tu, Enron?," *AdWeek Magazines' Technology Marketing*, April 2002, p. 33.
11. Sara Baase, *The Gift of Fire: Social, Legal and Ethical Issues in Computing* (Upper Saddle River, NJ: Prentice-Hall, 1997).
12. Trevor Moores, "Software piracy: a view from Hong Kong," *Communications of the ACM*, December 2000, pp. 88–93.
13. Trevor Moores, "Software piracy: a view from Hong Kong," *Communications of the ACM*, December 2000, pp. 88–93.
14. Peter Beruk, "Five years: $59.2 billion lost," Software and Information Industry Association site, May 24, 2000 <www.siia.net/sharedcontent/press/2000/5-24-00.html>, accessed November 14, 2002.
15. Geoffrey James, "Organized crime and the software biz," *MC Technology Marketing Intelligence*, January 2000, pp. 40–44.
16. Geoffrey James, "Organized crime and the software biz," *MC Technology Marketing Intelligence*, January 2000, pp. 40–44.
17. P. Thibodeau, "Canadian privacy law raises ante—complying may place burden on U.S. firms," *Computer World* December 4, 2000, available <www.computerworld.com/cwi/story/0,1199,NAV47_STO54674,00.html>.
18. David Rittenhouse, "Privacy and security on your PC," *ExtremeTech*, May 28, 2002 <www.extremetech.com>.
19. Hall Adams, III, "E-mail monitoring in the workplace: the good, the bad and the ugly," *Defense Counsel Journal*, January 2000, pp. 32–46.
20. Dana Corbin, "Keeping a virtual eye on employees," *Occupational Health & Safety*, November 2000, pp. 24–28.
21. Linda Pliagas, "Learning IT right from wrong," *InfoWorld*, September 29, 2000 <www.infoworld.com/articles/ca/xml/00/10/02/001002caethics.xml>, accessed November 1, 2002.
22. Brett Glass, "Are you being watched?," *PC Magazine*, April 23, 2002, available <www.pcmag.com/article2/0,4149,27974,00.asp>, accessed November 1, 2002.
23. Cassimir Medford, "Know who I am," *PC Magazine*, February 7, 2000, pp. 58–64.
24. Cassimir Medford, "Know who I am," *PC Magazine*, February 7, 2000, pp. 58–64.
25. Darren Charters, "Electronic monitoring and privacy issues in business-marketing: the ethics of the DoubleClick experience," *Journal of Business Ethics*, February 2002, pp. 243–254.
26. Mark Naples, "Privacy and cookies," *Target Marketing*, April 2002, pp. 28–30.
27. Frank Hayes, "Assault on privacy," *Computerworld*, May 13, 2002, p. 74.
28. Matthew P. Graven, "Leave me alone," *PC Magazine*, January 16, 2001, pp. 151–152.
29. Rachel Konrad and John Borland, "Guess what's in your hard drive?," *ZDNet News*, April 18, 2002 <zdnet.com.com/2100-1104-885792.html>, accessed November 14, 2002.
30. Dara Mirsky, "Tap your web site's log files to improve CRM," *Customer Inter@ction Solutions*, May 2001, pp. 42–43, available <www.tmcnet.com/cis/0501/0501estaff.htm>, accessed November 14, 2002.
31. Sara Baase, *The Gift of Fire: Social, Legal and Ethical Issues in Computing* (Upper Saddle River, NJ: Prentice-Hall, 1997).
32. J. Chua, "Identity theft: robbery in the new millennium," Special Reports, 2002, CBC News, available <www.cbc.ca/consumers/indepth/identity>.
33. The sources for this whole section were: "Canada enacts broad new privacy law, creating complex interplay with U.S. and EU," June 15, 2000, available <law.about.com/library/briefs/ucanadaprivacy.htm>; M. Gisler, "Canada's new privacy law creates tricky relationship with related EU legislation," available <www.wliaonline.com/publications/canadaprivacy.html>; N. d'Entremont. "Protection of privacy: the hype, the facts, and the government's role," *Government Information in Canada* 21(2000), available <www.usask.ca/library/gic/21/dentremont.html>.
34. Anna Shimanek, "Do you want milk with those cookies?: complying with the Safe Harbor privacy principles," *Journal of Corporation Law*, Winter 2001, pp. 455–477.
35. Peter Han and Angus Maclaurin, "Do consumers really care about online privacy?," *Marketing Management*, January/February 2002, pp. 35–38.
36. Elizabeth De Bony, "EU overwhelmingly approves U.S. data-privacy regulations," *Computerworld*, June 5, 2000, p. 28.
37. Russ Banham, "Share data at your own risk," *World Trade*, November 2000, pp. 60–63.
38. Bruce Caldwell, "We are the business," *InformationWeek*, October 28, 1996, pp. 36–50.
39. Don Mogelefsky, "Security turns inward," *Incentive*, May 2000, p. 16.
40. John Conley, "Knocking the starch out of white collar crime," *Risk Management*, November 2000, pp. 14–22.
41. George Hulme, "In lockstep on security," *InformationWeek*, March 18, 2002, pp. 38–52, available <www.informationweek.com/story/IWK20020315S0008>, accessed November 1, 2002.
42. George Hulme, "In lockstep on security," *InformationWeek*, March 18, 2002, pp. 38–52, available <www.informationweek.com/story/IWK20020315S0008>, accessed November 1, 2002.
43. Christine Chudnow, "Grid computing," *Computer Technology Review*, April 2002, pp. 35–36.
44. "Law enforcers target 'top 10' online scams: consumer protection cops from 9 countries, 5 U.S. agencies, and 23 states tackle Internet fraud," 2000, available <www.ftc.gov/opa/2000/10/topten.htm>; New Jersey Department of Law and Public Safety, "State targets 'top 10' cyber scams: New Jersey joins consumer protections cops worldwide," *Tackling Internet Fraud*, 2000, available <www.state.nj.us/lps/ca/press/cyber.htm>.

45. Deborah Radcliff, "Hackers, terrorists, and spies," *Software Magazine*, October 1997, pp. 36–47.
46. George V. Hulme and Bob Wallace, "Beware cyberattacks," *InformationWeek*, November 13, 2000, pp. 22–24.
47. "Hackers hit lucky streak with Net casinos," *USA Today* site, September 10, 2001 <www.usatoday.com/life/cyber/tech/2001/09/10/net-gambling-hackers.htm>, accessed November 13, 2002.
48. "Security you can live with: cooperation equals profit," *Fortune Tech Review* <fortune.cnet.com/fortune/0-5937473-7-7720726.html?tag=subdir>, accessed November 11, 2002.
49. "Fast Times," *Fortune*, Summer 2000, pp. 35–36.
50. Ron Zemke, "Tech-savvy and people-stupid," *Training*, July 2000, pp. 16–18.
51. Vikki Spencer, "Risk management: danger of the cyber deep," *Canadian Underwriter*, September 2000, pp. 10–14.
52. Lisa Meyer, "Security you can live with," *Fortune*, Winter 2002, pp. 94–99, available <www.lisameyer.ws/fortune3.html>, accessed November 13, 2002.
53. Brooke Paul, "How much risk is too much?," *InformationWeek*, November 6, 2000, pp. 116–124.
54. Alison Eastwood, "End-users: the enemy within?," *Computing Canada*, January 4, 1996, p. 41.
55. Deborah Radcliff, "Beyond passwords," *Computerworld*, January 21, 2002, pp. 52–53.
56. Robert Luhn, "Eliminate viruses," *PC World*, July 2002, pp. 94–95.
57. Maura Ammenheuser, "The business case for biometrics," *Bank Systems & Technology*, February 2002, p. 42.
58. John Wagley, "Tech detectives," *Institutional Investor*, August 2001, pp. 18–20.
59. "Airlines to offer faster services to attract passengers," *Biometric Digest*, September 1999, available <www.biometricgroup.com/a_bio1/biometric_digest/99sep.pdf>, accessed November 13, 2002.
60. T. Ouellette and T. Hoffman, "Ice storm freezes operations," *Computerworld* 32(3)(January 19, 1998).
61. Jim Hoffer, "Backing up business," *Health Management Technology*, January 2001, available <www.healthmgttech.com/archives/h0101backing.htm>, accessed November 1, 2002.
62. Stuart Kahan, "Hot sites: the solution when business interruption is fatal," *Practical Accountant*, July 1994, pp. 58–63.
63. Barbara DePompa, "Averting a complete disaster," *InformationWeek*, July 15, 1996 <www.informationweek.com/588/88mtdis.htm>, accessed November 1, 2002.

EXTENDED LEARNING MODULE B

1. Scott Bradner, "Your confession is good for us," *Network World*, April 15, 2002, p. 30.
2. Marcia Savage, "The white hats: security consultants," *Computer Reseller News*, November 13, 2000, pp. 137–138.
3. Pack Thomas, "Virus protection," *Link-Up*, January/February 2002, p. 25.
4. Jason Meserve, "People around the world bitten by 'Love Bug,'" *Network World*, May 8, 2000, pp. 14, 28.
5. Ron Zemke, "Tech-savvy and people-stupid," *Training*, July 2000, pp. 16–18.
6. Thomas York, "Invasion of privacy? E-mail monitoring is on the rise," *InformationWeek*, February 21, 2000, pp. 142–146.
7. Jason Meserve, "People around the world bitten by 'Love Bug,'" *Network World*, May 8, 2000, pp. 14, 28.
8. Sara Cox Landolt, "Why the sky isn't falling," *Credit Union Management*, October 2000, pp. 52–54.
9. Robert Luhn, "Eliminate viruses," *PC World*, July 2002, p. 94.
10. "Hackers attack *USA Today* web site," *Morning Sun*, July 13, 2002, p. 6.
11. Don Mogelefsky, "Security turns inward," *Incentive*, May 2000, p. 16.
12. George Hulme, "Vulnerabilities beckon some with a license to hack," *InformationWeek*, October 23, 2000, pp. 186–192.
13. Glenn Bischoff, "Fear of a black hat," *Telephony*, September 3, 2001, pp. 24–29.
14. Janet Kornblum, "Kournikova virus maker: no harm meant," *USA Today*, February 14, 2001, p. 3D.
15. Warren G. Kruse and Jay G. Heiser, *Computer Forensics: Incident Response Essentials* (New York: Addison-Wesley, 2002).

CHAPTER NINE

1. "Success stories: e-mail and more for people on the go," Canada's Innovation Strategy site, Government of Canada, April 23, 2002 <www.innovationstrategy.gc.ca/cmb/innovation.nsf/Success/RIM>, accessed November 14, 2002.
2. Elizabeth Corcoran, "The next small thing," *Forbes*, July 23, 2001, pp. 96–106.
3. J. Gallagher, "On the verge of voice commerce," InsuranceTech.com, March 8, 2001 <www.insurancetech.com/it2/story/specialReport/IST20010308S0009>.
4. Lisa Cavion, "Hubble telescope and the Canadarm," SpaceNet <www.spacenet.on.ca/stories/robotics/hubble/>, accessed November 14, 2002.
5. Nina Adams, "Lessons from the virtual world," *Training*, June 1995, pp. 45–47.
6. Laurie Flynn, "VR and virtual spaces find a niche in real medicine," *The New York Times*, June 5, 1995, p. C3.
7. "ARINC and Visionics will market face-recognition system for airport security," press release, ARINC Incorporated site, December 3, 2001, available <www.arinc.com/news/2001/12-03-01.html>, accessed November 13, 2002.
8. "Zensys closes over $15 million in funding, launches breakthrough home control technology," *Business Wire*, May 2, 2001, available <www.businesswire.com/webbox/bw.050201/211220321.htm>, accessed November 13, 2002.
9. Jennifer Lee, "Tailoring cellphones for teenagers," *The New York Times on the Web*, May 30, 2002 <www.nytimes.com/2002/05/30/technology/circuits/30TEEN.html>, accessed November 13, 2002.

EXTENDED LEARNING MODULE D

1. Steven Levy and Brad Stone, "The WiFi wave," *Newsweek*, June 10, 2002, pp. 50–53.
2. "How to revitalize host systems for client/server computing today and tomorrow," *Datamation*, April 1, 1995, pp. S1–S24.
3. Lisa Schalon, "Sales automation systems increase sales, productivity," *Best's Review—Life-Health Insurance Edition*, January 1996, pp. 100–102.

GLOSSARY

A

Ad hoc, or **nonrecurring, decision** one that you make infrequently (perhaps only once) and you may even have different criteria for determining the best solution each time.
Adaptive filtering asks you to rate products or situations and also monitors your actions over time to find out what you like and dislike.
Adaptivity for intelligent agents is discovering, learning, and taking action independently.
Adware software to generate ads that installs itself on your computer when you download some other (usually free) program from the Web.
Affiliate programs arrangements made between e-commerce sites that direct users from one site to the other and by which, if a sale is made as a result, the originating site receives a commission.
Alliance partner a company that you do business with on a regular business in a cooperative fashion, usually facilitated by IT systems.
Analysis phase involves end users and IT specialists working together to gather, understand, and document the business requirements for the proposed system.
Anonymous Web browsing (AWB) services, which in effect, hide your identity from the Web sites you visit.
Antivirus software detects and removes or quarantines computer viruses.
Application architects information technology professionals who can design creative technology-based business solutions.
Application generation subsystem contains facilities to help you develop transaction-intensive applications.
Application service provider (ASP) provides an outsourcing service for businesses software applications.
Application software the software that enables you to solve specific problems or perform specific tasks.
Arithmetic/logic unit (A/L unit) performs all arithmetic operations (e.g., addition and subtraction) and all logic operations (such as sorting and comparing numbers).
Artificial intelligence (AI) the science of making machines imitate human thinking and behaviour.
Artificial neural network (ANN) also called a **neural network**, an artificial intelligence system that is capable of finding and differentiating patterns.
ASCII (American Standard Code for Information Interchange) the coding system that most personal computers use to represent, process, and store information.
AutoFilter function filters a list and allows you to hide all the rows in a list except those that match criteria you specify.
Automatic speech recognition (ASR) system not only captures spoken words but also distinguishes word groupings to form sentences.
Autonomy the ability of an intelligent agent to act without your telling it every step to take.

B

B2B marketplace an Internet-based service which brings together many buyers and sellers.
Back office system used to fulfill and support customer orders.
Back-propagation neural network a neural network trained by someone.
Backup the process of making a copy of the information stored on a computer.
Bandwidth or capacity of the communications medium, refers to the amount of information that a communications medium can transfer in a given amount of time.
Banner ad a small ad on one Web site that advertises the products and services of another business, usually another dot-com business.
Barcode reader captures information that exists in the form of vertical bars whose width and distance apart determine a number.
Basic formatting tag HTML tag that allows you to specify formatting for text.
Benchmark a set of conditions used to measure how well a product or system functions.
Binary digit (bit) the smallest unit of information that your computer can process.
Biometrics the use of your physical characteristics—such as your fingerprint, the blood vessels in the retina of your eye, the sound of your voice, or perhaps even your breath—to provide identification.
Black-hat hackers cyber vandals.
Bluetooth technology provides entirely wireless connections for all kinds of communication devices.
Broadband high-capacity telecommunications pipeline capable of providing high-speed Internet service.
Browser-safe colours 216 colours that can be represented using 8 bits and are visible in all browsers.
Business intelligence knowledge—knowledge about your customers, your competitors, your partners, your competitive environment, and your own internal operations. Business intelligence comes from information.
Business process a standardized set of activities that accomplishes a specific task, such as processing a customer's order.
Business process reengineering (BPR) the reinventing of processes within a business.
Business requirement a detailed knowledge worker request that the system must meet in order to be successful.
Business to business (B2B) companies whose customers are primarily other businesses.
Business to consumer (B2C) companies whose customers are primarily individuals.
Buyer agent or **shopping bot** an intelligent agent on a Web site that helps you, the customer, find the products and services you want.
Buyer power high when buyers have many choices of whom to buy from, and low when their choices are few.
Byte a group of eight bits that represents one natural language character.

C

Cable modem a device that uses your TV cable to deliver an Internet connection.
Capacity planning determines the future IT infrastructure requirements for new equipment and additional network capacity.
Cat 5 (or **Category 5**) cable is a better-constructed version of the phone twisted-pair cable.
CAVE (cave automatic virtual environment) a special 3D virtual reality room that can display images of other people and objects located in other CAVEs all over the world.

CD-R (compact disk—recordable) optical or laser disk that offers one-time writing capability with about 800 MB of storage capacity.
CD-ROM optical or laser disk that offers no updating capabilities with about 800 MB of storage capacity. Most software today comes on CD-ROM.
CD-RW (compact disk—rewritable) offers unlimited writing and updating capabilities on the CD.
Central processing unit (CPU) the actual hardware that interprets and executes the software instructions and coordinates how all the other hardware devices work together.
Chief information officer (CIO) responsible for overseeing an organization's information resource.
Choice the third step in the decision-making process where you decide on a plan to address the problem or opportunity.
Class contains information and procedures and acts as a template to create objects.
Clicks-and-mortar a retailer, like Nordstrom, which has both an Internet presence and physical stores.
Clickstream records information about you during a Web surfing session such as what Web sites you visited, how long you were there, what ads you looked at, and what you bought.
Click-throughs count of the number of people who visit one site and click on a banner ad, and are taken to the site of the advertiser.
Client/server network a network in which one or more computers are servers and provide services to the other computers which are called clients.
Coaxial cable (coax) one central wire surrounded by insulation, a metallic shield, and a final case of insulating material.
Cold site a separate facility that does not have any computer equipment, but is a place where the knowledge workers can move after a disaster.
Collaboration software software that allows people to work together on a given project or document.
Collaboration system a system that is designed specifically to improve the performance of teams by supporting the sharing and flow of information.
Collaborative filtering a technique to enable a Web site to support personalization.
Collaborative planning, forecasting, and replenishment (CPFR) a concept that encourages and facilitates collaborative processes among members of a supply chain.
Collaborative processing enterprise information portal provides knowledge workers with access to workgroup information such as e-mails, reports, meeting minutes, and memos.
Collocation what happens when a vendor rents out space and telecommunication equipment to other companies.
Communications medium the path, or physical channel, in a network over which information travels.
Communications protocol (protocol) a set of rules that every computer follows to transfer information.
Communications satellite microwave repeater in space.
Communications service provider third party who furnishes the conduit for information.
Competitive advantage providing a product or service in a way that customers value more than what the competition is able to do.
Complementor a company that provides products and services that complement the offerings of another company and thereby extend its value-adding capabilities to its customers.
Composite primary key consists of the primary key fields from the two intersecting relations.
Composite relation represents the intersection of primary keys of two relations.
Computer-aided software engineering (CASE) tools are software suites that automate system development.
Computer crime is a crime in which a computer, or computers, plays a significant part.
Computer forensics is the gathering, authentication, examination, and analysis of electronic information stored on any type of computer media, such as hard drives, floppy disks or CDs.
Computer network (or a **network**) two or more computers connected so that they can communicate with each other and share information, software, peripheral devices, and/or processing power.
Computer virus (or simply a **virus**) software that is written with malicious intent to cause annoyance or damage.
Conditional formatting highlights the information in a cell that meets some criteria you specify.
Connectivity software enables you to use your computer to "dial up" or connect to another computer.
Control unit interprets software instructions and tells the other hardware devices what to do, based on the software instructions.
Conversion rate the percentage of customers who visit a site who actually buy something.
Cookie a small record deposited on your hard disk by a Web site containing information about you.
Copyright the legal protection afforded an expression of an idea, such as a song, video game, and some types of proprietary documents.
Counterfeit software software that is manufactured to look like the real thing and sold as such.
Cracker a hacker for hire who engages in electronic corporate espionage.
Crash-proof software utility software that helps you save information if your system crashes and you're forced to turn it off and then back on again.
Critical success factor (CSF) a factor critical to your organization's success.
Crossover part of a genetic algorithm where portions of good outcomes are combined in the hope of creating an even better outcome.
CRT a monitor that looks like a television set.
CRUD (create, read, update, delete) the four primary procedures, or ways, a system can manipulate information.
Culture the collective personality of a nation or society, encompassing language, traditions, currency, religion, history, music, and acceptable behaviour, among other things.
Custom AutoFilter function allows you to hide all the rows in a list except those that match criteria, besides "is equal to," you specify.
Customer-integrated system (CIS) an extension of a TPS that places technology in the hands of an organization's customers and allows them to process their own transactions.
Customer relationship management (CRM) system uses information about customers to gain insights into their needs, wants, and behaviours in order to serve them better.
Cyberterrorist is one who seeks to cause harm to people or destroy critical systems or information.

D

Data raw facts that describe a particular phenomenon.

Data administration the function in an organization that plans for, oversees the development of, and monitors the information resource.
Data administration subsystem helps you manage the overall database environment by providing facilities for backup and recovery, security management, query optimization, concurrency control, and change management.
Data cleansing ensures all information is accurate.
Data definition subsystem helps you create and maintain the data dictionary and define the structure of the files in a database.
Data dictionary contains the logical structure for the information.
Data manipulation subsystem helps you add, change, and delete information in a database and mine it for valuable information.
Data mart subset of a data warehouse in which only a focused portion of the data warehouse information is kept.
Data mining agent an intelligent agent that operates in a data warehouse discovering information.
Data mining tool software tool you use to query information in a data warehouse.
Data warehouse a logical collection of information—gathered from many different operational databases—used to create business intelligence that supports business analysis activities and decision-making tasks.
Database a collection of information that you organize and access according to the logical structure of that information.
Database-based workflow system stores the document in a central location and automatically asks the knowledge workers to access the document when it's their turn to edit the document.
Database administration the function in an organization that is responsible for the more technical and operational aspects of managing the information contained in organizational databases (which can include data warehouses and data marts).
Database management system (DBMS) helps you specify the logical organization for a database and access and use the information within the database.
DBMS engine accepts logical requests from the various other DBMS subsystems, converts them into their physical equivalent, and actually accesses the database and data dictionary as they exist on a storage device.
Decentralized computing an environment in which an organization splits computing power and locates it in functional business areas as well as on the desktops of knowledge workers.
Decision-processing enterprise information portal provides knowledge workers with corporate information for making key business decisions.
Decision support system (DSS) a highly flexible and interactive IT system that is designed to support decision making when the problem is not structured.
Demand aggregation combines purchase requests from multiple buyers into a single large order which justifies a discount from the business.
Denial-of-service (DoS) attack floods a Web site with so many requests for service that it slows down or crashes.
Design the second phase of the decision-making process. It's where you consider possible ways of solving the problem, filling the need, or taking advantage of the opportunity.
Design phase builds a technical blueprint of how the proposed system will work.
Desktop computer the most popular choice for personal computing needs.
Development phase takes all of your detailed design documents from the design phase and transform them into an actual system.
Digital cash (also called **electronic cash** or **e-cash**) an electronic representation of cash.
Digital divide the fact that different peoples, cultures, and areas of the world or within a nation do not have the same access to information and telecommunications technologies.
Digital economy marked by the electronic movement of all types of information, not limited to numbers, words, graphs, and photos but including physiological information such as voice recognition and synthesization, biometrics (your retina scan and breath for example), and 3D holograms.
Digital subscriber line (DSL) modem a high-speed Internet connection using phone lines, which allows you to use your phone for voice communications at the same time.
Direct material a material that is used in production in a manufacturing company or is placed on the shelf for sale in a retail environment.
Directory search engine organizes listings of Web sites into hierarchical lists.
Disaster recovery cost curve charts (1) the cost to your organization of the unavailability of information and technology and (2) the cost to your organization of recovering from a disaster over time.
Disaster recovery plan a detailed process for recovering information or an IT system in the event of a catastrophic disaster such as a fire or flood.
Disintermediation by using the Internet as a delivery vehicle, intermediate players in a distribution channel can be bypassed.
Disk optimization software utility software that organizes your information on your hard disk in the most efficient way.
Distributed denial-of-service (DDoS) attack attack from multiple computers that floods a Web site with so many requests for service that it slows down or crashes.
Distribution chain the path followed from the originator of a product or service to the end consumer.
Documentation management system manages a document through its life cycle.
Domain expert the person who provides the domain expertise in the form of problem-solving strategies.
Domain expertise the set of problem-solving steps; it's the reasoning process that will solve the problem.
Domain name identifies a specific computer on the Web and the main page of the entire site.
Dot pitch the distance between the centres of a pair of like-coloured pixels.
DVD-R optical or laser disk that offers one-time writing capability with upwards of 17 GB of storage capacity.
DVD-ROM optical or laser disk that offers no updating capabilities with upwards of 17 GB of storage capacity. The trend is now for movie rentals to be on DVD.
DVD-RW, **DVD-RAM**, or **DVD+RW** (all different names by different manufacturers) optical or laser disk that offers unlimited writing and updating capabilities on the DVD.

E

E-commerce commerce accelerated and enhanced by information technology, in particular the Internet.
E-government the application of e-commerce technologies in governmental agencies.

E-mail software (short for **electronic mail software**) enables you to electronically communicate with other people by sending and receiving e-mail.
E-tailer an Internet retail site.
ebXML a set of technical specifications for business documents built around XML designed to permit enterprises of any size and in any geographical location to conduct business over the Internet.
Electronic bill presentment and payment (EBPP) systems send us our bills over the Internet and give us an easy way to pay them if the amount looks correct.
Electronic catalogue designed to present products to customers or partners all over the world via the Web.
Electronic data interchange (EDI) the direct computer-to-computer transfer of transaction information contained in standard business documents, such as invoices and purchase orders, in a standard format.
Electronic job market consists of employers using Internet technologies to advertise and screen potential employees.
Electronic portfolio (e-Portfolio) collection of Web documents used to support a stated purpose such as demonstrating writing, photography, or job skills.
Encapsulation means information hiding.
Encryption scrambles the contents of a file so that you can't read it without having the right decryption key.
Enterprise application integration (EAI) the process of developing an infrastructure that enables employees to quickly implement new or changing business processes.
Enterprise application integration middleware (EAI middleware) allows organizations to develop different levels of integration from the data level to the business-process level.
Enterprise information portal (EIP) allows knowledge workers to access company information via a Web interface.
Enterprise resource planning (ERP) the method of getting and keeping an overview of every part of the business (a bird's-eye view, so to speak), so that production, development, selling, and servicing of goods and services will all be coordinated to contribute to the company's goals and objectives.
Enterprise software a suite of software that includes (1) a set of common business applications, (2) tools for modelling how the entire organization works, and (3) development tools for building applications unique to your organization.
Entity class a concept—typically people, places, or things—about which you wish to store information and that you can identify with a unique key (called the primary key).
Entity-relationship (E-R) diagram a graphic method of representing entity classes and their relationships.
Entry barrier a product or service feature that customers have come to expect from companies in a particular industry.
Ethernet card the most common type of network interface card.
Ethical (or **white-hat**) **hacker** a computer security professional who is hired by a company to break into its computer system.
Ethics are the principles and standards that guide our behaviour toward other people.
Executive information system (EIS) a highly interactive IT system that allows you to first view highly summarized information and then choose how you would like to see greater detail, which may alert you to potential problems or opportunities.
Expandability refers to how easy it is to add features and functions to a system.
Expansion bus moves information from your CPU and RAM to all of your other hardware devices such as your microphone and printer.
Expansion card a circuit board that you insert into an expansion slot.
Expansion slot a long, skinny socket on the motherboard into which you insert an expansion card.
Expert system, also called a **knowledge-based system**, an artificial intelligence system that applies reasoning capabilities to reach a conclusion.
Explanation module the part of an expert system where they "why" information, supplied by the domain expert, is stored to be accessed by knowledge workers who want to know why the expert systems asked a question or reached a conclusion.
extensible markup language (XML) a coding language for the Web that lets computers interpret the *meaning* of information in Web documents.
External information describes the environment surrounding the organization.
Extraction engine consists of smart software with a vocabulary of job-related skills that allows it to recognize and catalogue terms in your scannable résumé.
Extranet an intranet that is restricted to an organization and certain outsiders, such as customers and suppliers.

F

Fair Use Doctrine allows you to use copyrighted material in certain situations.
Feature analysis the step of ASR in which the system captures your words as your speak into a microphone, eliminates any background noise, and converts the digital signals of your speech in phonemes (syllables).
Feature creep occurs when developers add extra features that were not part of the initial requirements.
File transfer protocol (ftp) the communications protocol that allows you to transfer files of information from one computer to another.
File transfer protocol (ftp) server a computer that maintains a collection of downloadable files.
Financial cybermediaries Internet-based companies that make it easy for one person to pay another person over the Internet.
Financial EDI (FEDI) the use of EDI for payments.
Firewall hardware and/or software that protects a computer or network from intruders.
First mover the company first to market with a new IT-based product or service.
Five forces model a model developed to determine the relative attractiveness of an industry.
Flat-panel display thin, lightweight monitor that takes up much less space than a CRT.
Floppy disk storage device that is great for portability of information and ease of updating but holds only 1.44 MB of information.
Foreign key a primary key of one file (relation) that appears in another file (relation).
Forensic image copy an exact copy or snapshot of the contents of an electronic medium.
Front office system the primary interface to customers and sales channels.

G

Genetic algorithm an artificial intelligence system that mimics the evolutionary, survival-of-the-fittest process to generate increasingly better solutions to a problem.
Geographic information system (GIS) a decision support system designed specifically to work with spatial information.
Gigabyte (**GB** or **Gig**) roughly 1 billion characters.
Gigahertz (GHz) the number of billions of CPU cycles per second.
Global digital divide the term used specifically to describe differences in IT access and capabilities between different countries or regions of the world.
Global economy one in which customers, businesses, suppliers, distributors, and manufacturers all operate without regard to physical and geographical boundaries.
Global positioning system (GPS) a collection of 24 earth-orbiting satellites that continuously transmit radio signals to determine your current longitude, latitude, speed, and direction of movement.
Global reach the ability to extend a company's reach to customers anywhere there is an Internet connection, and at a much lower cost.
Glove an input device that captures and records the shape and movement of your hand and fingers and the strength of your hand and finger movements.
Government-to-business (G2B) the electronic commerce activities performed between a government and its business partners for such purposes as purchasing direct and indirect materials, soliciting bids for work, and accepting bids for work.
Government-to-consumer (G2C) the electronic commerce activities performed between a government and its citizens or consumers including paying taxes, registering vehicles, and providing information and services.
Government-to-government (G2G) the electric commerce activities limited to performing electronic commerce activities within a single nation's government focusing on vertical integration (local, city, state, and federal) and horizontal integration (among the various branches and agencies).
Graphical user interface (GUI) the interface to an information system.
Grid computing harnesses far-flung computers together by way of the Internet or a virtual private network to share CPU power, databases, and storage.
Group document database acts as a powerful storage facility for organizing and managing all documents related to specific teams.
Groupware the popular term for the software component that supports the collaborative efforts of a team.
GUI screen design the ability to model the information system screens for an entire system.

H

Hacker a very knowledgeable person who uses his or her knowledge to invade other people's computers.
Hacktivist a politically motivated hacker who uses the Internet to send a political message of some kind.
Hard disk storage device that rests within your system box and offers both ease of updating and great storage capacity.
Hardware the physical devices that make up a computer (often referred to as a computer system).
Heading tag HTML tag that makes certain information, such as titles, stand out on your Web site.
Headset a combined input and output device that (1) captures and records the movement of your head and (2) contains a screen that covers your entire field of vision and displays various views of an environment based on your movements.
Health Insurance Portability and Accountability Act in the United States, a law that forces the health care industry to install policies and procedures to maintain the confidentiality of patient information.
Help desk a group of people who responds to knowledge workers questions.
Hidden job market the collective term used to describe jobs that are not advertised. Up to 80 percent of new jobs fall into this category.
High-capacity floppy disk storage device that is great for portability and ease of updating and holds between 100 MB and 250 MB of information. Superdisks and Zip disks are examples.
Holographic device a device that creates, captures, and/or displays images in true three-dimensional form.
Home page the main page and entry point of a Web site.
Home PNA stands for **Home Phoneline Networking Alliance**; allows you to network your home computers using telephone wiring.
Horizontal market software application software that is general enough to be suitable for use in a variety of industries.
Hot site a separate and fully equipped facility where the company can move immediately after a disaster and resume business.
HTML document a file that contains your Web site content and HTML formatting instructions.
HTML tag specifies the formatting and presentation of information on a Web site.
Hypertext markup language (HTML) the language you use to create a Web site.
Hypertext transfer protocol (http) the communications protocol that supports the movement of information over the Web, essentially from a Web server to you.

I

Implant chip a technology-enabled microchip implanted into the human body.
Implementation the final step in the decision-making process where you put your plan into action.
Implementation phase distributes the system to all of the knowledge workers and they begin using the system to perform their everyday jobs.
Indirect material a material that is necessary for running a modern corporation, but does not relate to the company's primary business activities.
Inference engine the processing component of the expert system. It takes your problem facts and searches the knowledge base for rules that fit your problem facts.
Information data that have a particular meaning within a specific context.
Information age a time when knowledge is power.
Information decomposition breaking down the information and procedures into multiple classes for ease of use and understandability.
Information granularity refers to the extent of detail within the information.

Information partnership two or more companies cooperating by integrating their IT systems, thereby providing customers with the best of what each can offer.
Information supplier convergence the merging of all types of organizations that provide information and access to it.
Information technology (IT) any computer-based tool that people use to work with information and support the information and information-processing needs of an organization.
Information view includes all of the information stored within a system.
Information-literate knowledge workers can define what information they need, know how and where to obtain that information, understand the information once they receive it, and act appropriately based on the information to help the organization achieve the greatest advantage.
Infrared is a wireless communications medium that uses radio waves to transmit signals or information.
Inheritance the ability to define superclass and subclass relationships among classes.
Inkjet printer makes images by forcing ink droplets through nozzles.
Input device a tool you use to capture information and commands.
Insourcing a project means that IT specialists within your organization will develop the system.
Instance an occurrence of an entity class that can be uniquely described.
Integration allows separate systems to communicate directly with each other by automatically exporting data files from one system and importing them into another system.
Integrity constraints rules that help ensure the quality of the information.
Intellectual property intangible creative work that is embodied in physical form.
Intelligence the first step in the decision-making process where you find or recognize a problem, need, or opportunity (also called the diagnostic phase of decision making.
Intelligent agent software that assists you, or acts on your behalf, in performing repetitive computer-related tasks.
Interactive chat lets you engage in real-time typed exchange of information between you and one or more other individuals over the Internet.
Interface any device that calls procedures and can include such things as a keyboard, mouse, and touch screens.
Intermediary a specialist company that adds services.
Internal information describes specific operational aspects of the organization.
International government-to-government (IG2G) the electronic commerce activities performed between two or more governments including providing foreign aid.
International virtual private network (international VPN)—virtual private networks that depend on services offered by phone companies of various nationalities.
Internet a vast network of computers that connects millions of people all over the world.
Internet backbone the major set of connections for computers on the Internet.
Internet server computer computer that provides information and services on the Internet.
Internet service provider (ISP) a company that provides individuals, organizations, and businesses access to the Internet.
Internet telephony a combination of hardware and software that uses the Internet as the medium for transmission of telephone calls in place of traditional telephone networks.
Internet virtual private network a technology that enables establishment of a virtual network over the Internet consisting of a company, its suppliers, and its customers.
Interorganizational system (IOS) automates the flow of information between organizations to support the planning, design, development, production, and delivery of products and services.
Intersection relation (sometimes called a **composite relation**) a relation you create to eliminate a many-to-many relationship.
Intranet an internal organizational Internet that is guarded against outside access by a special security feature called a firewall (which can be software, hardware, or a combination of the two).
Intrusion-detection software looks for people on the network who shouldn't be there or who are acting suspiciously.
IRC (Internet relay chat) server supports your use of discussion groups and chat rooms.
IrDA (Infrared Data Association) port for wireless devices that work in essentially the same way as the remote control on your TV does.
IT infrastructure includes the hardware, software, and telecommunication equipment, that when combined, provides the underlying foundation to support the organization's goals.

J

Joint application development (JAD) occurs when knowledge workers and IT specialists meet, sometimes for several days, to define or review the business requirements for the system.

K

Key logger (or **key trapper**) **software** a program that, when installed on a computer, records every keystroke and mouse click.
Keyboard today's most popular input technology.
Knowledge acquisition the component of the expert system that the knowledge engineer uses to enter the rules.
Knowledge base stores the rules of the expert system.
Knowledge engineer the person who formulates the domain expertise into an expert system.
Knowledge worker works with and produces information as a product.
Knowledge-based system, also known as an expert system, an artificial intelligence system that applies reasoning capabilities to reach a conclusion.

L

Language processing the step of automatic speech recognition (ASR) in which the system attempts to make sense of what you're saying by comparing the word phonemes generated in the pattern classification step of ASR with a language model database.
Laser printer forms images using an electrostatic process, the same way a photocopier works.
Last-mile bottleneck problem occurs when information is travelling on the Internet over a very fast line for a certain distance and then comes near your home where it must travel over a slower line.
Legacy system a previously built system using older technologies such as mainframe computers and programming languages such as COBOL.

Link (the technical name is **hyperlink**) clickable text or an image that takes you to another site or page on the Web.
Linux an open-source operating system that provides a rich operating environment for high-end workstations and network servers.
List a collection of information arranged in columns and rows in which each column displays one particular type of information.
List table definition a description of a list by column.
Local area network (LAN) a network that covers a limited geographic distance, such as an office, building, or a group of buildings in close proximity to each other.
Logical view focuses on how you as a knowledge worker need to arrange and access information to meet your particular business needs.

M

M-commerce the term used to describe electronic commerce conducted over a wireless device such as a cell phone or personal digital assistant.
Mac OS the operating system for today's Apple computers.
Macro virus spreads by binding itself to software such as Word or Excel.
Mail server provides e-mail services and accounts.
Mainframe computer (sometimes just called a **mainframe**) a computer designed to meet the computing needs of hundreds of people in a large business environment.
Maintenance phase monitors and supports the new system to ensure it continues to meet the business goals.
Management information systems (MIS) deals with the planning for, development, management, and use of information technology tools to help people perform all tasks related to information processing and management.
Marketing mix the set of marketing tools that a firm uses to pursue its marketing objectives in the target market.
Mass customization when a business gives its customers the opportunity to tailor its product or service to the customer's specifications.
MD5 hash value a mathematically generated number that is unique for each individual storage medium at a specific point in time, because it's based on the contents of that medium.
Megabyte (**MB** or **M** or **Meg**) roughly one million bytes.
Megahertz (MHz) the number of millions of CPU cycles per second.
Message how objects communicate with each other.
Messaging-based workflow system sends work assignments through an e-mail system.
Meta tags a part of a Web site text not displayed to users but accessible to browsers and search engines for finding and categorizing Web sites.
Micro-payment a technique to facilitate the exchange of small amounts of money for an Internet transaction.
Microphone for capturing live sounds such as a dog barking or your voice (for automatic speech recognition).
Microsoft Windows 2000 Millennium (Windows 2000 Me) an operating system for a home computer user with utilities for setting up a home network and performing video, photo, and music editing and cataloguing.
Microsoft Windows 2000 Professional (Windows 2000 Pro) an operating system for people who have a personal computer connected to a network of other computers at work or at school.
Microsoft Windows XP Home Microsoft's latest upgrade to Windows 2000 Me, with enhanced features for allowing multiple people to use the same computer.
Microsoft Windows XP Professional (Windows XP Pro) Microsoft's latest upgrade to Windows 2000 Pro.
Microwave a type of radio transmission used to transmit information.
Minicomputer (sometimes called a **mid-range computer**) designed to meet the computing needs of several people simultaneously in a small to medium-size business environment.
Model management component of a DSS that consists of the DSS models and the DSS model management system.
Modelling the activity of drawing a graphical representation of a design.
Monitoring-and-surveillance agents (or **predictive agents**) are intelligent agents that observe and report on equipment.
Mouse today's most popular "pointing" input device.
Multidimensional analysis (MDA) tools slice-and-dice techniques that allow you to view multidimensional information from different perspectives.
Multifunction printer scans, copies, and faxes, as well as prints.
Multitasking allows you to work with more than one piece of software at a time.
Municipal area network (MAN) covers a metropolitan area.
Mutation part of a genetic algorithm; it's the process of trying combinations and evaluating the success (or failure) of the outcome.

N

Network two or more computers connected so that they can communicate with each other and possibly share information, software, peripheral devices, and/or processing power.
Network access point (NAP) a point on the Internet where several connections converge.
Network hub a device that connects multiple computers into a network.
Network interface card (NIC) an expansion card or a PC Card (for a notebook computer) that connects your computer to a network and provides the doorway for information to flow in and out.
Network service provider (NSP), such as MCI or AT&T, owns and maintains routing computers at NAPs and even the lines that connect the NAPs to each other.
Neural network (often called an **artificial neural network** or **ANN)** an artificial intelligence system that is capable of finding and differentiating patterns.
Nonrecurring, or **ad hoc**, **decision** one that you make infrequently (perhaps only once) and you may even have different criteria for determining the best solution each time.
Nonstructured decision a decision for which there may be several "right" answers and there is no precise way to get a right answer.
Normalization a process of assuring that a relational database structure can be implemented as a series of two-dimensional relations.
Notebook computer a fully functional computer designed for you to carry around and run on battery power.

O

Object an instance of a class.
Object-oriented (OO) approach combines information and procedures into a single view.

Object-oriented database works with traditional database information and also complex data types such as diagrams, schematic drawings, video, sound and text documents.
Object-oriented programming language a programming language used to develop object-oriented systems.
Objective information quantifiably describes something that is known.
Online training runs over the Internet or off a CD-ROM.
Online analytical processing (OLAP) the manipulation of information to support decision making.
Online transaction processing (OLTP) the gathering of input information, processing that information, and updating existing information to reflect the gathered and processing information.
Operating system software system software that controls your application software and manages how your hardware devices work together.
Operational database a database that supports OLTP.
Operational management manages and directs the day-to-day operations and implementations of the goals and strategies.
Optical fibre a telecommunications medium that uses a very thin glass or plastic fibre through which pulses of light travel.
Optical mark recognition (OMR) detects the presence or absence of a mark in a predetermined place (popular for multiple choice exams).
Output device a tool you use to see, hear, or otherwise accept the results of your information-processing requests.
Outsourcing the delegation of specific work to a third party for a specified length of time, at a specified cost, and at a specified level of service.

P

Palm Operating System (Palm OS) the operating system for Palm and Handspring PDAs.
Parallel connector has 25 pins, which fit into the corresponding holes in the port. Most printers use parallel connectors.
Pattern classification the step of ASR in which the system matches your spoken phonemes to a phoneme sequence stored in an acoustic model database.
Peer-to-peer network a network in which a small number of computers share hardware (such as a printer), software and/or information.
Performance measures how quickly an IT system performs a certain process.
Permission marketing when you have given a merchant your permission to send you special offers.
Personal agent (or **user agent**) an intelligent agent that takes action on your behalf.
Personal digital assistant (PDA) a small handheld computer that helps you surf the Web and perform simple tasks such as note taking, calendaring, appointment scheduling, and maintaining an address book.
Personal productivity software helps you perform personal tasks—such as writing a memo, creating a graph, and creating a slide presentation—that you can usually do even if you don't own a computer.
Personalization when a Web site can know enough about your likes and dislike that it can fashion offers that are more likely to appeal to you.
Physical view deals with how information is physically arranged, stored, and accessed on some type of storage device such as a hard disk.
Pirated software is the unauthorized use, duplication, distribution or sale of copyrighted software.
Pivot table enables you to group and summarize information.
Planning phase involves determining a solid plan for developing your information system.
PNA adapter card an expansion card that you put into your computer to act as an doorway for information flowing in and out.
Pocket PC OS (or **Windows CE**) the operating system for the PocketPC PDA.
Point-of-sale (POS) for capturing information at the point of a transaction, typically in a retail environment.
Pointing stick small rubberlike pointing device that causes the pointer to move on the screen as you apply directional pressure (popular on notebooks).
Polymorphism simply means "to have many forms."
Port the plug-in found on the outside of your system box (usually in the back) into which you plug a connector.
Portable document format (PDF) the standard electronic distribution file format for heavily formatted documents such as a presentation résumé because it retains the original document formatting.
Predictive agent (or **monitoring-and-surveillance agent**) is an intelligent agent that observes and reports on equipment.
Presentation résumé a format-sensitive document created in a word processor to outline your job qualifications in one to two printed pages.
Primary key a field (or group of fields in some cases) that uniquely describes each record.
Privacy is the right to be left alone when you want to be, to have control over your own personal possessions, and not to be observed without your consent.
Private network the communications media that your organization owns or exclusively leases to connect networks or network components.
Procedure manipulates or changes information.
Procedure view contains all of the procedures within a system.
Profile filtering requires that you choose terms or enter keywords to provide a more personal picture of you and your preferences.
Program a set of instructions that, when executed, cause a computer to behave in a specific manner.
Programming language the tool developers use to write a program.
Project manager an individual who is an expert in project planning and management, defines and develops the project plan, and tracks the plan to ensure all key project milestones are completed on time.
Project milestone represents a key date for which you need a certain group of activities performed.
Project plan defines the what, when, and who questions of system development including all activities to be performed, the individuals, or resources, who will perform the activities, and the time required to complete each activity.
Project scope clearly defines the high-level system requirements.
Project scope document a written definition of the project scope and is usually no longer than a paragraph.
Proof-of-concept prototype a prototype you use to prove the technical feasibility of a proposed system.
Prototype a model of a proposed product, service, or system.
Prototyping the process of building a model that demonstrates the features of a proposed product, service, or system.
Psychographic filtering anticipates your preferences based on the answers you give to a questionnaire.

Public key encryption (PKE) is an encryption system that uses two keys: a public key that everyone can have and a private key for only the recipient.
Public network a network on which your organization competes for time with others.
Pure play an Internet retailer such as Amazon.com that has no physical stores.
Push technology an environment in which businesses and organizations come to you with information, services, and product offerings based on your profile.

Q

Query-and-reporting tools similar to QBE tools, SQL, and report generators in the typical database environment.
Query-by-example (QBE) tool helps you graphically design the answer to a question.

R

RAM (random access memory) temporary storage that holds the information you're working with, the application software you're using, and the operating system software you're using.
Recovery the process of reinstalling the backup information in the event the information was lost.
Recurring decision a decision that you have to make repeatedly and often periodically, whether weekly, monthly, quarterly, or yearly.
Relation describes each two-dimensional table or file in the relational model (hence its name *relational* database model).
Relational database model uses a series of logically related two-dimensional tables or files to store information in the form of a database.
Repeater a device that receives a radio signal, strengthens it, and sends it on.
Report generator helps you quickly define formats of reports and what information you want to see in a report.
Request for proposal (RFP) a formal document that describes in detail your logical requirements for a proposed system and invites outsourcing organizations (which we'll refer to as "vendors") to submit bids for its development.
Requirements definition document defines all of the business requirements and prioritize them in order of business importance and place them in a formal comprehensive document.
Resolution of a printer the number of dots per inch (dpi) it produces, which is the same principle as the resolution in monitors.
Resolution of a screen the number of pixels it has. Pixels (picture elements) are the dots that make up an image on your screen.
Reverse auction the process in which a buyer posts its interest in buying a certain quantity of items, and sellers compete for the business by submitting successively lower bids until there is only one seller left.
Risk assessment is the process of evaluating IT assets, their importance to the organization, and their susceptibility to threats, to measure the risk exposure of these assets.
Risk management consists of the identification of risks or threats, the implementation of security measures, and the monitoring of those measures for effectiveness.
Rivalry among existing competitors makes an industry less attractive to enter when high and more attractive to enter when low.
Robot a mechanical device equipped with simulated human senses and the capability of taking action on its own.
Router a device that acts as a smart hub connecting computers into a network, and it also separates your network from any other network it's connected to.
Rule-based expert system the type of expert system that expresses the problem-solving process as rules.

S

Safe Harbor principles the set of rules to which U.S. businesses that want to trade with the European Union (EU) must adhere.
Sales force automation (SFA) system automatically tracks all of the steps in the sales process.
Satellite modem a modem that allows you to get Internet access from a satellite dish.
Scalability the ability of an information system to adapt to increased demands on its resources.
Scannable résumé (ASCII résumé, plain-text résumé) designed to be evaluated by skills-extraction software and typically contain all résumé content without any formatting.
Scanner captures images, photos, and artwork that already exist on paper.
Scope creep occurs when the scope of the project increases.
Script bunny (or **script kiddie**) people who would like to be hackers but don't have much technical expertise
Script kiddies (or **script bunnies**) people who would like to be hackers but don't have much technical expertise.
Search engine a facility on the Web that helps you find sites with the information and/or services you want.
Security auditing software checks out your computer or network for potential weaknesses.
Selection part of a genetic algorithm that give preference to better outcomes.
Self-organizing neural network finds patterns and relationships in vast amounts of data by itself.
Selfsourcing (also called **knowledge worker development** or **end user development**) the development and support of IT systems by knowledge workers with little or no help from IT specialists.
Selling prototype a prototype you use to convince people of the worth of a proposed system.
Serial connector usually has 9 holes but may have 25, which fit into the corresponding number of pins in the port. Serial connectors are often most used for monitors and certain types of modems.
Server farm a location that stores a group of servers in a single place.
Service level agreement (SLA) defines the specific responsibilities of the service provider and sets the customer expectations.
Shared information an environment in which an organization's information is organized in one central location, allowing anyone to access and use it as they need to.
Shopping bot or **buyer agent** an intelligent agent on a Web site that helps you, the customer, find the products and services you want.
Sign-off the knowledge workers' actual signatures indicating they approve all of the business requirements.
Skill words nouns and adjectives used by organizations to describe job skills which should be woven into the text of applicants' résumés.
Slack space the space left over when a file doesn't completely fill the last cluster of sectors.
Smart cards plastic cards the size of a credit card that contain an embedded chip on which digital information can be stored.

Sociability the ability of intelligent agents to confer with each other.
Social engineering conning your way into acquiring information to which you have no right.
Software the set of instructions that your hardware executes to carry out a specific task for you.
Software suite (or simply **suite**) a group of applications sold together by a software company.
Spam unsolicited e-mail from a company with whom you have never done business.
Spoofing forging the return address on an e-mail so that the e-mail message appears to come from someone other than the actual sender.
Spyware (also called **sneakware** or **stealthware**) software that comes hidden in free downloadable software and tracks your online movements, mines the information stored on your computer, or uses your computer's CPU and storage for some task you know nothing about.
Steganography the hiding of information inside other information.
Storage device a tool you use to store information for use at a later time.
Strategic management provides an organization with overall direction and guidance.
Structure tag HTML tag that sets up the necessary sections and specifies that the document is indeed an HTML document.
Structured decision a decision where processing a certain kind of information in a specified way so that you will always get the right answer.
Structured query language (SQL) a standardized fourth-generation query language found in most DBMSs.
Subjective information attempts to describe something that is unknown.
Supercomputer the fastest, most powerful, and most expensive type of computer.
Supplier power high when buyers have few choices of whom to buy from, and low when there are many choices.
Supply chain management (SCM) system tracks inventory and information among business processes and across companies.
Switch a device that connects multiple computers into a network in which multiple communications links can be in operation simultaneously.
Switching costs the costs that can make customers reluctant to switch to another product or service.
System bus consists of the electronic pathways which move information between basic components on the motherboard, including between your CPU and RAM.
Systems development life cycle (SDLC) a structured step-by-step approach for developing information systems.
System software handles tasks specific to technology management and coordinates the interaction of all technology devices.

T

Tactical management develops the goals and strategies outlined by strategic management.
TCP/IP (transport control protocol/Internet protocol) the primary protocol for transmitting information over the Internet.
Technical architecture defines the hardware, software, and telecommunication equipment required to run the system.
Technology-literate knowledge worker a person who knows how and when to apply technology.
Telecommunications device a tool you use to send information to and receive it from another person or location.
Telecommuting the use of communications technologies (such as the Internet) to work in a place other than a central location.
Telephone modem (or **modem**) a device that connects your computer to your phone line so that you can access another computer or network.
Temporary advantage an advantage that, sooner or later, the competition duplicates or even leapfrogs with a better system.
Terabyte (TB) roughly one trillion bytes.
Test condition a detailed step the system must perform along with the expected result of the step.
Testing phase verifies that the system works and meets all of the business requirements defined in the analysis phase.
Thin client a workstation with a small amount of processing power and costs less than a full-powered workstation.
Threat of new entrants high when it is easy for competitors to enter the market and low when it is difficult for competitors to enter the market.
Threat of substitute products or services alternatives to using a product or service.
Three-dimensional (3D) technology presentations of information give you the illusion that the object you're viewing is actually in the room with you.
Three generic strategies cost leadership, differentiation, or a focused strategy.
Thrill-seeker hacker a hacker who breaks into computer systems for entertainment.
Top-level domain three-letter extension of a Web site address that identifies its type.
Touch pad another form of a stationary mouse on which you move your finger to cause the pointer on the screen to move (popular on notebooks).
Touch screen special screen that lets you use your finger to point at and touch a particular function you want to perform.
Trackball an upside-down, stationary mouse; using it, you move the ball instead of the device (mainly for notebooks).
Traditional technology approach has two primary views of any system—information and procedures—and it keeps these two views separate and distinct at all times.
Transaction processing system (TPS) processes transactions that occur within an organization.
Transnational firm firm that produces and sells products and services in countries all over the world.
Trojan-horse software software you don't want hidden inside software you do want.
Trojan-horse virus hides inside other software, usually an attachment or download.
True search engine uses software agent technologies to search the Internet for key words and then places them into indexes.

U

Unallocated space the set of clusters that have been set aside to store information, but have not yet received a file, or still contain some or all of a file marked as deleted.
Uniform resource locator (URL) an address for a specific Web page or document within a Web site.
Uninstaller software utility software that you can use to remove software from your hard disk that you no longer want.

Universal serial bus (USB) becoming the most popular means of connecting devices to a computer. Most standard desktops today have at least two USB ports, and most standard notebooks have at least one.
User acceptance testing (UAT) determines if the system satisfies the business requirements and enables the knowledge workers to perform their jobs correctly.
User agent (or **personal agent**) an intelligent agent that takes action on your behalf.
User documentation highlights how to use the system.
User interface management of an expert system the part of the expert system that you use to run it.
Utility software software that provides additional functionality to your operating system.

V

Value-added network (VAN) a semipublic network that provides services beyond the movement of information from one place to another.
Value chain a tool that views the organization as a chain—or series—of processes, each of which adds value to the product or service for the customer.
Value network all of the resources behind the click on a Web page that the customer doesn't see, but that together create the customer relationship–service, order fulfillment, shipping, financing, information brokering, and access to other products and offers.
Vertical market software application software that is unique to a particular industry.
View allows you to see the contents of a database file, make whatever changes you want, perform simple sorting, and query to find the location of specific information.
Viral marketing encourages users of a product or service supplied by a B2C company to ask friends to join in as well.
Virtual private network uses software to establish a secure channel on the Internet for transmitting data.
Virtual private network (VPN) a public network that promises availability to your organization, but doesn't provide you with a dedicated line or communications media.
Virtual reality a three-dimensional computer simulation in which you actively and physically participate.
Virtual workplace a technology-enabled workplace with no walls and no boundaries. One can work anytime, anyplace, linked to other people and information, wherever they are.
Virus (or **computer virus**) software that is written with the intention to cause annoyance or damage.

W

Walker an input device that captures and records the movement of your feet as you walk or turn in different directions.
Wearable computer a fully-equipped computer that you wear as a piece of clothing or attached to a piece of clothing similar to way you would carry your cell phone on your belt.
Web browser software enables you to surf the Web.
Web farm either a Web site that has multiple servers, or an ISP that provides Web site outsourcing services using multiple servers.
Web page a specific portion of a Web site that deals with a certain topic.
Web portal a site that provides a wide range of services, including search engines, free e-mail, chat rooms, discussion boards, and links to hundreds of different sites.
Web server provides information and services to Web surfers.
Web Services software applications that talk to other software applications over the Internet using XML as a key enabling technology.
Web site a specific location on the Web where you visit, gather information, and perhaps even order products.
Web site address a unique name that identifies a specific site on the Web.
Web space a storage area where you keep your Web site.
White-hat (or **ethical**) **hacker** a computer security professional who is hired by a company to break into its computer system.
Wide area network (WAN) a network that covers large geographic distances, such as a province, a country, or even the entire world.
WiFi stands for **wireless fidelity** (also known as **IEEE 802.11b**) a way of transmitting information in wave form that is reasonably fast and is often used for notebooks.
Wired communications media transmit information over a closed, connected path.
Wireless communications media transmit information through the air.
Wireless Internet service provider (wireless ISP) does the same job as standard Internet service providers except that you don't need a wired connection for access.
Wireless network access point or **wireless access point** a device that allows computers to access a wired network using radio waves.
Workflow defines all of the steps or business rules, from beginning to end, required for a process to run correctly.
Workflow system automates business processes.
Workgroup support system (WSS) a system designed to support a work team and to enhance group performance and communication of information.
Workshop training set in a classroom-type environment and led by an instructor.
World Wide Web, or **Web**, a multimedia-based collection of information, services, and Web sites supported by the Internet.
Worm a type of virus that spreads itself, not just from file to file, but from computer to computer via e-mail and other Internet traffic.

X

XML (extensible markup language) a coding language for the Web that lets computers interpret the *meaning* of information in Web documents.

PHOTO CREDITS

CHAPTER ONE

Figure 1.9a Person using an ATM © Michael Newman/Photo Edit
Figure 1.9b Person paying for fuel at the pump © David Young-Wolf/Photo Edit

CHAPTER TWO

Figure 2.3a Man working in a manufacturing plant © Bob Daemmrich/The Image Works
Figure 2.3b Warehouse floor © Davis Barber/Photo Edit
Figure 2.3c Retailer shelf with PCs © Michael Newman/Photo Edit
Figure 2.3d Checkout clerk with customer © Spencer Grant/Photo Edit
Figure 2.3e Woman sitting in front of a computer © Ryan McVay/Photo Disc
Figure 2.3f Delivery man at a front door with a package © Leslye Borden/Photo Edit

CHAPTER NINE

Figure 9.5a Xybernaut Poma wearable computer Photo courtesy of Xybernaut Corporation
Figure 9.5b Levi Strauss computer jacket Photo courtesy of Levi Strauss Co.
Figure 9.5c Computer belt Photo courtesy of Charmed Technology

MODULE C

Figure C.1a Mouse/keyboard © Photo Disc/Nancy R. Cohen
Figure C.1b Flat-screen monitor Courtesy of International Business Machines Corporation. Unauthorized use not permitted.
Figure C.1c Stack of floppy disks © Corbis
Figure C.1e Intel Pentium 4 chip Photo courtesy of Intel Corporation
Figure C.1d Video card www.rage3d.com—The largest ATI fan site on the Net.
Figure C.3a PDA © Jason Reed/Ryan McVay Photo Disc
Figure C.3b Notebook computer © Hewlett-Packard
Figure C.3c Vertical desktop computer © Photo Disc/Siede Preis
Figure C.4a Minicomputer © Hewlett-Packard
Figure C.4b Mainframe computer © Steve Chenn/Corbis
Figure C.4c Supercomputer © Roger Russmeyer/Corbis
Figure C.8a Ergonomic keyboard © Photo Disc/Ryan McVay
Figure C.8b Flatbed scanner © Photo Disc/Siede Preis
Figure C.8c People at checkout. Courtesy of International Business Machines Corporation. Unauthorized use not permitted.
Figure C.8d Microphone © Eyewire
Figure C.8e Person using a touch screen. Courtesy of International Business Machines Corporation. Unauthorized use not permitted.
Figure C.8f Mouse/keyboard © Photo Disc/Nancy R. Cohen
Figure C.8g Computer touch pad © Eyewire
Figure C.9a Two monitors side by side. Courtesy of International Business Machines Corporation. Unauthorized use not permitted.
Figure C.9b Flat-screen monitor. Courtesy of International Business Machines Corporation. Unauthorized use not permitted.
Figure C.10 Personal laser printer © Photo Disc/Siede Preis
Figure C.12a Jazz Disk Photo courtesy of Iomega Corporation
Figure C.12b Hard disk drive. Courtesy of International Business Machines Corporation. Unauthorized use not permitted.
Figure C.12c CDs © Nance Trueworthy
Figure C.17a Serial connector Photo courtesy of Belkin Components
Figure C.17b Back of computer © Nance Trueworthy
Figure C.17c USB connector © Daisuke Morita/Photo Disc
Figure C.17d Parallel connector. Photo courtesy of Belkin Components.

MODULE D

Figure D.1 PCI network card for desktop computer © Nance Trueworthy
Figure D.2 LinkSys Home Router © 2001 Linksys Group Inc. All rights reserved.
Figure D.3 Ethernet cable with RJ-45 connectors © 2001 Linksys Group Inc. All rights reserved.
Figure D.4 Wireless network card. Courtesy Sierra Wireless
Figure D.5 Palm Pilot PDA © Photo Disc
Figure D.6 Coaxial cable © Spencer Grant/Photo Edit
Figure D.7 Cable. Courtesy of International Business Machines Corporation. Unauthorized use not permitted.

INDEX

C

E

F

I

N

O